Library of America, a nonprofit organization, champions our nation's cultural heritage by publishing America's greatest writing in authoritative new editions and providing resources for readers to explore this rich, living legacy.

JOHN MCPHEE

JOHN McPHEE

ENCOUNTERS IN WILD AMERICA

The Pine Barrens
Encounters with the Archdruid
The Survival of the Bark Canoe
Coming into the Country

David Remnick, *editor*

THE LIBRARY OF AMERICA

Published in the United States by Library of America,
14 East 60th Street, New York, NY 10022.
Visit our website at www.loa.org.

This paper exceeds the requirements of
ANSI/NISO Z39.48–1992 (Permanence of Paper).

Distributed to the trade in the United States
by Penguin Random House Inc.
and in Canada by Penguin Random House Canada Ltd.

The authorized representative in the EU for product safety
and compliance is eucomply OÜ, Pärnu mnt 139b-14, 11317 Tallinn, Estonia.
hello@eucompliancepartner.com

Library of Congress Control Number: 2025942877
ISBN 978–1–59853–842–7

First Printing
The Library of America—398

Manufactured in the United States of America

John McPhee: Encounters in Wild America
is published with support from

THE GIORGI FAMILY FOUNDATION

and

EDWIN S. MATTHEWS, JR.

Contents

THE PINE BARRENS

For Pryde
and for her father
Charles Mitchell Brown

Contents

Drawings by James Graves

I

The Woods from Hog Wallow

FROM THE fire tower on Bear Swamp Hill, in Washington Township, Burlington County, New Jersey, the view usually extends about twelve miles. To the north, forest land reaches to the horizon. The trees are mainly oaks and pines, and the pines predominate. Occasionally, there are long, dark, serrated stands of Atlantic white cedars, so tall and so closely set that they seem to be spread against the sky on the ridges of hills, when in fact they grow along streams that flow through the forest. To the east, the view is similar, and few people who are not native to the region can discern essential differences from the high cabin of the fire tower, even though one difference is that huge areas out in this direction are covered with dwarf forests, where a man can stand among the trees and see for miles over their uppermost branches. To the south, the view is twice broken slightly—by a lake and by a cranberry bog—but otherwise it, too, goes to the horizon in forest. To the west, pines, oaks, and cedars continue all the way, and the western horizon includes the summit of another hill—Apple Pie Hill—and the outline of another fire tower, from which the view three hundred and sixty degrees around is virtually the same as the view from Bear Swamp Hill, where, in a moment's sweeping glance, a person can see hundreds of square miles of wilderness. The picture of New Jersey that most people hold in their minds is so different from this one that, considered beside it, the Pine Barrens, as they are called, become as incongruous as they are beautiful. West and north of the Pine Barrens is New Jersey's central transportation corridor, where traffic of freight and people is more concentrated than it is anywhere else in the world. The corridor is one great compression of industrial shapes, industrial sounds, industrial air, and thousands and thousands of houses webbing over the spaces between the factories. Railroads and magnificent highways traverse this crowded scene, and by 1985 New

Jersey hopes to have added so many additional high-speed roads that the present New Jersey Turnpike will be quite closely neighbored by the equivalent of at least six other turnpikes, all going in the same direction. In and around the New Jersey corridor, towns indistinguishably abut one another. Of the great unbroken city that will one day reach at least from Boston to Richmond, this section is already built. New Jersey has nearly a thousand people per square mile—the greatest population density of any state in the Union. In parts of northern New Jersey, there are as many as forty thousand people per square mile. In the central area of the Pine Barrens—the forest land that is still so undeveloped that it can be called wilderness—there are only fifteen people per square mile. This area, which includes about six hundred and fifty thousand acres, is nearly as large as Yosemite National Park. It is almost identical in size with Grand Canyon National Park, and it is much larger than Sequoia National Park, Great Smoky Mountains National Park, or, for that matter, most of the national parks in the United States. The people who live in the Pine Barrens are concentrated mainly in small forest towns, so the region's uninhabited sections are quite large—twenty thousand acres here, thirty thousand acres there—and in one section of well over a hundred thousand acres there are only twenty-one people. The Pine Barrens are so close to New York that on a very clear night a bright light in the pines would be visible from the Empire State Building. A line ruled on a map from Boston to Richmond goes straight through the middle of the Pine Barrens. The halfway point between Boston and Richmond—the geographical epicenter of the developing megalopolis—is in the northern part of the woods, about twenty miles from Bear Swamp Hill.

Technically, the Pine Barrens are much larger than the thousand or so square miles of them that remain wild, and their original outline is formed by the boundaries of a thick layer of sand soils that covers much of central and southern New Jersey—down the coast from the outskirts of Asbury Park to the Cape May Peninsula, and inland more than halfway across the state. Settlers in the seventeenth and eighteenth centuries found these soils unpromising for farms, left the land uncleared, and began to refer to the region as the Pine Barrens. People in

New Jersey still use the term, with variants such as "the pine belt," "the pinelands," and, most frequently, "the pines." Gradually, development of one kind or another has moved in over the edges of the forest, reducing the circumference of the wild land and creating a man-made boundary in place of the natural one. This transition line is often so abrupt that in many places on the periphery of the pines it is possible to be at one moment in farmland, or even in a residential development or an industrial zone, and in the next moment to be in the silence of a bewildering green country, where a journey of forty or fifty miles is necessary to get to the farms and factories on the other side. I don't know where the exact center of the pines may be, but in recent years I have spent considerable time there and have made outlines of the integral woodland on topographic maps and road maps, and from them I would judge that the heart of the pine country is in or near a place called Hog Wallow. There are twenty-five people in Hog Wallow. Some of them describe it, without any apparent intention to be clever, as a suburb of Jenkins, a town three miles away, which has forty-five people. One resident of Hog Wallow is Frederick Chambers Brown. I met him one summer morning when I stopped at his house to ask for water.

Fred Brown's house is on an unpaved road that curves along the edge of a wide cranberry bog. What attracted me to it was the pump that stands in his yard. It was something of a wonder that I noticed the pump, because there were, among other things, eight automobiles in the yard, two of them on their sides and one of them upside down, all ten years old or older. Around the cars were old refrigerators, vacuum cleaners, partly dismantled radios, cathode-ray tubes, a short wooden ski, a large wooden mallet, dozens of cranberry picker's boxes, many tires, an orange crate dated 1946, a cord or so of firewood, mandolins, engine heads, and maybe a thousand other things. The house itself, two stories high, was covered with tarpaper that was peeling away in some places, revealing its original shingles, made of Atlantic white cedar from the stream courses of the surrounding forest. I called out to ask if anyone was home, and a voice inside called back, "Come in. Come in. Come on the hell in."

I walked through a vestibule that had a dirt floor, stepped up into a kitchen, and went on into another room that had several overstuffed chairs in it and a porcelain-topped table, where Fred Brown was seated, eating a pork chop. He was dressed in a white sleeveless shirt, ankle-top shoes, and undershorts. He gave me a cheerful greeting and, without asking why I had come or what I wanted, picked up a pair of khaki trousers that had been tossed onto one of the overstuffed chairs and asked me to sit down. He set the trousers on another chair, and he apologized for being in the middle of his breakfast, explaining that he seldom drank much but the night before he had had a few drinks and this had caused his day to start slowly. "I don't know what's the matter with me, but there's got to be something the matter with me, because drink don't agree with me anymore," he said. He had a raw onion in one hand, and while he talked he shaved slices from the onion and ate them between bites of the chop. He was a muscular and well-built man, with short, bristly white hair, and he had bright, fast-moving eyes in a wide-open face. His legs were trim and strong, with large muscles in the calves. I guessed that he was about sixty, and for a man of sixty he seemed to be in remarkably good shape. He was actually seventy-nine. "My rule is: Never eat except when you're hungry," he said, and he ate another slice of the onion.

In a straight-backed chair near the doorway to the kitchen sat a young man with long black hair, who wore a visored red leather cap that had darkened with age. His shirt was coarse-woven and had eyelets down a V neck that was laced with a thong. His trousers were made of canvas, and he was wearing gum boots. His arms were folded, his legs were stretched out, he had one ankle over the other, and as he sat there he appeared to be sighting carefully past his feet, as if his toes were the outer frame of a gunsight and he could see some sort of target in the floor. When I had entered, I had said hello to him, and he had nodded without looking up. He had a long, straight nose and high cheekbones, in a deeply tanned face that was, somehow, gaunt. I had no idea whether he was shy or hostile. Eventually, when I came to know him, I found him to be as shy a person as I have ever had a chance to know. His name is Bill Wasovwich, and he lives alone in a cabin about half a mile from Fred. First his father, then his mother left him when he was a young boy, and he grew up depending on the help of various people in the pines. One of them, a cranberry grower, employs him and has given him some acreage, in which Bill is building a small cranberry bog of his own, "turfing it out" by hand. When he is not working in the bogs, he goes roaming, as he puts it, setting out cross-country on long, looping journeys, hiking about thirty miles in a typical day, in search of what he calls "events"—surprising a buck, or a gray fox, or perhaps a poacher or a man with a still. Almost no one who is not native to the pines could do this, for the woods have an undulating sameness, and the understory—huckleberries, sheep laurel, sweet fern, high-bush blueberry—is often so dense that a wanderer can walk in a fairly tight circle and think that he is moving in a straight line. State forest rangers spend a good part of their time finding hikers and hunters, some of whom have vanished for days. In his long, pathless journeys, Bill always emerges from the woods near his cabin—and about when he plans to. In the fall, when thousands of hunters come into the pines, he sometimes works as a guide. In the evenings, or in the daytime when he is not working or roaming, he goes to Fred Brown's house and sits there for hours. The old man is a widower whose seven children are long since gone from Hog Wallow, and he is as expansively talkative and worldly as the young one is withdrawn and wild. Although there are fifty-three years between their ages, it is obviously fortunate for each of them to be the other's neighbor.

That first morning, while Bill went on looking at his outstretched toes, Fred got up from the table, put on his pants, and said he was going to cook me a pork chop, because I looked hungry and ought to eat something. It was about noon, and I was even hungrier than I may have looked, so I gratefully accepted his offer, which was a considerable one. There are two or three small general stores in the pines, but for anything as fragile as a fresh pork chop it is necessary to make a round trip from Fred's place of about fifty miles. Fred went into the kitchen and dropped a chop into a frying pan that was crackling with hot grease. He has a fairly new four-burner stove that uses bottled gas. He keeps water in a large bowl on a table in the kitchen and ladles some when he wants it. While he cooked the meat, he looked out a window through a stand of pitch pines and into the cranberry bog. "I saw a big buck out here last night with velvet on his horns," he said. "Them horns is soft when they're in velvet." On a nail high on one wall of the room that Bill and I were sitting in was a large meat cleaver. Next to it was a billy club. The wall itself was papered in a flower pattern, and the wallpaper continued out across the ceiling and down the three other walls, lending the room something of the appearance of the inside of a gift box. In some parts of the ceiling, the paper had come loose. "I didn't paper this year," Fred said. "For the last couple months, I've had sinus." The floor was covered with old rugs. They had been put down in random pieces, and in some places as many as six layers were stacked up. In winter, when the temperature approaches zero, the worst cold comes through the floor. The only source of heat in the house is a wood-burning stove in the main room. There were seven calendars on the walls, all current and none with pictures of nudes. Fading into pastel on one wall was a rotogravure photograph of President and Mrs. Eisenhower. A framed poem read:

> God hath not promised
> Sun without rain
> Joy without sorrow
> Peace without pain.

Noticing my interest in all this, Fred reached into a drawer and showed me what appeared to be a postcard. On it was a photograph of a woman, and Fred said with a straight face that she was his present girl, adding that he meets her regularly under a juniper tree on a road farther south in the pines. The woman, whose appearance suggested strongly that she had never been within a great many miles of the Pine Barrens, was wearing nothing at all.

I asked Fred what all those cars were doing in his yard, and he said that one of them was in running condition and the rest were its predecessors. The working vehicle was a 1956 Mercury. Each of the seven others had at one time or another been his best car, and each, in turn, had lain down like a sick animal and had died right there in the yard, unless it had been towed home after a mishap elsewhere in the pines. Fred recited, with affection, the history of each car. Of one old Ford, for example, he said, "I upset that up to Speedwell in the creek." And of an even older car, a station wagon, he said, "I busted that one up in the snow. I met a car on a little hill, and hit the brake, and hit a tree." One of the cars had met its end at a narrow bridge about four miles from Hog Wallow, where Fred had hit a state trooper, head on.

The pork was delicious and almost crisp. Fred gave me a potato with it, and a pitcher of melted grease from the frying pan to pour over the potato. He also handed me a loaf of bread and a dish of margarine, saying, "Here's your bread. You can have one piece or two. Whatever you want."

Fred apologized for not having a phone, after I asked where I would have to go to make a call, later on. He said, "I don't have no phone because I don't have no electric. If I had electric, I would have had a phone in here a long time ago." He uses a kerosene lamp, a propane lamp, and two flashlights.

He asked where I was going, and I said that I had no particular destination, explaining that I was in the pines because I found it hard to believe that so much unbroken forest could still exist so near the big Eastern cities, and I wanted to see it while it was still there. "Is that so?" he said, three times. Like many people in the pines, he often says things three times. "Is that so? Is *that* so?"

I asked him what he thought of a plan that has been developed by Burlington and Ocean Counties to create a supersonic jetport in the pines, connected by a spur of the Garden State Parkway to a new city of two hundred and fifty thousand people, also in the pines.

"They've been talking about that for three years, and they've never give up," Fred said.

"It'd be the end of these woods," Bill said. This was the first time I heard Bill speak. I had been there for an hour, and he had not said a word. Without looking up, he said again, "It'd be the end of these woods, I can tell you that."

Fred said, "They could build ten jetports around me. I wouldn't give a damn."

"You ain't going to be around very long," Bill said to him. "It would be the end of these woods."

Fred took that as a fact, and not as an insult. "Yes, it would be the end of these woods," he said. "But there'd be people here you could do business with."

Bill said, "There ain't no place like this left in the country, I don't believe—and I travelled around a little bit, too."

Eventually, I made the request I had intended to make when I walked in the door. "Could I have some water?" I said to Fred. "I have a jerry can and I'd like to fill it at the pump."

"Hell, yes," he said. "That isn't my water. That's God's water. That's God's water. That right, Bill?"

"I *guess* so," Bill said, without looking up. "It's good water, I can tell you that."

"That's God's water," Fred said again. "Take all you want."

Outside, on the pump housing, was a bright-blue coffee tin full of priming water. I primed the pump and, before filling the jerry can, cupped my hands and drank. The water of the Pine Barrens is soft and pure, and there is so much of it that, like the forest above it, it is an incongruity in place and time. In the sand under the pines is a natural reservoir of pure water that, in volume, is the equivalent of a lake seventy-five feet deep with a surface of a thousand square miles. If all the impounding reservoirs, storage reservoirs, and distribution reservoirs in the New York City water system were filled to capacity—from Neversink and Schoharie to the Croton basin and Central Park —the Pine Barrens aquifer would still contain thirty times as much water. So little of this water is used that it can be said to be untapped. Its constant temperature is fifty-four degrees, and, in the language of a hydrological report on the Pine Barrens prepared in 1966 for the United States Geological Survey, "it can be expected to be bacterially sterile, odorless, clear; its chemical purity approaches that of uncontaminated rain-water or melted glacier ice."

In the United States as a whole, only about thirty per cent of the rainfall gets into the ground; the rest is lost to surface runoff or to evaporation, transpiration from leaves, and similar interceptors. In the Pine Barrens, fully half of all precipitation makes its way into the great aquifer, for, as the government report put it, "the loose, sandy soil can imbibe as much as six inches of water per hour." The Pine Barrens rank as one of the greatest natural recharging areas in the world. Thus, the City of New York, say, could take all its daily water requirements out of the pines without fear of diminishing the basic supply. New Jersey could sell the Pine Barrens' "annual ground-water discharge"—the part that at the moment is running off into the Atlantic Ocean—for about two hundred million dollars a year. However, New Jersey does not sell a drop, in part because the state has its own future needs to consider. In the eighteen-seventies, Joseph Wharton, the Philadelphia mineralogist and financier for whom the Wharton School of Finance and Commerce of the University of Pennsylvania is named, recognized the enormous potentiality of the Pine Barrens as a source of water for Philadelphia, and between 1876 and 1890 he gradually acquired nearly a hundred thousand contiguous acres of Pine Barrens land. Wharton's plan called for thirty-three shallow reservoirs in the pines, connected by a network of canals to one stupendous reservoir in Camden, from which an aqueduct would go under the Delaware River and into Philadelphia, where the pure waters of New Jersey would emerge from every tap, replacing a water supply that has been described as "dirty, bacterial soup." Wharton's plan was never executed, mainly because the New Jersey legislature drew itself together and passed prohibiting legislation. Wharton died in 1909. The Wharton Tract, as his immense New Jersey landholding was called, has remained undeveloped. It was considered as a site for the United States Air Force Academy. The state was slow in acquiring it in the public interest, but at last did so in 1955, and the whole of it is now Wharton State Forest.

All the major river systems in the United States are polluted, and so are most of the minor ones, but all the small rivers and streams in the Pine Barrens are potable. The pinelands have their own divide. The Pine Barrens rivers rise in the pines. Some flow west to the Delaware; most flow southeast directly into the sea. There are no through-flowing streams in the pines—no waters coming in from cities and towns on higher ground, as is the case almost everywhere else on the Atlantic coastal plain. I have spent many weekends on canoe trips in the Pine Barrens—on the Wading River, the Oswego, the Batsto, the Mullica. There is no white water in any of these rivers, but they move along fairly rapidly; they are so tortuous that every hundred yards or so brings a new scene—often one that is reminiscent of canoeing country in the northern states and in Canada. Even on bright days, the rivers can be dark and almost sunless under stands of white cedar, and then, all in a moment, they run into brilliant sunshine where the banks rise higher and the forest of oak and pine is less dense. One indication of the size of the water resource below the Pine Barrens is that the streams keep flowing without great declines in volume even in prolonged times of drought. When streams in other parts of New Jersey were reduced to near or total dryness in recent years, the rivers in the pines were virtually unaffected. The characteristic color of the water in the streams is the color of tea—a phenomenon, often called "cedar water," that is familiar in the Adirondacks, as in many other places where tannins and other organic waste from riparian cedar trees combine with iron from the ground water to give the rivers a deep color. In summer, the cedar water is ordinarily so dark that the riverbeds are obscured, and while drifting along one has a feeling of being afloat on a river of fast-moving potable ink. For a few days after a long rain, however, the water is almost colorless. At these times, one can look down into it from a canoe and see the white sand bottom, ten or twelve feet below, and it is as clear as an image in the lens of a camera, with sunken timbers now and again coming into view and receding rapidly, at the speed of the river. Every strand of subsurface grass and every contour of the bottom sand is so sharply defined that the deep water above it seems, and is, irresistibly pure. Sea captains once took the cedar water of the Pine Barrens rivers with them on voyages, because cedar water would remain sweet and potable longer than any other water they could find.

According to the government report, "The Pine Barrens have no equal in the northeastern United States not only for magnitude of water in storage and availability of recharge, but also for the ease and economy with which a large volume of water could be withdrawn." Typically, a pipe less than two inches in diameter driven thirty feet into the ground will produce fifty-five gallons a minute, and a twelve-inch pipe could bring up a million gallons a day. But, with all this, the vulnerability of the Pine Barrens aquifer is disturbing to contemplate. The water table is shallow in the pines, and the aquifer is extremely sensitive to contamination. The sand soil, which is so superior as a catcher of rain, is not good at filtering out or immobilizing wastes. Pollutants, if they happen to get into the water, can travel long distances. Industry or even extensive residential development in the central pinelands could spread contaminants widely through the underground reservoir.

When I had finished filling the jerry can from Fred Brown's pump, I took another drink, and I said to him, "You're lucky to live over such good water."

"You're telling me," he said. "You can put this water in a jug and put it away for a year and it will still be the same. Water from outside of these woods would stink. Outside of these woods, some water stinks when you pump it out of the ground. The people that has dug deep around here claims that there are streams of water under this earth that runs all the time."

In the weeks that followed, I stopped in many times to see Fred, and saw nearly as much of Bill. They rode with me through the woods, in my car, for five and six hours at a time. In the evenings, we returned to Fred's place with food from some peripheral town. It is possible to cross the pines on half a dozen state or federal roads, but very little of interest is visible from them. Several county roads—old crown roads with uneven macadam surfaces—connect the pine communities, but it is necessary to get off the paved roads altogether in order to see much of the forest. The areas are spacious—fifty, sixty, and seventy-five thousand acres—through which run no paved roads of any kind. There are many hundreds of miles of unpaved roads through the pines—two tracks in the sand, with underbrush growing up between them. Hunters use them, and foresters, firefighters, and woodcutters. A number of these sand roads have been there, and have remained unchanged, since before the American Revolution. They developed, for the most part, as Colonial stage routes, trails to charcoal pits, pulpwood-and-lumber roads, and connecting roads between communities that have disappeared from the world. In a place called Washington, five of these roads converge in the forest, as if from star points, and they suggest the former importance of Washington, but all that is left of the town is a single fragment of a stone structure. The sand roads are marked on topographic maps with parallel dotted lines, and driving on them can be something of a sport. It is possible to drive all day on the sand roads, and more than halfway across the state, but most people need to stop fairly often to study the topographic maps, for the roads sometimes come together in fantastic ganglia, and even when they are straight and apparently uncomplicated they constantly fork, presenting unclear choices between the main chance and culs-de-sac, of which there are many hundreds. No matter where we were—far up near Mt. Misery, in the northern part of the pines, or over in the western extremities of the Wharton Tract, or down in the southeast, near the Bass River—Fred kept calling out directions. He always knew exactly where he was going. Fred was nearly forty when the first paved roads were built in the pines. Once, not far from the Godfrey Bridge on the Wading River, he said, "Look at these big pines. You would never think that I was as old as these big pines, would you? I seen all of these big pines grow. I remember this when it was all cut down for charcoal." A short distance away, he pointed into a high stand of pitch pines and scarlet oaks, and he said, "That's the old Joe Holloway field. Holloway had a water-powered sawmill." In another part of the woods, we passed a small bald area, and he said, "That's the Dan Dillett field, where Dan made charcoal." As the car kept moving, bouncing in the undulations of the sand and scraping against blueberry bushes and scrub-oak boughs, Fred kept narrating, picking fragments of the past out of the forest, in moments separated by miles: "Right here in this piece of woods is more rattlesnakes than anyplace else in the State of New Jersey. They had a sawmill in there. They used to kill three or four rattlesnakes when they was watering their horses at noon. Rattlesnakes like water. . . . See that fire tower over there? The man in that tower—you take him fifty yards away from that tower and he's lost. He don't know the woods. He don't know the woods. He don't know the woods. He don't know nothing. He can't even fry a hamburger. . . . I've gunned this part of the woods since I was ten years old. I know every foot of it here. . . . Apple Pie Hill is a thunderstriking high hill. You don't realize how high until you get up here. It's the long slope of a hill that makes a high one. . . . See that open spot in there? A group of girls used to keep a house in there. It was called Noah's Ark. . . . I worked this piece of cedar off here. . . . I worked this bog for Joe Wharton once. My father used to work for Joe Wharton, too. He used to come and stay with my father. Joe Wharton was the nicest man you ever seen. That is, if you didn't lie to him. He was quiet. He didn't smile very often. I don't know as I ever heard him laugh out loud. . . . These are the Hocken Lowlands." The Hocken Lowlands surround the headwaters of Tulpehocken Creek, about five miles northwest of Hog Wallow, and are not identified on maps, not even on the large-scale topographic maps. As we moved along, Fred had a name for almost every rise and dip in the land. "This is Sandy Ridge," he said. "That road once went in to a bog. Houses were there. Now there's nothing there. . . . This is Bony's Hole. A man named Bony used to water his horse here." Every so often, Fred would reach into his pocket and touch up his day with a minimal sip from a half pint of whiskey. He merely touched the bottle to his lips, then put it away. He did this at irregular intervals, and one day, when he had a new half pint, he took more than five hours to reduce the level of the whiskey from the neck to the shoulders of the bottle. At an intersection of two sand roads in the Wharton Tract, he pointed to a depression in the ground and said, "That hole in the ground was the cellar of an old jug tavern. That cellar was where they kept the jugs. There was a town here called Mount. That tavern is where my grandpop got drunk the last time he got drunk in his life. Grandmother went up to get him. When she came in, he said, 'Mary, what are you doing here?' He was so ashamed to see her there—and his daughter with her. He left a jug of whiskey right on the table, and his wife took one of his hands and his daughter the other and they led him out of there and past Washington Field and home to Jenkins Neck. He lived fifty years. He lived fifty years, and growed cranberries. He lived fifty years more, and he was never drunk again."

One evening, when it was almost dark and we were about five miles from Fred's place, he told me to stop, and he said, "See that upland red cedar? I helped set that out." Red cedar is not native in the Pine Barrens, and this one stood alone among the taller oaks and pines, in a part of the forest that seemed particularly remote. "I went to school there, by that red cedar," Fred said. "There was twenty-five of us in the school. We all walked. We wore leather boots in the winter that got soaked through and your feet froze. When you got home, you had to pull off your boots on a bootjack. In the summer, when I was a boy, if you wanted to go anywhere you rolled up your pantlegs, put your shoes on your shoulder, and you walked wherever you was going. The pigs and cows was everywhere. There was wild bulls, wild cows, wild boars. That's how Hog Wallow got its name. They call them the good old days. What do you think of that, Bill?"

"I wish I was back there, I can tell you that," Bill said.

2

The Vanished Towns

DRIVING ALONG a sand road between the vanished town of Calico and the vanished town of Munion Field, we passed a house that was so many miles from any other house that Fred said, with evident admiration, "He got well in away from everybody, didn't he? He got well in away from everybody." Fred made a similar remark every time we passed a house or cabin that was particularly deep and alone in the woods. Getting—or staying—away from everybody is a criterion that apparently continues to mean as much to many of the people in the pines as it did to some of their forebears who first settled there. Tories, for example, fled into the pines during the American Revolution. People with names like Britton and Brower, loyal to the King, and sometimes covered with feathers and tar, left their homes in Colonial cities and took refuge in the Pine Barrens. Also during the eighteenth century, when the farmlands of western New Jersey were heavily populated with Quakers, the Pine Barrens served as a catch basin for Quakers who could not live up to the standards of the Quaker code. A Quaker named Ridgway, for example, brought before a Quaker grand jury in west Jersey and found guilty of working on the Sabbath, was exiled to the pines, where Ridgways live in numbers today. Many young Quakers "went against the testimony" by fighting in the Revolutionary War, and when they came home after Yorktown they found that they were no longer welcome, so they built themselves cabins in the pines. Sooy is a German name more common in the pines than Smith. After the British defeats at Trenton and Princeton, Hessian soldiers deserted the British Army in considerable numbers, and some of them went into the Pine Barrens. Of all the stories of the origins of people in the pines, the one of the Hessian soldiers seems to have achieved the largest circulation elsewhere in New Jersey. Some New Jersey people who do not live in the Pine Barrens assume that everyone in the woods is a Hessian descendant, and the term

"Hessians" is often used in reference to all the people of the region. French Huguenots first settled Mt. Misery (Miséricorde), and Huguenot names, such as Bozarth, remain in the Pine Barrens. Some Negroes fled from slavery into the pines, but the Negro population there has always been close to nil. A Negro named James Still, who was born in the Pine Barrens in 1812, educated himself in medical botany, became known as the Doctor of the Pines, and eventually wrote an autobiography, which was published by J. B. Lippincott in 1877. Dr. Still treated piles with sassafras roots, and he made a "cough balsam" using the roots of spikenard and skunk cabbage. He treated hypochondria, on the other hand, with wit and wisdom, and thereby effected "cures" where many physicians failed. Of one such case, in which he had been called in to replace another doctor, Still wrote, "The doctor treated the case in a scientific manner, without success. I treated it according to the laws of nature." Among medical men in south-central New Jersey, Still was known as Black Jim. American Indians had almost no interest in the pinelands when the whole of the country was theirs, but in the seventeen-fifties they, too, sought asylum in the woods. At an interracial conference that followed a massacre in west Jersey, the tribesmen asked for land they could call their own, and they were given 3,258 acres in the Pine Barrens, where there had never been an Indian settlement of any size or duration. The place was called Brotherton, and was the first Indian reservation in North America. The Indians tried to make it work. They dammed a stream and set up a sawmill and a gristmill, but disease and poverty were the main results of the experiment, and in 1802 most of the Indians went off to northern New York and eventually to Indian Territory. Numerous people in the Pine Barrens today are descended, in part, from Indians who remained. A few are full-blooded, or something close to it. George Crummel, a charcoal-maker who lived in Jenkins Neck and died there in 1964, was the great-grandson of Isaac Cromo, a chief of the Leni Lenape. On the site of the Brotherton reservation is a hamlet called Indian Mills.

The Pine Barrens have been something besides a place of retreat, however. Isolation was not the goal of most of the early Englishmen, Welshmen, and Scots, who arrived, in large part, via New England, and whose names remain—Applegate, Wescoat, Jenkins, Brown, Cranmer (now Crammer or Cramer as well as Cranmer, a prodigious family that traces itself to Thomas Cranmer, the Archbishop of Canterbury), Bartlett, Leek, Leeds, Southwick, Wainwright. One thing that attracted people to the pines was good money in smuggling—a respectable business in Colonial America. The Pine Barrens were a smuggler's El Dorado, for all that wilderness so close to New York and Philadelphia was extraordinary even two hundred years ago, and through the inlets from the sea up the Pine Barrens rivers went hundreds of thousands of tons of sugar, molasses, tea, and coffee, while ships of the Royal Navy patrolled the roadsteads of Boston, New York, and Philadelphia. Cargoes were transferred to wagons and sent inland over the sand roads, often moving by night. One of the earliest of the merchant smugglers was John Mathis, whose contemporaries always called him Great John. His descendants are spread across the pine belt today. He sent lumber from the Pine Barrens to islands in the Caribbean, and when the ships came back he smuggled in his fortune in rum.

There was also iron in the pinelands. Most of the now vanished towns in the pines were iron towns—small, precursive Pittsburghs, in every part of the forest, where fine grades of pig and wrought iron were made. One of the geological curiosities of the Pine Barrens is that rainwater soaking down through fallen pine needles and other forest litter takes on enough acid to leach out iron from the sands below; the dissolved iron moves underground into the streams, where it oxidizes on contact with the air and forms a patch of scum on the surface that is partly rust brown and partly iridescent blue, and resembles an oil slick left by an outboard motor; drifting over to the edges of the streams, this iron-oxide film permeates the sands and gravels of the riverbanks and cements them together into a sandstone composite that has been known for centuries as bog iron. From it ironmasters of the Pine Barrens made cannonballs by the thousand and sent them by wagon over the sand roads and on to the Continental Army at Valley Forge and elsewhere. They brought in seashells for flux, and used charcoal from the pinewoods to fire their forges and furnaces. They made cannon as well as shot, and they ordnanced the

War of 1812 as well as the American Revolution. The twenty-four-pounders with which Stephen Decatur armed his flagship when he took his Marines to Algiers, Tunisia, and Tripoli were cast at Hanover Furnace, in the Pine Barrens, in 1814, and Decatur himself was there to supervise the casting and to test the product. Forty-five years later, an unsigned article in the May, 1859, *Atlantic* described the scene when the new guns came out of their molds: "Decatur ordered each one to be loaded with repeated charges of powder and ball, and pointed into the woods. Then, for miles between the grazed and quivering boles, crashed the missiles of destruction, startling bear and deer and squirrel and raccoon, and leaving traces of their passage which are even still occasionally discovered." Ironworkers in the pines made the steam cylinder for one of John Fitch's experimental steamboats, and they made the wrought-iron fence that once surrounded Independence Hall. They made nails, firebacks, sugar-mill gudgeons, Dutch ovens, and kettles that could hold as much as a hundred and twenty-five gallons. Bog iron is remarkably reluctant to rust. In some graveyards in the Pine Barrens, there are iron tombstones, and around old houses are walks made of iron flagstones. Iron stoves that bear the town name Atsion over their fuelling doors were made in a community that had a population of seven hundred in the early nineteenth century and has a population of fifteen today. A schooner named Atsion, loaded with stoves, made regular runs down the Mullica River and up the coast to New York and on to Albany. Atsion Forge was at one time owned by Samuel Richards, who built a glorious mansion in Atsion. The mansion is still there, off Route 206, in the Wharton Tract. It has iron windowsills. Atsion Forge had been established in 1765 by a man named Charles Read, who also built a furnace at Batsto, about ten miles away. In 1770, a Philadelphian named John Cox bought Batsto for twenty-three hundred and fifty pounds. Cox was a member of the first Committee of Correspondence and a member of the Council of Safety. With the coming of war, he became a lieutenant colonel and, eventually, assistant quartermaster general of the Continental Armies. His ironworks at Batsto flourished on war contracts from the Quartermaster Corps. In 1778, Cox sold Batsto for forty thousand pounds—a capital gain of about sixteen hundred per cent. The deal was exquisitely complicated, involving a number of new owners, among them Nathanael Greene, the quartermaster general under whom Cox served, and Charles Pettit, another assistant quartermaster general. Cox, furthermore, arranged to repurchase a one-twelfth share in Batsto for himself. Batsto was to reach its most developed stage in the eighteen-thirties and eighteen-forties, when the town had a population of eight hundred. Batsto, like Atsion, is one of the few iron towns that remain in the Pine Barrens. The headquarters of the Wharton State Forest is there, and the town, which was purchased in its entirety by Joseph Wharton in 1876, spreads out around the Batsto manor house much as it did a hundred years ago. The state has restored its water-powered sawmill, and sawyers cut white cedar there and make cedar shingles for use in restoration of Batsto buildings. Batsto is a functioning relic. In its gristmill, the great stones grind corn, and the miller sells cornmeal to the public.

The furnaces of the Pine Barrens were started up each year in the spring when the ice was gone and spillways from dammed streams again turned the waterwheels that powered giant bellows, which kept the furnaces in blast until winter froze them out. Men worked in twelve-hour shifts. There were no days off, and the happiest day of the year was the day the furnace went out of blast. In the furnace towns, bog iron was crushed under great stamping hammers, and in the forge towns pig iron was worked into anconies of wrought iron under forge hammers that weighed more than five hundred pounds. Miles away, teamsters coming over the sand roads with loads of shells from the coast could hear the din through the forest, as could ore raisers out in the bogs, and colliers—as charcoal-makers were known in the pines—working at their pits. Caleb Earle, company clerk in a furnace town called Martha, kept a semi-official diary from March 31, 1808, to April 27, 1815. It is terse and sporadic, averaging about sixty-five short entries a year, but it is the only contemporary record of life in a Pine Barrens town. Martha Furnace was built in 1793, a few miles southeast of Jenkins. The furnace has long since collapsed, and a large earth-covered mound remains where a high double-walled pyramid of bricks once stood. The spillway runs back to a broken dam on the Oswego River at Martha Pond. There were about fifty houses in the town, a central mansion, a school, and a small hospital—all interspersed with stands of catalpa trees, which were planted throughout the town and are about all that remains of it. With the exception of the furnace mound, there is not a trace of a structure in Martha now. The streets are bestrewn with green and blue glittering slag, but they are indistinguishable from the sand roads that come through the woods from several directions to the town, and if it were not for the old and weirdly leaning catalpa trees, it would be possible to pass through Martha without sensing its difference from the surrounding woodland.

> January 4, 1809—Frost stopped furnace wheel several times.
>
> January 7, 1809—Ore teams hauled hay. Blew the furnace out at eight o-clock P.M. All hands drunk.
>
> April 20, 1809—At twenty-five minutes past two o-clock P.M., put the furnace in blast. Delaney and Cox fillers. Hedger putting in the ore. Donaghau banksman.

Some of the ironworkers were indentured servants, and some of these had been English criminals. Most were not indentured. Each man's specialty fitted in somewhere on a scale of status, with colliers at the low end, founders at the top, and, somewhere between, blacksmiths, pattern-makers, and molders.

> July 28, 1809—Molders all agreed to quit work and went to the beach.
>
> July 30, 1809—Molders returned from the beach. J. Ventling drunk and eating eggs at the slitting mill. Josh Townsend wanting to fight J. Williamson. Furnace boiled and the metal consolidated in the gutter.
>
> July 31, 1809—Molders all idle.
>
> August 1, 1809—This month begins with good weather. Molders commenced molding for the first time since they came from the beach.

In the idiom of the community, a man who quit without giving notice was said to have made a clandestine retreat, and childbirth was spoken of as a muster or a general muster.

January 29, 1809—Terence Toole made a clandestine retreat from the chopping. Left his ax, blankets, etc.

December 6, 1810—The men begin to complain of beef. They want pork.

December 21, 1810—Rain. Furnace made very bad iron owing to the wet weather.

May 27, 1811—Cross carting logs for ore cabin. Mary Griffith made a muster.

July 4, 1811—Independence. May the name of Washington be immortal and the federal constitution may it never fail.

July 10, 1811—Mary Luker made a general muster and brought forth a daughter.

July 27, 1811—William Rose and his father both drunk and lying on the crossway.

February 18, 1812—Teams carting ore from Sassafras. Jane Hamilton conceived and brought forth a son. Women are all very fruitful, multiply, and replenish.

August 17, 1812—Molders a deer hunting. George Townsend shot one but did not get it. Mr. Evans surveying. Furnace making bad iron.

September 17, 1812—Jane Hamilton was this day tried by the synod of her church. The crime alleged against her was for using spiritual liquor, but acquitted.

October 13, 1812—Election at Bodine's. Hands chiefly there. Some very drunk.

October 30, 1812—Molders out a hunting. J. Townsend killed a deer.

December 16, 1812—Sarah Taylor brought down a load of cheese. William Rose died very sudden in the coaling, supposed drunk.

April 12, 1813—William Mick's widow arrived here in pursuit of J. Mick, who she says has knocked her up.

June 2, 1813—Great conflagration. The furnace and warehouse was this day entirely consumed, but fortunately no lives lost. John Craig got very much burnt.

August 23, 1814—Has a great fire in the pines.

November 14, 1814—The dam broke this morning. All the ore-raisers at work at it.

February 24, 1815—This day we had news of peace confirmed. Teams all standing still. Snowing and raining.

Bodine's Tavern, where the men of Martha went to vote on October 13, 1812, was a few miles south of Martha, on the

Wading River. The jug taverns of the pines—so called because rare was the traveller who passed by one without going in to top up his liquor jug—were places of assembly for many public events, from elections and town meetings to community suppers and the regular drills of the standing militia. On election days, the suffrage was exercised with abandon. Not only was the bar open, but the local candidates were there, and the winner—as a rule—was the man who stood the greatest number of drinks for the electorate. The voters drank metheglin (mead and water with a zest of herbs), cider royall (highly concentrated cider), mimbo (rum and muscovado sugar), straight rum, whiskey, gin, beer. The same men drank the same drinks when they turned up at the same tavern as militiamen assembling for Training Day, an antecedent of what today would be a National Guard meeting. Training Days tended to mock rather than to improve military skills and procedures. While the tavernkeepers kept making rounds with mimbo and metheglin, drums rolled and fifes put a sense of celebration into the air. Officers, wearing stunning blue American uniforms that were braided in gold and studded with brass, rapped out sharp orders, which no one obeyed. After a little more mimbo, fights began to occur in the ranks. There were casualties. Some men fell as a result of blows received, and many more toppled over without assistance. Nonetheless, it was apparently important that there be some simulacrum of command, for Captain Townsend, of Martha, was summarily court-martialled at Bodine's Tavern on April 1, 1814, a Training Day, for being too drunk to give orders.

Jug taverns were located at most of the important intersections of the sand roads, since the volume of freight and passenger travel was considerable in the eighteenth century and early nineteenth century in the pines. One major route ran from Philadelphia to Tuckerton, a coastal town on the edge of the Pine Barrens and the third officially established port of entry in the United States. The Philadelphia-Tuckerton stage stopped at Long-a-Coming, New Jersey (now Berlin), and then moved east through the pines, to Atsion, Quaker Bridge, Mount, and Washington, and on to the Wading River and eventually to Tuckerton. A large part of this road still exists, can be driven in an automobile, and has not been paved, oiled, or even scraped since it was cut through the woods when New Jersey was a royal colony. In some places between Atsion and Quaker Bridge, the road divides, because the wagon and stagecoach traffic was so heavy that it was necessary to have eastbound and westbound lanes in what may have been the first dual highway in North America. Bodine's Tavern was built where the Tuckerton Road crossed the Wading River. Similarly, a man named Arthur Thompson built Thompson's Tavern at Quaker Bridge, where a group of Quakers had put up a bridge over the Batsto River in 1772 in memory of numerous Quakers who had drowned while attempting to ford the stream. In 1805, four botanists who were staying at Thompson's Tavern went into the woods near Quaker Bridge and—in what proved to be a major botanical discovery—found an odd, small, beautiful fern (*Schizaea pusilla*, the curly grass fern), which grows almost exclusively in the Pine Barrens. Jonathan Cramer ran the tavern at Mount, where Fred Brown's grandfather had his last drink on earth. The tavern in Washington, in some ways the most important one in the pines, was used by the Committee of Safety during the Revolution as recruiting headquarters for the area. When a reasonably young and healthy-looking ironworker came through the door, a recruiting sergeant would clap him on the shoulder, buy him a drink, and attempt to persuade him to fight for his independence.

Weddings were held at Washington Tavern, and to one wedding during the Revolution came an uninvited guest named Joseph Mulliner, who, so the story goes, jabbed a pistol into the groom's ribs and told him to leave, which the groom did. Waving his pistol, Mulliner danced with the bride, and then, after drinking a yard or so of ale, retreated into the night alone. Mulliner, who became a legend in the pines, was the leader of a band of outlaws, and it was said that he recognized the groom as a fellow-outlaw and a deadly personal enemy. In general, Mulliner's biography has been cleaned up by romantic retelling, and it was even converted into fiction by Charles J. Peterson, whose novel *Kate Aylesford*, published in 1855, is set in the Pine Barrens during the Revolution and has for a villain a dashing character modelled on Mulliner, who kidnaps the heroine. Mulliner was actually one of a class of particularly brutal criminals who lived in numbers in the pines during the war and called themselves Pine Refugees. This was meant to suggest that they were Tories, like the Brittons and the Browers, and that they were taking refuge for their own safety, were loyal to the King, and were therefore serving the King when they murdered people committed to the Revolutionary cause. The Refugees, who travelled—frequently masked—in packs on the sand roads, actually killed and robbed as many Tories as Whigs. They were known also as Pine Robbers and Pine Banditti. Posses hunted them down. When a Pine Robber was shot, people assembled to celebrate. Richard Bird, a gang leader like Mulliner, was shot by a posse that had followed him to a cabin in the woods where he was visiting a girl. The shot that killed him was fired through a window, and when the posse went inside they found the girl going through his pockets. The Pine Robbers raped women of almost all ages, they killed clergymen, and they stabbed or shot many people who knelt before them and begged for life. In 1781, Joseph Mulliner was caught, dancing with a girl at another party he had crashed, and he was tried and hanged.

A considerable part of the goods that moved inland over the sand roads during the Revolution had been captured at sea by pirates from the pines who carried letters of marque from the Continental Congress authorizing them to attack, possess, and sell British ships and British cargoes. During the war, up and down the American coast, privateers captured well over a thousand British ships, worth upward of twenty million dollars. New Jersey pirates hauled so many of these ships into the Pine Barrens rivers that British hulls and scattered timbers are still in the riverbeds. There is a dam at Penny Pot, on the Great Egg Harbor River, that was made from salvaged ship timbers. It was built to be nothing more than a cranberry dam, but it has in it seventy-five thousand dollars' worth of teak. One New Jersey sailor went out to sea in a small whaleboat with nine other men and came back into the Mullica River with a British warship and a British brig, which were auctioned, like most of the New Jersey prizes, at The Forks, near Batsto. In 1778, England tried to put down the New Jersey privateers. A flotilla of ships and eight hundred soldiers surprised Chestnut Neck, a fort across the mouth of the Mullica from Tuckerton, and wiped it out. The force then moved upstream, intending to destroy the ships of privateers along the way and ultimately to raze the ironworks at Batsto. But a small boy warned Batsto that the British soldiers were approaching, and before they could do much of anything they were ambushed and their campaign was finished.

The iron industry in the Pine Barrens lasted for about half a century after the Revolution, and, curiously, reached its point of highest development just before it vanished. In the eighteen-thirties, the iron towns were as populous and productive as they would ever be, and other industries that had developed concomitantly were flourishing, too. Woodcutters supplied great amounts of cordwood to New York and to Philadelphia, as they had for a hundred years. Sawyers, working mainly with white cedar, made shingles, clapboards, lumber, lath, and shipboards. Cedar panelling from the Pine Barrens had been used since before the Revolution in the homes of the rich of Manhattan. Cabinetmakers kept up the high standards of their predecessor Benjamin Randolph, who lived in Speedwell, just north of Hog Wallow, and owned an iron furnace there. Randolph made the writing desk that Thomas Jefferson used when he wrote the Declaration of Independence, and he also made a wing chair that would be auctioned, in the twentieth century, for thirty-three thousand dollars. The era of iron in the pines ended after high-grade bituminous coal and iron ore were discovered in western Pennsylvania. The ore in western Pennsylvania was superior to the bog iron of New Jersey, not in the quality of the iron inside it but in the economy with which the iron could be got out. Coal had every advantage over charcoal. Iron smelting on a large scale began in Pennsylvania around 1840. Batsto Furnace blew out for the last time in 1848. Martha Furnace and Atsion Forge closed down about then, too. In less than twenty years, no ironworks of any kind were left in the pines. Depletion of the wood supply helped to force the closings. Each furnace used a thousand acres of pine per year, and the trees could not grow rapidly enough to permit an equilibrium. As early as 1846, the colporteur records of the American Tract Society reported, "The wood is generally gone, so the people are poorer than they were a few years ago and are likely to remain poor. Towns and populous neighborhoods can never be, on such barren sand." The pine towns did not give up at once, however. They tried to make other things. For example, the Wading River Forge & Slitting Mill, where pig iron from nearby Martha had been made into nails and other cut products, was converted into a paper mill. Heavy papers were manufactured there from marsh grasses. Some writing paper was produced as well, but it was yellow from the iron in the Wading River, and the line was discontinued. When four brothers named Harris bought the paper mill in 1855, the name of the community around it was changed from McCartyville to Harrisville. The Harrises were fussy but benevolent employers. Each man who worked for them got a rent-free house, a garden, horse-drawn-ambulance service, free ice, and a dollar and twenty-five cents a day for working from six until six. Harrisville was a neat little town, with picket fences, and with gas lamps lining its streets. If Richard Harris, one of the brothers, happened to see a gate ajar, he would look up the resident of the house behind the gate and tell him to try, please, not to be so unkempt. Ultimately, Harrisville could not compete with paper mills in other parts of the country. The ruins of the great paper factory—high, arched stone walls three feet thick—have gradually crumbled, but enough of them remains to suggest the scale of the original structure, which was seven hundred and fifty feet long. Of the town itself and the gas lamps there is nothing. Elsewhere in the Pine Barrens, glass factories were built in an attempt to find an industry that could replace iron. The first mason jar was made in the pines. Herman City, a hamlet in the Pine Barrens today, was given its name by visionary glassmakers who imagined tall buildings rising above the pine trees, financed by fortunes made in glass. Windowpanes were manufactured at Batsto, and also panes for gas street lamps, but by 1867 the surrounding forest was so cut over that the glassworks were forced to close for lack of fuel. The walls, before long, fell. Now, a hundred years later, a young archeologist named Budd Wilson has removed the sand and turf from the remains of the Batsto glass factories, no trace of which was above the surface. The project has the appearance of a dig on an island in the Aegean. Wilson has revealed the floors of the factories and the intricate brickwork, still intact, of the bases of glassmaking ovens. Perhaps on these foundations, or perhaps on replica foundations nearby, Wilson hopes to have glass factories again in operation in Batsto soon, as a part of the general restoration of the town.

3

The Separate World

IN 1859, when the population of the central Pine Barrens was about as large as it has ever been, the area had nonetheless remained wild enough for the *Atlantic* to report, "It is a region aboriginal in savagery, grand in the aspects of untrammelled Nature; where forests extend in uninterrupted lines over scores of miles; where we may wander a good day's journey without meeting half-a-dozen human faces; where stately deer will bound across our path, and bears dispute our passage through the cedar-brakes; where, in a word, we may enjoy the undiluted essence, the perfect wildness, of woodland life." The magazine feared, however, that accelerated development would soon clear this wild country. "It is scarcely too much to anticipate that, within five years, thousands of acres, now dense with pines and cedars of a hundred rings, will be laid out in blooming market-gardens and in fields of generous corn," the article concluded. "Five years hence, bears and deer will be a tradition, panthers and raccoons a myth, partridges and quails a vain and melancholy recollection, in what shall then be known as what was once the pines." The trend the *Atlantic* anticipated was the reverse of the one that actually took place. As the last of the iron furnaces gradually blew out and the substitute industries failed, people either left the pines or began to lead self-sufficient backwoods lives, and while the rest of the State of New Jersey developed toward its twentieth-century aspect, the Pine Barrens all but returned to their pre-Colonial desolation, becoming, as they have remained, a distinct and separate world. The people of the pines came to be known as pineys—a term that is as current today as it was at the turn of the century. After a generation or two had lived in isolation, the pineys began to fear people from the outside, and travellers often reported that when they approached a cabin in the pines the people scattered and hid behind trees. This was interpreted, by some, as a mark of lunacy. It was simply fear of the unknown.

The pineys had little fear of their surroundings, from which they drew an adequate living. A yearly cycle evolved that is still practiced, but by no means universally, as it once was. With the first warmth of spring, pineys took their drags—devices with tines, something like hand cultivators—and went into the lowland forests to gather sphagnum moss. This extraordinary material has such a capacity for absorbing water that one can squeeze it and twist it and wring it a dozen times and water will still come pouring out. Since the water is acidulous and somewhat antiseptic, sphagnum moss was used by soldiers during the Revolution when they lacked ordinary bandages. Florists provided a large part of the market for the pineys' moss. Boxes of cut flowers sent out by florists' shops all over the East used to contain—under and around the flowers—protective beds of sphagnum from the pines. Plastic moss has largely replaced sphagnum moss in the floral trade, but a market remains for it, and some people still gather it.

In June and July, when the wild blueberries of the Pine Barrens ripened on the bush, the pineys hung large homemade baskets around their necks, bent the blueberry bushes over the baskets, and beat the stems with short clubs. The berries, if just ripe enough, rained into the baskets. Fred Brown told me one day that he had knocked off his share of "huckleberries" in his time, and that many people still go out after them every summer. In the vernacular of the pines, huckleberries are blueberries, wild or cultivated. Huckleberries are also huckleberries, and this confuses outsiders but not pineys. Fred explained to me, when I pressed him, that "hog huckleberries" are huckleberries and "sugar huckleberries" are blueberries. He said, "Ain't nothing for a man to go out and knock off two hundred pounds in less than a day." In 1967, the average price for wild blueberries was fourteen cents a pound. People who gather wild blueberries now use No. 2 galvanized tubs instead of baskets. They beat the bushes with lengths of rubber hose. "Wild berries got a better taste than cultivated berries," Fred said. "Mrs. Wagner's Pies won't make pies with just cultivated berries." Millions of blueberry bushes grow wild in the pines, but when a forester who was doing field work for a doctoral thesis recently asked a piney assistant to cut one down, the piney refused.

Cranberries followed blueberries in the cycle of the pines. Cranberries grow wild along the streams and are white in the summer and red in the fall. In the eighteen-sixties and eighteen-seventies, people began to transplant them to the cleared and excavated bogs where ore raisers had removed bog iron, and that was the beginning of commercial cranberry growing in the Pine Barrens, where about a third of the United States total is now grown. Cranberry bogs are shallow basins, dammed on all sides, so that streams can fill them in late autumn and keep cold winter winds from drying out the vines. The older bogs were turfed out by hand, and the dams were built from the turf. In the fall, the berries were harvested by hand, with many-tined wooden scoops that went through the vines like large claws. Cranberry scoops are so primitive in appearance that they are sold as antiques in shops on Third Avenue and in Bucks County. In a few bogs in the Pine Barrens, scoops are still used, and only five years ago all bogs used them.

In winter, the cycle moved on to cordwood and charcoal. Woodcutters, in the seventeenth century, were among the first people in the pines. They were needed in the iron era, they remained when it was over, and they are still there. They are getting a good price for their pulpwood—seven dollars a cord. With a chain saw, a man can cut a cord of pine in less than an hour. "Oak isn't worth nothing, but the pine is way up," Fred Brown said one day. Charcoal burning also continued beyond the iron era and was actually a major occupation in the Pine Barrens until the Second World War. In the eighteen-fifties, fifty schooners made regular runs with charcoal from the Pine Barrens to New York. Countless four-mule teams hauled charcoal over the sand roads to Philadelphia in covered wagons. Eight-mule teams hauled larger wagons, full of the best grade, to the Philadelphia mint. Almost any piney knew how to make charcoal, and the woods were full of little clearings, which is one reason that so many culs-de-sac branch from the sand roads. Full-time colliers specialized in charcoal to the exclusion of most of the other occupations in the yearly cycle. They frequently made their pits with someone else's wood. They moved around a lot, nomadically, living in shacks that had no floors, or in tepee-shaped structures made of cedar poles and turf. They stored their supplies—mainly salt pork and apple whiskey—in turf-covered dugouts, in which they hid and sometimes died when wildfires overcame the forest. Charcoal pits were actually aboveground. They had the shape of beehives and were twenty feet high. To make them, colliers stacked cordwood in vertical tiers and covered the wood with chunks of sandy turf, known as floats. The colliers dropped burning kindling into a hole in the top and then sealed it over. They poked holes in the sides with a stick called a fagan, and kept watch over the pit day and night. If blue smoke came out, too much oxygen was involved in the combustion, and the colliers plugged a few holes. If white steam came out, the wood inside was charring perfectly. This went on for about ten days. The late George Crummel, the Indian collier of Jenkins Neck, had a dog that could watch a pit and would awaken him if the ventilating holes needed attention. With Crummel gone, there are only two or three colliers left in the Pine Barrens. The last important market was for bagged charcoal for back-yard cooking, but the modern briquette has all but eliminated that. Most "charcoal" briquettes are made in gasoline refineries as a petroleum by-product. On this subject, Fred Brown said one day, "These here charcoal brick-a-bats, or whatever you call them, that they sell—look at them, all you have to do is *look* at them. You *know* they didn't come from no tree."

Venison, of course, was available the year round to pineys, who have always felt detached about game laws. The sphagnum-blueberry-cranberry-wood-and-charcoal cycle was supplemented in other ways as well—most notably in December, when shiploads of holly, laurel, mistletoe, ground pine, greenbriar, inkberry, plume grass, and boughs of pitch pine were sent to New York for sale as Christmas decorations. Small birch trees were cut in short lengths and turned into candleholders. People who specialized in pine cones became known as pineballers, and the term is still used. The Christmas business continues to be an important source of income in the pines. Modern pineballers pick about three thousand cones in a day. They like to get them from the dwarf forests—the Plains, as they are called—because the trees there are shorter than men, and can be picked clean. At the moment, pineballing is not as remunerative as huckleberrying. Pineballers are getting only three dollars and seventy-five cents per thousand cones, or about eleven dollars for a day's work. Pineys once sold rosin, turpentine, pitch tar, and shoemaker's wax. They cut laurel stems to sell to makers of pipes. They dug the roots of wild indigo for medicinal use (wild indigo is, among other things, a stimulant), and they cut the bark of wild cherry (a tonic) and collected pipsissewa leaves (an astringent). They sold laurel, ilex, and rhododendron to landscape gardeners. They sent wild flowers into the cities—trailing arbutus, swamp pinks, wild magnolias, lupine, azaleas, Pine Barrens gentians. They made birdhouses out of cedar slabs, and they still do. They sold box turtles by the gross to people in Philadelphia, who used the turtles to keep cellars free of snails—a market that has declined.

While isolation in the woods was bringing out self-reliance, it was also contributing to other developments that eventually attracted more attention. After the pine towns lost touch, to a large extent, with the outside world, some of the people slid into illiteracy, and a number slid further than that. Marriages were pretty casual in the pines late in the nineteenth century and early in the twentieth. For lawful weddings, people had to travel beyond the woods, to a place like Mt. Holly. Many went to native "squires," who performed weddings for a fee of one dollar. No questions were asked, even if the squires recognized the brides and the grooms as people they had married to other people a week or a month before. Given the small population of the pines, the extreme rarity of new people coming in, and the long span of time that most families had been there, some relationships were extraordinarily complicated and a few were simply incestuous. To varying degrees, there was a relatively high incidence in the pines of what in the terms of the era was called degeneracy, feeblemindedness, or mental deficiency.

In 1913, startling publicity was given to the most unfortunate stratum of the pine society, and the effects have not yet faded. In that year, Elizabeth Kite, a psychological researcher, published a report called "The Pineys," which had resulted from two years of visits to cabins in the pines. Miss Kite worked for the Vineland Training School, on the southern edge of the Pine Barrens, where important early work was being done with people of subnormal intelligence, and she was a fearless young woman who wore spotless white dresses as she rode in

a horse-drawn wagon through the woods. Her concern for the people there became obvious to the people themselves, who grew fond of her, and even dependent upon her, and a colony for the care of the "feebleminded" was founded in the northern part of the Pine Barrens as a result of her work. Her report told of children who shared their bedrooms with pigs, of men who could not count beyond three, of a mother who walked nine miles with her children almost every day to get whiskey, of a couple who took a wheelbarrow with them when they went out drinking, so that one could wheel the other home. "In the heart of the region, scattered in widely separated huts over miles of territory, exists today a group of human beings as distinct in morals and manners as to excite curiosity and wonder in the mind of any outsider brought into contact with them," Miss Kite wrote. "They are recognized as a distinct people by the normal communities living on the borders of their forests." The report included some extremely gnarled family trees, such as one headed by Sam Bender, who conceived a child with his daughter, Mollie Bender Brooks, whose husband, Billie Brooks, sometimes said the child had been fathered by his wife's brother rather than her father, both possibilities being strong ones. When a district nurse was sent around to help clean up Mollie's house, chickens and a pig were found in the kitchen, and the first implement used in cleaning the house was a hoe. Mollie, according to Miss Kite, was "good-looking and sprightly, which fact, coupled with an utter lack of sense of decency, made her attractive even to men of otherwise normal intelligence." When Billie and all of their children were killed in a fire, Mollie said cheerfully, "Well, they was all insured. I'm still young and can easy start another family." Miss Kite reported some relationships that are almost impossible to follow. Of the occupants of another cabin, she wrote, "That May should call John 'Uncle' could be accounted for on the basis of a childish acceptance of 'no-matter-what' conditions, for the connection was that her mother was married to the brother of John's other woman's second man, and her mother's sister had had children by John. This bond of kinship did not, however, keep the families long together." Miss Kite also told of a woman who came to ask for food at a state almshouse on a bitter winter day. The people at the almshouse gave her a large burlap sack containing a basket of potatoes, a basket of turnips, three cabbages, four pounds of pork, five pounds of rye flour, two pounds of sugar, and some tea. The woman shouldered the sack and walked home cross-country through snow. Thirty minutes after she reached her home, she had a baby. No one helped her deliver it, nor had anyone helped her with the delivery of her nine other children.

Miss Kite's report was made public. Newspapers printed excerpts from it. All over the state, people became alarmed about conditions in the Pine Barrens—a region most of them had never heard of. James T. Fielder, the governor of New Jersey, travelled to the pines, returned to Trenton, and sought to increase his political momentum by recommending to the legislature that the Pine Barrens be somehow segregated from the rest of New Jersey in the interest of the health and safety of the people of the state at large. "I have been shocked at the conditions I have found," he said. "Evidently these people are a serious menace to the State of New Jersey because they produce so many persons that inevitably become public charges. They have inbred, and led lawless and scandalous lives, till they have become a race of imbeciles, criminals, and defectives." Meanwhile, H. H. Goddard, director of the research laboratory at the Vineland Training School and Miss Kite's immediate superior, had taken the genealogical charts that Miss Kite had painstakingly assembled, pondered them, extrapolated a bit, and published what became a celebrated treatise on a family called Kallikak—a name that Goddard said he had invented to avoid doing harm to real people. According to the theory set forth in the treatise, nearly all pineys were descended from one man. This man, Martin Kallikak, conceived an illegitimate son with an imbecile barmaid. Martin's bastard was said to be the forebear of generations of imbeciles, prostitutes, epileptics, and drunks. Martin himself, however, married a normal girl, and among their progeny were generations of normal and intelligent people, including doctors, lawyers, politicians, and a president of Princeton University. Goddard coined the name Kallikak from the Greek *kalós* and *kakós*—"good" and "bad." Goddard's work has been discredited, but its impact, like that of Governor Fielder's proposal to segregate the Pine Barrens, was powerful in its time. Even Miss Kite seemed to believe that there was some common flaw in the blood of all the people of the pines. Of one pinelands woman, Miss Kite wrote, "Strangely enough, this woman belonged originally to good stock. No piney blood flowed in her veins."

The result of all this was a stigma that has never worn off. A surprising number of people in New Jersey today seem to think that the Pine Barrens are dark backlands inhabited by hostile and semi-literate people who would as soon shoot an outsider as look at him. A policeman in Trenton who had never been to the pines—"only driven through on the way downa shore," as people usually say—once told me, in an anxious tone, that if I intended to spend a lot of time in the Pine Barrens I was asking for trouble. Some of the gentlest of people—botanists, canoemen, campers—spend a great deal of time in the pines, but their influence has not been sufficient to correct an impression, vivid in some parts of the state for fifty years, that the pineys are weird and sometimes dangerous barefoot people who live in caves, marry their sisters, and eat snakes. Pineys are, for the most part, mild and shy, but their resentment is deep, and they will readily and forcefully express it. The unfortunate people that Miss Kite described in her report were a minor fraction of the total population of the Pine Barrens, and the larger number suffered from it, and are still suffering from it. This appalled Elizabeth Kite, who said to an interviewer in 1940, some years before her death, "Nothing would give me greater pleasure than to correct the idea that has unfortunately been given by the newspapers regarding the pines. Anybody who lived in the pines was a piney. I think it a most terrible calamity that the newspapers publicly took the term and gave it the degenerate sting. Those families who were not potential state cases did not interest me as far as my study was concerned. I have no language in which I can express my admiration for the pines and the people who live there."

The people of the Pine Barrens turn cold when they hear the word "piney" spoken by anyone who is not a native. Over the years since 1913, in many places outside the pines, the stigma of degeneracy has been concentrated in that word. A part of what hurts them is that they themselves are fond of the word. They refer to one another freely, and frequently, as pineys. They have a strong regional pride, and, in a way that is not at all unflattering to them, they *are* different from the run of the people of the state. A visitor who stays awhile in the Pine Barrens soon feels that he is in another country, where attitudes and ambitions are at variance with the American norm. People who drive around in the pines and see houses like Fred Brown's, with tarpaper peeling from the walls, and automobiles overturned in the front yard, often decide, as they drive on, that they have just looked destitution in the face. I wouldn't call it that. I have yet to meet anyone living in the Pine Barrens who has in any way indicated envy of people who live elsewhere. One reason there are so many unpainted houses in the Pine Barrens is that the pineys believe, correctly, that their real-estate assessments would be higher if their houses were painted. Some pineys who make good money in blueberries or cranberries or in jobs on the outside would never think of painting their houses. People from other parts of New Jersey will say of Pine Barrens people, "They don't like to work. They can't seem to hold jobs." This, too, is a judgment based on outside values. What the piney usually says is "I hate to be tied down long to any one job." That remark is made so often in the pines that it is almost a local slogan. It expresses an attitude born of the old pines cycle—sphagnum in the spring, berries in the summer, coaling when the weather is cold. With the plenitude of the woodland around them—and, historically, behind them—pineys are bored with the idea of doing the same thing all year long, in every weather. Many of them have to, of course. Many work at regular jobs outside the woods. But many try that and give it up, preferring part-time labor—always at rest in the knowledge that no one who knows the woods and is willing to do a little work on his own is ever going to go hungry. The people have no difficulty articulating what it is that gives them a special feeling about the landscape they live in; they know that their environment is unusual and they know why they value it. Some, of course, put it with more finesse than others do. "I'm just a woods boy," a fellow named Jim Leek said to me one day. "There ain't nobody bothers you here. You can be alone. I'm just a woods boy. I wouldn't want to live in a town." When he said "town," he meant one of the small communities in the pines; he preferred living in the woods to living in a Pine Barrens town. When pineys talk about going to "the city," they usually mean Mt. Holly or the Moorestown Mall or the Two Guys from Harrison store on Route 206. When Jim Leek said "nobody bothers you" and "you can be alone," he was sounding two primary themes of the pines. Bill Wasovwich said one day, "The woods just look nice and it's more quieter. It's quiet anywhere in the pines. That's why I like it here." Another man, Scorchy Jones, who works for the state Fish and Game Division, said this to an interviewer from a small New Jersey radio station: "A sense of security is high among us. We were from pioneers. We know how to survive in the woods. Here in these woods areas, you have a reputation. A dishonest person can't survive in the community. You have to maintain your reputation, or you would have to jump from place to place. A man lives by his reputation and by his honesty and by his ambition to work. If he doesn't have it, he would be an outcast. These people have the reputations of their parents and grandparents ahead of them—and they are proud of them, and they want to maintain that same standard. They don't worship gold. All they want is necessities. They would rather live than make a lot of money. They live by this code. They're the best citizens in this country." Later in the interview, Jones said, "Unless these wild areas are preserved, we're going to get to the point where dense population is going to work on the nervous systems of the people, and the more that takes place, the poorer neighbors they become. Eventually, like birds or animals confined to too small an area, they will fight among themselves. Man is an animal as well." People known in the pines as "the old-time pineys"—those who lived wholly by the cycle, and seldom, if ever, saw an outsider—are gone now. When the United States Army built Camp Dix on the northwestern edge of the Pine Barrens during the First World War, civilian jobs were created, and many people of the pines first got to know what money was and how to use it. Paved roads first crossed the pines in the nineteen-twenties. Electrical lines, the Second World War, and television successively brought an end to the utter isolation of the pineys. But so far all this has not materially changed their attitudes. They are apparently a tolerant people, with an attractive spirit of live and let live. They seem to like hard work, if not steady work, and they like to brag about working hard. When they say they will do something, they do it. They seem shy, like the people who went before them, but when they get to know an outsider they are not shy and will generously share their tables, which often include new-potato stews and cranberry potpies. I have met Pine Barrens people who have, at one time or another, moved to other parts of the country. Most of them tried other lives for a while, only to return unreluctantly to the pines. One of them explained to me, "It's a privilege to live in these woods."

4

The Air Tune

THE VERNACULAR language of the pines is splendidly metaphorical. An outsider needs a glossary to follow simple directions—for example, "Go down here about a mile and turn left at the fingerboard." A fingerboard is a place where several roads come together. A point is a place where a road forks. When highway workers do anything to a road, they are said to be sciencing it. One day while I was driving along with Fred Brown, he said, "I didn't know this road was oiled all the way to here." The road was covered with pavement. Applejack is the laureate liquid of the pines. It is known as jack, and its effects are known as apple palsy. Pineys are much more imaginative than non-pineys with the common names of plants and flowers. There is a plant in the Pine Barrens that has velvety, magical leaves to which water absolutely will not adhere. Its common name is golden club. The pineys call it neverwet. Another plant, an *Arenaria*, is small and beautiful, and on its white flowers there is always a shining fluid. The plant's common name is sandwort. The pineys call it sparkle. They even have a better name than lady's-slipper. This small and exquisite orchid grows in the pines, where the natives call it a whippoorwill shoe. Of course, every last piney, shown a lady's-slipper, would not say, "That is a whippoorwill shoe." The Pine Barrens are too vast for that, and much of the pines vernacular is sub-regional. I doubt if Fred Brown would know a whippoorwill shoe from a lily of the valley; and, for all I know, he may be the only man in the pines who calls whiskey rum. At least, he is the only one I have ever heard call whiskey rum, but I have heard him say it many times. When he drinks his rum straight, or neat, he says he is drinking it clear. Fred refers to guardrails —the things that run along beside highways to protect cars —as guardrails. Many pineys call them bannisters. Soft sand is called sugar sand, and when a car gets stuck in it, the car is said to be set. The people say "thataway" and "tater" and "I ain't a-gonna." They also say "passed away." Homes are sometimes called homesteads. A native guide is a woodjin. Grouse are called pheasants. The pine trees themselves—the predominant pitch pines, at any rate—are called Old Jersey Bull Pines. Whenever Fred Brown referred to a man's wife—including, on one occasion, the wife of the President of the United States—he said "his woman." Fred says "spragnum" for "sphagnum," "braken" for "bracken," and "fastly" for "quickly," and when he was telling me that he had never flown in a plane he said, "I could of flewn lots of times, but I never cared to." In Tuckerton one day, he stopped a man to ask directions of him, and he said, "Excuse me, are you acquainted here?" In the vernacular, a low, wet area where the Atlantic white cedars grow is called a cripple. If no cedars grow there, the wet area is called a spong, which is pronounced to rhyme with "sung." Some people define spongs and cripples a little differently, saying that water always flows in a cripple but there is water in a spong only after a rain. Others say that any lowland area where highbush blueberries grow is a spong. With all this, it is no wonder that the names of places in the pines are so distinctive. In the nineteenth century, a man named Jacob Ong—whose name was pronounced conventionally, like "song" or "long"—went to a dance in a village in the northern part of the pines, and he somehow infuriated one of his partners, and she pulled Ong's hat from his head and crunched it under her feet. Ong is said to have taken the hat and tossed it up into a tree, where it caught on a branch and remained for months. The settlement below became known as Ong's Hat. It is one of the vanished towns, but cartographers find it irresistible, and it still appears on road maps. Once, in the eastern pines, there was a cranberry dam that kept giving way, and whenever it did one of the cranberry workers said, "Here's trouble." Then the dam gave way twice in a single week, and when this happened the man said, "Here's double trouble." That particular bog, which was run for years by the Double Trouble Cranberry Company, has been bought by the State of New Jersey, along with two thousand acres of surrounding land. It is now Double Trouble State Park.

Fred Brown told me one day that in modern times there have been certain adjustments in the ways that some of the older Pine Barrens families pronounce their names. "The Browers used to pronounce their name Brewer," he said. "They're still Brewers as far as I'm concerned, but they say they're Browers. It ain't changed them any, so far as I can see. The Jervises call themselves Jarvises now. The Salmons used to pronounce it Simons. Fifteen to twenty years ago, they started calling themselves Salmons." There is not much that Fred could do with the name Brown, even if he were inclined to, but his great-grandfather Zachariah Jenkins was the man for whom Jenkins and Jenkins Neck were named, and Fred is quick to point this out. Fred was born in Jenkins on June 29, 1887. His father did several things but was chiefly a cabinet-finisher. The school where Fred helped to plant the red cedar tree was near the Godfrey Bridge on the Wading River. "I made the fifth reader," Fred said. "That's the highest one there was in the school at that time. From what I've heard, it would be equal to the eighth grade today." He finished school at the age of fifteen. He worked with his father, as a carpenter, for a while. He also became skilled as a sawyer and worked in sawmills. "I cut cedar, I growed cranberries, I worked for construction companies, I gathered wild huckleberries, wild cranberries, moss—I pulled, I expect, two or three hundred carloads of moss," he said. "The only laws I ever used—if I was hungry and wanted a pheasant or a deer or something, I went out and killed it." When Fred was young, the now vanished towns were still vanishing, and he remembers the last people who lived in them. In Washington, for example, he said to me one day, "Jim Snow's was the last house. I went to school with Jim Snow's son and his daughter. It was a good house. Jim Snow's daughter runs Jennings' bar, in Indian Mills. She is two years older than I am. Right there is where she was born, and don't let her tell you she wasn't." In Martha once, standing under the old catalpa trees, with their long-podded seeds hanging down above us, Fred said, "The big mansion was there. I eat chicken potpie in that mansion. Aunt Katie Gunner was the last person to live here, in the mansion here under these bean trees." In 1910, Fred married a girl named Elizabeth Mick. They raised their seven children first in Jenkins and then in the house where Fred now lives in Hog Wallow. Elizabeth Brown died in 1948 and is buried in the pines, where Fred will be buried. Their children are now, in descending order of age, a housewife in a town on the edge of the pines, a retired state policeman, a guard in a juvenile home near the pines, a mechanic, a laborer for the state highway department, a wild-huckleberry picker and part-time junkman, and a beautician in Alexandria, Virginia. Fred himself was for many years —from 1915 to 1952—a cranberry broker. Dressed in overalls, he went around in horse-drawn wagons, then in Model Ts. He bought cranberries in the bogs and took them to canneries on the periphery of the Pine Barrens. "One was to New Egypt," he told me. "One was to Williamstown. One was to Folsom. One was to Egg Harbor. And one was to Landisville." These canneries eventually became part of the interstate coöperative Ocean Spray. Fred was also a blueberry broker, and he had his own small bogs and fields. "I just happen to be the one man in the State of New Jersey that growed seventeen straight crops of cranberries," he said once when we were riding along on a cranberry dam in my car. He explained that cranberry growers usually have to let their bogs be idle in one of every seven years. They do this by leaving the bogs flooded through blossom time, which is around the Fourth of July. Most bogs lose their vitality after about six years of growing and need a year of renewal.

"I believe they get that seven years out of the Bible," Bill Wasovwich said, from the back seat. "That seven years is in the Bible."

"I used fertilize and light sand," Fred said. "That will do it."

A fairly uncomplicated machine now knocks cranberries off the vines at harvest time, but the day of the hand cranberry scoop is so recent that Bill, at twenty-eight, is remembered as the last of the champion scoopers. He picks at his nails modestly when this is said, but it is apparently true. Growers told me Bill worked so hard that they had to go out into the bogs at dusk and actually take the scoop from his hands in order to force him to stop for the day. Fred says that he, too, was a great picker in his time. "I seen a Portugee scoop a half-barrel box in less than two minutes," he told me. "The best I could do was three minutes. There wasn't another man out of eighty that could scoop one in three minutes." Field, bog, and forest, Fred once owned five hundred and seventy-five acres, in Jenkins and in Hog Wallow. Now he owns one acre.

At Fred's house one day, Bill asked me if I would like to go down the road and see his bog. On the way, we stopped at his cabin. It is a small, sturdy saltbox in the woods, perhaps eighteen feet on a side. Bill had then lived in it for three years. It was clean within, and almost empty. An enamelled cabinet, a kerosene stove, and a small table were the only pieces of furniture in the room. Leaning against the doorjamb was a high-velocity rifle. A kerosene lamp on the table had been in the same position for a long time, for up the wall behind it went a wide and thick V of lampblack that pooled into a black hemisphere on the ceiling. Beside the lamp on the table was a huge book, larger than a Webster's New International Dictionary. It was open, and strewn all over it and the rest of the table were sheets of lined white paper covered with writing.

The first thing I asked Bill after we went into the cabin was where he slept, because there was no bed or cot.

"On the floor," he said. "I have a sleeping bag."

I then asked what the book was.

Bill said that it was a Bible and that he was taking a Bible correspondence course from Ambassador College. He was in the middle of the eighth course he had taken in Biblical studies. The enormous Bible was the largest he had been able to buy. He said it had cost twenty-seven dollars, and he explained that he needed large type so that he could read in the kerosene light at night. I picked up the heavy rifle and balanced it in my hands. Bill said it was a 44/40 Winchester, a model first built in 1873, and that it fired big, two-hundred-grain bullets. Unfortunately, he went on, the cartridges cost eight and a half dollars for a box of fifty, so he couldn't use the rifle very often. When he treats himself to a box of bullets, he does not space out the pleasure. He prefers to shoot up the whole boxful as rapidly as he can. The rifle has lever action and holds fifteen shells at a time. Bill selects a target, frequently nothing more than a pine tree, and rips it with fifty bullets. Sometimes the bullets cut the tree down. For other purposes, he said, he had only used the rifle three times—once to kill a dog, once to kill a deer, and once to frighten a reporter, who drove up in a car that had the name of a Trenton newspaper on it, got out, and peered through a window into Bill's cabin, in an attempt—Bill thought—to see how pineys live. Bill picked up the rifle, and the reporter ran to his car and drove away. "I'd have never shot to kill him," Bill told me. "But I'd have threw lead at him if I'd been scared enough. I wasn't scared enough."

Bill's bog is small—four acres. He only has time for it when he is not at work in other men's bogs, and for more than two years he has been clearing it and building up its dams by hand. The forest edges it on three sides, another bog on the fourth. Among the trees that line Bill's land are white birches and dark cedars. It is a pretty corner in the pines. Bill's hope is that he will marry, build a home there, and raise a family. "I intend to build a house down my bog or die trying it, I can tell you that," he said.

I asked him if the land was actually his.

He said that his employer had given it to him, but that he had no deed. "It's as good as my bog," he went on. "They can't take it away from me. They could, legally. But they'd have to get the state troopers. They take this bog, they take me with it. I'll get up here with my rifle. I took out stumps in here the size of chairs."

Bill spent one year in high school, in a town just outside the pines. For a number of years after that, while he was working in cranberry bogs and blueberry fields, he drove cars and pickup trucks without a driver's license. One day, when Bill was driving too fast in a pickup he had, he saw a state trooper approaching him from behind, and he put his foot to the floor and started a chase, which the trooper lost because Bill led him through a series of bogs and eventually set him in sugar sand. Unfortunately for Bill, the trooper had read his plates. Bill was soon arrested and put in jail for seventy days. Disgusted with life, Bill sold his pickup for a hundred dollars and caught a Greyhound bus for the pinelands of Georgia, where he cut pulpwood near Waycross and Fargo for about a year. He became so lonely that he took another Greyhound north to New Jersey. "When I came back, I was never so glad to see anything as these woods," he told me.

I asked him if he was going to be married soon.

"Who to?" he said. "I been looking for ten years. Like my father, I'm no good. I've always been ascared of girls, all my life." He went on to say that at one time there had been a girl he was fond of, but he had never taken her out. "The bravest

I got was to talk to her once," he said. Bill carves Indian dolls out of wood, and he would like to give them to a girl, but he knows no one he can give them to.

One day, Fred Brown told Bill and me that when he was eighteen he liked his women in the age range of fifteen to sixty-two. He also told us a story about a fight he once had over a woman. He said he had been "jumped by three guys" one night when he walked into the Peacock Inn, in Chatsworth, a pine town about six miles north of Hog Wallow. "The girl—they wanted her, she wouldn't have them," he said. "They couldn't go with her. I could. They had all tried me single-handed and they knowed they couldn't handle me one at a time. Ander Bozarth got his jaw broke. I throwed him across the pool table and his head hit the pocket that was iron. Bill Green—I throwed him over the bar and he went right into the big barrel full of bottled beer and ice. Bill Ford was next. Howard Sooy, who was watching—he was a friend of mine—he couldn't stand to see three on one. He grabbed Bill Ford and knocked him out. I was eighteen. I would say the girl was around forty." Fred brags winningly. One reason he is so good at it is that bragging is an honored craft where he lives, an element in the general art of storytelling, which was once of enough importance in the Pine Barrens to give rise to a class of local Homers, some of whom did nothing at all but travel through the woods telling tales. Big Bill Estell, who died in 1882, told stories for a living, and explained to people that he was too heavy for light work and too light for heavy work. Cracky Wainwright—whose name, in the pines, is pronounced Wineright—went around telling stories and stopped off at his own house once a year. Ander Bozarth, the fellow whose jaw Fred Brown disassembled in Chatsworth, was a male Scheherazade, known for his ability to tell a different story every night for months. Stories were told beside burning charcoal, and beside bonfires that used to blaze at night in cranberry-harvest time, when, before the automobile, pineys slept in the woods near the bogs they were working in. Most stories at least began with truth, but some never gave it a nod.

In the late nineteen-thirties and early nineteen-forties, a graduate student from the English Department of Indiana

University went around the Pine Barrens collecting stories. He was motivated in part by the somewhat melancholy knowledge that the development of broadcasting was going to wash away much of this part of regional American life. The student, Herbert N. Halpert, is now a professor of English at Memorial University, in Newfoundland. His doctoral dissertation was called "Folktales and Legends from the New Jersey Pines." He dated each story he heard. On June 19, 1941, a piney named Charles Grant told Halpert, "I heard old Cracky Wainright say he seen two black snakes come together, and they was both mad. He seen they was going to fight, so he stood and watched them. The one got ahold of the other one's tail and began to swallow it. And the other one got ahold of the other one's tail and began to swallow *him*. He said they kept on fighting and swallowing one another until both snakes was swallowed. There wasn't *any* snake left there at all." Grant also told Halpert a story about a piney who went around for a long time claiming that he had a pair of horns in his shack seventeen feet from tip to tip. People liked this brief story and kept asking the man to tell it. Eventually, as Grant remembered it, "He said no, that was one lie he had told so much he believed it himself. He said he had told about putting the horns up in the middle of his shack so much he believed they was there. So he said the last time he was there he made up his mind he would crawl up there and see if there was anything there. He said he went up there and there they was—seventeen foot from tip to tip." On June 26, 1941, a piney named George White told Halpert, "I heard of this old fellow travelling, and he had a jug of liquor with him. Come by this pond and he was taking a drink. And the frogs hollered, 'Jug-and-all, jug-and-all.' And he threw the jug and all in, because he thought the frogs wanted jug and all." On September 1, 1942, Stacy Bozarth, a collier, told Halpert about a man who had killed a deer. "He hit him with one shot and hit him in the hind foot and hit him in the ear," Bozarth said. "Now how could he do it? Can you tell me? Well, I can tell you. Well, the deer had his hind foot up scratching his ear."

After reading these stories, I repeated them to Fred Brown, who blew air through his teeth and said he had heard them all. He said *he* could tell me a *true* story. He asked if I had heard about a couple named Will and El Nichols. "Will and El Nichols dreamed three times—this ain't second-handed, this is first-handed—they dreamed three nights straight that there was an iron-handled drawer buried up to Tulpehocken, on the road that goes from the Joe Holloway Field and comes out to the High Crossing. They dreamed that there was a box there—with an iron drawer in it—near an old-fashioned walnut tree right along the road. Neither one told the other that they had dreamed anything. One morning, they got up and Will said to El, 'I'm going up to Tulpehocken.' 'So am I,' said El. They went up, and dug, and found a box full of buckskin bags full of gold coins. I've seen the hole where they dug that out. They would never tell how much gold they got, but they had nothing before and they had money the rest of their lives, and they had it when they died. They lived down here to Bulltown." Fred had an afterthought. "People used to put gold coins in buckskin bags and bury them all over these woods," he said.

The Pine Barrens have had two Paul Bunyans and one Merlin. Jesse Johnson is a local legendary figure who is said to have been seven feet tall and to have been capable of carrying two horseloads of stone. The other strongman hero was a woodchopper, and he is said to have been capable of cutting ten cords of wood in a day. His name was Salt Caesar. The wizard of the pines was Jerry Munyhon. He could make a cat's paw come through a keyhole. He could cause axes to chop wood by themselves. He could cause money to multiply. He was bulletproof. And he once caught a bullet that was fired at him and handed it to the man who had done the shooting. From some distance away, Munyhon could cause a man to stop in his tracks. Munyhon's cane was superior to Toulouse-Lautrec's. Munyhon's cane, on its own, could *go and get* whiskey. Munyhon is said to have lived in one of the iron towns, and to have died in the eighteen-sixties. Once, he asked for work at an iron furnace and was turned down. He stopped the furnace by causing it to fill with black and white crows. He got the job, and the crows flew away. Munyhon once came upon a six-mule team that was trying, unsuccessfully, to pull a wagon with a huge boiler on it up a hill. He had a Leghorn rooster under his arm, and he tied it to the tongue of the wagon and said, "Shoo!" The rooster pulled the load up and over the hill. Of all his powers, Munyhon's most widely celebrated one was a remarkable ability to create in the minds of women the illusion that they were walking in thigh-deep water when in fact they were walking on dry land. Up went their skirts.

Munyhon's water trick has parallels that go back as far as King Solomon, who pulled a similar trick on the Queen of Sheba. His horsepowered rooster has antecedents in the lore of several European nations. European sources can be found for many of the legends of the pines. In America, the Pine Barrens have been a kind of cultural middle ground, where regional traditions overlap. Halpert wrote in his dissertation, for example, "This region is the meeting place for the Northern and Southern folk-song traditions. Certain songs and ballads are found in New England and other Northern states. Others are encountered only in the Southern states. In South Jersey, the various tides of immigration met, and here one often finds a husband and wife, one singing the Northern variances and the other the Southern, each of course insisting that his or her version is the true one." Men who sing have always been particularly respected in the Pine Barrens, where the test of a singer's repertory is: Can he sing from morning until evening without repeating himself? Pineys once made violins out of red maple from the swamps. Sam Giberson (1808–84), known throughout the pines as Fiddler Sammy Buck, one night told a group of people that he thought he could beat any competitor both as a fiddler and as a dancer—"and," he went on, "I think I can beat the Devil." On his way home, Giberson met the Devil himself at a bridge. The Devil told him to play his violin, and while Giberson played the Devil danced. Then the Devil played the violin while Giberson danced. Giberson was the kind of dancer of whom people said things like "I seen him put a looking glass on the floor and dance on it—he was that light when he danced." But the Devil danced even more lightly and beautifully than Giberson, and the Devil played the violin more sweetly. Giberson conceded defeat. The Devil then said that he was going to take Giberson to Hell unless he could play a tune that the Devil had never heard. Out of the air, by Giberson's account, a tune came to him—a beautiful theme that neither Giberson nor the Devil had ever heard. The Devil let him go. That is what Giberson told people on the following day and for the rest of his life. The tune is known in the Pine Barrens as Sammy Giberson's Air Tune. No one, of course, knows how it goes, but the Air Tune is there, everywhere, just beyond hearing. Giberson drank a lot, like many of the fiddlers of his time.

Fred Brown said he might have competed with a man like Giberson once, but not at the age of seventy-nine. "I can't jig no more like I used to," he told me. "My legs won't twist around like they would. Wherever there was music, I used to jig. For years, we had a dance every Friday night to Chatsworth, in the hall. Now they go to a bar somewhere, and get half drunk, and go home. The younger people, they don't never waltz or two-step or time-and-a-half."

The Pine Barrens once had their own particular witch. Pineys put salt over their doors to discourage visits from the Witch of the Pines, Peggy Clevenger. It was known that she could turn herself into a rabbit, for a dog was once seen chasing a rabbit and the rabbit jumped through the window of a house, and there—in the same instant, in the window—stood Peggy Clevenger. On another occasion, a man saw a lizard and tried to kill it by crushing it with a large rock. When the rock hit the lizard, the lizard disappeared and Peggy Clevenger materialized on the spot and smacked the man in the face. Clevenger is a Hessian name. Peggy lived in Pasadena, another of the now vanished towns, about five miles east of Mt. Misery. It was said that she had a stocking full of gold. Her remains were found one morning in the smoking ruins of her cabin, but there was no trace of the gold.

The Pine Barrens also have their own monster. This creature has been feared in the woods—on a somewhat diminishing scale—from the seventeen-thirties to the present. It is known as Leeds' Devil, or the Jersey Devil, and a year or so ago the Trenton *Times* ran an article, with a Pine Barrens dateline, that said, "State Police from the Tuckerton Barracks today are searching for a wild beast. . . . Trooper Alfred Potter reported finding a footprint that was so large a man's hand could not cover it. . . . Many remember the legend of the Jersey Devil." From "a farm in a woodland swamp," the beast had carried away two large dogs, three geese, four cats, and thirty-one ducks. Remains of these animals were found, but that was all that was ever found. If the perpetrator was Leeds' Devil, the haul was modest, for Leeds' Devil had in the past been said to have devoured small children and to have mutilated strong young men. Over the years, the physical appearance and the personal history of the monster have been variously described. There are two main versions of its birth, which occurred early in the eighteenth century—one that a woman named Leeds so scornfully treated a preacher who was trying to convert her that the preacher told Mrs. Leeds her next child would be the offspring of Satan, and the other that Mrs. Leeds had so large a family that she cursed all unborn children and said she hoped she would give birth to the Devil, which she did. The Devil child's appearance was said to combine the features of a bat and a kangaroo. It was described in Cornelius Weygandt's book *Down Jersey* as "a leather-winged, steel-springed jumper of goat size that could clear a cranberry bog at a bound." (A variant was that it had a horse's head, the wings of a bat, and a serpent's tail.) It tore at its mother's flesh while it nursed. At the age of four, it killed its mother and its father and began its terrible wanderings, cutting the throats of hogs, horses, cattle, sheep, children, women, and men, and leaving cloven tracks. People used to hang up lanterns to scare the Jersey Devil away. Most people in the Pine Barrens now look upon the Jersey Devil as pure legend, but there are many who do not. Unexplained and sinister events will still cause its name to be spoken in serious voices.

Bill Wasovwich, for his part, is not certain whether he believes or disbelieves. "I was out in a swamp once on a moonlight night," he told me. "A mist came up, laying out in there like a blanket. You've seen those nights. Fog was rising up like a thing coming through water. Something screamed. My hat flew off my head. I ran home, through briars. My arms was all cut up when I got home."

Fred Brown believes. "The Jersey Devil is real," he told me. "That is no fake story. A woman named Leeds had twelve living children. She said if she ever had another one she hoped it would be the Devil. She had her thirteenth child, and it growed, and one day it flew away. It's haunted the earth ever since. It's took pigs right out of pens. And little lambs. I believe it took a baby once, right down in Mathis town. The Leeds Devil is a crooked-faced thing, with wings. Believe what you want, I'm telling you the truth."

5

The Capital of the Pines

CHATSWORTH, in Woodland Township, is the principal community in the Pine Barrens. It is six miles north of the approximate center of the pines at Hog Wallow, and is surrounded on all sides by deep forest. From the air, two miles away, Chatsworth is not visible under the high cover of oaks and pines. The town consists of three hundred and six people, seventy-four houses, ten trailers, a firehouse, a church, a liquor store, a post office, a school, two sawmills, and one general store. Somehow, Chatsworth is a half-tone more attractive than any other town in the pines. The people are apparently just a little competitive about the appearance of their houses, most of which are painted, and this gives Chatsworth a measure of distinction from its "suburbs"—the word used in Chatsworth for small settlements nearby in the woods, such as Leektown, Butler Place, Speedwell, and Jones Mill. People in Chatsworth pay twenty-four dollars a truckload to bring in topsoil so that they can grow lawns. That sort of thing notwithstanding, individualism and personal independence are as important there as they are in the rest of the pines. Two-thirds of Chatsworth's people make their living in Woodland Township—mainly from cranberries and blueberries and from "working for the state highway" and patrolling the woods as fire wardens or foresters. Half the people classify themselves as self-employed. Most of them are descended from English, Irish, and German ancestors who settled in the Pine Barrens in the eighteenth century, and the headstones in the Chatsworth cemetery bear names such as Brower, Bozarth, Dunfee, Leek, Applegate, Ritzendollar, and Buzby.

On the southwest corner of the town's principal intersection is the Chatsworth General Store, the entrance to which was cut into a corner of the building on an angle, so that the door itself, aproned with concrete steps, is the most prominent exterior feature of the building. The door was apparently designed to attract people from both intersecting streets, although the store has no competition for a ten-mile sweep in all directions. When I first stopped in there, I noticed on its shelves the usual run of cold cuts, canned foods, soft drinks, crackers, cookies, cereals, and sardines, and also Remington twelve-gauge shotgun shells, Slipknot friction tape, Varsity gasket cement, Railroad Mills sweet snuff, and State-Wide well restorer. Wrapping string unwound from a spool on a wall shelf and ran through eyelets across the ceiling and down to a wooden counter. A glass counter top next to the wooden one had been rubbed cloudy by hundreds of thousands of coins and pop bottles, and in the case beneath it were twenty-two rectangular glass dishes, each holding a different kind of penny candy. Beside the candy case was a radiator covered with an oak plank. Chatsworth loafers sat there. There were no particular loafers. Almost everyone who came into the store spent a little time on the oak plank. There were three Esso pumps on the sidewalk outside. Esso had been sold there since 1921. Just inside the door, a red kerosene pump was set in the floor. I was told that as many as four hundred gallons of kerosene had been sold through it in a week. Kerosene is widely used in the pines, both for heat and for light.

The general store was built in 1865. It was owned and run from 1894 until 1939 by Willis Jefferson Buzby, who was known as the King of the Pineys. After Buzby's death, the place was taken over by his son Willis Jonathan Buzby, who assumed his father's title, and who is still called the King of the Pineys, although he and his wife, Kate, recently sold the business to another Chatsworth couple and retired to their house across the street. "We're the original pineys," Mrs. Buzby said to me in the store one day. "People come here and say, 'We're looking for the pineys,' and I say, 'They're right here,' and they say, 'No, we mean the people who live in caves and intermarry,' and I say, 'I don't know of any such people. We're pineys. We live right here.'" Mrs. Buzby is a small woman with gray hair and bright eyes. "We've had electric in here since 1932," she went on. "People come here now and see all the electric fixtures and say, 'My goodness, I didn't know the pineys lived like this.' Some of these homes don't look so good on the outside, but in the inside they have everything—refrigerators, radios, television."

Her husband, who has a forward bend in his walk and is a man of quick motions, said over his shoulder as he moved off to fill an order, "I'm a piney and I'm proud of it."

"Live in caves and intermarry, hah," Mrs. Buzby went on. "No one ever lived in caves that I heard of. I don't know of anyone around here except one family that's intermarried, and I've lived here all my life. Illegitimacy is low. In the city, you can do what you like. Here, you make a misstep and everyone knows it. There are some drifters, but not many. We have very few new people in town—perhaps half a dozen."

Mrs. Buzby's maiden name was Ritzendollar. When she went to high school, in Pemberton, on the periphery of the pinelands, she stayed there during the week, and when the roads were bad in winter she had to stay in Pemberton for as much as a month without going home. Her husband went to a one-room school in Chatsworth and did not go on to high school. They have one daughter, Theresa, who married a boy she met at Pemberton High School. Their son-in-law now does acoustical research at the University of Michigan. The Buzbys have two granddaughters. One went to Radcliffe and majored in art, married a graduate of the Harvard Medical School, and lives in Palo Alto, California. The other is now at Wellesley. A Wellesley banner was tacked to a canned-goods shelf in the Chatsworth General Store.

On the store bulletin board was a proclamation signed by Peter T. Brower, mayor of Woodland Township, forbidding all men to shave for six weeks. Violators would be fined two dollars, which would be used to help cover the costs of a coming celebration of the centennial of the township's incorporation. Almost every man in Chatsworth had grown a grisly stubble. Buzby had let his own beard go for the better part of a week. Now he got out an electric razor and plugged it into an outlet. "I better shave," he said, rubbing the machine against his face. "I look like a God-damned Rip van Winkle. It costs you two bucks to shave now."

Out of a mud-colored 1948 De Soto came an old woman in a gray dress that reached her ankles. She bought two cans of beans and one slab of uncut bacon. She complained to Mrs. Buzby about a slab of bacon she had bought two weeks before, and she went out.

An old man in a straw hat, a faded blue shirt, and khaki trousers stopped in for his Philadelphia *Inquirer*. He reminisced with Mrs. Buzby. They talked of the school they went to, in Chatsworth, years ago. There was a big coal stove in the middle of the schoolroom. The oldest boys could throw erasers hard enough to knock the stovepipe out of the wall. When a doctor was scheduled to visit the school, the children ran into the woods to avoid vaccinations. The old man complained bitterly about a teacher who had whipped him for someone else's misdemeanor. As the old man was leaving, Mrs. Buzby drew him out on the origin of the word "pineys." He said, "Pineys is a freak name that was invented in New York City."

A Ford station wagon stopped at one of the Esso pumps, and Mrs. Peter Brower, the wife of the Mayor, pumped herself three dollars and seventy cents' worth of gas. She waved at Buzby and drove away. Buzby got out a book, read the pump from inside the store, and recorded what Brower owed.

An old blue-and-white Chevrolet succeeded Mrs. Brower at the pumps. In it was a tan and extremely tired-looking young woman with long tawny hair. She wore a green blouse. Two small children were crawling on her. Buzby went out. She undid two of her blouse buttons and reached inside. She removed a bill, unfolded it, and handed it to Buzby. He pumped a dollar's worth of gas.

A young man wearing a sleeveless shirt and dungarees asked Mrs. Buzby for a pack of cigarettes and a soft drink. "That will be fifty cents out of your jeans," she said.

Buzby, who frequently addressed remarks not to one person but to the loitering audience in general, announced that he had never had a drink or a smoke. "I got the thirty cents and I can do what I damned please with it," he said.

Charlie Applegate, custodian of the Chatsworth school and the husband of a teacher there, sat down on the oak plank for a while. In the course of a conversation, he told me that he once made seven hundred dollars in six weeks gathering wild blueberries. He is tanned, has gray hair, and speaks softly. He has a canoe, and loves to spend his free time on Pine Barrens rivers. "The woods are not built up, because they're so far from everything," he said. "In ten or fifteen years, they're going to build up. There's a proposal for a jetport. Most of the younger people are for it. The older people are not."

Buzby entered the conversation, saying, "As I look at it, damned if I'd want a jetport out there. It's going to be God-damned noisy."

"People from all over moving in would create problems," Applegate went on. "We have no crimes here. *That* would come to an end."

The statement—often heard in the Pine Barrens—that there is no crime in the pines is essentially true, with only a few exceptions, but among these exceptions some absorbing practices and events have been recorded. Fifty years ago, mounted state police patrolled the pines from barracks in Chatsworth. Now state police from barracks outside the woods patrol the pines, but only as a minor part of their work, which is almost wholly taken up with problems that arise elsewhere. A trooper at the Red Lion barracks, west of the woods, said to me one day, "There's no crime rate at all in the pines. They're loners in there. They don't bother you. You don't bother them. They take care of most of their troubles by themselves." Criminal events involving local people are infrequent. In 1912, a cranberry grower was returning to his bog with money to pay his scoopers when he came to a bridge that had been barricaded on the road from Atsion to Hampton Furnace. The men who had set up the barricade shot the grower and took the money. People still talk about it. Fred Brown once took me to the bridge and pantomimed the crime as he imagined it had happened. A man disappeared from Chatsworth in 1947, his bones were found in 1954, and the case has never been solved or explained. Two old men in Chatsworth fought over a woman in 1963, and one murdered the other. Stickups are all but unthinkable in the pines. Tavernkeepers and storekeepers say that the possibility almost never crosses their minds, and never did at all before the night in 1964 when a man with a silk stocking over his head and a gun in his hand walked into Hedger House, a bar isolated in the woods three miles north of Chatsworth. The man said that he wanted all the money in the cash register. By the accounts of those who were there, the men at the bar looked at the holdup man in surprise and disbelief. After a long

moment in which nothing happened, except that one man is said to have continued his drinking, there was an explosion of gunfire from the back of the room and the holdup man fell to the floor and died.

Moonshining has been practiced in the pines for more years than there has been an Internal Revenue Service, but it is done only on a mild scale today. The trooper at Red Lion told me, "All they have to do is dig a hole in the ground four feet deep and set up a still in a swamp. I've only been on two still raids in my life, but that's how they set it up. We don't go looking for moonshiners, to tell you the truth." Any fruit or grain will make whiskey, and the pineys use blueberries, apples, corn, or peaches. Sometimes outsiders come in—from places like Perth Amboy, Jersey City, Newark, or New York—and set up big-syndicate stills at dead ends of the sand roads. Such stills are highly efficient alcohol plants, which cost about fifty thousand dollars. They last a short time, usually, while Cadillacs move in and out of the pines carrying hoods who think they are alone in the remotest place they have ever seen. But all the time they are being watched by the pineys, who tell the police. Syndicate moonshiners could spoil the woods for small-scale, native moonshiners, and the moonshiners of the Pine Barrens have always made extraordinary efforts to keep their forest, for their purposes, free and clear. The age of blimps is over now, but not long ago blimps in great numbers were based at Lakehurst Naval Air Station, on the northeastern border of the central pinelands, and it was common for the big airships to return to Lakehurst with holes in their envelopes. As the blimps hung over the woods, moonshiners frequently shot at them, in the mistaken belief that the sailors in them were sweeping the woods with binoculars in search of stills.

I once asked David Harrison, the chief fire warden of the Pine Barrens area, how many moonshiners are in the pines today.

"We don't know," he said. "We leave them alone. They leave us alone. Look at it this way: If we go in there and report them and they get arrested, they might spend six months in jail; then when they come out—if they wanted to get even—they could burn down half of New Jersey."

When crime occurs in the Pine Barrens, it is usually the work of outsiders, for whom the woods hold sinister attractions simply because they are so vast. From a gangland point of view, it makes better sense to put a body in the Pine Barrens than in the Hudson River. Another state trooper said to me, "Anybody who wanted to commit a murder—all he'd have to do is ride back there with a shovel. They'd never find that body. I always did figure there's a lot of bodies in there. You get in those woods and you can get lost. You could kill a person very easily and throw the body in there, and within three or four weeks the buzzards would have taken care of everything except the bones, and they would be scattered. The sand roads attract suicides. They use shotguns, or hoses from their exhaust pipes. In there, since 1900, there have been gangland killings, lovers'-lane killings, feud murders, and bootleggers' shoot-outs. Three years ago, a body in city clothes was found near Hampton Furnace. The case is still under investigation."

At about three o'clock, one July afternoon, in the height of the blueberry harvest, Charlie Leek, the foreman of a blueberry field, came into the Chatsworth General Store to drink a bottle of soda and to cool off. Many people in Chatsworth have small blueberry fields of their own—two to twenty-five acres. A reasonable crop picked from fifteen acres will gross ten thousand dollars. Charlie works for one of the larger growers, looking after about a hundred acres of blueberries and cranberries. I had met him at Buzby's a week or so earlier. He is a big, good-looking man with big gestures, dark hair, a weathered face, flashing blue eyes, frequent smiles, and a solid but capacious middle. He is about fifty, and he has a manner that suggests that he is not afraid to work and not afraid not to work. That day, he wore a blue shirt, dark-blue trousers, and construction worker's shoes. Sitting on the oak plank, he got into a discussion with an old man about the bread their mothers used to make. Despite the considerable difference in the two men's ages, their mothers, Charlie told me, were sisters. "This is Horace Adams, my cousin," he said. "Everybody's a relation in this burg. Yes, Horace's mother and mine used to make their own yeast, too—out of potato water and hops. Modern women aren't up to that."

"They give you cold beans," Horace Adams said. "How is the picking going, Charlie?"

"I got so disgusted I just walked away for a while," Charlie said. "I don't know where they're getting the booze, but some of them got a bucket of water out there and I bet that water is ninety proof."

Blueberry pickers in the Pine Barrens are almost all brought in from outside, but they are not migrant workers. They come mainly from Philadelphia, in privately owned school buses that bear the words "Farm Labor Transport." For the most part, the buses are driven by the men who own them, and the drivers, like their passengers, come from the city. The drivers are mainly Negroes, and so are the passengers. The drivers read newspapers and magazines all day and get three cents a pint on the berries their passengers pick. It is up to the drivers to find the pickers, and they start cruising Philadelphia streets before dawn, offering a day's work to anyone they can find, sometimes picking up men who are so drunk that they have no idea what they are getting into and who sober up in the blazing sun of the Pine Barrens wondering how they got there. Busloads vary every day. About a third of the people are steady sober pickers who make daily trips in the same bus. There are always some who do almost no work and are simply taking advantage of a chance to have a day in the country. There is usually a high percentage of schoolchildren, some of whom appear to be too young to have working papers, but at least they seem to enjoy themselves and to be there by choice. Women in their eighties ride the farm-labor transports, too. So, occasionally, do prostitutes, who go with their customers out of the blueberry clearings into the woods. Some pickers spend more in this manner than they earn during the rest of the day. Some become so drunk in the fields that they fall down in the hot sand between the blueberry bushes and pass out. "We got everything from hoochy-coochy girls on up today," Charlie told me. Pickers are paid seven cents a pint. Picking begins when the dew dries on the bushes—and is not done on rainy days—because the blue of a blueberry is a protective wax, and it comes off on the hands if the berries are wet. Some of the wax comes off anyway, and pickers' hands are always blue. A real star can earn eighteen dollars in a day, but most pickers make about ten dollars, and those who do not pick steadily make less than that. Bus drivers clear from twenty-five to fifty dollars a day. Sometimes pickers of any sort are so scarce that growers have to compete for the favor of the drivers, and on days like that the drivers have been paid as much as ninety dollars. When the pickers get into the buses and start the ride back to Philadelphia, the drivers sell them wine. On arrival in the city, some people are drunk and have spent their day's pay in the buses. (This sorry scene is not repeated during the cranberry harvest in the fall, when the bogs are flooded an inch or so over the vines, and the cranberries, which float, are batted free by motorized water rakes until they form a great scarlet berry boom—hundreds of thousands of cranberries bobbing and drifting with the wind or on a slow drainage current to a corner of the bog, where they are hauled in.)

The cultivated blueberry was developed in the Pine Barrens. More cultivated blueberries are grown there than are grown in Michigan, the No. 2 blueberry state. In 1911, Miss Elizabeth White, one of four daughters of a cranberry grower who lived about ten miles north of Chatsworth, read a publication of the United States Department of Agriculture in which a Dr. Frederick Coville described the possibilities of crossing various wild blueberries and producing superior offspring. Miss White invited Dr. Coville to use Whitesbog, her family's property, for his experiments. She gave small boards with various-sized holes in them to all pineys who were interested, and said that she would pay for blueberry bushes at a rate scaled to the size of the largest hole that the berries would not go through. Of the first hundred and twenty bushes, she and Coville threw away a hundred and eighteen. From the remaining two, they eventually made thirty-five thousand hybrid cuttings. Of the resulting bushes, they threw away all but four, from which modern cultivated blueberries, in their numerous varieties, were developed. Some of the varieties were given the names of pineys who had collected for Miss White—Grover, Rubel, Sam, Stanley, Harding, Adams, Dunfee. Miss White was in her thirties when the experiments began, and the first commercial shipments were made in 1916. In 1952, she invited landscape architects from the state highway department to Whitesbog and showed them through her blueberry fields. Miss White was over six feet tall, she carried a cane and wore a Whistler's Mother dress that was as neat as a pin. Her ankles were black from the dirt of the fields, and her hands were midnight-blue from the wax of the berries. In her home, she served each of her visitors a blueberry that was the size of a baseball, as they recall it, heaped over with sugar and resting in a pool of cream. Then she asked them to consider planting blueberry bushes along the Garden State Parkway. Miss White died a few months after that. Blueberry bushes were planted later in profusion on the margins of the parkway where it runs along the edge of the Pine Barrens.

The Rubel blueberry was named for Charlie Leek's uncle Rube Leek. The Stanley was named for Charlie's older brother. Both varieties are grown in the blueberry patch where Charlie is foreman. He told me this in his pick-up truck on the way out there from Buzby's store. He had asked me if I would like to have a look at a packing house. On the way, we went past Charlie's home, in Leektown—a settlement of six houses, five of which are occupied by people named Leek. Charlie's place is low, miscellaneously built, dark, and tarpapered. There are many fragments of machinery and several defunct vehicles in the yard. "My son Jim lives in that white house across the road from me, where I was born," he said. Looking closely, I saw traces of the white paint that had apparently covered it when Charlie was a boy.

"What did your father do?" I asked him.

"Worked in the wildwoods," he said. "Sphagnum. Wild huckleberries. Cranberries." He said that he himself had tried working outside the pines once but that he couldn't stand it and had finally come back. While he was employed at an aluminum plant on the Delaware River, he used to drink a fifth of whiskey a day, on the job. "Working with hot metal, you sweat it out," he said. "But if you drink, you abuse your family. You'll abuse your best friend, if you don't look out. I haven't had a drink since I quit that place, in 1941. It's not hard for a man to make his living here in the pines, if he ever lived here. You got wealthy men here. No one bothers you. If you don't feel good, you don't have to work. If you want to get some food, you just take your gun and go out and get it—in season. I don't outlaw. I used to. My son does a little outlawing. He has a car with a sun roof, and he and a friend hunt with it. They go through the woods and they see a deer and they stand up through the sun roof and shoot. You can do what you want to do down here. Most jobs, you have somebody breathing down your neck when you're working. Most of your natives around here aren't used to that, I can tell you that."

We had come to a clearing where thousands of blueberry bushes grew. In the center of it was the packing house—a small, low building with open and screenless windows on all sides. In front of it was a school bus marked "Farm Labor Transport." The driver stood beside his bus. He was a tall and amiable-looking man, with bare feet. He wore green trousers and a T-shirt. The end of the working day had come. Pickers were swarming around a pump—old women, middle-aged men, a young girl. A line was waiting to use an outhouse near the pump. Inside the packing house, berries half an inch thick were rolling up a portable conveyor belt and, eventually, into pint boxes. Charlie's sister was packing the boxes. Charlie's daughter-in-law was putting cellophane over them. And Charlie's son Jim was supervising the operation. Charlie picked up a pint box in which berries were mounded high, and he told me with disgust that some supermarket chains knock off these mounds of extra berries and put them in new boxes, getting three or four extra pints per twelve-box tray. At one window, pickers were turning in tickets of various colors, and they were given cash in return. One picker, who appeared to be at least in his sixties, tapped Charlie on the arm and showed him a thick packet of tickets held together with a rubber band. "I found these," the man said. "They must have fallen out of your son's pocket." He gave the packet to Charlie, who thanked him and counted the tickets.

Charlie said, "These tickets are worth seventy-five dollars."

After loading for the return trip to Philadelphia, many buses stop in Chatsworth, so that the pickers can buy food and soft drinks at the general store. At 6 P.M. that day, they stood four and five deep all along the Buzbys' counters. One after another, they bought Coca-Cola in cold quart bottles and cookies in family-size boxes. One woman, short and middle-aged, wore a gray flannel skirt over a pair of blue-gray cotton slacks. One old man, who had swollen ankles, wore no socks, and parts of his shoes had been cut away to relieve his toes.

He bought a quart of orange soda and a bag of potato chips. Half of the crowd seemed to be teen-aged. Noise was high. When the pickers had gone to their buses, Mrs. Buzby said to me, "A couple of the drivers came in here earlier to buy soda water. They use it to cut the wine."

6

The Turn of Events

IN THE MEMORIES of the people of Chatsworth, three local events seem to stand out in the past fifty years—the Chatsworth Fire, in 1954; the crash and death in the woods, in 1928, of an aviator who was known as Mexico's Lindbergh; and a visit, in 1927, by S.E. il Principe Constantino di Ruspoli, an authentic Italian prince who happened to be a native of Chatsworth. The Prince's father, Prince Mario Ruspoli de Poggio-Suasa—an attaché at the Italian Embassy in Washington in the eighteen-nineties—had indirectly given Chatsworth its name. During his tenure in Washington, the senior prince married an American whose family happened to own seven thousand acres of the Pine Barrens. The property was near the town of Shamong, as Chatsworth was originally called, and the Prince became so fond of the area that he and the Princess built a villa there, beside Lake Shamong, less than a mile from the middle of the town. Their son was born in the villa, and the present Mr. Buzby's mother worked as a nursemaid there. The Ruspolis entertained on the level that might be expected of a diplomat-prince. Into the pines they brought Astors, Drexels, Goulds, Armours, Morgans, Vanderbilts, the Marquise de Talleyrand-Périgord, Don Giovanni del Drago, Prince Brancaccio, and Levi P. Morton, the Vice-President of the United States. Morton (1824–1920), a Vermonter who had become a New York banker on a grand scale, was Vice-President under Benjamin Harrison and was later elected governor of New York. Like most guests of the Prince and Princess, he developed an affection for the Pine Barrens, and, with the Prince and others, he formed a syndicate that built, next to the Prince's villa, a prodigious Tudor manor house. It was three stories high, with oak half timbers, brooding gables, and five huge chimneys. This new phenomenon in the pines was named the Chatsworth Country Club—after Chatsworth House, the country seat of the Duke of Devonshire, a friend of various members of the syndicate. Before long, the piney colliers and sawyers of Shamong agreed to change the name of the town itself to Chatsworth and the name of the lake to Chatsworth Lake. The Chatsworth Country Club had seven hundred members around the turn of the century, but its era was to be a short one. When the Prince was sent by his government to another country, the woodland retreat lost much of its appeal. By 1912, an Italian real-estate firm was trying—with no success—to promote it as an attraction for Italian tourists in the United States. Buzby has a pamphlet, published in Italian, that speaks stirringly of the great hall and of the Prince's splendid *palazzina* beside it, in a setting where the air is forever *profumata* with the scent of a million pines. The villa and the manor house stood empty for many years and slowly disintegrated. Draperies hung in place for decades and gradually moldered. Red silk that covered the walls fell away in strips. When the native prince came to Chatsworth to see his birthplace, that is how it appeared to him. He spent one afternoon in the town. He is now dead. Nothing whatever remains of the Chatsworth Country Club—not even a discernible trace of its outlines—and where the villa stood the only remnants are a few scattered bricks.

Near the headwaters of Tulpehocken Creek is a small clearing where a monument stands, twelve feet high, made of cement in the shape of a pylon. There are two tall flagpoles near it. Out there in one of the wildest parts of the Pine Barrens, trees have been cleared to make three crescent-shaped parking lots behind the monument, although the road that runs by it is untravelled for hours and sometimes days at a time. An Aztec falling eagle stands out in relief on one side of the monument, and Spanish words spill down another, in memory of "*capitan aviador Emilio Carranza, muerto tragicamente el 13 de julio 1928.*" Carranza was twenty-three when he died. He had been a Mexican hero since he was eighteen, when he strafed Yaqui Indians in Sonora while helping to put down the de la Huerta rebellion. Once, one of his wings caught fire and he flew into a thunderhead, where rain put out the flames. His hair was parted in the middle, and he had a long, thin, sad face, more Andalusian than Mexican. After a crash in Sonora, his face bones were set with platinum screws. He was a great-nephew of President Venustiano Carranza, who was assassinated in 1920. With the Carranza name and his military honors, he was the logical choice of the Mexican government to make a good-will flight, in 1928, from Mexico City non-stop to Washington. This was a formal response to a good-will flight made in the reverse direction by Charles Lindbergh the previous December. Carranza, who took off on June 11, 1928, flew a Ryan monoplane, as Lindbergh did, and newspapers called him "Mexico's Lone Eagle." Fog overcame Carranza in Mooresville, North Carolina, and his non-stop flight to Washington included a stop there until the fog lifted. This detail was politely deëmphasized in the warm flurry of inter-presidential telegrams that celebrated his trip, and in the speeches and parades that welcomed him to Washington and, later, New York. His heroism was acknowledged by Secretary of Commerce Herbert Hoover and Mayor Jimmy Walker. Nonetheless, he had failed to carry out his mission as planned, and he intended to redress the failure by flying home non-stop from New York to Mexico City. Getting away from newsmen, he left Manhattan earlier than he had said he would, and went out to Roosevelt Field on Long Island on July 13th. It was a day of thunderstorms. He waited for one to let up, then took off and headed south before another one closed in. There was, however, a thunderstorm over the Pine Barrens, and it apparently killed him. People in Chatsworth still stand around in the general store and say they heard a plane in difficulty in the sky that day, and some say they heard it crash, but no search party went out, and it is unlikely that the crash or even the sound of the plane—in the rumbling thunder—was ever heard at all. Henry Carr, of Chatsworth, and his wife, Marie, were out gathering wild blueberries a couple of days later and came upon the wreckage—at the site of the present memorial, in Tabernacle Township, six miles from Chatsworth. "The men who went out and got him brought Carranza over to our garage and put him on Mother's ironing board," Buzby tells people. A few days later, a thirty-two-gun salute was fired on the front steps of Pennsylvania Station as the body left New York by rail for Mexico City, where three hundred thousand people followed Carranza's cortege to the Dolores Cemetery.

On a Saturday in July, an annual ceremony is held at the graveside in Mexico, and at the same time a ceremony is held in the Pine Barrens at the Carranza Memorial. I was present a summer ago, on an overwhelmingly hot day with a cloudless sky. Three hundred people were there, half of them Mexican. The Mexicans came from as far away as Chicago, but most of them were from New York, northern New Jersey, or Pennsylvania. They were in costume, in the main, and before the ceremony began they played strident arrangements of Mexican songs, like "Mi Patria Es Lo Primero" and "Mi Lindo Monterrey," on a record-player that was set on the tailgate of a Chevrolet station wagon. Girls in florid skirts and white blouses took thirty minutes to make up, combing and spraying one another's hair and swaying to the sound of the phonograph. Little boys wore frilled shirts and straw hats. One man wore a green-white-and-orange sombrero, a red bandanna around his neck, and a black shirt. A Mexican colonel, tall and trim in a deep-green uniform, walked through the crowd and took a seat in a folding chair under a canopy, where people from Chatsworth and other places in the pines sat quietly in the heat, waiting. Two trucks from the state Forest Fire Service arrived, a bus and a truck from Fort Dix, and an ambulance. A fire warden came out of the woods carrying a six-foot pine snake. Mexican children formed a circle around him, and he told them that a group of Boy Scouts had cut the head off a rattlesnake in that same part of the woods three days before. An Army band from Fort Dix put the Mexican phonograph to shame with a soft and beautiful flow of Mexican melodies, notably "La Paloma" and the "Zacatecas March." There were thirty-five men in the band, including a blond soldier with a bowl haircut who had the touch of Granada with a pair of castanets. American Legionnaires with red-veined, waxy faces walked around saying, "Where's the beer?" The beer was on ice in a large blue garbage can under a pitch pine, and the Legionnaires—who came from the Mt. Holly area, outside the pines—shared it with the Tabernacle Township police, one of whom was so heavy that he could not reach down into the garbage can. Brigadier General William C. Doyle, of Fort Dix, gave an address, and said, "Here in New Jersey's pine country, the gallant airman was grounded forever. He was not dess-tined to complete his mission." The Honorable Donald E. Johnson, Immediate Past National Commander of the American Legion, said in the course of

his speech that he had recently spent "an unprecedented hour with the President of Mexico." He also spoke about the war in Vietnam, saying, "Anyone who tells you this is a civil war is either ill-informed or uninformed or deliberately deceptive." There was no discernible reaction from either the Mexicans or the pineys. Finally, he mentioned Emilio Carranza, saying, "Had Captain Carranza lived, his name might be forgotten today—such are the imponderables of life and death." Another Legionnaire informed the crowd that men of the American Legion had hacked a trail twenty-five miles through the wilderness to carry Carranza's body out to Mt. Holly. Actually, Carranza crashed beside a sand road, and his body was removed easily to Chatsworth. What the Mt. Holly Legionnaires have done, though, is to organize and maintain the annual ceremony. Ten large floral wreaths were placed around the memorial. Six United States soldiers raised rifles, a second lieutenant said, "Sergeant of the firing squad, prepare to salute the dead," and three rounds were fired. A soldier played "Taps." From the two flagpoles, the flags of Mexico and the United States descended. There was a contrail fifty thousand feet above this scene, and at a lower altitude a Navy jet fighter passed over it as well. A young man named Antonio Huitron, who had a child in his arms, and who lived on 176th Street in New York and had been in the United States for six years, said to me at this moment, "It was very sad, because everyone in Mexico was expecting him to come back."

Three or four days after the ceremony, I went again to the memorial, this time with Fred Brown. The wreaths, which were on stands, had fallen over in a wind. All papers, cups, and beer cans had been taken away, and the memorial clearing, wreaths aside, looked just as it had when I first saw it—desolate and improbable. "I heard him," Fred said. "I heard him when he went down. That was in an awful thunderstorm. I heard him circling. I said to my wife, 'There's an airplane in trouble.' Then I didn't hear it no more. I knew from the sound that it was out in the Hocken Lowlands where he crashed. I come out here the next day. This was tall timber here. It's burnt since he went down." Fred walked to a large pine that had been left standing in the cleared area, and he paced out four yards from the tree. "Carranza's wing fell three hundred yards up that way," he said, gesturing to the east. "The rest of the airplane hit this tree, and right here is where his head was. There wasn't no blood where he laid. What do you suppose —he just bled inside? There was no blood. He had a flashlight still in his hand, an ordinary nickel flashlight, no more than a two-cell." Carranza's widow visited Chatsworth some years after her husband's death. She wore a purple blouse and a purple skirt, and protruding from her sandals were purple toenails. Carranza's sister also came. She flew over the monument and scattered roses from the air. The road that leads into the pines through Tabernacle Township and goes past the memorial and on to Speedwell is not marked with a name, even on topographic maps. For almost thirty years, however, the people of the Pine Barrens have called it Carranza's Road.

The lookout watcher in the fire tower on Apple Pie Hill, which is about three miles north of Carranza's Road and three miles west of Chatsworth, is a man named Eddie Parker. He has held the job for twenty-four years, manning the tower when the woods are dry, and he finds it disagreeably lonely. He does not use a particular technique, such as a grid system for periodic checking. Day after day, he just watches the woods. He can see hundreds of square miles of the pinelands, but even small amounts of smoke will quickly attract his eyes. "If a fire starts, it is like someone put a new chair in my living room," he explains to people who visit his tower. "I see it right away." He has seen a lot of fires, for the Pine Barrens are particularly flammable, as woodlands go, and they are the scene of some of the most spectacular forest fires that occur in the United States.

July 12, 1954, was a hot day in a time of drought. The woods of the greater Chatsworth area were "loaded with fuel," as foresters put it, for there had been no large fires in that section for some years. The Chatsworth Fire, as it eventually came to be known, started in a cedar swamp nine miles southwest of the town. Eddie Parker saw it at 4:04 P.M. and called it in. In a short time, twenty-five men had reached the cedar swamp. They had back tanks and other portable equipment, and also three four-wheel-drive trucks carrying two-hundred-gallon water tanks. When the men arrived, only three acres had burned. At 7:30 P.M., they reported the fire under control. The ground was so dry, however, that the fire was burning down into the turf of the swamp. By morning, it had spread over about twelve acres, and had gone so deep that it could not be put out. It was surrounded by firefighters, but sometime in the forenoon of July 13th it escaped. The flames began to move east before brisk winds. The strategy and number of the firefighters had to expand with the fire. By 3 P.M., fire lines were being plowed and backfires set in an effort to contain the destruction within an area of six hundred acres. Winds grew in force and began to shift. Spot fires from flying embers appeared all over the woods downwind. By midnight, new lines had been established and the new area of containment was five thousand acres. A forest fire moves in a V, like the wake of a ship. The point of the V is called the head fire, and if it gets up into the tops of the trees it is also called a crown fire. The sides of the V, which burn slowly outward, are called lateral fires, and they have to be fought by men with back tanks and shovels, for if lateral fires get far enough out to catch a wind of their own with fresh fuel in front of them, they can become new head fires. At 8 A.M. on July 14th, a fire warden named William Phoenix flew over the fire in a light plane and reported that it seemed to be pretty much under control. That afternoon, however, winds even higher than those of the two previous days came up, and, before them, several new head fires developed, in broadly separated places. These new head fires jumped the previous lines of containment. They crowned, and, like warships converging, they moved toward Chatsworth. By this time, some two hundred fire trucks had come from all over central and southern New Jersey, and even from Pennsylvania. The United States Army had arrived. Many women in Chatsworth packed what they could and left the town. People buried things. A man who lived in the woods north of Chatsworth buried his refrigerator.

"The whole earth was burning up," Mrs. Buzby said. "Everybody thought the town was going to be burned out. The fire jumped the lake. You could see nothing but dense smoke. The sand was burned black. The wind was terrific. Fire creates wind, you know. The sky overhead was all afire. A piece of the roof of the Coopers' house blew off, burning, and went a quarter of a mile through the air. It landed on a house and burned it up. Everybody thought the world was coming to an end, I guess. It looked like the heavens had lit up. We were all scared to death. We were all praying pretty hard. After the fire jumped through the town one time, the wind shifted and it started to come back. They say that a fire can't go back over ground it has already crossed, but this one did. A neighbor and I stood here on the steps of the store and watched. 'The town's going,' she said. 'Let's go for the lake.' I said, 'No, I'm going to stick.'"

By nightfall, the winds were moving at seventy miles an hour, and Chatsworth did seem to be doomed. Sparks from the returning fire were actually showering into the streets when rain began to fall. A brief but extremely heavy rainstorm drenched Chatsworth. People who watched the fire from distant hills say that the storm moved across the woods like a dark, reaching arm and, coming to the reddest part of the fire, killed it. Segments burned on for three weeks more, but most of the destruction had been ended by the storm over Chatsworth, which saved the town. Twelve buildings were burned, and nineteen thousand five hundred acres of land.

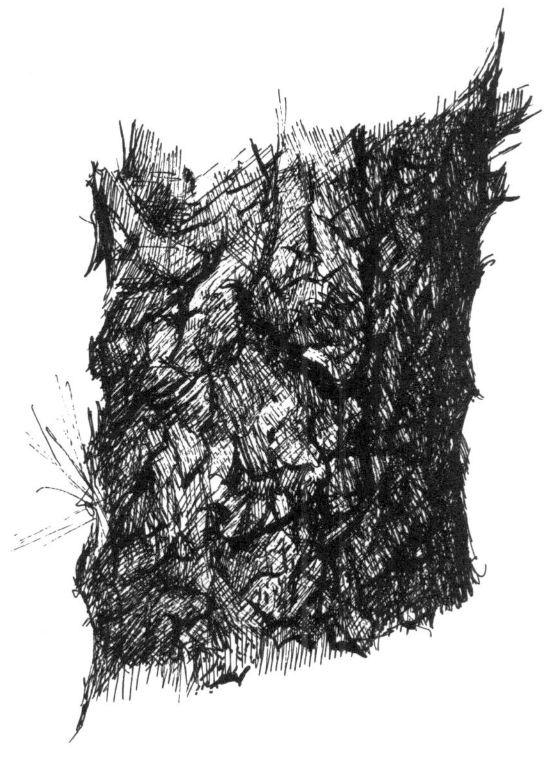

7

Fire in the Pines

WHATEVER ELSE they do, men in the Pine Barrens are firefighters throughout their lives. There are about four hundred forest fires in the pinelands every year, and fifteen or twenty of them are major ones (more than a hundred acres). It has been theorized that the pineys are defeatists because of the constant presence of the danger of fire. They are, at any rate, extremely fire-conscious, and they know what to expect of a fire when one moves through the woods. Head fires can be as little as ten feet deep. A person overtaken by a head fire can turn, go through it, and get onto safe, burned ground. One of the first lessons in forest-fire survival is: Get onto burned ground. But this is not always easy. Head fires can also be as much as half a mile deep. Lateral fires can be only a foot deep, but they can also be a hundred feet deep. In 1936, a cousin of the fire watcher Eddie Parker was caught in the middle when a head fire and a backfire came together. He had no time to get to burned ground. The last living thing he did was to kneel, as he burned, and embrace a pine tree.

Some fires are hotter than others. What makes the difference between a standard blaze and an inferno is something called fuel continuity. This is the ladderlike arrangement of litter, understory, and overstory that naturally builds up, with time, in the forest. It begins with leaves and pine needles and other litter on the forest floor, moves up to sheep laurel and blueberries and huckleberries, on up to scrub oaks and laurel and young pines, on up to trees of intermediate age, and finally to the crowns of the tallest trees. In order to remove the lower part of this ladder, the litter and the understory may be burned under control in winter, and where this has been done the results have been dramatic. Wildfires have raced through the forest and, upon reaching control-burned areas, have stopped dead. Unfortunately, there is not manpower enough to do a really significant amount of controlled burning. As much is done in Wharton State Forest as anywhere, and of its ninety-six thousand acres only about seven thousand are control-burned each winter. Wildfires have burned more than a third of the Wharton Forest since 1954.

"I like fire. I like to fight fire," the chief Wharton forester, Sydney Walker, said to me one day. "Fire is the key down here." Equipment is, to a considerable extent, mechanical now. Hand fighting with shovels and rakes has largely been supplanted by the use of tractor-drawn plows to cut forty-eight-inch swaths through the woods, along which backfires are set with kerosene torches. The big water trucks, some of which can hold five hundred gallons, are making back tanks obsolete. Aerial techniques are improving steadily. Airdrops, from light planes, used to be made with volclay, a fine clay mixed with water. Well placed, a clay airdrop could retard a fire. Now, liquid fertilizer (nitrogen and phosphorus, one to three) has replaced volclay, and when the fertilizer hits in the right place it will smother a modest fire altogether. Airdrops require skillful and nervy flying. About a hundred and eighty gallons of mixture are laid down, necessarily from a low altitude, and the target is the head fire. Done properly, a drop will cover an area of about a half acre. Pilots with experience in combat sometimes lack whatever it is that will make a man run a slow plane in close over a crown fire. A typical report of the Forest Fire Service in such a case said, "The pilot was a retired Air Force lieutenant colonel with no previous experience in fire-bombing. Although he was repeatedly advised that it was of major importance that we get to the fire swiftly before it could build up, he took an inordinately long time in takeoff. His helmet and goggles took a long time to adjust and he appeared slower than other pilots in starting his motor. Although his pilot's reports show from fifty to one hundred feet as being the height from which he dropped his load of retardant, the ground crew in general reported that he was much higher. One warden remarked, 'He will never put out any fire dropping from that height.' And another warden said, 'He was so high he looked like a sparrow.'"

Fire in the pines is never spontaneous, and lightning sets only about one per cent. There is an area in the northeastern part of the woods where most of the lightning fires begin, probably because there is a concentration of iron deposits there. It is supposed that the Chatsworth Fire started when a cigarette was tossed away by one of a group of woodcutters who were clearing the cedar swamp where the fire began. Carelessness is the cause of many fires, but not to the overwhelming extent that one might imagine. A remarkably common cause of fire in the pines is arson. Standing in all that dry sand, the forests glisten with oils and resins that—to some people—seem to beg for flame. Oak leaves in forests that are damp and rich are different from Pine Barrens oak leaves, which have so much protective oil concentrated within them that they appear to be made of shining green leather. The ground soaks up rainfall so efficiently that the litter on its surface is, more often than not, as dry as paper. In the sand soil, there are no earthworms and few bacteria to consume the litter, and it piles up three and four inches deep. In all, the Pine Barrens respond explosively to flame, and thus they appear to be irresistible to incendiaries of many kinds. Of the thirty-seven fires that occurred in the Wharton Forest in 1966, for example, the foresters say that twenty-four were definitely set by arsonists and three others probably were. The year before that, elsewhere in the pines, one man alone set sixty-nine fires. He was, at the time, a policeman in a town on the edge of the woods. After his actions became known, he was described by surprised neighbors as "a good family man" and "a nice guy." He himself "discovered" and reported all sixty-nine fires, usually calling them in on the police radio, and when he had been placed under arrest he couldn't explain why he had felt compelled to set the woods ablaze. Another man, in recent years, stole an arm patch from a fire warden and turned up at forest fires as a participant in the fighting. Wherever he was working, spot fires would break out, until the pattern of coincidences entangled him. After a fire, men from the Forest Fire Service go through the area where the burning began, often on their hands and knees, sifting through the ashes for evidence of the cause. Sometimes they find bits of railroad flares. More often, they find the remains of an ordinary matchbook with a wire wrapped around it. Incendiaries use the wire to add weight to the matchbook so that it will carry some distance into the woods when they toss it flaming from their automobiles. That way, they don't have to get out and walk. Almost without exception, arson in the pines is committed by people who come in from the outside. Pineys *have* set grudge fires from time to time, and colliers used to set fires because charred wood was good only for charcoal and they could buy it cheaply from the owners of the burned land. Pineys also used to make "skeeter smoke" by burning a mixture of pine needles, pine cones, pine chips, and charcoal in pans on their stoves. The smoke permeated their houses, and mosquitoes stayed away. Sometimes these smudge fires jumped off the stoves, burned down houses, and expanded into forest fires. Years ago, the pineys deliberately set fires in blueberry lowlands, because wild blueberry bushes will come back strong after a fire and produce more berries than they yielded before. This practice is still carried on by gatherers of wild blueberries in Maine, Vermont, and New Hampshire, but is forbidden in the Pine Barrens, where it was once given as the cause of a tenth of all forest fires. A relatively new cause of fire in the pines is burning automobiles. Foresters make their way through the smoldering aftermath of a headlong fire and at the source they find a blackened automobile. Teen-age hoods steal cars in cities, take them into the pines, strip them, ignite them, and leave the scene.

The Forest Fire Service has indices that show when the woods are least and most vulnerable to fire. There may be fires almost any day of the spring, summer, and fall, but when the indices are high the fires tend to be big. First, there is something called the buildup index, which takes into account the ground moisture and also whether the vegetation is cured, transitional, or green. When wind velocities, barometric readings, and fuel-moisture levels are added in, the result is the burning index. The scale of the burning index goes from zero to two hundred. On April 20, 1963, the day of the worst forest fire in the recorded history of the Pine Barrens, the burning index shot past two hundred into the indeterminable beyond. It was not a particularly hot day, but the vegetation was still in the cured stage, winds were blowing at about fifty miles an hour, and there was a drought. Once a fire got started, there was not much chance that it could be controlled. Actually, twelve non-contiguous major fires started on that day. The big one began after a man who was burning brush about seven miles west of Mt. Misery left his fire because he thought it was out. It was brought under control about thirty miles to the east at midnight on April 23rd, and it was finally pronounced out on May 1st. Smoke from this fire palled the air and deeply reddened the sun as far away as Princeton. The men who fought the fire made stand after stand—first at a state highway and later at county roads, sand roads, and plowed lines—only to have the flames burst over them and force them to regroup farther east. Embers went into the upper wind and advanced as much as two miles at a jump, starting new fires where they landed. Several crown fires were spread out over a six-mile front, and rolling white heat was trailed by streaks of orange flame. The fire was so hot that it caused the surfaces of macadam roads to form bubbles. Overhead, white piles of smoke went up hundreds of feet, and against this white background, now and again, appeared black twisters of smoke from pitch. Multiple airdrops were made but did not significantly help. Finally, the crews were forced back all the way to the Garden State Parkway, where, forming long lines and working with shovels and back tanks, they made a last try to control the fire. They held it there, but it had only a few miles to go anyway before it would have reached the sea. One man died. As in the Chatsworth Fire, the damage to buildings was relatively light, but only because there were so few buildings to damage. The fire crossed the Pine Barrens from one side to the other, and burned seventy-five thousand nine hundred and twenty-five acres.

A color photograph taken of a section of woods just after the 1963 fire shows about what you would expect—blackened spars above a smoldering forest floor. A photograph taken from the same spot two months later presents to the viewer a forest panoply of summer green. Of all the natural phenomena of the Pine Barrens, the most startling one is the speed with which the vegetation comes back from fire. There has been so much fire in the pines for so many centuries that, through the resulting processes of natural selection, the species that grow there are not only highly flammable but are able to tolerate fire and come back quickly. There are only three kinds of pines in the United States that respond to fires by putting forth sprouts. Two of these—the pitch pine and the shortleaf pine—predominate in the Pine Barrens. (The other, the Chihuahua pine, grows in New Mexico.) The sprouts develop from dormant buds in the trunks and larger limbs, and soon after the fire dies down, out they come. All over the woods are pine trees with splendid green crowns and trunks that are still black from old fires. Oaks that are burned usually die at the top, but they reshoot from the roots. Chestnut oaks put out so many sprouts all around their trunks that in time the shoots form palisaded enclosures resembling jails, and drunken pineys were once incarcerated in them and left there until they sobered up. Almost every woody species in the Pine Barrens has the ability to sprout after fire. The understory starts right up again, and bracken fern and sheep laurel are particularly fast. Scrub oaks put out so many acorns after a fire that they look like overdecorated Christmas trees. This helps to increase, among other things, the communities of deer and grouse.

It is because of fire that pines are predominant in the Pine Barrens. There is thought to be a progression in the development of any forest from pioneer species to climax trees. Most ecologists agree that if fire were kept out of the Pine Barrens altogether, the woods would eventually be dominated by a climax of black oaks, white oaks, chestnut oaks, scarlet oaks, and a lesser proportion of hickories and red maples. In some areas, oaks dominate now. Fire, however, has generally stopped the march of natural progression, and the resulting situation is one that might be called biological inertia—apparently endless cycles of fire and sprouting. Fire favors the pine trees because they have thick bark that provides insulation from high temperatures, and also because burned ground is just about perfect for pine seedbeds. Oaks lose vigor when they are repeatedly burned. They develop heart rot, and they die. Scarlet oaks go first, then chestnut oaks, then white oaks, then black oaks. Blackjack oaks are an exception and after a fire come back strong. In an area where a fire has been extremely hot, the pines die and the blackjack oaks put out basal sprouts that grow to be the predominant trees in that section. But, for the most part, fires are not that intense, and, working in behalf of the pitch and shortleaf pines, they clear out the competition. It would be an error, however, to think of forest fires as magic wands that clean the woods. Controlled burning can have this effect, but wildfires leave an ugly trail. Oak spars and—if the fire was hot enough—pine spars stick up everywhere. There are sprouts, but for a time there is no shade. Even when pines develop new crowns, several seasons must go by before the crowns are full. The white cedars, which are the most beautiful trees in the Pine Barrens, are killed outright if they are burned, and for years—standing feathery and dead—they commemorate the wildfire that took them. Foresters can cut an old pine and read in its occasional dark rings the dates of fires that have gone through the area in which it stands; 1930, 1927, 1924, 1922, 1916, 1910, 1905, 1894, 1885, and 1872 are the dates of dark rings that can still be read in some trees. Causes differed, but fires were frequent in the pines in the eighteenth and seventeenth centuries, and before that Indians burned the woods to improve conditions for hunting and travel. Almost certainly, the role of fire in the development of the Pine Barrens has been of importance since post-Wisconsin time, when the patterns of the present vegetation began to form as the great Wisconsin ice sheet receded.

The glacier reached only about as far south as Morristown, which is fifty miles north of the pines, but the torrents that poured from it as it melted carried southward prodigious loads of gravel that mounded here and there into what are now some of the hills of the Pine Barrens. As the early vegetation developed, the climate of the area was still arctic. The Pine Barrens were then a cold desert of permafrost and tundra—a scene that I found myself imagining at one point while I was spending some time with three men from the National Park Service who were making a general survey of the pinelands area. One man had recently returned from two years in Alaska. Standing on the observation platform of the fire tower on Bear Swamp Hill, he remarked that the Pine Barrens reminded him very much of Alaska, going on to say that the evergreen species were different but that their general appearance—and the appearance of the undulating land—was much the same from that high perspective. There is a theory that the Hudson River once flowed much farther south than it does now, and that it passed through the Pine Barrens, leaving more gravels, which eventually became more hills. Helderberg limestone from the upper Hudson Valley is found in the pines. When white men first saw the region, many of the pitch and shortleaf pines were about two hundred years old and about twenty inches in diameter. The white cedars, in their swamps, were larger. Some of them were six feet thick at the base and a thousand years old. When these great trees fell, some of them sank beneath the sphagnum moss and deep into the swamps, where they were sealed away from oxygen and were also protected from fungi by the acidulous muck. They were thus preserved. The mining of ancient cedar logs was once a source of income to some people in the pines, and even today the logs are occasionally found and removed. From them come the most durable of all cedar boards and shingles. During the Second World War, wood from sunken cedar logs taken from Pine Barrens swamps was used in the hulls of patrol torpedo boats. In Lebanon State Forest, which is four miles north of Chatsworth, foresters have put on display a pair of mined cedar logs, each about four feet thick.

No one has yet determined with certainty how the dwarf forests of the eastern Pine Barrens developed, but there have been many hypotheses, and, as one after another has been shown to be unsound, the process of elimination has led back to fire. Frequent as fires are everywhere in the pines, they are more frequent in the dwarf forests than anywhere else. The dwarf forests occur in two upland areas, which do not quite touch one another. The Upper Plains and the Lower Plains, as they are called, cover about twenty thousand acres. Pitch pines predominate there, as they do elsewhere in the Pine Barrens, but instead of rising fifty or sixty feet into the air they rise five feet. A snapshot of the Plains will often seem to take in huge expanses of forest, as if the picture had been made from a low-flying airplane, unless a human being happens to have been standing in the camera's range, in which case the person's head seems almost grotesque and planetary, outlined in sky above the tops of the trees. There is aluminum in the soil of the Plains, and one prominent hypothesis was that aluminum toxicity stunts the trees. Equal amounts of aluminum have been found, however, in Pine Barrens soils where trees grow high. Another hypothesis, long in vogue among botanists and soil scientists, was that a layer of hardpan a short distance beneath the surface was stunting the vegetation. But a graduate student from Rutgers dug three hundred well-spaced holes a few years ago and concluded that there is little or no hardpan under the Plains. Because the Plains are on high ground and winds are fierce there, it has been thought that the little trees are wind-stunted. But the Plains are not on the highest ground in the Pine Barrens. Winds are at least as fierce on the higher ground elsewhere, and the trees there are of normal height. According to the Nantucket-tip-moth theory, a small creature in the Plains eats into the pine trees' terminal shoots and cuts them back, dwarfing the trees. The tip moth, however, does not eat oaks, and twenty-two per cent of the trees in the Plains are oaks and they are just as tiny as the pines. Fred Brown gave me his own explanation for the existence of the Plains when we went there one day. "This ground is so poor a pismire can't live on it," he said. "If you found a pismire here, he'd be half starved to death." Studies have shown that the soil of the Plains is about the same as the soil of the rest of the Pine Barrens. What remains is fire. Wildfires have completely swept the Plains on an average of once every seven years for centuries. Young trees there that have not yet been hit by fire are apparently normal and have taproots, but after the trees have burned they lose their taproots, and their lateral roots spread abnormally far out—from twenty to thirty feet —forming a great mat with the lateral roots of other trees, all of which are dwarfs. The correlation with fire is apparent, but no one can say how fire causes the stunting. Another curiosity apparently brought about by fire is the type of pine cone that develops in the Plains. There are two races of pitch pines. One race has open cones (these are the familiar pine cones that have gaps between their scales) and the other race has closed cones (the scales fit tightly together, and the surfaces of the cones are smooth). Open cones drop from the trees once a year, but closed cones hang on until a fire comes, or until so many years have passed that they are finally squeezed off by other cones. In either case, aloft or on the ground, closed cones remain closed until they are opened by fire. Taxonomically, the open-cone race and the closed-cone race are not distinguished. In the Pine Barrens outside the Plains, the great majority of the pitch pines are of the open-cone race. In the Plains, ninety-nine per cent of the dwarf pitch pines produce closed cones. This, again, does not indicate why the trees are stunted, but it seems to point to the exceptional frequency of fire in the Plains, where the closed-cone race has been selected. Jack McCormick, who is chairman of the Department of Ecology and Land Management at the Academy of Natural Sciences of Philadelphia, spent an afternoon with me in the Plains, where he explained these hypotheses and phenomena. His doctoral dissertation was a study of two watersheds elsewhere in the Pine Barrens, and when he was working on it he lived in a trailer in the woods for two years. He feels that the Plains are ecologically unique, and he says that they are somewhat analogous to the chaparral of southern California. He hopes that the Plains will be left as they are. "From studies made here, we can add to our fund of information about the behavior of species under the influence of fire," he said. "Heaven knows what we'll find out. The average frequency of fires—once every six or seven years—means nothing in itself. Rapid sequence of fires—say, when three occur in six years—may have something to do with dwarfism. Also, at least to my knowledge, no one has planted an open-cone pitch pine and a closed-cone pitch pine side by side to see what would happen. Nor has anyone cross-pollinated open- and closed-cone pines. We don't know which is dominant. We don't know what a hybrid would do. We don't know a God-damned thing."

Near Warren Grove, in the Lower Plains, the Navy has a target area for skip bombers and dive bombers. The planes dive soundlessly, like toys on strings, all but hitting the five-foot trees as they pull out of their dives and simultaneously drop their payloads in the target area, usually with a concerted accuracy—plane after plane after plane—that is almost unbelievable. After each plane has gone and is moving up into the sky as if it were on the inside rim of a wheel, the sound of its jet comes to a ground observer—much too late to be connected in any sensible way with its source. Three years ago, one pilot did not pull out of a dive, and his exploding plane started a major forest fire.

8

The Fox Handles the Day

TWENTY-THREE KINDS of orchids grow in the Pine Barrens —including the green wood orchid, the yellow-crested orchid, the white-fringed orchid, the white arethusa, the rose pogonia, and the helleborine—and they are only the beginning of a floral wherewithal that botanists deeply fear they will someday lose. One day, I heard a lady botanist say, with gentle anguish in her voice, "If Sim Place were developed, what would happen to *Habenaria integra* then?" *Habenaria integra*, the yellow southern fringeless orchid, grows mainly around Sim Place, a semi-ghost town several miles east of Hog Wallow. The people the lady was addressing could, of course, give no answer; they simply looked more or less distressed. The occasion was a summer field trip of the Philadelphia Botanical Club, on a day so debilitatingly hot that only a loyal core of about a dozen people had met at a Pine Barrens crossroads and proceeded as planned through several areas of woods. Six hundred and fifty thousand acres of wilderness were spread out around them, but they moved virtually on tiptoe to avoid hurting plants underfoot. One of the first species they examined was the threadleaved sundew, which grows in boggy depressions and, like several Pine Barrens plants, is insectivorous. There is little nitrogen in Pine Barrens soil, and the region has selected some plant species that get their nitrogen elsewhere —mainly from the bodies of insects. The filiform leaves of the sundews were spread out like the spines of umbrellas, and their glands were covered with a glutinous secretion that sparkled in the sun. Brooks Evert, an insurance executive, whose wife had organized the outing, carefully scooped up a sundew in a large handful of the wet sand it was growing in. He showed it to the group. Caught in the shining fluid on the sundew's glands, several winged creatures were struggling and dying. Evert carefully set the plant back in the ground as he had found it. Mrs. Evert said, "As a rule, we take nothing and we leave nothing." The group moved onward through the bog, passing thousands of additional sundews. "Oh, my goodness," another woman said. "I'm stepping on them."

In the group were, among others, a physician, a horticulturist, a management consultant, and, most notably, Edgar T. Wherry, professor emeritus of botany at the University of Pennsylvania. Wherry is the author of *The Wild Flower Guide* and *The Fern Guide*, each work the standard of its field, and he also developed the method that is used today to test the alkalinity and acidity of soil. He is a tall man in his eighties, quite thin and frail-looking. When someone, greeting him, asked him how he was, he said, "Still around, somehow." Even when he spoke, he seldom looked at anything but the ground, in his search for specimens that might be of particular interest to the others. He wore a green eyeshade. He seemed to care a little less than some of the others for the life-span of an individual plant, and he also seemed less respectful of Latinate, scientific names. "This is candy root," he said, pulling a plant out of the ground. "Taste it." The root of the plant had the taste of a sweet peppermint candy cane. "I like regular names better than scientific names—they don't mean anything to people," Wherry went on. "When I got up a book on wild flowers, I tried to find the colloquial names, if any, rather than the scientific names."

"What is this, Dr. Wherry?" someone asked him, pointing to a small plant with greenish-white leaves.

"Dogbane," he said. "Why 'dogbane' no one knows. I never saw a dog pay any attention to it."

Asked what plants in the Pine Barrens are botanically most important, Wherry said that the curly-grass fern, which was discovered there and grows almost nowhere else, is in a class by itself. "After that, there are several plants of special interest," he went on. "*Narthecium*, the bog asphodel, is isolated here. It's disjunct. You don't see it again until you get to the North Carolina mountains. Goldcrest grows here, too, and its nearest relative is in Australia. *Lycopodium carolinianum*, the slender club moss, ranges from the Pine Barrens to Florida, then jumps to South Africa. Any plant that is able to do that has a great geological history. To me, that's one of the most remarkable ranges of all the plants that are here." The group found and examined the curly-grass fern, bog asphodel, and club moss. Wherry pulled up another kind of moss and pointed out its spores, saying, "This is foxtail moss. The spores are explosive. The Chinese used them for gunpowder." He showed the group mountain mint and cat briar. "Cat-briar shoots are tender and taste like fresh peas or asparagus," he said. "Deer like cat briar."

Mrs. Evert called out to her husband, "Brooks, keep your eyes open and see if you can see the adder's-tongue fern over there." Someone else found an adder's-tongue fern, and all the others assembled around it, on their hands and knees, as they did, moments later, around an orchid called Loesel's twayblade. This was in Martha, and the orchid was growing on the site of the mansion that had stood in the middle of the now vanished town. Overhead, crowded down by the pines, were the strangely twisted catalpa trees that had been planted by the people of Martha in the first half of the nineteenth century.

"The catalpa trees sure don't look happy," said one woman.

"They are weeds of civilization," said Wherry. "So is ebony spleenwort," he added, and he pulled up an ebony spleenwort, which is a small fern, and explained that it is not native to the Pine Barrens, nor could it be, because the soil there is too acid for it. Wherever man has used lime to build structures, however, ebony spleenwort can be found. Spores come in on the wind from heaven knows what distances. Often this alien plant is the only existing sign that a house—or a town—once stood where it grows. Ebony spleenwort is found in abundance around the building sites in all the vanished towns, but it is found nowhere else in the pines. Wherry moved on to a patch of velvet grass and said that it was "another invader as a result of man's activities." He also said that there is no poison ivy in the Pine Barrens except where man has made clearings and disturbed the earth.

Leading the group into wide bogs that were once Martha Pond, Mrs. Evert said, "Come look for *Utricularia resupinata*. The best way to find it is to squat. Then you're on your own." Everyone squatted on his own. A lady in a blue hat, a blue blouse, blue slacks, and blue sneakers found a pink orchid (*Calopogon pulchellus*) instead.

"Would anyone like my lens?" Mrs. Evert said. Through her lens, the orchid appeared to be made of crystal foam covered with patches of purple glazing.

The sphagnum surface of the bogs seemed to quake. Wherry said that in the United States quaking bogs are almost unique to the Pine Barrens—that there are some quaking bogs in the pinelands of North Carolina, but they are dry and firm in summer. He added that the flora of the pinelands of New Jersey and North Carolina "are related but not identical in any sense."

"When you spend a day in these bogs, it's a good idea to bring a change of feet," Mrs. Evert said.

Wherry pointed out rattlesnake ferns, cinnamon ferns, papery bluish-gray marsh ferns, bold and lacy royal ferns. Before the outing was over, the group had found Indian shoestrings, Turk's-cap lilies, some rare spreading pogonias, swamp azaleas, swamp hyacinths, wild magnolias, cassandras, and prickly pears—the only cactus that is native east of the Mississippi River. Walking out of the woods at the end, Wherry said, "To have all this destroyed by a jetport, or by anything else, would be an ecological disaster."

I once met a man from the New Jersey state geologist's office, in Trenton, who has made hundreds of trips through the Pine Barrens. He told me that one of the most remarkable things about the region is that the great silence there is not broken by so much as a birdcall, since the pines are so barren that there is nothing for birds to eat. That one ranks high in the large catalogue of misconceptions that people elsewhere in New Jersey have about the Pine Barrens, for the trees there are full of noisy birds, and the whippoorwills cry all night. The whippoorwills also dust themselves in the sand roads, and when they are approached at night their eyes blaze red. Nighthawks dive in the evening, and when they come out of the dive their wings open and make an explosive sound, like a sonic boom. Great-crested flycatchers hang snakeskins outside their holes in hollow pines. Eighty-four different kinds of birds breed in the Pine Barrens, not to mention the ones that make stopovers there, and the natives include Cooper's hawks, alder flycatchers, brown creepers, Henslow's sparrows, red crossbills, Baltimore orioles, green herons, black ducks, yellow-billed cuckoos, sharp-shinned hawks, great horned owls, screech owls, bobwhites, woodcocks, ruby-throated hummingbirds, white-breasted nuthatches, indigo buntings, scarlet tanagers, brown-headed cowbirds, Carolina chickadees, bluebirds, blue jays, brown thrashers, turkey vultures, meadowlarks, yellow-breasted chats, hooded warblers, prairie warblers, pine warblers, yellow warblers, chestnut-sided warblers, blue-winged warblers, black-and-white warblers, parula warblers, prothonotary warblers, red-eyed vireos, white-eyed vireos, cedar waxwings, Carolina wrens, catbirds, and robins. The most common bird in the Pine Barrens is the towhee. When a man from the National Park Service asked a state forester, "What is your biggest bird, your most dramatic bird?," the forester answered, "I would say the bald eagle."

Ducks make their skid-in landings on Pine Barrens rivers and swim along alertly, heads high, looking out for themselves, when suddenly and involuntarily they disappear beneath the surface. "Snappers lie under the water and wait for ducks," Fred Brown said one day when he and I and Bill Wasovwich had gone out for a drive in the pines. "The snappers grabs the ducks by the feet and pulls them right under there, and in two or three minutes they drown and the snappers eats them. The snappers catch big ducks." Snapping turtles in the Pine Barrens are sometimes a foot and a half long and almost as wide. They weigh fifty pounds. Pineys trap them in fykes, and fry their delicious white meat. Minks and muskrats are also trapped, for their pelts. Beaver dams are frequent in the pines. Beaver lakes attract ducks and encourage expansion in the communities of pickerel, muskrats, minks, and otters. The beavers are big and surprisingly fierce.

"I don't believe there's an animal in these woods could take on a beaver," Bill said.

Fred seemed to disagree. "A fish otter is a fighter," he said. "A fish otter can kill a dog."

Some of the pickerel are more than three feet long. It is said that people used to drift down the rivers and catch thirty or forty in a morning. The pickerel are not quite that plentiful anymore. With catfish, they are the only large fresh-water fish in the rivers. The acid content of the water is too high for trout. In addition to green frogs, sphagnum frogs, leopard frogs, and swamp-chorus frogs, there is a tree frog in the pines that has considerable status. This is *Hyla andersoni*, Anderson's tree frog, a rare creature prized by naturalists and found almost nowhere else. Anderson's tree frogs live in the Pine

Barrens in abundance. They are only one and three-eighths inches long with their legs stretched out. At night, they go *wonk*, *wonk*, *wonk*, and the art of stalking them is to follow the sound and, at the key moment, surprise them with light. This is not simple, because the frogs are ventriloquists. But they are worth seeing, for their skins are a brilliant green, trimmed with white, and they have lavender stripes down the sides of their legs. They look like state troopers. The rattlesnake community is small in the Pine Barrens, and consists wholly of timber rattlesnakes. It is said to be centered at Mt. Misery. A man known as Rattlesnake Ace Pittman once lived in that area. He made his living collecting rattlesnakes for zoos and shoe manufacturers. There are puff adders in the pines, and beautiful corn snakes, five feet long, with red eyes, red tongues, and red bodies. While I was riding along one of the sand roads with the three men from the National Park Service, we came upon a mottled brown-and-white snake that was more than six feet long and about two inches in diameter. The Park Service men jumped out of the car, and one of them set up a tripod and began to photograph the snake while another, using a snake stick, played with it. The snake coiled. It raised its forward third in an S curve, as if preparing to strike, and it took an enormous breath that filled its body with air from one end to the other and swelled it to the diameter of a fire hose. Then it exhaled with a sensational hiss, so loud and menacing that everyone jumped backward. With the hiss came a rattling sound. The snake was really furious. None of the men from the Park Service knew what kind of snake it was, although at the time we were on the southwestern slope of Bear Swamp Hill, in the middle of the Pine Barrens, and it was a pine snake.

The gray fox climbs like a cat. He goes up leaning cedars. He hides in the forks of oaks. In the daytime, he sometimes sleeps in a crow's nest. Red foxes are rare in the pines. It is the gray fox that the native hunters hunt. The hunters follow their hounds in pickup trucks. "I used to have the best dogs that you ever heard run in the woods," Fred Brown once told me. "American foxhounds. I never had no big packs of twelve or fifteen, like some people. I had six, or four, sometimes only two." A mother foxhound can listen to her puppies hunting and by the sound of their cries she can tell what they are after.

If the puppies are chasing a rabbit, she doesn't move. If they have smelled a fox, she gets up and joins them. She will not go after deer. Deer are a nuisance to foxhunters, and their good dogs are, as they put it, deer-broke. For a hunt, several packs are brought together, since one object of the sport is to see who has the best dogs. Experienced hounds know how to "cold-trail," and they are turned loose first, while the younger hounds stay in the backs of the pickup trucks. Three or four cold-trailing dogs move around for a while, and soon, as the trail becomes hot, their voices change. What began as a long, drawling bay becomes shorter and shorter as the scent grows stronger, until the sound of the hounds becomes what the hunters call a chop. The chop intensifies, and when it reaches a certain pitch and tempo the hunters know that the hounds are about to "jump a fox"—the moment when the chase begins. The younger hounds are released, and off goes the pack through the woods, while the men in pickup trucks race up and down the sand roads, frequently stopping to listen, then gunning flat out in the shifting direction of the sound. The idea is to anticipate where the fox and the pack are going, get there first, and catch sight of the fox as he crosses a sand road. The man who scores the most sightings has proved himself to be the most skillful hunter, so there is a great deal of lying about who saw the fox how many times. A good, and lucky, hunter might see the fox three times in a four-hour chase. When the fox is sighted, a point of even greater importance is: Whose dog is first on the fox's trail? There is a great deal of lying about that, too. A strung-out pack can spoil a chase, since concentrated sound is essential to the hunters, and when the dogs "pack up" on a fox the ideal is that they run so close together that a blanket thrown over them would cover them all. The hunters' wives ask their husbands why they go to so much effort just to hear a pack of dogs bark, and the hunters say that it is not barking they hear but music. They say that the sound of a pack of hounds is as musical as the sound of a flight of wild geese. Each dog apparently yells in a different key. The hunters also say that they learn more from foxes than foxes learn from them. The fox handles the day. The fox knows the age and experience of the dogs that are chasing him. The fox maintains his lead position in the chase, but if the dogs are slow and inept he himself slows down and keeps things interesting for the hunters. The chase finally ends when the fox is treed. None of the foxhunters of the Pine Barrens would dream of killing such a creature. One of them climbs the tree with a bag and, as gently as possible, puts the fox inside. The fox is then driven to a place in the woods that is safe and distant from the hounds. The bag is opened and he jumps out.

In Atlantic City not long ago, a man bit into a hamburger and found that it was full of buckshot. He was really eating a venisonburger, and the meat had come from the Pine Barrens, where deer poaching has been going on for exactly as many years as there have been fish-and-game laws. One day when I stopped in to see a family I know in Washington Township, the woman of the house excused herself at one point and made a phone call, and she said to the person who answered, "Charlie, do you know where I can get some deer meat now? Is Butch poaching? He's in jail? Is Petrosch poaching? No? Well, you think it over overnight. The meat's O.K., right? No ticks? No worms? O.K., you think it over." This was in August, and she explained to me that from the middle of May until about the first of August deer have ticks under their skins, which heavily spot the meat. "And you can get fevers," she said. "I know. I've had them." The kind of order she was placing was for small-scale poaching, for home consumption, and it was a negotiation between one piney and another. "I don't call it poaching when you're putting meat on the table," the woman went on. Most people in the Pine Barrens would agree with her. They know that it is against the law to kill deer out of season—the shooting season is six days long and comes in December—but they seem to feel that the law was made to control sportsmen hunters, and not to deny a native right to the people of the woods. Market hunting, as they call commercial poaching, is something else. The state police told me of one deerjacker who used to kill over three hundred deer a year. Deerjackers are not all pineys. Some are from towns outside the Pine Barrens. One, who was arrested a short time ago, was a city youth from Philadelphia. When a deerjacker goes out poaching, the first thing he does is to stop at one of several gin mills on Route 206, which runs north and south through the western part of the pines. There he meets a contact man. Over beers, the two discuss current prices. Carcasses have been bringing about twenty-five dollars in recent years. Then the poacher leaves. It is night, and he moves into the woods in his automobile on the sand roads. He has with him a hand spotlight that plugs into the car's cigarette lighter. A permanent, mounted spotlight would be too much of a signal to police. He also has a 30-30 rifle or a shotgun. He drives, as often as not, to a deer-diversionary strip, where he stops his car and waits. Deer-diversionary strips are swaths in the pines, miles long and only a few yards wide, where crops such as soybeans and lespedeza are planted by the state so that deer will eat there and do less damage to blueberry fields and cranberry bogs, and to farm crops on the periphery of the woods. A bit unintelligently, the state put these diversionary strips beside sand roads, thus establishing some of the world's most convenient poaching grounds. If the strips had been cleared even a few hundred yards from the roads, the annual kill by poachers would be much smaller. Fish-and-game men say that modern poachers, for the most part, will not go after deer if they have to walk. When a poacher has made his kill, or kills, he goes back to the gin mill and has another drink with the contact man. They go outside and exchange the meat for the money. Then the poacher goes back inside, as often as not, and drinks up more of his profit.

Last year, in Toms River, which is just outside the Pine Barrens, Fred Brown went into a short-order restaurant and ordered a hamburger. When it came and he had taken a bite of it, he said to the man behind the counter, "That hamburger wasn't raised on corn."

"What *was* it raised on?" the man said.

"Acorns."

"Keep quiet," the man said, and he gave Fred a second deerburger on the house.

"The second one was deer and pork mixed," Fred told me. "And that is good. Hell, yes."

Pineys have a curious regard for the New Jersey state law that forbids hunting with rifles. They generally use shotguns, like the thousands of hunters who come into the pines in hunting season, but they sometimes perform alterations that turn the shotguns at least partway into rifles. Fred once took a ball bearing from a pump engine, "crimped" it into a brass shotgun shell, and killed a deer. Some men string buckshot together with wire, after drilling holes in the shot, so that the connected pellets will carry farther and stay close together, like the flying chains of cannon days. All over the woods, gun clubs have cabins, full of cots, for men who spend one week in the pines each year. The legitimate deer kill is large there. More deer are harvested in Washington Township than in any other township in New Jersey, and New Jersey as a whole is among the best deer-hunting states in the country. There are more deer per square mile in the woods of New Jersey than there are in the woods of Maine. An American Indian from Kingston, New Jersey, goes into the pines every fall and hunts deer the way his forebears did. He waits in a tree until a deer passes beneath, then he drops on it with a knife in his hand and slits its throat. Few among the autumn throng are in that kind of shape. They walk for miles and miles, eat too much, drink too much, and frequently suffer heart attacks. The state police used to keep a jeep on patrol just to remove heart-attack patients from the woods. "They eat so heavy it's just too much for their body," one trooper told me. "They want to be woodsmen one week of the year." For every man who has a heart attack, fifty get lost. The forest perspectives are so deceptive that even the natives get lost, but they at least know what to do. Charlie Leek told me, "If I'm lost, I sit right down. A piney gets lost, he'll sit down. You take your native who lives around here, he'll sit, and he'll think. On the south side of the tree you find the longest branches. Most all your streams here runs north and south. On a clear day, you've got your sun. The worst I've ever been lost was over near Atsion. They got a fern bush over there high as your head. Everything looks the same. I been lost in the Plains, too. Deer play games with hunters there. The Plains are not like the big woods, where it's more open between the trees. Deer walk right by you in the Plains, ten feet away. In the Plains, they can hide from you, don't you think that they can't."

The director of New Jersey's Fish and Game Division, Lester MacNamara, was born and grew up in the San Joaquin Valley of California. He went to the University of California, and after that, in 1929, to the Game Conservation Institute in Clinton, New Jersey, a school that no longer exists. He is a big, soft-spoken man with a splendidly weatherworn face. Before reaching his present position, he wandered the state for years as chief of the Bureau of Wildlife. "When I left California, I thought I was coming to a place that would be just one line of houses," he once told me. "I found it entirely different. New Jersey has always been very interesting to me, not only from the point of view of wildlife but of its wilderness, too. I went back to California in 1950. Places I used to hunt when I was a kid, you couldn't hunt. I hurried back here. The Fish and Game Division has purchased a lot of land down in the Pine Barrens. I hate to think of losing the pines to industry."

9
Vision

IN EVERY DECADE for more than a century, there have been men of vision who could see, and somehow could make others see, urban skylines in the pines—with beautiful, pine-scented subdivisions set close to throbbing factories. Roughly five hundred major real-estate promotions based on these intracranial panoramas have been set in motion since 1850, and the selling points have always been irresistible. After all, industry once prospered in the pines. It could prosper again. No matter what a buyer pays per acre, the land values seem certain to rise, and the purchase of land is an excellent speculative investment. The long succession of instant paradises has made the Pine Barrens the scene of what is perhaps the country's only permanent nonexistent land boom. In the eighteen-sixties, the name of Atsion was changed to Fruitland and the surrounding woods were divided into small lots. Pamphlets titled "Cheap Lands, Homes for the Homeless, the Wild Lands of New Jersey" were handed out on New York City sidewalks. "The New Jersey wilderness shall be transformed into farms and fields of grain," the pamphlets said. "A large population should take the place of a few scattered families of woodchoppers and coal-burners and their concomitants of ignorance, sin, and wretchedness. Let all this forest be made flagrant with fruit blossoms!" In a short time, the name of Fruitland was changed back to Atsion, and the woods remained unflagrant. A New York doctor once started a clinic on Apple Pie Hill. He bottled and sold water from a spring, and he divided the slopes into five-acre lots and sold them, too. Almost nothing was built, and the only structure there now is the fire tower. A mile or so west of Apple Pie Hill was Paisley, the Magic City. Paisley was an instant Athens, where, according to advertisements that ran in the New York *World* in 1889, "Your neighbors are great artists, authors, composers, medical men, lawyers." Wavering buyers were warned against delay: "Grasp this last opportunity. We will never sell lots in Paisley at these prices again." The

Magic City covered fourteen hundred acres and included thirteen thousand lots. The promoters bought the land for three dollars and sixty-seven cents an acre and sold it, usually, for three hundred and seventy-five dollars an acre, although to get things moving they gave lots away. There were Paisley offices in New York, Philadelphia, Washington, and Chicago. More than three thousand people bought Paisley land, and nearly all of them, in expectation of turnover profits, sat back and waited for the others to build. The nutrient-free soils of Paisley were advertised as "the finest farmland in central New Jersey," and the town itself was described as "a manufacturing center with an academy of music, conservatories, schools, and colleges." At Paisley's peak of development, in 1890, the Magic City consisted of twelve wooden buildings. Nothing is there now but a stucco gun club that was built in recent times. Over the years, more than a million people have bought or otherwise acquired lots in the Pine Barrens on which no houses have ever been built. There were once twenty-two thousand proposed houses on proposed roads in Bass River Township alone. The lots were twenty feet wide and eighty feet deep, or roughly the size of a brownstone lot in Manhattan. Prosperity Park, outside Chatsworth, consisted of eighteen thousand lots, twenty-five by a hundred feet. In the nineteen-twenties, lots were given away as premiums with new subscriptions to a Philadelphia newspaper. In the Depression, deeds to lots in the Pine Barrens were given away as door prizes at movie theatres and to purchasers of encyclopedias. The selling price at the time was five dollars a lot. When prospective buyers actually came to see the land, promoters tied pears and apples to the limbs of pine trees and stationed fishermen in small boats in Pine Barrens lakes with dead pickerel on the ends of their lines and instructions to pull the fish out of the water every ten minutes. The typical development never existed on anything but paper. Some subdivisions were cleared but never built, and the vegetation soon moved back in to cover almost all the evidence. In one lonely place in the woods today is a street sign marked Fifth Avenue

In many areas of the Pine Barrens, titles are so cloudy—as a result of all the speculation—that about twelve thousand acres of the woods are virtually a no man's land. Modern real-estate sharks have further complicated the situation by faking the signatures of "original owners" in order to gain title to pieces of land. It has been said of one such realtor that he is able to disappear into empty woods and emerge moments later with a signed deed. When four thousand four hundred acres of land were offered for sale a few years ago, the state looked into the property and found that the would-be sellers owned only twelve hundred acres. In other places, the land-ownership picture is clearer. There are two hundred and fifty square miles of state forest in the central Pine Barrens, in areas that are not contiguous. The Plains are, for the most part, privately owned, and so are all the woods for several miles around Chatsworth in every direction. More than half the private land is in absentee ownership. Speculators think no less of the pines now than they did in the days of the Magic City. They are just a little quieter about it. They are waiting. The Pine Barrens were bypassed by the farmers of the seventeenth century, but they are unlikely to be bypassed now. The simple facts of all that space and all that subsurface water increase in importance with each new nail that goes into the megalopolis of which the Pine Barrens are the geographical center. Many private owners have more than a thousand acres, and a number of corporations have been organized for the purpose of real-estate speculation in the pines. One man in North Jersey owns five thousand acres near Chatsworth and wants to turn them into an industrial park. There are individual holdings in the same area of four thousand acres, two thousand acres, and fifty-five hundred acres. The Rutherford Stuyvesant estate, known as the Lacey Tract, contains fourteen thousand five hundred acres in the northeastern pines and is owned now by a syndicate. A nine-thousand-acre property nearby is owned by another syndicate. Pineland sells, on the average, for a hundred and fifty dollars an acre. There is a sign on a tree on Carranza's Road that says "2,150 Acres—For Information Call New York City, TRafalgar 3-9111." Some people in the pines say that they wouldn't mind seeing industry come in, since they could use the tax money. Others have refused to sell land even for small roadside refreshment stands, because of the changes such things effect in the nature of the woods.

Of all the schemes that have ever been created for the development of the Pine Barrens, the most exhaustive and expensive one is the proposal for a jetport and a new city. Under this plan, a spur of the Garden State Parkway would take off into the woods from Toms River, soon passing beneath the central business district of a city of two hundred and fifty thousand people. Beyond the city, the road would go through a green belt, then through an industrial park, and then under the runways and past the terminal building of the largest airport on earth—four times as large as Newark Airport, LaGuardia, and Kennedy put together. As a supersonic jetport, it would serve a third of the United States, and supersonic jets would land there ninety minutes after leaving Paris. Shuttle jets would fly passengers to inland airports, and hundred-and-fifty-mile-an-hour trains would take travellers to Philadelphia in twenty minutes and to New York in thirty. All this was worked out by Herbert H. Smith Associates, of Trenton, under contract to the Pinelands Regional Planning Board, a group consisting of representatives of Burlington and Ocean Counties. The study cost a hundred and twenty thousand dollars and was largely paid for by the federal government. It was published in 1964, and since then it has been drawing abuse from conservationists, hunters, campers, and pineys—along with studious disregard from the Port of New York Authority. The Federal Aviation Administration has said that the jetport would interfere with present air-traffic patterns but that if the state wanted to build it F.A.A. approval could be secured. The New Jersey legislature has displayed some interest in the project, and the governor has appointed a committee of businessmen to study the feasibility of a jetport in the pines.

Forked River Mountain, in the Lacey Tract, is in the center of the proposed city. With Herbert Smith, the planner, I went up there one morning to have a look at the site. It was a clear summer day, with big clouds in the sky and a cool wind blowing. The view from the top of the hill was spacious, and unbroken pineland reached away for miles, streaked with dark lines of cedars. "I hope I don't start to cry," Smith said. "This is a planner's dream. From this elevation, we could move right out onto the central-business-district platform—two hundred and forty acres of stores and plazas and high buildings in the middle of the city, for pedestrians only. The parkway goes under the platform, and there is parking space down there for twenty thousand cars. Battery-operated taxis and battery-operated scooters are permitted on the platform. The sidewalks move, too. Even outside the platform, underpasses and bridges make it possible for you to walk from any part of the city to any other part without crossing a street. This area of the pinelands simply begins to jump out at you if you're going to go for urbanization. It's magnificent. It's just magnificent. I can see those goldarn structures now, surrounded with green."

Smith is a trim, likable, red-headed man in his forties. He comes from Mayfield, Kentucky. He was educated at the University of Cincinnati, got an M.A. in planning from Cornell, and worked in the planning office of the State of New Jersey before setting up his own practice. In my car, we drove a short distance to a dry, flat area that had been badly burned not long before. The spiky remains of the trees were grotesque. Smith remarked that we were in the middle of the campus of the city college. As we drove on, along a sand road, he said, "We've come through the city college into the high-density low-income housing area." The car was bumping over a corduroy surface of cedar logs, but I imagined myself cruising along Avenue D on the lower East Side of Manhattan. A burned-up 1949 Chrysler, which had been abandoned in the high-density low-income housing area of the proposed city, was sieved with bullet holes and had ninety-three bullet holes in the driver's door alone. "There are two elementary schools nearby," Smith said, studying a map on his knees. "Now we are in a neighborhood of town houses and garden apartments. . . . Now we are just about to pass over the Garden State Parkway connection. We are between a high-rise area and the city-center core. . . . Now we're in the middle of the lake—twenty feet deep, two miles long. That's the country club over there. . . . Now we're right in the middle of the hoity-toity housing." In the middle of the hoity-toity housing was the only building we had seen in two hours of driving around the city. It was made of purplish-tan bricks and had a corrugated roof, and its name was over the door—Ironside Gun Club.

Smith sees his plan as "a happy marriage between conservation and economic development," since—in concert with the new city, the jetport, and the industrial park—it calls for five hundred square miles of state forest, or twice the amount of state forest that is now set aside in the pines. He believes that no unilateral conservation plan could accomplish as much. He suggests also that a possible alternative to the new city would be three new towns with populations of about eighty thousand each. "What we're pleading for is that a pinelands area be defined and then developed according to a single, controlled plan," he said. "It goes against my political philosophy, but sovereign government can do it, and I don't know of another area where both economic and conservation potential can be realized so completely. In this situation right here, we have the epitome of the problem of planning in a democratic society. We can make the plan, but then we run into conflict with all the people who want to profit from the land by exploitation. Private enterprise *could* do a hell of a lot. If, say, Esso and Portland Cement and Johns-Manville saw the potential, a development corporation could be formed and the new city could be developed by free enterprise. Private enterprise needs to prove that it can do this. Or the state could create a Pinelands Development Authority, with the right of eminent domain and the right to sell bonds with state credit pledged behind them. This is the way the Garden State Parkway Authority was set up. To do this, you have to declare a public purpose—in this case, water potential, conservation of an open area, and a new city with a decent way of life for people in a region that has economic potential. Planning has to be statewide for the pines. Otherwise, you have local planning boards coming up with controlled hodgepodge. I will predict that if nothing at all is done in terms of planned development here, within twenty years the area will be so spotted with exploitative development that it will be impossible to assemble the land into something that is sensibly planned. The state has about five years in which to act."

We moved on to see the site of the jetport, which would cover thirty-two thousand five hundred acres and would eliminate virtually all of the Upper and Lower Plains, several ponds, a lake, an entire state forest, and Bear Swamp Hill. The dual runways, forming a great square, would each be two miles wide. The over-all cleared area for each runway—including overrun areas at the ends—would be five miles long. "You get a hell of a lot less fog here than you do at the New York airports," Smith said. "This one would be open fifty per cent more than Newark, Kennedy, and LaGuardia." We were standing on the observation platform of the fire tower on Bear Swamp Hill. The ranger, in the cabin above us, was listening to rock 'n' roll. Looking out over the immense forest, Smith went on to say, "One of our problems is that you can't get people to believe that this area is as big as this. They can't believe that you could come down here and build a fifty-one-square-mile airport and not have a structure problem—not even one building visible from here to the horizon. Bear Swamp Hill is in the terminal-service area, where the planes would come in and unload. I can just see those supersonic transports coming in here now. Gorgeous! And when they take off, you can get them out over the ocean before they break the sound barrier. Here comes Flight 424, which left London one and a half hours ago. Brisbane is five hours away."

Many people would like to see the conservation part of Smith's plan developed wholly on its own. A group called the Pine Barrens Conservationists has advanced a proposal that ninety thousand acres—including all of the Plains—be preserved under the administration of the National Park Service. The area would be called a national reserve, would lie between existing state forests, including the Wharton Forest, and would effectively keep one big segment of the central pines perpetually wild. The New Jersey Audubon Society has a proposal for a national monument that encompasses even more land. In a general way, the National Park Service has offered encouragement to these plans, but some of the Park Service people I talked with seemed to think that the state should preserve the Pine Barrens. They pointed out that the laws are uncompromising under which various federal preserves are established, and that making even a part of the woods a national domain might limit too severely the uses to which the land could be put. State people, for their part, said frankly that no land is safe in the hands of the state. New Jersey's Forest Park Reservation Act is among the most elastic conservation laws ever written. The state can use its forest land for any purpose it chooses. There is no guarantee that state forests will be preserved. In

1951, a small state park was sold outright to Western Union. In 1961, a large piece of a state forest, including a section of the Appalachian Trail, was sold to the New Jersey Power & Light Co. On the other hand, federal law would prohibit the removal of subsurface water from a Pine Barrens national monument, no matter how badly it was needed. Controlled burning would be forbidden, and so would hunting, although ecologists who have studied the Pine Barrens feel that the deer count has to be kept down or the balance of nature will be seriously upset. In a Pine Barrens national park, these limitations would be identical. Calling the area a national reserve might solve the problem. Another alternative might be a national recreation area, but when this is mentioned National Park Service people say that new lakes would have to be made, big enough for powerboats; cabins, tent-platform cities, and even airfields would have to be built. "You can't make a national recreation area just for a few people who have canoes," one man told me. "People who go to a national recreation area want to play in the water and drink beer and eat hot dogs and that sort of deal. Orchids? Eagles? If they happen to be there, O.K.—but they have to be there along with the other things. The Pine Barrens probably should be state-managed."

Given the futilities of that debate, given the sort of attention that is ordinarily paid to plans put forward by conservationists, and given the great numbers and the crossed purposes of all the big and little powers that would have to work together to accomplish *anything* on a major scale in the pines, it would appear that the Pine Barrens are not very likely to be the subject of dramatic decrees or acts of legislation. They seem to be headed slowly toward extinction. In retrospect, people may one day look back upon the final stages of the development of the great unbroken Eastern city and be able to say at what moment all remaining undeveloped land should have been considered no longer a potential asset to individuals but an asset of the society at large—perhaps a social necessity. Meanwhile, up goes a sign—"Whispering Pines, Two and Three Bedrooms, $11,900"—and down go seventy-five acres of trees. Up goes another sign: "Industry!! Jackson Township Has an Abundance of Water!," and another: "Dreamwood Acres, from $13,900," and another: "Deer Hollow Estates, Five Models," and another: “Sav-Cote, Inc., Manufacturers of Liquid Plastic Coatings,” and others: “Buck’s Outlet Store,” “Pine Tree Inn —Dinners, Snacks, Package Goods,” “A. G. Weller, Landscaping, Bulldozing,” “Will Build to Suit.” At the rate of a few hundred yards or even a mile or so each year, the perimeter of the pines contracts.

ENCOUNTERS WITH THE ARCHDRUID

To Robert Bingham

Contents

PART I

A Mountain

A SMALL CABIN stands in the Glacier Peak Wilderness, about a hundred yards off a trail that crosses the Cascade Range. In midsummer, the cabin looked strange in the forest. It was only twelve feet square, but it rose fully two stories and then had a high and steeply peaked roof. From the ridge of the roof, moreover, a ten-foot pole stuck straight up. Tied to the top of the pole was a shovel. To hikers shedding their backpacks at the door of the cabin on a cold summer evening—as five of us did—it was somewhat unnerving to look up and think of people walking around in snow perhaps thirty-five feet above, hunting for that shovel, then digging their way down to the threshold. Men from the Chelan County Snow Survey use the cabin in winter while they measure snow depths and snow densities, and figure how much runoff to expect at the time of thaw. Because of the almost unbelievable amount of snow that can accumulate in that part of the State of Washington, what they do there is a vital matter to the people below and even far beyond the mountains.

What we were doing there was something else again. We were tired. We had walked seven and a half miles uphill since three that afternoon. One of us was in his sixties, another in his fifties, and all of us saw the cabin as a haven from what obviously would have been very cold ground. Until midsummer, the trails had been impassable, and to make the trip we had had to wait for the winter snows to melt. An entry in the register in the cabin said that snow had fallen one week earlier, August 5th. But we had been drawn to the Cascades in part because a great many people believed that they were the most beautiful mountains in the United States. A somewhat smaller and, on the whole, more parochial group felt that these huge, conical peaks, raised in volcanic fire and later carved by moving ice, were the most beautiful mountains in the world. In 1964, the United States Congress set aside this region and others as permanent wilderness, not to receive even the use given a national park, not to be entered by a machine of any kind except in extreme emergency, not to be developed or altered or lumbered—forevermore. Within the structure of this so-called Wilderness Act, however, was a provision known as "the mining exception": all established claims would remain open to mining, and new claims could be made in any wilderness until 1984. At the foot of Glacier Peak, in the center of this particular wilderness, is a copper lode that is half a mile from side to side. The Kennecott Copper Corporation has a patented claim on this deposit and could work it any time. We wanted to have a look at the region while it was still pristine. The others left it to me to add their names to the register in the cabin: Charles Park, geologist, mineral engineer, who believes that if copper were to be found under the White House, the White House should be moved; David Brower, who has been described by Stewart Udall as "the most effective single person on the cutting edge of conservation in this country," leader of a conservation organization called Friends of the Earth; and Larry Snow and Lance Brigham, medical students from the University of Washington, who were along to help with the logistics of the trip and perhaps incidentally to give first aid.

A mouse ran out from under the cabin, made a fast move among the packs, and went back under the cabin. We collected firewood and water. There was a cascade, white and plummeting, beyond the cabin. We changed into warmer clothes and lighter shoes. Brower, who hiked in twill shorts and a T-shirt and soft gray Italian boots, put on a long plaid shirt, trousers, and a pair of basketball shoes. Although he was out of shape, Brower was a prepossessing figure. He was a tall man. He had heavy bones, thick wrists, strong ankles. And he had a delicate, handsome, ruddy face, its features all finely proportioned but slightly too small, too refined, for the size of his frame, suggesting delicacy. His voice was quiet and persuasively mellifluous. He had an engaging smile and flashing white teeth. He was in his late fifties, and he had a windy shock of white hair. Brower had dropped out of college when he was nineteen, and disappeared into the Sierra Nevada. He had spent his life defending mountain ranges and what, by extension, they symbolized to him, and one of the ironies of his life was that his love of the mountains had long since drawn him away from them and into buildings impertinently called skyscrapers, into congressional corridors, into temporary offices in hotel rooms, into battle after battle, and out of shape. (In the idiom of conservation, "battle" is the foremost term for what conservationists do, and conservationist publications are "battle tracts.") Brower's skin was pink from the work of the climb, and when he was taking off his soaked T-shirt he had revealed a fold across his middle. The mouse ran out again from under the cabin, looked around, its nose vibrating, and retreated.

Lance Brigham said, "Stick your head out once more, mouse, and it's curtains for you."

Brower said softly, "It's we who are the intruders."

Park had been taking off his boots—made in Canada, of heavy leather—and was putting on a pair of sandals. He grinned cryptically. He, too, had a shock of white hair. He was in his sixties, and he was as trim and hard as a college athlete, which he had once been, and nothing about him suggested that he had ever been out of breath. From his youth to the present, he had spent a high proportion of his life in the out-of-doors, and a high proportion of that in wilderness. Going up the trail that afternoon, with his geologist's pick in his hand, he whacked or chipped at half the boulders and rock faces we passed, and every once in a while, apparently for the sheer hell of it, he rapped the pick's hammer end on the stump of a tree that had been taken to clear the trail.

"That's a habit I developed long ago—banging on rocks and stumps," he said.

"Why?"

"Kodiak bears. I never wanted to take one by surprise. The same is true in Africa of leopards and gorillas. In other words, never take an animal by surprise."

Park spoke slowly, not because he was hesitant but simply in a measure that seemed compatible with geologic time. He had an almond face, alert gray eyes, and a mobile smile that tended to concentrate in one or the other corner of his mouth. He was even taller than Brower, and he wore khaki from head to foot. He had a visored khaki cap.

Not far into the mountains from their eastern extremity, at Lake Chelan, we had come to an oddly formal landmark. It was a sign that said, "You Are Now Entering the Glacier Peak Wilderness Area." In other words, "Take one more step and, by decree, you will enter a preserved and separate world, you will pass from civilization into wilderness." Wilderness was now that definable, that demonstrable, and could be entered in the sense that one enters a room.

Park said, "Will they let me carry my pick in there?"

"Until 1984," said Brower.

We stepped across the line. I said, "If we get lost in here with that pick, we may discover a new copper deposit."

Brower said, "If you make a new discovery, I'm here to see that you don't get out."

We moved on into the wilderness. The trail was dusty. It was covered with a light-brown powder too fine to be called sand. Park said it was glacial flour—finely ground rock coming out of the ice, ice of the past and ice of the present. Far above us in the high cirques were glaciers—the Lyman Glacier, Isella Glacier, Mary Green Glacier, and, perhaps prophetically, the Company Glacier on Bonanza Peak. The sky was blue and cloudless, a day to remember in the Cascades. Brower said he was disappointed that it was not raining. He explained that he did not like dry duff but preferred the feel and the beauty of a wet and glistening forest, vaporous and dripping. He said that he hoped we would be fortunate enough to have a good rain before the trip was over. He labored slowly up the trail, taking it conservatively, eating thimbleberries and huckleberries as he moved along.

"There are no really old rocks in the Cascades," Park said, nicking a rock in passing. He picked up and admiringly turned in his hand a piece of pistachio-green epidote. Two hundred yards up the trail, he rapped at an outcropping with his pick and said, "That is volcanic." Minutes later, he swung again, sent chips flying, and said, "That is contact rock." This in some way entertained Brower, who laughed and shook his head. I remembered once driving through the Black Hills with Park, and how he would stop his car from time to time and just sit there looking at rocks. As a boy in Delaware, Park used to collect rocks and think about the West. While he was still in Wilmington High School, he had fifty ore minerals in his collection—hematite, malachite, galena, chromite. "I wanted to study mining, not particularly geology—mining," he said. "I just wanted to get into rocks. Mining has always appealed to me. It's in the out-of-the-way places."

A serrated ridge several miles from the trail had a reddish

glow in the late-afternoon light. "See that color? That's pyrite," Park said, pointing. "Copper often comes with it. If I were in here looking for copper, that's where I'd head." The copper terrain we wanted to see was still more than ten miles away, however, and we stayed on the trail.

We passed a big Douglas fir, at least six feet in diameter, that had crashed to earth in the recent past, and Brower said how nice it was to see it there, to know that some lumber company had never had a chance at it, to see the decay stage of a natural cycle—the forest reclaiming its own. If dead trees are not left to rot, he said, the ecology of the wilderness is disturbed. Park kept his reactions to himself. His eye wandered to a square hole in a cedar stump. He waved his pick in the direction of the stump and said, "Pileated woodpecker." We moved on.

After a series of switchbacks had lifted us seven hundred feet in less than a quarter of a mile, we stopped to rest by a stream that was alternately falling through the air and racing down the mountainside. Everywhere, from every slope, the Cascades cascade. Water shoots out of cracks in the rock, it falls over the edges of cliffs, it foams, sprays, runs, and plunges pure and cold. Enough snow and rain fall up there to irrigate Libya, and when water is not actually falling from the sky the sun is melting it from alpine ice. Down the dark-green mountainsides go streamers of white water, and above the timberline water shines against the rock. In every depression is a tarn, and we had passed a particularly beautiful one a little earlier and, from the escarpment, were looking back at it now. It was called Hart Lake and was fed by a stream that, in turn, fell away from a high and deafening cataract. The stream was interrupted by a series of beaver ponds. All around these free-form pools were stands of alder, aspen, Engelmann's spruce; and in the surrounding mountains, just under the summits, were glaciers and fields of snow. Brower, who is an aesthetician by trade and likes to point to beautiful things, had nothing to say at that moment. Neither did Park. I was remembering the words of a friend of mine in the National Park Service, who had once said to me, "The Glacier Peak Wilderness is probably the most beautiful piece of country we've got. Mining copper there would be like hitting a pretty girl in the face with a shovel. It would be like strip-mining the Garden of Eden."

Park wiped his forehead with his hat. I dipped a cup into the stream and offered him a drink. He hesitated. "Well, why not?" he said, at last. He took the cup and he drank, put the cup down with a smile, wiped his lips, and said, "That's good stuff."

"It's melted glacier ice, isn't it?"

Park nodded, and swallowed a little more.

Brower drank from a cup that was almost identical to mine —stainless steel, with low, sloping sides, a wide flat bottom, a looped wire handle—with the difference that in raised letters on the bottom of Brower's cup were the words "Sierra Club." Brower for seventeen years had been the executive director of the Sierra Club—its leader, its principal strategist, its preëminent fang. In the mountains, a Sierra Club mountaineer eats and drinks everything out of his Sierra Club cup, and in various wildernesses with Brower I had never seen him eat or drink from anything else. In the past, in the High Sierra, he had on occasion rubbed pennyroyal-mint leaves over the embossed letters in the bottom of his cup and added snow and whiskey for a kind of high-altitude julep, but he rarely drinks much in the mountains and there was no whiskey at all on this trip. That night at the snow cabin, we ate our dinner from our cups —noodles, beef, chocolate pudding—and hung our packs on high rafters and were asleep before nine. We slept on bunks that had been tiered in the improbable cabin. At two in the morning, we were all awake, with flashlight beams crisscrossing from various heights in the compact blackness.

"What the hell is going on?"

"What is it?"

"What's there?"

"Four very beautiful little tan-and-white meadow mice," Brower said.

"Aw, for heaven's sake," Park said, and he went back to sleep.

Park, throughout his career, had not made a religion of camping out, and he had been particularly pleased when we found the cabin and its bunks, although they were little more than stiffly woven wire in frames. His general practice on trips of exploration for minerals had been to sleep in a bed if there was one within five miles, so he had managed to keep his lifetime total down to something like nineteen hundred nights on the ground. On foot and alone, he had hunted for copper in the Philippines, in Cuba, in Mexico, in Arizona, in Tennessee. He had hunted for silver in Nevada and Greece, for gold in Alaska, gold in South Dakota, and—on one curious assignment for the United States Geological Survey—gold in Alabama, Georgia, South Carolina, North Carolina, Virginia, and the District of Columbia. He had found what he was looking for. During the Second World War, there was a working gold mine in Rock Creek Park, in Washington, D.C. Such is Park's feeling for where ore bodies are that some of his friends think he has occult powers. For fifteen years or so, he used his skills in the name of the Geological Survey. Then, in the late nineteen-forties, he began to teach geology and mineral engineering at Stanford University, where he eventually became Dean of the School of Earth Sciences. From one base or the other—Washington or Palo Alto—he has never stopped hunting the earth for metal, sometimes as a consultant to various companies. He has looked almost everywhere for iron and manganese. He once set up a base camp at fifteen thousand feet in the Chilean-Bolivian Andes and, working up from there, found iron at seventeen thousand feet. In 1956, he was taken in a pirogue up the Ivindo River, in Gabon, to a point from which he took compass bearings and walked for two weeks through jungle. On relatively high ground, elephant trails were so wide and hard they were like roads, but in swamps the elephants' footprints were like postholes. The canopy was so thick it obscured the sky. Park had had serious back trouble for some time, and one day he fell to the ground and could not get up. He lay there for two hours until something jelled, and he got slowly to his feet again and moved on. He was hunting for iron, and he found a part of what is now called the Belinga Deposit. Even in the United States, he usually stayed out, alone, for about two weeks at a time. He went light, eating out of his frying pan and drinking from a small tin cup. He has used the same pick for twenty years. He speaks of the rootlessness of the life of an exploration geologist and says that many people tend to be discouraged by it. "You're just wandering. You're on the loose." He has planted gardens spring after spring and never seen his plants in bloom. Instead, he has drawn from the earth its mercury, lead, zinc, uranium, fluorspar, phosphate, nickel, molybdenum, manganese, iron, lithium, tin, copper, silver, and gold.

In the morning, soon after we were again on the trail, we went around the north edge of a lake that had a surface of at least ninety acres and was almost as big as the glacier that was dripping into it from fourteen hundred feet above. The effect of glacial flour in still water is to turn it green. As we moved uphill, and looked back, we saw that there were three other green lakes, closer to the glacier. In them, small icebergs were drifting. Ahead of us, and far above, was a ridge that ran north-south and dipped at one point to form a shallow notch. This was our immediate destination, and it had been named Cloudy Pass, because the most distant view a person usually has there is of his own groping hands. On this day, though, the sky was without clouds anywhere. The climb was steep toward the pass and we tended to string out. Brower, in the lead, said again that he wished it were raining.

I asked him if, by his own standards, he would describe the terrain we were in as wilderness. "Yes, it is wilderness," he said. "The Sierra is what I love, but these mountains are perhaps the most beautiful we have." Then he accelerated his pace and was soon far ahead. He seemed to be feeling good, getting into rhythm with the mountains.

A mosquito bit Park on the wrist, and he slapped it. "They follow the snow," he said. "The higher we get, the more mosquitoes there are."

We climbed on in silence for a while, and then he asked why Brower had gone on so far ahead.

"I don't know. He seems to want to be alone," I said.

"He certainly is—let's say—reserved," Park said. "I don't see how anyone could ever break through it. I almost called him yesterday when he said the big trees ought to be left to rot in the forest. Long before they fall, they are dying from the inside out. It's a shame not to use big trees like that." He waved his pick at a stand of spruce. "I am not a member of the Sierra Club," he went on. "I don't approve of their policy. To me, they are preservationists, not conservationists. You can't avoid change. You can direct it, but you can't avoid it. I like Sierra Club books, though."

In 1960, in Yosemite Valley, Brower helped put together an exhibit of landscape photographs and accompanying swatches of prose. Then he developed the idea of circulating the exhibit in book form. The result was the Sierra Club's Exhibit-Format series—big, four-pound, creamily beautiful, living-room-furniture books that argue the cause of conservation in terms, photographically, of exquisite details from the natural world and, textually, of essences of writers like Thoreau and Muir. Brower was editor and publisher. He selected the photographs. He wrote the prefaces. In this way, as in others, he brought the words "Sierra Club" into the national frame of reference. He published Exhibit-Format books on everything from the Maine islands (*Summer Island—Penobscot Country*) to the Grand Canyon (*Time and the River Flowing*), the region of his own youth (*Gentle Wilderness—the Sierra Nevada*), and the mountains we were now crossing (*The Wild Cascades*). Within nine years, people had paid ten million dollars for Exhibit-Format books, and Brower said he had been surprised to find that people were willing to pay that much for beauty. Brower himself was certainly willing to spend money on it. Once, a set of picture proofs did not look quite right to him and he had ten thousand dollars' worth of plates thrown out. Udall gave *Time and the River Flowing* to Lyndon and Lady Bird Johnson for Christmas, 1964. At twenty-five dollars a copy, the books were, in a sense, investments, and rich conservationists bought them in round lots. Struggling conservationists could buy them in compacted form as three-dollar-and-ninety-five-cent paperbacks.

With Brower as its executive director, the Sierra Club grew from an organization of seven thousand members to an organization of seventy-seven thousand members. The figure seems both large and small. There are more people in Cedar Rapids than there are in the Sierra Club. Nonetheless, under Brower the club became a truly potent force, affecting legislation that had to do with the use of the land, the sea, and the atmosphere. Brower was not the leader in every battle. He concentrated on certain foes, and many were in the Department of the Interior. To the Bureau of Reclamation, he is the Antichrist. They say there that Brower singlehandedly prevented the construction of two major dams in the

Grand Canyon for at least two generations and possibly for all time. On the Green River in Utah, Brower stopped cold a dam that would have inundated parts of Dinosaur National Monument. In the cause of mountains, he and lieutenants in the State of Washington fought loggers, miners, and hunters, and won a North Cascades National Park. For nearly twenty years, Brower has crossed and recrossed the United States campaigning for conservation before every kind of audience. The federal government's Outdoor Recreation Resources Review was his idea. He was a primary force in the advancement of the Wilderness Act. His counterparts in other conservation organizations long ago acknowledged him as "*the* spokesman for protected wilderness." Once, when Brower had driven for several hours through wretched fog and rain to attend a meeting and make a speech in Poughkeepsie, I asked him if he could say why he did all this, and he said, "I don't know. It beats the hell out of me. I'm trying to save some forests, some wilderness. I'm trying to do anything I can to get man back into balance with the environment. He's way out—way out of balance. The land won't last, and we won't."

Having moved above the trees into a clear area, Park stopped to look back over the forest, the green lakes, the glacier, the snowfields, and the white peaks beyond. I asked him if, from his experience, he would call this wilderness. "No," he said. "Not with this trail in it." He agreed that what we were looking at was almost incomparable, and he said he doubted if Brower saw anything he didn't see. "That is a beautiful view," he went on. "And these are magnificent mountains. They remind me of the Chilean Andes. But how is a mining company operating a pit on the other side of this ridge going to hurt all this? I don't see it. My idea of conservation is maximum use. I think preserving wilderness as wilderness is a terrible mistake. This area is one of the few places in the country where copper exists now in commercial quantities, and we just have to have copper. The way things are set up, we can't do without it. To lock this place up as wilderness could imperil the whole park system, because in ten years or so, when copper becomes really short, people will start yelling and revisions will have to be made. Any act of Congress can be repealed." Park was speaking slowly, and we were making our way up through open alpine meadows that were splayed with streams and full of heather, lupine, horsemint, daisies, and wild licorice. "I'm in favor of multiple use of land," he continued. "Have you ever been in the Harz Mountains? With proper housekeeping, you can have a mine and a sawmill and a primitive area all close together. When the Kerr-McGee Corporation wanted to mine phosphate on the coast of Georgia, conservationists howled. A hearing was held, and twenty-six people, most of them representing groups, testified against Kerr-McGee. *No one* testified for them. This shocked me. It was like people standing around watching a man get beat up. When Texas Gulf Sulphur drilled three holes and found an ore body in Ontario, people accused them of hiding information. I testified before the S.E.C. on their behalf. The image of copper companies is bad today, with all this conservation poop. There's a Clark's nutcracker!" The nutcracker, in flight, was a hundred feet above us.

We were now about to top the final rise to Cloudy Pass, where Brower was waiting. We looked back again over the eastward view—lakes, peaks, beaver ponds, cascades, snow, ice, white-ribbon streams, and dark-green forests. Again Park said, "I don't see it. I don't see how a mine on the other side of this ridge is going to affect that." Park lives in a trim, attractive, solid-looking one-level house on a dead-end street in Palo Alto, and beside his front door is a decorative grouping of green rocks—copper ore—and an old pick with a broken handle. With his present pick, he swung at an outcropping with what seemed to me to be unusual curiosity and force.

"What are you looking for?" I said.

A grin came into the corner of his mouth. "Nothing," he said. "I just haven't hit one in a long time."

Most of the pass was covered with snow, but there were some patches of bare ground, and these were blue, green, red, yellow, and white with wild flowers. The air felt and smelled like the first warm, thaw-bringing day in spring in Vermont, and, despite the calendar, spring was now the season at that altitude in the North Cascades, and summer and fall would come and go in the few weeks remaining before the first big snow of September. Brower had dropped his pack and was sitting on a small knoll among the flowers. Park and I and Brigham and Snow dropped our own packs, and felt the sudden coolness of air reaching the sweatlines where the packs had been—and the inebriate lightness that comes, after a long climb, when the backpack is suddenly gone. The ground Brower was sitting on was ten or fifteen feet higher than the ground on which we stood, and as we went up to join him our eyes at last moved above the ridge-line, and for the first time we could see beyond it. What we saw made us all stop.

One of the medical students said, "Wow!"

I said slowly, the words just involuntarily falling out, "My God, look at that."

Across a deep gulf of air, and nearly a mile higher than the ground on which we stood, eleven miles away by line of sight, was Glacier Peak—palpable, immediate, immense. In the direction we were looking, we could see perhaps two hundred square miles of land, and the big mountain dominated that scene in the way that the Jungfrau dominates the Bernese Alps. Glacier Peak had originally been a great symmetrical cone, and that was still its basic shape, but it had been monumentally scarred, from within and without. It once exploded. Pieces of it landed in what is now Idaho, and other pieces landed in what is now Oregon. The ice sheet mauled it. Rivers from its own glaciers cut grooves in it. But it had remained, in silhouette, a classic mountain, its lines sweeping up beyond its high shoulder—called Disappointment Peak—and converging acutely at the summit. The entire upper third of the mountain was white. And below the snow and ice, black-green virgin forest continued all the way down to the curving valley of the Suiattle River, a drop of eight thousand feet from the peak. Spread around the summit like huge, improbable petals were nine glaciers—the Cool Glacier, the Scimitar Glacier, the Dusty Glacier, the Chocolate Glacier—and from each of these a white line of water ran down through the timber and into the Suiattle. To our right, on the near side of the valley, another mountain—Plummer Mountain—rose up about two-thirds as high, and above its timberline its snowless faces of rock were, in the sunlight, as red as rust. Around and beyond Glacier Peak, the summits of other mountains, random and receding, led the eye away to the rough horizon and back to Glacier Peak.

Brower said, without emphasis, "That is what is known in my trade as a scenic climax."

Near the southern base of Plummer Mountain and in the deep valley between Plummer Mountain and Glacier Peak —that is, in the central foreground of the view that we were looking at from Cloudy Pass—was the lode of copper that Kennecott would mine, and to do so the company would make an open pit at least two thousand four hundred feet from rim to rim.

Park said, "A hole in the ground will not materially hurt this scenery."

Brower stood up. "None of the experts on scenic resources will agree with you," he said. "This is one of the few remaining great wildernesses in the lower forty-eight. Copper is not a transcendent value here."

"Without copper, we'd be in a pretty sorry situation."

"If that deposit didn't exist, we'd get by without it."

"I would prefer the mountain as it is, but the copper is there."

"If we're down to where we have to take copper from places this beautiful, we're down pretty far."

"Minerals are where you find them. The quantities are finite. It's criminal to waste minerals when the standard of living of your people depends upon them. A mine cannot move. It is fixed by nature. So it has to take precedence over any other use. If there were a copper deposit in Yellowstone Park, I'd recommend mining it. Proper use of minerals is essential. You have to go get them where they are. Our standard of living is based on this."

"For a fifty-year cycle, yes. But for the long term, no. We have to drop our standard of living, so that people a thousand years from now can have any standard of living at all."

A breeze coming off the nearby acres of snow felt cool but not chilling in the sunshine, and rumpled the white hair of the two men.

"I am not for penalizing people today for the sake of future generations," Park said.

"I really am," said Brower. "That's where we differ."

"Yes, that's where we disagree. In 1910, the Brazilian government said they were going to preserve the iron ore in Minas Gerais, because the earth would run short of it in the future. People—thousands and thousands of people in Minas Gerais —were actually starving, and they were living over one of the richest ore deposits in the world, a fifteen-billion-ton reserve. They're mining it now, and people there are prospering. But in the past it was poor consolation to people who were going hungry to say that in the future it was going to be better. You have to use these things when you have them. You have to know where they are, and use them. People, in the future, will go for the copper here."

"The kids who are in Congress in the future should make that decision, and if it's theirs to make I don't think they'll go for the copper here," Brower said.

"Sure they will. They'll have to, if people are going to expect to have telephones, electric lights, airplanes, television sets, radios, central heating, air-conditioning, automobiles. And you *know* people will want these things. I didn't invent them. I just know where the copper is."

Brower swung his pack up onto his back. "Pretend the copper deposit down there doesn't exist," he said. "Then what would you do? What are you going to do when it's gone?"

"You're trying to make everything wilderness," Park said.

"No, I'm not. I'm trying to keep at least two per cent of the terrain as wilderness."

"Two per cent is a lot."

"Two per cent is under pavement."

"Basically, our difference is that I feel we can't stop all this —we must direct it. You feel we must stop it."

"I feel we should go back, recycle, do things over again, and do better, even if it costs more. We mine things and don't use them again. We coat the surface of the earth—with beer cans and chemicals, asphalt and old television sets."

"We *are* recycling copper, but we don't have enough."

"When we knock buildings down, we don't take the copper out. Every building that comes down could be a copper mine. But we don't take the copper out. We go after fresh metal. We destroy that mountain."

"How can you ruin a mountain like Glacier Peak?" Park lifted his pick toward the mountain. "You *can't* ruin it," he went on, waving the pick. "Look at the Swiss mountains. Who could ruin *them*? A mine would not hurt this country—not with proper housekeeping."

Brower started on down the trail. We retrieved our packs and caught up with him. About five hundred feet below us and a mile ahead was another pass—Suiattle Pass—and to reach it we had to go down into a big ravine and up the other side. There were long silences, measured by the sound of boots on the trail. From time to time, the pick rang out against a rock.

Brower said, "Would America have to go without much to leave its finest wilderness unspoiled?"

We traversed a couple of switchbacks and approached the bottom of the ravine. Then Park said, "Where they are more easily accessible, deposits have been found and are being—or have been—mined."

We had seen such a mine near Lake Chelan, in the eastern part of the mountains. The Howe Sound Mining Company established an underground copper mine there in 1938, built a village and called it Holden. The Holden mine was abandoned in 1957. We had hiked past its remains on our way to the wilderness area. Against a backdrop of snowy peaks, two flat-topped hills of earth detritus broke the landscape. One was the dump where all the rock had been put that was removed before the miners reached the ore body. The other consisted of tailings—crushed rock that had been through the Holden mill and had yielded copper. What remained of the mill itself was a macabre skeleton of bent, twisted, rusted beams. Wooden buildings and sheds were rotting and gradually collapsing. The area was bestrewn with huge flakes of corrugated iron, rusted rails, rusted ore carts, old barrels. Although there was no way for an automobile to get to Holden except by barge up Lake Chelan and then on a dirt road to the village, we saw there a high pile of gutted and rusted automobiles, which themselves had originally been rock in the earth and, in the end, in Holden, were crumbling slowly back into the ground.

Park hit a ledge with the pick. We were moving up the other side of the ravine now. The going was steep, and the pace slowed. Brower said, "We saw that at Holden."

I counted twenty-two steps watching the backs of Brower's legs, above the red tops of gray socks. He was moving slower than I would have. I was close behind him. His legs, blue-veined, seemed less pink than they had the day before. They were sturdy but not athletically shapely. Brower used to put food caches in various places in the High Sierra and go from one to another for weeks at a time. He weighed two hundred and twelve pounds now, and he must have wished he were one-eighty.

Park said, "Holden is the sort of place that gave mining a bad name. This has been happening in the West for the past hundred years, but it doesn't have to happen. Poor housekeeping is poor housekeeping wherever you find it. I don't care if it's a mine or a kitchen. Traditionally, when mining companies finished in a place they just walked off. Responsible groups are not going to do that anymore. They're not going to leave trash; they're not going to deface the countryside. Think of that junk! If I had enough money, I'd come up here and clean it up."

I thought how neat Park's house, his lawn, and his gardens are—his roses, his lemon tree, his two hundred varieties of cactus. The name of the street he lives on is Arcadia Place. Park is a member of the Cactus and Succulent Society of America. He hit a fallen tree with the hammer end.

"It's one god-awful mess," Brower said.

"That old mill could be cleaned up," Park said. "Grass could be planted on the dump and the tailings."

Suiattle Pass was now less than a quarter mile ahead of us. I thought of Brower, as a child, on his first trip to the Sierra Nevada. His father drove him there from Berkeley in a 1916 Maxwell. On the western slopes, they saw both the aftermath and the actual operations of hydraulic mining for gold. Men with hoses eight inches in diameter directed water with such force against the hillsides that large parts of the hills themselves fell away as slurry.

"Holden was abandoned in 1957, and no plants of any kind have caught on the dump and the tailings," Brower said.

Holden, in its twenty years of metal production, brought out of the earth ten million tons of rock—enough to make a hundred thousand tons of copper, enough to wire Kansas City.

Park said, "You could put a little fertilizer on—something to get it started."

When we reached the pass, we stood for a moment and looked again at Glacier Peak and, far below us, the curving white line of the Suiattle. Park said, "When you create a mine, there are two things you can't avoid: a hole in the ground and a dump for waste rock. Those are two things you can't avoid."

Brower said, "Except by not doing it at all."

In a bottle gentian, Brower found a butterfly drinking. With a quick but precise move of his hand, he picked it up. He said it was a monarch and that it had a flying range of two thousand miles. "Monarchs almost have a sense of humor," he went on. "They play with the wind." He let the butterfly go, and it went up into the wind, looped, dipped, and sailed off on an oblique tack through voids of air against the backdrop of the big mountain. Noting patterns, habits, frequency of wingbeat, Brower can identify butterflies in flight. He will be moving along a trail and his eyes will be attracted by flutterings sometimes hundreds of yards away, and he will say, for example, "Parnassian." I was with him once near Piute Pass, in the Sierra, when he saw a Parnassian beating its way west, and he said he was impressed by its being at that altitude, which was twelve thousand feet. On the same day, he found a California tortoiseshell butterfly—orange, black, and yellow—sitting on a rock. He picked it up. It was so cold it couldn't move. Brower warmed it up, and it flew from his hand.

There is a butterfly called *Anthocharis sara reakirtii broweri*. Brower discovered it, when he was fifteen years old. He was a solitary boy, a collector of butterflies, and he knew he had something unusual when he saw that its primaries were black and white and the undersides of its secondaries were green. He found it near Grizzly Peak, in the Berkeley Hills, where he used to go for long walks after school as a boy, sometimes leading his mother by the hand. She was blind, and he would describe to her the terrain they were moving through and the plants and animals he saw. His mother was a tall, attractive woman. She had an advanced degree in English literature. An inoperable brain tumor had blinded her when he was eight.

Brower was born in Berkeley, in 1912. When he was a year old, his mother went shopping one day at a Red Front store and left him for a few minutes in a baby carriage on the sidewalk. Squirming around, he fell to the pavement, and smashed out several of his front teeth, damaging also the wall of the gums. His second set of front teeth did not come in until he was twelve, and when they did they were awry. He was ashamed, embarrassed, unsure of himself, shy. He was afraid to smile. In school, he was known as the Toothless Boob. He withdrew into the Berkeley Hills—which are now covered with houses, including his own house, but were wild then. He also liked to go to Two Rock Valley, some fifty miles north of Berkeley, to the chicken ranch where his mother had grown up. The place was a haven for both of them. Brower avers that he could hear the chickens growing there. He also says he learned to talk with chickens. He believes that tones cross the barriers of species. There was a mare at Two Rock Valley that no one could handle, but whenever Brower went near her she whinnied cordially and did as she was told.

Brower's father taught mechanical drawing at the University of California. He was a small man (five seven), with a rock-ribbed face and stern habits. His first name was Ross. He never smoked. He did not drink, even coffee. One traumatic day, he came home with the news that he had lost his instructorship. Home was 2232 Haste Street, where the family had two frame houses, one behind the other, that had been partitioned into eleven apartments. For the rest of his life, Brower's father managed and janitored the apartments. Things became, in Brower's words, "pretty thin," and he remembers holes in his sweaters, holes in his shoes, and paper routes. His father's mother moved in to help with the apartments. She was a high-momentum Baptist who had seen to it that her grandson David was underwater when presented to God. She also saw to it that he always had plenty of housework to do. He washed clothes. She banned card games. She permitted the drinking of hot Jello.

The family's escape zone was the Sierra Nevada. Ross Brower had made something he called a camping box. It fitted on the running board of the Maxwell—and, later, of the Willys Knight—and it held food and utensils; one side of it let down on chains and became a table. In Berkeley, the camping box was kept in the basement, and frequently young David would go down there just to look at it. To Donner Summit was a three-day drive. (It is now a three-hour drive.) They would spend the first night in a campground in what is now metropolitan Sacramento, and the second near Colfax, on the American River. The river was potable then. As if he were there still, Brower remembers lying on the ground inside an arrangement of blankets and blanket pins—his mother at one end, his father at the other, his two brothers and his sister with him in the middle—listening to the elegiac whistling of the big Mallet engines of the Southern Pacific. He developed an extraordinary affection for trains. Malapropos as it may seem at this point in his career, he still has it. The force of nostalgia in Brower is such that it can in some instances bend logic. A railroad over the Sierra is all right. It was there. An interstate highway is an assault on the terrain.

At Donner Summit, Brower once pointed out to me the road he and his family had used. It was a dirt road seven feet wide and as tortuous as the contours of the mountains. On almost every trip, they camped in the wild country at the south end of Lake Tahoe, in a forest of big pines, white fir. He would wade in the cold, clear, notoriously blue lake and catch minnows. He stood there one day not long ago and took in the scene as it is now. Just up the street were Jimboy's Tacos, Pettyjohn Realty, Shakey's Pizza Parlor, Harrah's casino, Harrah's Thrifty Gambler, Shell, Texaco, Phillips 66, Standard, Enco, Stoddard the Jeweler ("Wedding Rings"), and the south-shore offices of O. R. "Bode" Martin, Real Estate. We went into Harrah's Thrifty Gambler, where Brower dropped a dollar and five cents at nickel roulette and ten-cent craps, then on into the big casino. "These people were perfectly happy in Las Vegas, Carson City, and Reno," Brower said, looking around. "They didn't have to come to this lake."

I remarked that the people in Harrah's looked young and fresh-faced, and not made of ochre suède, like the people in downtown Las Vegas.

Brower said, "Maybe that's because they go out and look at the lake once in a while."

On the precise spot where Brower and his family used to camp when he was a boy now stands the Royal Valhalla Motor Lodge—Diners Club, BankAmericard, Carte Blanche, Master Charge, American Express, sunbathing balconies, and an eight-foot Anchor fence to keep undesirables away from the lake. People with oil-glistening skins were languid on the balconies.

"These are people who got on the wrong subway and missed Coney Island," Brower said. "This is Jones Beach West. I'm glad there's a Jones Beach. I'm sorry this happened to Lake Tahoe."

Brower was standing by the Anchor fence, which had barbed wire along its top, and through it a stiff north wind was whistling. Visible through the fence were high whitecaps on the lake. The water was noticeably green. By a process called eutrophication, algae build up as a result of the accumulation of various human wastes, and even lakes that are famous for being blue will turn green. Brower said, "When Lake Erie started to die, it went in twelve years. This lake is a lot smaller than that. I can't think of a scenic climax in the world more polluted, and in more ways, than this one. Oh, is this ever grim!"

I asked him, "What do you think would happen if you were to address an audience collected out of these motels?"

"They would understand. They would be with me," he said. "People love the land."

"Do you really believe that?"

"Yes," he said. He pointed to a small bush. "Look at that plant," he said. "There has been *some* attempt at landscaping here."

"It's plastic."

"O.K.," Brower said, "I take it back. This long ago ceased to be my country anyway. You can see into my country." He pointed. "Pyramid Peak is just visible, in the Desolation Wilderness."

"Have you been up Pyramid Peak?"

"Seven times. Three times in the winter, on skis. But by the time I was twenty even *that* was behind me. I found bigger peaks, wilder places, higher country."

As a child, he had at times been frightened in that country. The family had always headed south after Tahoe, into the higher mountains, higher than the Rockies—the High Sierra, tallest mountain range in the contiguous United States. To minor summits—Gaylor Peak, Sentinel Dome, Vernal Fall—the family would scramble, but David was afraid to go, and he sat in the car, sometimes trembling, while the others were away. At Glacier Point, a look-off reachable by road—and three thousand two hundred and fifty-four feet up a cliff face from the floor of Yosemite Valley—the family always went out to the lip to have a look. David stayed behind, terrified even by the thought of looking over the rim. Not many years later, though, with rope and pitons, he started up that cliff from the bottom, and he was two thousand feet off the valley floor when rocks and beer cans started to fall around him, tossed down by tourists above. Afraid for his life, he shouted until his voice was gone, but the tourists did not hear him. He says that beer cans in that situation make a light and Christmassy tinkle, while rocks go by with a Doppler effect—*peeeeenyow*. By pure luck, nothing hit him, but he was discouraged and gave up the climb.

Theodore Roosevelt, when he was President of the United States, slept one night at Glacier Point, a bit of blanket over him, and when he awoke in the morning he was covered with four inches of snow. He said later that it was the greatest day of his life. Brower told me this while we ourselves were standing at Glacier Point one day. A bronze map there shows what you are looking at—Mount Starr King, Grizzly Peak, Mount Clark, Mount Lyell, Mount Maclure, Half Dome, North Dome, Clouds Rest, Mount Hoffmann, Mount Watkins, Mount Broderick, Liberty Cap. Brower had been to the summits of all these mountains. Glacier Point is a scenic climax and a half—fathoms and fathoms of air down to the green valley and up the granite on the far side to Yosemite Falls and beyond to the sharp outlines of the peaks. We shared the scene with a cluster of tourists, all adults, who were making paper airplanes and sailing them to the valley. By paper airplane, that is a long flight; and for ten, fifteen, twenty minutes at a time all these people, some of whom had driven three thousand miles to be there, kept their attention fixed on the paper airplanes. A National Park Service ranger tried to persuade them to have a look at the view. He also politely noted that what they were doing was against the law. To Brower he said that there were worse troubles than that, up there. The trail out to Glacier Point is lighted at night by fixtures placed in clefts and crevices of rock. Tourists unscrew the bulbs and throw them over the cliff.

By the time Brower reached high school, he thought that he wanted to be an entomologist, but he gave up that ambition, because at Berkeley High School people who were interested in things like entomology were considered odd. Brower had had enough of that. He was still afraid to smile, because of his teeth. As manager of the lightweight football team, he had found the beginnings of a kind of social life, and he feared losing it. He was sixteen, though, when he entered the University of California. He felt out of step, too young. Quiescent sensitivities renewed. He kept "trying for approvals here and there." He lived at home, and when he was eligible for fraternity rushing he saw from within his house one day a group from a fraternity coming up the street. They stopped and looked at the place in apparent dismay—a narrow lot in a poor section, an ersatz-Victorian clapboard-and-shingle rundown embarrassing house. The boys from the fraternity moved on without coming up the walk. Brower dropped out of the university in his sophomore year. "Because of the Depression," he said. "The Great Depression—it was a convenient excuse." He went into the mountains. Before ten years had passed, it was being said of him that if he were to be set down at night anywhere in the Sierra Nevada, with the coming of morning he would know just where he was.

Now, at Suiattle Pass, Brower was still talking about butterflies. He said he had raised them from time to time and had often watched them emerge from the chrysalis—first a crack in the case, then a feeler, and in an hour a butterfly. He said he had felt that he wanted to help, to speed them through the long and awkward procedure; and he had once tried. The butterflies came out with extended abdomens, and their wings were balled together like miniature clenched fists. Nothing happened. They sat there until they died. "I have never gotten over that," he said. "That kind of information is all over in the country, but it's not in town."

We left the trail and went off to the right, toward Plummer Mountain, in order to attempt to find our way to the center of the area of the copper lode, and to see for ourselves—if possible—evidence of its presence. Park took the lead. The problem was to try to stay on a contour and still move in a generally westerly direction in landscape that was full of thick vegetation, ledges, ravines, and cliffs. It quickly became apparent that Brower thought Park had no idea where he was going. Our feet hurt—at least, Park's and mine did. I had developed a bone spur under one heel earlier in the year, and Park had made a bad choice with his new Canadian boots, which were stiff and were beginning to wear away parts of his ankles and feet. This fact emerged later. He said nothing at the time. Picking the shortest or easiest route—and assessing the one against the other—was of obvious importance to all of us. Although Brower seemed to be getting stronger with every added mile, he nonetheless was hardly indefatigable. Park had simply assumed command—aggressive, perhaps, because he was so uncomfortable—and we followed him, but Brower kept craning toward other possibilities, other routes. So close up, and so rough in character, the terrain was hard to read. Two or three times, Brower suggested that we try a gulch or a ridge that Park was having no part of, but Park kept moving and paid no attention, perhaps because he does not hear well. What we all feared was that we would come out onto some impossible ledge or up against a cliff face and have to turn back and add perhaps miles to our day. After a time, we got into the beginnings of what appeared to be a descending, curving cul-de-sac; at least, it appeared that way to me and to Brower. We imagined that if we were to go down into it, we would end up facing cliffs and have to climb back out the way we went in. Brower said he wanted to stay on high ground and go to even higher ground to get around the problem. Park kept on walking, downhill and to his right, around the curve, whacking boulders with his pick. With no trail to keep us threaded together, we had to follow. Around the bend, the "cul-de-sac" came open, and the landscape spread out into broad alpine meadows interspersed with stands of spruce and reaching out in gentle gradients toward the talus slopes of Plummer Mountain.

This place had been named the Golf Course, apparently by explorers for Kennecott—or so we gathered from a crude property map we had with us, the "property" being the corporation's patented claims. With very little bulldozing, the Golf Course could in fact become one of the seven wonders of sport, with the red wall of Plummer Mountain above it, the deep valley of the Suiattle falling away beside it, and the sparkling, spectacular imminence of Glacier Peak in full view from every tee, fairway, and green. Brower's response to this conception was that each and every round would have to be played over his remains.

Park said that we had apparently reached the outermost lens of the copper deposit. He looked up at Plummer Mountain, all rusty and tawny and jagged in the air, and described what he was looking at as intrusive rock impregnated with pyrite and, he assumed, with copper—a porphyry of disseminated copper in granitic intrusive material. He said this mountain glacial topography reminded him of Greenland—sharp peaks sticking up through the ice pack. He could almost see the ice that had been there in the past.

Brower said he could see the hole in the ground that would be there in the future. He said that it would be a man-made crater so large it would be visible from the moon.

"Aw, Dave, it wouldn't be that bad," Park said.

While Brower was executive director of the Sierra Club, the organization became famous for bold full-page newspaper ads designed to arouse the populace and written in a style that might be called Early Paul Revere. One such ad called attention to the Kennecott Copper Corporation's ambitions in the Glacier Peak Wilderness under the headline "AN OPEN PIT, BIG ENOUGH TO BE SEEN FROM THE MOON." The fact that this was not true did not slow up Brower or the Sierra Club. In the war strategy of the conservation movement, exaggeration is a standard weapon and is used consciously on broad fronts. Beneath the headline was an aerial photograph of an open pit that Kennecott has created in Bingham Canyon, Utah. It would be difficult to exaggerate that one. Bingham Canyon is the largest copper mine in the United States. Two miles from rim to rim, it goes down into the earth in some fifty concentric circular terraces, so that from the air it looks very much like a thumbprint pressed into the ground—the thumbprint, it works out, of a man well over a hundred miles tall. The Internal Revenue Service eventually reacted to the Sierra Club ads by declaring contributions to the Sierra Club no longer tax deductible. Organizations that tried to influence legislation could not have tax-deductible status. That didn't slow up Brower, either. He went right on with the ads.

"Well, with a small telescope," Brower said.

We moved up the fairways toward Plummer Mountain, walking through buttercups and vetch. Park said cheerfully, "I wouldn't object at all to seeing a nice open pit here, improving the standard of living."

"Improving the standard of living for a short time," Brower said.

"For a hundred years," said Park. "And fifty years after that it's all covered over. There's a beach in New South Wales where the deep sands have rutile, zircon, and other rare things. National Lead and some Australian companies got permission to mine the beach. There was a hullabaloo. They mined it, and now the beach is *better* than it was before. It's been rebuilt. Swamps and mosquitoes are gone. The shorebird habitats were untouched. The Australian government wants more beaches to be mined elsewhere."

Brower let the beach go. He once wrote and narrated a film about the North Cascades, and, with "America the Beautiful" softly rendered behind his own soft-toned voice on the sound track, he said that these mountains were among "the few surviving samples of a natural world, to walk and rest in, to see, to listen to, to feel the mood of, to comprehend." The narration continued, "There isn't much of it left. What there is is all all men will ever have, and all their children. It is only as safe as people want it to be." That must have been more or less what he was thinking at that moment. At length, he said, "The pit is only a small part of what else they do."

"Every mine in the country has someone objecting to it," Park said. "Where are you going to get your metals?"

"Nevada, Arizona—Bingham Canyon."

"People object *there*."

We stepped around several piles of fresh dung. Brower said he didn't know what it was. Park said, "It's bear dung."

A pluming waterfall, hundreds of feet high, fell from the east face of Plummer Mountain, and, for lack of a more specific goal, we were homing on it.

"This scenic climax is of international significance," Brower said.

"That may be, but as long as you've got copper here, pressure to mine is going to continue."

"Well, I'll give up when copper has to be used as a substitute for gold. The kids will decide then. And I think they'll decide not to mine it."

"A mine would remove the mining area from wilderness—anyone in his right mind would admit that," Park said. "You're going to have people, equipment, machinery. You're going to blast. You're going to have a waste dump. You're also going to get copper, which contributes to the national wealth and, I think, well-being. And all that can't possibly affect Glacier Peak."

"The mine will affect anybody in this whole area who *looks* at Glacier Peak. One of the last great wildernesses in the United States would have been punctured, like a worm penetrating an apple. There would not only be the pit but also the dumps, the settling ponds, the tailings, the mill, machine shops, powerhouses, hundred-ton trucks. Good Lord! The mood would go. Wilderness defenders have to get into abstract terms like mood and so forth, but that is what it is all about. How are the people and equipment going to get in and out of here? A road? A railroad?"

"I think cost would have to enter into that."

"O.K. I put a price of ten billion dollars on the Glacier Peak Wilderness. Actually, that is facetious. There is no price. The price of beauty has never been evaluated. Look at that mountain! What would it *cost* to build an equal one?"

A galvanized pipe rising about a foot out of the earth stopped the conversation, and stopped us where we stood. Only three inches from rim to rim, it seemed somehow, to me, in the surprise of coming upon it, to reach far out into the surrounding wilderness, to be the mine itself. It had been marked as Kennecott's Drill Site No. 3. Park said it probably went down about five hundred feet, and that the core samples that had been removed through it must have been three-quarters of an inch in diameter. The core samples would have shown not only whether copper was there, in that spot, but also the concentration of it in the porphyry. Earlier in this century, if copper ore was not at least two or three per cent copper it was bypassed. Now if it is seven-tenths of one per cent copper it is mined. We sat down, roughly in a circle, around the pipe. We each had a plastic bag full of a mixture of peanuts, raisins, and chocolate, and we opened the bags and ate while we looked at the pipe, although there was so little to see. Around it spread the meadow grass, the vetch, and the buttercups, undisturbed.

"What per cent of the world's known copper is under here?" Brower asked.

"I don't know," Park said. "Kennecott hasn't told me."

For a time, the only sound was from the wind and from the waterfall on the mountain. Then Brower said, "We don't know the size of the reserve."

"That's true."

"If you start with point seven per cent and work down, say, to point three five—if that level becomes commercially feasible, then there's no telling *how* big the pit will be."

"That's true."

"The theory of economic growth is doomed on a finite planet."

"It has to be."

"We have to figure out how to cool it. I think a major change in thinking is around the corner."

Park took off his cap and smoothed his hair. "I hope your optimism holds," he said. "I'm a pessimist."

"I *have* to be an optimist. It keeps me in business. Otherwise, I'd open a waffle shop."

Of all the things Brower swallows, the two he seems to like

most in the world are Tanqueray gin and whipped-cream-and-strawberry-covered waffles.

"Copper affects the international balance of payments," Park said. "We are net importers of copper."

"I can't get excited about that."

"Again, what you're saying is that you're willing to lower the standard of living."

"Very much so."

"Then you increase ghetto problems in cities."

"There is a gap between a lowered standard and the ghetto," Brower said. "One thing we could do, to begin with, is stop copper roofing."

"That's not a great amount. It's mostly in wiring."

"A lot of copper goes into coinage. Quarters are sandwiches of nickel and copper."

"Yes. We could get rid of that."

"We could use aluminum coins."

"Aluminum coins are horrible," Park said. "They're dirty."

"Well, then, I'd rather have a hole in a coin than a hole in Plummer Mountain. A mine in this wilderness is horrible, too."

"The mine has to come. Population pressure is irresistible."

"Population is pollution spelled inside out."

"I agree. At least, I agree that it is a very real problem."

"Families with more than two children should be taxed," Brower said.

"I agree with that, too. Everything is hopeless without population control."

"How many children do you have?"

"Three. How many do you have?"

"Four," Brower confessed.

They both turned to me.

"Four," I said.

The medical students looked on with interest.

"Seven billion people are going to be on the earth in the year 2000," Park said.

"It is wrong to assume so. Demographers make a projection like that and then we all assume it's inevitable and we go ahead and make it so."

Brower has a metaphysical or perhaps superstitious belief in the idea of the self-fulfilling prophecy. He also has no regard for the extrapolations of social scientists.

"India? Africa? Have you seen the figures?" Park asked him.

"I think there will be a massive pestilence."

"Perhaps so, but meanwhile population pressure is irresistible."

"Central Park and the Adirondacks have resisted it pretty well."

Adirondack State Park is the largest park, state or federal, in the United States. It was created in 1892, principally as the result of the efforts of a group of conservationists in Brooklyn, who put into the constitution of the State of New York this guarantee: "The Forest Preserve shall be forever kept as wild forest lands."

Park put on his cap. "There was a titanium mine in the Adirondacks during the Second World War," he said.

Around the galvanized pipe, there was no evidence that copper ore had in fact come through it. We moved on. Our eyes began to hunt—in a sense, to forage—for green rock. The alpine meadows ended abruptly at the edge of an extremely steep escarpment above the stream that ran from the waterfall off Plummer Mountain. We picked our way down the face of the escarpment. Park was wielding his pick with more intent than whimsy, and when he hit something we all looked around, as if we were expecting him at any moment to crack open the vaults of the Glacier Peak Wilderness. Halfway down the incline, he split off a hunk of gray rock about the size of a book and looked with interest at the part of it that was newly exposed to light.

"What did you find?"

"Nothing. Just a good streak of mineral. We're in the mineralized area."

"But no copper."

"None there. Copper is water soluble. It leaches out and precipitates below. This is certainly your ore horizon."

"Will we actually see copper ore?"

"Maybe. Who knows?"

We inched on down toward the stream, which had the pools, the clear water, the smooth water-magnified rocks, and the airy white rips of a perfect trout stream. A spring spilled into it from a ledge about eight feet above it. We paused there. Looking far up to the level where we had begun our descent to the stream, Park said, "We're locked in here now. I wouldn't go back up there for anything." Our intent was to cross the brook and try to work our way around the mountainside along a kind of welt that was known as Miner's Ridge—so named for prospectors who had worked small claims there in an era when open pits were ten feet deep.

Brower filled his Sierra Club cup and offered it to Park, who thanked him, drank the water, and said, "If you stuck a nail in that spring and came back in two years, I think you'd have a copper nail."

"Is there copper in seawater?" I asked him.

"Very little," Park said.

"Harrison Brown thinks seawater is a viable source of copper," Brower said. "And he is considered a leading authority on resources for the future."

"That depends on who you talk to," Park said. "Anyway, I'm sure he doesn't think there is that much copper in seawater."

One of the medical students said, "Who is Harrison Brown?"

Park and Brower described Brown as a geochemist at the California Institute of Technology who believes that in energy lies the answer to the problem of diminishing resources. Minerals are almost everywhere for the taking if we can develop the energy and technology to extract them. In a mere cubic mile of seawater, for example, is more magnesium than has yet been mined in the history of metallurgy. According to Brown, uranium can be drawn from the granite of mountains. Thus, said Brower with irony, a kind of total mine could be made of the Sierra Nevada, starting at one end and consuming the entire mountain range until the area between the Nevada Desert and the orchards and vineyards of California consisted only of a vast gray peneplain.

I said that a conservationist in Seattle had told me that one method Kennecott might use to extract the copper from where we stood was to insert a nuclear bomb in Plummer Mountain, bring the mountain down in shards into the

Suiattle Valley, then pour rivers of chemicals over it to leach out the copper.

"Operation Plowshare," Park said. "It wouldn't level the mountain. That's a gross exaggeration. It would hardly show on the surface. But it wouldn't work well, either. They can't direct their blast. They make a cylinder. Most ore deposits are not cylindrical, to say the least. They're on an angle. The nuclear blast goes straight up."

Brower said, "If Harrison Brown can get so much out of granite, he ought to be able to get something out of concrete. He could start with the Embarcadero Freeway."

I once drove across the Mojave Desert with Brower; and to help pass the time in the hundred-degree heat I asked him if he could make a list of places for Harrison Brown to grind up. Where, if anywhere, would Brower find such mega-mining acceptable? "The Mojave Desert," Brower said, and then fell silent in thought. Brower's son Ken, who was twenty-three, sat up in the back seat and said, "He's hard-pressed. It's going to be a short list. He likes everything." The list was less than short. Brower began to look around the Mojave, his eyes taking in the plumbing-fixture weirdness of the Joshua trees, the zigzag fissures in the earth, the curls and crests of desiccated waves. "I take that back," he said. "There are some nice shapes here."

In the streambed we found another galvanized pipe. This one had been bored into the earth at a forty-five-degree angle. Again there was no tangible evidence of copper. Other than the pipe, the only evidence that men had been there was a number of crushed fuel cans among the boulders in the stream. A helicopter must have delivered the drill, later flying away heavy with core samples, cuprous and green. I noticed that Park was limping, and, as it happened, I was limping, too. We had a long way to go even to return to the trail, let alone to reach the place where we had planned to stop for the night, a scenic climax of much renown—Image Lake, a mirror-surfaced mountain tarn so situated that it reflects and even magnifies Glacier Peak. Park was not much interested in going there, since a detour would be involved. Brower felt that the lake should not be missed. Meanwhile, we would hunt for copper along Miner's Ridge, which at that point was the most uninviting piece of terrain I had ever seen, being thickly vegetated, trailless, chopped with rock walls and ravines, and generally so steep that the use of hands would obviously be necessary most of the way. Park moved quite slowly, hunting the best route, making his way downhill, breaking through meshed branches, and continually chipping at rocks. Somehow, he and I became separated from the others. We shouted and heard them shout back. They were above and behind us. We waited for them to join us.

Park said, "Dave lives in a house, doesn't he?" Park had a grin in the corner of his mouth, and I developed one in mine. I told him I had once heard a man in an audience in Scarsdale tell Brower that to be consistent with his philosophy he should wear a skin and live in a cave.

I thought of Brower's house and how it clings to a steep hillside far above the campus at Berkeley. It is a simple structure, made of redwood. Although it is far from large, it almost completely fills Brower's lot, which he acquired in 1946, at the start of the postwar building boom. He sketched a plan on the back of an envelope, showed it to a contractor, and told him to build what he saw—thus the first house in what quickly became a neighborhood. There is almost no front yard—just a concrete apron for Brower's Volvo and his Volkswagen bus. In back is a patch of ground, Brower's private claim on the out-of-doors—the eighty-seventh part of an acre. Filled with vegetation—loquat, lemon, fuchsia, apricot, peach, camellia —it is an infinitesimal jungle. From the front windows of Brower's house the view of San Francisco Bay is panoptic—the Golden Gate, the Bay Bridge, the Marin Peninsula, the white city—and would be a breathtaking view were it not for a high telephone pole, directly across the street, where lines come in from four or five directions and have been looped and bunched into something that suggests a huge tumbleweed hanging in the air, an enormous ganglion of copper wires.

"Yes, he does live in a house," I said.

We could hear Brower and the medical students crashing through the undergrowth and coming closer to us.

"Is it painted?" Park asked. "Most people don't think about pigments in paint. Most white-paint pigment now is titanium. Red is hematite. Black is often magnetite. There's chrome yellow, molybdenum orange. Metallic paints are a little more permanent. The pigments come from rocks in the ground. Dave's electrical system is copper, probably from Bingham Canyon. He couldn't turn on a light or make ice without it. The nails that hold the place together come from the Mesabi Range. His downspouts are covered with zinc that was probably taken out of the ground in Canada. The tungsten in his light bulbs may have been mined in Bishop, California. The chrome on his refrigerator door probably came from Rhodesia or Turkey. His television set almost certainly contains cobalt from the Congo. He uses aluminum from Jamaica, maybe Surinam; silver from Mexico or Peru; tin—it's still in tin cans—from Bolivia, Malaya, Nigeria. People seldom stop to think that all these things—planes in the air, cars on the road, Sierra Club cups—once, somewhere, were rock. Our whole economy—our way of doing things, most of what we have, even our culture—rests on these things. Oh, gad! I haven't even mentioned minerals like manganese and sulphur. You won't make steel without them. You can't make *paper* without sulphur. By a country's use of sulphuric acid you can almost measure its industrial capacity. The top of Mount Adams has been prospected by sulphur companies. Did you know that?"

Mount Adams is one of the great beauties of the Cascades, a volcano of the storybook kind, its curving lines sweeping to a white summit. The mountain is owned by the government of the United States, but its apex could be mined. The top is where the sulphur is.

Brower and the medical students caught up with us, and Brower asked how we were doing.

"Fine," said Park. "But, to tell you the truth, I wish these boots were still in Canada. My feet are in bad shape."

"Did you find any copper?" one of the medical students asked.

Park shook his head. "It's down in here, though," he said, pointing straight down. "That's for sure." With no trail, and without much energy, we continued along the face of Miner's Ridge, and the going became even slower as we encountered a greater concentration of ravines, but no copper. The desire to see evidence of the copper lode was mere curiosity—no one doubted that copper was inside the mountain—but the curiosity, the sense of hunting, was compelling nonetheless.

Park talked about minerals. Few minerals are found in their native state, or, as he put it, free in nature; among them are silver, platinum, and gold. Zinc comes from sphalerite, tin comes from cassiterite, cobalt comes from smaltite, mercury comes from cinnabar. Each year, in the United States, about fifteen hundred tons of silver—about a third of all that is used—goes into photographic film and paper. For the price of a pound of hamburger, you can buy ten pounds of steel, and if it were not that cheap there would be economic problems all over the earth. Vanadium comes from sedimentary rock and may be an answer to air pollution; vanadium somehow defeats the toxicity in exhaust fumes. Titanium exists in the rutile of Georgia and Florida beaches, and is needed for the skins of supersonic aircraft, because aluminum without titanium would melt in the friction heat. Almost all mercury comes from three places: Almadén, Idria, Monte Amiata (Spain, Yugoslavia, Italy). Mercury is essential to any instrument intended to measure or control temperature or pressure. There is no known substitute for it, and there is very little of it. Japan buys iron ore from Nevada and coal from strip mines in West Virginia. In many places in the United States, it is impossible to buy nails that were not made in Japan. No nation has an adequate supply of all the minerals it uses. Since 1900, more minerals have been used than in all previous time.

Park had recently published all this, in less random form, in a book titled *Affluence in Jeopardy*, which is in part a primer on minerals and their uses and significance and in part an exhortation to mankind to husband what we have. Introducing minerals one by one, he says in clear and fascinating detail what they are, where they come from, what we do with them, and, ultimately, how we are locked into a system of living that is fuelled by them and founded upon them and would collapse without them. He quotes Lord Dewar, who said, "Minds are like parachutes. They only function when they are open," and he goes on to define conservation (at least with regard to minerals) as the complete use of natural resources, with as little waste as possible, for the benefit of all the people, and not merely for industrialists, on the one hand, or preservationists, on the other. He says that the search for energy, being vital to the extraction of minerals, and thus to the survival of the society, is far more important than exploration of the back of the moon, and he says that each nation should have a mineral policy that involves the intelligent exploration and development of mineral resources and an acceptance of fully reciprocal international trade. Copper, he reports, is used in the United States at the rate of at least two million tons a year. "As we look at the nonferrous metals, we note that, in spite of the value of mercury and the great demands for aluminum, copper remains the giant of the group. There has been an unbelievable amount of searching for copper, much of it in recent years, and there are entire nations whose economies depend upon this metal. . . . No substitute for copper is as satisfactory as the metal itself."

At about half past three that afternoon, we came to a small stream that ran straight down the steep mountainside. We shook off our packs, removed our boots, and set our feet in the water. "Oh, gad, that feels good," Park said. Our feet were as white as fish flesh in the cold water—so cold that I could barely stand it. This was a way to keep going, though. A cold stream offers a kind of retread. The pain goes away for a while afterward, and miles can be added to a day. Reaching upstream, Brower dipped himself a cupful of water. "Wilderness is worth it, if for no other reason than it is the last place on earth where you can get good water," he said. No one else said anything. We were too tired. We stared into the stream, or looked across the deep Suiattle Valley at the virgin forests on the lower slopes and the snow and ice on the upper slopes of Glacier Peak. Park's attention became fixed on the pebbles at the bottom of the stream, and after a moment he leaned forward and reached into the water, wetting his sleeve. He removed from the water a blue-and-green stone about the size of a garden pea. He set it on the palm of one hand and passed it before us. "We have been looking all day for copper," he said. "Here it is."

The beauty of the mountain across the valley was cool and absolute, but the beauty of the stone in Park's hand was warm and subjective. It affected us all. Human appetites, desires, ambitions, greeds, and profound aesthetic and acquisitional instincts were concentrated between the stone and our eyes. Park reached again into the stream, and said, "Here's another one.

The blue is chrysocolla—copper silicate. The rest is malachite—green copper carbonate."

All of us, Brower included, knelt in the stream and searched for stones. Brower found one. He was obviously excited by it. Brigham found one. Snow found one. Park found one as large as a robin's egg, mottled blue and green, with black specks of cupric oxide.

"My God, look at that!"

"Malachite and chrysocolla in altered intrusive rock," Park said.

"I've got another one," Brower said. "Good Lord, look at them all!"

"Hey, there are even more up here!" Snow called out.

"The rock is probably monzonite—a granite with equal parts of potash and soda feldspars—altered by hydrothermal solutions. I'd have to take it into a lab to know for sure. The copper came way up out of the earth's core when these mountains were fluid."

Larry Snow was shouting from above. He had a green rock in his hand the size of a golf ball. The slope and the streambed were as steep as a ladder, and ten minutes earlier the thought of going up there would have filled me with gloom and inertia. Now I put on my boots and followed him, scrambling hand over foot for the copper.

The higher we went, the larger were the green rocks—two inches, three inches, four inches thick. On a ledge about a hundred yards above Park, Brower, and Brigham, who were still assembling green pebbles, Snow picked up a rock that he could barely manage with one hand. Others like it were all over the ledge—cuprous green and aquamarine.

I held one high in my right hand and shouted down to Brower, "Dave, look at this! Look at this rock! Don't you think it would be a crime against society not to take this copper out of here?"

"Stay up there! Don't come back down!" Brower shouted. He was a small figure, from that high perspective. He was waving Snow and me away. "Stay up there! We'll send a party for you next spring!"

At the back of the ledge was the source of the copper. A deep, narrow hole had been blown into the side of the mountain, making what appeared to be a small cave—a nick in the wilderness, exposing and fragmentarily spilling its treasure. Snow and I filled a small canvas bag with perhaps twenty pounds of ore and made our way back down the streambed.

No one seemed anxious to move. I again took off my boots and put my feet in the stream. Brower had made an attractive collection of green pebbles. He looked with interest and feigned contempt at the big stones we had brought down. Brower is a collector of rocks. Behind his desk in his office in San Francisco were rocks he had collected from all over, and notably from the canyons of the Colorado—Glen Canyon, Grand Canyon. In most cases, he did not know what these rocks were, nor did he appear to care. He had taken them for their beauty alone.

Park was contemplating Glacier Peak. We were as close to it as we would ever be. It was right there—so enormous that it seemed to be on top of us, extending upward five thousand feet above our heads. "That's the sort of thing that draws people into geology," he said. "Geologists go into the field because of love of the earth and of the out-of-doors."

"The irony is that they go into wilderness and change it," Brower said.

Park appeared to be too tired to be argumentative. "There are some silly things about the mining laws," he said after a time, and he went on to explain that once a mining company or anyone else establishes a patented claim on public land they have complete rights to do anything they want, just as if they —and not the people of the United States—were owners of the property. Within federal law, they can cut down all the trees, they can build skyscrapers. If Kennecott wants to, Kennecott can put up a resort hotel in the Glacier Peak Wilderness. This law, enacted in 1872, makes no sense now to Park. He said he thought that mining companies should be given leases, and that these leases should include strong restrictions on mining practice and use of the land. In his view, something like that would go a long way toward eliminating the dichotomy that currently exists between conservationists and miners. While he was saying all this, he dried his feet in the air. I noticed for the first time that Park's heels were so raw red they were all but bleeding. He pulled on his socks and, with care, his boots. He got up—we all got up—and moved west along the ridge. He was forced to trudge, even after we rejoined the trail. Going to Image Lake would add several miles to the trip, involve an extra climb, and, the next day, a precipitous descent, but when the trail forked, Park headed for Image Lake.

Above Park's desk at Stanford was a picture of a jackass, with the caption "Can I help? Or do you want to make your own mistakes?" Near it was a photostatic blowup of a five-cent postage stamp showing cherry boughs and the Jefferson Memorial over the legend "Plant a More Beautiful America." Park's great-grandfather was a Minuteman. His grandfather was a guide on the Santa Fe Trail. His father had a real-estate and travel agency in Wilmington. His older brother went off and became a cowpuncher for the Bell Ranch, in New Mexico, and this in part established the draw to the West that Park felt throughout his youth. Tall, loose, rangy, and graceful, Park was a basketball player—a very good one—and he loved the game so much that he played not only for Wilmington High School (he was in the Class of 1922) but also, on the side, for various churches. His father told him that he had to worship at any church for which he played basketball, so for a long time he went to church at least twice each Sunday. He says he hasn't been to church since, except on the day that he was married. Also in those days, he made camping trips along the Brandywine, fished with a drop line in Chesapeake Bay, collected rocks that people sent him from beyond the hundredth meridian, and waited for the day when he could go beyond it himself.

When he was eighteen, he went to New York and shipped out in steerage on a Matson Line steamer for Galveston. It was the cheapest way West. He was not sure where he was going. He thought he might go to Golden (the Colorado School of Mines), or possibly to Socorro (the New Mexico School of Mines). "In those days, if you wanted to go to one of those places all you had to do was show up," he once explained to me. Eventually, he showed up at Socorro. He was the captain of his college basketball team, and he learned his mineralogy, and went on to get his master's degree at the University of Arizona and his Ph.D. at the University of Minnesota. In mining camps in those years, he became known as Chas (pronounced "chass"), specifically because the nickname distinguished him from the numerous Chinese in the mining camps, who, to a man, were known as Charlie. For a time, he worked as a mine surveyor for the New Jersey Zinc Company in Hanover, New Mexico, where he met a girl from Colorado—Eula Blair—who eventually became his wife and the mother of his two sons and his daughter. His daughter is a teacher of physical education. His sons are both working geologists—one with Humble Oil, the other with Hanna Mining. Mining geology is not widely taught anymore, and across the years students have come from all over the earth to Stanford because—in term, anyway, when he was not in equatorial Africa or the Andes or the Great Basin or the Black Hills—Park has been there, to teach them courses with names like Ore Genesis 101.

We were about a mile east of Image Lake. Park stopped, picked up a stone, split it in half with his pick, and said, "We are well past the mineral deposit. The mine won't come anywhere near Image Lake. The rock here is not intrusive. It's completely volcanic."

"Of course, it could be a volcanic overburden," said Brower, to suggest the possibility that far beneath the earth's surface the copper might spread to untold dark horizons.

"That's true. It could," Park said, with a tired shrug, and he trudged on.

We were a somewhat bizarre group on arrival at Image Lake. Park and I could scarcely place one foot after the other. The medical students appeared to be as fresh as they had been in the morning. And Brower was yodelling with pleasure. Brower yodels badly. The happier he seems to be, the more and the worse he yodels. He is Antaeus in the mountains, and he was clearly feeling good.

Image Lake is very small—a stock-water pond in size—and it stands in open and almost treeless terrain. Slowly, we went around it, looking for a place to sleep. The sun was just setting, and we had arrived much too late. We walked past tents along the shore—blue tents, green tents, red tents, orange tents. The evening air was so still that we could hear voices all around the lake. We heard transistor radios. People greeted us as we went by. The heaviest shadows were in the northwest arc of the shore, so the air was particularly cold there, and space had been left. We took the space. We had come into the mountains from the east. These people had come in from the west. It had not been an easy trip for them, to be sure. The nearest roadhead was fifteen miles west of us and some four thousand feet below. Nonetheless, the lake that night had the ambience of a cold and crowded oasis. Shivering, I climbed up a slope to witness in the water the fading image of the great mountain. Objectively, the reflection was all it was said to be. But a "No Vacancy" sign seemed to hang in the air over the lake.

A real sign pointed the way to a privy. We collected firewood, which was very hard to find, and when we had something of a blaze going and had all drawn in close around it for warmth, I said to Park and Brower, "Do you feel that you're in a wilderness now?"

"Yes," Brower said. "All these people certainly diminish the wilderness experience, but I've seen crowds in wilderness before. I know that they'll go away, and when they go they haven't really left anything."

Once, on a trail in the Sierra, Brower and I passed numerous hikers coming in the other direction, and because there were so many of them they disturbed him. They weren't riding Bonanza Trail-Bikes and they didn't have transistor radios and they weren't tossing beer cans away. They were disturbing to him only because they were there. Brower kept asking them if we were likely to find "too many" people in Humphreys Basin, which lay ahead of us, and when he concluded that Humphreys Basin—an area of several thousand acres—was going to contain too much of humankind he left the trail and struck off overland for another part of the mountains. Once, also, Brower and I were approaching the Sierra from the west on Route 198, and it happened to be the evening of the final day of a holiday weekend, and a river of cars was coming in the other direction. Brower drove without hurry. "The longer we wait, the more people we'll get out of the mountains," he said.

Now, at Image Lake, Park said, "This is no wilderness to me. My idea of wilderness is not to walk a quarter of a mile to a biffy. There's just too many people here."

Brower said, "It's hard to believe that this many people would walk this far."

"Population pressure," Park said. "You can't stop it. I don't really understand why they come here, though. This is a very ordinary little mountain lake."

We put our dinner into a single pot, boiled the food, ate it; and no one noticed what it was. Park was the first to speak again. "The more I see of this country, the more I fail to see what that copper mine would do to it. When we started, I was under the impression it might do something, but, golly, I can't see that now."

"The excavation would be within a mile of here and would effectively remove even this lake from wilderness. Right now it has more impact than it can bear. The ecosystem is delicate here. Recovery rates are fast, but nonetheless it is getting pounded. And the disruption would go all the way to Suiattle Pass, so the Glacier Peak Wilderness would effectively be cut in half."

"There would be a mining company here on business, and that's what they'd be doing—that's all. The miners would stick to the mine. Some would go off hiking or fishing, sure, but they would be doing that anyway. Miners like wilderness."

"The trouble is they want to dig it up and take it home."

"Awww."

"Logging follows mining."

"You can control that."

"That's what I'm hoping."

"Your idea of control is to keep it out."

"All a conservation group can do is to defer something. There's no such thing as a permanent victory. After we win a battle, the wilderness is still there, and still vulnerable. When a conservation group *loses* a battle, the wilderness is dead."

"It doesn't have to be."

"It's dead by definition."

"I don't agree with that concept of wilderness—to just take a big block of land and say you're going to keep it for the future. I can't see it."

"Wilderness was originally a nice place to go to, but that is not what wilderness is for. Wilderness is the bank for the genetic variability of the earth. We're wiping out that reserve at a frightening rate. We should draw a line right now. Whatever is wild, leave it wild."

"I would take a certain area and make part of it accessible and part of it inaccessible. Taking very large areas out of the country and keeping them as they were a thousand years ago —you can't do it. The population pressure is too great."

"A wilderness is a place where natural forces can keep working essentially uninterrupted by man. If ten per cent is still wild, we should tithe with it. Man has taken enough for himself already. We should pretend the rest doesn't exist. It's there for a different purpose."

"What purpose?"

"Not man's purpose. Man is a recent thing in the time scale here."

The moon had risen, pale and gibbous. We looked up at it. Men had been there recently and were going back in a few weeks. "There may be possibilities in the moon, but I can't see it," Park said.

"Apollo 11 proved the capability, and that was quite enough," Brower said. "Now let's spend the money on something else. We need to save the earth."

"Moon walking is silly," Park agreed. "There are too many things about the earth that we don't know, that would improve our lot, and that cost a lot of money."

"We're not so poor that we have to spend our wilderness or so rich that we can afford to. That kind of boxes it in nicely. Newton Drury said it."

"I don't believe you can stop expansion of the consumption of raw materials."

"You stop when you run out," said Brower. "Meanwhile, you make it less wasteful."

"Waste is criminal."

"If we recycled enough copper annually, we could do without this mine. Now that we know that we ourselves are on a spaceship, we have to get into our heads a concept of limits. Some things must stop or the world will become repugnant. There are limits everywhere, whether we are dealing with an island, a river, a mountain, with people, or with air. Living diversity is the thing we're preserving."

The fire had subsided almost to nothing, and the conversation subsided with it. The air was quite cold. We dispersed and got into our sleeping bags. Brower had arranged his pallet on top of a high promontory above the lake-shore. As a mountaineer, he knew that less dew condenses on high ground, and also that the air is warmer there. Park and I felt too achingly sore in the feet to bother making the climb. We stretched out below. As Park adjusted himself to the ground beneath him, he said, "I know half a dozen lakes like this that I can drive to and where I would find less people. I'll give you my interest in Image Lake for a piece of a counterfeit penny." Then he fell asleep. It was 8:30 P.M.

Once, in the Black Hills, Park had taken me with him into the deepest mine in the Western Hemisphere. The descent took one hour—first in a wire cage down a shaft almost a mile deep, then a level mile or so on a narrow-gauge railway, then on down in another cage, until we were six thousand eight hundred feet beneath the earth's surface. Heat increases in that area about two degrees for every three hundred feet you go down into the earth. The rock down there was a hundred and twenty degrees Fahrenheit, but the temperature in the tunnels we walked through had been brought down into the nineties by air pumped from the surface in long cloth tubes. The tunnels are known as drifts. Wearing coveralls, rubber boots, lamps, hard hats, and shatterproof glasses, we followed one drift to its end—to the deepest and remotest working face in the mine. Park hit away with his pick. Sparks came off the wall, and so did pieces of rock, basically dark gray with shining seams of pyrite and nodular insets of white quartz. I still have the pieces of rock that he knocked off that wall, and I have often shown them to people—particularly to children—and asked them what they thought they were looking at. What is in that rock? Why would men dig a hole that deep? What would make them go six thousand eight hundred feet underground? What could they possibly be seeking? The answer seldom comes quickly, perhaps because the rock is truly prosaic. "Iron?" they say. "Copper?" "Silver?" No. Keep going. It is the sum and symbol of why we mine anything, the base substance of the economies of nations, the malleable, ductile, most saint-seducing mineral in the crust of the earth. Something happens in their eyes when at last they say, "Gold."

Another day, on the surface, Park went out to look for greenstone pillows in a hill of amphibolite. Someone in the Geological Survey had suggested that these rock pillows, by the way they were positioned in the folds of the Black Hills, could indicate the direction of gold. Park walked along a ledge on the face of an escarpment, nagging at the pillows with his pick. Finally, he said, "Pretty inconclusive, I'd say." We were on high ground, and we could see around that beautiful country, with its big pines and its Engelmann's spruce so dark, dark green that the Sioux called the hills black. Surrounded by hot, dry terrain—the South Dakota Badlands on one side of them and Wyoming on the other—the Black Hills reach seven thousand feet and are cool and moist, with green valleys and clear-stream waterfalls and beaver ponds and deer and trout. "The Sioux loved this country," Park said. "No wonder they didn't want to give it up."

Land was a form of religion to the Indians, and the Black Hills, in this sense, were the religion of the Sioux. With all the fish, game, and beauty any man could want, the Black Hills fed the Sioux in body and spirit. Indians had no sense of private property, private land. The idea of individual human beings' owning pieces of the earth was to them at first incomprehensible and, when comprehended, a form of sacrilege. With the white man and his sense of property and the rights of property came the inequities and paradoxes that eventually led to the need for a conservation movement. Meanwhile, in 1851 the Sioux were promised by treaty that they could keep their Black Hills forever. In 1874, white men found gold there, and in 1875 white men entered the Black Hills in staggering numbers—white trash, in the main, like Wild Bill Hickok. It was the last gold rush in the United States. The promise to the Sioux was permanently broken, and the Sioux expressed their grief by destroying General Custer and his soldiers. "The Sioux are now a hundred miles east of here on a flat reservation in the Badlands," Park said to me. "There are no Sioux in the Sierra Club."

As we walked through a narrow swale filled with lilies, daisies, horsemint, and yellow vetch, we passed depressions in the ground that appeared to be graves that had been dug but not filled. Kinnikinnick berries grew in these depressions, and in one grew an aspen, tall and spreading, and in all likelihood nearly a hundred years old. "Prospectors," Park said. "A man would have come here and spent a day or a day and a half digging that hole in the ground. If he found anything, that would be his discovery-point pit, around which he would stake his claim. It was hit or miss. He had little to go on but the association of gold with quartz and pyrite. Sometimes prospectors found nuggets the size of peanuts. But that was extremely rare. Mining, and panning in the streams, was generally very hard work." There was a cool wind in the ponderosas, and a long view down through the stands of aspen below them. The rock formation before us stood on end. "It's Pre-Cambrian," Park said. "It's between three and four billion years old, probably. There are some old Pre-Cambrian flows like this up in Michigan—old pillow flows. There's some Pre-Cambrian rock in the Berkshires. There's also some in the bottom of the Grand Canyon. Look there! There are two good pillows! Maybe that boy has something."

The Black Hills are veined with unpaved roads. One of them was the stage route, a hundred years ago, from Telegraph Gulch to Deadwood. Driving his car along it one afternoon, Park said, "This is what I like about my profession. You see so much beautiful country. If I were starting over again, I'd do the same thing." In the next few miles, he saw a night hawk, a white-winged junco, a vesper sparrow, a western flycatcher, and a Townsend solitaire. He is a member of the American Ornithologists Union. He is a man who knows what he is looking at in wild country. I have never spent time with anyone who was more aware of the natural world, and he seemed to find in the land and landscape of the Black Hills an expression of almost everything he had come to believe about that world. He said, "People have a tendency to get a little bit emotional about preservation of the environment, I'm afraid. There are a couple of sawmills in here. They take mature trees. What harm do they do? They don't hurt the country. I don't see it. While I love the out-of-doors, I have no use for wilderness. We need to lumber. We need to mine. People don't realize what mining is. They don't realize the contributions that minerals and metals make to their lives. You can't live without industry. But that is what preservationists will say. Sawmills, mines, and forests *can* live together. These forests are beautiful here. They really are. The Black Hills are an example of where industry has not ruined an environment." In Park's view, about all that has been ruined in the Black Hills is Mount Rushmore, where the face of a mountain was blasted away and replaced with the faces of four American Presidents. It happens that Jefferson's nose is cracking. So is Lincoln's chin. And there are water stains on George Washington. But all that is just added insult. No face should be there except the face of the mountain. Even now, the face of Chief Crazy Horse is being sculpted on a mountain nearby. The Sioux need no monuments. Their monuments are seven thousand feet high and have been there since Pre-Cambrian time.

The deep gold mine is all that lives on from the legends of Deadwood Gulch. Park, a director of the mining company, was in the Black Hills to make a model—a sort of cubic map—of the mine. Three metamorphic-rock formations, called Homestake, Ellison, and Poorman, are folded together there like three kinds of ice cream. The gold is in the Homestake. From established drifts, narrow drills "feel" their way into the rock, sometimes as far as fifteen hundred feet—strange antennae. With data so obtained, Park was reproducing on stacked plastic sheets all the streaks, striations, bands, and brindles in several cubic miles of rock.

Down on the Sixty-eight—as the sixty-eight-hundred-foot level of the mine is called—Park looked with admiration at the walls of a drift and said, "These miners can look at a turn in a drift and tell who made it. They're proud of a good drift, clean walls. These are hard-rock miners, not coal miners. And they want you to know the difference. There are advantages in mining. Conditions are fixed. Man has control of the environment. People who work in a mine figure they are creating something. They feel that they are creating wealth. They all think they're geologists. There isn't a miner here who doesn't have a favorite place he wants to blast into."

Park drew a couple of miners into the conversation, which was spoken in high voices, because of the noise of the air pumps and the working drills. "I prefer working underground to on the surface," one of them said. "Conditions are set. You're not going to get caught in a thunderstorm. If I didn't like it, I wouldn't be doing it. We're tearing apart solid rock."

The rock, Park explained, is taken to the surface and crushed until it is fine sand. Mercury is poured through the sand. The mercury adroitly picks up gold, and nothing else. The mercury is then boiled away. Cyanide is poured into the sand and dissolves from it even more gold. Zinc is then put into the gold-cyanide solution. The zinc dissolves, and replaces the gold, which falls as metal to the bottom. The sand is put back in the mine, where concrete is poured on it to make platforms for upward mining. Thus, the mine consumes its own tailings, sparing in large measure the beauty of its environment—but not sparing it entirely. Because crushed rock expands in volume, all cannot be put back into the mine, and one of the Black Hills is a flat-topped mountain of black sand. And, as it happens, Whitewood Creek flows black after it passes the mine.

Park said that three tons of rock yield only one ounce of gold—a bit of gold about the size of a drop of rain. There is only about a third of an ounce of gold to back the financial wherewithal of each person now on earth. The very name Fort Knox implies vast vaults and armories full of piled gold, but actually the gold in Fort Knox could be formed into a twenty-foot cube. All the gold in all the monetary reserves of the world could be stacked on a single tennis court and scarcely reach over the fence.

Now, on the ground by Image Lake in the North Cascades, Park had begun to snore. To block the dew, we had stretched a clear-plastic tarpaulin over our heads, and I lay on my back and looked up through it at the disrupted constellations. I remembered walking into Park's living room once in Palo Alto. What I had noticed first, on a coffee table, was a book called *Gold, Its Beauty, Power, and Allure.*

In the morning, we went down to the Suiattle River—a drop of three thousand feet from Image Lake down the face of Miner's Ridge on a grassy incline so steep that Brower began telling stories about what happens to people on slopes like that if they fall. They apparently start to tumble, and sometimes can't stop. Park said he didn't care whether he fell or not—he was that uncomfortable. He finally took off his boots and put on his open leather sandals, deciding that bruises all over his feet would be preferable to the pain in his heels. His difficulty notwithstanding, he kept knocking rocks apart all day. After the big drop, the trail, for something like ten miles, ran roughly parallel to the river. The more altitude we gave up, the larger were the trees, the deeper the forest, until we were walking among big Douglas firs six feet thick. The air was warm and sunlit, and even when we could not see the river through the dense trees, the Suiattle was something to hear. It had the overbearing sound of rock sliding in a steel chute. As the afternoon lengthened, the sound grew louder. Park said he had known rivers in Alaska that could be crossed in the morning but by afternoon were unfordable torrents of melted glacier ice. "This one is like them," he said. Coming into view, the Suiattle was a headlong chaos of standing waves and swirling eddies, white with spray and glacial flour. "This one is a really wild river," Park went on. "Look at that rush of glacier milk."

The lower reaches of the trail had been scarred and battered by an improvement project commissioned by the United States Forest Service. Dynamite had torn great rocks apart, and some of the big trees had been felled to make the trail wider and the grade easier. Brower began to say unflattering things about the Forest Service, which he described as a collection of timber engineers who have no concept of ecology and whose idea of selective logging is to select a mountain and cut all the trees down. He said, "We conservationists would like to keep the Forest Service out of wilderness, and, for that matter, the National Park Service, too. They build too many things for their own convenience—for rangers who have forgotten how to range."

Brower had scarcely said this when we came upon a man who had three horses with him and several empty dynamite boxes. He was about thirty-five, strongly built and in excellent condition, solid muscles under his T-shirt, short-cropped hair, pale-gray eyes. His name was Don Dayment, and he told us he had been the foreman of the crew that improved the trail. Brower complained bluntly about the desecration of the trail. Dayment looked from Brower to Park to me to the medical students, and he said, "You wilderness-lovers are all the same."

"You foresters are all the same," Brower said.

Dayment cinched his horses. "Wherever man goes, whatever he does, he scars the land," he said. "That's the way things are. We were told to make a ten-per-cent grade here with a two-foot tread and eight feet of clearance. If we had to chop a six-foot fir, too bad."

I asked him where he lived, and he said he had been born twenty miles from where we stood.

I asked him how he felt about the copper mine.

"I don't like it, and I'll tell you why," he said. "I don't like the class of people that would come with it. I've seen their camps—in Wallace, Idaho, and Butte, Montana. They're dirty and run-down, and so are the people. I wouldn't want my children growing up around them."

Over the last five miles, each of us went at his own pace; we gave up all cohesion as a group. I walked with Brower, who was moving fast, because I had the almost drunken, rubber-legged feeling you get toward the finish of a long, long walk, and the roadhead at the end of the trail had become for me a repeating mirage. The trail ran closer and closer to the Suiattle—right beside it in some stretches—and the sound of the water was deafening. Over what proved to be the last thousand yards, though, we became aware of a sound even louder than the sound of the river—a higher-pitched roar, coming in jugular gusts, and increasing in volume as we moved down the trail. We came to the roadhead. There in the river, in the middle of the river, the white torrents crashing over it, was a bulldozer. Half submerged, its purpose obscure, it heaved, belched, backed, shoved, and lurched around on the bottom of the Suiattle as if the water were not there. The bulldozer was stronger than the river.

I took off my boots and sat alone on a ledge where my feet could reach the water. For a couple of hours, I had been able to think of almost nothing but feet. Now the cold milk of glaciers dispelled that, and as I watched the bulldozer my mind went back over the day—all the way back to its beginning. Miner's Ridge, as it extended westward from Image Lake, was a ridge indeed. The terrain fell away as steeply on the north side as it did toward the Suiattle, and we had walked for a mile or so—before beginning the descent—along the ridgeline of a topographical configuration that was like a sharply pitched gable roof. There was no timber up there, and in the early morning the ridge was isolated from the land below by huge bodies of cloud that filled up the river valleys on either side almost to our shoes. Above the clouds, the air was clear and the sky blue, and nothing else broke into that world but Glacier Peak, seven miles away—all ice and snow, and almost too dazzling to look at as it sprayed sunlight in every direction. Big blueberries were growing along the trail, and we began to eat them as if we had had no breakfast. Some were a half inch in diameter. Filling his Sierra Club cup with berries, Brower said, "I'm just taking the renewable crop. Only bears will object."

Park ate his blueberries straight from the bushes. His eyes lifted suddenly and followed a bird in flight above the ridge. He said, "Look at that marsh hawk. What's *he* doing up here?" The hawk canted to its left and soared in the direction of Glacier Peak. Streamers of cloud began to rise from the Suiattle Valley, cross the face of the mountain, and above the summit disappear, sparkling, into the blue. Park said it was a shame that more people couldn't see Glacier Peak—in fact, he thought people had a right to see it—and a nice little mining road would take care of that.

Brower said that a view of Glacier Peak, to mean much of anything, ought properly to be earned, and that the only way to earn it was to get to it on foot.

"What about people who can't walk?" Park said.

"They stay home. Ninety-nine point nine per cent can walk —if they want to."

"The other one-tenth per cent includes my wife."

Without hesitating, Brower said, "I have a friend named Garrett Hardin, who wears leg braces. I have heard him say that he would not want to be able to come to a place like this by road, and that it is enough for him just to know that these mountains exist as they are, and he hopes that they will be like this in the future."

"The future can take care of itself," Park said. "I don't condone waste, but I am not willing to penalize present people. I say they're penalized if they don't have enough copper. Dave says they're penalized if they don't have enough wilderness. Right?" He smacked a stone with his pick.

"Right," said Brower. "But I go further. I believe in wilderness for itself alone. I believe in the rights of creatures other than man. And I suppose I accept Nancy Newhall's definition: 'Conservation is humanity caring for the future.' It is the antithesis of 'Eat, drink, and be merry, for tomorrow we die.'"

"These are the best blueberries I've ever seen," Park said. "Here on Miner's Ridge."

Brower's cup was up to its brim, and before he ate any himself he passed them among the rest of us. It was a curious and surpassingly generous gesture, since we were surrounded by bushes that were loaded with berries. We all accepted.

"I just feel sorry for all you people who don't know what these mountains are good for," Brower said.

"What are they good for?" I said.

"Berries," said Brower.

And Park said, "Copper."

PART 2

An Island

DAVID BROWER, who talks to groups all over the country about conservation, refers to what he says as The Sermon. He travels so light he never seems far from home—one tie, one suit. He calls it his preacher suit. He has given the sermon at universities, in clubs, in meeting halls, and once in a cathedral (he has otherwise not been in a church for thirty years), and while he talks he leans up to the lectern with his feet together and his knees slightly bent, like a skier. He seems to feel comfortable in the stance, perhaps because he was once a ski mountaineer.

Sooner or later in every talk, Brower describes the creation of the world. He invites his listeners to consider the six days of Genesis as a figure of speech for what has in fact been four billion years. On this scale, a day equals something like six hundred and sixty-six million years, and thus "all day Monday and until Tuesday noon, creation was busy getting the earth going." Life began Tuesday noon, and "the beautiful, organic wholeness of it" developed over the next four days. "At 4 P.M. Saturday, the big reptiles came on. Five hours later, when the redwoods appeared, there were no more big reptiles. At three minutes before midnight, man appeared. At one-fourth of a second before midnight, Christ arrived. At one-fortieth of a second before midnight, the Industrial Revolution began. We are surrounded with people who think that what we have been doing for that one-fortieth of a second can go on indefinitely. They are considered normal, but they are stark, raving mad."

Brower holds up a photograph of the world—blue, green, and swirling white. "This is the sudden insight from Apollo," he says. "There it is. That's all there is. We see through the eyes of the astronauts how fragile our life is, how thin is the epithelium of the atmosphere."

Brower has computed that we are driving through the earth's resources at a rate comparable to a man's driving an automobile a hundred and twenty-eight miles per hour—and he says that we are accelerating. He reminds his audiences that buffalo were shot for their tongues alone, and he says that we still have a buffalo-tongue economy. "We're hooked on growth. We're addicted to it. In my lifetime, man has used more resources than in all previous history. Technology has just begun to happen. They are *mining* water under Arizona. Cotton is subsidized by all that water. Why grow cotton in Arizona? There is no point to this. People in Texas want to divert the Yukon and have it flow to Texas. We are going to fill San Francisco Bay so we can have another Los Angeles in a state that deserves only one. Why grow to the point of repugnance? Aren't we repugnant enough already? In the new subdivisions, everybody can have a redwood of his own. Consolidated Edison has to quadruple by 1990. Then what else have you got besides kilowatts? The United States has six per cent of the world's population and uses sixty per cent of the world's resources, and one per cent of Americans use sixty per cent of that. When one country gets more than its share, it builds tensions. War is waged over resources. Expansion will destroy us. We need an economics of peaceful stability. Instead, we are fishing off Peru, where the grounds are so rich there's enough protein to feed the undernourished of the world, and we bring the fish up here to fatten our cattle and chickens. We want to build a sea-level canal through Central America. The Pacific, which is colder than the Atlantic, is also higher. The Pacific would flow into the Atlantic and could change the climate of the Caribbean. A dam may be built in the Amazon basin that will flood an area the size of Italy. Aswan Dam, by blocking the flow of certain nutrients, has killed off the sardine fisheries of the eastern Mediterranean. There is a human population problem, but if we succeed in interrupting the cycle of photosynthesis we won't have to worry about it. Good breeding can be overdone. How dense can people be?"

More than one of Brower's colleagues—in the Sierra Club, of which he was for seventeen years executive director, and, more recently, in his two new organizations, Friends of the Earth and the John Muir Institute for Environmental Studies—has compared him to John Brown. Brower approaches sixty, but under his shock of white hair his grin is youthful and engaging. His tone of voice, soft and mournful, somehow concentrates the intensity of his words. He speaks calmly, almost ironically, of "the last scramble for the last breath of air," as if that were something we had all been planning for. "There is DDT in the tissues of penguins in the Antarctic," he says. "Who put the DDT in Antarctica? We did. We put it on fields, and it went into streams, and into fish, and into more fish, and into the penguins. There is pollution we know about and pollution we don't know about. It took fifty-seven years for us to find out that radiation is harmful, twenty-five years to find out that DDT is harmful, twenty years for cyclamates. We're getting somewhere. We have recently found out that polychlorinated biphenyls, a plastic by-product, have spread throughout the global ecosystem. At Hanford, Washington, radioactive atomic waste is stored in steel tanks that will have to be replaced every fifteen years for a thousand years. We haven't done *anything* well for a thousand years, except multiply. An oil leak in Bristol Bay, Alaska, will put the red salmon out of action. Oil exploration off the Grand Banks of Newfoundland will lead to leaks that will someday wreck the fisheries there. We're hooked. We're addicted. We're committing grand larceny against our children. Ours is a chain-letter economy, in which we pick up early handsome dividends and our children find their mailboxes empty. We must shoot down the SST. Sonic booms are unsound. Why build the fourth New York jetport? What about the fifth, the sixth, the seventh jetport? We've got to kick this addiction. It won't work on a finite planet. When rampant growth happens in an individual, we call it cancer."

To put it mildly, there is something evangelical about Brower. His approach is in some ways analogous to the Reverend Dr. Billy Graham's exhortations to sinners to come forward and be saved now because if you go away without making a decision for Christ coronary thrombosis may level you before you reach the exit. Brower's crusade, like Graham's, began many years ago, and Brower's may have been more effective. The clamorous concern now being expressed about conservation issues and environmental problems is an amplification—a delayed echo—of what Brower and others have been saying for decades. Brower is a visionary. He wants—literally—to save the world. He has been an emotionalist in an age of dangerous reason. He thinks that conservation should be "an ethic and conscience in everything we do, whatever our field of endeavor"—in a word, a religion. If religions arise to meet the most severe of human crises, now and then religions may come too late, and that may be the case with this one. In Brower's fight to save air and canyons, to defend wilderness and control the growth of population, he is obviously desperate, an extreme and driven man. His field, being the relationship of everything to everything else and how it is not working, is so comprehensive that no one can comprehend it. Hence the need for a religion and for a visionary to lead it. Brower once said to me, "We are in a kind of religion, an ethic with regard to terrain, and this religion is closest to the Buddhist, I suppose." I have often heard him speak of "drawing people into the religion," and of being able to sense at once when people already have the religion; I also remember a time, on a trail in the Sierra Nevada, when he said, "We can take some cues from other religions. There is something else to do than bang your way forward."

Throughout the sermon, Brower quotes the gospel—the gospel according to John Muir ("When we try to pick out anything by itself, we find it hitched to everything else in the universe"), the gospel according to Henry David Thoreau ("What is the good of a house if you don't have a tolerable planet to put it on?"), the gospel according to Buckminster Fuller ("Technology must do more with less"), and the gospel according to Pogo ("We have met the enemy and he is us"). A great deal of the sermon is, in fact, a chain of one-liners from the thinking sector: "The only true dignity of man is his ability to fight against insurmountable odds" (Ignazio Silone), "Civilization is a thin veneer over what made us what we are" (Sigurd Olson), "Despair is a sin" (C. P. Snow), "Every cause is a lost cause unless we defuse the population bomb" (Paul Ehrlich), "The wilderness holds answers to questions man has not yet learned how to ask" (Nancy Newhall).

Brower has ample ideas of his own about what might be done. He says, "Roughly ninety per cent of the earth has felt man's hand already, sometimes brutally, sometimes gently. Now let's say, 'That's the limit.' We should go back over the ninety and not touch the remaining ten per cent. We should go back, and do better, with ingenuity. Recycle things. Loop the system." When he sees an enormous hole in the ground in the middle of New York City, he says, "That's all right. That's part of the ninety." In non-wilderness areas, he is nowhere happier than in places where the ninety has been imaginatively gone over—for example, Ghirardelli Square in San Francisco, a complex of shops and restaurants in a kind of brick Xanadu that was once a chocolate factory. When someone asks him what one person can do, Brower begins by mentioning Rachel Carson. Then he tells about David Pesonen, a young man in California who stopped a nuclear-power station singlehanded. Then he sprays questions. "Are you willing to pay more for steak, if cattle graze on level ground and not on erodable hills? Are you willing to pay more for electricity, if the power plant doesn't pollute air or water?" He taunts the assembled sinners. "You are villains not to share your apples with worms. Bite the worms. They won't hurt nearly as much as the insecticide does. You are villains if you keep buying automobiles. Leave these monsters in the showroom." Invariably, he includes what must be his favorite slogan: "Fight blight, burn a billboard tonight!"

The cause is, in a sense, hopeless. "Conservationists have to win again and again and again," he says. "The enemy only has to win once. We are not out for ourselves. We can't win. We can only get a stay of execution. That is the best we can hope for. If the dam is not built, the damsite is still there. Blocking something is easiest. Getting a wilderness bill, a Redwoods Park bill, a Cascades Park bill, is toughest of all."

Brower is somewhat inconvenienced by the fact that he is a human being, fated, like everyone else, to use the resources of the earth, to help pollute its air, to jam its population. The sermon becomes confessional when he reveals, as he almost always does, that he has four children and lives in a redwood house. "We all make mistakes," he explains. His own mistakes don't really trouble him, though, for he has his eye on what he knows to be right. After he gave a lecture at Yale once, I asked him where he got the interesting skein of statistics that six per cent of the world's population uses sixty per cent of the world's resources and one per cent of the six per cent uses sixty per cent of the sixty per cent. What resources? Kleenex? The Mesabi Range?

Brower said the figures had been worked out in the head of a friend of his from data assembled "to the best of his recollection."

"To the best of his *recollection*?"

"Yes," Brower said, and assured me that figures in themselves are merely indices. What matters is that they feel right. Brower feels things. He is suspicious of education and frankly distrustful of experts. He has no regard for training per se. His intuition seeks the nature of the man inside the knowledge. His sentiments are incredibly lofty. I once heard him say, "It's pretty easy to revere life if you think of all the things it's done while it was onstage." He is not sombre, though. Reading a newspaper, he will come upon a piece by a conservation writer and say, "I like that. He's neutral the right way."

Brower is a conservationist, but he is not a conservative. I have heard him ask someone, "Do you like the world so much that you want to keep it the way it is?"—an odd question to be coming from David Brower, but he was talking about the world of men. The world of nature is something else. Brower is against the George Washington Bridge. He is against the Golden Gate Bridge. He remembers San Francisco when the bridge was not there, and he says the entrance to the bay was a much more beautiful scene without it. He would like to cut back the population of the United States to a hundred million. He has said that from the point of view of land use the country has not looked right since 1830. There are conservationists (a few, anyway) who are even more vociferous than Brower, but none with his immense reputation, none with his record of battles fought and won—defeater of dams, defender of wilderness. He must be the most unrelenting fighter for conservation in the world. Russell Train, chairman of the President's Council on Environmental Quality, once said, "Thank God for Dave Brower. He makes it so easy for the rest of us to be reasonable. Somebody has to be a little extreme. Dave is a little hairy at times, but you do need somebody riding out there in front."

The office of Charles Fraser, the developer, is in a small building about halfway between an undeveloped jungle and an alligator pond on Hilton Head Island, South Carolina. Alligators sometimes crawl along the sidewalk between the jungle and the pond. The alligators are natives and Fraser is not. Fraser was anxious lest the alligators be disturbed when, in 1957, he began building roads and golf courses and clearing homesites on some five thousand acres of the island, so he fed them great hunks of raw beef to lull them into acceptance of his bulldozers. The alligators swallowed it. They live now in water hazards and other artificial ponds throughout Fraser's Sea Pines Plantation. On his office wall Fraser has a picture of himself, in a white suit and a panama hat, walking an alligator. Signs along the fairways say, "Please do not molest the alligators." Fraser tried something similar with the bald eagles that were there, but the eagles would have none of it, and they flew away.

Fraser is a short man, heavyset, prominent in the forehead, dark curly hair wisping out behind. The first time I saw him, he was standing on a floating dock at his Sea Pines marina, drinking Portuguese rosé and wearing tennis shoes, white trousers, and a blue striped shirt. Those who know him would not instantly recognize such a snapshot, for although Fraser has built one of the creamiest resorts in America, he himself is not the resort type. He drinks little and plays less. Recreation is his business, and business seems to be his recreation. He almost always wears a plain dark suit. He tucks his chin in and sits straight when he is saying something important, and the more important it is, the straighter he sits. He talks about "marketing-acceptance factors" and about how "public money floats better than joint-venture money." His conversation is predominantly about money—its flows, its freezes, its cataracts, its sources, its deltas. He speaks in a clear, authoritative voice, very slowly, as if he were writing a contract as he goes along.

When Fraser first saw Hilton Head Island, rimmed with beaches and the ocean, it was a wilderness of palmettos, live oaks, Sabal palms, egret rookeries, and tupelo swamps shimmering with rattlesnakes and cottonmouths. What he saw there horrified him. Fraser is a visionary. He did not see the rattlesnakes. He saw Coney Island rising from the swamps. He saw what he calls "visual pollution." He saw Myrtle Beach, Asbury Park, Seaside Heights, and Atlantic City. He saw the whole sorry coastline of the Atlantic states—two thousand miles of used flypaper. The flies had missed here and there—Blackbeard Island, Cape Fear, Hilton Head—leaving pristine and visible some segments of one of the longest and most beautiful chains of barrier beaches in the world. Fraser, who was twenty-one, felt that development of some kind was inevitable at Hilton Head, and that it need not look like Myrtle Beach, and need not be done in dissonance with nature. He went to Yale Law School, and the course that most absorbed him was Myres McDougal's Land Use Planning and Allocation by Private Agreement. The gist of what McDougal had to say was that the use of property ought to be planned, because when development is allowed to occur without control the result can be a form of destruction. Throughout his years in New Haven, Fraser was obsessed with a desire to create on Hilton Head Island a resort community over which he would retain absolute aesthetic control, and he was in a position to do so, since his family owned much of the island.

Fraser's father, Lieutenant General Joseph B. Fraser, was a lumber king in Hinesville, Georgia, whenever there was not a war. He and several partners had bought the island for its timber and its speculative potentialities. Charles Fraser worked in summer with the timbering teams and successfully urged that no cutting be done in oceanfront stands of virgin pine. He also drove up and down the coastline from Virginia Beach to Miami seeking out the original developers of beachfront properties wherever he could find them and asking, "If you had it to do over again, what would you do differently?" From *haut monde* to honky-tonk and back again, they told him what a shortsighted mistake it had been to line up a row of houses along a beach and then put a road just behind the houses, creating a safety hazard and reducing the value of all the lots on the inland side of the road. They told him that large houses have a way of becoming boarding houses. They told him that control is quickly lost if it is not ironclad. Fraser regularly read almost all the journals of architecture. He went to the National Archives, in Washington, and looked up surveyors' notebooks from the eighteen-sixties, because he wanted his development to be of a piece with history, and he tried to locate old cotton fields, wartime fortifications, and vanished Taras. In 1956, with no development experience and not much money, he returned permanently to Hilton Head, where he began to sketch in the air with his hands scenes that he alone could see. Locally, he was considered a major and absolute nut. To his mother he confided, "I may never make any money, but I want to create something beautiful." She told him he was going to waste his time and his legal talent. She says now, "Of course, a person doesn't often have a chance to take wilderness and make something of it. Charles has a sense of beauty and balance. He saw the possibilities there. I think he would have been a painter if he hadn't chosen to do something else."

Sea Pines Plantation appears to be something painted by a single hand, in greens, grays, and browns. Its roads, meandering among the live oaks and Sabal palms, were bent wherever necessary to miss the big trees. All stop signs are green. Private roadside mailboxes are all green. Fireplugs are green. So far there are five hundred and fifty private houses, built by five hundred and fifty individual owners, yet most of the houses have cedar-shake roofs and bleached-cypress siding, the intention being that they should blend into their environment like spotted fawns. Some houses are set back in the woods along the fairways. (There are fifty-four fairways.) Other houses are on narrow drives that lead toward the beach from the principal roads, which are considerably inland. No one in the plantation lacks convenient access to the sea, because Fraser left dozens of fifty-foot public swaths between his arterial roads and the beach, and he has built walkways through the swaths. Neither the beach nor the line of primary dunes behind it has been built upon. Fraser spent fifty thousand dollars to save one live oak when he built a seawall for a harbor he dredged. Trees crowd the roads—dangerously in some places—but Fraser will not remove a tree until automobiles have crashed into it at least twice. He has one section of about a thousand acres that he calls the Main Wildlife Sanctuary and Woodland Recreation Area, and he has legally committed himself to leave twenty-five per cent of the plantation in its natural state. When prospective buyers used to ask about snakes, Fraser would say amelioratively, "Snakes? We'll show you a couple this afternoon." But the snakes eventually received the message, and now they do not show anymore. Alligators are packed up and sent to zoos when they become six feet long. Fraser has a private police force that spends most of its time protecting alligators and deer from poachers. The alligator hides are worth a hundred dollars apiece. Fraser's live oaks were once Methuselan with moss, but after he discovered that rain-soaked Spanish moss can get so heavy it cracks limbs, crews of barbers were sent into the trees to create an overhead garden of Vandykes.

An aerial view of Sea Pines Plantation reveals the great number of houses there, and how close to one another they really are, whereas an observer on the ground—even in the most densely built areas—feels that he is in a partly cleared woodland with some houses blended into it, nothing more. Fraser accomplished this in a region where people have traditionally liked to proclaim their prominence by piling red bricks into enormous cubes and placing before them rows of white columns. He did it—although he occasionally met strong opposition from buyers, bankers, and even subordinates in his own organization—by writing some forty pages of restrictions to attach to every deed. It was a reverse bill of rights (ironclad), a set of ten times ten commandments—take it or leave. The first restriction in the long list gives a suggestion of the whole: it says that any plan or specification can be disallowed by Fraser for any reason whatever. In the early days, when Fraser was operating more on hope than on money (and in full knowledge that half the bankers in South Carolina thought he would soon go under), he was nonetheless so uncompromising that he was ready without hesitation to reject the house plans even of a textile king. If the king refused to conform, Fraser bought back his land. One giddy homeowner tried to paint his house yellow—a historic moment at Sea Pines Plantation—but Fraser backed him down, blending him into the landscape along with his house.

Fraser is cruising through Sea Pines in an air-conditioned green Dodge. A man who is opening a green mailbox marked "H. F. Scheetz, Jr." looks up and waves hello. Fraser lowers the window. "Hi, Henry!" he says as he glides by. Up goes the window. "I operate as nonelected mayor, so I have to act as if I were elected," he explains. "There is democracy of communication here but autocracy of decision-making. Our corporate contracts and deed covenants are the constitution and bylaws of the community. The only way you can have aesthetic control is through the power of ownership. We have more power than a zoning board has. I have centralized the decision-making process, but I'll listen to anybody." The marvel is not whom he listens to but who listens to him. The car passes some of the nation's most authoritative mailboxes—McCormack of Comsat, Hipp of Liberty Life, Taylor of New York State wine, Twining of the Air Force, Simmons of the mattress, Close of Springs Mills. Fraser calls the plantation "a high-quality destination resort," and it has proved to be the destination of a fairly extensive variety of people—not just the barons of war and commerce but also retirees with wan incomes, golfers of most incomes and all handicaps, tennis players of the wider levels, a few painters, a few writers, and rich widows from the North, who bring their late husbands to Fraser's graveyard and then build homes for themselves in the plantation. What these people have in common is Fraser. He is Yahweh. He is not merely the mayor and the zoning board, he is the living ark of the deed covenant. He is the artist who has painted them into the corners he has sold them. A few owners have put sums like two hundred and fifty and three hundred thousand dollars into their houses, but most are in the forty- to fifty-thousand-dollar range, and Fraser has also built condominium villas that sold originally for as little as nineteen thousand—a minimum that has since risen to thirty-eight thousand. He has also built a small town, shops and all, with apartments that rent for two hundred and fifty to three hundred dollars a month. He figures he can blend fifteen hundred more houses into the trees, and one more golf course.

The chairman of the Continental Mortgage Forum recently introduced Fraser as "one of the two finest developers in the United States," not mentioning his peer. Lyndon Johnson appointed him to the Citizens' Advisory Committee on Outdoor Recreation and Natural Beauty. Fraser is also Commissioner of Parks, Recreation, and Tourism for the South Carolina coast. Now forty-one, he has made twenty million dollars in the past ten years, but he, his friends, and his enemies all agree that personal profit is not paramount among his motives. Fraser's drive seems to have been directed toward accomplishment for its own sake, toward aesthetics for the sake of an aesthetic criterion. Sea Pines has evolved, perhaps, as a kind of monument.

Fraser considers himself a true conservationist, and he will say that he thinks of most so-called conservationists as "preservationists" but that he prefers to call them "druids." "Ancient druids used to sacrifice human beings under oak trees," he says. "Modern druids worship trees and sacrifice human beings to those trees. They want to save things they like, all for themselves." He is aware of the importance of the larger environment. He says he would like to establish a College of the Oceans—"you know, pot, ecology, the whole bag." He reads the newsletter of the Conservation Foundation. He knows the vital position of salt marshes in marine ecology. "Salt marshes are productive feeding grounds for seafood," he says. "In the immediate marsh boundaries of Hilton Head Island, in the marsh flood plain, we save seventy-five per cent of the marsh, as a balanced approach between the interests of recreation and the interests of the druids. Man has to use some of the salt marsh if he is going to live near the sea. A few years ago, anybody would have said it was O.K. to build anything in a salt marsh. Now the society has so much money that we can afford to wonder. The druids get emotional and say you are upsetting ecology if you as much as touch the salt marsh, and you *have* to be polite. But you can't take the position that production of seafood is the most important issue in America. The druids dismiss me as a quote developer unquote, and that makes me mad."

There must be a very remarkable druid at Hammond, Inc., in New York, for Hammond has published a large map that seems particularly notable for what can only be a deliberate omission. It happens that the longest undeveloped beach on the Atlantic coast of the United States forms the eastern shoreline of a very large island, no part of which appears on this map—Hammond's Superior Map of the United States, four feet wide, one inch to seventy miles—although the map shows clearly such islands as Ocracoke, Hatteras, Assateague, Long Beach, and Manhattan, all of which are smaller. The name of the missing island is Cumberland. Virtually uninhabited, it lies off the coast of Georgia. It is the largest and the southernmost of the Georgia sea islands, and on the map the place where Cumberland Island should be is filled with nothing but blue Atlantic, although other sea islands—St. Simons, Sapelo, Ossabaw—stand forth in bold outline to the north. Clearly the work of a druid cartographer.

Cumberland Island, a third larger than Manhattan, has a population of eleven. Its beach is a couple of hundred yards wide and consists of a white sand that is fine and soft to the touch. The beach is just under twenty miles long, and thus, although there are no obstructions whatever, it is impossible to see from one end of it to the other, because the beach itself drops from sight with the curve of the earth. Wild horses, gray and brown, roam the beach, apparently for the sheer pleasure of the salt air. Poachers round them up from time to time and sell them to rodeos for fifteen dollars apiece. Wild pigs seem to like the Cumberland beach, too. The figure of a man is an unusual thing there. New, young dunes rise behind the beach, and behind the dunes are marshes, fresh or tidal. In some of the marshes and in ponds and lakes elsewhere on the island live alligators fourteen feet long. The people of the island will not say specifically where the alligators are. They are fond of their tremendous reptiles. Poachers, commando-fashion, come for them by night, kill them, and take just the hides. Behind the marshes stand the old dunes, high, smooth as talc, sloped precipitously like lines of cresting waves, and covered with pioneer grasses. At the back of the dunes begins a live-oak forest. The canopies of the oaks nearest the beach have been so pruned by the wind that they appear to have been shaped by design in a medieval garden. Among the oaks are slash pines and red cedars —trees also tolerant of salt. Sand-lane roads wind through the forest. Poachers use them in pursuit of white-tailed deer. Hotels in Jacksonville pay thirty-five dollars a deer. Through the woods run thousands of wild pigs. Now and again, a piglet is stopped by a diamondback.

A generally high bluff rims the western shore of the island, and along it are irregular humps—Indian burial mounds that have never been opened. Watched from the bluff, sunsets gradually spread out over a salt marsh five miles wide. This distance from the mainland in part explains why Cumberland Island remains as it is at this apparently late date in the history of the world. There is no bridge. The salt marsh is the most extensive one south of the Chesapeake. It is dominated by cord grass that rises higher than a man's head. The higher the tide, the higher the grass in a tidal marsh, and the Georgia coast has seven-foot tides. An acre of that marsh is ten times as fertile as the most fertile acre in Iowa. Roots of the cord grass reach down into the ooze and mine nutrients. When the grass dies and crumbles, it becomes high-protein detritus. Shrimp spend a part of their life cycle in there eating the crumbled grass. In the marsh, too, is a soup of microscopic plants, of phosphorus, nitrogen, calcium. Oysters grow there. Fish feed in the marshes and on marsh foods washed by the tides. If a quarter acre of marsh could be lifted up and shaken in the air, anchovies would fall out, and crabs, menhaden, croakers, butterfish, flounders, tonguefish, squid. Bigger things eat the things that eat the marsh, and thus the marsh is the broad base of a marine-food pyramid that ultimately breaks the surface to feed the appetite of man.

Tidal creeks penetrate Cumberland Island, and along their edges, when the tide is low, hundreds of thousands of oysters are exposed to view. Shrimp, fast-wiggling and translucent, feed between the beds of oysters. No wonder the Indians wanted to be buried on Cumberland Island. The only wonder is that the island now is much as it was when the Indian mounds were built. It has not always been so. There are stands of virgin pine and virgin live oak on Cumberland, but the island as a whole is a reclaimed wilderness. Orange and olive groves stood there once, and plantations of rice, indigo, and cotton. At the outbreak of the Civil War, the sea islands were abandoned. Later, rich Yankees began competing with one another in the acquisition of Georgia islands, and nearly all of Cumberland was bought by a Carnegie—Andrew's brother Thomas. His family, as it increased, built several enormous houses, and two or three of these are still in fair condition, but the others make Cumberland the world's foremost island in salt-sprayed baronial ruins. The Carnegie heirs are in the third, fourth, and fifth generations, and their number is so large that they went to court not long ago and had the island divided. Conservationists, noting this, and realizing that not all Carnegies could afford to hold land anymore, began to move toward finding a way to keep the island from being developed. They spoke of Cumberland as—in the words of one of Brower's colleagues in the Sierra

Club—"a spot in our eyes, a dream that may not come true." Then, in October, 1968, three Carnegies—Tom, Andrew, and Henry—sold three thousand acres of Cumberland Island for one and a half million dollars to Charles E. Fraser.

There was an expression that had been in the air there since the days of the rice and indigo plantations, and now it rose again to currency: "The Devil has his tail wrapped around Cumberland Island."

With "the purchase of lands on Cumberland Island," as Fraser termed the event, the issue was joined for one of the great land-use battles of recent times. Remaining Carnegie heirs closed ranks against him. All over the coast and, in fact, all over the South—particularly in Atlanta, Augusta, Columbia, and Athens (the University of Georgia)—people began talking intensely about Fraser.

"He walked into the Cloister at Sea Island and he said, 'I'm the golden boy of the Golden Isles, and I've just bought three thousand acres of Cumberland Island.'"

"I want to shoot the son of a bitch."

"He is a visionary young man who has learned that conservation can pay."

"No. Charlie is a conservationist in the real sense. He wants to harmonize a modern environment with all the endowments of nature."

"Conservation to Charlie means, in great part, that Charlie should not be bitten by a mosquito."

"He thinks he's a home boy with a lot of clout in Georgia, but he'll find out what he can do with his pink-sock golfers."

"Charles himself is interested in power. That's what motivates him. Everybody thinks he will go into politics."

"He would dearly love to be governor of South Carolina, and he would be fabulous."

"He doesn't have the stomach for it. In politics, there's a lot you can't control. Where he is, he controls everything."

"I'm an ecosystems man. It's not the island alone that interests me. It's the island, the marsh, and the sea. If the marshes are saved, there would not be much ecological loss with development. If you're going to have a developer, I'm all for Fraser. Unplanned development would spoil it."

"I don't think his declared intentions are always his true intentions."

"He's a demon. He has no principles."

"He is a little man walking empty with a cartoon balloon before his mouth, talking and talking as if to create a Charles Fraser who isn't there."

"Fraser says he wants to make these islands available to the people. Horse manure. He means taking it from the old rich and giving it to the new rich. Let's just be straight. A fifty-thousand-dollar investment ain't too many of the people."

"He does things no other developer would. Those concrete bulkheads at Hilton Head cost him three-quarters of a million dollars. He could have had steel for two hundred thousand."

"Steel bulkheads are an eyesore."

"Mr. Fraser does preserve environment. The university hopes that most of Cumberland can become a National Seashore, so people can enjoy it. It can't be all wilderness. We think it should be a mix—people in nature."

"The guy is tearing off an island just as if it were a postage stamp. He's behaving like a hunter knocking off buffaloes. We'll challenge anyone who wants to be the Buffalo Bill of the Georgia coast."

"He has half-baked, two-bit ideas. He's thinking very small. I challenge Charlie Baby to come up with something exciting. We are going to come into an age when people want more than a bag of sticks and some white balls."

"We can't afford to think in Colonial land-grab terminology anymore. We could set a precedent on Cumberland Island for recreational land use in America. Let's do something imaginative. Fraser's plans are not big enough. The golf-course bit should go to the mainland. There could be three planned communities on the mainland, with Cumberland their open space."

"You come in to the coast slowly. It grows on you. River mouths, marshes, tidal creeks, islands, the continental shelf, and the continental slope are really an integral unit, a single system. We have had integration of the races in the sixties, and we are going to have integration of man and the land in the seventies, or we'll all be gone in the eighties."

On a cold but sunlit November day, a small airplane, giving up altitude, flew down the west shore of Cumberland, banked left, crossed the island, and moved out to sea. Sitting side by side behind the pilot were Brower and Fraser. The plane turned, still descending, and went in low over the water and low over the wind-pruned live oaks and down into a clearing, where the ground was so rough that the landing gear thumped like drumfire. A man in khaki trousers and a wild-boarskin shirt waited at the edge of the woods. The aircraft wheeled around at the far end of the clearing and taxied back toward him through waist-high fennel.

Fraser and Brower had met only the evening before, at Hilton Head, and Fraser, in his direct way, had begun their relationship by giving Brower a dry Martini and then telling him what a conservationist is. Fraser said, "I call anyone a druid who prefers trees to people. A conservationist too often is just a preservationist, and a preservationist is a druid. I think of land use in terms of people. At Hilton Head, we have proved that you can take any natural area and make it available to people while at the same time preserving its beauty." Brower listened and, for the moment, said nothing. He had not expected so young a man. Fraser's dynamism impressed him, and so did Sea Pines Plantation. Fraser, for his part, was surprised by what he took to be, in Brower, an absence of thorns. Expecting an angry Zeus, he found instead someone who appeared to be "unargumentative, quiet, and shy."

Now, on Cumberland Island, the pilot cut the props, and into the resulting serenity stepped Fraser and Brower. Fraser wore a duck hunter's jacket and twill trousers that were faced with heavy canvas. Brower had on an old blue sweater, gray trousers, and white basketball shoes. The name of the man in the boarskin shirt was Sam Candler. Hands were shaken all around. Brower said it was "nice to be aboard the island." The weather was discussed. Amiability was the keynote.

Candler, who was thirty-eight, had spent much of his life on the island. He grew up on its oysters and shrimp. His children were doing the same. Candler knew where the alligators were, and he had a boxful of diamondback rattles, from snakes he had killed with a hackberry stick. Notches on the stick corresponded to rattles in the box, and Candler would have dearly loved to be able to make an additional notch that corresponded to Charles E. Fraser. There was native gentility in Candler, however, and he did not permit his darker sentiments to surface in the presence of his new neighbor. Candler spoke even more softly than Brower did, and the accents of Atlanta were in his voice. He was a slim man of medium height, with dark hair. He owned, with others in his family, the part of Cumberland Island that Thomas Carnegie did not buy. The Candler property, about twenty-two hundred acres at the north end, was the site of a rambling wooden inn (now Candler's house) in which business flourished around the turn of the century but atrophied after causeways were built to other islands. Candler's great-grandfather was the pharmacist who developed and wholly owned the Coca-Cola Company; his son, Candler's grandfather, bought the Cumberland property in 1928.

The pilot said goodbye. The airplane waddled into position and took off.

"An airport is essential here," Fraser said.

"But it's not a nice neighbor," Brower told him.

"Yes, but ours would be just large enough for small private jets, no more," Fraser said. "Let's go see Cumberland Oaks."

Cumberland Oaks was Fraser's working title for the development he intended to build on Cumberland Island. To get to the site, we drove about ten miles on narrow sand-lane roads, Fraser at the wheel of a Land Rover that belonged to his company. Sunlight came down in slivers through the moss in the canopies of huge virgin oaks. We stopped near one, and Brower paced the ground under it. The limbs reached out so far that, bent by their own weight, they plowed into the ground, from which they emerged farther out, leafily. Yucca grew in a crotch twenty feet high. Brower computed that the canopy covered fifteen thousand square feet of ground.

We drove on, through long stretches that were straight to the end of perspective. "This is a vast island," Fraser said. "It can absorb dozens of different kinds of uses. You won't even be able to *find* the uses, it's so vast—if it is handled with discretion." Brower was silent. "By going into islands, I tarnish my shining image, because I irritate so many druids," Fraser said.

Brower smiled. The Land Rover raced along at forty miles per hour and occasionally bounced over a corduroy bridge. Eventually Fraser said, with both humor and sarcasm in his voice, "Now we're on my property. Don't it look lovely?" Brower said sincerely that lovely was how it looked, with its palmettos, its live oaks, its slash and longleaf pines. To Fraser, it was obviously raw and incomplete, but even now he could clearly see before his eyes finished villas and finished roads. So complete was this vision, in fact, that Fraser turned off the existing road and began to zip through the trees, rounding imaginary corners and hugging subdivisional curves. Spiky palmettos rattled against the Land Rover's sides like venetian blinds. Pine branches smacked against the windshield, making explosive noises and causing us all, instinctively, to blink and cover our heads with our arms. A buck and two does leaped away from the oncoming vehicle, and Candler, raising his voice above the din, commented pointedly that on an island heavy with deer they were the first we had seen. "Variety of wildlife increases sharply with variety of food," Fraser said, accelerating. "A place like Sea Pines Plantation has more wildlife than an untouched forest—more browsing, more habitat variation."

The western edge of Fraser's property was a high bluff over the Cumberland River, a tidal lagoon separating the island from the broad marsh, and as we stood there looking down at the water and across to the distant mainland Fraser said, "We'll have slides here, so kids can slide down the bluff."

"You could have swings here on these cedars," Brower offered.

Fraser said that some of the cedars on his property had been planted by Scottish soldiers who had built and manned a stockade there in the early eighteenth century. Development was thus nothing new around Cumberland Oaks. Looking west across the water and the marsh, he confided that he was envisioning a seven-hundred-and-fifty-thousand-dollar system of towers, cables, and aerial gondolas to carry people to Cumberland Oaks from the mainland. "Brunswick Pulp & Paper owns those forests over there," Fraser said. "I would describe Brunswick Pulp & Paper as 'friendly.'"

Wild grapevines as thick as hawsers hung from the high limbs of Fraser's pines, and as we moved east through the woods

Brower found them irresistible. Fraser stopped the Land Rover so Brower could get out and swing on one—fifty feet in an arc through the air. He crashed into a palmetto.

Between the deep woods and the beach, among the secondary dunes of Cumberland Oaks, was a freshwater lake—Whitney Lake—so clear and lustrous that it gave Fraser's property a slight edge over all other parts of the island. Set in all the whiteness of the big hills of powder sand, the lake was so blue that day it paled the blue sky. Near the north end of the lake, three skeletal trees protruded from the slopes of sand—branches intact, but spare and dead. A buzzard sat in each tree. The trees were dead because the dunes were marching. Slowly, these enormous hills, shaped and reshaped by the wind, were moving south. They had already filled up half of Fraser's lake, and, left alone, they would eventually fill it all. Five buzzards stood at the edge of the water. Fraser stood there, too, with the unconcealed look on his face of a man watching a major asset disappear. "We've got to stabilize these dunes," he said.

Brower, for his part, was moved by the lyricism of the scene. If destruction is natural, Brower is for it. "I think it's just fine to see it happen," he said.

Fraser said, "I've got to restore dune-grass vegetation here. I've got to put the lake back to its original size. I'm an advocate of lakes."

"There's a place for development and there's a place for nature," said Candler.

"What would you move the dunes with?" I asked Fraser.

"Spoons, hoes, shovels—earthmoving equipment. You change natural gradings very cheaply with a bulldozer," he said.

Fraser went on to tell us that the lake had been named for Eli Whitney. Planters on the island had given Whitney financial support toward the development of the cotton gin. "This lake shouldn't be allowed to disappear," Fraser said. "There should be canoes on it for children. Children should be fishing here for bream. There is nothing here now but buzzards and dead trees."

Thinking of his three thousand acres as a whole, I asked him privately what he would like to build there by Whitney Lake.

"Houses!" he whispered.

The northernmost tip of the ocean beach was a long spit owned by Candler. We drove up there, inadvertently filling the sky with sandpipers and gulls. Then we turned and, in the late-afternoon light, went south all the way. The big beach ran on and on before us, white and dazzling in the clear sunlight. No other human beings were there. Of the several houses on Cumberland Island, the one nearest to the beach was a half mile back in the woods. We had been driving for a while when Candler remarked that we were nearing the end of his property. He has two and a half miles of beach. He said, "The only thing wrong with this beach—the traffic's so bad." Shells crunched under the wheels and salt foam flew out behind us. Plastic jugs, light bulbs, bottles, and buoys had drifted up along the scum line, but nowhere near enough of them to defeat the wild beach. I remembered the shoreline of the Hudson River at Barrytown, New York. A photographer from *Sports Illustrated* had caught up with Brower near there, and they had gone to some difficulty to get down to the river's edge, so that Brower could be photographed with the wind tousling his white hair against a background of natural beauty. For the occasion, Brower had changed from a topcoat into a ski parka, and the picture was successful—this ecological Isaiah by the wide water. It was just a head-and-shoulders shot, so it did not include the immediate environment of Brower's feet. The shore of the Hudson River, a hundred miles upstream from Manhattan, was literally obscured by aerosol cans, plastic bottles, boat cushions, sheets of polyethylene, bricks, industrial scum, globs of asphalt, and a tattered yacht flag. Now, on the Cumberland beach, Fraser, for the moment, was sounding much like a hard-line real-estate man. He was saying that we had beside us "the finest, gentlest breakers on the Atlantic coast." Brower said that where he came from such ripples were not called breakers. We got out of the Land Rover and walked for a while. Brower paused and studied the reflection of the falling sun on the surfaces of the breakers. This was what mattered to him—the play of light. He saw a horseshoe crab and had no idea what it was. He picked up a whelk shell and a clamshell and asked the names of the creatures that had lived in them. He wondered what made the holes of fiddler crabs. Shrimp boats were working offshore. Brower said he liked the look of them, bristling with spars. Brower seems to think in scenes. He seems to paint them in his mind's eye, and in these scenes not everything made by man is unacceptable. Shrimp boats on a bobbing sea are O.K. On the waterfront in San Francisco, he and I once drove at dusk past a big schooner that is perennially moored there, and its high rigging was beautiful in the fading light. "There should be more masts against the sky," Brower said. And now, back in the Land Rover, he looked up at high cumulus that was assembling over the ocean and he spoke of "sky mountains," while Fraser looked the other way and said that the primary dunes were in a process of severe disintegration, and the Land Rover moved on at forty miles per hour, crunching Paisley-spotted shells of the tiger crab.

"Have you ever been on a shrimp boat to see how they work?" Brower said.

"I have—when I was twelve," said Fraser. "I want a shrimp boat out of Cumberland Oaks, taking four or five kids a day."

The distance was so great across the beach and the dunes to the woods that I asked Fraser how far back he thought the nearest of his houses ought to be.

"The mainland," said Candler.

"That's a real dilemma here," Fraser said. "If the houses are set back in the trees, it's bad for recreation. What we need is an extensive tree-planting program to build up destroyed areas by the shore."

"Destroyed?"

"Destroyed. These dunes are not ordinary."

"They have always looked all right to me," Candler said.

"Pine trees grow exceedingly fast down by the ocean," Fraser went on.

Brower was silent.

"Within thirty years, there need to be fifty thousand more points for a week's visit on the Georgia coast," Fraser said. "You don't decrease the number of Americans taking a vacation by sealing off a particular land area. Surveys show that seventy-five per cent of Americans prefer beaches to all other places of recreation. I believe in human enjoyment of beaches, but, of course, the druids think it would be a shame and a crime to have people on this beach—a shame and a crime."

Acres of ducks darkened the swells of the ocean. A wild brown mare and her gray colt stood ankle-deep in a tidal pool. "Sam, why didn't you buy the property I bought?" Fraser said.

"I didn't have enough money," Candler said.

A line of pelicans—nineteen of them—flew south just seaward of the breakers. Pelicans fly single file, and Candler said he could remember them going by in lines a hundred pelicans long. That was in an era that seems to be gone. DDT has got into the bodies of pelicans and eventually into the shells of their eggs, and its effect on the shells is that they come out so thin they crack before chicks are ready to be born. Brower remarked that the pelican is one of the earth's oldest species. He quoted Robinson Jeffers, saying that pelicans "remember the cone that the oldest redwood dropped from." We were nearing the end of the beach, and we could see Florida across the mouth of the St. Mary's River. The pelicans kept going, like flying boxcars, across the river. "They're doomed," Brower said. "Maybe we're lined up behind those pelicans."

Fraser is descended from the Frasers of Inverness and the Bacons of Dorchester, who began their existence in the New World as Puritans of seventeenth-century New England and gradually moved in a southerly direction, establishing Dorchester, Massachusetts; Dorchester, South Carolina; and, eventually, Dorchester, Georgia. The Bacons and the Frasers were on the original roll of the Midway Church Settlement, a seat of Presbyterian enlightenment important in the history of Georgia and the South. The Frasers regularly sent their sons to Edinburgh to be educated. The 1810 census showed the Frasers to be among the ten foremost slaveholders in the state. One distinguished Fraser voted against secession, and another used a slingshot against troops of General Sherman. For two hundred years, the family has had what Fraser calls "substantial amounts of land," and the family's "social antennae" (as he would phrase it) have developed a length and sensitivity commensurate with the family's history and standing. Consequently, nothing makes Fraser sit straighter and tuck his chin in deeper than the assertion—often repeated in gossip—that his acquisition of property on Cumberland Island was something straight out of Chekhov: the capitulation of a fine old family under inexorable pressure from a *nouveau-riche* developer.

Having returned to the middle of the island, Fraser stopped at a small graveyard, not by chance. Its walls were made of tabby—lime, sand, and oyster shells—and it was only twenty feet square. Dusk had come and was now heavy, and Brower grew rhapsodic about the penumbral grays, the deep shafts of varied gloom under the high trees. Fraser, meanwhile, was intently pointing to a stone, and there was still enough light to reveal what was written there: "Thomas Morrison Carnegie, born Dunfermline, 1843, died Pittsburgh, 1886." What Fraser wanted us to note was that the Carnegies are comparatively recent immigrants. He referred to them as "upstarts," and said, "I have no patience with them. They have no sense of history. They think the history of the island is the history of their occupancy. They think history began when they arrived. Look there." He was pointing to another stone. The inscription said, "In memory of Catherine Miller, widow of Major General Nathaniel Greene, Commander-in-Chief of the American Revolutionary Army in the Southern Department, 1783, who died November 2, 1814, aged 59 years. She possessed great talents and exalted virtues." "More talents and more virtues than all the Carnegies put together," Fraser said. "Her friend General Lighthorse Harry Lee died here on Cumberland Island. Did you know that, Sam?"

"Yes, I did, Charles."

"The family of my friend Brailsford Nightingale, in Savannah, owned parts of this island when the Carnegies were still herding sheep. The Nightingales have been elegant for more generations than you can count. They are descendants of General Greene. They had subdivided this island and were going to make it a rich man's retreat before the Carnegies had ever heard of it, but the Nightingales were thwarted by history. Reconstruction was a brutal wipeout. And now the Carnegie druids do not wish to share the island with other people. They think only Carnegie eyes are sensitive enough to appreciate the beauties of that beach out there. On any list of America's hundred most selfish families these poor new-rich Carnegies must be placed very high."

On the way in from the beach we had passed another kind of graveyard—a place where at least twenty automobiles and pickup trucks were disintegrating in flakes of rust. It was this scene that had set off Fraser's ridicule and fulminating scorn. Here, he said, was a family posing as conservationists, attempting at this very moment to enlist the support of the federal government in protecting their island with them on it, and this junk heap was their idea of preserving natural beauty. He said he would like to bring a bulldozer to the island and cover the junk up. And he said, "How about your place, Sam? You must have some things up there that need covering up. Could I give you a neighborly hand?"

"I have nothing to hide," Candler said.

"You haven't got anything one day with a bulldozer won't cure."

Fraser's relationship with the Carnegies had not always been as clearly defined as it now appeared to be. The Carnegie heirs were a diffuse group. Most of them spent little or no time on the island. Two or three of them lived there. During early negotiations, the Carnegies' attitudes toward Fraser varied considerably. Then a social event framed the nature of things to come. A few days after Fraser was given the deed to his new lands, one of the Carnegie heirs, a pretty girl in her twenties, was married on Cumberland Island. The groom, a junior executive in Fraser's Sea Pines Plantation Company, had been assigned to the Cumberland Island project and had met his bride there. That should be plot enough for a Deep South Lorca, but there was more: The bride was the author of a Sierra Club book. Fraser arrived for the wedding, as various Carnegies recall the scene, wearing an ascot and carrying an enormous leather map case. They say that he unstrapped his case in the middle of the reception and displayed plats and plans for his new utopia on Cumberland Island. They say he called them idiots not to understand the concept of conservation easements. Moreover, they say, he burped in front of ladies. According to the bride, Fraser "galvanized the Carnegies into unanimity." They united in order to block Fraser in any way possible, most notably by promoting a Cumberland Island National Seashore, with "inholding" or "life-time-estate" provisions for established residents. The groom, for his part, defected. He quit the Sea Pines Plantation Company, the better to live happily ever after.

And now, by the little graveyard, in the near-darkness, Fraser said to Candler, "Sam, what do you think of that line about the hundred most selfish families? Do you think I can get some mileage out of that? Shall I hone it?"

Candler said, "You don't want to develop that line, Charles. You might spoil it."

"All right, I'll leave it as it is, but did you know that one of the older Carnegie ladies told Stewart Udall that only blooded heirs of Thomas and Lucy Carnegie should ever be allowed to set foot on this island?"

"How do you know that?"

"I was told by someone present. She wagged her finger under Udall's nose and said, 'Only blooded heirs of Thomas and Lucy Carnegie should ever set foot on Cumberland Island.' You know, during all the present talk about National Parks and National Seashores the Carnegies have been keeping something under the table. A few years ago, most of them were in favor of strip-mining the beach. The sand is full of ilmenite, zirconium, and rutile. I have no patience with the Carnegies. All they want to do is maximize their dollar, either through the mining industry or through the federal government or by piggybacking on me. Now look at one more headstone."

The inscription said, "Thomas Hutchison, Golf Professional, eldest son of William and Helen H. of St. Andrews, Scotland. Born October 6, 1877. Died December 8, 1900."

"He was surely the first golf pro to be buried in America," Fraser said. "When this property was bought by the Carnegies, there were no golf courses in the United States. A golf club had once been in operation in Charleston and another in Savannah, but they had long since ceased. The oldest continuing golf organization in the United States is St. Andrews of Yonkers. It was built in 1888, and from then to 1900 golf swept the country. Hundreds of courses were built, including one here on Cumberland Island—where we landed in the airplane. The Carnegies brought this young man from St. Andrews, Scotland, and he died here when he was twenty-three."

Fraser had already made something out of his research into the history of golf in the South. He had arranged with the

Professional Golfers Association a new hundred-thousand-dollar tournament, to be held at Sea Pines, and to be called the Heritage Classic, because the first golf club in America had been built in South Carolina. The first Heritage Classic was won by Arnold Palmer, and because Palmer had not won a tournament in more than a year this was major news in the sporting world, and the names of Sea Pines and Hilton Head were publicized throughout the United States. As we stood there in the graveyard on Cumberland Island, I looked at the tombstone and then at Fraser, feeling a kind of awe for his luck. Someday, if he had his way, there would surely be a hundred-thousand-dollar First Pro Classic on the Thomas Hutchison Memorial Golf Course, Cumberland Oaks.

Reflectively, Fraser placed a hand on the tombstone and said, "Druids hate golf. I keep telling them golf was here seventy-five years ago. Dave, you wouldn't mind if I built a little golf course here on Cumberland Island, would you?"

"I suppose not, if you don't take too many trees," Brower said.

"You know I don't take too many trees, Dave," Fraser said. He turned to Candler. "Sam, Dave is going to let us have a golf club here."

"He is?"

"Yes."

"That's damned white of him."

That night, in a place called Greyfield, before a big fireplace that glowed with burning logs and coals of oak, Fraser and Brower spread out on the floor a map of Cumberland Island twelve feet long. Together they crawled around on it, pushing cocktails from one part of the island to another. Antlers hung above them, and portraits of Carnegies, and a portrait of George Washington, while the skull of a loggerhead turtle, huge and primordially human—or so it seemed—faced them from a cluttered shelf. The map was about twenty years old and bore the names of quick and dead Carnegies—Thomas M. Carnegie, Jr., Florence Carnegie Perkins, Carter C. B. Carnegie, Lucy Ricketson Ferguson, Nancy Carnegie Johnston, Andrew

Carnegie II. Greyfield, with high porch and high columns and a need of paint, belonged to Lucy Ferguson's son Rick, who once ran a plastics factory in Jacksonville and was now running Greyfield as an inn for selected guests. Fraser could hardly be said to have been selected, but he was made welcome at Greyfield, and nearly all the inimical things said about him were said behind his back. Meanwhile, on his hands and knees on the big map, a Martini at his fingertips, Brower was saying, "When you get onto a floor with a big map, something happens. You think you're in an airplane."

Fraser said to Brower, "Dave, suppose you owned this island. Suppose you were the dictator and were under no financial pressure whatever. How do you think this island ought to be used in the last thirty years of this century?"

Brower said, "I'd have one feeder point to the beach per mile."

Fraser seemed to levitate, to float above the map. He might have been a skin diver who had just picked up a doubloon. The excitement he felt was almost, but not quite, palpable. Was this the David Brower of Friends of the Earth and the Sierra Club —the slayer of environmental dragons, the uncompromising defender of wilderness? Fraser's face was a mask. He tucked in his chin and said unflickeringly, "I call them 'beach social points.'"

The conversation was semi-private. Several duck hunters and the odd Carnegie or two moved around it. Beyond the firelit room was a long hall, and off this was a small room where Rick Ferguson had set up a self-service bar. He was there, a short man, wiry and strong, in tennis shoes, khaki trousers, an old blue oxford-cloth button-down shirt—the great-grandson of Thomas Carnegie. Ferguson's wife, in a long hostess gown, was with him.

"Cumberland Island is going down the drain," Ferguson said.

"Fraser's drain," said his wife.

"I feel like a man who has just been told his block is up for urban renewal. We seem to be on the sidelines while this big show is going on. All I want to protect here is my children's inheritance."

"We have no rights except what the majority lets us do."

"I was giving Charles the benefit of the doubt once when I called him insensitive. I think his rudeness is an inherent characteristic."

"Charles is over-self-righteous. He thinks he is absolutely right and is doing good—and that is his mistake."

"No one is interested in this island but the family, basically."

Ferguson excused himself and went off to slice a roast of beef.

On the floor in the big room, Brower was leaning on his elbows. Fraser was on his knees.

"How many people would you, as dictator, permit on the island July 4, 1980?" Fraser asked.

"I don't know," Brower said. "An answer is needed, but if on the evening I come here I come up with an answer, I'm an ass."

"Ninety per cent of Americans want bedrooms when they are on vacation," Fraser went on. "Ten per cent want to camp with automobiles. Only five per cent of that ten per cent—or five people in a thousand—want wilderness camping. How many would you permit on this island, and how would you accommodate them?"

"Let's keep Cumberland Island for the five per cent of the ten per cent who want wilderness," Sam Candler said.

"I think I'd recommend the Yosemite formula," Brower said. "Seven square miles of Yosemite bears heavy and concentrated use. The rest is open."

Brower has deep affection for the Yosemite, which is, or was once, the most beautiful valley in the Sierra Nevada. He has spent whole years there, and a great deal of time in or around the valley throughout his life. When he is in the Yosemite, he seems to be packed in nostalgia, and he appears to be unaffected by the valley's peeled-log Levittowns, its tent cities, its bumper-to-bumper traffic, and its newsstands—all results of what has been described as the fatal beauty of Yosemite. In all likelihood, he accepts Yosemite whole because the valley was already urbanized when he was young. And now, on Cumberland Island, he was recommending something similar. "I would cluster all development in one place," he said to Fraser. "People could walk elsewhere. Walking on the beach is the most important thing a person can do here. If you were going to develop just one spot on the entire island, where would that be?"

"To be very explicit, my tract has tremendous diversity," Fraser said. "I have Whitney Lake, the Scotch fort, the marching dunes. But we're pretending *you're* the dictator. The island as a whole is twenty miles long. How many people can your area of concentration absorb?"

"You mean at night?"

"Yes, at night."

"They do have to be there at night," Brower mused. "People will want to see what the sky is saying. It's their last contact with Mother Earth."

"How many people?" Fraser said again.

"It's their last chance to listen to the sun and the moon."

"How many people?"

Brower shrugged. He said, finally, "I wouldn't mind having a population of twenty thousand here."

"Twenty thousand?"

"Twenty thousand."

Brower got up and went in to make himself another drink. When he came back, he and Fraser agreed that if a National Park or Seashore could surround Fraser's place on Cumberland Island, that would be very good. Brower said that what worried him was that if Fraser were to go ahead and develop his land without some such federal protection of the rest of the island, the value of the remaining properties would rise so sharply that the neighbors might have to let the land go to less capable developers. Fraser said that worried him, too.

"Whatever happens to this island, the automobile should be ruled out," Brower went on.

"I agree," said Fraser.

"No tourist vehicles. No bridge. No private automobiles or other vehicles on the beach."

"I agree."

"How would you get people around?"

"Perhaps jeep trains."

"How would you bring in food and services?"

"In sky vans—mini flying boxcars."

"Whatever you do, don't give the island to Detroit. Zermatt is carless. Stehekin, in the State of Washington, is carless. It is good conservation practice, if you are going to develop, to concentrate people and leave wild land around them. People need earning territory—territory they have to earn by walking, limping, crawling, or whatever they can do. With that around them, the concentrated area is important, and I wouldn't mind so many people. Not at all. When you get out of the city, you hear the planet talk, and here it is talking. If the dunes want to march, they ought to march. I know how you feel, but the land itself should not be controlled."

"The Brower Plan is economically sound," Fraser said. "I could live within the constraints imposed by the Brower dictatorship. As the island is now, birds enjoy it but nobody's swimming here. Nobody's in the woods. There are no people. The island's stable population is eleven. That comes to one person per mile and three-quarters of beach."

Rick Ferguson had come into the room to say the roast beef was ready. "One person per mile and three-quarters of beach is just about right," he said.

"Why do you think the family have kept it this way?" said Mrs. Ferguson. "Because they *feel* so strongly."

"If you can keep it the way it is, fine," Brower told her. "But I don't think that is one of your choices."

Not long after Fraser acquired his property on Cumberland Island, he established a public campsite there. He admitted privately that he had several motives. For one thing, it was a way to acquaint the public with the island. For another, it would set a precedent for public use of the island at a fee. Finally, and most ingeniously, it would put Stewart Udall in a position where he might have to criticize camping—for Udall had been employed by the Carnegies as a conservation consultant, or, as Fraser insisted on putting it, as "a hired mudslinger." Udall said of Fraser, "I want to push Charlie into a corner where he has to face the truth. He is good news as a developer and bad news for Cumberland Island. He is not interested in having a reputation as a spoiler, but he can't have it both ways. He tries to incorporate conservation with economic development, but it doesn't work."

One motive Fraser emphatically did not have for establishing his campsite was a desire to camp on Cumberland Island himself. Fraser is not in any sense a woodsman or a man of the outdoors, as he will acknowledge without shame. Nonetheless, under urging from Brower and from me, he had agreed to sleep in his own campsite. And now, after dinner at Greyfield, the three of us went out into the black, cold night and headed for the campsite, which Brower was eager to see. After we had gone some distance through the woods, Fraser said, "I'm most happy to go along with this, but, frankly, you are taking me out of my element."

It would be difficult to say whose element the campsite was. It consisted of fifteen so-called recreation vehicles—tent-covered, two-wheeled automobile trailers, with electric lights, electric heat, and four-burner gas stoves. A central toilet facility had hot showers, an ice machine, and a cedar-shake roof in the Sea Pines manner. Fraser said he believed in "use," and that this was a good way to start. He said he planned to build a small store at the campsite and, eventually, to rent jeeps by the day. Meanwhile, he was charging five dollars a night for the mobile tents—loss leaders if ever there were any, for they cost him fifteen hundred dollars apiece.

Two of the vehicles had been set up for us, and they faced each other, like canvas tourist cabins, across an area filled with palmettos and cast-iron grills that were mounted on galvanized pipes. Brower went into one tent and Fraser and I into the other. While we were unrolling our sleeping bags, Fraser said, "Very interesting, his views. They're so different from what I thought they would be." Spreading out the contents of a briefcase on a Formica-topped table, Fraser looked through them. Then he got out a pen and began to read and make marginalia. He read an article in the *Yale Law Journal* on large-lot zoning; he read a piece from the Beirut *Daily Star* on a new kind of sewage-disposal system; and in an issue of *American Forests* he read something called "The Destiny of Conservation Depends Upon Truth." "At the moment, I am rather aggravated about the distruth of statements made by certain druids," he commented. "But Dave is not a druid—not the way he was talking. Arthur D. Little would get ninety thousand dollars for the consultancy Dave did tonight." For morning, Fraser set aside a copy of *Audubon* magazine, a book called *Land, People, and Policy*, and the first draft of a prospectus for the first public issue of stock in his company. He shut off the light. "The highest and best use of this island is for children," he said as he was settling to sleep. "I believe, however, that the struggle here is too complicated, and therefore hopeless, and that no reasonable development will ever go on here."

Brower called out from across the palmettos, "Good night, and sleep well if your conscience is good."

Fraser called back, "My conscience is always bad, and I always sleep very well. Good night."

"Good night."

Sleep was not all that easy, in part because the bunks folded out and were cantilevered from either end of the mobile unit. Fraser and I were balanced on a kind of rubber-tired seesaw. Every time he rolled to his right, I went up a little, and every time he rolled to his left I went down. I lay there long into the night thinking mainly about the peculiar pattern of the relationship developing between him and Brower.

A beach is for children, Fraser had said. I didn't think he was just groping for a key to a bank vault. I had seen swings of various kinds all over Sea Pines Plantation—swings hanging from the eaves of covered walkways, swings hanging from the limbs of trees. He had bought tricycles and scattered them around. He had strung hammocks at the height of children. Walking among the fresh foundations of his new town, he had once said to me, "Landscape architects won't hang swings. They say swings are not a strong enough design statement. I'll wait until the landscape architects are finished, and then I'll hang a hundred swings from the live oaks. I'll have a vender selling watermelon, too—roasted oysters in the winter, ice-cold slices of watermelon in the summer." Fraser and his wife, Mary, lived in a glass-and-cypress Sea Pines house. Gardeners took care of the environment. The Frasers had two daughters, aged four and two. The Frasers believed that the direction of a life was established almost at the beginning—that no years were as telling as the earliest ones. Hence, among other things, the Montessori School (where Mary Fraser worked) and the swings all over the plantation.

Brower was reverent toward the young. His faith had told him that the young would do better with the earth. He did not associate lumber companies, motor companies, chemical companies, or mining companies with youth. He admired Young Turks while he attacked Old Philistines. By his ready admission, he had learned a great deal from his own children, all of whom were college age or older. Brower himself looked almost unnaturally young, his white hair notwithstanding. He sometimes seemed to trust young people's judgment over his own. He often said, "I'm impressed with what young people can do before older people tell them it's impossible." Any number of times since we had come to Cumberland Island, he had commented on the youth of Charles Fraser. "I didn't know he was so young. . . . What energy! I didn't expect so young a man."

Out through a picket fence and down a deeply shaded street Fraser, as a boy, had walked every day to school. He was blond then, and had curly hair. His mother and father used to buy athletic equipment for him, but he would give it all away and sit on the porch reading books while his friends—endangering the camellias—played football or baseball on his family's lawn. His family owned nearly half of Hinesville. Their house had been the first in Liberty County to have running water, inside toilets, and two pianos. The land for the First Presbyterian Church had been a gift from his grandmother. His father had been moderator of the Presbyterian Church of the State of Georgia and president of the Men of the Presbyterian Church of the United States of America. The church was the Frasers' locus of being. "Holy, holy, holy," Fraser had chanted one day at Hilton Head, waving his hands like a choir leader as he revealed these credentials. "As a Calvinist, I was told that you're not supposed to do all the pleasurable things in life. But eventually I realized that I would be part of the elect no matter what sins I might commit." He said that at the age of thirteen he had been a newspaper entrepreneur. Under his ironclad managerial control, his entire Boy Scout troop sold papers. He fished the creeks, hunted squirrels, collected buckeyes. He became the first Eagle Scout in the history of Liberty County. Now the executives of the Sea Pines Plantation Company included a high proportion of former Eagle Scouts. On the Sea Pines boardroom wall was a life-size portrait of Fraser's father, in uniform, and beside this portrait stood two flags—a United States flag and the three-star flag of a lieutenant general. General Fraser commanded the first ground troops to land on New Guinea. He went into France with Patton. Charles Fraser, at the age of ten, had been quite relieved when his father's unit was converted from cavalry to anti-aircraft. Charles hated horses and did not want to ride them. His interests were elsewhere. In becoming an Eagle Scout, he won merit badges in birds, reptiles, conservation. He loved beautiful objects and had a gift for design. He painted his family's coat of arms on a mug, applying the paint with toothpicks. His brother, Joe, was an athlete. Liberty was a coastal county, and one thing Charles particularly liked to do was to go to the beaches and build castles in the sand.

Fraser's mother-in-law, before she became that, used to send newspaper clippings about him and his plantation to her daughter wherever she might be—at Stephens College, in Columbia, Missouri, for example, or, later, in Washington, D.C., where she worked for Senator Thurmond. "Mary's mother is a very sensible Southern mother, who knows that her daughter's standard of living depends on her husband's income," Fraser once explained. "Mary was accustomed to a very elegant standard. She had a Cadillac to drive to school when she was sixteen—and that was just the leftover car around the place." Mary, in her college days, had not so much as met him. He was twelve years older than she, and he lived two hundred miles from Greenville, her home town. Nonetheless, she dutifully read and saved the clippings. Eventually, she would more or less save Fraser. Small details not being his forte, she had assumed responsibility for looking after them. He forgot everything—his money, his briefcase, his topcoat, his whereabouts. He lost every hat he ever owned. "Hats are a nuisance and an absurdity," he complained. He was not absentminded, his wife decided. He was simply not interested in petty detail.

He read all the time. He read walking upstairs, he read until his food was cold, and he rigged up extra lights in the car so he could read while she drove. He forgot his raincoat but remembered facts. Three minutes after he walked into a room, it was a shambles. "Have you read this? What did you think of it? What do you think about that?" Newspapers hit the floor. Sixteen books came off the shelves. "Charles says there is so little time, and never a convenient time for anything, so if you want to do something you have to just do it," Mary once said. "He applies this to a trip to Europe, to conceiving a child—to anything." Mary, dark-haired, dark-eyed, slender, was collaterally descended from a family named Lawton that once grew cotton on Hilton Head Island—in fact, on the site of Sea Pines Plantation. When Fraser's archival researches yielded this fragment, he was most pleased. He and Mary began to refer to it as "the heritage." He would talk about it with a detached grin, but he was obviously happy that he had something like that to be detached about. "The Lawtons were planters," he liked to say, invoking images of antebellum wealth and antebellum elegance. He once introduced his four-year-old daughter, Laura Lawton, to a stranger.

"Hello, Laura," said the stranger.

"It will have to be Laura Lawton, I'm afraid," said Fraser. "Laura Lawton, say 'My great-great-great-great-great-granddaddy planted cotton here.'"

In an office at the University of California Press, in 1941, Anne Hus had demonstrated to David Brower that she could lean over and pick a newspaper off the floor with her teeth. She wondered if he could do the same. They shared the office. Both were editors, working on what she called "rewarmed dissertations with the scaffolding taken out." He said stiffly, about the newspaper stunt, that one does not do that sort of thing in an office, and he refused to try. Brower as an editor made her jealous. "He was so much better than I. I have never understood where he got his feel for words. He is a great editor. He liberates what is good in an author's work. It just infuriates me that anyone who has read so little can do that. I have been reading since I was four. He has never read anything. He hasn't read novels. He knows very little about English literature. Yet he has a remarkable sense of language."

Anne had been born in Oakland. Her father was a man who failed at so many jobs that he said he should go into undertaking in order to prolong human life. Her grandfather John P. Irish, editor and politician, was the man who was debating with William Jennings Bryan when Bryan said, "You shall not crucify mankind upon a cross of gold." Brower was in the 10th Mountain Division when, in 1943, he proposed to Anne by mail. Before he went overseas, they lived in Colorado for a time, and then in West Virginia, where Brower taught climbing to the mountain troops, on the Seneca Rocks. He spent so much time on bivouac that she despaired and went to Washington, where she edited combat narratives for Army Intelligence. Later, she went back to the University of California. She was still an editor there when I met her, in 1969. A gentle person, she seemed almost complacent—an impression that belied her sharpness of ear and eye. I remembered her telling him once, "I never see people I'd rather be married to than you—especially in National Parks." Brower obviously needed her guidance. Away from her, he could scarcely pass a phone booth without getting into it and calling her. At the Press, in their early days, he had dropped from sight now and again and gone off to the Sierra Nevada. After he had been doing this for a while, she told him he was getting away with murder. Leaning over, he picked a newspaper off the floor with his teeth and said he had to practice somewhere. He asked her to go with him to the mountains. She loved the sea and didn't like the mountains. "Edna Ferber said mountains were beautiful but dumb, and that is how I felt, too. Finally, I went on a Sierra Club trip just to fill in. To get through it, I took a bottle, and took nips. After three days, I really loved the trip—such incredible country. Until you've seen him up there, you don't know him."

I thought of Brower in the Sierra Nevada, in the Valley of the Mineral King. To conservationists, the Mineral King had become an Agincourt, a Saratoga, an El Alamein. Walt Disney Productions wanted to string the slopes with lifts and build enough hotels there to draw a million people a year. Mineral King had been mentioned as an excellent setting for the Winter Olympics of 1976, celebrating the two-hundredth anniversary of the birth of the nation. Brower and I went to Mineral

King together. My impression was that—all other considerations aside—it was an extraordinarily good site for a skiing resort. A stream ran through the middle of the valley, and if you stood beside it and looked up and around you saw eleven conical peaks, the points of a granite coronet. The steep slopes of these mountains were covered with red fir, juniper, aspen, and foxtail pine. Great rising swaths were treeless and meadowed. Hannes Schneider had called it the best potential ski area in California. So much snow had been there the winter before that avalanches had sheared off many hundreds of trees twenty feet above the ground—the snow was that deep. The avalanches had been so powerful that they had not stopped at the bottom of the valley but had climbed the other side, smashing trees. In the geological history of the Sierra Nevada, Mineral King was an old valley. The Sierra Nevada had been a minor mountain range of about four thousand feet when it began the great upheaval that made it higher than the Rockies. New streams cut through the new uplift and created valleys like the Yosemite, with wide, flat floors and sheer walls. The Mineral King was lifted with the mountains and remained intact, a V-shaped valley—alpine, ancestral—and it caught snow like nothing else in a mountain range that was named for the snow that fell there. Brower had done a ski survey of Mineral King once, long ago, and had said that he favored limited development. He said now that he essentially felt the same way. Sitting under a big cottonwood with his feet in the stream, he pointed out that the valley was, for one thing, not wilderness. A road reached into it. A couple of dozen buildings were there, a sawmill, and corrals belonging to a pack station. Listening to him, a surprised conservationist might have thought that the Antichrist had come to the Mineral King disguised as David Brower. But to the Disney interests Brower would not have seemed like much of an advocate. Looking around at the Mineral King peaks, he decided that although he was for limited development, he was against ski lifts. He said he preferred to see people earn their ski runs by climbing with skins attached to their skis. Moreover, he was against improvement of the existing access road, an incredibly twisting cliff-hanger so narrow and serpentine that a million people trying to use it would grow old before they reached the valley. Brower said

Disney Productions should build a hundred-million-dollar tunnel, or fly people in—save the approaching mountains, hang the cost. Told he was being almost poetically impractical, Brower responded that the Disney people were going to change something forever, so they could amortize the changes over a thousand years.

Fraser rolled over and sighed in his sleep. I wondered if in the day to follow he would find that Brower's apparent tolerance for the development of Cumberland Island was equally tied in string. He sighed again. Possibly he was dreaming of Badische Anilin-& Soda-Fabrik Aktiengesellschaft, a name, of all names, that haunted him. Fraser was hoist on a most ironic petard. Badische Anilin-& Soda-Fabrik Aktiengesellschaft, known as BASF, was a company that made, among other things, petrochemicals and dyes for the textile and furniture industries, and not long before they had decided to expand beyond Ludwigshafen and into the American South. They searched in several states for a site for a new plant. There were plenty of possibilities. What in the end attracted the Germans most in all the South was Sea Pines Plantation. German chemical kings apparently liked golf and the good life, too. They had found a plant site on Victoria Bluff, three miles from Hilton Head Island. Air and water pollution would surely follow. Fraser, meanwhile, had become the unlikely leader of a battalion of druids, whose war cry was "BASF—Bad Air, Sick Fish!" Ultimately, Fraser and his druids would drive the Germans away, but he had learned that even in the beauty of Sea Pines Plantation there could be something fatal.

One night of camping out, even in a fifteen-hundred-dollar mobile tent, was quite enough for Fraser, and the following evening we transferred our gear to a motorship called the *Intrepid*, which had slipped quietly down the coast from Hilton Head and into the Cumberland River. The size of Fraser's yacht was proportionate to his distaste for wilderness. The yacht was ninety feet long. It contained five staterooms and a floor-through saloon. Its bar was stocked with Tanqueray gin. Fraser's Southern antennae had reached out unobtrusively, suprasocially, and their research had shown that Tanqueray is Brower's gin of gins. With the moral support of a friendly doctor, Brower once used gin as his principal weapon in humbling a stomach ulcer, and he was so successful that he has ever since been a friend of the preventive Martini. With something beatific in his eyes, he ritually asks for "a Martini with Tanqueray gin, straight up, with nothing in it." Lemon, he feels, changes the taste, while only a madman would accept an olive, for an olive displaces two cubic centimetres of gin. It had been a long, full day on the island, and Brower now settled back with a drink innocent of additives and watched the sun fall behind the Georgia mainland. Fraser sipped bourbon and Calvinistically worked on his stock prospectus—for several hundred thousand shares of something he was calling Recreational Environments, Inc., at twenty-five dollars a share. He needed money for expansion—not only to Cumberland Island but to half a dozen other places he was interested in, from North Carolina to Hawaii. He had just bought six miles of beautiful and undeveloped white beach under coconut palms on the east coast of Puerto Rico, and only the week before he had gone as far as Kuwait looking for funds. "I'm just an oyster catcher from South Carolina begging for money," he said, moving a blue pencil over the prospectus. "A million dollars. A million dollars. Can you spare a million dollars?"

"Look at that sun on that smog!" Brower said. Shining low through the air over the paper-mill country, the sun tended to embarrass Georgia. It appeared to be setting in black-bean gumbo. "American industry never asked my permission to shorten my life," Brower went on. "They have taken two years off my life and will take seven years off my children's. These are figures I can't support, but I believe them."

"Let's put a paper mill over here on Cumberland Island and get the smell away from the cities," Fraser said, looking at Sam Candler, who went on looking at the sunset.

"Whatever their economy is, they haven't paid for the people's air," Brower said. "They should be given six months to clean up or go out of business. Roll, you earth. I swear the sunset is slower than the sunrise."

On the beach at six-fifty-seven that morning, we had watched the sun jump into the clear sea air like a rubber ball released from a hand below the ocean's surface. Fraser, over breakfast, read an article called "The Dying Marsh" in *Audubon* magazine, and throughout the day he pelted Brower with sachets and nosegays. Hurtling along a narrow, curving sand road through the forest, Fraser said, "We'll call this the David Brower Scenic Drive." And later, approaching an attractive swamp, he said, "We'll call this the David Brower Wildlife Sanctuary and Woodland Recreation Area." In a small skiff on a tidal creek, Fraser stood in the bow like George Washington and spoke what were apparently the first words of a press release he was forming in his mind: "Charles Fraser announced today the results of a detailed study for the use of Cumberland Island." Sam Candler had one hand on the skiff's tiller and with the other he was bailing. Flights of ducks passed overhead. The tide was low. Using a small anchor as a kind of oyster rake, Fraser knocked hundreds of oysters loose from an exposed bed. He was clearly feeling very good. On the beach, he drove at fifty-five miles an hour and said gleefully that he had decided to name his new development the Cumberland Island Conservation Association.

Brower was feeling good, too—obviously enjoying himself on the island. Why he did not rise up and clout Fraser, verbally, seemed a little odd to me, but I had seen him before in situations where he was getting the sense and feel of something, and while his mind was working toward a settled attitude he had vacillated or lapsed into an uncharacteristic passivity. In the North Cascades, he had known where he was. He had been there before, and had fought for the wilderness there. He had never before set foot on Cumberland Island. Fraser, ebullient, was finding Brower so docile that he wouldn't even call him a druid, and in a sense Fraser was right, for the rote behavior of an ordinary member of the priesthood should be simple to predict. This, however, was—as Fraser apparently did not grasp—no ordinary member of the priesthood. This was the inscrutable lord of the forest, the sacramentarian of *ecologia americana*, the Archdruid himself. Fraser's difficulties with druids were anything but over.

Lacking a target in the invisible Brower, Fraser eventually attacked Candler. Candler, whose original intention had been merely to help show Brower around the island, had tried to hold off from saying much, but now there was a gun-fusillade argument.

"Sam, you just don't want people on this beach, do you?" Fraser said.

"I didn't say that," Candler said.

"A man has no more right to personal private property on a beach than he has to a highway, an Army camp, a railroad, a school, a hospital, an airport, a valley to be flooded for a dam. A fundamental part of the pursuit of happiness is one's annual vacation. Hence this beach is for a public purpose."

"Your purpose. I'm happy to have people use the island now, if they make the effort to get over here and to enjoy it."

We happened to be at the southern boundary of Fraser's proposed development. Fraser said that a National Seashore should begin just there and extend all the way to the southern tip of the island—about fifteen miles—and that the north end, above his property, should become "an environmental-protection zone." The development, he promised, would include nothing that would pollute the environment.

"What *would* it have?" Candler asked.

"Houses, a marina, an airport, a store."

"That is not my idea of conservation."

"Tell me, Sam, which Carnegies will break ranks and sell out next?"

No answer.

"How many Carnegies will rub their hands with glee when prices go up because of development?"

No answer.

"Those snobs—high on the list of the hundred most selfish families."

"I'd like to make a list of island destroyers," Candler said.

Fraser said, "The government has a perfect right to condemn my land here if it thinks its use is wiser than mine."

It emerged that a Cumberland Island Conservation Association already existed.

"Name all organizations that exist on the island," Fraser said.

"What do you mean?" Candler asked him.

"Every time I pick up a paper, I read about another organization."

"You mean like your Cumberland Island Holding Company?"

"Name another one."

"The Cumberland Island Conservation Association is the only one I know about," Candler said.

"Is it incorporated?"

"I believe so."

"You *believe* so?"

"Yes."

"Who is the president of the Cumberland Island Conservation Association?"

"I am."

"Is it incorporated?"

"I'm not real sure."

"The light is nice on the water there," Brower said. "The light is getting good."

Brower and Fraser climbed a high dune. Candler stayed on the beach. From the dune, he appeared a lonely figure—the only person on twenty miles of white sand. "People develop passionate attachments to these islands, and any change from the way they have known them since childhood is emotionally disturbing to them," Fraser said. "It's a jolt to them to have any of their property used by strangers."

One afternoon in Atlanta, Candler had told me what Cumberland Island meant to him. "Changes come slowly there, and leave marks on one another," he said. "There is a blending from one era to the next. Indian mounds are there. When I am on Cumberland Island, I see the same things the Indians saw. I would like to live where the Indians lived. They were closer to the earth, a part of the environment. Fraser said that after the hurricane there were no sea oats on Cumberland. The island teaches you the value of patience. The sea oats came back. Dunes that are washed down will return. You've got to have some places that are hard to get to. I don't think this is a selfish thought. I think it's thoughtful."

Fraser, for his part, had told me that nothing would please him more than to develop his property in consonance with a National Seashore that would take up the rest of the island. In fact, he would be hesitant—even unlikely—to develop his land without knowing what might happen around it. Another Sea Pines freshly rising among the live oaks could so enhance the value of the island as a whole that the Carnegies and Candler might find irresistible the offers of ticktack developers. There was so much of Cumberland that, even for a man of Fraser's resources, protective buying was out of the question. So he dreamed of a beautiful enclave in various shades of income, with forever-protected wildernesses stretching away from either side and rationed quantities of the public wandering the great beach.

Now, on the dune, Brower and Fraser—Columbus and Cortez—stood high above the wild and pristine seascape. Fraser said, "I think it is wise public policy for the government to take a place like this from private owners. Don't you agree?"

"Yes."

Candler, who had moved farther down the beach, was an even smaller figure. From the dune, he could be framed between a thumb and forefinger a quarter inch apart. His hands were in his pockets.

"I would like to reverse my ninety-ten here," Brower said. "I would like to see ten per cent developed here and ninety not."

Fraser said, "I hope that can be arranged."

Oysters on the half shell, when they are as fresh as the ones we ate for lunch that day, are so shining and translucent, so nearly transparent, that if you were to drop one on a printed page you could read words through the oyster. I had lived beside tidal creeks at various times in the past, and had once set up my own amateur oyster farm, from which I regularly removed a hundred and forty-four oysters each day to eat before lunch, but even the memory of my oyster farm was turned slightly opaque by the quality of the oysters from Candler's tidal creek. Mantle to palpi, each vitrescent blob was a textural wonder. We ate at least five hundred of them, raw or roasted (over an oak fire)—*Ostrea virginica*, better than the best oysters of Bordeaux, and, as it happened, long-range appetizers to the roasted game hens that were spread before us that evening on Fraser's yacht.

On the yacht, Brower held up his glass and studied the prismatic coupling of gin and light. He then looked off into the rouge afterglow over the marshes to the west. "The outdoor life is all right," he said. "But don't knock the amenities." Pale wines escorted the game hens, and brotherhood bobbed on the water with the yacht, while the dark mass of Cumberland Island stood beside the boat with what Joseph Conrad once described as "the stillness of an implacable force brooding over an inscrutable intention." No one was looking at the island. On a color-television set inside the yacht, the San Francisco 49ers were bombing the Baltimore Colts. Brower said, "Long live the instant playback—the nicest thing technology has given us!"

"We will create a conservation conference center here on the island," Fraser said.

"That will require an airport," said Brower. "I'm Machiavellian enough to know that if you are going to have a conference center you have to have a way to get there."

"We'll let druids land free," Fraser said. "If you were dictator, what would you do with that marsh?"

"Save it! Save the greenery! I can make noise, but you can make deeds," Brower said. "Save the marsh! Grasses are one of the nicest ways the green thing works. The green giant is chlorophyll, really. When I come back in another life, I am going to spend my whole life in grasses. I'm addicted to the entire planet. I don't want to leave it. I want to get down into it. I want to say hello. On the beach, I could have stopped all day long and looked at those damned shells, looked for all the messages that come not in bottles but in shells. Life began Tuesday noon, and the beautiful organic wholeness of it developed over the next four days. At three minutes before midnight, man appeared. At one-fourth of a second before midnight, Christ arrived. At one-fortieth of a second before midnight, the Industrial Revolution began. You, Charles Fraser, have got to persuade the whole God-damned movement of realtors to have a different kind of responsibility to man than they have. If they don't, God will say that man should be thrown away as an experiment that didn't work. I have seen evidence of what you can do. Now make others do it. The system must be used to reform the system."

Fraser had been listening with his hands clasped behind his head. When Brower finished, Fraser said nothing and sipped his wine.

In the early morning, in the yacht's saloon, Brower performed his matins. He spilled out and sorted the contents of his briefcase—an old and thick one, jammed with books, notebooks, magazines, clippings—and he read for an hour or so, as if to put himself in context. He read a Sierra Club tract called *Machiasport: Oil and the Maine Coast.* He read a copy of a letter from Earl Bell, the planner, to Senator Henry M. Jackson, asking how the island Amchitka could still be called a National Wildlife Refuge since it had become a military missile dump, a military garbage dump, and a site for atomic testing. Simultaneously, Brower made cryptic notes for a talk he would give at Harvard: "Loop the system . . . Ravisher of the Month . . . SST . . . Signs . . . Dams . . . Sawlogs." Reading on, he piled up newsclips on the table before him: "JOIN POLLUTION FIGHT, NATO TOLD," "BP OIL ESTIMATES ALASKA TRACT AT FIVE BILLION BARRELS," "DROWNING AN ECOLOGICAL PARADISE," "CAN ANYONE RUN A CITY?," "PLANNER URGES TWO-CHILD LIMIT," "SLOW DOWN THE OIL RUSH," "BAN ON ABORTION STRUCK DOWN," "THE MAZE OF HAZE THAT SPOILS OUR DAYS," "WE ARE SUBVERSIVES IN THE STATE OF NATURE," "NORTHWEST PASSAGE TO WHAT?" He had heretical material, too: "ALARMISTS IGNORE THE FACTS," "MAN MUST CONTROL NATURE," "THE POPULATION FIRECRACKER" (William Buckley arguing that there is no population explosion), and an editorial from the *New Scientist* mocking the excessive excitability and the platitudes and dogmas of "ecological high priests." Brower next examined a dummy for a conservation newsletter to be called the *National Hammer*, an article from the *Stanford Law Review* called "The SST: From Watts to Harlem in Two Hours," and a list of proposals—to him as publisher—for a series of Suppose We Didn't books, on things that would be best left undeveloped: the SST, the oil refinery in Machiasport, the Alaska pipeline, the sea-level canal through Central America. He read the Leopold Report ("Land drainage . . .

will destroy inexorably the South Florida ecosystem") and an article from *Trial* called "Can Law Reclaim Man's Environment?" Finally, he read a piece on architectural ravages in New York City's West Village, and he waved in the air a *Business Week* article—"The War That Business Must Win"—and said, "Here is the first faint streak of dawn coming up over the business world. They are at last finding out that environment is not only to sell."

From below, Fraser appeared, dressed in a dark suit and tie. After breakfast, he was going to leave Cumberland Island in order to do battle with druids in other parts of the South. The rest of us would stay on for a while. Fraser clearly felt that Cumberland was safe, for the moment. In the Land Rover, he drove to the primitive airstrip. The same small plane was waiting in the field of fennel. Fraser walked confidently away from an atmosphere of cordial farewells and climbed into the plane. The pilot advanced the engines to maximum r.p.m. Four wild horses slowly walked off the runway. The plane raced through the fennel and into the air. Watching it rise and turn, Brower said softly, "What makes Sammy run in the South?"

We got into Candler's jeep and spent the day slowly reviewing the island. At Candler's speed—ten to twenty miles per hour—details came into focus that, at Fraser's speed, had previously tended to blur. The jeep, for one thing, was open, and we felt the island around us in a way that we had not in Fraser's Land Rover, which was closed in. "You can't see the whole island anyway—it's too big—so you might as well enjoy what you can see," said Candler. "Going along in Fraser's Land Rover was like going over Niagara Falls in a barrel."

"I've never run into anybody quite like that," Brower said.

"Are you sorry or glad that he developed Hilton Head Island?"

"I don't know. I think probably I'm not glad. I'd rather have more wilderness on the coast than there is. But if it had to be developed, I'm glad it was developed by him."

As we moved along, deer walked across the road in front of us. Candler showed us a place where he had often found arrowheads at low tide and a place where we picked wild grapefruit. We went to the south end of the island, which was ribbed with hummocks and was full of freshwater ponds and tall magnolias.

A jetty there had been built ninety years ago at what was then the southernmost point of the island. The jetty was now at least two thousand feet inland from the southern shore. Land had simultaneously been eroding from the north end. Cumberland Island was gradually migrating to Florida, and had already crossed the state line. A sonic boom hit us with a report so loud that Brower staggered as if he had been shot, and tens of thousands of birds—oyster catchers, pelicans, sandpipers, gulls—rose screaming into the air between the Cumberland shore and the Florida mainland. They stayed up there, flapping in panic, for ten minutes, clouds and clouds of shrieking birds. Candler showed us where he had once dug into a mound and found a skeleton in a sitting position, and he told us how as a boy he used to play with muzzled alligators. We visited a tame buzzard at Lucy Ferguson's place, where a rusting automobile engine hung from a tree and no one but the buzzard was home. The buzzard's eyes glittered like the running lights of an airplane. The buzzard nibbled at Brower's basketball shoes. Brower stroked the bird and talked gently to it. The buzzard nibbled at his fingers and draped a talon over his hand. We saw blue herons, bluebills, and egrets in the marshes, and cacti hanging like strings of sausages from live oaks in the woods. At Candler's place, we ate a foot-high pile of shrimp from the tidal creek—under a big kitchen clock on which red lettering said, "Things Go Better With Coke." Shrimp, like oysters, are as transparent as clear gelatine when they come out of the creek. On the beach, Candler noticed the remains of a leatherback turtle, its back as large as a steamer trunk. It had been there for days, but we, whipping by, had not seen it before. We saw wild pigs in the tidal marshes eating seafood, and a flight of seventy cormorants, in imprecise formation, passing overhead.

"What are they trying to spell to us?" Brower said.

"Pepsi-Cola," said Candler.

As far as I could see, though, the message in the sky over Cumberland Island was "Finis." We drove up a marching dune and snowplowed down the other side, leaving fresh tracks in the powdery white sand. The wind would cover them. But how many tracks could the wind cover? Since early morning—in fact, for three days—we had roamed an island bigger than Manhattan and had seen no one on its beach and, except at

Candler's place and Greyfield, no one in its interior woodlands. In the late twentieth century, in this part of the world, such an experience was unbelievable. The island was a beautiful and fragile anachronism. We were, as Candler had said, seeing what the Indians saw, and it was not at all difficult to understand why he wanted to "live where the Indians lived . . . closer to the earth, a part of the environment." We, too, had eaten from the tidal creeks and had gone where and how we pleased—a privilege made possible in our time by private ownership. That was the irony of Cumberland Island and the index of its fate. The island was worth nothing when the Muskhogean Creeks lived and fished there. Now it was worth at least ten million dollars, a figure that could swell beyond recognition. Need, temptation, and realistic taxes would eventually wrest the island from its present owners. They would not be able to afford it. The question whether it was right for a few individuals to own twenty miles of beach had already been bypassed by these inexorable facts of economics.

Actually, the resolution was to arrive swiftly. In months to come, druids in massed phalanx were to create so many pressures—social, political, financial—and so much ecological propaganda that Fraser would give up his Cumberland territory, selling Cumberland Oaks to the National Park Foundation. Money for the purchase was to be made available to the Park Service by the Andrew Mellon Foundation, with enough left over to acquire the rest of the island from the other owners. Thus Fraser, in his coming and going, was in the end to be the catalyst that converted Cumberland Island from a private enclave to a national reserve. The other owners, as Brower had said, were without choice, really. They would have preferred to keep the island the way it was—and no wonder. It was Earth in something close to its original state. The alternatives—private development, public park—came nowhere near that, and never would. In the battle for Cumberland Island, there could be human winners here or there, but—no matter what might happen—there could be no victory for Cumberland Island. The Frasers of the world might create their blended landscapes, the Park Service its Yosemites. Either way, or both ways, no one was ever to be as free on that wild beach in the future as we had been that day.

PART 3

A River

FLOYD ELGIN DOMINY raises beef cattle in the Shenandoah Valley. Observed there, hand on a fence, his eyes surveying his pastures, he does not look particularly Virginian. Of middle height, thickset, somewhat bandy-legged, he appears to have been lifted off a horse with block and tackle. He wears blue-jeans, a white-and-black striped shirt, and leather boots with heels two inches high. His belt buckle is silver and could not be covered over with a playing card. He wears a string tie that is secured with a piece of petrified dinosaur bone. On his head is a white Stetson.

Thirty-five years ago, Dominy was a county agent in the rangelands of northeastern Wyoming. He could not have come to his job there at a worse time. The Great Drought and the Great Depression had coincided, and the people of the county were destitute. They were not hungry—they could shoot antelope and deer—but they were destitute. Their livestock, with black tongues and protruding ribs, were dying because of lack of water. Dominy, as the agent not only of Campbell County but of the federal government, was empowered to pay eight dollars a head for these cattle—many thousands of them—that were all but decaying where they stood. He paid the eight dollars and shot the cattle.

Dominy was born on a farm in central Nebraska, and all through his youth his family and the families around them talked mainly of the vital weather. They lived close to the hundredth meridian, where, in a sense more fundamental than anything resulting from the events of United States history, the West begins. East of the hundredth meridian, there is enough rain to support agriculture, and west of it there generally is not. The Homestead Act of 1862, in all its promise, did not take into account this ineluctable fact. East of the hundredth meridian, homesteaders on their hundred and sixty acres of land were usually able to fulfill the dream that had been legislated for them. To the west, the odds against them were high. With local exceptions, there just was not enough water. The whole region between the hundredth meridian and the Rocky Mountains was at that time known as the Great American Desert.

Still beyond the imagination were the ultramontane basins where almost no rain fell at all.

Growing up on a farm that had been homesteaded by his grandfather in the eighteen-seventies, Dominy often enough saw talent and energy going to waste under clear skies. The situation was marginal. In some years, more than twenty inches of rain would fall and harvests would be copious. In others, when the figure went below ten, the family lived with the lament that there was no money to buy clothes, or even sufficient food. These radical uncertainties were eventually removed by groundwater development, or reclamation—the storage of what water there was, for use in irrigation. When Dominy was eighteen years old, a big thing to do on a Sunday was to get into the Ford, which had a rumble seat, and go out and see the new dam. In his photo album he put pictures of reservoirs and irrigation projects. ("It was impressive to a dry-land farmer like me to see all that water going down a ditch toward a farm.") Eventually, he came to feel that there would be, in a sense, no West at all were it not for reclamation.

In Campbell County, Wyoming, the situation was not even marginal. This was high, dry country, suitable only for free-ranging livestock, not for farming. In the best of years, only about fourteen inches of rain might fall. "Streams ran water when the snow melted. Otherwise, the gulches were dry. It was the county with the most towns and the fewest people, the most rivers with the least water, and the most cows with the least milk in the world." It was, to the eye, a wide, expansive landscape with beguiling patterns of perspective. Its unending buttes, flat or nippled, were spaced out to the horizons like stone chessmen. Deer and antelope moved among them in herds, and on certain hilltops cairns marked the graves of men who had hunted buffalo. The herbage was so thin that forty acres of range could reasonably support only one grazing cow. Nonetheless, the territory had been homesteaded, and the homesteaders simply had not received from the federal government enough land for enough cattle to give them financial equilibrium as ranchers, or from the sky enough water to give them a chance as farmers. They were going backward three steps for each two forward. Then the drought came.

"Nature is a pretty cruel animal. I watched the people there—I mean good folk, industrious, hardworking, frugal—compete with the rigors of nature against hopeless odds. They would ruin their health and still fail." Without waiting for approval from Cheyenne or Washington, the young county agent took it upon himself to overcome nature if the farmers and ranchers could not. He began up near Recluse, on the ranch of a family named Oedekoven, in a small bowl of land where an intermittent stream occasionally flowed. With a four-horse Fresno—an ancestral bulldozer—he moved earth and plugged the crease in the terrain where the water would ordinarily run out and disappear into the ground and the air. He built his little plug in the classic form of the earth-fill dam—a three-for-one slope on the water side and two-for-one the other way. More cattle died, but a pond slowly filled, storing water. The pond is still there, and so is Oedekoven, the rancher.

For two and a half years, Dominy lived with his wife and infant daughter in a stone dugout about three miles outside Gillette, the county seat. For light they used a gasoline lantern. For heat and cooking they had a coal-burning stove. Dominy dug the coal himself out of a hillside. His wife washed clothes on a board. On winter mornings when the temperature was around forty below zero, he made a torch with a rag and a stick, soaked it in kerosene, lighted it, and put it under his car. When the car was warm enough to move, Dominy went off to tell ranchers and farmers about the Corn-Hog Program ("Henry Wallace slaughtering piglets to raise the price of ham"), the Wheat Program (acreage control), or how to build a dam. "Campbell County was my kingdom. When I was twenty-four years old, I was king of the God-damned county." He visited Soda Well, Wild Cat, Teckla, Turnercrest—single-family post offices widely spaced—or he followed the farmers and ranchers into the county seat of the county seat, Jew Jake's Saloon, where there was a poker game that never stopped and where the heads of moose, deer, elk, antelope, and bighorn sheep looked down on him and his subjects, feet on the rail at 9 A.M. Dominy had his first legitimate drink there. The old brass rail is gone—and so is Dominy—but the saloon looks just the same now, and the boys are still there at 9 A.M.

There was an orange scoria butte behind Dominy's place and an alfalfa field in front of it. Rattlesnakes by the clan came out of the butte in the spring, slithered around Dominy's house, and moved on into the alfalfa for the summer. In September, the snakes headed back toward the butte. Tomatoes were ripe in Dominy's garden, and whenever he picked some he first took a hoe and cleared out the rattlesnakes under the vines. Ranchers got up at four in the morning, and sometimes Dominy was outside honking his horn to wake them. He wanted them to come out and build dams—dams, dams, dams. "I had the whole county stirred up. We were moving! Stockpond dam and reservoir sites were supposed to be inspected first by Forest Service rangers, but who knows when they would have come? I took it upon myself to ignore these pettifogging minutiae." Changing the face of the range, he polka-dotted it with ponds. Dominy and the ranchers and farmers built a thousand dams in one year, and when they were finished there wasn't a thirsty cow from Jew Jake's Saloon to the Montana border. "Christ, we did more in that county in one year than any other county in the country. That range program really put me on the national scene."

In the view of conservationists, there is something special about dams, something—as conservation problems go—that is disproportionately and metaphysically sinister. The outermost circle of the Devil's world seems to be a moat filled mainly with DDT. Next to it is a moat of burning gasoline. Within that is a ring of pinheads each covered with a million people—and so on past phalanxed bulldozers and bicuspid chain saws into the absolute epicenter of Hell on earth, where stands a dam. The implications of the dam exceed its true level in the scale of environmental catastrophes. Conservationists who can hold themselves in reasonable check before new oil spills and fresh megalopolises mysteriously go insane at even the thought of a dam. The conservation movement is a mystical and religious force, and possibly the reaction to dams is so violent because rivers are the ultimate metaphors of existence, and dams destroy rivers. Humiliating nature, a dam is evil—placed and solid.

"I hate all dams, large and small," David Brower informs an audience.

A voice from the back of the room asks, "Why are you conservationists always against things?"

"If you are against something, you are for something," Brower answers. "If you are against a dam, you are for a river."

When Brower was a small boy in Berkeley, he used to build dams in Strawberry Creek, on the campus of the University of California, piling up stones in arcs convex to the current, backing up reservoir pools. Then he would kick the dams apart and watch the floods that returned Strawberry Creek to its free-flowing natural state. When Brower was born—in 1912—there was in the Sierra Nevada a valley called Hetch Hetchy that paralleled in shape, size, and beauty the Valley of the Yosemite. The two valleys lay side by side. Both were in Yosemite National Park, which had been established in 1890. Yet within three decades—the National Park notwithstanding—the outlet of Hetch Hetchy was filled with a dam and the entire valley was deeply flooded. Brower was a boy when the dam was being built. He remembers spending his sixth birthday in the hills below Hetch Hetchy and hearing stories of the battle that had been fought over it, a battle that centered on the very definition of conservation. Should it mean preservation of wilderness or wise and varied use of land? John Muir, preservationist, founder of the young Sierra Club, had lost this bitter and, as it happened, final struggle of his life. It had been a battle that split the Sierra Club in two. Fifty-five years later, the Sierra Club would again divide within itself, and the outcome of the resulting battle would force the resignation of its executive director, David Brower, whose unsurprising countermove would be to form a new organization and name it for John Muir.

Not long after Brower's departure from the Sierra Club and his founding of the John Muir Institute, I went to Hetch Hetchy with him and walked along the narrow top of the dam, looking far down one side at the Tuolumne River, emerging like a hose jet from the tailrace, and in the other direction out across the clear blue surface of the reservoir, with its high granite sides—imagining the lost Yosemite below. The scene was bizarre and ironic, or so it seemed to me. Just a short distance across the peaks to the south of us was the Yosemite itself, filled to disaster with cars and people, tens of thousands of people, while here was the Yosemite's natural twin, filled with water. Things were so still at Hetch Hetchy that a wildcat walked insolently across the road near the dam and didn't even look around as he moved on into the woods. And Brower—fifty-six years old and unshakably the most powerful voice in the conservation movement in his country—walked the quiet dam. "It was not needed when it was built, and it is not needed now," he said. "I would like to see it taken down, and watch the process of recovery."

During the years when Brower was developing as a conservationist, many of his most specific and dramatic personal accomplishments had to do with proposed dams. Down the tiers of the Western states, there are any number of excellent damsites that still contain free-flowing rivers because of David Brower—most notably in the immense, arid watershed of the Colorado. Anyone interested, for whatever reason, in the study of water in the West will in the end concentrate on the Colorado, wildest of rivers, foaming, raging, rushing southward—erratic, headlong, incongruous in the desert. The Snake, the Salmon, the upper Hudson—all the other celebrated white torrents—are not in the conversation if the topic is the Colorado. This is still true, although recently (recently in the long span of things, actually within the past forty years) the Colorado has in places been subdued. The country around it is so dry that Dominy's county in Wyoming is a rain forest by comparison. The states of the basin need water, and the Colorado is where the water is. The familiar story of contention for water rights in the Old West—Alan Ladd shooting it out with Jack Palance over some rivulet God knows where—has its mother narrative in the old and continuing story of rights to the waters of the Colorado. The central document is something called the Colorado River Compact, in which the basin is divided in two, at a point close to the Utah-Arizona line. The states of the Upper Basin are allowed to take so much per year. The Lower Basin gets approximately an equal share. And something gratuitous is passed on to Mexico. The Colorado lights and slakes Los Angeles. It irrigates Arizona. The odd thing about it is that all its writhings and foamings and spectacular rapids lead to nothing. The river rises in the Rockies, thunders through the canyons, and is so used by mankind that when it reaches the Gulf of California, fourteen hundred miles from its source, it literally trickles into the sea. The flow in the big river and in its major tributaries—the Green, the Yampa, the Escalante, the San Juan, the Little Colorado—is almost lyrically erratic, for the volume can vary as much as six hundred per cent from one year to the next. The way to control that, clearly enough, is storage, and this is accomplished under programs developed and administered by the federal Bureau of Reclamation. The Bureau of Reclamation, all but unknown in the American East, is the patron agency of the American West, dispenser of light, life, and water to thirty million people whose gardens would otherwise be dust. Most of the civil servants in the Bureau are Westerners—from the dry uplands as well as the deserts of the Great Basin. They have lived in the problem they are solving, and they have a deep sense of mission. There are many people in the Bureau of Reclamation—perhaps all nine thousand of them—who hope to see the Colorado River become a series of large pools, one stepped above another, from the Mexican border to the Rocky Mountains, with the headwaters of each succeeding lake lapping against the tailrace of a dam. The river and its tributaries have long since been thoroughly surveyed, and throughout the basin damsites of high quality and potentiality stand ready for river diversion, blast excavation, and concrete. Three of these sites are particularly notable here. One is near the juncture of the Green and the Yampa, close to the Utah-Colorado border. The two others are in northern Arizona—in the Grand Canyon. A fourth site would belong in this special list if it were still just a site, but a dam is actually there, in northernmost Arizona, in Glen Canyon. David Brower believes that the dam in Glen Canyon represents the greatest failure of his life. He cannot think of it without melancholy, for he sincerely believes that its very existence is his fault. He feels that if he had been more aware, if he had more adequately prepared himself for his own kind of mission, the dam would not be there. Its gates closed in 1963, and it began backing up water a hundred and eighty-six miles into Utah. The reservoir is called Lake Powell, and it covers country that Brower himself came to know too late. He made his only trips there—float trips on the river with his children—before the gates were closed but after the dam, which had been virtually unopposed, was under construction. Occasionally, in accompaniment to the talks he gives around the country, Brower shows an elegiac film about Glen Canyon, "the place no one knew." That was the trouble, he explains. No one knew what was there. Glen Canyon was one of the two or three remotest places in the United States—far from the nearest road, a hundred and twenty-five miles from the nearest railhead. The film records that the river canyon and its great trellis of side canyons was a deep and sometimes dark world of beauty, where small streams had cut gorges so profound and narrow that people walking in them were in cool twilight at noon, and where clear plunges of water dropped into pools surrounded with maidenhair fern in vaulted grottoes with names like Cathedral in the Desert, Mystery Canyon, Music Temple, Labyrinth Canyon. With all their blue-and-gold walls and darkly streaked water-drip tapestries, these places are now far below the surface of Lake Powell. "Few people knew about these canyons," Brower says quietly. "No one else will ever know what they were like."

The lost worlds of Utah notwithstanding, if conservationists were to label their heroes in the way the English label their generals, David Brower would be known as Brower of the Colorado, Brower of the Grand Canyon. In the early nineteen-fifties, he fought his first major campaign—in his capacity as the first executive director of the Sierra Club—against the dam that the Bureau of Reclamation was about to build near the juncture of the Green and the Yampa. The reservoir would have backed water over large sections of Dinosaur National Monument. In the view of Brower, the Sierra Club, and conservationists generally, the integrity of the National Park system was at stake. The Dinosaur Battle, as it is called, was a milestone in the conservation movement. It was, to begin with, the greatest conservation struggle in half a century—actually, since the controversies that involved the damming of Hetch Hetchy and led to the debates that resulted in the creation, in 1916, of the National Park Service. The Dinosaur Battle is noted as the first time that all the scattered interests of modern conservation—sportsmen, ecologists, wilderness preservers, park advocates, and so forth—were drawn together in a common cause. Brower, more than anyone else, drew them together, fashioning the coalition, assembling witnesses. With a passing wave at the aesthetic argument, he went after the Bureau of Reclamation with facts and figures. He challenged the word of its engineers and geologists that the damsite was a sound one, he suggested that cliffs would dissolve and there would be a tremendous and cataclysmic dam failure there, and he went after the basic mathematics underlying the Bureau's proposals and uncovered embarrassing errors. All this was accompanied by flanking movements of intense publicity—paid advertisements, a film, a book—envisioning a National Monument of great scenic, scientific, and cultural value being covered with water. The Bureau protested that the conservationists were exaggerating—honing and bending the truth—but the Bureau protested without effect. Conservationists say that the Dinosaur victory was the birth of the modern conservation movement—the turning point at which conservation became something more than contour plowing. There is no dam at the confluence of the Green and the Yampa. Had it not been for David Brower, a dam would be there. A man in the public-relations office of the Bureau of Reclamation one day summed up the telling of the story by saying, "Dave won, hands down."

There are no victories in conservation, however. Brower feels that he can win nothing. There is no dam at the Green and the Yampa now, but in 2020 there may be. "The Bureau of Reclamation engineers are like beavers," he says. "They can't stand the sight of running water." Below the Utah-Arizona border, in Marble Gorge, a part of the Grand Canyon, there is likewise no dam. The story is much the same. The Bureau of Reclamation had the dam built on paper, ready to go. A battle followed, and Brower won, hands down. In the Lower Granite Gorge, another part of the Grand Canyon, there is also no dam, and for the same reason. These Grand Canyon battles were the bitterest battles of all. The Bureau felt that Brower capitalized on literary hyperbole and the mystic name of the canyon. He implied, they said, that the dams were going to fill the Grand Canyon like an enormous bathtub, and that the view from the north rim to the south rim would soon consist of a flat expanse of water. Brower's famous advertising campaigns reached their most notable moment at this time. He placed full-page ads in *The New York Times* and the *San Francisco Chronicle*, among other places, under the huge headline "SHOULD WE ALSO FLOOD THE SISTINE CHAPEL SO TOURISTS CAN GET NEARER THE CEILING?" Telegrams flooded Congress, where the battle was decided. The Bureau cried foul, saying that it was intending to inundate only a fraction of one per cent of what Brower was suggesting. The Internal Revenue Service moved in and took away from the Sierra Club the tax-deductibility of funds contributed to it. Contributions to lobbying organizations are not tax-deductible, and the ads were construed as lobbying. The Sierra Club has never recovered its contributions-deductible status, but within the organization it is felt—by Brower's enemies as well as his friends—that the Grand Canyon was worth it. There are no dams in the Grand Canyon, and in the Bureau of Reclamation it is conceded that there will not be for at least two generations. The defeat of the high dams is frankly credited, within the Bureau, to David Brower. "He licked us." "He had all the emotions on his side." "He did it singlehanded."

Popular assumptions to the contrary, no federal bureau is completely faceless—and, eyeball to eyeball with David Brower, there was a central and predominant figure on the other side of these fights, marshalling his own forces, battling in the rooms of Congress and in the canyon lands of the West for his profound and lifelong belief in the storage of water. This was the Bureau's leader—Floyd E. Dominy, United States Commissioner of Reclamation.

In the District of Columbia, in the labyrinthine fastnesses of the Department of the Interior, somewhere above Sport Fisheries and Wildlife and beyond the Office of Saline Water, there is a complex of corridors lined with murals of enormous dams. This is Reclamation, and these are its monuments: Flaming Gorge Dam, Hungry Horse Dam, Hoover Dam, Glen Canyon Dam, Friant Dam, Shasta Dam, Vallecito Dam, Grand Coulee Dam. I remember the day that I first saw these murals. In the moist and thermoelectric East, they seemed exotic, but hardly more so than the figure to whom the corridors led, the man in the innermost chamber of the maze. The white Stetson was on a table near the door. Behind a magisterial desk sat the Commissioner, smoking a big cigar. "Dominy," he said, shaking hands. "Sit down. I'm a public servant. I don't have any secrets from anybody."

He wore an ordinary Washington suit, but capital pallor was not in his face—a hawk's face, tanned and leathery. He had dark hair and broad shoulders, and he seemed a big man—bigger than his height and weight would indicate—and powerful but not forbidding. "Many people have said of me that I never meet a stranger," he said. "I like people. I like taxi-drivers and pimps. They have their purpose. I like Dave Brower, but I don't think he's the sanctified conservationist that so many people think he is. I think he's a selfish preservationist, for the few. Dave Brower hates my guts. Why? Because I've *got* guts. I've tangled with Dave Brower for many years."

On a shelf behind Dominy's desk, in the sort of central and eye-catching position that might be reserved for a shining trophy, was a scale model of a bulldozer. Facing each other from opposite walls were portraits of Richard M. Nixon and Hoover Dam. Nixon's jowls, in this milieu, seemed even more trapeziform than they usually do. They looked as if they, too, could stop a river. Seeing that my attention had been caught by these pictures, Dominy got up, crossed the room, and stood with reverence and devotion before the picture of Hoover Dam. He said, "When we built that, we—Americans—were the only people who had ever tried to put a high dam in a big river." He said he remembered as if it were his birthday the exact date when he had first seen—as it was then called—Boulder Dam. He had taken a vacation from Campbell County, Wyoming, and driven, with his wife, into the Southwest, and on January 2, 1937, reached the Arizona-Nevada border and got his first view of the dam as he rounded a curve in the road descending toward the gorge of the Colorado. "There she was," he said, looking at the picture in his office. "The first major river plug in the world. Joseph of Egypt learned to store food against famine. So we in the West had learned to store water." He went on to say that he felt sure that—subconsciously, at least—the outline of his career had been formed at that moment. He had begun by building dams seven feet high, and he would one day build dams seven hundred feet high.

The rancher Fred Oedekoven, on whose place Dominy built his first dam, is nearly eighty years old. A tall man, bent slightly forward, he lives in a peeled-log house on the land he homesteaded when he was twenty. I met him once, when I was in the county, and talked with him in the sitting room of his house. Two pictures hung on the walls. One was of Jesus Christ. The other was the familiar calendar scene of the beautiful lake in Jackson Hole, Wyoming, with the Grand Tetons rising in the background. Jackson Lake, as it is called, was built by the Bureau of Reclamation. "When Dominy come here, he took aholt," Oedekoven said. "I hated to see him go. They wanted him to go to Washington, D.C., to go on this water-facilities program, and I advised him to do it, for the advancement. He really clumb up in life."

Dominy had stayed up there as well, becoming the longest-running commissioner in the Department of the Interior. Appointed by Eisenhower, he adapted so well to the indoor range that he was able to keep his position—always "at the pleasure of the President, without term of office"—through two Democratic Administrations, and now he was, in his words, "carrying the Nixon hod." He winked, sat down on the edge of his desk, and pronounced his absorbing code: "Never once have I made a decision against my will if it was mine to make." He had learned to plant creative ideas in senators' and congressmen's minds ("Based on your record, sir, we assume . . ."), when to be a possum, and when to spring like a panther ("'You get out of my office,' I said. The average bureaucrat would have been shaking, but I wasn't the least bit scared. No member of Congress is going to make me jump through hoops. I've never lost my cool in government work unless I thought it was to my advantage"). He had given crucial testimony against the proposed Rampart Dam, on the Yukon River, arguing that it was too much for Alaska's foreseeable needs; Rampart Dam would have flooded an area the size of Lake Erie, and Dominy's testimony defeated it. He had argued for federal—as opposed to private—power lines leading away from his big dams, thus irritating the special interests of senators and congressmen from several states. "I have been a controversial bastard for many years," he explained, lighting another cigar. Dominy knew his business, though, and he could run a budget of two hundred and forty-five million dollars as if he were driving a fast bus. He had cut down the Bureau's personnel from seventeen thousand to ten thousand. And he had built his stupendous dams. On the wall of his office there was also a picture of Dominy—a bold sketch depicting his head inside a mighty drop of water. It seemed more than coincidence that in an age of acronyms his very initials were FED.

Dominy switched on a projector and screened the rough cut of a movie he had had prepared as an antidote to the Sierra Club's filmed elegy to the inundated canyons under Lake Powell. Dominy's film was called "Lake Powell, Jewel of the Colorado," and over an aerial shot of its blue fjords reaching into the red desert a narrator said, "Through rock and sand, canyon and cliff, through the towering formations of the sun-drenched desert, the waters of the Colorado River pause on their way to the sea." Water skiers cut wakes across the water.

"Too many people think of environment simply as untrammelled nature," Dominy commented. "Preservation groups claim we destroyed this area because we made it accessible to man. Six hundred thousand people a year use that lake now."

The film showed a Navajo on horseback in a blazing-red silk shirt. "Into his land came Lake Powell, which he has woven into his ancient ways," said the narrator.

"Right," said Dominy. "Now people can fish, swim, water-ski, sun-bathe. Can't you imagine going in there with your family for a weekend, getting away from everybody? But Mr. Brower says we destroyed it."

"The canyon lay isolated, remote, and almost unknown to the outside world," said the narrator, "until"—and at that moment a shot of the red walls of Glen Canyon came on the screen, and suddenly there was a great blast and the walls crumbled in nimbuses of dust. Ike had pressed a button. Bulldozers followed, and new roads, and fifty thousand trucks. Cut to dedication of dam, ten years later. "I am proud to dedicate such a significant and beautiful man-made resource," said Lady Bird Johnson. "I am proud that man is here."

Dominy blew smoke into the scene as Lady Bird dissolved. "The need for films of this kind, for public information, is great, because of those who would have all forests and rivers remain pristine," he said. "People ignore facts and play on emotions."

There were more scenes of the blue, still water, lapping at high sandstone cliffs—panoramic vistas of the reservoir. An airplane now appeared over the lake—twin-engine, cargo. "Watch this," Dominy said. "Just watch this." What appeared to be a contrail paid out behind the plane—a long, cloudy sleeve that widened in the air. "Trout!" Dominy said. "Trout! Those are fingerling trout. That's how we put them in the lake."

Montages of shots showed the half-filled lateral canyons—Forgotten Canyon, Cascade Canyon, Reflection Canyon, Mystery Canyon—with people swimming in them, camping beside them, and singing around fires. "In this land, each man must find his own meanings," said the narrator. "Lake Powell, Jewel of the Colorado, offers the opportunity."

"Reclamation is the father of putting water to work for man—irrigation, hydropower, flood control, recreation," Dominy said as he turned on the lights. "Let's *use* our environment. Nature changes the environment every day of our lives—why shouldn't *we* change it? We're part of nature. Just to give you a for-instance, we're cloud-seeding the Rockies to increase the snowpack. We've built a tunnel under the Continental Divide to send water toward the Pacific that would have gone to the Atlantic. The challenge to man is to do and save what is good but to permit man to progress in civilization. Hydroelectric power doesn't pollute water and it doesn't pollute air. You don't get any pollution out of my dams. The unregulated Colorado was a son of a bitch. It wasn't any good. It was either in flood or in trickle. In addition to creating economic benefits with our dams, we regulate the river, and we have created the sort of river Dave Brower dreams about. Who are the best conservationists—doers or preservationists? I can't talk to preservationists. I can't talk to Brower, because he's so God-damned ridiculous. I can't even reason with the man. I once debated with him in Chicago, and he was shaking with fear. Once, after a hearing on the Hill, I accused him of garbling facts, and he said, 'Anything is fair in love and war.' For Christ's sake. After another hearing one time, I told him he didn't know what he was talking about, and said

I wished I could show him, I wished he would come with me to the Grand Canyon someday, and he said, 'Well, save some of it, and maybe I will.' I had a steer out on my farm in the Shenandoah reminded me of Dave Brower. Two years running, we couldn't get him into the truck to go to market. He was an independent bastard that nobody could corral. That son of a bitch got into that truck, busted that chute, and away he went. So I just fattened him up and butchered him right there on the farm. I shot him right in the head and butchered him myself. That's the only way I could get rid of the bastard."

"Commissioner," I said, "if Dave Brower gets into a rubber raft going down the Colorado River, will you get in it, too?"

"Hell, yes," he said. "Hell, yes."

Mile 130. The water is smooth here, and will be smooth for three hundred yards, and then we are going through another rapid. The temperature is a little over ninety, and the air is so dry that the rapid will feel good. Dominy and Brower are drinking beer. They have settled into a kind of routine: once a day they tear each other in half and the rest of the time they are pals.

Dominy is wearing a blue yachting cap with gold braid, and above its visor in gold letters are the words "LAKE POWELL." His skin is rouge brown. His nose is peeling. He wears moccasins, and a frayed cotton shirt in dark, indeterminate tartan, and long trousers secured by half a pound of silver buckle. He has with him a couple of small bags and a big leather briefcase on which is painted the great seal of the Bureau of Reclamation —snow-capped mountains, a reservoir, a dam, and irrigated fields, all within the framing shape of a big drop of water. Dominy has been discoursing on the multiple advantages of hydroelectric power, its immediacy ("When you want it, you just throw a switch") and its innocence of pollution.

"Come on now, Dave, be honest," he said. "From a conservationist's point of view, what is the best source of electric power?"

"Flashlight batteries," Brower said.

Brower is also wearing an old tartan shirt, basically orange, and faded. He wears shorts and sneakers. The skin of his legs and face is bright red. Working indoors and all but around the clock, he has been too long away from the sun. He protects his head with a handkerchief knotted at the corners and soaked in the river, but his King Lear billowing white hair is probably protection enough. He travels light. A miniature duffelbag, eight inches in diameter and a foot long—standard gear for the river—contains all that he has with him, most notably his Sierra Club cup, without which he would be incomplete.

Dominy and Brower are both showing off a little. These organized expeditions carry about a dozen people per raft, and by now the others are thoroughly aware of the biases of the conservationist and the Commissioner. The people are mainly from Arizona and Nevada—schoolteachers, a few students, others from the U.S. Public Health Service. On the whole, I would say that Dominy so far has the edge with them. Brower is shy and quiet. Dominy is full of Irish pub chatter and has a grin as wide as the river.

Cans of beer are known as sandwiches in this red, dry, wilderness world. No one questions this, or asks the reason. They just call out "Sandwich, please!" and a can of Coors comes flying through the air. They catch the beer and drink it, and they put the aluminum tongues inside the cans. I threw a tongue in the river and was booed by everyone. No detritus whatever is left in the canyon. Used cans, bottles—all such things—are put in sacks and go with the raft all the way. The beer hangs in the water in a burlap bag from the rear of the raft, with Cokes and Frescas. The bag is hauled onto the raft before a heavy rapid but rides through the lighter ones.

The raft consists of, among other things, two neoprene bananas ten yards long. These pontoons, lashed to a central rubber barge, give the over-all rig both lateral and longitudinal flexibility. The river sometimes leaps straight up through the raft, but that is a mark of stability rather than imminent disaster. The raft is informal and extremely plastic. Its lack of rigidity makes it safe.

This is isolation wilderness: two or three trails in two hundred miles, otherwise no way out but down the river with the raft. Having seen the canyon from this perspective, I would not much want to experience it another way. Once in a rare while, we glimpse the rims. They are a mile above us and, in places, twelve miles apart. All the flat shelves of color beneath them return the eye by steps to the earliest beginnings of the world—from the high white limestones and maroon Hermit Shales of Permian time to the red sandstones that formed when the first reptiles lived and the vermillion cliffs that stood contemporary with the earliest trees. This Redwall Limestone, five hundred feet thick, is so vulnerable to the infiltrations of groundwater that it has been shaped, in the seas of air between the canyon rims, into red towers and red buttes, pillars, caverns, arches, and caves. The groundwater runs for hundreds of miles between the layers of that apparently bone-dry desert rock and bursts out into the canyon in stepped cascades or ribbon falls. We are looking at such a waterfall right now, veiling away from the Redwall, high above us. There is green limestone behind the waterfall, and pink limestone that was pressed into being by the crushing weight of the ocean at the exact time the ocean itself was first giving up life—amphibious life—to dry land. Beneath the pink and green limestones are green-gray shales and dark-brown sandstones—Bright Angel Shale, Tapeats Sandstone—that formed under the fathoms that held the first general abundance of marine life. Tapeats Sea was the sea that compressed the rock that was cut by the river to create the canyon. The Tapeats Sandstone is the earliest rock from the Paleozoic Era, and beneath it the mind is drawn back to the center of things, the center of the canyon, the cutting plane, the Colorado. Flanked by its Bass Limestones, its Hotauta Conglomerates, its Vishnu Schists and Zoroaster Granites, it races in white water through a pre-Cambrian here and now. The river has worked its way down into the stillness of original time.

Brower braces his legs and grips one of the safety ropes that run along the pontoons. He says, "How good it is to hear a living river! You can almost hear it cutting."

Dominy pulls his Lake Powell hat down firmly around his ears. He has heard this sort of thing before. Brower is suggesting that the Colorado is even now making an ever deeper and grander Grand Canyon, and what sacrilege it would be to dam the river and stop that hallowed process. Dominy says, "I think most people agree, Dave, that it wasn't a river of this magnitude that cut the Grand Canyon."

Brower is too interested in the coming rapid to respond. In this corridor of calm, we can hear the rapid ahead. Rapids and waterfalls ordinarily take shape when rivers cut against resistant rock and then come to a kind of rock that gives way more easily. This is not the case in the Grand Canyon, where rapids occur beside the mouths of tributary creeks. Although these little streams may be dry much of the year, they are so steep that when they run they are able to fling considerable debris into the Colorado—sand, gravel, stones, rocks, boulders. The debris forms dams, and water rises upstream. The river is unusually quiet there—a lakelike quiet—and then it flows over the debris, falling suddenly, pounding and crashing through the boulders. These are the rapids of the Grand Canyon, and there are a hundred and sixty-one of them. Some have appeared quite suddenly. In 1966, an extraordinarily heavy rain fell in a small area of the north rim, and a flash flood went down Crystal Creek, dumping hundreds of tons of rock into the river at Mile 99. This instantly created the Crystal Rapids, one of the major drops in the Colorado. In rare instances—such as the rapid we are now approaching—the river has exposed resistant pre-Cambrian rock that contributes something to the precipitousness of the flow of white water. The roar is quite close now. The standing waves look like blocks of cement. Dominy emits a cowboy's yell. My notes go into a rubber bag that is tied with a string. This is the Bedrock Rapid.

We went through it with a slow dive and climb and a lot of splattering water. We undulated. The raft assumed the form of the rapid. We got very wet. And now, five minutes later, we are as dry and warm as if we were wearing fresh clothes straight out of a dryer. And we are drinking sandwiches.

We have a map that is seven inches high and fifty feet long. It is rolled in a scroll and is a meticulously hand-done contemporary and historical portrait of the Colorado River in the Grand Canyon. River miles are measured from the point, just south of the Utah line, where the Paria River flows into the Colorado—the place geologists regard as the beginning of the Grand Canyon. As the map rolls by, it records who died where. "Peter Hansbrough, one of two men drowned, Mile 24, Tanner Wash Rapids, 1889. . . . Bert Loper upset, not seen again, Mile 24, 1949. . . . Scout found and buried in talus, Mile 43, 1951. . . . Roemer drowned in Mile 89, 1948." The first known run of the river was in 1869, and the second shortly thereafter—both the expeditions of Major John Wesley Powell—and even by 1946 only about a hundred people had ever been through the canyon by river. With the introduction of neoprene rafts—surplus from the Second World War—the figure expanded. Five hundred a year were going through by the middle nineteen-sixties, and the number is now in the low thousands.

"As long as people keep on taking out everything that they bring in, they're not going to hurt the Grand Canyon," Brower says. "Rule No. 1 is 'Leave nothing—not even a dam.'"

Dominy does not hear that. He is busy telling a pretty young gym teacher from Phoenix that he played sixty minutes a game as captain of the ice-hockey team at the University of Wyoming. "I liked the speed. I liked the body contact. I developed shots the defense couldn't fathom."

Dominy is in his sixtieth year and is planning an early retirement, but he looks fifty, and it is not at all difficult to imagine him on a solo dash down the ice, slamming the Denver Maroons into pulp against the boards and breaking free to slap the winning shot into the nets. He once did exactly that. He has the guts he says he has, and I think he is proving it now, here on the Colorado. He may be an athlete, but he can't swim. He can't swim one stroke. He couldn't swim across a goldfish pond. And at this moment it is time for us to put things away and pull ourselves together, because although we are scarcely dry from the Bedrock Rapid, the crescendoing noise we hear is Deubendorff, an officially designated "heavy rapid," one of the thirteen roughest in the canyon. Brower goes quiet before a rapid, and he is silent now. He says he is not much of a swimmer, either. We all have life vests on, but they feel as if they would be about as effective against these rapids as they would be against bullets. That is not true, though. Once in a great while, these rafts turn over, and when they do the people all end up bobbing in the calmer water at the foot of the rapid like a hatful of spilled corks. Riding a rigid boat, Seymour

Deubendorff was claimed by this rapid on the Galloway-Stone expedition, in 1909. This we learn from our map. Looking ahead, we see two steep grooves, a hundred and fifty yards apart, that have been cut into the south wall of the river gorge. They are called Galloway Canyon and Stone Canyon, and the streams in them are not running now, but each has thrown enough debris into the river to make a major rapid, and together they have produced Deubendorff. Directly in front of us, a mile ahead and high against the sky, is a broad and beautiful Redwall mesa. The river disappears around a corner to the left of it. Meanwhile, the big, uncompromising mesa seems to suggest a full and absolute stop, as if we were about to crash into it in flight, for spread below it in the immediate foreground is a prairie of white water.

There is a sense of acceleration in the last fifty yards. The water is like glass right up to where the tumult begins. Everything is lashed down. People even take hats and handkerchiefs off their heads and tie them to the raft. Everyone has both hands on safety ropes—everyone but Dominy. He giggles. He gives a rodeo yell. With ten smooth yards remaining, he lights a cigar.

There is something quite deceptive in the sense of acceleration that comes just before a rapid. The word "rapid" itself is, in a way, a misnomer. It refers only to the speed of the white water relative to the speed of the smooth water that leads into and away from the rapid. The white water is faster, but it is hardly "rapid." The Colorado, smooth, flows about seven miles per hour, and, white, it goes perhaps fifteen or, at its whitest and wildest, twenty miles per hour—not very rapid by the standards of the twentieth century. Force of suggestion creates a false expectation. The mere appearance of the river going over those boulders—the smoky spray, the scissoring waves—is enough to imply a rush to fatality, and this endorses the word used to describe it. You feel as if you were about to be sucked into some sort of invisible pneumatic tube and shot like a bullet into the dim beyond. But the white water, though faster than the rest of the river, is categorically slow. Running the rapids in the Colorado is a series of brief experiences, because the rapids themselves are short. In them, with the raft folding and bending—sudden hills of water filling the immediate skyline—things happen in slow motion. The projector of your own existence slows way down, and you dive as in a dream, and gradually rise, and fall again. The raft shudders across the ridgelines of water cordilleras to crash softly into the valleys beyond. Space and time in there are something other than they are out here. Tents of water form overhead, to break apart in rags. Elapsed stopwatch time has no meaning at all.

Dominy emerged from Deubendorff the hero of the expedition to date. Deubendorff, with two creeks spitting boulders into it, is a long rapid for a Grand Canyon rapid—about three hundred yards. From top to bottom, through it all, Dominy kept his cigar aglow. This feat was something like, say, a bumblebee's flying through a field of waving wheat at shock level and never once being touched. Dominy's shirt was soaked. His trousers were soaked. But all the way down the rapid the red glow of that cigar picked its way through the flying water from pocket to pocket of air. Actually, he was lucky, and he knew it. "Lucky Dominy," he said when we moved into quiet water. "That's why they call me Lucky Dominy." The whole raftload of people gave him an organized cheer. And he veiled his face in fresh smoke.

We have now moved under and by the big mesa. Brower watched it silently for a long time, and then softly, almost to himself, he quoted Edith Warner: "'This is a day when life and the world seem to be standing still—only time and the river flowing past the mesas.'"

Wild burros stand on a ledge and look at us from above, right. All burros are on the right, all bighorns on the left. Who knows why? We have entered the beauty of afternoon light. It sharpens the colors and polishes the air.

Brower says, "Notice that light up the line now, Floyd. Look how nice it is on the barrel cactus."

"Gorgeous," says Dominy.

The river is in shadow, and we have stopped for the night where a waterfall arcs out from a sandstone cliff. This is Deer Creek Falls, and it is so high that its shafts of plunging water are wrapped in mist where they strike a deep pool near the edge of the river. The campsite is on the opposite bank. Brower has half filled his Sierra Club cup with water and is using it as a level with which to gauge the height of the falls.

His measuring rod is his own height at eye level. Sighting across the cup, he has painstakingly climbed a talus slope behind us, adding numbers as he climbed, and he is now a small figure among the talus boulders at the level of the lip of the waterfall across the river. He calls down that the waterfall is a hundred and sixty feet high. With the raft as a ferry, we crossed the river an hour or so ago and stood in the cool mist where the waterfall whips the air into wind. We went on to climb to the top of the fall and to walk above the stream through the gorge of Deer Creek. The creek had cut a deep, crenellated groove in the sandstone, and for several hundred yards, within this groove, we moved along a serpentine ledge high above the water, which made a great deal of sound below, within the narrow walls of the cut. Brower walked along the ledge—it was sometimes only a foot wide—as if he were hurrying along a sidewalk. At the beginning, the ledge was perhaps fifty feet above the foaming creek, and gradually, up the gorge, the ledge and the creek bed came closer together. Brower just strode along, oblivious of the giddy height. In that strange world between walls of rock, a butterfly flickered by, and he watched it with interest while his feet moved surely forward, never slowing. "Viceroy," he said.

I am afraid of places like that, and my legs were so frozen that I couldn't feel the ledge underfoot. I suggested that we stop and wait for Dominy, who had started later and had said he would catch up. This would obviously provide a good rest, because where Dominy comes from the narrowest ledge is at least three hundred miles wide, and I thought if he was still coming along this one he was probably on his hands and knees. Just then, he came walking around a shoulder of the rock face, balanced above the gorge, whistling. We moved on. Where the ledge met the creek bed, the walls of the gorge widened out and the creek flowed in clear, cascading pools among cactus flowers and mariposa lilies under stands of cottonwood. A scene like that in a context of unending dry red rock is unbelievable, a palpable mirage. Brower walked in the stream and, after a while, stopped to absorb his surroundings. Dominy, some yards behind, had an enamelled cup with him, and he dipped it into the stream. Lifting it to his lips, he said, "Now I'll have a drink of water that has washed Dave Brower's feet."

The water was cold and very clear. Brower scooped some for himself, in his Sierra Club cup. "Any kind of water in country like this is good, but especially when man isn't hogging it for his own use," he said.

Watercress grew around the plunge pools of the short cascades—watercress, growing in cool water, surrounded by thousands of square miles of baking desert rock. Brower took a small bunch in his hand. Bugs were crawling all over it, and he carefully selected leaves and ate them, leaving the bugs behind. "I don't mind sharing my cress with them," he said. "I hope they don't mind sharing it with me."

Brower's snack appealed to Dominy. He waded into the same pool, picked two handfuls of cress, and ate them happily, bugs and all. "Paradise," he said, looking around. "Paradise."

Half obscured in the stream under a bed of cress was the distinctive shimmer of a Budweiser can. Brower picked it up, poured the water out of it, and put it in his pocket.

"When people come in, you can't win," Dominy said, and Brower looked at him with both approval and perplexity.

Inside Dominy's big leather briefcase is a bottle of Jim Beam, and now, at the campsite, in the twilight, with the sun far gone over the rimrocks, we are going to have our quotidian ration—and Dominy is a generous man. After dinner, if patterns hold, he and Brower will square off for battle, but they are at this moment united in anticipation of the bourbon. Big steaks are ready for broiling over the coals of a driftwood fire. There is calm in the canyon. The Commissioner steps to the river's edge and dips a half cup of water, over which he pours his whiskey. "I'm the nation's waterboy," he says. "I need water with my bourbon."

Over the drinks, he tells us that he once taught a German shepherd to climb a ladder. We believe him. He further reminisces about early camping trips with his wife, Alice. They were in their teens when they married. He was state Master Counsellor for the Order of DeMolay, and she was the Queen of Job's Daughters. They had married secretly, and she went with him to the University of Wyoming. "We lived on beans and love," he said. "Our recreation was camping. We went up into the Snowy Range and into the Laramie Peak country, where there was nothing but rattlesnakes, ticks, and us. We used to haul wood down from the mountains to burn for heat in the winter."

Jerry Sanderson, the river guide who has organized this expedition, calls out that dinner is ready. He has cooked an entire sirloin steak for each person. We eat from large plastic trays—the property of Sanderson. Brower regularly ignores the stack of trays, and now, when his turn comes, he steps forward to receive his food in his Sierra Club cup. Sanderson, a lean, trim, weathered man, handsome and steady, has seen a lot on this river. And now a man with wild white hair and pink legs is holding out a four-inch cup to receive a three-pound steak. Very well. There is no rapid that can make Sanderson's eyes bat, so why should this? He drapes the steak over the cup. The steak covers the cup like a sun hat. Brower begins to hack at the edges with a knife. Brower in wilderness eats from nothing but his Sierra Club cup.

10 P.M. The moon has moved out in brilliance over the canyon rim. Brower and Dominy are asleep. Dominy snores. Just before he began to snore, he looked at the moon and said, "What's the point of going there? If it were made of gold, we couldn't afford to go get it. Twenty-three billion dollars for landings on the moon. I can't justify or understand that. One, yes. Half a dozen, no. Every time they light a roman candle at Cape Canaveral, they knock four hundred million off other projects, like water storage."

Tonight's fight was about siltation. When Brower finished his steak, he looked across the river at the flying plume of Deer Creek Falls and announced to all in earshot that Commissioner Dominy wished to fill that scene with mud, covering the riverbed and the banks where we sat, and filling the inner gorge of the Colorado right up to within fifty feet of the top of the waterfall.

"That's God-damned nonsense," Dominy said.

Brower explained quietly that rivers carry silt, and that silt has to go somewhere if men build dams. Silt first drops and settles where the river flows into still water at the heads of reservoirs, he said. Gradually, it not only fills the reservoir but also accumulates upstream from the headwaters, and that might one day be the story here at Deer Creek Falls, for Dominy wanted to create a reservoir that would begin only seven miles downstream from our campsite.

"They said Hoover Dam was going to silt up Lake Mead in thirty years," Dominy said. "For thirty years, Lake Mead caught all the God-damned silt in the Colorado River, and Hoover has not been impaired."

"No, but when Mead is low there are forty miles of silt flats at its upper end, and they're getting bigger."

"Not appreciably. Not with Lake Powell three hundred miles upstream."

"Yes, Lake Powell will fill up first."

"When? Tell me *when*?" Dominy was now shouting.

"In a hundred to two hundred years," Brower said quietly.

"That's crap! The figures you work with aren't reliable."

"They come from reliable people."

"Nonsense."

"Oh."

The Colorado, Brower reminded us, used to be known as Old Red. This was because the river was full of red mud. It would never have been possible for Dominy to dip his cup in it in order to get water to go with his bourbon unless he wished to drink mud as well. On arriving at a campsite, rivermen used to fill their boats with water, so that the mud would settle to the bottom of the boats and they would have water for drinking and cooking. Except after flash floods, the Colorado in the Grand Canyon is now green and almost clear, because Lake Powell is catching the silt, and Glen Canyon Dam—fifteen miles upstream from the beginning of the Grand Canyon—is releasing clean water. "Emotionally, people are able to look only two generations back and two generations forward," Brower said. "We need to see farther than that. It is absolutely inevitable, for example, that Lake Powell and Lake Mead will someday be completely filled with silt."

"Nonsense, nonsense, complete nonsense. First of all, we will build silt-detention dams in the tributaries—in the Paria, in the Little Colorado. And, if necessary, we will build more."

"Someday the reservoirs have to fill up, Floyd."

"I wouldn't admit that. I wouldn't admit one inch!"

"Someday."

"*Some*day! Yes, in geologic time, maybe. Lake Powell *will* fill up with silt. I don't know how many thousands of years from now. By then, people will have figured out alternative sources of water and power. That's what I say when you start talking about the geologic ages."

Brower then began to deliver a brief lecture on the phenomenon of aggradation—the term for the final insult that follows when a reservoir is full of silt. Aggradation is what happens to the silt that keeps on coming down the river. The silt piles up and, in a kind of reverse ooze, reaches back upstream many miles, following an inclined plane that rises about eighteen inches per mile—a figure reckoned from the site of the now mud-packed and obsolete dam.

Brower was scarcely halfway through sketching that picture when Dominy ended his contributions with a monosyllabic remark, walked away, put on his pajamas, delivered to the unlistening moon his attack on the space program, and, forgetting Brower and all the silt of years to come, fell asleep. He sleeps on his back, his feet apart, under the mesas.

5 A.M. The sky is light. The air temperature is eighty degrees. Brower sleeps on his side, his knees drawn up.

7 A.M. Eighty-eight degrees. We will soon be on the river. Dominy is brushing his teeth in the green Colorado. Sam Beach, a big, bearded man from White Plains, New York, just walked up to Dominy and said, "I see God has given us good water here this morning."

"Thank you," Dominy said.

And Brower said to Beach, "I imagine that's the first time you ever heard Him speak."

And Beach said, "God giveth, and God taketh away."

What seemed unimaginable beside the river in the canyon was that all that wild water had been processed, like pork slurry in a hot-dog plant, upstream in the lightless penstocks of a big dam. Perspective is where you find it, though, and with this in mind Dominy had taken Brower and me, some days earlier, down into the interior of his indisputable masterpiece, the ten-million-ton plug in Glen Canyon. We had seen it first from the air and then from the rim of Glen Canyon, and the dam had appeared from on high to be frail and surprisingly small, a gracefully curving wafer wedged flippantly into the river gorge, with a boulevard of blue water on one side of it and a trail of green river on the other. No national frontier that I can think of separates two worlds more dissimilar than the reservoir and the river. This frontier has a kind of *douane* as well, administered by men who work in a perfectly circular room deep inside the dam. They wear slim ties and white short-sleeved shirts. They make notes on clipboards. They sit at desks, and all around them, emplaced in the walls of the room, are gauges and dials, and more gauges and dials. To get to this control room, we rode about five hundred feet down into the dam in an elevator, and as we descended Dominy said, "People talk about environment. We're doing something about it." His eyes gleamed with humor. He led us down a long passageway and through a steel door. The men inside stood up. From the devotional look in their eyes, one might have thought that Marc Mitscher had just walked into the engine room of the carrier *Lexington* on the night after the Battle of the Philippine Sea. This was, after all, the man they called the Kmish. Throughout Reclamation, Dominy was known as the Kmish. Standing there, he introduced each man by name. He asked the elevation of Lake Powell.

"Three thousand five hundred and seventy-seven point two zero feet, sir."

Dominy nodded. He was pleased. When the level of the surface is lowered, a distinct band, known to conservationists as "the bathtub ring," appears along the cliff faces that hold the reservoir. Three thousand five hundred and seventy-seven point two zero would eliminate that, and a good thing, too, for on this day—one hundred years to the sunrise since the day Major Powell reached Glen Canyon on his first expedition—Lake Powell was to be dedicated.

"What are we releasing?" Dominy asked.

"Four thousand three hundred and fifty-six point zero cubic feet per second, sir."

"That's about normal," Dominy said. "Just a little low."

At their consoles, turning knobs, flicking switches, the men in the control room continually create the river below the dam. At that moment, they were releasing something like fourteen hundred tons of water every ten seconds—or, in their terminology, one acre-foot.

"We have eight generating units," Dominy went on. "When we want to make peaking power, we turn them up full and send a wall of water downstream. The rubber rafts operate with licenses, and the guides know the schedule of releases."

Dominy then took us all the way down—down in another elevator, down concrete and spiral stairways, along ever-deeper passageways and down more stairways—until we were under the original bed of the Colorado and at the absolute bottom of the dam, seven hundred and ten feet below the crest. "I don't want Dave Brower to be able to say he didn't see everything," Dominy said—and I could not help admiring him for it, because the milieu he had taken us into could easily be misunderstood. Water was everywhere. Water poured down the spiral staircases. It streamed through the passageways. It fell from the ceilings. It ran from the walls. In some places, sheets of polyethylene had been taped to the concrete. At the bottom, Glen Canyon Dam is three hundred feet thick, but nearly two hundred miles of reservoir was pressing against it, and it had cracked. The Colorado was pouring through. "We may have to get some Dutch boys in here with their thumbs," Dominy said. "The dam is still curing. It hasn't matured yet. So we aren't doing much of anything about this now. We will soon. We have a re-injectionable grouting system; it's an idea I picked up in Switzerland. The crack water is declining anyway. The crack may be sealing itself. It's not serious. You just cannot completely stop the Colorado River."

Brower seemed unable to decide whether he should be shocked by the crack in the dam or impressed by the unvanquishable river. Stalactites had formed on the ceilings of the passageways. I reached up and broke one off. "Don't let Dave Brower see you do that," Dominy said. "You're interrupting nature." Obviously in love with his dam, he scrambled all over it. "When a dam is being built, the concrete is *placed*, not poured," he said, rubbing a hand over a smooth interior wall. "The concrete is barely wet—too dry for pouring. It's put in place with vibrators. We regularly take core samples and send them to Denver for testing—to see if the contractor is meeting specifications. Dave, just to cement our friendship, I'm going to have a pair of bookends made from some of those old core samples for you. Nothing could support a set of Sierra Club books better than a couple of pieces of Glen Canyon Dam. Would you accept that?"

"I'll accept the bookends," Brower said. "Thank you very much, Floyd."

Under the generator room, Dominy led us onto a steel platform inches away from a huge, shining steel generator shaft. The shaft was spinning at who knows how many revolutions per minute, yet the platform around it was scarcely trembling. "Balance," he said proudly. "The secret is balance. In Russia, these platforms vibrate so much they practically knock you down. I know. I've stood on them there." He pointed out sections of giant pipe—penstocks—that contained the Colorado in its passage from reservoir to riverbed. The mighty rapids of the Grand Canyon were now inside that pipe.

Dominy opened a door that led to a strange exterior space—a wide, flat area at the base of the main wall of the dam. Six hundred feet of acutely angled concrete—white and dazzling in the sun—soared up from this level, where Dominy, for purely aesthetic reasons, had somehow imported tons of soil and had planted a smooth and elegant lawn. He called it "the football field," and it was more than large enough to hold one. When visitors peer over the crest of the dam, they look far down its white face to this incongruous lawn, unique in the cosmetics of high dams. From the lawn itself, the thought of the great wall of water on the other side of the dam is unnerving, but no more so than the ten acres of concave concrete up which the eye is led to fragments of red cliff where power-line towers claw at off-plumb angles into a blue swatch of sky. "You don't really appreciate this dam unless you're down on the transformer deck looking up," Dominy said. "Looking down is no way to look at life. You've got to be looking up. Suicides come down that wall sometimes. They don't realize how unvertical it is. When they're found at the bottom, there isn't a God-damned bit of flesh left on them."

Brower said, "My advice to suicides is 'If you've got to go, take Glen Canyon Dam with you.'"

"Read *Desert Solitaire*," Dominy said. "Page 165. The guy who wrote it is way ahead of you."

I eventually bought a copy of *Desert Solitaire*, and found that on page 165 its angry author—Edward Abbey—imagines "the loveliest explosion ever seen by man, reducing the great dam to a heap of rubble in the path of the river. The splendid new rapids thus created we will name Floyd E. Dominy Falls. . . ."

On an overlook not far from the dam, Lake Powell was dedicated by men, white and red, who addressed much of what they said to an unseen enemy, assuming that he was a thousand miles away; he happened to be standing right there. "The Sierra Club to the contrary, I *like* dams," said Governor John Williams of Arizona. When the dam was begun, Williams was a radio announcer, and it was he who broadcast the play-by-play of the original blasting ceremony.

"The Sierra Club notwithstanding, this is a beautiful lake," said Governor Calvin Rampton of Utah, sweeping an arm toward the reservoir. Red cliff walls met the dark-blue water, big buttes stood high in the background, and above it all—immense and alone in the distance—was sacred Navajo Mountain. Far below the overlook, boats wove patterns on the water. Skiers cut crescent wakes. Bunting hung from the speakers' platform in symbolic blue and brown—blue for Lake Powell and brown for the old Colorado.

"A conservationist is one who is content to stand still forever," said Raymond Nakai, of Window Rock, the head of the Navajo Tribal Council. "Major Powell would have approved of this lake. May it ever be brimmin' full." Brower remained silent, but was having difficulty doing so. It was not hard to guess his thoughts. Major Powell—explorer, surveyor, geographer—was not alive to say how he might feel, in English or Navajo.

Then Dominy spoke. "Dave Brower is here today," he said, and the entire ceremony almost fell into the reservoir. "Brower is not here in an official capacity but as my guest," Dominy went on. "We're going to spend several days on Lake Powell, so I can convert him a little. Then we're going down the river, so he can convert me."

Seven years earlier, we could have flown north through Glen Canyon at an altitude of four hundred feet over the riverbed, and that, in a way, is what we did now. We got into a nineteen-foot gray boat—its hull molded for speed, a Buick V-6 engine packed away somewhere, a two-way radio, and the black-lettered words *United States Government* across the stern—and up the lake we went at twenty knots, for three days spraying arches of clear water toward red-and-black-streaked tapestry walls, pinnacle spires, and monument buttes. The Utah canyonland had been severed halfway up by a blue geometric plane, creating a waterscape of interrupted shapes, spectacularly unnatural, spectacularly beautiful. If we stopped for lunch, nudging up to a cool shadowing wall, we were in fact four hundred feet up the sheer side of what had been an immense cliff above the river, and was still an immense cliff—Wingate, Kayenta, Navajo Sandstones—above the lake. The boat sped on among hemispherical islands that had once been mountainous domes. It wheeled into Caprian bays. Arched overhangs formed grottoes in what had once been the lofty ceilings of natural amphitheatres.

Above the sound of the engine, Dominy shouted, "Who but Dominy would build a lake in the desert? Look at the country around here! No vegetation. No precipitation. It's just not the setting for a lake under any natural circumstances. Yet it is the most beautiful lake in the world."

"A thousand people a year times ten thousand years times ten thousand years will never see what was there," Brower said. He pointed straight down into the water. Then he opened a can of beer. The beer was in a big container full of ice. The ice had been made from water of the reservoir—reclaimed pellets of the Colorado. The container held dozens of cans of beer and soft drinks, enough for ten men anywhere else, but even on the lake the air was as dry as paper and the sun was a desert sun, and we held those cans in the air like plasma, one after another, all day long. Brower, the aesthetician, likes beer cans. Not for him are the simple biases of his throng. He really appreciates the cans themselves—their cylindrical simplicity, their beautifully crafted lithography. Brower's love of beauty is so powerful it leaps. It sometimes lands in unexpected places. Looking out over the lake at canyon walls flashing in reflected light, he slowly turned his Budweiser in his hand, sipped a little, and then said, "Lake Powell does not exist. I have never seen anything like it before. It's an incredibly beautiful reservoir. It must be the most beautiful reservoir in the world. I just wish you could hold the water level where it is now, Floyd."

Dominy smiled. The lake would become more and more beautiful as it continued to fill, he said. It would go up another hundred and twenty feet, revising vistas as it rose, and the last thirty-five feet would be the most dramatic, because the water at that elevation would reach far into the canyonland.

"You can't duplicate this experience—this lake—anywhere else," Brower said. "But neither can you enjoy the original experience. That's the trouble. I camped under here once. It was a beautiful campsite. The river was one unending campsite. The ibis, the egrets, the wild blue herons are gone. Their habitat is gone—the mudbanks along the river."

"We've covered up a lot of nice stuff, there's no question about that, but you've got to admit that as far as views are concerned we've opened up a lot. Look. You can see mountains."

"The Henry Mountains," Brower said. "They were the last mountain range discovered in the lower forty-eight."

For my part, I kept waiting to see the lake. "Lake," as I sensed the word, called to mind a fairly compact water-filled depression in high terrain, with bends and bays perhaps obscuring some parts from others, but with a discernible center, a middle, a place that was farther from shore than any other, and from which a sweeping view of shoreline could be had in all directions. This was a provincialism, based on a Saranac, a Sunapee, a Mooselookmeguntic, and it had left me unprepared for Lake Powell, a map of which looks like a diagram of the human nervous system. The deep spinal channel of Glen Canyon, which was once the path of the Colorado, is now the least interesting part of Lake Powell. The long, narrow bays that reach far into hundreds of tributary canyons are the absorbing places to enter—the boat rounding bends between ever-narrowing walls among reflections of extraordinary beauty on wind-slickened rock. These were the places—these unimaginably deep clefts in the sandstone—that most stirred and most saddened Brower, who remembered wading through clear pools under cottonwood trees four hundred feet below the arbitrary level on which we floated.

In Face Canyon, the boat idled slowly and moved almost silently through still water along bending corridors of rock. "There used to be pools and trees in this little canyon," Brower said. "Cottonwoods, willows."

"Poison ivy, jimsonweed," Dominy said.

"Little parks with grasses. Water always running," Brower went on.

The rock, dark with the oxidation known as desert varnish, appeared to be a rich blue. Desert varnish somehow picks up color from the sky. The notes of a canyon wren descended the pentatonic scale. "That's the music here—the best there is," Brower said. "There used to be paper shells of surface mud on the floor of this canyon, cracking, peeling. Damn it, that was handsome."

"On balance, I can't lament what's been covered up," Dominy said.

In Cascade Canyon, on a ledge that had once been hundreds of feet high, grew a colony of mosses and ferns. "Now there's a hanging garden that's going to get water beyond its wildest dreams," Dominy said. "But unfortunately, like welfare, the water is going to drown it."

In Brower's memory, the most beautiful place in all the region of Glen Canyon was a cavernous space, under vaulting rock walls, that had been named the Cathedral in the Desert. The great walls arched toward one another, forming high and almost symmetrical overlapping parabolas. They enclosed about an acre of ground, in which had grown willows, grasses, columbine, and maidenhair fern. The center of this scene was a slim waterfall, no more than a foot in diameter, that fell sixty feet into a deep and foaming pool. From it a clear stream had flowed through the nave and out to the Colorado. The government boat now entered the Cathedral. Dominy switched off the engine. Water was halfway to the ceiling, and the waterfall was about ten feet high. It was cool in there, and truly beautiful—the vaulted ceiling, the sound of the falling water, the dancing and prismatic reflections, the echo of whispers.

It had been beautiful in there before the reservoir came, and it would continue to be so, in successive stages, until water closed the room altogether.

A cabin cruiser came into the Cathedral. In it were a middle-aged couple and an older man. They asked what branch of the government we represented.

"I'm the Commissioner of Reclamation," Dominy said.

"Holy mackerel!" said the younger man.

"This lake is beautiful," the woman said.

"Thank you," Dominy said.

Back in the sunlight, Dominy worried about Brower's lobstering skin. "It would be a terrible thing to get this wildlife enthusiast out here and burn him up," he said.

"I'm red-faced not from the sun but from anger," Brower said.

"Red-faced with anger at my destructive tactics," said Dominy. "See that buoy? That's the Colorado River under water. The buoy is exactly over the original riverbed. Fabulous. Fabulous." The buoy floated on fifty or sixty fathoms of water.

The boat's radio crackled with heavy static as Park Service rangers made contact with one another. One ranger commented on "the unusual companionship" that was loose on the lake.

Dominy gave his cowboy yell, and said, "Hell, if those rangers could see us now! Dave, in spite of your bad judgment, you're a hell of a nice guy."

"I have nothing but bias," Brower said.

Skiers whipped by, going south. "Some of these bastards come up here and ski for fifty miles," Dominy said.

We cruised into the vicinity of a large natural rock span called Gregory Arch, which was now thirty-five feet beneath us. "If I could swim, I would want to go down and lay a wreath on Gregory Arch, because we've covered it up," Dominy said. "Dave, now that we've cemented our friendship, let me ask you: Why didn't you make a fuss about Gregory Arch?"

"We didn't know about it."

"No one else did, either. No one could have helped you."

"The public's evaluation of a place they may not have ever seen is what will save a place—it is what saved Grand Canyon. It's what might have saved Glen Canyon."

"Saved? For every person who could ever have gotten in here when this place was in its natural state, God damn it, there will be hundreds of thousands who will get in here, into all these side canyons—on the water highways. It's your few against the hundreds. Kids can see this place. Eighty-year-olds. People who can't walk."

"Ninety-nine per cent of the population can walk."

"Before I built this lake, not six hundred people had been in here in recorded history."

"By building this lake," Brower said, "mankind has preëmpted a hundred and eighty-six thousand acres of habitat for its own exclusive use."

"I'm a fair man," said Dominy. "Just to show you how fair I am, I'll say this: When we destroyed Glen Canyon, we destroyed something really beautiful. But we brought in something else."

"Water."

"You can lament all you want what we covered up. What we got is beautiful, and it's accessible."

The boat, in Labyrinth Canyon, drifted in a film of tamarisk needles, driftwood, bits of Styrofoam, bobbing beer cans, plastic lids. "We conservationists call this Dominy soup," Brower said.

On ledges above the soup were dozens of potholes, some of them very large, and Brower silently drew circles in the air to indicate how, over centuries, these enormous holes in the sandstone had been made by small rocks in swirling water. He and Dominy climbed out of the boat onto a ledge and lowered themselves into a pothole that was eleven feet in diameter and fifteen feet deep. There they began to argue about evaporation—through which, inevitably, a percentage of water in storage will be lost. Six hundred thousand acre-feet of water would annually evaporate from the surface of Lake Powell when full, Brower asserted, and Dominy did not like being baited on his own ground. Something spiralled in his mind like the stones that had cut the hole he was standing in, and eventually he burst out, "Don't give me that evaporation crap! If we didn't store the water, it wouldn't be here."

Brower danced away, came back, and jabbed lightly. "The water is stored only to produce kilowatts anyway," he said.

"We don't release one God-damned acre-foot of water from Lake Powell just to produce kilowatts," Dominy said.

Brower nodded solemnly in disbelief. He moved in again, shifting his grounds of complaint, and mentioned the huge aeolian sand deposits—millions of tons of fine sand clinging to hollows in the cliffsides—that regularly plop into Lake Powell as the rising water gets to them. Conservationists had suggested that Lake Powell was all but filling with these sands and that the very shores of the lake were crumbling into the water.

"The stuff melts on contact!" Dominy shouted. "You know you're exaggerating! Stretch the truth, that's all you conservationists do. When water hits it, that stuff melts like powder. The unstable material goes, but the walls of Jericho won't come down. The cliffs aren't coming down." He climbed out of the pothole.

Brower pointed to strange striations in jagged shapes on the opposite canyon wall. "That is hieroglyphic, written centuries ago by God Himself," he said.

"Yeah? What does it say?" said Dominy.

"It says, 'Don't flood it.'"

Inevitably, the buoys and the floating directional signs of Lake Powell lead to the Rainbow Bridge Marina, the only source of food or fuel within a radius of fifty miles—a floating hamlet where merchants and Park Service rangers live in structures built on pontoons and drums. No other design solution was possible in a place where the lake surface keeps rising, and sometimes temporarily falling, between shores of sheer stone wall. On the decks of this marina, the people of Lake Powell congregate—campers, skiers, rangers, Reclamation men—and it was here that the sway of Dominy, if it had not been altogether evident before, was displayed in full. From cabin cruiser to cabin cruiser, his name spread everywhere within moments of his arrival, and as he moved along the nonskid marina decks he was regarded as a kind of god, creator of the unending blue waters. A child asked for his autograph. People thanked him repeatedly for the lake. The Kmish winked, and told them they were welcome. He also handed me his camera, put his arm around Brower, and said he wanted a visual record that such a moment had actually happened.

Brower captioned the picture, "Brower gives up."

Moving on from the marina, we tied up the boat at a small wooden dock where the water of Lake Powell met the dry bed of Aztec Creek, and we walked a mile or so uphill among the boulders of the arroyo. Now Brower and Dominy stood under Rainbow Bridge, and there they reopened a running battle they had fought for ten years.

Rainbow Bridge was formed—in an era when the land was uplifting—by waters that raced off Navajo Mountain and punched through a sandstone wall. Pushing gravel and boulders through the opening, cutting down and cutting wide, the creek, in centuries, made the gigantic stone span that crosses it now. Thick and red, immense against the sky, it would fit over the national Capitol dome. It is the largest known natural bridge on earth. When Lake Powell is full, still water will reach into the deep groove of the creek bed below Rainbow Bridge and will fill it to a level twenty-two feet below the base of the span. To Brower, this is simple sacrilege. To Dominy, it is a curious and agreeable coincidence that the water will stop just there.

There have been fly-ins, hike-ins, Congressional hearings. Brower wants a cutoff dam to keep the lake out of the creek bed under the bridge, a diversion dam above the bridge to make the creek—when it runs—run elsewhere, and a diesel pumping station to move the diverted water. Dominy and Brower were standing like two chinch bugs under the enormous stone arch. In a curious reversal of roles, Dominy told Brower that he was "a pyramid builder," that his cutoff dam and diversion dam would cost twenty-five million dollars, and that a little still water beneath the bridge would do far less damage to the natural setting that Brower was trying to preserve than would a pair of flanking dams. Brower said that water under the bridge would undermine its foundations. Dominy said geologists had told him that still water would do far less damage over the years than the flash floods that now go through there. Brower said he did not believe Dominy's geologists. Moreover, he said, Dominy had not taken into account the eventual problem of aggraded silt, which would one day pack the pillars of the bridge in mud.

If there was one concept Dominy had had enough of for a lifetime, it was aggraded silt—all these conservationists telling him about the high-piling ooze that was inescapably going to rise above his clotted reservoirs.

"It won't build back into here, God damn it!" he shouted.

"Yes, it will," Brower said, in a low, firm voice.

"What are you talking about—two hundred years from now?"

"No. About three hundred and fifty. Luna Leopold says that silt aggradation will be eighty feet here."

"That's what he says. I say it's crap. You conservationists say we are destroying Rainbow Bridge simply because we are making it available to people."

The two men walked around for a while, not saying anything, looking up in awe at the bridge. The spanning rock is forty feet thick. It could support a highway. Curiously, it is in more danger from sonic booms than from water. It shakes when booms hit it.

Two hikers appeared from up the creek bed. They had on backpacks, and had come to the bridge overland from Navajo Mountain, an extremely rugged journey. They were college age. One was from Bethesda, the other from St. Louis. We all shook hands, each person giving his name. One of the hikers said, "Did you say 'Dave *Brower*'?"

"Yes," said Brower.

"Dave *Brower*?" the boy repeated. Then, almost to himself, he said it again. "Dave Brower."

I wondered if the hiker was going to bend over and draw a picture of a fish in the sand.

Dominy said, "You're happy to meet *him*? How would you like to meet the Commissioner of Reclamation?"

Perhaps because they were from Missouri and Maryland, neither of the young men had any idea what the term meant, or where the commissioner of whatever it was might be, nor did they ask.

"Dave *Brower*."

They went with us all the way down the trail to the waterhead and the government boat. They stood there, watching Brower, as we pulled away. Without moving, they watched him until we passed out of sight around a bend. Briefly, we came into their view again. They were still watching.

"His supporters believe that the prophet can do no wrong."

"Conservation is a religious movement. So you get sects. And then you have the art of exposition of the individual creed. Each sectarian knows that he is right. Dave Brower has been the prophet leading the faithful."

"The Sierra Club itself is a religious movement."

"If the prophet goes off the straight and narrow course, he becomes more of an adversary than the adversary in the distance."

"He has been bitten by the worm of power."

"He has jumped in front of a moving car, which he was driving."

"Dave *had* to violate orders of the board, in order to get done what he had to do."

"He once said he had thousands of volunteers working with him and that if he ever tried to do things himself there would be one person instead of thousands. And that, tragically, is what has happened in recent years."

"The power structure broke down, or there was insubordination, depending on how you want to look at it."

"He has become, over the years, increasingly less tolerant of the conservation opposition. He used to be far more flexible in his attitude toward the conservation problem."

"This is why the Sierra Club membership has grown, however. He has built it from seven thousand to seventy-seven thousand. People, particularly younger people, flock to the cause. They are fed up with traditional attitudes. Brower once had a willingness to see the other point of view, but now he is a flaming firebrand, and he has split the Sierra Club right down the middle."

"He wasn't arrogant once, but he is now."

"I think that's a fair statement."

"I don't think 'arrogant' is really the right word. You wouldn't associate arrogance with Jesus Christ, for example. I don't mean to make a comparison there."

"With tact, he could have avoided his present trouble. He is stubborn. He's just God-damned stubborn."

"His concern is wilderness. He doesn't really care what happens to people."

"There is a pre-Eden strain in Dave—no question."

"I will say this: I prefer Dave's vices to the virtues of his enemies."

"They are crucifying him, and they are self-congratulating bourgeoisie."

The people who said these things eddied in the Empire Room of the Hotel Sir Francis Drake, in San Francisco, where—four or five hundred in all—they awaited the gavel that would begin the most momentous meeting of the directors of the Sierra Club in the fifty-five years since the defeat of John Muir. There were bearded men in open shirts who appeared to have walked directly in from the trail. There were good-looking women with hairbands, an advertising writer with a Beethoven haircut, at least twenty members of the press, a television-news crew. There were a preponderant number of old people, very local, very San Franciscan people—old bankers in vested suits, with fine memories of Sierra Club high trips in the nineteen-twenties, old men on canes who had reached into low reserves of energy just to be there, because they felt that Brower had expanded their club beyond recognition and had therefore, in a sense, usurped it. They had come in for the kill.

"He is financially reckless."

"He has impugned the motives of the opposition."

"He has disobeyed the directives of the board."

"There has been a growth in ecological sophistication in the United States over the past twenty years, and Dave has in part caused it."

"He is a high-risk politician, that's all. He risked his neck and he lost."

"He has a death wish."

"He's been edging toward it all the time."

"He loved his job, and was always pushing things to the point where he might lose it."

"He is a great practitioner of brinkmanship, and this time he went much too far."

"He is a shy man who thrusts himself forward—onstage. He is a freewheeling, farseeing visionary when he is not trapped, and he is a rigid personality when he is trapped."

"Sometimes he seems paranoid. He believes that the Park Service, the Forest Service, the Pacific Gas and Electric Company are out to get him. We always told him, 'No one outside the Sierra Club is going to get you. The only person who'll get you is you.'"

"What will he do? Do you think he would ever go into private industry?"

"He would open his own waffle shop first."

There was a U-shaped table at one end of the room, faced by hundreds of funeral chairs. People read the *Chronicle* while they waited. A celebrated tree in the Sierra Nevada—a giant sequoia with a roadway running through it—had crashed to the ground. The paper reprinted on the front page Ansel Adams' famous old photograph of the tree—the Wawona Tunnel Tree, as it was called—with a Pierce-Arrow nosing into it and a couple of figures standing beside the Pierce-Arrow. No one seemed to be getting much past the front page. Although the outcome of the meeting was a foregone conclusion, the atmosphere was tense. David Brower was going to be ejected as executive director of the Sierra Club. A last-minute resignation notwithstanding, "ejected" was the word. The executive director was an employee of the board of directors, and the board of directors was going to throw him out. The actual showdown had come in a mail-ballot election of new members of the board. Brower himself and a slate of his allies had been candidates, and they had lost, hands down. Supporters of Brower remained on the board, but the balance of power was now against him. Right to the end, Brower held on to the hope that somehow a majority of the fifteen directors would—all their expressed attitudes and commitments to the contrary—decide to keep him on, but he was the only person in the Sir Francis Drake Hotel who was that naïve. Whatever the terms might be, today's event would be a rite of expurgation.

"As his success grew, he paid less and less attention to what people in the club were thinking and saying. I don't think the man changed so much as he developed. He began to think, I *am* the Sierra Club."

"He is a combination poet, naturalist, and politician, a generalist in the fight to save the environment. He is tough enough to get into the thick of back-alley fights. He thinks that to win fights you have to have uncompromising militancy. The tax-exemption thing illustrates the risks he has been willing to take."

"No one in the Sierra Club faults him for that."

"I think Dave is right in feeling that militancy is the stance the Sierra Club should take if it is to be true to the spirit of John Muir."

"He started on five-sevenths pay and he worked seven-fifths of the time. His trouble was that he could not take direction. He was unapproachable. He tried to claim all the rights of an individual while representing an organization."

"He was the most effective single force in the conservation effort in this country. And he still is."

The gavel rapped. The room fell silent. Seated at the U-shaped table was the high tribunal of the Sierra Club.

Martin Litton, writer. Portola Valley, California. Big, outspoken man, bitter for the cause. Courageous. He goes down the Colorado in rigid boats. Pro-Brower.

Patrick D. Goldsworthy, biochemist. University of Washington. Wilderness mountain man but not a rope-and-piton climber. Defender of the North Cascades. Pro-Brower.

Eliot Porter, one of the two great wilderness photographers in the world. Tesuque, New Mexico. Medical doctor. Never practiced. Pro-Brower.

Larry Moss, nuclear engineer. Tanzania, California. White House Fellow. No outdoor specialty. Pro-Brower.

Raymond Sherwin, Superior Court judge. Vallejo, California. No outdoor specialty. Anti-Brower.

August Frugé, director of the University of California Press, Berkeley. Brower's boss when Brower worked there. No outdoor specialty. Anti-Brower.

Will Siri, biophysicist. University of California, Berkeley. Mountaineer. Co-leader in 1954 of the Makalu expeditions in the Himalayas. Cordillera Blanca, Peru, 1952. Everest, 1963. Anti-Brower.

"Say what you will about financial irresponsibility or insubordination, what's really going on here is a deep death struggle between mountaineers. Siri and others. Mountaineers are individualists—loners. Brower is an individualist, a loner."

"Brower is a mountaineer."

"Not a single climber he grew up with is still a friend of his."

"They've all turned on him."

"There is no love-hate like the love-hate that exists among mountaineers."

Philip Berry, lawyer, climber, mountaineer. Age, thirty-one. Grew up in Berkeley. Frequent visitor, throughout his youth, in Brower's home. Brower taught him climbing techniques. Brower and Berry once attempted a new route up Mount Clarence King, in the Sierra. Brower loosened a rock that hit Berry. Duck hunter. Anti-Brower.

Richard Leonard. Former president of the Sierra Club. Four years older than Brower and long his closest friend. Neighbor of Brower in Berkeley, and in the Mills Tower office building, San Francisco. Original proposer of Brower for membership in the Sierra Club. Nominator of Brower as executive director. Anti-Brower. Said to be the mastermind of the anti-Brower forces. Lawyer, climber, mountaineer.

From the bottom of the U, Leonard looked out into the room without expression. He appeared to be a man who had never lost, or even mislaid, his composure. Leonard did not so much as turn his head when Martin Litton grabbed a microphone and shouted, "This election has been rife with perjury, calumny, and fraud!" Leonard, short and unprepossessing, cleared his throat at regular intervals. Nothing of his climbing past showed in his legal present. He and Brower

—tied together—had climbed more mountains than either could remember. Among the people Leonard could see from his seat at the U-shaped table was Brower, standing at the edge of the crowd, his chin up, his white hair focal in the room. What Leonard was thinking then is anyone's guess, but it may have been something close to a commentary he had made in private only hours before.

"In the early years, Dave was absolutely magnificent as the leader of the club. He fought vigorously, aggressively, and—the point I want to emphasize—courteously. In later years, he started into his philosophy that Nice Nelly could never do the job. He impugned the motives of Forest Service people, Park Service people, congressmen. He seemed to feel that the end justified the means. The board passed resolutions insisting that he wage campaigns on demonstrable facts. Repeatedly, he has disregarded what the board has told him to do. He seems to think that it is he who knows what is best for the Sierra Club and for conservation in the long run, and that the board of directors is just standing in his way. The basis of his drive is that the earth is going to hell fast and something has to be done about it. Because of this, Dave will spend the resources of any organization he is with in unlimited fashion. 'We're not trying to save money, we're trying to save the world,' he will say, and then he will put thirty thousand dollars or so into another newspaper advertisement, without being authorized to do so by the board. I want you to know this, though: He has never taken one dime for himself. One look at his house shows that—how shabby it is, aluminum pans catching the rain. His ideals are good, but his naïveté would eventually destroy the organization. He believes that if he bankrupts the Sierra Club it is in a glorious cause. He was, incidentally, an excellent climber. We began to climb together when he was twenty-one and I was twenty-five. My life depended on his judgment and ability for weeks at a time. We once spent three weeks together on a glacier in British Columbia, sleeping on ice two thousand feet deep. Dave went snow-blind. He thought it was a weakness to use dark glasses. He was convinced that he could adjust his eyes to the sun. The sun's rays will congeal albumin, like cooking an egg. Dave's eyes were closed for two or three days. I think he feels the need to decide medical and optical questions for himself. He also believes, as you know, in self-fulfilling prophecies. The snowball theory of action. Things will work out. Providence has always looked after the Sierra Club and always will, Dave thinks. I have no personal animosity toward Dave. We just have to save the Sierra Club, that's all."

Richard Sill, physicist. University of Nevada. No outdoor specialty. Anti-Brower.

Paul Brooks, writer on conservation subjects. Lincoln, Massachusetts. Retired executive editor of Houghton Mifflin. Canoeman. Refers to his wife as "the bow paddle." At home, she puts up the storm windows. Anti-Brower.

Edgar Wayburn, San Francisco physician, who grew up in Macon, Georgia. President of the Sierra Club, and long its principal voice of conciliating reason. Describes Brower as "a creative genius." Anti-Brower.

Maynard Munger, realtor. Lafayette, California. No outdoor specialty. Campaigned for the board of directors with a photograph of himself in a kayak. Feels that the Sierra Club enhances his image as a realtor. Anti-Brower.

Ansel Adams, the other great wilderness photographer in the world. Carmel, California. Met Brower on a knapsack trip in the High Sierra in 1933. Strong personal and professional relationship with Brower over the years. Anti-Brower.

Adams, a burly, black-bearded man, knew a detail of which only one other person in the room was in all likelihood aware. Under the big tree, beside the Pierce-Arrow, in the Ansel Adams photograph that was on the front page of that day's *Chronicle* stood David Brower—indistinguishable, unidentified, but present, in a picture that was captioned "A Fallen Giant."

Luna Leopold, hydrologist. Washington, D.C. Sharp mind, sharp tongue. Expert on the Colorado. Expert on river sedimentation. Snowshoe hunter. Son of Aldo Leopold, who wrote *A Sand County Almanac* and *Round River*, literary touchstones of modern conservation-ecology. Pro-Brower.

The event of the day occurred in less time than it would take to tack a notice to a wall. President Wayburn recognized Siri, and Siri said that David Brower was "the greatest spiritual conservation leader of this century." He added, "However, two giants are in conflict—the body of the Sierra Club and the embodiment of David Brower. I move that his resignation be accepted."

Richard Leonard seconded the motion and was hissed as he did so.

Perhaps incredibly, Brower, standing in the back of the room, still felt hopeful. There could be a change of heart.

All in favor? Ten. Opposed? Five. Carried.

In a soft, emotional voice, Brower read a farewell speech that contained no pumice. From its tone, he might have been reading a story to children around a campfire. Then he left the room.

"Expansion cracking" was his term for what had happened. A small, local organization had grown into a major national and international force in the conservation movement, and at each stage there had been people who had wanted to stop. Brower had come to see conservation as inescapably a global and supranational matter, with pollution control and population control its first concerns, *sine qua non* to the preservation of wilderness. The best of his opposition, not necessarily disagreeing, felt that the Sierra Club should have more limited objectives if it was to reach any objectives at all, but Brower, meanwhile, was reaching into the endangered stratosphere and beyond it for the sun and the stars. The money would come from somewhere. It always had.

In the months that followed the meeting at the Sir Francis Drake, Brower went off whenever he could into wilderness areas where, in his words, he put himself back in touch with his purposes. On one of these trips, an aimless wandering through the Sierra Nevada, he found himself drawn, perhaps not so aimlessly, to the grove in the southern Yosemite where the giant sequoia had fallen.

The crash had been sudden and cataclysmic, the impact so great that the enormous tree had broken into pieces as if it were made of crockery. In several places, at intervals of about fifty feet, the trunk had broken clean through. The wood inside looked like red brick. Upper limbs had been driven deep into the ground. Sequoia cones were everywhere, and Brower picked some up. "I am forced to say it was a rough winter on both of us," Brower said to the tree. He climbed the side of the fallen trunk and stood on it, three stories off the ground. He shook a seed out of one of the cones. The cone was no larger than a walnut, and the tiny seed, encased in a winglike fibre, was nothing but a sliver, three-sixteenths of an inch long. "This seed can grow fifty thousand cubic feet of wood that can live for thirty-five hundred years," Brower said, speaking down from the trunk. "This seed knows how to shape an arrowhead canopy, how to design a root system to combat siltation, how to pump water three hundred feet up. This seed has worked for ninety million years and has not been to forestry school." He looked around to see, if he could, why the big tree had fallen. The tunnel in its base had been cut through a burn scar in 1881, and was wide enough for horse-drawn carriages and, until the middle of the twentieth century, for automobiles. But automobiles in recent years had grown too wide, so another roadway had been paved around the tree for cars that could not go through it, and this additional roadway was on the side away from the fall—on the side where the roots had broken. "Too much encroachment on the vitality of a living thing," Brower concluded. "It must have been a hell of a noise, a gorgeous crash. Detroit wins again."

Mile 141. We are in a long, placid reach of the river. The Upset Rapid is eight miles downstream, but its name, all morning, has been a refrain on the raft. People say it as if they were being wheeled toward it on a hospital cart. We have other rapids to go through first—the Kanab Rapid, the Matkatamiba Rapid—but everyone has been thinking beyond them to Upset.

"According to the *River Guide*, there hasn't been a death in the Upset Rapid for a little over two years," someone joked.

"The map says Upset is very bad when the water is low."

"How is the water, Jerry?"

"Low."

"Under today's controlled river, we're riding at the moment on last Sunday's releases," Dominy explained. "This is as low as the river will get under controlled conditions. Tomorrow, Monday's conditions will catch up with us, so things will improve."

"Thank you very much, Commissioner, but what good will Monday's releases do us today?"

"Let's camp here," someone put in.

"It's ten-thirty in the morning."

"I don't care."

"The river has its hands tied, but it's still running," said Brower. "If the Commissioner gets very wet today, it's his own fault."

Jerry Sanderson has cut the engine—a small, cocky outboard that gives the raft a little more speed than the river and is supposed to add some control in rapids. We drift silently.

Brower notices a driftwood log, bleached and dry, on a ledge forty feet above us. "See where the river was before you turned it off, Floyd?"

"I didn't turn it off, God damn it, I turned it on. Ten months of the year, there wasn't enough water in here to boil an egg. My dam put this river in business."

Dominy begins to talk dams. To him, the world is a tessellation of watersheds. When he looks at a globe, he does not see nations so much as he sees rivers, and his imagination runs down the rivers building dams. Of all the rivers in the world, the one that makes him salivate most is the Mekong. There are chances in the Mekong for freshwater Mediterraneans—huge bowls of topography that are pinched off by gunsight passages just crying to be plugged. "Fantastic. Fantastic river," he says, and he contrasts it with the Murrumbidgee River, in New South Wales, where the Australians have spent twenty-two years developing something called the Snowy Mountains Hydroelectric Scheme—"a whole lot of effort for a cup of water." Brower reminds Dominy that dams can break, and mentions the disaster that occurred in Italy in 1963. "That dam didn't break," Dominy tells him. "That dam did *not* break. It was nine hundred feet high. Above it was a granite mountain with crud on top. The crud fell into the reservoir, and water splashed *four hundred feet* over the top of the dam and rushed down the river and killed two thousand people. The dam is still there. It held. Four hundred feet of water over it and it held. Of course, it's useless now. The reservoir is full of crud."

"Just as all your reservoirs will be. Just as Lake Powell will be full of silt."

"Oh, for Christ's sake, Dave, be rational."

"Oh, for Christ's sake, Floyd, *you* be rational."

"Have you ever been *for* a dam, Dave? Once? Ever?"

"Yes. I testified in favor of Knowles Dam, on the Clark Fork River, in Montana. I saw it as a way to save Glacier National Park from an even greater threat. Tell me this, Floyd. Have you ever built a dam that didn't work?"

"Yes, if you want to know the truth. I'm not afraid to tell you the truth, Dave. On Owl Creek, near Thermopolis, Wyoming. Geologic tests were done at one point in the creek and they were O.K., and then the dam was built some distance upstream. We learned a lesson. Never build a dam except exactly where tests are conducted. Cavities developed under the dam, also under the reservoir. Every time we plug one hole, two more show up. Plugs keep coming out. The reservoir just won't fill. Someday I'll tell you another story, Dave. I'll tell you about the day one of our men opened the wrong valve and flooded the *inside* of Grand Coulee Dam."

"I've heard enough."

Dominy and Brower call for sandwiches, open them, and dutifully drop the tongues inside. Brower now attacks Dominy because a dam project near Ventura, California, is threatening the existence of thirty-nine of the forty-five remaining condors in North America. "We've got to get upset about the condor," Brower tells him. "No one likes to see something get extinct."

"The condor was alive in the days of the mastodons," Dominy says. "He is left over from prehistoric times. He can't fly without dropping off something first. He is so huge a kid with a BB gun can hit him. He's in trouble, dam or no dam. If you give him forty thousand acres, he's still in trouble. He *is* in trouble. His chances of survival are slim. I think it would be nice if he survived, but I don't think this God-damned project would have any real bearing on it."

Dominy draws deeply on his beer. He takes off his Lake Powell hat, smooths his hair back, and replaces the hat. I wonder if he is thinking of the scale-model bulldozer in his office in Washington. The bulldozer happens to have a condor in it—a rubber scale-model condor, sitting in the operator's seat.

Dominy's thoughts have been elsewhere, though. "Who was that old man who tried to read poetry at Kennedy's Inaugural? With the white hair blowing all over the place."

"Robert Frost."

"Right. He and I went to Russia together. I was going to visit Russian dams, and he was on some cultural exchange, and we sat beside each other on the plane all the way to Moscow. He talked and talked, and I smoked cigars. He said eventually, 'So you're the dam man. You're the creator of the great concrete monoliths—turbines, generators, stored water.' And then he started to talk poetically about me, right there in the plane. He said, 'Turning, turning, turning . . . creating, creating . . . creating energy for the people . . . for the people. . . .'

"Most of the day, Frost reminisced about his childhood, and he asked about mine, and I told him I'd been born in a town so small that the entrance and exit signs were on the same post. Land as dry and rough as a cob. You'll never see any land better than that for irrigating. God damn, she lays pretty. And he asked about my own family, and I told him about our farm in Virginia, and how my son and I put up nine hundred and sixty feet of fence in one day. I told my son, 'I'll teach you how to work. You teach yourself how to play.'"

We have been through the Kanab Rapid—standing waves six feet high, lots of splash—and we are still wet. It is cold in the canyon. A cloud—a phenomenon in this sky—covers the sun. We are shivering. The temperature plunges if the sun is obscured. The oven is off. Clothes do not quickly dry. Fortunately, the cloud seems to be alone up there.

Mile 144.8. "Here we are," Brower says. He has the map in his hand. Nothing in the Muav Limestone walls around us suggests that we are anywhere in particular, except in the middle of the Grand Canyon. "We are entering the reservoir," Brower announces. "We are now floating on Lake Dominy."

"Jesus," mutters Dominy.

"What reservoir?" someone asks. Brower explains. A dam that Dominy would like to build, ninety-three miles downstream, would back still water to this exact point in the river.

"Is that right, Commissioner?"

"That's right."

The cloud has left the sun, and almost at once we feel warm

again. The other passengers are silent, absorbed by what Brower has told them.

"Do you mean the reservoir would cover the Upset Rapid? Havasu Creek? Lava Falls? All the places we are coming to?" one man asks Dominy.

Dominy reaches for the visor of his Lake Powell hat and pulls it down more firmly on his head. "Yes," he says.

"I'd have to think about that."

"So would I."

"I would, too."

Our fellow-passengers have become a somewhat bewildered —perhaps a somewhat divided—chorus. Dominy assures them that the lake would be beautiful, like Powell, and, moreover, that the Hualapai Indians, whose reservation is beside the damsite, would have a million-dollar windfall, comparable to the good deal that has come to the Navajos of Glen Canyon. The new dam would be called Hualapai Dam, and the reservoir—Brower's humor notwithstanding—would be called Hualapai Lake.

"I'm prepared to say, here and now, that we should touch nothing more in the lower forty-eight," Brower comments. "Whether it's an island, a river, a mountain wilderness—nothing more. What has been left alone until now should be left alone permanently. It's an extreme statement, but it should be said."

"That, my friend, is debatable."

The others look from Brower to Dominy without apparent decision. For the most part, their reactions do not seem to be automatic, either way. This might seem surprising among people who would be attracted, in the first place, to going down this river on a raft, but nearly all of them live in communities whose power and water come from the Colorado. They are, like everyone, caught in the middle, and so they say they'll have to think about it. At home, in New Jersey, I go to my children's schoolrooms and ask, for example, a group of fourth graders to consider a large color photograph of a pristine beach in Georgia. "Do you think there should be houses by this beach, or that it should be left as it is?" Hands go up, waving madly. "Houses," some of the schoolchildren say. Others vote against the houses. The breakdown is fifty-fifty. "How about this?

Here is a picture of a glorious mountain in a deep wilderness in the State of Washington. There is copper under the mountain." I list the uses of copper. The vote is close. A black child, who was for houses on the beach, says, "Take the copper." I hold up the Sierra Club's Exhibit-Format book *Time and the River Flowing* and show them pictures of the Colorado River in the Grand Canyon. Someone wants to build a dam in this river. A dam gives electricity and water—light and food. The vote is roughly fifty-fifty.

After Brower ran his ad about the flooding of the Sistine Chapel, Dominy counterattacked by flying down the Colorado in a helicopter, hanging by a strap from an open door with a camera in his hand. He had the pilot set the helicopter down on a sandbar at Mile 144.8, and he took a picture straight down the river. The elevation of the sandbar was eighteen hundred and seventy-five feet above sea level. Taking pictures all the way, Dominy had the pilot fly at that exact altitude down the river from the sandbar to the site of Hualapai Dam. ("That pilot had the God-damned props churning right around the edge of that inner-gorge wall, and he was *noivous*, but I made him stay there.") At the damsite, the helicopter was six hundred feet in the air. Dominy took his collection of pictures to Congress. "Brower says we want to ruin the canyon. Let's see whether we're going to ruin it," he said, and he demonstrated that Hualapai Lake, for all its length, would be a slender puddle hidden away in a segment of the Grand Canyon that was seven miles wide and four thousand feet deep. No part of the lake would be visible from any public observation point in Grand Canyon National Park, he told the congressmen. "Hell, I know more about this river than the Park Service, the Sierra Club, and everyone else," he says, finishing the story. "I took my pictures to Congress because I thought that this would put the ball in their court, and if they wanted to field it, all right, and if they wanted to drop it, that was all right, too."

We have gone through Matkatamiba and around a bend. Jerry Sanderson has cut the motor again, and we are resting in the long corridor of flat water that ends in the Upset Rapid. There is a lot of talk about "the last mile," the low water, "the end of the rainbow," and so on, but this is just fear chatter, dramatization of the unseen.

"Oh, come on, now. One of these rafts could go over Niagara Falls."

"Yes. With no survivors."

Brower hands Dominy a beer. "Here's your last beer," he says. It is 11 A.M., and cool in the canyon. Another cloud is over the sun, and the temperature is seventy-seven degrees. The cloud will be gone in moments, and the temperature will go back into the nineties.

"Here's to Upset," Brower says, lifting his beer. "May the best man win."

The dropoff is so precipitous where Upset begins that all we can see of it, from two hundred yards upstream, is what appears to be an agglomeration of snapping jaws—the leaping peaks of white water. Jerry cannot get the motor started. "It won't run on this gas," he explains. "I've tried river water, and it won't run on that, either." As we drift downstream, he works on the motor. A hundred and fifty yards. He pulls the cord. No sound. There is no sound in the raft, either, except for the *psss* of a can being opened. Dominy is having one more beer. A hundred yards. Jerry starts the motor. He directs the raft to shore. Upset, by rule, must be inspected before the running.

We all got off the raft and walked to the edge of the rapid with Sanderson. What we saw there tended to erase the thought that men in shirtsleeves were controlling the Colorado inside a dam that was a hundred and sixty-five river miles away. They were there, and this rapid was here, thundering. The problem was elemental. On the near right was an enormous hole, fifteen feet deep and many yards wide, into which poured a scaled-down Canadian Niagara—tons upon tons of water per second. On the far left, just beyond the hole, a very large boulder was fixed in the white torrent. High water would clearly fill up the hole and reduce the boulder, but that was not the situation today.

"What are you going to do about this one, Jerry?"

Sanderson spoke slowly and in a voice louder than usual, trying to pitch his words above the roar of the water. "You have to try to take ten per cent of the hole. If you take any more of the hole, you go in it, and if you take any less you hit the rock."

"What's at the bottom of the hole, Jerry?"

"A rubber raft," someone said.

Sanderson smiled.

"What happened two years ago, Jerry?"

"Well, the man went through in a neoprene pontoon boat, and it was cut in half by the rock. His life jacket got tangled in a boat line, and he drowned."

"What can happen to the raft, Jerry?"

"Oh, parts of them sometimes get knocked flat. Then we have to stop below the rapid and sew them up. We have a pump to reinflate them. We use Dacron thread, and sew them with a leather punch and a three-inch curved needle. We also use contact adhesive cement."

"Wallace Stegner thinks this river is dead, because of Glen Canyon Dam, but I disagree," Brower said. "Just look at it. You've got to have a river alive. You've just got to. There's no alternative."

"I prefer to run this rapid with more water," Sanderson said, as if for the first time.

"If you want to sit here twenty-four hours, I'll get you whatever you need," said Dominy.

Sanderson said, "Let's go."

We got back on the raft and moved out into the river. The raft turned slightly and began to move toward the rapid. "Hey," Dominy said. "Where's Dave? Hey! We left behind one of our party. We're separated now. Isn't he going to ride?" Brower had stayed on shore. We were now forty feet out. "Well, I swear, I swear, I swear," Dominy continued, slowly. "He isn't coming with us." The Upset Rapid drew us in.

With a deep shudder, we dropped into a percentage of the hole—God only knows if it was ten—and the raft folded almost in two. The bow and the stern became the high points of a deep V. Water smashed down on us. And down it smashed again, all in that other world of slow and disparate motion. It was not speed but weight that we were experiencing: the great, almost imponderable, weight of water, enough to crush a thousand people, but not hurting us at all because we were part of it—part of the weight, the raft, the river. Then, surfacing over the far edge of the hole, we bobbed past the incisor rock and through the foaming outwash.

"The great outdoorsman!" Dominy said, in a low voice. "The great outdoorsman!" He shook water out of his Lake Powell hat. "The great outdoorsman standing safely on dry land wearing a God-damned life jacket!"

The raft, in quiet water, now moved close to shore, where Brower, who had walked around the rapid, stood waiting.

"For heaven's sake, say nothing to him, Floyd."

"Christ, I wouldn't think of it. I wouldn't dream of it. What did he do during the war?"

The raft nudged the riverbank. Dominy said, "Dave, why didn't you ride through the rapid?"

Brower said, "Because I'm chicken."

A Climber's Guide to the High Sierra (Sierra Club, 1954) lists thirty-three peaks in the Sierra Nevada that were first ascended by David Brower. "*Arrowhead.* First ascent September 5, 1937, by David R. Brower and Richard M. Leonard. . . . *Glacier Point.* First ascent May 28, 1939, by Raffi Bedayan, David R. Brower, and Richard M. Leonard. . . . *Lost Brother.* First ascent July 27, 1941, by David R. Brower. . . ." Brower has climbed all the Sierra peaks that are higher than fourteen thousand feet. He once started out at midnight, scaled the summit of Mount Tyndall (14,025) by 3 A.M., reached the summit of Mount Williamson (14,384) by 7 A.M., and was on top of Mount Barnard (14,003) at noon. He ate his lunch—nuts, raisins, dried apricots—and he went to sleep. He often went to sleep on the high peaks. Or he hunted around for ice, removing it in wedges from cracks in the granite, sucking it to slake his thirst. If it was a nice day, he would stay put for as much as an hour and a half. "The summit is the anticlimax," he says. "The way up is the thing. There is a moment when you know you have the mountain by the tail. You figure out how the various elements go together. You thread the route in your mind's eye, after hunting and selecting, and hitting dead ends. Finally, God is good enough. He built the mountain right, after all. A pleasant surprise. If you don't make it and have to go back, you play it over and over again in your mind. Maybe this would work, or that. Several months, a year, or two years later, you do it again." When Brower first tried to climb the Vazquez Monolith, in Pinnacles National Monument, he was stopped cold, as had been every other climber ever, for the face of the monolith was so smooth that Brower couldn't even get off the ground. Eventually, someone else figured out how to do that, but, as it happened, was stopped far shy of the summit. When Brower heard about this, he went to his typewriter, wrote a note identifying himself as the first man to ascend Vazquez Monolith, and slipped the note into a small brass tube. In his mind, he could see his route as if he were carrying a map. He went to Pinnacles National Monument, went up the Vazquez Monolith without an indecisive moment, and, on top, built a cairn around the brass tube. When Brower led a group to Shiprock in 1939, at least ten previous climbing parties had tried and failed there. Shiprock is a seven-thousand-foot monadnock that looks something like a schooner rising in isolation from the floor of the New Mexican desert. Brower studied photographs of Shiprock for many months, then planned an ornately complicated route—about three-quarters of the way up one side, then far down another side, then up a third and, he hoped, final side, to the top. That is how the climb went, without flaw, start to finish. Another brass tube. "I like mountains. I like granite. I particularly like the feel of the Sierra granite. When I climbed the Chamonix Aiguilles, the granite felt so much like the granite in the Yosemite that I felt right at home. Once, in the Sierra, when I was learning, I was going up the wall of a couloir and I put both hands and one knee on a rock. The rock moved, and fell. It crashed seventy-five feet below. One of my hands had shot upward, and with two fingers I caught a ledge. I pulled myself up, and I sat there on that ledge and thought for a long while. Why was I that stupid—to put that much faith in one rock? I have an urge to get up on top. I like to get up there and see around. A three-hundred-and-sixty-degree view is a nice thing to have. I like to recognize where I've been, and look for routes where I might go."

Mile 156. Already the talk is of Lava Falls, which lies twenty-four miles ahead but has acquired fresh prominence in the aftermath of Upset. On the table of rated rapids—copies of which nearly everyone is at the moment studying—categories run from "Riffle" through "Heavy" to "Not Recommended." Upset was a "Heavy" rapid, like Deubendorff. In the "Not Recommended" category there is only Lava Falls.

"Do you agree with that, Jerry?"

Sanderson grins with amusement, and speaks so slowly he seems wistful. "It's the granddaddy of them all," he says. "There's a big drop, and a lot of boulders, and several holes like the one at Upset. You have to look the rapid over carefully, because the holes move."

In the stillness of a big eddy, the raft pauses under an overhanging cliff. Lava Falls fades in the conversation. Twenty-four miles is a lot of country. Through a cleft that reaches all the way down through the overhanging cliff a clear green stream is flowing into the river. The cleft is so narrow that the stream appears to be coming straight out of the sandstone. Actually, it meanders within the cliff and is thus lost to view. The water is so clear that it sends a pale-green shaft into the darker Colorado. The big river may no longer be red with silt, but it carries enough to remain opaque. In the small stream, the pebbles on the bottom are visible, magnified, distinct. "Dive in," Brower suggests. "See where it goes."

Brower and I went into the stream and into the cliff. The current was not powerful, coming through the rock, and the water was only four feet deep. I swam, by choice—the water felt so good. It felt cool, but it must have been about seventy-five degrees. It was cooler than the air. Within the cliff was deep twilight, and the echoing sound of the moving water. A bend to the right, a bend to the left, right, left—this stone labyrinth with a crystal stream in it was moment enough, no matter where it ended, but there lay beyond it a world that humbled the mind's eye. The walls widened first into a cascaded gorge and then flared out to become the ovate sides of a deep valley, into which the stream rose in tiers of pools and waterfalls. Some of the falls were only two feet high, others four feet, six feet. There were hundreds of them. The pools were as much as fifteen feet deep, and the water in them was white where it plunged and foamed, then blue in a wide circle around the plunge point, and pale green in the outer peripheries. This was Havasu Canyon, the immemorial home of the Havasupai, whose tribal name means "the people of the blue-green waters." We climbed from one pool to another, and swam across the pools, and let the waterfalls beat down around our shoulders. Mile after mile, the pools and waterfalls continued. The high walls of the valley were bright red. Nothing grew on these dry and flaky slopes from the mesa rim down about two-thirds of the way; then life began to show in isolated barrel cactus and prickly pear. The cacti thickened farther down, and below them was riverine vegetation—green groves of oak and cottonwood, willows and tamarisk, stands of cattail, tall grasses, moss, watercress, and maidenhair fern. The Havasupai have lived in this place for hundreds, possibly thousands, of years, and their population has remained stable. There are something like two hundred of them. They gather nuts on the canyon rim in winter and grow vegetables in the canyon in summer. They live about twelve miles up Havasu Creek from the Colorado. Moss covered the rocks around the blue-and-green pools. The moss on dry rock was soft and dense, and felt like broadloom underfoot. Moss also grew below the water's surface, where it was coated with travertine, and resembled coral. The stream was loaded with calcium, and this was the physical explanation of the great beauty of Havasu Canyon, for it was the travertine—crystalline calcium carbonate—that had both fashioned and secured the all but unending stairway of falls and pools. At the downstream lip of each plunge pool, calcium deposits had built up into natural dams, and these travertine dams were what kept Havasu Creek from running freely downhill. The dams were whitish tan, and so smooth and symmetrical that they might have been finished by a mason. They were two or three feet high. They sloped. Their crests were flat and smooth and with astonishing uniformity were about four inches thick from bank to bank. Brower looked up at the red canyon walls. He was sitting on the travertine, with one foot in a waterfall, and I was treading the green water below him. He said, "If Hualapai Dam had been built, or were ever built, this place where you are swimming would be at the bottom of a hundred feet of water." It was time to go back to the Colorado. I swam to the travertine dam at the foot of the pool, climbed up on it and dived into the pool below it, and swam across and dived again, and swam and dived—and so on for nearly two miles. Dominy was waiting below. "It's fabulous," he said. "I know every river canyon in the country, and this is the prettiest in the West."

Mile 171. Beside the minor rapids at Gateway Canyon, we stop, unload the raft, and lay out our gear before settling down to drinks before dinner. Brower is just beyond earshot. Dominy asks me again, "What did Dave do during the war?"

I tell him all I happen to know—that Brower trained troops in climbing techniques in West Virginia and Colorado, and that he later went with the 10th Mountain Division to Italy, where he won the Bronze Star.

Dominy contemplates the river. Brower goes to the water's edge and dips his Sierra Club cup. He will add whiskey to the water. "Fast-moving water is a very satisfying sound," Dominy says to him. "There is nothing more soothing than the sound of running or falling water."

"The river talks to itself, Floyd. Those little whirls, the sucks and the boils—they say things."

"I love to see white water, Dave. In all my trips through the West over the years, I have found moving streams with steep drops to them the most scenic things of all."

Over the drinks, Brower tells him, "I will come out of this trip different from when I came in. I am not in favor of dams, but I am in favor of Dominy. I can see what you have meant to the Bureau, and I am worried about what is going to happen there someday without you."

"No one will ever say that Dominy did not tell anyone and everyone exactly what he thinks, Dave."

"I've never heard anything different, Floyd."

"And, I might say, I've never heard anything different about you."

"I needed this trip more than anyone else."

"You're God-damned right you did, with that white skin."

Dominy takes his next drink out of the Sierra Club cup. The bottle of whiskey is nearly empty. Dominy goes far down into his briefcase and brings out another. It is Jim Beam. Dominy is fantastically loyal to Jim Beam. At his farm in Virginia a few weeks ago, he revived a sick calf by shooting it with a hypodermic syringe full of penicillin, condensed milk, and Jim Beam. Brower says he does not believe in penicillin.

"As a matter of fact, Dave Brower, I'll make a trip with you any time, anywhere."

"Great," Brower mutters faintly.

"Up to this point, Dave, we've won a few and lost a few—each of us. Each of us. Each of us. God damn it, everything Dave Brower does is O.K.—tonight. Dave, now that we've buried the hatchet, you've got to come out to my farm in the Shenandoah."

"Great."

To have a look at the map of the river, Dominy puts on Brower's glasses. Brower's glasses are No. 22s off the counter of F. W. Woolworth in San Francisco. Dominy rolls the scroll back to the Upset Rapid.

"How come you didn't go through there, Dave?"

"I'm chicken."

"Are you going to go through Lava Falls?"

"No."

"No?"

"No, thank you. I'll walk."

Upstream from where we sit, we can see about a mile of straight river between the high walls of the inner gorge, and downstream this corridor leads on to a bold stone portal. Dominy contemplates the scene. He says, "With Hualapai Dam, you'd really have a lake of water down this far."

"Yes. A hundred and sixty feet deep," notes Brower.

"It would be beautiful, and, like Lake Powell, it would be better for *all* elements of society."

"There's another view, and I have it, and I suppose I'll die with it, Floyd. Lake Powell is a drag strip for power boats. It's for people who won't do things except the easy way. The magic of Glen Canyon is dead. It has been vulgarized. Putting water in the Cathedral in the Desert was like urinating in the crypt of St. Peter's. I hope it never happens here."

"Look, Dave. I don't live in a God-damned apartment. I didn't grow up in a God-damned city. Don't give me the crap that you're the only man that understands these things. I'm a greater conservationist than you are, by far. I do things. I make things available to man. Unregulated, the Colorado River wouldn't be worth a good God damn to anybody. You conservationists are phony outdoorsmen. I'm sick and tired of a democracy that's run by a noisy minority. I'm fed up clear to my God-damned gullet. I had the guts to come out and fight you bastards. You're just a bunch of phonies and you'll stoop to any kind of God-damned argument. That's why I took my pictures. You were misleading the public about what would happen here. You gave the impression that the whole canyon was going to be inundated by the reservoir. Your weapon is emotion. You guys are just not very God-damned honorable in your fights."

"I had hoped things would not take this turn, Floyd, but you're wrong."

"Do you want to keep this country the way it is for a handful of people?"

"Yes, I do. Hualapai Dam is not a necessity. You don't even want the water."

"We mainly want the power head, but the dam would be part of the over-all storage project under the Colorado Compact."

"The Colorado Compact was not found on a tablet written on Mount Sinai. Hualapai Dam is not necessary, and neither was Glen Canyon. Glen Canyon Dam was built for the greater good of Los Angeles."

"You're too intelligent to believe that."

"You're too intelligent not to believe that."

"For Christ's sake, be objective, Dave. Be reasonable."

"Some of my colleagues make the error of trying to be reasonable, Floyd. Objectivity is the greatest threat to the United States today."

Mile 177, 9:45 A.M. The water is quite deep and serene here, backed up from the rapid. Lava Falls is two miles downstream, but we have long since entered its chamber of quiet.

"The calm before the storm," Brower says.

The walls of the canyon are black with lava—flows, cascades, and dikes of lava. Lava once poured into the canyon in this segment of the river. The river was here, much in its present form. It had long since excavated the canyon, for the volcanism occurred in relatively recent time. Lava came up through the riverbed, out from the canyon walls, and even down over the rims. It sent the Colorado up in clouds. It hardened, and it formed a dam and backed water two hundred miles.

"If a lava flow were to occur in the Grand Canyon today, Brower and the nature lovers would shout to high heaven that a great thing had happened," Dominy said, addressing everyone in the raft. "But if a man builds a dam to bring water and power to other men, it is called desecration. Am I right or wrong, Dave? Be honest."

"The lava dam of Quaternary time was eventually broken down by the river. This is what the Colorado will do to the Dominy dams that are in it now or are ever built. It will wipe them out, recover its grade, and go on about its business. But by then our civilization and several others will be long gone."

We drift past an enormous black megalith standing in the river. For eighty years, it was called the Niggerhead. It is the neck of a volcano, and it is now called Vulcan's Forge. We have a mile to go. Brower talks about the amazing size of the crystals on the canyon walls, the morning light in the canyon, the high palisades of columnar basalt. No one else says much of anything. All jokes have been cracked twice. We are just waiting, and the first thing we hear is the sound. It is a big, tympanic sound that increasingly fills the canyon. The water around us is dark-green glass. Five hundred yards. There it is. Lava Falls. It is, of course, a rapid, not a waterfall. There is no smooth lip. What we now see ahead of us at this distance appears to be a low white-washed wall.

The raft touches the riverbank. Sanderson gets out to inspect the rapid, and we go, too. We stand on a black ledge, in the roar of the torrent, and look at the water. It goes everywhere. From bank to bank, the river is filled with boulders, and the water smashes into them, sends up auroras of spray, curls thickly, and pounds straight down into bomb-crater holes. It eddies into pockets of lethal calm and it doubles back to hit itself. Its valleys are deeper and its hills are higher than in any other rapid in North America. The drop is prodigious—twenty-six feet in a hundred yards—but that is only half the story. Prospect Creek, rising black-walled like a coal chute across the river, has shoved enough rock in here to stop six rivers, and this has produced the preëminent rapid of the Colorado.

When Dominy stepped up on the ledge and into the immediacy of Lava Falls, he shouted above the thunder, "Boy, that's a son of a bitch! Look at those *rocks*! See that hole over there? Jesus! Look at that one!"

Brower said, "Look at the way the water swirls. It's alive!"

The phys.-ed. teacher said, "Boy, that could tear the hell out of your bod."

Brower said, "Few come, but thousands drown."

Dominy said, "If I were Jerry, I'd go to the left and then try to move to the right."

Lava protruded from the banks in jagged masses, particularly on the right, and there was a boulder there that looked like an axe blade. Brower said, "I'd go in on the right and out on the left."

My own view was that the river would make all the decisions. I asked Sanderson how he planned to approach what we saw there.

"There's only one way to do it," he said. "We go to the right."

The raft moved into the river slowly, and turned, and moved toward the low white wall. A hundred yards. Seventy-five yards. Fifty yards. It seems odd, but I did not notice until just then that Brower was on the raft. He was, in fact, beside me. His legs were braced, his hands were tight on a safety rope, and his Sierra Club cup was hooked in his belt. The tendons in his neck were taut. His chin was up. His eyes looked straight down the river. From a shirt pocket Dominy withdrew a cigar. He lighted it and took a voluminous drag. We had remaining about fifteen seconds of calm water. He said, "I might bite an inch off the end, but I doubt it." Then we went into Lava Falls.

Water welled up like a cushion against the big boulder on the right, and the raft went straight into it, but the pillow of crashing water was so thick that it acted on the raft like a great rubber fender between a wharf and a ship. We slid off the rock and to the left—into the craterscape. The raft bent like a V, flipped open, and shuddered forward. The little outboard—it represented all the choice we had—cavitated, and screamed in the air. Water rose up in tons through the bottom of the raft. It came in from the left, the right, and above. It felt great. It covered us, pounded us, lifted us, and heaved us scudding to the base of the rapid.

For a moment, we sat quietly in the calm, looking back. Then Brower said, "The foot of Lava Falls would be two hundred and twenty-five feet beneath the surface of Lake Dominy."

Dominy said nothing. He just sat there, drawing on a wet, dead cigar. Ten minutes later, however, in the dry and baking Arizona air, he struck a match and lighted the cigar again.

THE SURVIVAL OF THE BARK CANOE

To John Kauffmann

Contents

WHEN HENRI VAILLANCOURT goes off to the Maine woods, he does not make extensive plans. Plans annoy him. He just gets out his pack baskets, tosses in some food and gear, takes a canoe, and goes. He makes (in advance) his own beef jerky—slow-baking for many hours the leanest beef he can find. He takes some oatmeal, some honey, some peanut butter. Not being sure how long he will be gone, he makes only a guess at how much food he may need, although he is going into the Penobscot-Allagash wilderness, north of Moosehead Lake. He takes no utensils. He prefers to carve them. He makes his own tumplines, his own carry boards. He makes his own paddles. They have slender blades, no more than five inches across. He roughs them out with his axe and carves them with his crooked knife, a tool well known in the north woods, almost unknown everywhere else. And—his primary function—he makes his own canoes. He carves their thwarts from hardwood and their ribs from cedar. He sews them and lashes them with the split roots of white pine. There are no nails, screws, or rivets keeping his canoes together—just the root lashings, in groups spaced handsomely along the gunwales, holding the framework to the bark.

Vaillancourt built his first canoe in 1965, when he was fifteen. He had tried to make other canoes in earlier years, always working by trial and error, until error prevailed. He had never paddled a canoe, had not so much as had a ride in one. In a passionate way, he had become interested in Indian life, and the aspect of it that most attracted him was the means by which the Indians had moved so easily on lakes and streams through otherwise detentive forests. He wanted to feel—if only approximately—what that had been like. His desire to do so became a preoccupation. He has said that he would have settled gladly for a ride in a wood-and-canvas canoe, or even an aluminum or a Fiberglas canoe—any canoe at all. But no one he knew had one. His town—Greenville, in southern New Hampshire—was small and had suffered from closing mills and regional depression. Greenville had ponds but no canoes. So far as he could see, there was only one way to achieve his wish. If he wanted to ride in a canoe, he would have to make one, and from materials at hand. White birches were all through the woods around the town. After his first couple of failures, a cousin who had become aware of his compulsion sent him an old copy of *Sports Afield* in which an article described, without much detail, how the Indians had done it. Henri laid out a building bed, went out and cut bark and saplings, and began to grope his way into a technology that had evolved in the forest under anonymous hands and—as he would learn—was much too complex merely to be called ingenious. His standards were—where else?—in their nascent stages, and he made his ribs out of unsplit saplings. What came up off the bed, though, was a finished, symmetrical, classical canoe. He picked it up and took it to a pond. He is lyrical (uncharacteristically lyrical) in describing that moment in that day and the feel of the canoe's momentum and response. "The first canoe I ever got into was one of my own. I can launch the best ones now and they don't thrill me one-tenth as much. It was the glide, the feel of it, just the sound as it rustled over the lily pads."

He took the canoe home and, before long, destroyed it with an axe. "It was a piece of junk," he explains. "I didn't want it around to embarrass me. Pieces of it still crop up here, now and then, and they go into the stove." He had had his initial thrill, and it had felt good, but his standards had gone shooting skyward, and that first canoe would never do. He formed an ambition, which he still has, to make a perfect bark canoe, and he says he will not rest until he has done so. He says that some of his canoes may look perfect to other people but they don't to him, because he sees things other people cannot discern. He has built thirty-three birch-bark canoes. He is in his mid-twenties now, and—with the snowshoes and paddles he makes in winter—he does nothing else for a living. Three or four Indians in Canada are also professional makers of bark canoes, and one old white man in Minnesota. All the rest—the centuries of them—are dead. With a singleness of purpose that defeats distraction, Henri Vaillancourt has appointed himself the keeper of this art. He has visited almost all the other living bark-canoe makers, and he has learned certain things from the

Indians. He has returned home believing, though, that he is the most skillful of them all.

What he learned from the Indians was minor detail, such as using square pegs instead of round ones to secure his gunwale caps. His actual teacher (through the printed sketch and the printed word) was Edwin Tappan Adney, who died in the year that Vaillancourt was born. Without Adney, Vaillancourt might today be working in a plastics factory. Adney was an American who went to New Brunswick in the eighteen-eighties and built a bark canoe under the guidance of a Malecite. He was twenty, and he recorded everything the Malecite taught him. For the next six decades, he continued to collect data on the making and use of bark canoes. He compiled boxes and boxes of notes and sketches, and he made models of more than a hundred canoes, illustrating differing tribal styles, differences within tribes, and differences of design purpose. A short, low-ended canoe was the kindest to portage, and the best to paddle among the overhanging branches of a small stream. A canoe with a curving, rocker bottom could turn with quick response in white water. A canoe with a narrow bow and stern and a somewhat V-sided straight bottom could hold its course across a strong lake wind. A canoe with a narrow beam moved faster than any other and was therefore the choice for war. Adney so thoroughly dedicated himself to the preservation of knowledge of the bark canoe that he was still doing research, still getting ready to write the definitive book on the subject, when, having reached the age of eighty-one, he died. Over the next dozen years or so, Howard I. Chapelle, curator of transportation at the Smithsonian Institution, went through Adney's hills of paper and ultimately wrote the book, calling it *The Bark Canoes and Skin Boats of North America*. Large in format, it has two hundred and forty-two pages containing drawings, diagrams, photographs, and a text that frequently solidifies with technical density:

> When the bark has been turned up and clamped, the gores may be trimmed to allow it to be sewn with edge-to-edge seams at each slash. This is usually done after the sides are faired, by moving the battens up and down as the cuts are made, then replacing them in their original position. The gores or slashes, if overlapped, are not usually sewn at this stage of construction.

The U.S. Government Printing Office released the book in 1964, and Henri Vaillancourt first heard of it a couple of years later, when someone passing through town happened to mention it. He sent for a copy. The book enabled him, while still in his teens, to take a big step toward the perfection he was imagining when he hacked his first boat to pieces. His second completion was, in his words, "a very tolerable canoe."

He enrolled for a while in the forestry program at the University of New Hampshire, but in a sense Adney and Chapelle had already supplied him with his college, and the one in Durham interested him less than the one he could carry anywhere under his arm. So he went home to Greenville after his freshman year (1969) and began what in all likelihood will prove to be a life's career, since he appears to be interested in almost nothing else. Nothing much enters his time, his thought, or his conversation that does not have to do with the making and use of birch-bark canoes. He is unmarried and lives with his parents. He works in a small room that was his grandfather's shop—nine by fourteen feet—in a tarpapered shed that stands separate from the house. The shed is old, and light comes in at places other than the windows, but he has an iron stove with a chimney pipe that bends shy of the ceiling and makes a long horizontal trip through the room before penetrating to the outside. This rig is more than equal to the New Hampshire winter, and Vaillancourt, eight to twelve hours a day, sits below the long chimney in his shirtsleeves, feeding the stove, and stringing snowshoes or carving paddles or shaping the ribs, thwarts, and stempieces of the next summer's canoes. A picture on a wall shows hunters in a birch-bark canoe on Long Lake in the Adirondacks in 1880. Another is a Frederic Remington print of Chippewas in a canoe with high-swept ends, riding a big tail wind on the lakelike St. Lawrence. Stored on racks are long strips of split cedar, brought from Maine, which by spring will be resplit and split again to appropriate size, then tapered and finished with the crooked knife until they are ready to be lashed together as the gunwales of a started canoe. Vaillancourt, whittling, or rough-shaping wood with an axe, sits on a rocking chair over which is draped the hide of a deer. New paddles stand against the walls, and some are inlaid with deer bone, which looks like mother-of-pearl and is set in designs of eastern Canadian tribes. He bends hickory for his snowshoes, and he strings them—in a painstaking fineness of pattern—with rawhide that he scrapes and cuts. He is not a hunter, but there is no lack of hunters in Greenville, and they give him the skins he needs. He never uses power tools. He uses a froe, an axe, an awl, a crooked knife—and with the last three alone could build a canoe. The crooked knife is the finishing instrument, the tool whose ten thousand touches yield the artistry he seeks. One does not drive to a shopping center in search of a crooked knife. Tacked to the inside of the shed door is the address where Vaillancourt sends for his: Hudson's Bay Co., Pointe Claire, P.Q.

When the weather warms and the thaw is gone, Vaillancourt comes out of the shop and works in the yard. He has built a canvas-covered lean-to against a wall of the house, and under the lean-to he starts the canoes. After some weeks, he may have as many as four under construction, each in a different stage of the process. Music falls on him from a second-story window. He keeps his stereo up there, playing country-and-Western and Beethoven symphonies. Sometimes he becomes so absorbed in the music he makes mistakes on the canoes. He can build seven a year. Most are around sixteen feet long, and for that size he charges eight hundred and fifty dollars. Even after they are gone, he remains ferociously proprietary about them. He has made them for customers as far away as Idaho, but he seems to regard each canoe as his own forever, and his profoundest hope is that it will survive its owner and then be passed on to a museum. When he can, in his travels, he visits his canoes. This satisfies his longing to know how they are doing. He is pleased also to get one "back in the yard," so he can touch it up, repair it, perhaps even improve it in the light of his continually rising skills. He refers to "the yard" as someone else might refer to the Newport News Shipbuilding & Dry Dock Company.

"The yard" is on the edge of town. A state road runs close by, and a blinking light hangs overhead: the intersection of New Hampshire 31 and Mill Street, Greenville—population sixteen hundred, a mill town sitting on hillsides, divided by a stream. Since the mills folded, smaller businesses have been set up within their walls: plastics, apples, herbs. Three of

Vaillancourt's grandparents came from farms along the south bank of the St. Lawrence, in the Eastern Townships of Quebec. They came south for the money to be made in the mills, as did so many others, and not much about Greenville is English except its name. Stones in the cemetery say Rousseau, Blanchette, Bergeron, Fournier, Souliers, Chuinard, Bourgeois, Charrois, Desrosiers, McMillan, Beausoleil, Robichaud, Charbonneau, Baillargeon, Caron, Martin, Vaillancourt. French, as Henri grew up, was the language of the table at home, the language —although fading now—of the street. When Henri started school, French was used there. The change to English came soon after. Henri's mother and father (who works in a yarn mill in another town) refer to the people in surrounding towns, counties, and the rest of the United States as "*les Américains*." Henri's name, in French, is said the way it looks. In English, he is "Henry Vallenkort" to everyone in town.

A number of completely finished canoes might be strewn around the yard at any one time, for Vaillancourt is slow to ship them out, or if people are coming to get them he is in no hurry to notify them that the canoes are ready. He likes to keep his canoes awhile—use them some, test them out. Whatever the excuse may be, he does not like to let them go. Two were there when I first saw the yard. Their bark, smooth and taut, was of differing shades of brown, trellised with dark seams. I guess I had expected something a little rough, rippled, crude, asymmetrical. These things, to the eye, were perfect in their symmetry. Their color was pleasing. Turn them over—their ribs, thwarts, and planking suggested cabinetwork. Their authenticity seemed built in, sewed in, lashed in, undeniable. In the sunlight of that cold November morning, they were the two most beautiful canoes I had ever seen. All this—when what I had frankly feared encountering were outsize, erratic souvenirs.

I had spent a good part of my early summers in canoes and on canoe trips, and all the canoes I used in those years were made of wood and canvas. They were Old Towns and E. M. Whites—lake canoes, river canoes, keeled, and keel-less. The bark canoe was gone, but not as long gone as I then—in the nineteen-thirties and forties—imagined. Now, in the nineteen-seventies, wood-and-canvas canoes were gradually becoming extinct, or seemed to be. They were seen about as frequently on canoe trails as bark canoes apparently were fifty years ago. What had replaced the wood and canvas were new generations of aluminum, Fiberglas, and plastic—canoe simulacra that lacked resonance, moved without elegance, fairly lurched through the forest. Some of them—white streaked with black—were designed to suggest birch bark. The sport in white water—where runs are made against a stopwatch—had been taken over by small Fiberglas boats that were called canoes but looked like kayaks. And now here was Henri Vaillancourt, whom I had heard of through a note in a newsletter of the Canoe Cruisers Association, standing in his yard beside bark-covered canoes—in full-time resolve to preserve them in the world—shyly and with what I then took to be modesty answering a most obvious question. Oh, don't worry, they were quite strong, really strong. They could take quite a blow. The ribs and planking were flexible, the bark elastic and durable. All the wood in them had been split, none of it sawn. Split wood had more flexibility and more strength. If you hit a rock with sawn wood in your canoe you were more likely to crack the ribs and the planking. He cocked his arm and drove his fist into the bottom of one of the canoes with a punch that could have damaged a prizefighter. He is six feet tall and weighs a hundred and seventy-five pounds. The bottom of the canoe was unaffected. He remarked that the bark of the white birch was amazing stuff—strong, resinous, and waterproof. He said there was, in fact, virtually nothing the Indian canoe-makers did that was not as good as or better than what could be done with modern tools and materials.

His shyness was in his eyes—looking away, almost always, from the direction in which his voice was travelling—but not in his speech. He talked volubly, with nasal, staccato inflections, and if the subject was bark canoes he seemed in no hurry to stop. I stayed around the yard for a couple of days, and before I left we took one of the canoes and—as Vaillancourt likes to put it—"went for a spin" on a local pond. After paddling half a mile or so over rustling lily pads and open water, we rounded a point at one end of an island and Vaillancourt warned that the pond was shallow there and we might hit a rock. Crunch. We hit one. The canoe glanced off. It was moving fast—slicing, planing the water with much momentum and glide. Crunch. "Look out! There could be more!" Crunch.

The canoe moved on—dry, sound in the ribs. When we landed, we turned it over. On the bark, a couple of marks were visible of the sort that a fingernail might make on a piece of hide. "We hit a stump head on once, in Maine," he said. "And the stump, you know, split in two." He was happy enough, though, to have people go on thinking—as people apparently did—that bark canoes were fragile. Any canoe could be damaged, and the general welfare of bark canoes might be helped by this common misconception. Bark canoes were actually so strong and flexible that Indians had used them not only in heavy rapids but also on the ocean. "But they're so rare today, you know, I wouldn't sell them to people who do white water. It's not the canoes I don't trust. I fully trust the canoes to go down white water. I don't trust the people who are paddling them. Bark canoes are so rare. There's no sense in wrecking even one."

IN THE MIDDLE of one morning, Vaillancourt left the shop, got into his car, drove two or three miles down the road, and went into woods to cut a birch. The weather was sharp, and he was wearing a heavy red Hudson's Bay coat. His sandy-brown hair, curling out in back, rested on the collar. He carried a sheathed Hudson's Bay axe and a long wooden wedge and a wooden club (he called it a mallet) of the type seen in cartoons about cave societies. His eyes—they were pale blue, around an aquiline nose over a trapper's mustache—searched the woodlot for a proper tree. It need not be a giant. There were no giants around Greenville anyway. He wanted it for its sapwood, not its bark—for thwarts (also called crosspieces and crossbars) in a future canoe. After walking several hundred feet in from the road, he found a birch about eight inches in diameter, and with the axe he notched it in the direction of a free fall. He removed his coat and carefully set it aside. Beneath it was a blue oxford-cloth button-down shirt, tucked into his blue-jeans. He chopped the tree, and it fell into a young beech. "Jesus Christ!" he said. "It is so frustrating when Nature has you beat." The birch was hung up in the beech. He heaved at it and hauled it until it at last came free.

What he wanted of the tree was about six feet of its trunk, which he cut away from the rest. Then he sank the axe into one end of the piece, removed the axe, placed the wedge in the cut, and tapped the wedge with the mallet. He tapped twice more, and the entire log fell apart in two even halves. He said, "You get some birch, it's a bastard to split out, I'll tell you. But, Christ, this is nice. That's good and straight grain. Very often you get them twisted." Satisfied, he shouldered the tools and the wood, went back to the road, and drove home.

In the yard, he split the birch again, and he now had four pieces, quarter-round. One of these he cut off to a length of about forty inches. He took that into the shed. He built a fire, and in minutes the room was warm. He sat in his rocking chair and addressed the axe to the quarter-round log—the dark heartwood, the white sapwood. Holding the piece vertically, one end resting on the floor, he cut the heartwood away. He removed the bark and then went rapidly down the sapwood making angled indentations that caused the wood to curve out like petals. He cut them off, and they fell as big chips to the floor. A pile began to grow there as the axe head moved up and down, and what had been by appearance firewood was in a short time converted to lumber—a two-by-three, knotless board that might almost have been sawn in a mill.

He then picked up his crooked knife and held its grip in his upturned right hand, the blade poking out to the left. The blade was bent near its outer end (enabling it to move in grooves and hollows where the straight part could not). Both blade and grip were shaped like nothing I had ever seen. The grip, fashioned for the convenience of a hand closing over it, was bulbous. The blade had no hinge and protruded rigidly—but not straight out. It formed a shallow V with the grip.

Vaillancourt held the piece of birch like a violin, sighting along it from his shoulder, and began to carve, bringing the knife upward, toward his chest. Of all the pieces of a canoe, the center thwart is the most complicated in the carving. Looked at from above, it should be broad at the midway point, then taper gradually as it reaches toward the sides of the canoe. Near its ends, it flares out in shoulders that are penetrated by holes, for lashings that will help secure it to the gunwales. The long taper, moreover, is interrupted by two grooved protrusions, where a tumpline can be tied before a portage. The whole upper surface should be flat, but the underside of the thwart rises slightly from the middle outward, then drops again at the ends, the result being that the thwart is thickest in the middle, gradually thinning as it extends outward and thickening again at the gunwales. All of this comes, in the end, to an adroit ratio between strength and weight, not to mention the incidental grace of the thing, each of its features being a mirror image of another. The canoe's central structural element, it is among the first parts set in place. Its long dimension establishes the canoe's width, and therefore many of the essentials of the canoe's design. In portage, nearly all of the weight of the canoe bears upon it.

So to me the making of a center thwart seemed a job for a jigsaw, a band saw, a set of chisels, a hammer, a block plane, a grooving plane, calipers, templates, and—most of all—mechanical drawings. One would have thought that anyone assertive enough to try it with a knife alone would at least begin slowly, moving into the wood with caution. Vaillancourt, to the contrary, tore his way in. He brought the knife toward him with such strong, fast, heavy strokes that long splinters flew off the board. "Birch is good stuff to work with," he said. "It's almost as easy to work as cedar. This feels like a hot knife going through butter. I used to use a drawknife. That God-damned thing. You've got to use a vise to hold the work. With the crooked knife, I can work in the woods if I want. I saw an Indian on TV in Canada using one. I got one, and I worked and worked with it to get the knack. Now it almost feels as if it's part of me. If anybody ever comes out with a tool that will rival a crooked knife, I'd like to hear about it." He sighted along the wood, turned it over, and began whipping splinters off the other side. He said that steel tools had come with the white man, of course, and that most people seemed to imagine that Indian workmanship had improved with steel tools. "But I doubt it," he continued. "With bone and stone tools, it just took longer. The early Indians relied more on abrasion. With the exception of the center thwart, there is no fancy carving in a canoe. It's all flatwork. In fact, I'm doing experiments with bone tools." He stopped carving, reached to a shelf, and picked up a bone awl. "Make two holes with a bone awl in a piece of cedar, take out the wood between the holes with a bone chisel, and you have a mortise for a thwart to fit into." He reached for a piece of cedar (wood debris was all over the shop), made two holes, picked up a wooden mallet and a bone chisel, and made a mortise in the cedar. Then he picked up the long, curving incisor of a beaver. "I made a knife last winter out of a beaver's tooth," he said. "The original crooked knife was made out of a beaver's tooth." He sat down and continued to carve. The strokes were lighter now as he studied the wood, carved a bit, studied the wood, and carved some more. The piece was beginning to look roughly like a thwart, and the gentler motions of the knife were yielding thin, curling shavings that settled down on the bed of chips and splinters around his feet.

"Where the crooked knife was, the bark canoe was," he said. "People from Maine recognize the crooked knife. People from

New Hampshire do not. All they knew was the drawknife. The God-damned drawknife—what a bummer."

The bark canoe was also where the big white birches were, and that excluded a good part of New Hampshire, including Greenville. Vaillancourt goes north to find his bark. The range of the tree—*Betula papyrifera*, variously called the white birch, the silver birch, the paper birch, the canoe birch—forms a swath more than a thousand miles wide (more or less from New York City to Hudson Bay) and reaches westward and northwestward to the Pacific. Far in from the boundaries of this enormous area, though, the trees are unlikely and always have been unlikely to grow large enough for the building of good canoes, and this exclusion includes most of the West, and even the Middle West. The biggest trees and the best of Indian canoes were in what are now New Brunswick, Nova Scotia, Maine, Quebec, and parts of Ontario. Even within this region, the most accomplished craftsmen were concentrated in the east. Of these, the best were the Malecites. So Henri Vaillancourt builds Malecite canoes. Before all other design factors, he cares most about the artistic appearance of the canoes he builds, and he thinks the best-looking were the canoes of the Malecites. The Malecites lived in New Brunswick and parts of Maine. Vaillancourt builds the Malecite St. John River Canoe and the Malecite St. Lawrence River Canoe. He builds them with modifications, though. Toward the end of the nineteenth century, tribes started copying one another and gave up some of the distinctiveness of their tribal styles, and to varying extents, he said, he has done the same.

His carving became even slower now, and he studied the piece carefully before making his moves, but he measured nothing. "There's really no need for feet and inches," he said. "I know more or less what's strong and what isn't. If I want to find the middle of this crosspiece, I can put a piece of bark across it from end to end, and then fold it in half to find the center." He had measured the length—thirty-five inches—and had cut to it exactly. In the spring, when the time came to make the gunwales, he would measure them as well. But that is all he would measure in the entire canoe. According to the prescript passed on by Adney and Chapelle, the center thwart he was working on should taper

> slightly in thickness each way from its center to within 5 inches of the shoulders, which are 30 inches apart. The thickness at a point 5 inches from the shoulder is ¾ inch; from there the taper is quick to the shoulder, which is ⁵⁄₁₆ inch thick, with a drop to ¼ inch in the tenon. The width, 3 inches at the center, decreases in a graceful curve to within 5 inches of the shoulder, where it is 2 inches, then increases to about 3 inches at the shoulder. The width of the tenon is, of course, 2 inches, to fit the mortise hole in the gunwale.

Yet the only instruments Vaillancourt was using to meet these specifications were his eyes.

He finished off the tumpline grooves. The thwart appeared to be perfect, but he picked up a piece of broken glass and scraped it gently all over. Fine excelsior came away, and the surface became shiningly smooth. It was noon. He had cut the birch in the woods at half past nine. Now he held the thwart in his hand, turning it this way and that. It was a lovely thing in itself, I thought, for it had so many blendings of symmetry. He said he could have done it in an hour if he had not been talking so much. And he was glad the tree in the woods had turned into this thwart instead of "all the chintzy two-bit things they make out of birch—clothespins, dowels, toothpicks, Popsicle sticks." As he worked, he had from time to time scooped up handfuls of chips and shavings and fed them into the stove. Even so, the pile was still high around him, and he appeared to be sitting in a cone of snow.

He soon added more to the pile. From the rafters he took down a piece of cedar and, with the knife, sent great strips of it flying to the floor. He was now making a stempiece, the canoe part that establishes the profile of the bow or the stern. "Sometimes, when there are, you know, contortions in the grain, you can get into a real rat's nest," he said. "Around a knot, there will be waves in the grain. You cut to the knot from one side, then the other, to get a straight edge. At times like that, I'm tempted just to throw the thing out."

The wood he was working now, though, was clear and without complications, and after a short while, in which most of it went to the floor, he had made something that looked very much like a yardstick—albeit a heavy one—a half inch thick. Its corners were all sharp, and it seemed to have been machine-planed. Then he pressed the blade of the crooked knife into one end of the stick and kept pressing just hard enough to split the stick down fifty per cent of its length. He pressed the knife into the end again, near the first cut, and made another split, also stopping halfway. Again and again he split the wood, going far beyond the moment when I, watching him, thought that further splitting would be impossible, would ruin the whole. He split the board thirty-one times—into laminations each a half inch wide and a sixteenth of an inch thick. And all the laminations stopped in the middle, still attached there; from there on, the wood remained solid. "You split cedar parallel to the bark," he commented. "Hickory you can split both ways. There are very few woods you can do that with."

He plunged the laminated end of the piece into a bucket of water and left it there for a while, and then he built up the fire with scraps from the floor. In a coffee can he brought water to a boil. He poured it slowly over the laminations, bathing them, bathing them again. Then he lifted the steaming cedar in two hands and bent it. The laminations slid upon one another and formed a curve. He pondered the curve. It was not enough of a curve, he decided. So he bent the piece a little more. "There's an awful lot of it that's just whim," he said. "You vary the stempiece by whim." He liked what he saw now, so he reached for a strip of basswood bark, tightly wound it around the curve in the cedar, and tied it off. The basswood bark was not temporary. It would stay there, and go into the canoe. Bow or stern, the straight and solid part of the stempiece would run downward from the tip, then the laminated curve would sweep inward, establishing the character of the end—and thus, in large part, of the canoe itself.

The canoe-end profile was the principal feature that distinguished the styles of the tribes. The Ojibway Long-Nose Canoe, for example, had in its bow (and stern) an outreaching curve of considerable tumblehome (an arc—like a parenthesis—that turns more than ninety degrees and begins to come back on itself). The end profiles of the Algonquin Hunter's Canoe were straight and almost vertical, with a small-radius ninety-degree curve at the waterline. The departure from the vertical was inward, toward the paddler. The end profiles of certain Malecite canoes were similar, but the departure from vertical was outward. Other Malecite canoes had long-radius, "compass sweep" bows and sterns.

I mentioned to Vaillancourt that, before and during college years, I had spent a lot of time around a place in Vermont that still specializes in sending out canoe trips, and a birch-bark canoe hangs in the dining hall there.

"Near Salisbury," he said. "Lake Dunmore—am I right?" He took down a worn, filled notebook and began to whip the pages. "Let's see. Yeah. Here. Keewaydin. Is that it?"

That was it. He had not been there, but he would stop by someday. He hoped to see every bark canoe in existence. There were, for example, sixteen bark canoes in Haliburton, Ontario; one in Upper Canada Village, near Morrisburg, Ontario; a couple at Old Jesuit House, in Sillery, Quebec. In his notebook he had the names and addresses of museums, historical societies, and individuals from Maine to Minnesota, Nova Scotia to Alberta, and as far south as Virginia. Peter Paul, a Malecite in Woodstock, New Brunswick, had one. Vaillancourt had been to see him. The most skillfully built birch-bark canoe he had ever seen was made in Old Town, Maine, and was signed "Louis P. Sock." "I've seen only two or three canoes that were near perfect," he said. "But I've never seen a bark canoe that wasn't graceful. I've never seen an Eastern Cree canoe or a Montagnais. Most of the canoes I've seen did not have a definite tribal style. There's a bark canoe on Prince Edward Island. A sign says it's a Micmac canoe. It isn't."

I told him I'd long ago been told that the bark canoe at Keewaydin was an Iroquois.

He said he doubted that very much, because the Iroquois, except in early times, had had limited access to good birch, and had made their canoes—when they made canoes at all—out of elm or hickory bark. Various tribes had also used the bark of the spruce, the basswood, the chestnut. But all were crude compared to birch. If they wanted to get across a river, they might—in one day—build an elm-bark canoe, and then forget it, leave it in the woods. "You couldn't, by any stretch of the imagination, compare an elm-bark or a hickory-bark canoe to a birch canoe," he said. "Barks other than birch bark will absorb water the way wood will. Canoes made from them—even well made—got waterlogged and heavy. Most were just, you know, rough shells. Good for nothing, like automobiles. Automobiles last, you know, five or six years. A birch-bark canoe lasted the Indians ten."

I asked him how much experience he had had by now in more modern canoes. He said he had been in an aluminum canoe twice and in wood-and-canvas canoes only a few times in his life. Otherwise, he had never paddled anything but a birch-bark canoe. He did not paddle much around home, he said, because when he went canoeing he wanted to go to Maine.

"Where in Maine?"

"Oh, up north of Moosehead Lake. The Penobscot River. Chesuncook Lake. Caucomgomoc Lake. It's not just to get out in the canoe—it's to get out and see wildlife. A moose, you know, thirty feet away. Next time I go, I'm going down the Penobscot and on to the Allagash lakes."

I said, "Next time you go, I'd like to go with you."

He said, "Bring your own food."

I had been yearning to make a trip into that region for what was now most of my life. Keewaydin had run trips there, but one circumstance or another had always prevented me from going. Just the thought of making a journey there in a birch-bark canoe was enough to make me sway like a drunk. I thought of little else through the winter and the spring.

IT IS FIVE-FIFTEEN in the morning, August 12th, and Henri is up splitting cedar. The lake is smooth. The far shore is indistinct in rising mist. A loon, attracted to the sound of the axe, cruises near. When the axe stops, the loon laughs. Two tents. Two canoes—resting on their sides. The firewood, which is driftwood, is so dry that the fire is almost as quiet as the sun, which is still too low to cut through the mist. The air is cold.

Henri is splitting out pieces eighteen feet long. He cut the tree green two years ago and left it in the woods here—seven miles from the roadhead—to season. Now he has begun this trip by coming to retrieve the cedar, to carry it out the seven miles across the gunwales of his canoe. The split strips, which themselves will become gunwales in months ahead, will ride more stably than would a solid log.

There are five of us. The Blanchette brothers—Rick and Mike, friends of Henri's from Greenville—are eating oatmeal for breakfast. Warren Elmer and I have tea and dried fruit. Warren and I are from the same town in New Jersey. He is a teacher of environmental studies at Washington International School. He is a backpacker by choice and experience, and this is his first long canoe trip.

Henri, finished with his work, opens a paper bag and eats jerky. That is his breakfast. Last night, he ate jerky for dinner. The Blanchettes have their food. Warren and I have ours. Henri has his. He insists on this arrangement. He says that on one canoe trip he made he tried eating the communal way but "that was a real bummer; someone always ate all the food," and he will never do it again.

The Blanchettes' tent is small, low, nylon. It weighs three and a half pounds, and somewhat bulgingly sleeps two. They own a larger one, but Henri insisted that they leave it home, to eliminate the extra weight. The other tent is mine, sleeps three, and is a pavilion you can stand up in. Henri, when he first saw it, said not to bring it, that it was too heavy, and too bulky.

In the yard in Greenville, we had a general weed-out of equipment. The back of my car was full of stuff, and Henri looked it over. I showed him my candle-powered folding lantern.

"Forget it," he said. "You don't need it. You can get around, you know, about as well in the dark as you can in the daylight."

"How about just a candle or two?"

"They're not necessary."

I showed him my reflector baker.

"Hang it up," he said.

How about Warren's gas-powered emergency trail stove?

"Forget it."

My white-water paddle?

"If we need a spare, I can make one."

My fishing rod?

"Forget it. Who wants to carry, you know, all that junk on a portage?"

I showed him the tent. Rolled up, it was a cylinder eight inches in diameter and four feet long. It weighed eighteen pounds.

"Hang it up," he said. "The idea is to travel light."

How much equipment goes on a canoe trip is a reflection of the criteria that go along as well. Young Indians of the Maine woods, several centuries ago, went off alone for upward of a year—to prove their skills and their ability to survive. They took a canoe, a spear, some bone tools, a crooked knife, snowshoes, and a blanket. Today, if someone's criterion is to play at being an Indian, that is how to do it. Henri knew too much about the Indians to pretend to be one. He was a craftsman—an artist, really—with a historical purpose, not a boy with a feather in his hair. His professed criteria were to take it easy, see some wildlife, and travel light with his bark canoes—nothing more—and one could not help but lean his way. I had known of people who took collapsible cots, down pillows, chain saws, outboard motors, cases of beer, and battery-powered portable refrigerators on canoe trips—even into deep wilderness. You set your own standards. Travel by canoe is not a necessity, and will nevermore be the most efficient way to get from one region to another, or even from one lake to another—anywhere. A canoe trip has become simply a rite of oneness with certain terrain, a diversion of the field, an act performed not because it is necessary but because there is value in the act itself; and what you take along depends on what you can afford (Henri could not afford to buy beef jerky, so he had to make it) and on how you see yourself in the setting.

Indians slept in pairs under their canoes—feet touching in the center, heads toward the ends. Henri had tried sleeping under a canoe once, too, but would never try it again. Ultimately, he changed his mind and decided that it would be a good idea to take my tent after all, because he could fit into it with Warren and me. I needed the reflector baker. Much of the food I had brought depended on its use. So I stowed it where he wouldn't see it. Deep in my pack basket I had a small flashlight. I decided not to tell Henri it was there.

I unrolled a set of topographic maps I had bought, and asked him to show us our route. He said he had no idea what the route would be and didn't care to think about it. We would leave a car at each of two roadheads—one at North East Carry, the other at Caucomgomoc Lake—but the trip we made between these two points would not be direct and would not be pressured by a plan. There would be no big rush. There was no point in rushing. Travel light. Take it easy. See the wildlife. I rolled up the maps.

Rick Blanchette was bringing his own canoe—one of the early ones that Vaillancourt had made. Henri, for himself, had selected a small one from the inventory then in the yard. It was narrow of beam, nine inches deep, and only thirteen and a half feet long. It was particularly attractive—covered almost wholly with a single sheet of bark—and it was light to carry. Rick Blanchette was worried, though, that the canoe was too small to bear two men and their gear, so Henri took it to the pond to try it out. With a single paddler in it, and no gear, it was a poised and responsive canoe, but with three of us in it—aggregating five hundred pounds—it showed too much instability and very nearly ate the pond. Henri decided to leave it home. He chose a longer canoe instead—a canoe he had made for Idaho State University and would crate for shipment in a moon or two. He put it on sawhorses, right side up, and poured into it a couple of buckets of water. Almost none dripped through.

Our packs, in final form, pleased Henri, and he said so. The Blanchettes each had a pack frame. Warren and I each had a pack basket. Henri stuffed his personal food and gear into two pack baskets, tied the canoes to my car and his, and in early morning we started north. He led the way, and we drove ten hours without stopping for food.

Between Rockwood, Maine (about halfway up Moosehead Lake), and Allagash, Maine (at the confluence of the Allagash and St. John Rivers), there is an area of about five thousand square miles in which is neither a paved nor a public road. What few roads there are "north of the Moosehead" have dirt-and-gravel surfaces and are travelled by the public, at the public's risk, courtesy of the paper companies that own the land. We drove the last hour into the woods on these roads, and put the canoes into the West Branch of the Penobscot River at six in the evening. The current was strong but unbroken, flowing between walls of spruce. Swiftly moving, loaded, the canoes looked superb—their duffel, compactly secured, implying days and distances of travel, implying less an excursion than a *modus vivendi*. Henri and Warren were one crew, the Blanchettes and I the other. Warren, as he paddled, looked Norse, his billowing beard projecting downriver under a tumult of blond hair. Our canoe, all things included, had between six and seven hundred pounds in it. Rick Blanchette—slight, not particularly tall, dark hair, a modest mustache—looked weightless, but his brother, well over six feet and athletically built, seemed to make up the difference. The total poundage in Henri's canoe was around four hundred and fifty. It was the shorter of the two—about fifteen and a half feet—and it had a low freeboard. In the center, three inches separated the top of the gunwale from the surface of the river. The canoe's interior depth was only ten and a half inches. It glided, though, with momentum and balance. Our canoe was nearly a foot deep, from center thwart to ribs, and it was sixteen feet long. It bore its heavier load with a higher freeboard and moved well under the paddles. Each paddle was decorated with incised line pictures of moose or with various Indian vine-and-leaf designs, and each was signed on its grip "H.A.V."—Henri Armand Vaillancourt.

Each canoe had a fleur-de-lis on its stern, and Blanchette's had as well a complex abstract design done in porcupine quills. After French priests converted the Malecites, fish designs began appearing on Malecite canoes that were launched on Fridays. On some Malecite canoes, a lynx would be drawn on one side and on the other a rabbit smoking a pipe. The rabbit symbolized the tribe. The lynx was the rabbit's mortal enemy. That the rabbit could calmly smoke a pipe so near the lynx showed the cool of the Malecite in the presence of enemies. These pictures were generally created by scraping away rind from the bark. And that is how Vaillancourt had made the fleurs-de-lis on his canoe. The bark of a birch-bark canoe is always inside out. The side that touched the wood of the tree is the side that touches the river. Rind clings only to bark that is taken in winter. There was a practical function in the designs the Indians scraped into it. The designs were a way to indicate the bow or the stern. Birch-bark canoes are not—like their progeny—reversible, because where one piece of bark is sewn to another there is a slight overlap, and the overlap faces the stern, so the seams will not be torn open when the canoe scrapes over a rock.

The evening was cool, and there was much laughing and joking as we moved along. After half an hour, we checked the canoes for leaks. They were all but completely dry.

"I have a small leak in back here," Rick said.

"*C'est dommage*," said Henri.

We turned into a small tributary. The lake where Henri had hidden the cedar was less than two miles upstream.

The sky after dark was as clear as a lens. There was no moon. We stood on the shore, tilted back our heads, looked up past the branches of the jack pines, and watched for shooting stars. One after another they came, at intervals too short to require patience. All the stars in the canopy seemed closer. We were so far out into the clear. There is more to Maine than exists in the imagination. Henri's house in New Hampshire is a lot closer to New York City than it is to this lakeshore in Maine. Maine is half of New England. It is as large as New Hampshire, Vermont, Connecticut, Rhode Island, and Massachusetts put together. And most of Maine is in the north woods, reaching embarrassingly far into Canada. Our trip would move in a northerly direction, and we had scarcely begun it, yet the lake we were camped by was a good bit north of Montreal. A shooting star burst with almost frightening brightness, illuminating our faces, lighting the sky like a flare. A loon wailed, long and mournfully. We stayed up late—to ten-thirty—too pleased with Maine to go to sleep.

We had hoped to see a moose even by now, but none has yet appeared in lake, stream, or river. Meanwhile, the loon will do. He is out there cruising still, in the spiralling morning mist, looking for fish, trolling. He trolls with his eyes. Water streams across his forehead as he moves along, and he holds his eyes just below the surface, watching the interior of the lake. He is gone. He saw something, and he is no doubt eating it now. When he dives, he just disappears. As a diver, there is nothing like him. Not even mergansers can dive like the loon. His wings close tight around his body, condensing everything—feathers, flesh—and he goes down like a powered stone, his big feet driving. He is known as the great northern diver. He can go two hundred feet down. He can swim faster than most fish. What he catches he eats without delay. His bill is always empty when he returns to the surface, and fifteen fish might be in his stomach. Because loons eat trout and young salmon, sportsmen (so-called) have been wont to shoot them—a mistaken act in any respect, because loons eat as well the natural enemies (suckers, for example) of salmon and trout.

He is up again now, not far from where he disappeared. When a loon dives, you never know where to look for him next. In what seems no time, he may break the surface far down the lake, or he may come up where he made his dive. This one is not about to go far. He is too interested in us. He cruises now with only his head and neck above the water—his conning tower. If something scares him, he can swim with only his beak out, a straw in the air—invisible if there's a ripple on the lake. Now his body is up again, and he laughs. If the laugh were human, it would be a laugh of the deeply insane. The bird's lower jaw opens and claps shut five times in each laugh. If, from where you watch, he is swimming in silhouette, you can count the movements of the jaw. He can laugh two or three ways, and he can also squeal like a puppy. But it is with another sound—a long cry in the still of the night—that the loon authenticates the northern lake. The cry is made with the neck stretched forward, and it is a sound that seems to have come up a tube from an unimaginably deep source—hardly from a floating bird. It is a high, resonant, single unvaried tone that fades at the end toward a lower register. It has caused panic, because it has been mistaken for the cry of a wolf, but it is far too ghostly for that. It is detached from the earth. The Crees believed that it was the cry of a dead warrior forbidden entry to Heaven. The Chipewyans heard it as an augury of death. Whatever it may portend, it is the predominant sound in this country. Every time the loon cry comes, it sketches its own surroundings—a remote lake under stars so bright they whiten clouds, a horizon jagged with spruce.

The loon here is laughing again, so I laugh back. He laughs. I laugh. He laughs. I laugh. He will keep it up until I am hoarse. He likes conversation. He talks this way with other loons. I am endeavoring to tell him that he is a hopeless degenerate killer of trout. He laughs.

His flesh is tough. The Indians boiled him until he fell apart in shreds. He looks like a big duck, a small goose. His back, in summer, is a tessellation of white squares and dots on a black field. His head is black and forest green, and so is his neck, which is surrounded with vertical white stripes. His eyes are red. In the air, he could be part flamingo—long neck extended, feet behind, back humped. His maximum airspeed is sixty miles an hour, and his stall-out speed must be fifty-nine. Anyway, he scarcely slows up, apparently because he thinks he will fall. He lands on his stomach (not feet first, like a duck), and at sixty miles an hour his landing is something to see. Ashore, he flops helplessly, vulnerably. His nest is a foot or two from water. Takeoff is a considerable problem for him. With, say, ten fish in him, he needs a runway at least a quarter of a mile long. He runs over the surface of the lake on his big feet and beats the water with his wings. Heavily, he goes into the air. With fifteen fish in him, he has no chance whatsoever. For takeoff, he needs, as well, a breeze to head into—sometimes a pretty stiff one. From a calm lake—even if he has an empty stomach—he cannot fly.

He sleeps on the water. *St. Nicholas* magazine, in 1910, told a story of a man—a white man, a summer camper—who in early morning paddled across a northern lake, silently approached a sleeping loon, and captured it with his hands. The article was illustrated, and showed the man reaching for the loon—from a bark canoe.

THE DAYS ARE hot, and we often dip our cups in the river. Henri prefers Tang. He has the powder in his pack and a plastic jug by his feet as he paddles. He also has a supply of white bread—several loaves of it—and when he is hungry he pours honey onto the bread. In five minutes, he can prepare and finish a meal. Then he is ready to move on. We are in no hurry, like the shooting stars.

The river has many riffles, too minor to be labelled rapids. Nonetheless, they are stuffed with rock. The angle of the light is not always favorable. The rocks are hidden, and—smash—full tilt we hit them. The rocks make indentations that move along the bottom of the canoe, pressing in several inches and tracing a path toward the stern. It is as if the canoe were a pliant film sliding over the boulders. Still, I feel sorry and guilty when we hit one. I have been in white water and Rick has not, so he has asked me to paddle in the stern—to steer, to pick the route, to read the river—and I reward his confidence by smashing into another rock. Nothing cracks. If this were an aluminum canoe, it would be dented now, and, I must confess, I would not really care. Of all the differences between this canoe and others I have travelled in, the first difference is a matter of care about them. The canoes can take a lot more abuse than we give them, but we all care. Landing, we are out of the canoes and in the water ourselves long before the bark can touch bottom. We load and launch in a foot of water. The Indians did just that, and the inclination to copy them is automatic—is not consciously remembered—with these Indian canoes.

Once, on the upper Delaware, in a fifteen-foot rented Grumman canoe, I ran through a pitch of white water called Skinner's Falls. On a big shelf of rock at the bottom of the rapid, a crowd of people watched. When the canoe came through dry, they gathered around and asked how that was done. They said they were novices—a ski club on a summer outing—and none of them had been able to run the rapid without taking in quantities of water. "Well," said my wife, getting out of our canoe, "if you think you've seen anything yet, just wait until you see what is going to happen now. My husband spent his whole childhood doing this sort of thing—and so did that man up there in the other canoe. The two of them are now going to run the rapid together."

I walked up the riverbank. When I joined my friend and got into his canoe (also a fifteen-foot aluminum), I saw that one of the skiers had set up a tripod on which was mounted a sixteen-millimetre movie camera. My wife later told me she had said to them that it was good that they had the camera, because they would be able to study the film and learn a great deal. Skinner's Falls is easiest on the right. It gets worse and worse the farther to the left you go. So, for the rash hell of it, we dug in hard, got up to high speed, and went into the extreme left side of the rapid. The canoe bucked twice before the bow caught a rock that swung us broadside to the current and into a protruding boulder with a crash that threw us into the white river and bent the canoe into the shape of the letter C.

I have chosen not to tell that story to Rick Blanchette, for no one has ever cared more for a fifteen-thousand-dollar sports car (or, for that matter, for a work of sculpture) than he cares for his birch canoe.

Henri hits a rock; slides right; hits another. "I'd venture to say it would be easier to rip a wood-and-canvas canoe than a birchbark," he says. "Anyhow, I've never, you know, ripped one." Henri paddles like an Indian. His stroke is a short, light, rapid chop. White people tend to take longer, harder strokes, which use a great deal more energy, he says. He appears relaxed in the stern of his canoe—leaning back, looking for wildlife, his paddle in motion like a wire whisk. Warren, in the bow, digs a large hole in the river with every stroke, contributing to the over-all effort the higher part of the ratio of power. We kneel, of course, and lean against the thwarts. There are no seats in these canoes. Kneeling is the natural paddling position anyway. It lowers the center of gravity, adds to the canoe's stability, brings more of the body into the stroke. Arms don't ache. You don't get tired.

We are seeing only ducks and muskrats on the big river, so we go into small streams in search of moose. These tributaries, tortuous and boggy, have all the appearance of moose country—Pine Stream, Moosehorn Stream. Moose tracks are everywhere—great cloven depressions in the mudbanks.

Paddling silently, we move upstream—half, three-quarters of a mile. No moose. Henri is good at the silent paddle—the blade feathered on the recovery from each stroke and never coming out of the water. However, he is having difficulty travelling in the channel. The stream is only a few yards wide and has many bends. The canoes keep hitting the banks and sticking in the mud. With some trepidation, I suggest that there are bow strokes—draw, cross-draw, draw-stroke, pry, cross-pry—intended to help the canoe avoid the banks of the river. Trepidation because it is astonishing how people sometimes resent being told how to paddle a canoe. I have paddled on narrow, twisting rivers in New Jersey with good friends—easygoing, even-tempered people—who got royally incensed when I suggested that if they would only learn to draw and cross-draw they would not continue to plow the riverbanks. The look in their eyes showed a sense of insult, resting on the implication that every human being is born knowing how to use a canoe. The canoe itself apparently inspires such attitudes, because in form it is the most beautifully simple of all vehicles. And the born paddlers keep hitting the banks of the rivers. Mike Blanchette, though, in the bow of our canoe, to my relief, is not offended. Nor is Warren. They quickly pick up the knack of the pry and the draw—ways of moving the bow suddenly to left or right. Henri shows interest, too, inadvertently revealing that he knows almost nothing about paddling in the bow. His interest is genuine but academic. The bow is the subordinate position in a canoe. The person in the stern sets the course, is the pilot, the captain. The Blanchettes and I regularly change positions in our canoe, but Henri never leaves the stern.

Eventually, we give up the mooselook and go back to the main stream. Henri says it is all but impossible to go down the West Branch of the Penobscot River from North East Carry to Chesuncook Lake without seeing a number of—not to mention one—moose. Deriding us, a screaming seagull flies high above the river. We are two hundred river miles from the sea. Some substitute. In lieu of a moose, a seagull.

The Abnakis lived here. And the first whites to come into this lake-and-river country were hunters. They went back with stories of white pines so big that four men, grasping hands, could not reach around them. The next whites who came were timber cruisers. They made trips not unlike the one we are making—wandering at will in bark canoes—noting, and marking on inexact maps, the stands of pine. The big trees were there for the taking. They tended to cluster on the shores of the lakes. Loggers and log drivers followed, of course. Indian, hunter, cruiser, lumberer—this progression, in such beautiful country, could not help but lead to the tourist, the canoe-tripping tourist, and among the first of these (in all likelihood, *the* first tourist in the Maine woods) was Henry David Thoreau. He made two bark-canoe trips here, in 1853 and 1857, each time with an Indian guide. He went down this river. He went to the lake where Henri Vaillancourt—a hundred and twenty years later—would hide the felled cedar. Looking for moose in the night, he went up Moosehorn Stream. No moose. He had in his pack some pencils and an oilskin pouch full of scratch paper—actually letters that customers had written to his family's business, ordering plumbago and other printing supplies. On the backs of these discarded letters he made condensed, fragmentary, scarcely legible notes, and weeks later, when he had returned home to Concord, he composed his journal of the trip, slyly using the diary form, and writing at times in the present tense, to gain immediacy, to create the illusion of paragraphs written—as it is generally supposed they were written—virtually in the moments described. With the advantage of retrospect, he reconstructed the story to reveal a kind of significance that the notes do not reveal. Something new in journalism. With the journal as his principal source, he later crafted still another manuscript, in which he further shaped and rearranged the story, all the while adhering to a structure built on calendar dates. The result, published posthumously in hardcover form, was the book he called *The Maine Woods.*

Henri Vaillancourt's familiarity with books appears to be narrow, but he has read Thoreau—from *Walden* to *Cape Cod*, and most notably *The Maine Woods.* Rick Blanchette is saturated in Thoreau. In every segment of the river, they remember things Thoreau did there—places where he camped, where he collected flora, where he searched for moose. "I'm into Thoreau, too," Mike has said. "He writes about pickerel fishing, turtle hunting—the things I know and do."

Vaillancourt is transfixed by the knowledge that Thoreau, at North East Carry, actually watched a group of Indians making bark canoes. "All of them sitting there whittling with crooked knives! What a life! I'd give anything to have been there."

Back and forth between our two canoes, bits of Thoreau fly all day.

"Thoreau said the nose of the moose was the greatest delicacy, and after that the tongue."

"Thoreau said it is a common accident for men camping in the woods to be killed by a falling tree."

"Do you remember during the Allagash and East Branch trip when he said that all heroes and discoverers were insane?"

"No, that was in *Cape Cod*."

"Some people think he was humorless, you know. I disagree."

"Thoreau said . . ."

"Thoreau believed . . ."

"Do you remember the passage where . . ."

When it is not my turn to paddle and I am riding in the center of the canoe, I read to catch up. Thoreau's trips were provisioned with smoked beef, coffee, sugar, tea, plum cake, salt, pepper, and lemons for flavoring the water. His tent was made from cut poles and cotton cloth. He had one blanket. He carried his gear in India-rubber bags, and it included an extra shirt, extra socks, two waistcoats, six dickies, a thick nightcap, a four-quart tin pail, a jackknife, a fishline, hooks, pins, needles, thread, matches, an umbrella, a towel, and soap. For foul weather, he had an India-rubber coat, in which he sweated uncomfortably and got wetter than he would have in the rain. He ate his meals from birch-bark plates, using forks whittled from alder. For relief from mosquitoes, he wore a veil; he also threw damp leaves onto the fire and sat in the smoke. He slept in smoke, too—burning wet rotting logs all night.

Thoreau's guide on the first canoe trip was Joe Aitteon, and, on the second, Joe Polis—both Penobscots from Indian Island in Old Town, Maine. Henri Vaillancourt is at least as interested in these Indians as he is in Thoreau—particularly in Polis, who made his own canoes. Polis and Aitteon travelled light—no changes of clothing. Aitteon was a log driver. Polis was the better woodsman. Polis had represented his tribe in Washington. He had visited New York. He said, "I suppose, I live in

New York, I be poorest hunter, I expect." Thoreau hired him for eleven dollars a week, which included the use of his canoe. Some eighteen feet in length, thirty inches wide, and a foot deep in the center, it was a longer, narrower canoe than the Vaillancourt canoes we are using. Thoreau's first canoe—on the 1853 trip with Aitteon—was more than nineteen feet long, and the bark was painted green. Our paddles are made from birch. Thoreau's were made from sugar maple. Thoreau was discomforted by the confinement of the paddling position, and he used the word "torture" to describe it. Sometimes he stood up in the canoe to stretch his legs. He appreciated nonetheless the genius of canoe technology. "The canoe implies a long antiquity in which its manufacture has been gradually perfected," he wrote in his journal. "It will ere long, perhaps, be ranked among the lost arts."

When Thoreau, from Mt. Katahdin, saw neither clearings nor cabins across huge domains of forest, lake, and river, he said, "It did not look as if a solitary traveller had cut so much as a walking-stick there." On closer view, though, from water level, he saw the stumps of timber a great deal larger than walking sticks. He saw dry-ki, too. The first dams (small dams, built to raise the lakes a few feet to serve, in various ways, the convenience of logging companies) had been built in 1841, and now, after a dozen years and more, "great trunks of trees stood dead and bare far out in the lake, making the impression of ruined piers of a city that had been—while behind, the timber lay criss-a-cross for half a dozen rods or more over the water." Dry-ki (the syllables rhyme) apparently derives from "dry kill": wood killed as a result of the dams and now, as dry as bone —gray, resins gone—crudely fencing the shores of open water. Thoreau always hoped to see some caribou but saw none. Of the caribou, Polis said, "No likum stump. When he sees that he scared."

The stumps that scared Thoreau were the stumps of the giant pines. To cut and take those trees was "as if individual speculators were to be allowed to export the clouds out of the sky, or the stars out of the firmament, one by one." If the attitudes behind such rapine were to go on unchecked, he said (a century and a quarter before the great ecological uprising), "we shall be reduced to gnaw the very crust of the earth for nutriment." And what of the remaining "stately pines"? Twenty years before the first national park, and more than a century before the Wilderness Act, he asked, "Why should not we . . . have our national preserves, where . . . the bear and panther . . . may still exist, and not be 'civilized off the face of the earth'?" The Maine of his bark-canoe trips was the deepest wilderness Thoreau would see in his lifetime. Today, astonishingly, it looks much the same as it did when he saw it. Lake and river, many thousands of miles of shoreline are unbroken by human structures and are horizoned only with the tips of spruce. The lakes are still necklaced with dry-ki, some of it more than a century old. Dry-ki has come to be regarded as charming. It certainly makes good firewood, a smokeless fire.

After forty-odd miles of Penobscot River, we are impatient for a change. For all its big bends and deadwaters—larger dimensions the farther we go—the river is now hemming us in, and we anticipate Chesuncook Lake, a burst of space. The skyline is opening up some. The lake must be around the next, or the next, bend. Thoreau said that in this same reach of the river he found himself approaching the big lake "with as much expectation as if it had been a university." The river debouches. The lake breaks open. We move out onto it and look to the right down miles of water and far beyond to the high Katahdin massif. Katahdin is a mile high. The lake's elevation is less than a thousand feet. Katahdin stands alone. The vast terrain around it is the next thing to a peneplain. Wherever you paddle through this country, when you move out onto the big lakes you can look to the southeast and see Katahdin.

A steady wind is blowing from the direction of the mountain, and since we are heading north we hold the canoes together and put up an improvised sail. Supported by two paddles as masts, the sail is the largest plastic bag I have ever seen—five by five feet. It is something called a Gaylord liner and comes from the small plastics factory in Greenville, where both Blanchettes work. The canoes move smartly before the wind. Indians used great sheets of bark as sails, and moose hide as well. According to *The Bark Canoes and Skin Boats of North America*, Indians of prehistory "may have set up a leafy bush in the bow of their canoes to act as a sail with favorable winds." At any rate, "the old Nova Scotia expression 'carrying too much bush,' meaning over-canvassing a boat, is thought by some to have originated from an Indian practice observed there by the first settlers." Thoreau sailed using a blanket. Our plastic sail sets Henri Vaillancourt off on a long, surprising tirade against the mills and factories of Greenville, which he says are sweatshops, exploiters of immigrant labor. "I'm glad I don't have to work in one of those places," he says. "Particularly that plastics shop. What a rip-off!" For Mike, the plastics shop is a summer job. He is a student at the University of New Hampshire. His brother, Rick, who is already a college graduate, wants to be a librarian in a New England college. He works full time in the plastics shop and also takes graduate courses in library science at Fitchburg State. Water rushes by and between the canoes. Holding the polyethylene sail, Rick quotes one of his favorite lines from Thoreau, which was occasioned by Thoreau's first night here on Chesuncook. He had moose meat for dinner and afterward went for a walk. "For my dessert," he said, and Rick is now quoting him, "I helped myself to a large slice of the Chesuncook woods, and took a hearty draught of its waters with all my senses."

Vaillancourt sneers. "Some dessert," he says. "Thoreau was a great guy, but a little far-flung there at times. What a crackpot —a real featherbrain, a very impractical person."

Blanchette is annoyed. Vaillancourt is amused. Blanchette says, "Yes? Well, the most influential man of this century will turn out to be Thoreau, who lived in the century before."

"He was extreme," Vaillancourt goes on. "He would not cut down a live tree. You can use nature without destroying it. I have an aunt in Concord. I asked her what people there thought of Thoreau, and she said, 'He was a real bum.'"

"Thoreau actually started a couple of forest fires in his time," Blanchette admits. "One in Concord. The other on Mt. Washington. When the fires went out of control, Thoreau just walked away."

"He said he thought he could make a bark canoe," Vaillancourt adds. "I doubt very much if he could have. That Aitteon, for an Indian, didn't know much, either. Thoreau asked him about the canoe, how the ribs were attached to the gunwales, and he said, 'I don't know. I never noticed.' Aitteon saw a porcupine once and thought it was a bear."

The Gaylord liner is pulling us up the west side of Gero, a big island. Near the island shore, Vaillancourt sees two, three, four tall specimen birches, paper birches—perfection trees. He decides in an instant to camp below them tonight.

IT IS MORNING now, after a tormented, insectile night. The mosquitoes were the least of it, the no-see-ums infernal. The wind never stirred enough to take them away. No-see-ums are so small they go right through the screening of the tent. They home on flesh. They cover the hands, the arms, the neck, the face. Like an acid, they eat skin. They are not ubiquitous, but they have been with us now two nights in a row. At 3 A.M., I got up and went out of the tent and down to the shore. I went into the water like a fly-crazed moose. I stayed in the lake in the dark for an hour, as I had in the river the night before, only the nose out—dozing.

"No-see-um" was an Indian word—red skin vulnerable as white. To the early Indian, coming here to make a warm-weather camping trip would have seemed the act of a fool: Thoreau, with his veil, his smoke from rotting logs; we, with our Off and our Cutter. When the tribes lived here—before the logging whites came—they left in the summer. When the blackflies, the mosquitoes, and the no-see-ums hatched, the Indians departed, and they did not come back until the bugs were gone. They went to the coast—to what is now Kennebunkport, Northeast Harbor, Fortunes Rocks—and there they steamed clams and lobsters in hot seaweed and ate them the summer long. Between feasts, they dried clams and lobsters to take home for the winter. These were thoughts for the night, underwater.

Henri's beef jerky has begun to turn green. He dips it into peanut butter and eats it for breakfast. The one taste envelops the other.

I make my notes as I watch the bread rise in my reflector oven. The dough began as Bisquick, and it is turning golden brown. Last night we had spice cake; gingerbread the night before. In my own porings through *The Maine Woods*, I have found something that has apparently never arrested Henri Vaillancourt's eye. Thoreau refers a couple of times to a cooking device known as a Yankee-baker. ("A shed-shaped tent will catch and reflect the heat like a Yankee-baker, and you may be drying while you are sleeping.") So Thoreau himself would have recognized my reflector oven—an endorsement that might have been helpful when Vaillancourt was saying "hang it up" but is hardly necessary now. Henri likes the gingerbread, and if his beef jerky gets any greener he plans to use the reflector to reroast it. The baker is a small, collapsible lean-to of shining tin, with a shelf in it for holding a rectangular pan. You fill the pan with dough or batter and set the oven close to the fire. Level it. Watch to see that it is not picking up too much or too little heat. It reflects heat into the pan from the interior—back, sides, top, and bottom. Henri's way of cooking Bisquick is to wrap a gluey mass around a green stick and then jab the stick into the ground near the fire. The Blanchettes tried that, and when the Bisquick began to plop off the stick they removed their dough to the baker.

This is a fine campsite, looking north over the water to the end of Chesuncook, and growing here is everything that goes into a bark canoe: feasible birch, dense stands of tall cedar, hard maple, white pine, white and black spruce. Henri would like to contrive to be put in the Maine woods someday (dropped in, somehow, out of nowhere) without a canoe or a paddle but with some food and gear and just three tools: an axe, an awl, and a crooked knife. He says they are everything he would need in order—three weeks later—to paddle out in a new canoe. This island is the sort of place where he could do it, and that is why he has stopped here, to take a long, wistful look around.

After unloading his canoe last night, he went straight to one of the big birches and took a sample of its bark. He cut it from near the base of the trunk—a piece six inches high and a foot long, the size of a shingle. Along the grain he bent the sample, steadily applying pressure with his fingers as the bark formed the shape of a U. Gradually, he increased the pressure until the bark cracked. It was pretty good bark, he said. It had good relative elasticity. Its layers did not tend to separate. In these respects, as in others, bark will vary a great deal from tree to tree. The eyes—the dotted lines that run in the direction of the grain—were not too close together. The closer the eyes, the weaker the bark. He cut a sample from another tree, with the same results. The third birch he came to was better still —a remarkably straight and columnar tree, with a usable segment of bark that was long enough in itself for a sixteen-foot canoe. Henri said, "There are trees in the White Mountains that put these trees to shame. For Maine, though, these are all right. They're acceptable trees."

He finds his bark, usually, in the White Mountains, and in New Hampshire woods that are north of the White Mountains, and in forests of southwestern Maine. He leaves his car by the side of the road and wanders through the woods—searching, sampling. The trees have to be clean-lined and free of blemishes. The slightest, barely detectable bend in a trunk will cause puckers—welts—in the bark of a finished canoe. He walks on sometimes for many miles, looking not just for good trees but for good big trees. A single tree once gave him two fourteen-foot canoes and most of an eighteen-footer as well. When he finds the sort of quality he is looking for, appreciation registers in his mind and he moves on. These are scouting trips. He will return for the bark when he needs it. He remembers regretfully the best white birch he ever saw. "It was like a palm tree, it was so straight." When he was ready for the bark and went back for it, all he found was a stump. A timber company had taken the tree for spindles and spools. No matter how far off in the woods a tree may be, he does not mark its location on a map or otherwise assist his memory. "When you are in this business, a good birch will make an impression on you," he says. "You remember where it is."

His range has increased, and so has his capacity for guessing where to look. "I've been finding better bark in recent years," he says. "Better bark, that's for damned sure."

I ask him where.

"Near Canada," he says.

"Where near Canada?"

"I don't want to mention too specifically where I get the bark."

"Why not?"

"I just don't care to, that's all."

"Are you worried about the law?"

"The law? Oh, no. Oh hell, no."

"So, what is it that troubles you?"

"I don't want anyone horning in on my birch. If there's one thing I'm possessive about, it's where the good bark is.

I wouldn't sell a sheet of good bark for anything—even for a price greater than the price of the canoe I could make from it."

When he goes to take the bark from a tree, he enters the forest with a wooden ladder. He slits the bark vertically and begins to peel it back. If the month is June or early July, the bark will "almost pop off by itself"—will, at any rate, easily come free. Bark taken at this time of the year is called summer bark, and on a canoe it gradually turns a lighter and lighter brown, until it is high buff. Bark that is peeled before the sap flows is called winter bark, and on a canoe it gradually turns a darker and darker brown, until it is a rich cordovan. Canoe coverings usually include several pieces of bark, and they can be attractively quilted with mixtures of the two kinds, as are the hulls of both of our canoes.

"Winter bark is really tight, I'm telling you. You need a special tool, a type of spud, to get it off."

Henri makes the peeling tool from bark itself—stiff bark with a bevelled edge. With much effort, he—in effect—chisels the winter bark off the tree. Winter or summer, when he is done he has something like a long piece of linoleum. He rolls it up the short way, brown side out. Norwegians roof houses with birch bark. Lapps make clothing with it. In Siberia, birch bark has been found—unchanged through all the centuries since it grew—clinging to petrified wood. Henri's long searches are not the result of a modern scarcity of appropriate trees. The search always took time. Indians spent as much as a week roving birch-filled woods looking for a perfect tree. Henri ties the roll of bark with a pine root, or with a length of spruce or cedar bark, or with his belt or a string. He shoulders the ladder and walks out of the woods, leaving behind him a standing but slaughtered tree.

The parts of a bark canoe—in the general order in which they are assembled—are these:

center thwart —

quarter thwarts (2) —

end thwarts (2)

inwales (2)

wedges
pegs
bark
split roots of black spruce or white pine
outwales (2)
wulegessis (2)
stempieces (2)
pitch
planking
ribs (40 *or* 50)
headboards (2)
dry cedar shavings or dry moss
gunwale caps (2)
porcupine quills (*optional*)

Inwales and outwales are collectively called gunwales. The inwale, a strip of cedar running the length of the canoe, is about an inch and a half square in the center and tapers toward the ends. The outwale is a thinner strip and also runs the length of the canoe. The edge of the bark and the tips of the ribs are pinched between the inwale and the outwale.

The *wulegessis* is a flap of bark that forms a deck over the bow (or the stern) and extends a short way down the sides of the canoe.

The headboards are ovate slabs of cedar that are wedged

vertically into the bow and the stern to contribute both support and form.

If Henri were to build a canoe here on Gero Island, he would start by felling cedar, splitting it out, and whittling and forming various parts. He would cut young birch or maple for thwarts. Always, he prepares the wooden pieces first. Ribs, planking, stempieces, gunwales, and headboards are made from cedar. After carving rib boards in varying lengths, he dips them in boiling water and then bends them around his knee to an appropriate shape, which, for the center of the canoe, is much like the letter C lying on its back. To hold the tension and the shape, he ties a strip of cedar bark from tip to tip, and a rib is made. As the ribs progress from the center of the canoe toward the ends, they must become not only shorter but also more sharply bent. Some are actually cracked a bit to approach the shape of a V. He racks up several dozen subtly graduated ribs, like auto parts awaiting delivery to an assembly line.

That is the building bed—a section of ground about twenty feet long, free of rocks and roots. The soil has to be firm enough to hold driven stakes. If the bed is level, the canoe will come off it with a slight rocker in the profile of the bottom. Henri likes it that way, and here on the island he would clear a level bed.

No one knows how the canoe's design began, centuries ago. I venture to guess that the structure of the hull was modelled on the thoracic structure of vertebrates—of men and animals, reptiles and birds. The skin is bark. The flesh is planking. A cage of bent-cedar ribs gives the craft its skeletal form. Between a wood-and-canvas canoe and a bark canoe there is an elemental difference in the order in which the hull is assembled. In the more modern canoe, the canvas comes last. It is stretched across an essentially completed and rigid frame. The Indian, on the other hand, began the assembly with bark. He rolled it right out on the building bed, white side up, and built the canoe from there. Lashing the bark to the gunwale frame, he made—in effect—an elongated birchbark bag. Then he lined the bag with planking. Then—one by one—he forced in the ribs. The resulting canoe was lithe, supple, resilient, strong. And if something cracked, it could easily be replaced.

When, at the outset, the bark was folded upward from the building bed, a template was needed to guide the bark toward the shape of a canoe. The Indians used two kinds of template. The one gave the canoe bulging tumblehome sides. The other made the sides flare. Henri Vaillancourt uses both kinds. The template that will lead to pronounced tumblehome is actually the completed gunwale frame of the canoe itself—all thwarts in place, mortised into the inwales, which are lashed together at the ends. The gunwale frame (looked at from above) is the outline of the intended canoe. The other kind of template, which does not end up as part of the canoe, is called a building frame and is simply a smaller (shorter and narrower) version of the gunwale frame.

Henri places on the building bed whatever frame he is using and drives stakes into the ground in outline around it. He removes the stakes. He rolls out the bark, white side up. He sets the frame on top of the bark. He centers it—bark protruding on all sides—and he tries as best he can to line up the frame with the stake holes below, which are now hidden by the bark. Satisfied, he weights down the frame with rocks.

The bark that protrudes outside the frame is to be bent upward, but it cannot be bent without forming pronounced wrinkles. So, from the edges, wedge-shaped indentations —gores—are cut into it in a number of places to within an inch of the frame. Then the bark is folded upward all around the frame. As the builder works along, he puts the stakes back into their holes, and when all stakes are in place they form a confining palisade around the upturned bark, which has now begun to assume the appearance of a canoe—ragged, lumpy, flat-bottomed, but still a canoe. A much greater breadth of bark is required in the middle, of course, than at the ends, so, unless the bark came from a tree of extraordinary girth, the sides of the canoe for several feet amidships have to be "pieced out" with additional bark, which Henri now sews on with split roots.

It is better that all this happen in good shade, which is deep and abundant here on Gero Island, because in direct sunlight the bark becomes less flexible, and it needs all the elasticity it can retain during the building process. Indians would choose a site like this—with its available water, shade, and materials—and build canoe after canoe in the one place for many generations.

As Henri works, he is not worried about an irretrievable error. Nothing can go so disastrously wrong that he has no alternative but to junk the whole thing and begin again. "Nothing about it is, you know, that dramatic," he says. The Indian methodology was in no sense haphazard, and a canoe will result every time if the method has been understood and mastered. Within tolerable margins, the results do vary, however, and no two canoes are alike. Some, in the end, please him more than others. "They don't always come out exactly the way you want them to."

The bark is clamped to the surrounding palisade of stakes by short half-rounds of wood tied to the stakes with strips peeled from basswood. Pinched between stake and half-round, the birch bark will stay put while the gunwale frame is lashed in its proper place. The gunwale frame, now lifted a foot or so off the ground in the center, and more at the ends, is temporarily supported by wooden posts that have been cut to varying lengths so they will establish the profile curve of the gunwales—the upsweep toward the ends, the sheer of the canoe. When the sheer is just right, the deck flaps—*wulegessis*—are placed on the ends, the outwales are added (secured by pegs that go through the bark and into the inwales), and lashing of the gunwales begins. The split roots go around the gunwales and through awl holes in the bark, around, around, around again, each pass snug beside another. It is necessary, however, to do this in groups—to stop the lashing, leave a space, and start again, for the space eventually accommodates the tip of a rib, poking up between inwale and outwale. The grouped lashings, handsome to look at, are evenly spaced along both gunwales. The decorative dividend is high. The gunwale lashings contribute considerably to the beauty of the canoe. Yet they are vital and, in pattern, completely functional.

The canoe is about ready to come off the building bed. Stakes have been removed while the lashing progressed. The edges of the gores are sewn together, making neat seams. The thwarts, which are mortised into the gunwales, are further secured by lashings that run through awl holes near their ends. The canoe is lifted, turned upside down, and placed on wooden horses.

Lumpish and battered-looking, it appears to be covered not so much with smooth birch bark as with parts of a used tin roof. The canoe is so crooked that it is difficult even to guess where the centerline might be. The stempieces are now tied in, and they at least suggest the profiles of the ends. Wherever sewing remains undone, it is completed. The canoe is then set on the ground again, upright—ready to be gummed, planked, and ribbed.

Inside the hull, all seams are "payed with gum." Indian gum was mainly the pitch of white or black spruce. Indians tapped trees in a way analogous to the collection of maple sap; they boiled the pitch and strained it, and at tribal campgrounds they had communal pitch pots where anyone could go for sealant to touch up a canoe. Henri Vaillancourt has used spruce gum on a number of his canoes, but his preference of late has been to use mineral pitch—plain asphalt roofing cement. Asphalt and dark spruce pitch are almost identical to the eye and the touch, but there is an incongruity here that I cannot to my own satisfaction resolve. Why would someone who had used spruce gum with the same good results the Indians got, someone who would drive hundreds of miles and then walk tens of miles to select a single tree, someone who would disdain power tools and elect to work twelve hours a day with an axe and a crooked knife, someone who would put no metal in a canoe whatsoever (not so much as a carpet tack), although Indians used nails in their canoes even before 1850, someone who would travel to outposts of Ontario just in the hope of learning a detail or two from an Indian, someone to whom authenticity was an otherwise primal value—an artist, for that by style and temperament is what he is—seal his canoes with mineral pitch? His own (quick) answer is that he would unhesitatingly use anything—nails, wire, buzz saws, vinyl tile—that might be an improvement on Indian materials or technology, but for canoe-making nothing modern *is* an improvement, except, in a small way, asphalt, because to collect and boil spruce pitch involves unnecessary tedium. Whether the pitch is vegetable or mineral, the seams of bark canoes have to be touched up with some frequency. The Indians mixed animal fat into the spruce gum to keep it from cracking in cold weather, and they had to be careful to repitch their canoes in warm weather so the pitch would not weep. With all this, Henri won't be bothered. So he carries in his pack a small pan that contains a cupful of hard asphalt.

As planking and ribs are installed, a bark canoe takes its final form. The planking—also called sheathing—lines the bark: fifteen (or so) random-width cedar boards running from each end to the middle, and overlapping there by about six inches. Pressure from the ribs is all that holds the planking in place. Temporary ribs—bent saplings, or ribs rejected in the making of other canoes—are used to hold the planking before the permanent ribs are installed. Nearly three weeks have by now gone into the assembly of the canoe, and the time of completion has come, as fifty ribs, give or take a few, are pounded into position with a mallet. "I've heard one or two people call them 'floating ribs,'" Henri says. "They're not anchored. They can move a little. You work from the ends toward the middle, putting the ribs in. You pour very hot water on the bark to keep it flexible at this stage." To install a rib, it is necessary to tilt it a bit and put its tips in place in the gunwales. Then the rib is firmly tapped with the mallet, and as it moves toward the vertical it presses ever more tightly against the planking and the bark. If the rib is too large, it will split the bark. If it is too small, it will not offer the pressure needed to create and maintain the hull form. Where a rib is not quite right, Henri tries another. When he taps the last one in, it is below the center thwart.

He trims the bark at the ends and sews roots around the stempieces. He fills out the bow and stern by stuffing them with shavings or moss, kept in place by the headboards, which are installed next. He pegs on the gunwale caps—long, narrow strips of cedar that cover the top of the gunwales and protect the grouped lashings from wear. He turns the canoe over again and pitches the seams on the outside. The canoe is done now—ready to take its maker home from an island in Maine, or the reverse, whichever the case may be. All that is left is to find a porcupine. Take some quills. Commence the decorations.

WHEN WHITE explorers first came to northeastern North America, they looked in wonder at such canoes—as well they might, for nothing like them existed in Europe. There was eloquence in the evidence they gave of the genius of humankind. The materials were simple, but the structure was not. An adroit technology had come down with the tribes from immemorial time, and now—in the sixteenth, the seventeenth century—here were bark canoes on big rivers and ocean bays curiously circling ships from another world. Longboats were lowered, to be rowed by crews of four and upward. The sailors hauled at their oars. The Indians, two to a canoe, indolently whisked their narrow paddles and easily drew away. In their wake they left a stunning impression. Not only were they faster. They could see where they were going.

White explorers got out of their ships and went thousands of miles in bark canoes. They travelled in them until the twentieth century, for bark canoes were the craft of the north continent. Nothing else, indigenous or imported, could do what they could do. The explorers in the main were not seeking the advancement of geophysical knowledge, chimeric routes to the Orient. They were looking for fur. Fur sources around the Baltic Sea were diminishing, and prices there had risen to prohibitive levels, so the attention of Western Europe had turned to the American woods. The demand for fur was intense, because it was used not only in pelt form but also, and to a much greater extent, in the making of felt and other materials. Most wanted of all was the fur of the beaver. The underhair, or "beaver wool," had minute barbs, and when the hair was compressed the barbs would hold fabric together.

The fur trade began in the estuaries of rivers. White traders soon followed the Indians upstream to complete their transactions nearer the sources of the fur. What the whites brought to offer were not merely clothes, blankets, beads, and copper kettles but also steel traps, spears, knives, and guns, with which the Indians could vastly increase the collection of fur. Red and white hands were clasped in enterprise. Some Canadians savor the thought that while Americans to the south—intoxicated with their "Manifest Destiny"—were killing Indians and stealing their land, Canadians red and white were developing warm interracial relationships bonded by a business that was conducted to the advantage of all. All but the beaver. Where Indian families might once have taken just a few pelts for their own use, whole lodges were destroyed. Beaver populations declined toward zero with proximity to the outlets of commerce. Thus the Ojibway, the Cree, the Algonquin—Canadian tribes across the woods—were in on the beginnings of the end of their own environment. They were willing partners, profiteers. Down the river they sold the beaver, the mink, the marten, the lynx, the otter. They sold the hides of deer, moose, caribou. They even sold the skin of the wild goose. They sold anything with hair, almost anything that moved—and to keep the whole bonanza going they sold their birch canoes.

The fur trade, as it lengthened, manifested its own destiny and Canada's, too. The fur trade established canoe routes to the far northwest, and conjoined the segments of a continental wilderness. It is possible to cross Canada by canoe, to crisscross Canada, to go almost anywhere. Canada is twenty-five per cent water. The quantity of it outreaches belief. A sixth of all the fresh water that exists on earth is in Canadian lakes, Canadian ponds, Canadian streams, Canadian rivers. A friend of mine who grew up in Timmins, a remote community in Ontario, once told me about an Indian friend of his in boyhood who developed an irresistible urge to see New York City. He put his canoe in the water and started out. From stream to lake to pond to portage, he made his way a hundred miles to Lake Timiskaming, and its outlet, the Ottawa River. He went down the Ottawa to the St. Lawrence, down the St. Lawrence to the Richelieu, up the Richelieu to Lake Champlain, and from Lake Champlain to the Hudson. At the Seventy-ninth Street Boat Basin, he left the canoe in the custody of attendants and walked on into town. Reversing that trip, and then some, one could go by canoe from Seventy-ninth Street to Alaska, and down the Yukon to the Bering Sea. By the Rat-Porcupine route (up the Rat, down the Porcupine), the length of the portage over the Rocky Mountains is half a mile. Between the Atlantic and the Pacific, anywhere on the routes that were used by the fur trade, the longest portage is thirteen miles (and even that is an exaggeration, because the trail is interrupted by a mile-long lake). In 1778, a white trader for the first time crossed that portage. It is Methye Portage, in what is now northern Saskatchewan. His name was Peter Pond. Beyond the portage, in the region of Lake Athabasca, he encountered a crowded population of beaver whose fur (as a result of the mean temperature there) was as long and rich as any yet found in North America. The discovery extended to its practical limit the distance that fur could travel in the unfrozen season by canoe from the source to Montreal. Transatlantic ships could navigate the St. Lawrence to the Lachine Rapids, near Montreal. At the head of the rapids, the fur-trade canoe routes began. The distance from Lachine to Lake Athabasca was three thousand miles. Unsurprisingly, the men who did the paddling were known as the *voyageurs.*

Some stayed in the far-northern outposts for the winter, others in Montreal. With the spring breakup, they started from both ends, and by midsummer had met in the middle. They exchanged cargoes. These were some of the things in the packs bound west and north: false hair, garters, tomahawks, rolls of bark from the birches of the East. The *voyageurs* returned—the survivors returned—whence they had come. Crosses marked their routes, sometimes many crosses in a single place. Packs weighed ninety pounds, and a *voyageur* on a portage was responsible for six. Generally, two packs were portaged at a time, and sometimes three. The largest recorded burden carried by one man in one trip across a portage was six hundred and thirty pounds. It has been reported that the *voyageurs* liked to show off. They were, on the whole, small men; large ones were not worth their extra weight in fur. Even under the hundred-and-eighty-pound weight of a standard two-pack load, they were more or less forced to run if they wanted to move at all, so they took off at a trot at the start of a portage—uphill, downhill, over rough or boggy terrain. They died of strangulated hernias, and of heart attacks, sometimes. Five hundred mink skins would fit in one pack. *Voyageurs* also drowned in rapids.

When they started out in the spring from Montreal, they were blessed by a priest, and each canoe was given a summer-ration eight-gallon keg of brandy. The *voyageurs* drank most of it the first night out. They went virtually nowhere the next day. Sober again, they sang their way to Lake Superior. All day, they sang *chansons* of the Loire Valley, which gave them their rhythm and their distraction. They went up the Ottawa and up the Mattawa and across the Height of Land. They went down the French River from Lake Nipissing to Georgian Bay. They circled the north rim of Lake Superior. They averaged fifty miles a day. When rivers became too shallow for paddling, they shoved upcurrent with poles. When they could not pole, they got out and lined—hauled the canoes, barge-like, from the shore with ropes. When they could not line, they dragged. They would do anything to avoid a portage or reduce its length. There were more than a hundred portages between Lake Athabasca and Montreal.

They wore plumed hats, billowing shirts, bright-colored sashes. Their paddle blades were brilliant red, green, blue. They stopped once an hour for a churchwarden smoke, and they measured big lakes not in miles but in pipes. They got up in the morning at two or three. Hours of paddling preceded breakfast. They made their camp at nine, even ten, at night. In the north, they ate pemmican—pounded buffalo or caribou meat, sometimes with berries in it, dried in the sun. In the Middle West, they ate wild rice and maize. Toward the East, they ate pork and hardtack, peas and beans.

They came in large numbers from the Quebecois farm country east of Montreal, like the forebears of Henri Vaillancourt. From the fur trade the *voyageurs* got almost nothing but a change of scene, in a business that for its owners was unimaginably profitable. An investment of, say, eight hundred pounds could bring back sixteen thousand. The *voyageurs* worked for the North West Company and, ultimately, for the Hudson's Bay Company, which merged the North West Company out of existence in 1821.

Bark canoes the Indians made for themselves seldom exceeded twenty feet, and were generally shorter than that, on down to nine-foot and ten-foot hunter canoes. Canoes they built on order for the fur trade were thirty-six feet long and could carry four tons. It took four men to portage them. Wet, they weighed six hundred pounds. They were known as *canots de maître*. They travelled in brigades—usually four, but sometimes as many as ten, in a line. The bowman, the *avant*, had the captain role. In white water, the sternman, the *gouvernail*, was too far back to see what the *voyageurs* called the *fil d'eau* —the place to shoot the rapid. Paddlers in the middle worked two abreast. Personnel shifts (advancement, transfer, death) caused a crew to vary considerably, and as many as fifteen men sometimes paddled a *canot de maître*. Eight or ten was the usual number. The crew slept under the overturned canoe and an attached tarpaulin, and to make this arrangement as spacious as possible the canoes were designed with high, curling ends. For the more northerly runs through what is now Manitoba and Saskatchewan, the trade developed the *canot du nord*, which was narrower and shorter—twenty-five feet. Some of the streams of the northern route were too small for the *canot de maître*. The companies appropriated the art from the Indians, set up their own factories, and made bark canoes. On spruce-plank building beds with permanent stake holes, the plant at Trois-Rivières, Quebec, could produce in a year twenty *canots de maître*. Certain white names ultimately acquired celebrity in the field, notably L. A. Christopherson, who for almost forty years built, and in part designed, Hudson's Bay Company fur-trade canoes. High on their curling sterns were the letters "HBC." This, in company argot, meant "Here Before Christ."

Inevitably, after working for some years in the sixteen-foot range, Henri Vaillancourt developed an ambition to build a fur-trade canoe. He needed an order, though. It was not the sort of thing he could just stop and do, since he was laden with commitments and was taking orders a year and more ahead. Meanwhile, on a reconnaissance trip in northern New Hampshire he had found one of the largest birches he had ever seen. It had suitable, elastic bark. He decided not to use the bark for sixteen-foot canoes. It would stay there on the living tree until he got an order for a *canot du nord*, or even a *canot de maître*.

All through his building history, Vaillancourt has experimented with aspects of the craft, going through phases that have been less pragmatic than artistic in their shifts and choices. Some of his early canoes were very sharp-ended. "I had a thing for sharp ends," he explains. "The sharp-ended ones were fast canoes. They looked good." They were narrow in the bow and stern to the point of seeming hollow-cheeked. It was difficult to turn them. They could not be called responsive. They cut a fine, deep line into the water, and straight ahead was the direction in which they wanted to go. Compared with an apple-cheeked Grumman canoe, Henri's canoes still look like cutlery, but of late the ends have markedly amplified. Why? "I like it that way. I think it looks good." The criterion is always the same: "It looks good." His canoes were once narrower in beam as well. They have always been shallow—rarely deeper than a foot. He has generally preferred straight profiles at the ends. "But sometimes I'll give it some heel toward the bottom, or undercut it a little bit. It depends on your mood when you build it." He used to overlap his planking, like clapboard, in the Abnaki manner. Then, some years ago, in his travels he saw a Malecite canoe with edge-to-edge planking. "It was so neat-looking. So sophisticated. I just had to do it. It's much harder to do." With the edge-to-edge planking, he began making wider and thicker ribs. They look good against the planking.

The largest canoe dealer in the East uses a Vaillancourt canoe as a conversation piece in a showroom full of Old Towns. A woman named Jean Newton, who lives in a shed in the Palouse mountains of Idaho, has a Vaillancourt tumblehome canoe that was made from a single piece of bark. She saw Henri's name in *The Last Whole Earth Catalog*, to which he once wrote a letter promoting trade. Her canoe hangs from the shed rafters, on cinches. The canoe Henri is using on this trip was ordered by Idaho State University for a course on Indian canoeing and for the making of an educational film. John Farrell, of Warren, New Jersey, discovered Henri in the "Small Business & Crafts" section of *Yankee* magazine and ordered a fourteen-foot Vaillancourt canoe, which he uses for fishing and duck hunting on the upper Passaic River. Warren Soderberg, who owns a hardware store in Dresser, Wisconsin, bought an eighteen-foot Vaillancourt canoe so that, among other things, he could make fifteen-day canoe trips in Ontario during moose season in the fall. "I'd like to shoot a moose out of my birchbark canoe with a bow and arrow," he said. "Why? Just to say that I've done it." Henri made a nine-foot hunter canoe for a woman in New Jersey who wanted one that small so she could lift it herself. It weighs twenty pounds.

Then, finally, an order came for a fur-trade canoe. The customer's name was Kent Reeves. He lived in Shokan, New York, and he was a professor of environmental education whose classroom was a forest (called the Ashokan Field Campus). It belonged to a subdivision of the State University. Reeves had conceived, and was in the process of organizing, a graduate course that would be one long field trip on the route of the *voyageurs*, mainly west of Superior. It would be called Frontier Life on the Voyageurs' Trail—six credits toward a master's degree. Beyond Reeves' considerable library on the fur-trade era, what the course needed most was a *canot du nord*. Reeves had sought out the names of people who could make one. He had visited them and had examined their work. He had arrived at an opinion of Henri that exactly coincided with Henri's opinion of himself: Henri was, by a considerable margin, the best. The two main considerations that brought Reeves to this conclusion were, in his words, "quality and authenticity." Henri wanted three thousand dollars. Reeves flinched, but he produced the money. The students who signed up for the course made their own paddles, sawing them out of basswood and finishing them with draw-knives. They sewed their own billowy shirts and wove bright-colored sashes. They made *voyageur* hats, and they made moccasins with moose skin from the HBC. Meanwhile, Henri made the *canot du nord*. The bark was all it had appeared to be when it stood in the forest, and the canoe was representative of the best work he could do. He was still tapping in ribs as the course was about to begin, and the day he finished the canoe someone sent by Reeves arrived to take it away. Henri could not stand to see it go, and he was in an ugly mood for the rest of the summer. Finished in the morning, gone in the afternoon—never again would he let that happen, he decided. He was never going to be deadlined by a day, or even a month—the year alone was enough of a promise. He wanted his canoes around for a while when they were done. Wistfully, he wondered if the North Canoe would ever come back to Greenville for a touchup in "the yard." Meanwhile, in the Quetico-Superior, it went up the Pigeon River on the route of the *voyageurs*. It was poled upstream and lined up rapids. It was a dry, sound, stable canoe—beautiful in sheer, smoothly seamed, with high, Christopherson ends. The graduate students sprayed themselves with Off and carried freeze-dried food, but they also learned and sang Loire Valley songs, ate some pork and dried peas, and drank from eight-gallon kegs of brandy. The course, moving northward, was a total success. It established itself in the curriculum. It left nothing in its wake but a lonely master of arts.

HENRI VAILLANCOURT once had a dead bear in his room at college. This emerges as we move north on the northernmost arm of Chesuncook Lake. Between the canoes, idle conversation is for us what the *chansons* were for the *voyageurs*. Up at six, we have been on the water since seven-forty-five. The wind has not yet come up for the day. The canoes tend to separate. One or the other moves wide or falls behind. The gap extends until it reaches a kind of psychological apogee, at which moment binding forces begin to apply, and the two canoes—alone on hundreds of acres of water—draw slowly together until they all but touch.

Rick Blanchette says to Henri, when the gap is narrow, "So. How are you?"

"Fine. How are you? Still working down at the plastics shop?"

"Yes. Still building canoes?"

"Yes."

"How are the wife and kids?" Henri has no wife and kids.

"Fine. How are *your* wife and kids?"

Rick has none, either, but this ritual occurs at least twice a day.

I have told them they sound like Kordofan Arabs, who say to one another:

"God bless you."

"How is your health?"

"Thanks be to God, well."

"God bless you."

"How are your camels?"

"Thanks be to God, well. How are your camels?"

"Thanks be to God, well. How are your cattle?"

"Thanks be to God, well." And so on through any living thing in sight or mind.

And now Henri says to Rick, "How are your camels?"

And Rick says, "Thanks be to God, well. How are your cattle?"

And—to put a stop to it—I say, "God bless you. How is your dead bear?"

Henri explains that it was a cub and did not take up much space in the room.

"A *cub*!" Warren Elmer says, and his paddle stops.

"Someone had shot it, and my roommate got it from a butcher. I wanted to have the skin."

"I'd like to have the skin of the person who shot it," Warren says, and with his paddle rips a hole in the lake.

"If someone shot it, you know, someone might as well make use of it," Henri says, with a dismissive shrug. The gap begins to widen again. He takes the lead. He likes to be in the lead. He crosses our bow—so close that we have to stop to let him pass.

There has been an inordinate amount of talk this morning about Mud Pond Carry, which is only a mile or so ahead of us, and which comes back into the conversation now as we make the first portage of the trip—although "portage" is hardly the word for it. A scant fifty feet separates Chesuncook Lake from Umbazooksus Stream, across the low remains of an earthfill logging dam. The topographic map indicates that Mud Pond Carry, two miles long, is a straight walk with a gentle rise of seventy feet followed by a gentle drop of sixty. There is tension, though, in Henri's voice when he talks about it, and in Rick's as well—a lot of verbal flexing and dancing around, with tremors at the mention of the name. I don't understand why. Perhaps it is because Thoreau got lost there—wandered right off into the woods, and was found, by his guide, many miles away.

We move on up Umbazooksus Stream, which is almost a deadwater—a current so light it can scarcely bend grass. We have come into a quiet, somewhat eerie chamber in the woods. Inaccurately, it puts forth a sense of lurking harm, and someone mentions *Deliverance*. We have all read the book or seen the movie—about four men on a canoe trip, one of whom is sexually abused at gunpoint by a stubbly-bearded mountain man—and among us *Deliverance* has become a sort of standing joke, like the plastics shop and the camels. *Deliverance* may have been set at the far end of the Appalachian chain, but its thought-wave effects seem to have reached to wherever canoes may float, and in one way or another we have all been warned not to go on canoe trips. Were we crazy? Did we realize what could *happen* out there? Had we seen *Deliverance*?

James Dickey, author of the novel and of the script of the film, lives on an artificial lake in Columbia, South Carolina. He teaches creative writing at the university there. He owns an aluminum canoe, and, by the report of colleagues, has logged in it journeys of impressively short distance. Students gather around him, and he says, "We need white water!," and they address the canoe to the shore of the flat brown lake. Dickey goes into the house and comes back with a half-gallon bottle of bourbon, glasses, and ice. He goes in again, and comes out with his bow and arrow, his Martin guitar, and more duffel and cargo, until the canoe, loaded and launched, is low in the freeboard with students, writer, and gear. The canoe goes over the water. Then the water goes over the canoe. The canoe rolls, spills everyone. The guitar floats away. Dickey struggles to his feet. The lake comes up to his knees.

Such germinal scenes, transmuted in the treasuries of the author's imagination, have led to the impression that this mildest, gentlest, safest of outdoor activities—pursued for generations by summering teachers and Explorer Scouts—is a fear-shot thing to do. We decide that Umbazooksus Stream is James Dickey country, and around the next bend we will encounter the Umbazooksus Stationary Rapist, who, truth be told, is flown in each day from Boston. With thumbless hands, he strums a banjo while he waits.

From time to time, we encounter on the rivers and lakes other people in canoes. Warren and I, on a long walk in the woods one day in the hope of seeing wildlife, see instead two travelling canoemen in yellow slickers drinking canned beer by their beached canoe. As we emerge from the woods and walk toward them, incredible fear comes into their eyes. We are hairy—I with a stubble, Warren with a Visigoth's beard. We have no apparent canoe. We look "native" enough to rape a stone. One of the men has cherubic cheeks and fair hair and a fat tummy and small eyes, and he seems to be aware of his unfortunate resemblance to the victim in *Deliverance.* The closer we move, the beadier the eyes become. The beer can is up like plasma. We are now on top of these men, and there is nothing warm in their regard, which seems to say, "One more step and we'll scream."

"Hello," Warren says.

"Hi," I insert.

Warren speaks to them of routes and the weather. It is at once apparent that he has been miscast. His voice is all wrong to bear freight of danger, ignoble tones of any kind. The beer descends. The eyes de-bead. The scene uncreates itself.

Facts fulfill fiction sometimes, though. The river in the South that is most often identified as *Deliverance* country has attracted many hundreds of people who might otherwise have never in their lives stepped into a canoe. With some apparent sense of secondhand macho and shared novelistic experience, they have set out in canoes on the river; and, like boys from Hotchkiss and Groton being gored in the streets of Pamplona, a few of them have been killed—the ultimate adventure—but not by the gun of a strange aggressor. They have been killed by fast-moving water, with which their experience was limited to having seen it on film.

Dickey is not responsible, of course. He did not create foolhardiness. All he created was an imaginative book full of wildly impossible canoeing scenes—canoes diving at steep angles down breathtaking cataracts, and shooting like javelins through white torrents among blockading monoliths—and a film that was faithful to the book. A canoe trip is a society so small and isolated that its frictions—and everything else about it—can magnify to stunning size. When trouble comes on a canoe trip, it comes from the inside, from fast-growing hatreds among the friends who started. Perhaps Dickey delivered less than he might have when he brought trouble in from the outside.

Henri says that his reaction to *Deliverance*, while seeing the movie, was that he couldn't care less who was doing what to whom but he was shocked and alarmed by what was happening to the canoes.

Dingbat Prouty, a hundred years ago, was a logger who worked in this region of the woods, and one noted day he nearly drowned in a multiple tragedy in fast water, at a pitch on the Penobscot that took the lives of three of his companions. Prouty, swimming to safety, pulled himself up on a huge log that was floating in an eddy, and there he searched his soaked clothing, found his pipe and some tobacco that was dry, and had himself a quiet, contemplative smoke while the corpses went on downriver. "Ain't he a James Dickey bird!" said another logger, who watched him sitting there. The year was 1870. "Now, ain't he a James Dickey bird!" The expression was used to describe any person whose words or actions were filled with striking incongruities; and here, north of the Moosehead, it was universally understood.

We take a clearer look at the stream. If ever there was moose country, it is Umbazooksus Stream—with its broad meanders through fields of sedge, its occasional dead standing trees. The stream is quiet and protected, surrounded by forest. We decide that we are going to see a moose here. We will stop paddling, stop talking, and stay until a moose shows up or the stream freezes. We settle down to wait. Stillness envelops us. It is the stillness of a moose intending to appear.

Thoreau was here on the twenty-seventh of July. Polis, his guide, told him that "Umbazooksus" meant "Much Meadow River." Thoreau described it in his journal as "a very meadowy stream, and deadwater. . . . The space between the woods, chiefly bare meadow . . . is a rare place for moose." He described the sedges, the wool grass, the abundant colonies of common blue flag. The year was 1857, and nothing has discernibly changed since then. "It was unusual for the woods to be so distant from the shore," he continued. "There was quite an echo from them, but when I was shouting in order to awake it, the Indian reminded me that I should scare the moose, which he was looking out for, and which we all wanted to see. The word for echo was Pockadunkquaywayle."

It is, of course, possible that a long brown snout will appear, a rack of antlers—unfortunately, a buck. We have seen no deer, but there are enough around—five per square mile of the Maine forest. Deer are so suburban, however, that for me they would frankly disturb the atmosphere of this remote northern stream. Deer intensely suggest New Jersey. One of the densest concentrations of wild deer in the United States—fifty per square mile—inhabits the part of New Jersey that, as it happens, I inhabit, too. Deer like people. They like to be near people, and New Jersey has more people per acre than any other state. People move out of the city to a New Jersey town and turn rhapsodic at the sight of deer. They write letters, songs, poems implying that they now live on the edge of wilderness. ("There were *deer* outside the window this morning.") Thoreau mentions a "deer that went a-shopping" in the streets of Bangor, explaining that deer "are more common about the settlements." Deer use the sidewalks in the heart of Princeton. A year or so ago, I saw a buck with a big eight-point rocking-chair rack looking magnificent as he stood between two tractor-trailers in the Frito-Lay parking lot in New Brunswick, New Jersey. When the buckshot season comes, New Jersey's deer know it, and at the sound of the first blast they get up on people's porches or stand around on lawns, waiting it out. The season lasts a week, in December. If the deer are patient, they die of old age. Meanwhile, they love apples. They like alfalfa, soybeans, clover, and lettuce. They like much of the truck in the gardens of man. In long files, they move through woodlots from orchards to gardens to the edges of fields. When the squirrels stop playing on the ground and run up into the trees, the herd is coming, travelling into the wind. A doe appears. Another. Another. Sometimes twenty go by, and then there is a skip in time. Now the main buck, the king of the herd, steps out of the woods. Hunters—watching from cover or from tree stands—will choose a buck in summer and take movies of him through the fall, waiting for December. Deer particularly gravitate to semi-rural research centers, of which there are many around Princeton, spaced like moons through the wooded countryside. The hunters know the size and special characteristics of each herd: the Squibb herd, the Dow Jones herd, the Western Electric herd, the Mobil Oil herd. The Institute for Advanced Study has extensive woodlots, and the smartest deer on earth are in the Institute herd.

If a deer would degrade this place slightly, a moose, on the other hand, would stir the morning. Our patience endures, though, no more than an hour. Like Thoreau before us, we fail to see a moose on Much Meadow River. Above us, a loon flies, laughing. We move on up the stream to its source—Umbazooksus Lake. A strong north wind has come up, and we have to fight it across the lake to the beginning of the carry.

Henri is edgy before the start. With considerable meticulousness, he slowly ties his tumpline to the center thwart and adjusts his carry board, which is tied to the thwart with a rawhide thong. The tump will fit across his forehead and pick up some of the canoe's weight. The carry board, a flat piece of cedar, a modified shingle, will place weight on the back of his head and the middle of his shoulders. Thoreau described such a carry board in *The Maine Woods*, and Henri has made this one from Thoreau's description. I ask him if the carry board generally helps a lot, and he says he will soon find out.

"You've always done without one?"

"I've never made a portage before."

With the exception of the fifty-foot carry we made into Umbazooksus Stream, he says, this is the first portage of his life.

In astonishment, I ask him, then, how many canoe trips he has made, and he says four—all short ones, and all without portages. I remember the little thirteen-foot canoe he was determined to bring on this trip, and I now understand why. He is well prepared, though, with his tump and carry board, and with two paddles tied to the thwarts so the flat of the blades will rest on his shoulders. He flips the canoe and holds it by the gunwales above him, the bow tip resting on the ground. He lowers the canoe into place on his shoulders. The bow swings upward to a point of balance. He adjusts the tump on his forehead. The over-all rig rides lightly. He starts off fast, almost at a trot, and disappears up the trail. His manual is in his head. "The Indian started off first with the canoe and was soon out of sight, going much faster than an ordinary walk," wrote Thoreau in his journal, describing the start of this portage.

Mud Pond Carry is the way of traffic north, and has been, apparently, since a time soon after the invention of the canoe. So many feet have scuffed across these two miles that the trail is a worn trench, lying well below the surrounding terrain, just as roads in Somerset, many centuries old, run in deep grooves between the fields around them. It is impossible to imagine how Thoreau could have got lost here, how he got out of the long ditch and wandered away, for in his time it was already deep. He called it "a loosely paved gutter" and a "very wet and rocky path through the universal dense evergreen forest . . . where we went leaping from rock to rock and from side to side, in the vain attempt to keep out of the water and mud." If Mud Pond Carry were more ample, we could paddle across it in the canoes, for it is a trail full of water. From one end to the other, bullfrogs live in the portage.

Rick, lighter than Henri and with the heavier canoe, has no tumpline or carry board, and the paddles, almost from the start, cut into his shoulders. With a pack basket and other gear, I walk in front of him and test the footing, so he can avoid following where I sink in deep. The water in the portage is not just standing there in pools. It actually runs—a man-made (foot-made) stream. As we cover the first mile, the current is coming toward us. I keep calling back to Rick, telling him when to step up on "the bank," because the mud is too deep, and when to step back into the trail, because the canoe would otherwise strike the encroaching trees. Now and again, the strain of the canoe's bulk and the knee-wrenching slipperiness underfoot cause him to stop and rest, but he declines all offers of assistance. It is clearly quite important to him that he carry the canoe to the far end by himself. It is his first portage, too.

In the second mile, we notice that the current in the carry is now moving away from us. We have crossed the height of land. The water that ran toward us was on its way to the Penobscot River and Penobscot Bay. The water now running away from us is by nature Allagash flow, headed north to Canada, to go down the St. John to the Bay of Fundy. For some sixty years after Yorktown, Great Britain was under the impression that this height of land was the boundary between the United States and Canada—a viewpoint that contained within it an excuse for war, but the king of Holland was called upon as mediator and the opportunity passed. The king saw the Mud Pond Carry only on a map, and Thoreau thought this a pity, because "the king of Holland would have been in his element" here.

At the Mud Pond end of the carry, Henri combs and recombs his hair. He shows no inclination to go back and get his packs. By conventional procedure, the person not carrying the canoe takes some of the duffel halfway and then goes back for the rest; meanwhile, the canoe carrier goes to the far end, then returns for the gear that has been left at the halfway point. Henri, who has worked out so many of his skills empirically, obviously means to do the same with portaging, and the precedent he sets now is that carrying the canoe is all he will do. Someone else will have to go back for his packs. Warren does so, with a cheerful shrug.

FOR THIRTY MILES up the Allagash lakes—Chamberlain, Eagle, Churchill Lake—we fight the north wind. Much of the time, we lose. For hours it stops us—blows so hard that we can't move. It brings frustration and fans dissension. It's a real muzzler, a nose-ender. Henri's advertised philosophy—"Take it easy, see some wildlife"—has long since shrivelled, and now blows completely away. Nothing can distract him—neither a mink nor a marten nor a buff-colored hawk clinging to a swaying fir—from his apparent need not to take it easy. When the wind defeats us and we have to wait, he prowls, fidgets, and swears. At home, he can carve for ten straight hours, but here he cannot sit still.

Even Mud Pond, which is only one mile by two, is a brownish froth, uncrossable, and to get to the other side we have to make a high circle in the lee of the northern shore. Henri, whose talents do not include map reading, wanders up the inlet stream. The Blanchettes call him back. The outlet stream is too shallow for riding, so we walk down it with our hands on the floating canoes. We enter a bay of Chamberlain Lake. The bay is small—only two or three hundred acres—and almost completely landlocked. At the far end is a gap in the trees, beyond which is open water. It is fairly hard work just to traverse this little bay, for the oncoming waves are high enough to wash into the canoes—into Henri's in particular. Finally, we near the gap, and through it can more clearly see the main body of the lake—storied, wind-ridden Chamberlain. For thirty-odd years, I have been hearing tales of this lake and how it is a whistling groove whose waves stand up like the teeth of a saw. The lake surface out there now is as white as a fast rapid. The waves are two feet high. We pause in the narrows, watch the big rollers, and take out on the shore beside them. The sun is falling. We will wait for morning and hope for calm.

Warren and I jump into the water and—to get the grit of travel out of our hair—shampoo with Lava soap. Henri unloads his canoe and takes Mike Blanchette in his bow, and they go out to play with the big waves. The canoe nearly broncos them into the water, and they run for shore. Clean, feeling good, Warren and I build a bonfire of dry-ki in the lee of the forest and beside a big rock on the beach. Henri and the Blanchettes make their fire back in the woods. I go down in my pack for my pharmaceutical bottles, which are white and plastic and contain bourbon and gin. Henri makes himself a gin-and-Tang. There are worse things in life than stopping early for the day, surveying whitecapped water across the rim of a tin cup, standing in a wind where no-see-um no fly. Warren and I cook dried hamburgers in a bucket of noodles. Henri eats his green jerky and gray oatmeal. Facing the big dry-ki fire, a trayful of gingerbread rises to unprecedented heights in my reflector oven. Henri wolfs it when the tray is passed to him. He announces that he has decided to buy a reflector oven.

Some years ago, with his college roommate, Henri went camping in chill weather. He had an old, thinned-out sleeping bag, in which he nearly froze, while his roommate slept comfortably in a down bag. Henri is frugal, and he generally gets along on things he makes or adapts, but when he does decide to buy he invariably seeks out things extraordinarily good of their kind. After that trip, he bought himself an Eddie Bauer down bag—a Cadillac with feathers in it. He still has it, and has kept it in excellent condition. "I hate to even mention what I used to bring into the woods, I was so ill-equipped," he says. Before he discovered pack baskets, he used plastic garbage bags. They developed holes, and water soaked his gear. He has encased his pack baskets in waterproofed canvas. As a raincoat, he still uses a plastic garbage bag with holes cut in it for his arms and head. He paid seventy-five dollars for his Hudson's Bay jacket, though. He has bought a color-television set for his shop. His stereo equipment is of an expensive order. And when his work presses in on him and he has to get away from it, he will bolt out of town sometimes on his new ten-speed Schwinn Le Tour.

At five-thirty in the morning, Henri is up and ready to go. He wants to move while the lake is relatively calm, to be ahead of the wind. There are scattered whitecaps even now. The Indians called Chamberlain Apmoojenegamook, and no one could argue with that description. If the human race has one common denominator, it is hatred of head winds, and the Indian assessment seems to have been that no one of sound mind would counterattack the winds of this long, finger-shaped lake, so they called it "Lake That Is Crossed." Apmoojenegamook: get across it and away from it as quickly as possible; used as a thoroughfare, it is too dangerous and, moreover, too much work. We move north against the morning wind, intending to make the crossing where the lake is narrowest, reducing the risk if the wind should rise. But the going is slow, and we cover less than two miles in an hour. The wind has already grown considerably when we reach the narrows, where almost a mile separates the shores. What lies between them looks like broken glass.

There are two choices. On the opposite shore is a stream that leads to Eagle Lake. We can wait out the wind, and when it dies cross to the stream. Or, staying close to shore, we can continue against the wind all the way to the north end of Chamberlain, where, according to the topographic map, there is a portage that also leads to Eagle. Henri does not hesitate. We push on to the north.

The waves are just as high close in as they are in the center of the lake, but we are safer near shore, and where points of land protrude there is respite in the lee. Neither one of these canoes is very good in heavy wind. They do not hold course easily. Henri's takes in appalling amounts of water. With our drinking cups, we continually bail. Bailing is not altogether sufficient to keep Henri's canoe afloat, and twice he has to go ashore to empty it completely. His canoe was just not designed for a lake like Chamberlain. The three-inch freeboard and the ten-and-a-half-inch depth at the center thwart are inadequate dimensions for big lake waves. Moreover, the holes through which the root lashings pass—holes made in the bark below the gunwales—are less than two inches above the waterline when the canoe is loaded, and every wave that rolls by sends a bit of water through these holes. When Henri notices this, he goes into a long, revolutionary harangue about root lashings in bark canoes. If the canoes had nails in them, he says, the holes would not be there to take in the water. The only reason he does root lashings is that they look good, he says ruefully. He turns on his art. He says he wishes he had used nails. He will recover.

A wave slops over his knees. He bails. He curses the wind and praises nails. The wind is now coming down the lake in black squalls. "What a bummer!" he shouts, finally, above the wind. "What a God-damned bummer! That's all! I'm not going any farther!"

In shallow water, we get out of the canoes, steady them, and pass the gear ashore. We spread our clothes to dry, and sit in the sun. Mike discovers a leech on his ankle and pulls it away, and, stranded on a warm rock, it dies. We build a fire. We bake coffee cake, cook Cream of Wheat, and make tea. I open Thoreau and read, "A wave will gently creep up the side of the canoe and fill your lap, like a monster deliberately covering you with its slime before it swallows you, or it will strike the canoe violently and break into it. The same thing may happen when the wind rises suddenly, though it were perfectly calm and smooth there a few minutes before; so that nothing can save you, unless you can swim ashore, for it is impossible to get into a canoe again when it is upset. . . . We rarely crossed even a bay directly, from point to point, when there was wind, but made a slight curve corresponding somewhat to the shore, that we might the sooner reach it if the wind increased."

In six hours we have travelled five miles, and the wind—under the noon sun—has risen even more since we stopped. There is something cyclical but unpredictable about the rise and fall of lake winds. They decline in force, and decline a little more, and soon the water seems negotiable. So we collect our gear and start to load up. Then, like a siren, the wind goes high. We settle back. Watch the lake. The wind subsides. Again we load the canoes—only to be pushed ashore by a heavy squall.

On this same lake where we have been trying to paddle canoes with a loaded weight of several hundred pounds into heavy winds, log drivers a century ago were—by hand—moving booms that weighed many thousands of tons. They fought such winds for days and nights. They could not stop to sleep, or the wind would shove the boom backward, possibly breaking it open against the rocky shore and hopelessly scattering the logs. The boom was a teardrop enclosure of floating timber, its periphery a set of logs joined together. The boom was attached to a log raft. In a batteau (a modified dory), a three-hundred-pound anchor was carried roughly a thousand feet ahead of the raft and dropped into the lake. On the raft was a capstan, which had been made from a segment of log, with capstan bars protruding like the stubs of branches. Men on the raft strained against the capstan bars and, trudging in a circle, slowly spooled in a thousand feet of rope. Then they stood around gasping while the anchor was pulled up and taken forward another thousand feet. Even into the wind, the big boom had enough momentum to keep moving while the anchor went out again. Then the raft crew returned to the capstan bars, and the boom continued toward Bangor, at a sixth of a mile an hour.

Out of the lakes and down the Penobscot, boom crews and rivermen drove two hundred million board feet of lumber a year. They wore red shirts and caulked boots, and stepped from log to log carrying peaveys, pickpoles, pickaroons. The logs averaged sixteen feet, and those of greatest girth—the first-cut logs from the giant pines—were too big for the float down the river and were left in the forest to rot. By damming the Allagash lakes and raising them a scant twenty feet, the loggers in 1842 spilled some Allagash water into the Penobscot watershed through the Telos Cut, near the foot of Chamberlain, and timber that might have had to go to Canada could now go to the sawmills of Bangor. Down the river in spring ran waters of frightening weight—in rapids, through gorges, over falls—and in the fast water the logs ran free. Sometimes they jammed—thousands in crisscross, plugging the river. Up front, at the focus of pressure, were certain key logs. To pick them free was to "pick the jam" and send the tumult on its way. The river drivers now and then worked from boats, but more often from the banks, on foot. A wing jam was tough to pick. To pick a middle jam was sometimes fatal. If these men had been shooting each other instead of shooting rapids, their light would now shine with the cowboys'. "Go down and pick a jam on the Heater," their boss would tell them, and without a quiver they went off to die. When they attempted rescues, they enhanced the art of suicide. "Drown ten men to save two" was the accepted code of the river. They were white and Indian, and the whites on the whole were wilder—more coarse—than the Indians. Those who believed in God for the most part respected Him, but of Noah they were outspokenly critical. They thought his ark had been "a Jim Dickey house," because Noah used too much pitch.

Fortunately, the log drivers had a chronicler—a magazine writer, naturalist, and free-lance historian, whose name was Fannie Hardy Eckstorm. Her father was a Maine fur trader, and she grew up in the presence of the rivermen. She idolized them, saw them as heroes of grand dimension. She sold stories about them to the *Atlantic Monthly*, and in 1904 published the *Atlantic* stories and other pieces on the subject in a collection called *The Penobscot Man*. "It has always been the glory of the West Branch Drive that it had so many such men, every one of whom placed the welfare of those logs above his own life," she wrote. They were "supple young foam-walkers," in her eyes, and they could "traverse the froth of those white rapids without wetting a shoe-tap." Upriver they went—as many as two hundred of them—to start the drive with the spring high water, and, come what may, it was a matter of pride to have the logs in Bangor by the end of June. For two months, they ate "sow-belly an' Y.E.B.'s" (pork and yellow-eyed beans), and they drank themselves to heaven on the Fourth of July.

Joe Aitteon worked the West Branch Drive. He was only twenty-four when, in September 1853, he made his trip with Thoreau. In his thirties, he was elected governor of his tribe, and in 1870, aged forty-one, he died on the drive. Paddle in hand, he drowned in the Heater, where the water ran so white, the river drivers said, "a brick would swim." In command of a full batteau crew, a mixture of whites and Indians, he had been sent to pick a jam, and the boat was staved in and swamped and carried on into even heavier rapids. Aitteon was a swimmer, and by leaving the boat he might have survived—as did others, including Dingbat Prouty. Aitteon, however, died with the nonswimmers, whom he was trying to save. Far below the rapids was a calm, still stretch of the river, and a crew of drivers working the banks there suddenly saw a long stern paddle—unmistakably Aitteon's, with its blue blade and its carved eagle—rise vertically halfway out of the water.

It was Eckstorm's opinion that Thoreau was "lacking in penetration" and had "failed to get the measure" of Aitteon. Thoreau had missed a chance to sketch a character of considerable worldliness and with a gift for leadership—never mind that Aitteon was young when Thoreau knew him. "Thoreau hired an Indian to be aboriginal," she explained, and he tended to ignore anything that did not accord with his preconceptions. Aitteon said "By George!" too much when he should have been talking pidgin. His true character failed to emerge in *The Maine Woods.* Thoreau had a "luckless knack of blundering," according to Eckstorm, and "when he came in contact with men, in his own phrase, 'he improved his opportunity to be ignorant.'" He was, after all, the "hermit of Walden," she said. He was "naïve," and he could not grasp a "truly strange" and "subtle matter" when one was brought to his attention. For example, a mysterious death had taken place at a riverine landmark called the Gray Rock of Abol, and Joe Polis, Thoreau's other Indian guide, tried to tell him the story. Thoreau deflected the conversation before Polis could get to the point, and thus Thoreau, in Eckstorm's words, "bungled utterly" what she called "the most significant incident that ever came under his observation while he was in the Maine woods." Fortunately, though, the Indian had told at least a fragment of the story to this "man who wrote everything down, even the things he did not understand," and, equipped with Thoreau's thin clue, Eckstorm herself went to the rivermen and uncovered the full, long tale. The gray rock is flat and stands in quiet water. Reduced to essentials, the story concerned a log driver who suddenly disappeared from the rock, never again to be seen alive. The day was clear. He was not killed by man or nature. He died because he was in the act of cursing God:

> The man who had seen this told the others. "I seen him stand there like he was on a barn floor, and I seen him lift up his fist an' shake it right stret in the face of old Katahdin, an' I hearn him holler like his voice would rattle lead inside him, 'To hell with God!' An' then when I looked the Gray Rock was all empty, an' in the water I seen only his two sets of fingers movin' slow-like in the mist that sticks close to the black slick of the falls. I seen 'em open once, an' then they shut an' was gone."
>
> "That was a judgment," said the men one to another.

It never occurred to Eckstorm to question what she saw as the high purpose of the West Branch Drive. Moving those logs downstream was pure epic to her, and the goal—beyond challenge—was the common good. One suspects, therefore, that Thoreau annoyed her less by what he failed to say than by what he said most strongly. One imagines her reaching for a pickpole when, in *The Maine Woods*, she came upon this:

> The reader will perceive that the result of this particular damming about Chamberlain Lake is, that the head-waters of the St. John are made to flow by Bangor . . . thus turning the forces of nature against herself, that they might float their spoils out of the country. . . . The wilderness experiences a sudden rise of all her streams and lakes, she feels ten thousand vermin gnawing at the base of her noblest trees. . . . The chopper . . . speaks of a "berth" of timber, a good place for him to get into, just as a worm might. When the chopper would praise a pine, he will commonly tell you that the one he cut was so big that a yoke of oxen stood on its stump; as if that were what the pine had grown for, to become the footstool of oxen.

Henri Vaillancourt's great-great-grandfather was a river driver, and he drowned on the job.

WELL BEYOND noon, we are still held fast by the wind. It has subsided a little, but the lake remains a whitecapped sea. One senses that we will be on it soon. Henri is using the word "bummer" at about double the rate he was using it an hour or two ago. The wind and Henri's patience are drawing lines across the day, and when the lines converge we will load up and go.

Just a few feet inside the treeline on the shore, the wind is filtered and calmed. Looking out on the lake from between two trees is like looking through a window at a storm. It is pleasant here, and warm. I could stay here for a week, not to mention the hours that are left in this day. I would very much like to sleep and read and—no matter how much time it takes—outlast the wind. But that would be the Indians' way, and Henri is not an Indian. Restless, impatient to move forward and cover ground, he paws the beach. He throws a rock in the water. He curses the wind. He says, "Christ, it's quiet enough. Let's go." It would take a meteorologist to tell us whether the wind is stronger or weaker than it was when we put in to shore. The waves are rolling hard, but the waiting, apparently, has built the case for going. We load the canoes and shove off.

We dig into the lake. We paddle and bail, bail and paddle—draining the bilge with drinking cups. We are struggling to get to the north end, about three miles away, and gambling that the wind will not rise to an even higher level before we are in the lee of the north-end woods. Why do we need these miles now? Why does Henri have this compulsion to move? Is he Patton? Sherman? Hannibal? How *could* he be, when the only regimentation he can tolerate is the kind he creates as he goes along? These are thoughts not composed in tranquillity but driven into the mind by the frontal wind. Why do we defer to him? Why do we look to his decisions? Is it only because he made the canoes, because the assumption is that he knows what is best for them and knows what they can do and ought not to do? His judgment draws attention to itself, right enough. On the Penobscot River, he went "out for a spin" in heavy, gray dusk and was gone long after dark—much longer than he wished or intended. What was he doing? He was struggling to pick his way through boulders and up a set of minor rapids he could not see. A camper on the riverbank, that same day, asked him if his canoe was not too low in the freeboard for paddling on open lakes, and he said, "Not really. They don't really ride low. You can design a canoe to do anything." But here he is on Chamberlain Lake, bailing six inches of water from between his knees and whisking with his paddle, while Warren, like a tractor, pulls the canoe. A suspicion that has been growing comes out in the wind: Henri's expertise stops in "the yard"; out here he is as green as his jerky.

After two hours of paddling, we have gone a mile and three-quarters, but we are at least not going backward. We begin to feel the protection of the land ahead of us, and Rick and I point off the wind and head more directly for the carry at the northeast corner of the lake. Mike, though, does not like rolling in the troughs of the waves. He says to his older brother, "Do you think we'll have trouble taking these waves broadside, Rick?"

"We'll head out a little," Rick answers.

"No. Follow Henri, Rick. Follow Henri."

Mike is a pessimistic soul, and he is convinced that—as he puts it—"if the canoe turns over, you're a goner." All the more touching is his belief that Henri will see him through.

Rick defers to Henri, too, but less so. Rick is Henri's lifelong friend. The differences between them must attract the one to the other. Rick is self-effacing and thoughtful, and he is less impressed than he might be with his own intelligence. He has no apparent special talent, and he admires greatly Henri's single-minded dedication, his artistry, and his adroitness with his tools. Rick introduced Henri to Beethoven and, in all likelihood, to Thoreau. Subtly, in one way or another, he seems to have been helping Henri along for years. Rick seems to sense frailty and unsureness under Henri's carapace of bluntness, and is always ready to give him the benefit of the doubt. Rick is sensitive to Henri's insensitivities—to his opinionated arrogance, to his inconsiderate manner, to his platoon-leading orders. In Rick's long, contemplative glances, Warren and I can see him weighing the effect of Henri's directives.

Warren, who has the misfortune to be paddling in Henri's bow, is by now suffering from acute propinquity, and, being a silent man, takes it out on the lake. His strokes are delivered with killing strength, and in their canoe it is Warren who is defeating the wind. The more Henri orders him around, the harder Warren must work to work off his anger. It is an asset to have such an engine in the bow. Warren and I are more or less guests on this trip, so we defer to Henri. We have, however, tried to make suggestions—where to stay, when to go, what to head for—but the results have been dismal, and we have learned that suggestions are challenges to the tacit commander. We go when he is ready. We stop when he wants to stop. We stay where he wants to stay. He does not seek out the consensus of the group, and when it comes his way he almost automatically rejects it.

Some of these thoughts subside with the wind as we move in among the sedges in the corner of the lake. We are finished at least with the winds of Chamberlain, having climbed ten miles through them an inch at a time.

An isthmus half a mile wide separates Chamberlain from Eagle, and a steam-powered continuous cable once ran across it, hauling logs from one lake to the other on little steel trucks. All the thousands of bolts, steel clamps, steel saddle, steel tracks, and fourteen tons of cable were brought into the woods over winter ice or in canoes and other boats, following the route we have followed. The conveyor lasted about six years—at the beginning of the twentieth century. Beside what is left of it we portage now. The track is still there, upgrown with trees. The portage trail is firm and open, and easy going all the way. Just before the shore of Eagle, we drop our packs, set down the canoes, and stare in disbelief at what may be the most incongruous sight any of us has ever seen: two full-scale steam locomotives, alone in the woods, abandoned. They, too, were brought in here in fragments and assembled in the woods. Standard-gauge track—seventy-five miles from the nearest railroad—was laid so that logs could be moved a few miles over the height of land. The trains began running in 1927 and were used for only a season or two. The track they ran on has been all but closed over by the woods.

We go down to the shore and look at Eagle Lake. It is a big one, and four miles of it stretch north in front of us before it bends to the west and out of sight. The wind and the white-caps are worse than they were on Chamberlain—a forbidding gale. Henri sucks on a blade of grass and paces around saying, "Christ, what a bummer." It is as clear to him as to the rest of us that there will be no moving into such a wind. We eat lunch. It is four-thirty in the afternoon. The wind will drop soon, Henri tells us. Meanwhile, Henri's packs are still at the other end of the carry. The Blanchettes go back to fetch them for him.

After two more hours, big gray waves are still coming down the lake, rolling before the wind. Unfortunately, this is a bad place to spend a night, because the mechanized loggers gave it a century's fouling and the century isn't over yet. Rust is everywhere—rusty spikes, rusty hunks of the conveyor. To accommodate incoming logs, landfill was shoved into the lake, so the shore is artificial and swampy and strewn with boulders and still jagged with the corpses of water-killed trees. Mike wants to stay here, in this oxidized hole of commerce. He is so tired that it looks good to his eyes. He says it is as good as any campsite we've seen. Rick watches Henri and says nothing. Warren and I move our packs up the portage trail, planning to sleep there and avoid the junk yard. When we return to the lakeshore, Henri says the wind is declining. It is seven-thirty now, and the lake is indeed calming down. We will paddle at night, Henri says, and take advantage of the absence of the wind. Warren looks around with incredulity, and even apprehension, in his eyes. He appears to be wondering how to make a straitjacket. We got up at five today. We have paddled ten miles into blistering wind and followed that with a portage. Now we are told that we are going to set out on another big lake for God knows where in the dark of night. Under the influence of the wind, our affection for our leader has been waning all day, and it now levels out at zero. We turn without comment and walk away.

Warren, who was recently discharged from the Marine Corps, says, "I feel as if I were back in uniform." We go up the trail to our packs and our tent, and pick them up, and carry them back to the lake. It is Henri's trip. We will paddle tonight.

There is a cut, a sluiceway, a small canal, that penetrates the shore. It was used to float logs to the conveyor. Henri and Warren load their canoe in the sluiceway and push off toward the open lake. Rick and Mike and I fill our canoe, and while we are handling the packs a six-inch leech excitedly swims among us, trying to get in on the fun. With everything aboard, the three of us prepare to step in. We do not know that two iron spikes, set in timber, stand upright underwater, the tip of each less than an inch from the underside of the floating canoe. We step in, one at a time, and we give the canoe a shove. It does not move. Water spurts upward in fountains, fast enough to swamp us instantly.

Jumping out, we shout for Henri. We unload the canoe, lift it ashore, and roll it over. Rick is struggling to control his distress. His canoe, a treasure to him, has two ugly holes in it, large enough and ragged enough to make one wonder how it can continue the trip. Henri, examining the wounds, curses Rick for negligence, for irresponsibility, for failure as custodian of a bark canoe. Rick does not try to demur.

Now, all at once, Henri stops his harangue and changes utterly. The man who has been pouting, sucking grass, and cursing the wind all afternoon is suddenly someone else—is now, in a sense, back in his yard, his hands on a torn canoe. The lacerations are broad, and the bark around them is in flaps with separating layers. "Make a fire," he says, and Warren and I move off for wood. "Rick, Mike, get bark. Get strips of bark. And cut a green stick."

Henri goes down into his pack for the small paper bag in which he keeps his pot of pitch. He has been touching up the canoes from time to time since we started, and now has about six ounces left.

The fire is going. He sets the pot on two burning sticks. It seems so vulnerable. What if the pitch spills or blazes up? Where are we then, with one canoe?

Thirty minutes ago, we were standing apart in groups, tense to the edges of rage, some of us committing verbal mutiny. Now we are all bustling in service to Henri—his surgical nurses, offering instruments to his hand. First—with his crooked knife—he cuts away what appears to me to be a considerable amount of bark, trimming the split and flapping laminations. He does not cut all the way through, for with the exception of the actual punctures most of the damage is in the outer layers. He cuts a wide, shallow crater around each wound—four to five inches in diameter—taking away about half the bark's layers.

He asks for the green stick and the fresh bark, and with them he makes a torch. He lights it, and moves it close to the bottom of the canoe. He takes a deep breath and steadily blows flame into and around one of the punctures. Gradually, the bark there lightens in tone and becomes bone-dry. Henri says it is not impatience but necessity that causes him to use the torch. Even if he were to wait many hours, the rent bark would not completely dry; and "if bark is not absolutely dry the pitch won't stick."

It is now too dark for him to see. He calls for the flashlight, and I get it from my pack and shine it on the canoe as he works. He removes the pot from the fire and—with a flat stick—paints the entire damaged area with pitch while the Blanchettes, one at each end, hold the canoe level. Henri pulls out the tail of his shirt and cuts it off. It is broadcloth, and he cuts out of it a circular piece, which he presses down onto the pitch. Calling for the pot again, he paints on more pitch, until the cloth is completely covered. Then, as the pitch cools, he presses it repeatedly with his thumb, licking his thumb as he goes along to keep it from sticking. The finished patch is a black circle, about six inches in diameter. It is in the center of the bottom of the canoe. "At home I'll cut an eye of bark and put a rim around it," Henri says. "Then the patch, you know, will look better."

It is too late to move now. We sleep beside the canoes and get up at five-thirty to continue the repair. The pitch, heating up in the morning fire, bursts into flame. Henri runs to it and smothers it with a coffeepot lid, but some is lost. Minutes later, the pitch catches fire again.

"Our pitch after this is going to be nil," Henri says. "That's no problem, though. I should have brought more pitch, but we can always get spruce gum. There's plenty of it around here."

Applying what is left to the other rip in the canoe, he says casually, "I've never had this happen before. I've never had to patch a canoe before." He pauses, and licks his thumb. "You could break a whole end off in the woods and still fix the canoe —that is, if you'd built a canoe before," he says. "If you hadn't, I think you'd be in trouble."

Mike says, "I wonder what will happen if those patches let go in the middle of the lake."

And Henri says, "I don't think they will."

THE LAKE IS flat calm—mirror condition—and the sky cloudless. It is seven-thirty. We load up and go. Early in the trip, we tied almost nothing to the canoes, but now every pack is secured with thongs, ropes, and strings. Our boots are tied to the thwarts, since we launch and paddle without them.

The canoe is dry, and sound, and it seems to slide on oil. It cuts an arrow of a wake directly north across the open water—four, five miles—with an ease that launches jokes again, canoe to canoe.

"So. How are you?"

"And how are your wife and camels?"

Now, though, in the last half mile before the end of Eagle, a cruising loon leans forward and gives its long, lamentful cry. When, on a dead-calm day, a loon breaks a silence with such a cry, it is almost invariably a signal that a wind—not a breeze but a sudden, heavy wind—is coming. A minute passes. Two. There is no sign of it. Three. Four. On the last stretch of lake before us, the surface suddenly appears scratched, like rubber prepared for a patch. Moments later, a stiff wind ruffles our shirts. It is not a puff but a steady push. Waves rise quickly, and minutes later they are capped white.

"Mother."

"God."

"Damn."

"Bitch."

We have to fight to finish the lake.

Fortunately, narrow waters lead on to the north for three miles—dam-drowned stretches, actually, of the Allagash River. The riparian forests temper the wind somewhat, but still it comes at us hard down the alley.

"What a—"

"Bummer."

Long before we reach and slide through them, the wind brings the sweet scent of a rich purple grove of pickerelweed.

Henri has begun to bail with exceptional vigor. His canoe is showing trouble—taking in more water than before. The land widens again to either side, and we move onto Churchill Lake, where the waves are as high and the wind as strong as they were at any time on Chamberlain. The lake inclines to the northeast, and the wind is quartering on us now. A thousand yards out, Henri turns to face it. He cannot take even the small amount of extra water that comes with quartering waves. His canoe is filling up. Racing a serious leak, he and Warren cut straight through the wind. Ahead of them is a strip of sand-and-pebble beach. Bailing as they go, they make it. We are two and a half hours, and nine miles, from breakfast —not bad against a rising head wind and with another sick canoe.

We eat an early lunch—Rick, Warren, Mike, and I—and lie on the beach and take the sun, and watch Henri fix the canoe. He is collected and professional. He does not rail at his canoes as he rails at the wind. His problem now is no less serious than the one after the accident last night, and in the repair the degree of difficulty appears to be, if anything, greater. A longitudinal seam connecting two pieces of bark below the waterline has broken its sewing, and a gap has opened. When he made the canoe, he sewed that area too close to the edge of the bark, and the root stitching has now broken through to the edge. It is a wonder the canoe did not founder.

Henri's confidence is undisturbed, and he goes into the forest for a fresh root. He digs a spruce root—five or six feet, which is more than he needs—and returns to the beach. With his crooked knife he rubs the bark off the root until it looks, and wriggles, like a cord of white rubber. (Indians used roots for fishing lines.) He bites one end, splitting it, and then—with a shaking, shivery manipulation—pulls the root into halves from one end to the other. The splitting, as it goes along, will tend to favor one side. The idea is to sense which way it wants to go and to correct the split in favor of the other side. A novice could dig up roots by the dozen and not split one successfully, but Henri refuses to be praised for his swift execution of the trick. "There's nothing to it," he says. "You get the knack quickly. You feel them going one way or the other and you just correct it." Around Greenville, he has found white-pine roots twenty-five feet long. Like the roots of the black spruce, they run close to the surface and are easy to collect. White spruce will not do. Joe Polis once said of the roots of white spruce, "No good, break, can't split 'em." And they run too deep in the ground.

Henri takes a close look at the position of the break in the seam and is pleased to find that it is directly under a rib. "Good," he says. "The repair won't show." And he taps the rib aside. His awls are at home, but he has picked up a nail somewhere, and he uses it now to bore holes through the planking and the bark. The root is soon moving through the planking and out through the bark and back again in a set of cobbler's stitches—Henri reaching around the canoe, hugging it, to draw the sewing tight. He is sewing not only bark to bark (near the original seam) but also bark to planking, to give the repair increased authority. When the sewing is finished and tied off, bright sutures mar the planking, but Henri taps the rib back in, and—as he said it would—it completely hides the job.

Warren, sitting up on one elbow, tugs his beard, looks at me, and says, "I have a question. What in the name of hell would we ever do without him?"

We are about as far north as we are going to go. On Thoreau's canoe trips in the Maine woods, his most northern campsite was on Pillsbury Island, in Eagle Lake. "We did not intend to go far down the Allegash," he wrote in his journal, "but merely to get a view of the great lakes which are its source." Henri may have taken his cue from this, for his own intention has been much the same: to scour the scenes of the big Allagash lakes and then to bend off in another direction and go upstream to the highest sources of the river—and to Allagash Lake itself, the best and remotest of them all.

To the north, meanwhile, we have some five more miles to paddle—to Churchill Dam, which raised the water here enough to boom logs, there to see (but not to shoot) the Chase Rapids of the Allagash River. We shove off and round a point and buck the head wind all the way. Henri's canoe is as good as ever; that is to say, it takes in the usual amount of wave lap but nothing through the re-sewn seam.

There is a Maine state ranger station at Churchill Dam. The ranger comes out and looks in wonder at the two birchbark canoes. He is short and dark, with a creased face and a quick smile. He says that he has seen thousands of canoes in his time on the Allagash Wilderness Waterway but none, ever, like these. The canoes are exquisite, he agrees. Those paddles, though, those little Indian paddles—"now, they would drive you foolish." He, in his turn, has something to show—three fresh bullet holes in his cabin door, through which, last night, he fired three fresh bullets at bears that were crowding his porch trying to claw their way in.

In broad bends of white water, the Allagash River flows away from the dam and the cabin. The rapids, continuous for several miles, are not heavy but are broad, shallow, and rocky. Henri says if he were going on downriver he would portage around them.

I ask him why.

"The canoes would be all right," he says. "I'd trust them. I just wouldn't trust myself. I've never been in rapids before."

The ranger controls the river. Each evening around five, he says, when people downriver are presumably camped for the night, he closes the gates—turns off the water. Suddenly, the Chase Rapids are no longer white or rapid. They become a set of island pools, as does the rest of the river. In the morning at six, before the campers are up, the ranger opens the gates. The river fills while the campers are cooking breakfast. When they are ready to shove off, there is water to float them. We ourselves shove off—heading back, for the time being, in the direction from which we have come.

For a while, we sail down Churchill Lake, pleased to have foxed the wind, but the wind, the anthropomorphic wind, will not be so tricked and cheated. It quickly dies behind the sail—dies as fast as it rose in the morning—and leaves us to paddle under the glare of the sun. Three, four, five hours we paddle, until the sun is almost down. The rate of jokes flying between the canoes declines steadily with the lengthening of the afternoon. We hint, suggest, urge, and ultimately beg Henri to stop for the day, which he does, with good grace, at sundown. Even with the time spent patching and sewing two disabled canoes, we have paddled twenty-five miles since we slept. There is an ice-cold spring in the woods near the campsite. The spring water gives altitude to gin in a way that the tepid water of these shallow lakes can never do. Even before the stars are bright, we are half asleep. The canoes are overturned by the shore.

I remember that books say never to leave canoes overturned in bear country, because a bear wondering what's inside may smash its way in. Too late, too tired, to worry about bears. Warren snores through the night like a bear—a bass to the treble of the loons.

ALLAGASH STREAM, the highest reach of the river, drops to the head of Chamberlain Lake from the west-northwest. Recrossing the isthmus carry, we go in the morning to the mouth of the stream. By noon, we are literally in the water. As it pours toward us, it is too shallow to be paddled, too shallow to be poled. There is nothing to do but frog it—get out of the canoes and walk them up the current. If it is this shallow here, it is not in all likelihood going to get any deeper as we go along; therefore, as the map informs us, the best we can hope for is a seven-mile walk in the water.

Alternative routes are, for various reasons, less attractive, and do not include Allagash Lake, whose remoteness is written in its approaches: from the east, seven miles' sloshing up a rocky stream; from the west, a portage of three miles, by far the longest in the Allagash woods. So we drag the canoes—in two, three inches of water, jumping, bubbling, rushing at us. We lift them at the gunwales to reduce the draw. Now and again, we slide and fall on rock shelves covered with algae. In pools, we go in to the hips, to the chest, all the way. The cool water feels good coming on. It feels good rushing around the ankles. It feels good closing overhead. I would prefer to frog fifty miles up a forest stream than paddle ten against a big lake head wind.

Often, it is necessary to heave rocks aside to create a channel wide enough for the canoes. On many of the rocks are heavy streaks of paint or aluminum left by hundreds of canoes that have come banging down this river in varying levels of water under the care of people who did not give a damn what they hit. What comes home once more at the sight of those aluminum-covered rocks is the world of difference in the way we feel toward our canoes, and it is the central pleasure of this trip: we care so much about them. We scrape a little, too, and it can't be helped. *Tant pis*, as Henri says. Bark leaves no marks behind. Warren, leading, voraciously sculpts the river—kicking stones aside, lifting rocks so large they appear to be ledges and stuffing them into the banks. Then he hauls the canoe up the freeways he has made. Henri walks behind with a rope in his hand. It is tied to the stern, which he moves from side to side, as if the canoe were a horse on a halter.

The stream is a white-water primer, for it is flowing much like a riverine rapid, which is what it is, scaled down. All in miniature, the haystacks, the standing waves, the souse holes, the eddies, the satin-water pillows are here, and usually there is a place to go—a *fil d'eau*—that is deeper and better than anywhere else. One learns to read the stream. After four hours, we have gone two miles.

Henri remarks that he is now hungry enough to eat a moose, and wouldn't mind trying if one were to appear.

"You have to see one before you can eat one, Henri."

"And how are your wife and your cattle?"

"God bless you, well."

A windfall fir lies across the stream now and stops us altogether, but Henri unsheathes his axe and sends flotillas of chips down the current. The log drops into the water. We shove it out of the way. The air is chill. The sky, all but unnoticed by us, has clouded over, and the afternoon is almost gone. Even Henri is ready to stop. The map shows a waterfall ahead, a place to camp beside it. I see a clam, pick it up, and toss it into the canoe—another, another, beds of them in the eddies of the stream. I remember a time when I was hungry on the Susquehanna River and hunted it for miles for freshwater clams, peering down over the side of a canoe, finding nothing but an empty shell. These clams of the Allagash are squirting, vigorous, living, lovely freshwater clams. Warren and I have been eating freeze-dried food, which I, having had little of it before, was interested in trying; and, having tried it days on end, I look forward all the more to the clams.

"Why are you picking those things up?" Henri wants to know.

"We're going to eat them. Do you want some?"

"Not really."

Glances are exchanged between Vaillancourt and the Blanchettes. Madness will out, and they are sure they have seen it now.

Others have preceded us to Little Allagash Falls—a man in his twenties, his wife, their malamute puppy, and their twenty-foot wood-and-canvas Old Town canoe. It is new, green, undeniably beautiful. Twenty feet is a lot of canoe, and the hull has many fresh scratches, despite his care. He is in the wilderness business, he says, with an outfitting shop and a dealership in canoes—an interest that developed in his boyhood, when he made long canoe trips with Keewaydin in Canada in terrain where portages sometimes did not exist and had to be scouted and cut. Where on earth, he wonders, did we get those canoes?

"I make them."

"You *make* them?"

"Full time," Henri says, his eyes averted toward the falls.

"May I photograph them?"

"Oh, sure."

We carry around the falls and pitch our tents near the upstream side, before it begins to rain. It rains hard. Henri brings up one of the canoes and turns it over near the fire and runs his tarp from the canoe to a pair of trees. The shelter gives some protection to the fire and more than some to us, and we wait out the worst of the rain.

"Just a shower," I say.

"I don't know," Mike says. "I don't know" means "I disagree."

We steam the clams open in a four-quart pot, and remove them from their shells. We sprinkle them with salt and roll them in Bisquick and fry them in very hot Crisco. Henri says they are *moules frites.* "*Frites,*" on his tongue, is "*frètes.*"

"Clam? Have a clam?"

Everyone is hungry. The Blanchettes are hungry and Henri is hungry, but they will have no part of the clams.

The larger clams are chewy, go down with some resistance. But the smaller ones are crisp, succulent, tender, delicious, Allagash-Ipswich, golden brown.

"Clam?"

"Not really. Not yet, anyways."

"What are you waiting for—to see if we die?"

The three of them—Rick, Mike, Henri—are to varying extents wavering, but they still refuse. They eat their jerky and their boiled dinners. Warren and I alone are eating the clams. There are two left.

"I'll take one."

Out comes the hand of Henri. In all the culinary spectrum, there is not much he likes, but one great exception is clams.

He has told us how he drives to favorite places to buy pints and quarts of fried clams. Now he eats this one. He eats the other.

Rain again—heavy rain. We go into the tents at half past seven, and get into our bags to sleep it away. The rain sounds good, if nothing else, and it should put more water in the stream. It comes in torrents down through the trees.

Warren outsnores the sound of the rain. Henri, too. The harder the day, the more vibrant the snore. I kick them. I pick up a loose boot and hit them. The effort is wasted.

Lake, portage, and stream, we covered only ten miles today —in twelve hours of travel. I will confess that, on the whole, I don't mind these long days. I like the purpose in the motion, the clear possession of a course to follow, the sense of journey. I like to go to sleep early and rise with the sun. In these respects, I guess, I am much like Henri.

At eleven, there is a cry from Rick Blanchette—from out of the rain and the black. He wants to know—this politest of all people—if he can come to our tent, since his tent is not functioning to the end toward which it was designed. When he arrives, the flashlight discovers that he is totally soaked. His hair is matted and dripping. His clothes are as wet as they would be if he had fallen into a lake. He shivers. His brother's long frame now comes in as well, clothes and body equally drenched. They report that their sleeping bags are soaked through, and all their personal gear. The rain pours hard as ever. It is impossible for five people to lie down in our tent except in a stack, like cordwood. So the Blanchettes sit up through the night, silently. Hours go by. They doze on their haunches, and shiver. Henri, before returning to sleep, observes with mild remonstrance in his voice that they made a mistake in bringing that tent, which has the appearance of something sent for with a hunk of a cereal box. It would have been much better, he says, to bring their other tent, no matter that it was larger and heavier. Toward five in the morning, with dawn breaking and the rain so light now it is almost mist, Warren and I get up and go out, putting the Blanchettes in our bags, where they drop at once to sleep.

They sleep until eight. Warren and I meanwhile nurse up the fire and bake bread for the day. Henri, up around seven, pulls on his river-stiff leather shoes. (They are all he has, and he wears no socks.) He makes his breakfast. He then picks up a clamshell and rubs the bark off a cedar. He seems to be testing the effectiveness of the shell as a tool, and its score must be high, for he has swiftly denuded a part of the tree. Less than ten miles ahead of us, after Allagash Stream and at the far end of Allagash Lake, is the long carry. Rick, who is determined to carry his canoe himself all the way, will need something more than the paddles on his shoulders to absorb the weight. With cedar bark, Henri makes for him a tumpline. It is eight feet long and is broad and soft in the center, where it will cross his forehead. "When the canoe was lifted upon his head bottom up," wrote Thoreau, describing Polis on a carry, "a band of cedar-bark, tied to the crossbar . . . passed round his breast, and another longer one, outside of the last, round his forehead."

By nine, we are back in the stream, which must have been helped by the rain but is nonetheless shallower than it was below the falls, so the going is slower. It is necessary to stop more often to make a channel among the shelves and gravels and small cascades. Conversation is scarce and inclined to be snappish. The rain has stopped, though. The overcast is cracking, and we are more than halfway up the stream. Three more miles will kill it.

In late morning, as a kind of energizer, I eat some freeze-dried vanilla ice cream. It sticks in my teeth like white cement. As candy, it is not bad, despite its texture—tough meringue—but, no matter what its origins may have been, it is bunkum to call it ice cream. With breakfast, Warren and I had freeze-dried pears. Semi-permeable, they had soaked for hours, but the water got through only halfway, so what we ate might have been pear-covered chewing gum. Freeze-dried peaches, a day or so ago, had the consistency of garden slugs. The ecological insurrection has yielded some pyrrhic triumphs, and one of them is commercial freeze-dried food. Whose idea of wilderness travel could be embodied, enhanced, or even faintly expressed in Mountain House Freeze Dried Raspberry Apple Crunch? Mountain House Freeze Dried Tuna Salad? Rich-Moor "Astro" Freeze-Dried Eggs? Yet it moves. Moves off the shelf and into the wilderness, sold. It creates, apparently, a sense of hardtack and pemmican within a gourmet context. On a canoe trip, the weight of food is not of crucial importance. There is something to be said for the lighter weight of freeze-dried food on the trail, but not enough to justify Mountain House Freeze Dried Shrimp Creole, Mountain House Freeze Dried Beef Stroganoff, Tea Kettle Freeze Dried Turkey Tetrazzini—violations of the rites of the wild. They are expensive, these shining foil packets from the rugged boutiques. They represent a return to nature—with money. Next time out, I'm going back to beans and bacon, prunes, rice—macaroni, too. I have had enough for a lifetime of freeze-dried "chunk chicken" and freeze-dried "beef almondine." I would prefer to eat emerald jerky in peanut-butter sauce.

I appear to be the only one who likes Allagash Stream. Warren is cursing and hauling; so are the Blanchettes. Henri's vocabulary has collapsed, condensed; "bummer" is the only remaining word. We have covered three miles in five hours, but the sun is warm, and ahead is a break in the trees. The trip up the Rat, in the Northwest Territories, involves nine days of this—hauling canoes a foot at a time into oncoming water that is not merely cool, as it is here, but ice-cold, pouring from Arctic mountains. The yield is a remote and beautiful height of land among the mountains, then the short carry, the long run down the Pacific side. It may seem a strange way to travel, walking uphill with a canoe along as a kind of packhorse, but, given enough water to float the canoe, the experience is not disagreeable, and I wish we could all do it for those nine northern days.

The lake is close, and clams proliferate in the last bends of the stream. Henri, as he goes along, scoops them up, and so do we all, making piles of them in the canoes.

Now, after fourteen hours in the stream, a night of naps, and a soaking rain, we stand in the outlet of Allagash Lake. The most distant point we can see is perhaps four miles away—a clear shot down open water past a fleet of islands. The lake is broad in all directions, and is ringed with hills and minor mountains. Its pristine, unaltered shoreline is edged with rock—massive outcroppings, sloping into the water, interrupting the march of the forest. It is a reward, this lake—handsome, natural, serene, remote, the long stream and the long portage holding it aloof on either end.

We unload the canoes near a huge slope of rock, which has baked for some hours in steady sun. Tents, sleeping bags, clothes, shoes—everything we have is soon spread out there like wash on a Spanish hillside. We swim with soap and then spread ourselves out, too. The heat in the rocks rises into the bones and drifts us into sleep. An hour dries it all. Even the Blanchettes' sodden sleeping bags are dry and warm and light as fluff.

Out on the lake is the glint of a metal canoe. It approaches unsteadily. The paddlers ask for Allagash Stream. They wear bathing suits, and their bellies are pale and fat. They appear to have stepped out of an airplane and into the canoe. Unbelievably, that is exactly what they have done. A float plane has set them down with their canoe on a pond near a corner of the lake, and they have come down a stream from there. What a travesty! What a majestic bummer! It is the law of the state that no plane can land in this lake, an airplane being an affront to the Allagash Wilderness Waterway. At least, no airplane is going to help these two drag seven miles downstream to Chamberlain. More aluminum for the rocks.

Naturally, the wind has risen, for we have come into its purview again. No doubt because we are heading southwest, the wind is coming from that direction. We load and go. It is three in the afternoon. The wind accelerates, and the waves rise high. Now we are digging again, as hard as ever—more work than we might have hoped for. Henri informs us there is even more ahead. He wants to make the long carry today. He wants to paddle against this head wind the six miles to the end of the lake, take out the canoes, and portage three miles. Return trips included, the carry should take four hours. That would bring us to the far side—all going well—at 9 or 10 P.M. The great beauty of this lake apparently means nothing to him. He has worked for two days to get to it, and now wants to rush across it and portage away from it in the dusk and dark. He is paddling hard. He is piqued at the discord his plan evokes. Sentiment against it runs four to one.

The benevolent wind attempts the rescue, blasting us so hard it is all we can do to fight to the lee of an island. Henri's canoe nearly swamps. We dash to another island, and work its lee, and another. Wind and mutiny in the end prevail. We pitch our tents beside Allagash Lake.

Henri rigs the tarp over the Blanchettes' tent, and they dig a trench around it that could divert a river. Warren and I steam open the clams. We fry them, as before, and this time Henri squats near, waiting for the clams to be done. The Blanchettes approach and wait beside him, also on their haunches, a little behind him. Onto a plate on the ground by the fire Warren tosses a clam. Henri picks it up and eats it. He praises it. Warren flips more clams onto the plate. Henri eats them. The eyes of the Blanchettes follow the clams from pan to plate to Henri's mouth. But toward the plate they do not make a move. Warren and I are not particularly hungry now, and, in any case, are too absorbed with this tableau to enter it and break it. Henri is the alpha wolf. The others in the pack, no matter how hungry they may be, will watch but not budge while the alpha dines. In time, the Blanchettes do get some clams—each about an eighth of the total—and they eat them hungrily, for they are running out of food.

Henri, after dinner, carves by the campfire, working on a piece of balsam and a piece of cedar until each is a lath that seems perfectly squared. He tests for tensile strength, slowly bending each length of wood until it strains and cracks. "The cedar is all right," he says. "But this balsam is nowhere. Hang it up."

THERE IS A time of change in a wilderness trip when patterns that have been left behind fade beneath the immediacies of wind, sun, rain, and fire, and a different sense of distance, of shelter, of food. We made that change when we were still in the Penobscot valley, and by now I, for one, would like to keep going indefinitely; the change back will bring a feeling of loss, an absence of space, a nostalgia for the woods. The end has come, though. Henri has run out of Tang. Tang is his halazone, his palate's defense, his agent conversional for pure lakes and streams. Without Tang, he is without water.

The Caucomgomoc roadhead is about twenty miles away—prospectively a long day's journey, since three of the twenty miles are forest portage trail. We are up in the morning at half past four.

On the water, in the post-dawn light, the canoes slide across a mirror so nearly perfect that the image could be inverted without loss of detail. The lake is absolutely still, and mist thickens its distances and subdues in gray its islands and circumvallate hills. Warren and Henri are perhaps a hundred feet farther out than we are, and appear to be gliding through the sky: Henri's back straight, his hand moving forward on the grip of his paddle, his dark knitted cap on his head, his profile French and aquiline; Warren under the bright tumble of hair, his back bending. Their canoe was alive in the forest only months ago, and now on the lake it is a miracle of beauty, of form and symmetry, of dark interstitial seams in mottled abstractions of bark. The time is the present, of course—effectively, and importantly, now—yet without changing a grain of the picture this could be the century before, or the century before that, or the century when the whites first came here in Indians' bark canoes. Two straight wakes trace the way in silence toward the southern end of the lake.

The silence, after a time, is torn apart by a congress of loons: ten loons, racing in circles on the surface of the water, screaming, splashing, squealing like dogs, taxiing in long half-flying runs. For a full ten minutes they keep it up—a ritual insanity, a rampant dance of madness, a convincing demonstration that every one of them is as crazy as a loon.

The long carry has about every obstacle a carry can have, short of German shepherds trained to kill. It has quagmires, slicks of rock, small hills, down trees, low branches, and, primarily, distance. Three miles, even on flat ground, is a long way. In sheer ooze and muck, this portage is as wretched as the Mud Pond Carry. Warren departs first, with a large pack and the tent, to cross, return, and cross again—nine miles. Moving alone, he escapes the compass of tension. Mike follows soon after. Henri tells me not to go on my own but to stay back with Rick and guide and help him. "Stay close to Rick. . . . Stay with Rick. . . . Help Rick," he keeps saying as the three of us go up the trail. The implication is that Rick may collapse, and this is not lost on Rick, who is tight in the throat but seems all the more determined to carry the canoe the whole distance alone. Henri's canoe weighs sixty pounds, Rick's seventy. It is not the weight but the bulk that brings difficulty. Light branches of balsam springily push the hulls, staggering the walker beneath. With the slightest stumble, the canoes lurch forward, straining the muscles of the legs, neck, and back.

"Help Rick!"

Henri shows no inclination to move ahead by himself. To them both I call out the story of the terrain: "Watch a hole here! . . . The mud is a foot deep here! . . . Low branches here! . . . Step to the left of this little swamp!"

After a mile, Rick's resolve declines. He doubts if he can make it. He rests his canoe on an overhanging branch and asks me if at the halfway point I will give him my pack basket and other gear and take the canoe from there. With that to look forward to, he moves on.

Henri now steps into mud up to his knee and, with a cry, falls. On the way down, he twists his body and spreads his elbows to cushion—as far as is possible—the canoe. He does not seem to care if he cracks every bone in his body as long as he cracks not a rib of the canoe, which lands on top of him and squashes him into the mud.

He gets up cursing me. The fault is mine. I did not tell him where not to step.

I stay closer to him, the better to guide him. He lifts the canoe, moves on a short distance, then puts the canoe down. His Indian carrying board is hurting his head. "Give me your jacket," he says. I give him my jacket. "Get me some string." From my pocket I give him some cord. Terse, angry, he fashions a pad for his head. At this point, Henri seems frightened and shaken with doubt.

Rick, for his part, seems to be, if anything, stronger. Much of the strain has left his face. His vitality, his endurance seem to rise a bit with each part of Henri that comes unstuck.

Warren passes us, going the other way. It is Warren, really, who is defeating the portage—outwalking, outcarrying everyone else. He tells us we are more than halfway. The news is surprising and tonic. I look to Rick. My turn now? He has no thought of giving up his canoe.

After another half mile of narrating the trail, I have become both restless and guilty. I tell Henri I feel pinned down, leading him through the woods, slowly, while Warren is doing so much of the work.

"Well, I'm carrying my share," Henri answers emphatically. Apparently, he wants to believe it. "Anyways," he adds, "Warren is a backpacker. He likes what he is doing."

Not far from the portage end—two hours after the start—Henri calls a halt at a stream for a drink. I am about to go back to help Warren, but Henri insists that I stay—that it is more important to guide the canoes safely to the end of the carry. Raspberry bushes are in fruit around the stream. At leisure, he eats from them. Now and again, he combs his hair. Rick notices moose tracks, large and fresh. We look around. No moose. Henri finds pin cherries and eats them, too. Twenty minutes go by. Warren by now is in his seventh mile. On his back is one of Henri's packs. The other is clutched in his arms.

Henri is a hero of the portage ends, for at such places we encounter other travellers passing through, and they are generally awestruck by the bark canoes. Henri overcomes his constitutional shyness. He moves in close. He fixes his eyes on one of his elbows and answers questions, quaffs the commentary, until the supply is gone.

"Your canoes look Indian, but you don't."

"Did you make them from a kit?"

"Is that real birch bark?"

"Where do you buy them?"

"They looked too fakey to be fake, so I figured they had to be the real thing."

"I've always thought it was painted on."

"Those are old ones, aren't they? All patched up like that?"

"They don't make them like that anymore."

"Congratulations. That's the best imitation of a birch-bark canoe I've ever seen."

("Our little canoe, so neat and strong, drew a favorable criticism from all the wiseacres among the tavern loungers along the road," wrote Thoreau as he approached the woods.)

Henri seems disappointed at portage ends if no one is there. He is not disappointed now. Six men in plastic canoes arrive to begin the carry.

"Are they real?" one of them asks.

"Do you mind if we look them over?"

"You *made* them?"

"*Really?*"

They, in turn, have something to tell us. In Ciss Stream, which lies between the long portage and Caucomgomoc Lake, they saw, thirty minutes ago, a cow moose. Warren arrives with the packs. We load and go.

Ciss Stream, from the portage to the lake, does not drop one inch, and is a deadwater with meanders so curving that they almost form oxbows. In near silence, we steal around its unending bendings through the sedge. Everything is right. The breeze is toward us. The bends conceal us. And the so-called stream is a bog of dry-ki and water-standing grasses —a phreatophytic meadowland, a magnification of Umbazooksus Stream. Our chances thus seem one in one. Another bend. Another scene. No moose. No moose—just the craggy spars of the dry-ki pointing lifeless into the sky. Thousands of trees, dead a century, fill the swamps here, and they are eerily beautiful, silver gray. The logging dams on Caucomgomoc destroyed them so long ago that they are now thought picturesque, their root structures webbing upward thirty feet above the sedge-meadow plain. People came here and killed these trees, and created this unearthly beauty. Another bend. No moose.

A mother merganser races squawking out of the sedge and starts down the stream before the two canoes. Screaming, feigning injury, displaying an awkward wing, she leads us around another bend. She will not give up. She will not shut up. She keeps her position, about a hundred feet in front of the canoes, for fully half a mile, raucous all the way. She wrecks the mooselook for good and all. At last, she rises flippantly into the air and flies back to her chicks where she left them.

We round the last bend, and swing into Caucomgomoc. It is two miles wide, and we have about six miles to go—to its far, northwestern corner. Coming directly at us across the lake are the highest waves we have seen yet, driven by a western wind. Henri, in his own drive for the finish, moves straight out onto the water and begins to plow headlong for the farther shore. His caution—what there was of it on Eagle and Chamberlain—is gone. To me, it seems a certainty that we are going to swamp, that we will complete the day with a long, slow swim, dragging the canoes to shore. I check my boots, my pack, to make sure they are firmly tied. I am ready to shrug and see what happens. Warren, however, is not. Having absorbed Henri in silence for something like a hundred and fifty miles, he now turns suddenly and shouts at the top of his lungs, "You God-damned lunatic, head for the shore!" The canoes turn, and head for the shore.

We are pinned down for the rest of the afternoon, squatting among boulders, eating chocolate in the wind—watching the whitecaps, the rolling, breaking, spraying waves. Then, with amazing suddenness after the fall of the sun, the wind subsides and dies. The lake becomes still, smooth, a corridor of glass. We venture out, timid, remembering the wind, then forget it and go straight down the middle the last six miles, mirrored as in the early morning, and under cumulus mountains, in alpenglow, scarlet.

As we touch shore, a young couple with a Grumman canoe are preparing to leave, to paddle into the evening to camp who knows where. She grips her paddle as if it were a baseball bat. He instructs her to separate her hands. Practicing paddling, she strokes the air, pulling the blade past her the narrow way. Stepping into the canoe, she sits in the bow seat, ready to go. But the canoe is beached, fifteen feet from the water. She gets out.

He shoves it over the gravel. They get in and paddle off. They go down the lake half a mile, then turn around and come back. They have left standing open all the doors of their car, which is covered with fresh white letters: "JUST MARRIED. BUZZ ON."

Henri cuts poles to support both canoes on the rooftop of his car. Fifteen miles down the dirt-and-gravel road, in what is now the black of night, we are blinded by the oncoming headlights of a many-ton truck, a logging truck—the immense, roaring descendant of the West Branch Drive. The lights are so bright that Henri pulls to the side. On and on the truck approaches, an omnivorous machine, swallowing earth and sky. In the blackness, it dominates all—all light, all sound. Suddenly, though, there is another sound, distinct from the engine's churning. The truck is forcing something up the road, something moving in flight before it, that now, within inches of our windows, pounds by. A hoofbeat clatter, a shape as well, a stir of dust, a glimpse of a form, a terrored eye, a spreading rack—a moose. A bull moose.

It is many hours to the end of Maine. The last glimpse of Henri must wait until then. He has—in Greenville, New Hampshire—one final thing to say to Warren, one farewell remark. He says, "Thanks for taking care of the canoe."

A PORTFOLIO OF THE SKETCHES AND MODELS OF EDWIN TAPPAN ADNEY (1868–1950)

EDWIN TAPPAN ADNEY, who died in the year Henri Vaillancourt was born, spent much of his life collecting material on the art of the making of the bark canoe. He was a journalist, a lecturer, and, ultimately, a consultant on Indian lore to the Museum of McGill University, in Montreal. In 1897, he covered the Klondike for *Harper's Weekly*, and three years later he was *Colliers'* man in Nome. For the most part, though, he lived and worked in eastern Canada. Born in Ohio, he had married a New Brunswick Canadian, and eventually he became a Canadian citizen.

When he was twenty, Adney made a birch-bark canoe, under the guidance of a Malecite builder. Writing down the methodology as he learned it, he began the central work of his life—making sketches, making notes, and traveling to Indian outposts to absorb and record both the basic craftsmanship and the differences in tribal styles. He understood Indian languages. The material he assembled, over decades, had not been gathered in anything like such detail and scope before, nor could it ever be again, for in Adney's lifetime the number of makers of bark canoes declined from the thousands to a scattered, vestigial few. Alone, Adney preserved this immemorial technology; but when he died he had—with the exception of a couple of short articles that appeared in 1890 and 1900—published none of it.

The collection, in hundreds of folders in long file boxes, went into a library storeroom in the Mariners Museum, in Newport News, Virginia. Howard Chapelle, who was Curator of Transportation at the Smithsonian Institution, went through Adney's papers and—adding where necessary his own research—published in 1964 *The Bark Canoes and Skin Boats of North America*, the book that became Henri Vaillancourt's vocational college.

What follows here is a selection of Adney's sketches and models, some of which are included in the Adney-Chapelle book. Most are being published for the first time. They are not intended to be a manual on bark-canoe-building (Adney-Chapelle is all of that and more), but merely to suggest in one more way the complexity of the craft—to give the reader a sense of what Adney did, and, through Adney's pen, a sense of what the Indians did for centuries before.

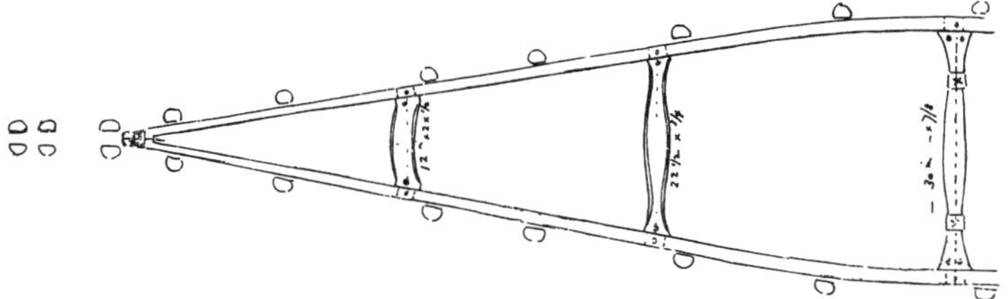

The first seven sketches show the development of a bark canoe from an outline on a building bed to a boat near completion. In this one, stakes have been driven into the ground around the building frame.

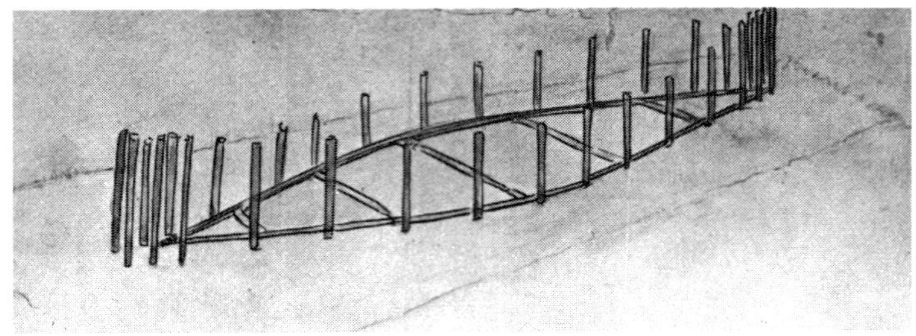

The peripheral lines are not meant to suggest bark, but merely the dimensions of the bed, the carefully chosen and smoothed-out patch of ground where one canoe after another was built—not just for years, but, in some places, for many generations.

Now the stakes are out and the bark is down. The building frame —weighted with rocks—has been lined up as accurately as possible with the stake holes invisible beneath the bark.

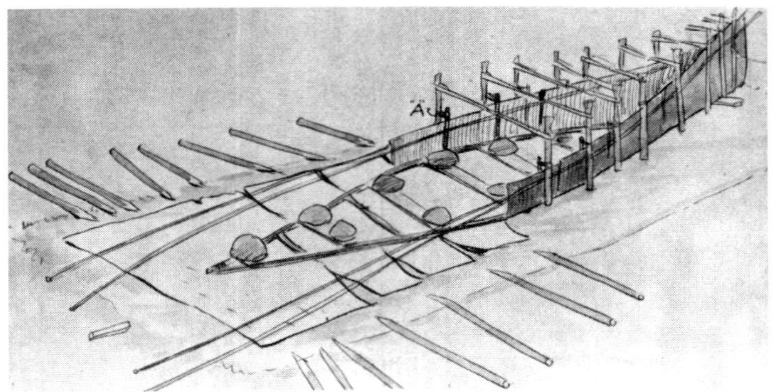

Folding up the bark, the builder gradually replaced the stakes in their holes. Small sticks, tied to the stakes, pinched the bark and held it in place. Without the V-shaped cuts in the bark—known as gores—the bark would not fold properly. Like all seams in the canoe, the gores would be sewn with the split roots of black spruce or white pine. Long strips of cedar—not to remain in the finished canoe—were sometimes (as here) inserted between the small sticks and the bark to influence the fairing of the sides.

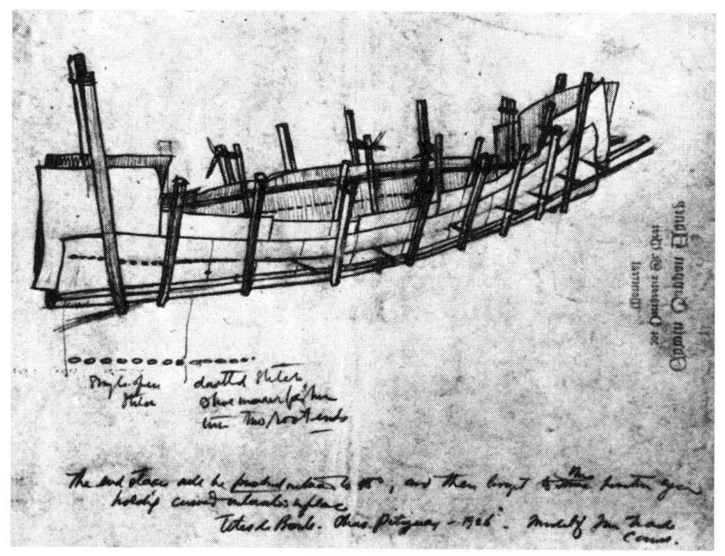

It was rare that any canoe could be covered with bark from a single tree—least of all a great fur-trade canoe, which, in a nascent stage, is the subject of this particular sketch. Fur-trade canoes had high ends, curving back upon themselves with tumblehome; hence extra bark was needed there. Even a relatively small canoe generally had to be "pieced out" with additional bark, one roll being sufficient to cover the ends but not the middle, where the span was considerably greater.

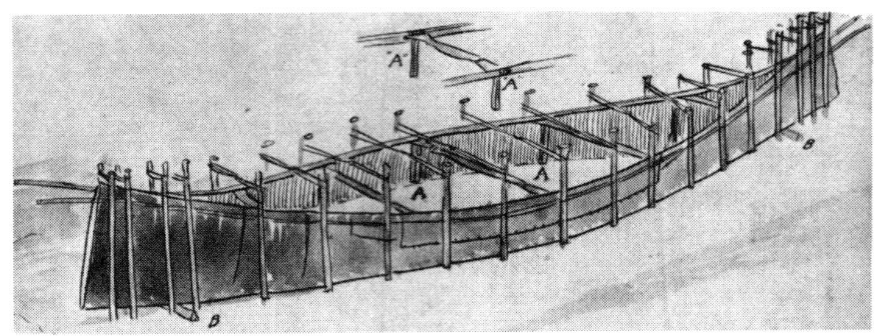

This is a conventional canoe again—about sixteen feet long. The basic roll of bark has covered the ends. The middle has been pieced out. The gunwales and thwarts are in place, establishing the upper profile, or sheer, of the canoe. The bark has, for the most part, been trimmed, and is ready for lashing to the gunwales. If the gunwales and thwarts were used as the building frame around which the bark was folded, the sides of the canoe will bulge with tumblehome. If the building frame was narrower (a separate construction, termed by Adney a "false frame"), the sides of the canoe will flare.

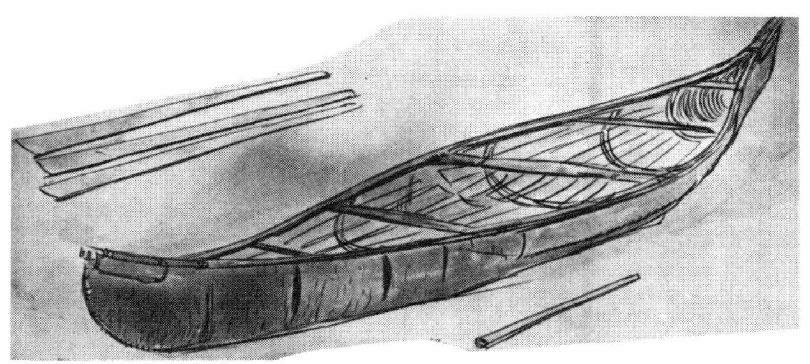

Now the canoe is virtually complete. All seams and gores are sewn. Stempieces (not visible) have been stitched in place to form the ends. A bark deck flap (*wulegessis*) has been laid across the gap at each end where gunwales join, then held in place by the gunwale caps. Cedar planking (in lengths that run from ends to middle) has been arranged as lining to the bark, and is being pressed against the bark by temporary ribs. From the ends, the tapping in of the permanent ribs has begun. They will meet in the middle when the final rib is tapped in, under the center thwart.

Adney tried to miss nothing, as this typical sketch, and its rush of notes, indicates. This is what he came away with after a look at a canoe he had not previously seen—in this case, a "two and a half fathom" Algonquin canoe. (Its overall length was fifteen feet six inches.) Adney's scrawled observations cover everything from the depth of the end stitching to the fact that the ribs of this canoe would be the same as those found in a large Ojibway canoe. The depth of the gores indicated to him that the canoe had been shaped around a false frame.

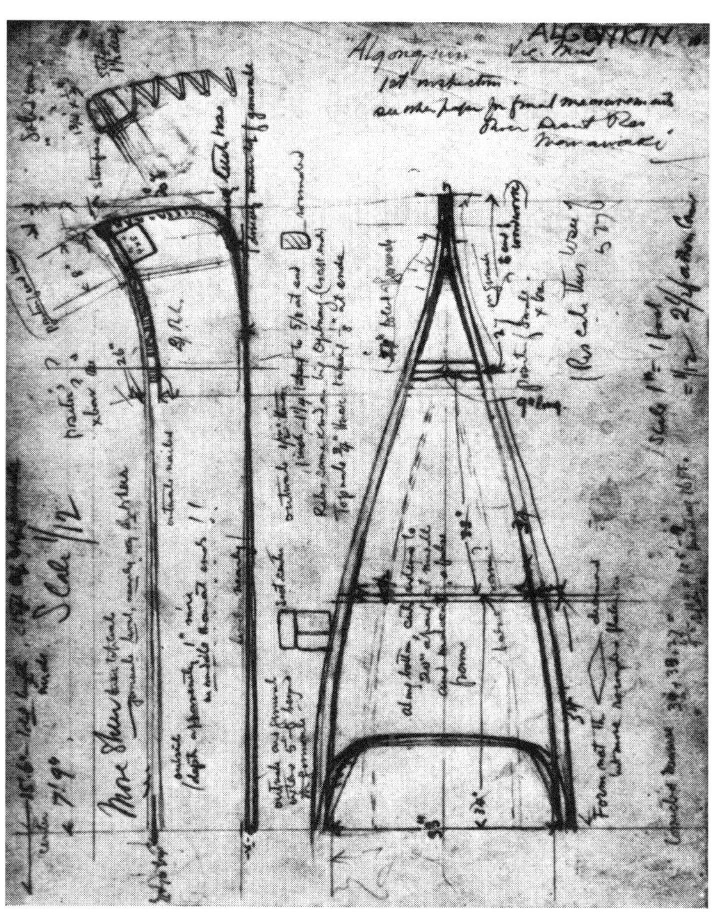

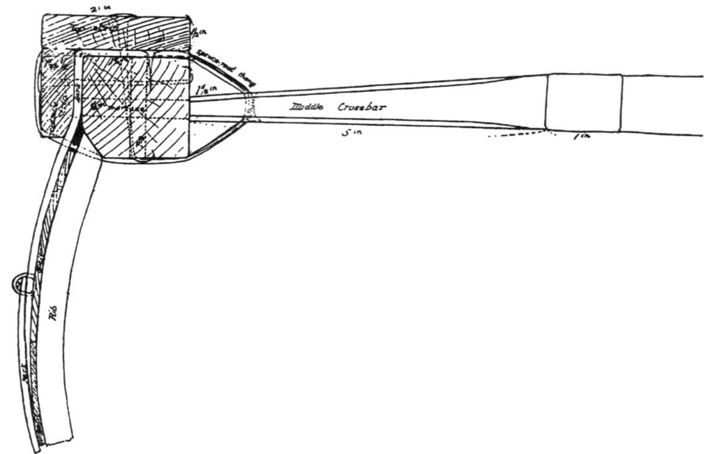

Adney submitted this sketch with an article that was published in *Harper's Young People* in 1890. It shows parts as they fit together at the gunwale. The large block, beveled in one corner, is a sectional view of the inwale, into which is mortised the center thwart, or, as Adney labels it here, the "middle crossbar." The bark comes up between the inwale and the outwale ("outside strip") and is protected from above—as are the root lashings—by the gunwale cap ("top strip"). Between the bark and the rib is the planking. The ringlike configuration to the left of the rib is a bit of split root, sewing two pieces of bark together.

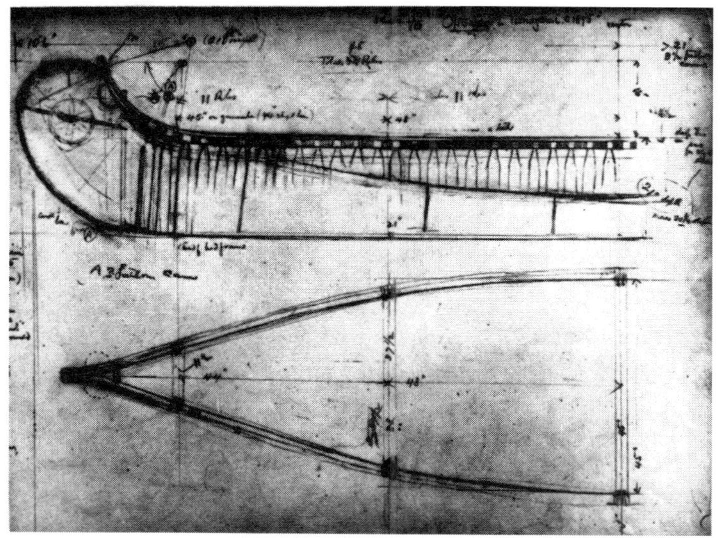

These details of a three-fathom Ojibway canoe nicely show the relationship between ribs and group lashings, which must be discontinuous in order to allow the tips of the ribs to fit into the gunwales.

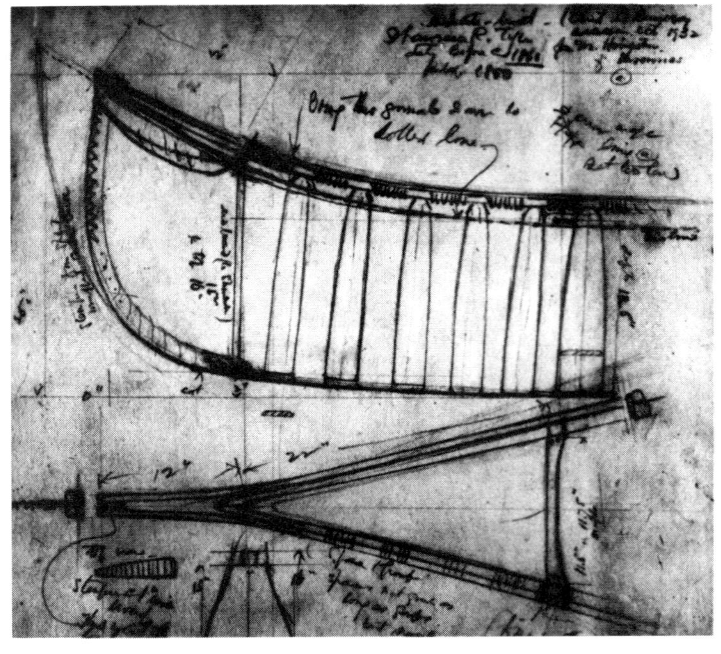

The harplike configuration of the end of the canoe was formed by the ends of the gunwales, the curving stempiece, and the vertical headboard (or endboard). The plan-view sketch shows how the inwales were placed together and held within the outwales.

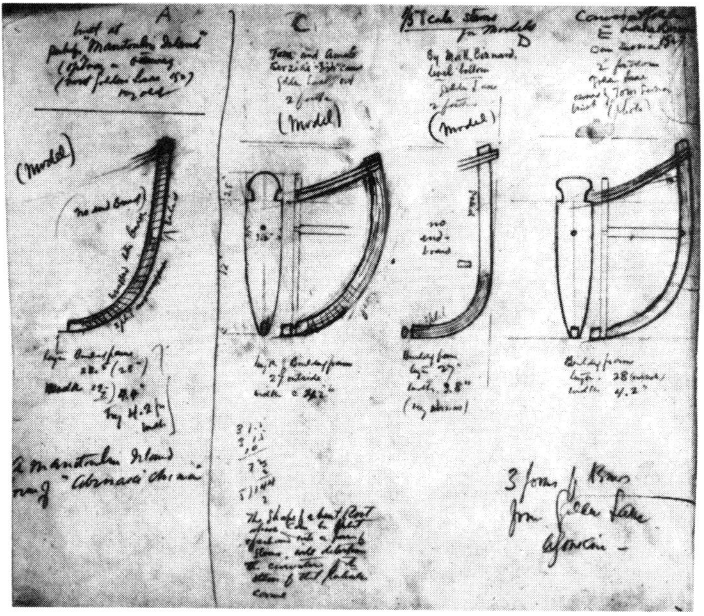

The relationship of headboard to stempiece is shown more clearly here, in the second and fourth sketches from the left. The headboard took over from the ribs and filled out the narrowest parts of the canoe. The stempiece third from the left best illustrates how stempieces were made. The part that was to be curved was delicately split into many laminations. The rest remained solid wood. After soaking in water, the laminations were bent to a desired curve, then tied in place with basswood bark.

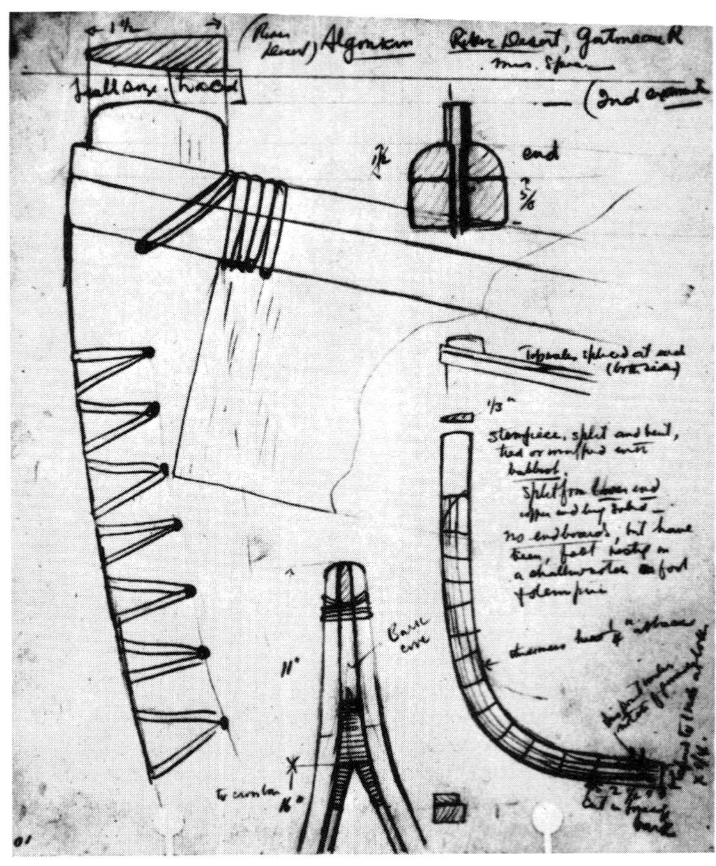

Henri Vaillancourt's canoes do not have protruding stempieces, as does this Gatineau River Algonquin canoe. Note the long laminations of the stempiece, and the lashings of the inwales.

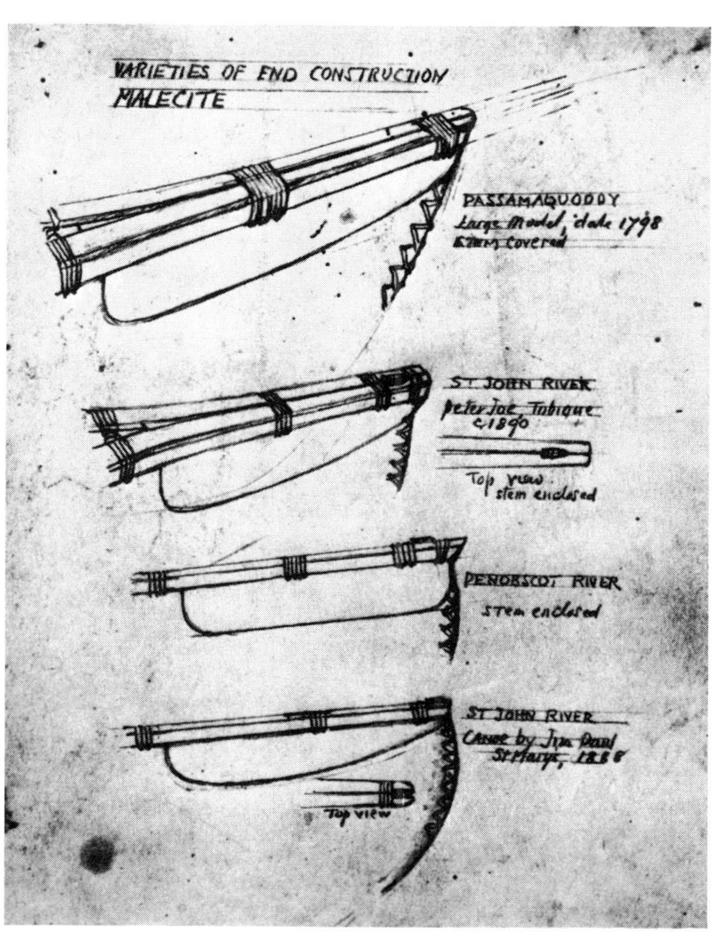
VARIETIES OF END CONSTRUCTION
MALECITE
PASSAMAQUODDY
Large Model, date 1798
Stem covered
ST JOHN RIVER
Peter Joe, Tobique
c1890
Top view
stem enclosed
PENOBSCOT RIVER
stem enclosed
ST JOHN RIVER
Canoe by Jim Paul
Top view

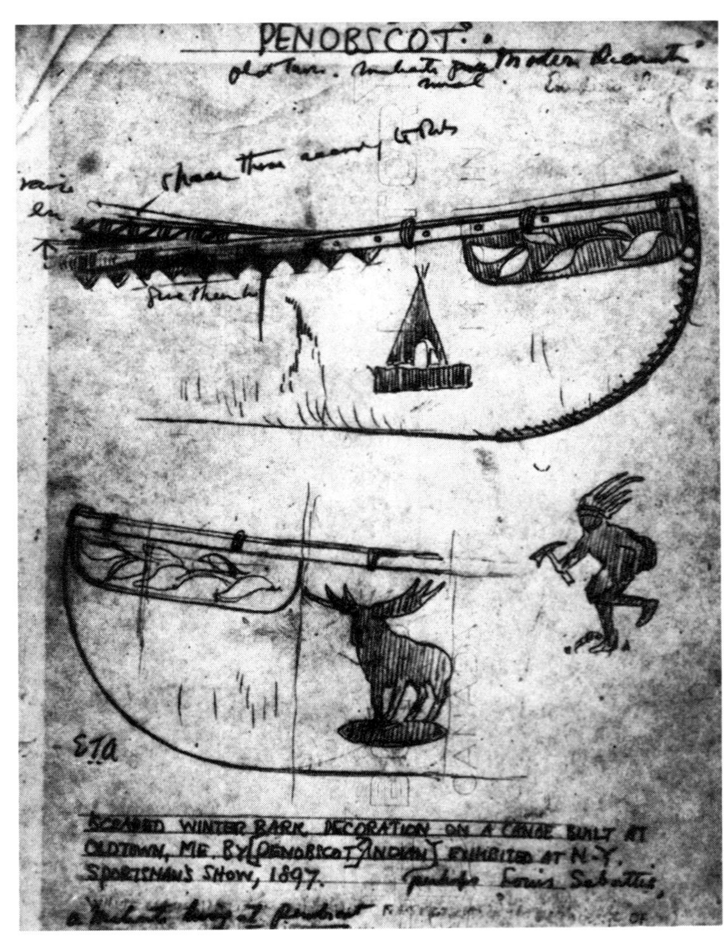
PENOBSCOT.
ETA
SCRAPED WINTER BARK DECORATION ON A CANOE BUILT AT
OLDTOWN, ME. BY PENOBSCOT INDIAN EXHIBITED AT N.Y.
SPORTSMAN'S SHOW, 1897.

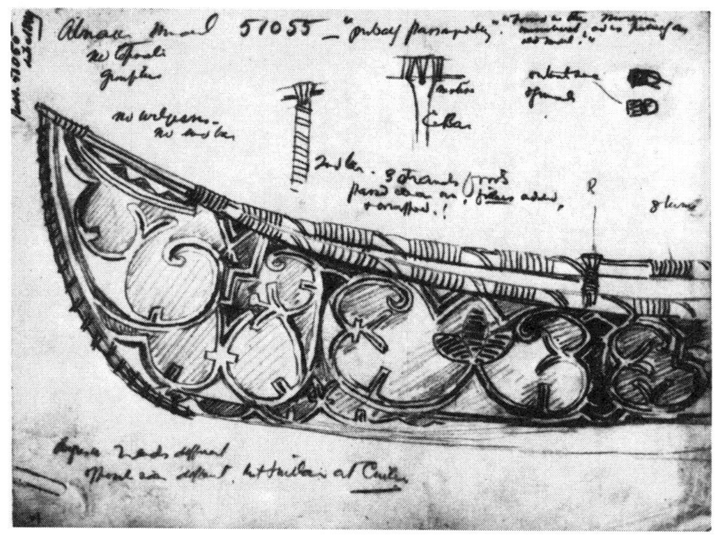

The inside of the bark was the outside of the canoe. Bark removed in winter had a rind in which decorations—sometimes elaborate—could be scraped.

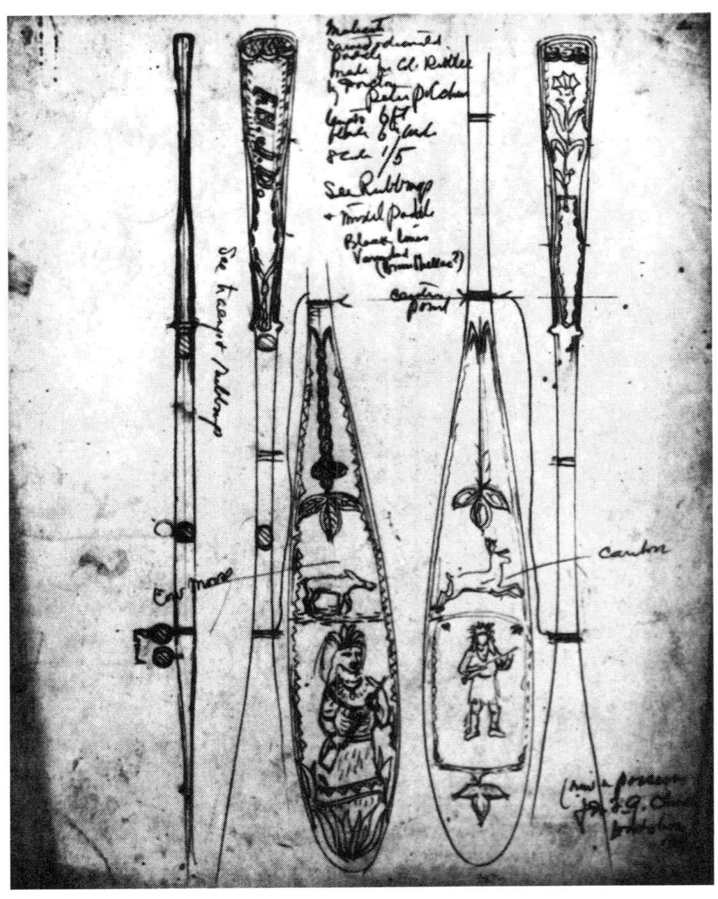

These are Malecite paddles, showing, among other things, a cow moose, a caribou, and rifle-bearing braves. Henri Vaillancourt, decorating his own paddles, usually follows simpler designs: a moose here and there, vine leaves covering the blade and the grip.

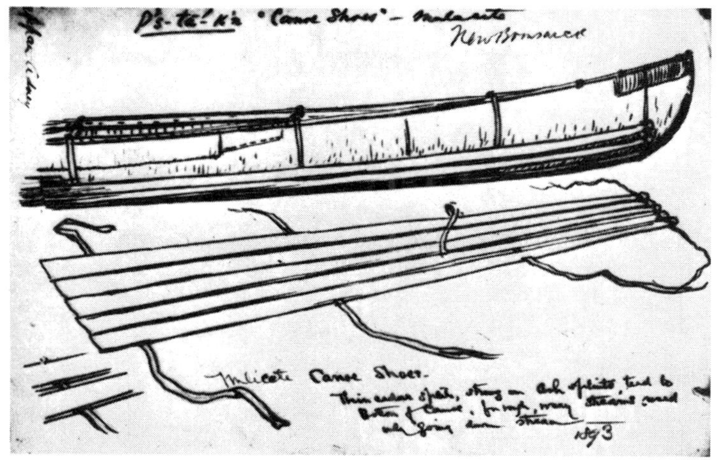

Bark canoes lasted ten years, in part because they were tough and in part because they were respected. Here is an inventive Malecite idea. Slats, collectively called "canoe shoes," were tied onto canoes' bottoms as fenders against rocks in rapids.

The Micmac Rough-Water Canoe (above) was built for use on, among other places, the ocean. It could be rigged for sail. For portaging, the Algonquin Gatineau River Canoe (opposite) was equipped with reinforcing bars. The sketch also exemplifies clearly the way a midsection was generally pieced out. Note the differences between the profiles of its ends and those of the Ojibway canoe below it.

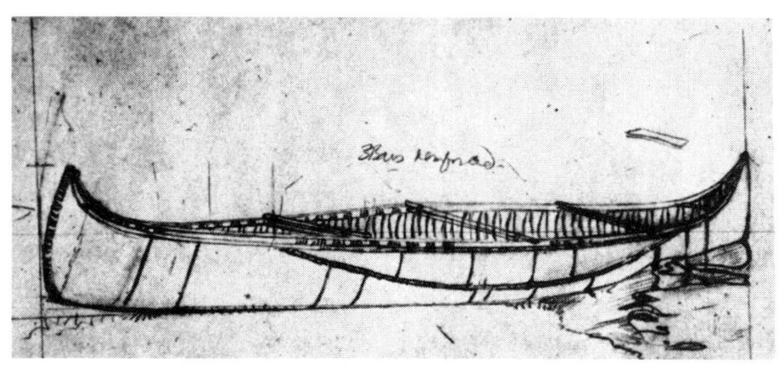

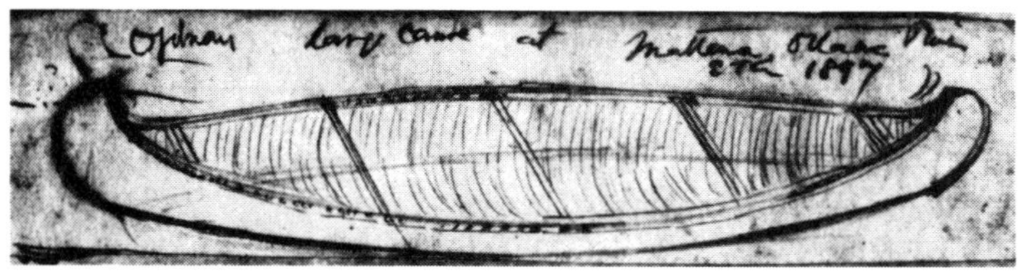

Adney kept his records with models, too. He was an accomplished builder who had once made military-equipment training models for the Canadian army, and his model canoes were beautiful studies in precision and form—complex, detailed, in every way reflecting the art they copied. He built well over a hundred, from many tribes and styles. Most were between two and three feet long. He built a fur-trade-canoe model that was over seven feet. Unlike the silly boats that come out of northland roadside shops, his models were—of the ages they represented—authentic souvenirs. A selection of fifteen follows. All are in Newport News, at the Mariners Museum, where—it is hoped—some of Henri Vaillancourt's canoes will one day be collected, too.

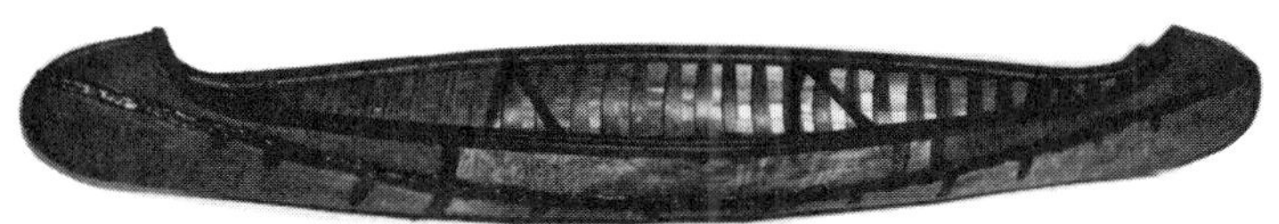

An Ojibway four-thwart rice-harvesting canoe.

The Naskapi Crooked Canoe—built of many pieces of bark, because birches are small where these canoes were made, near Hudson Bay.

The Chipewyan Mackenzie River Canoe.

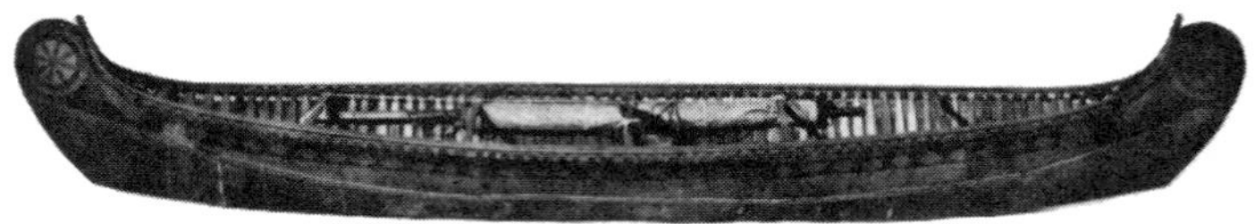

A Têtes de Boule canoe.

The Micmac Woods Canoe—with the personal mark of Old Joe Pictou (the crescent moon).

Iroquois hickory-bark canoe. Where birches were inadequate or unavailable, other barks could be used—but not for much more than crossing a river.

Cree.

Montagnais.

Canot de Maître—a six-fathom, fur-trade, birch-bark canoe. Cargo: four tons. The white spirals and rayed figures painted on the ends were copied by Indians from designs of European immigrants and are related to the rayed discs that still appear on Pennsylvania Dutch barns.

Among canoes of all tribes and styles, the ones that most attracted Adney were the varied canoes of the Malecites. The tribe lived in New Brunswick and parts of Maine, in the center of the terrain where the best white birches grew. In a Malecite canoe—the bark ones, anyway—beauty and function each came through at very high levels, and in balance. This one, of origins in eastern Maine, was a typical Malecite river canoe.

And this was a Malecite racing canoe.

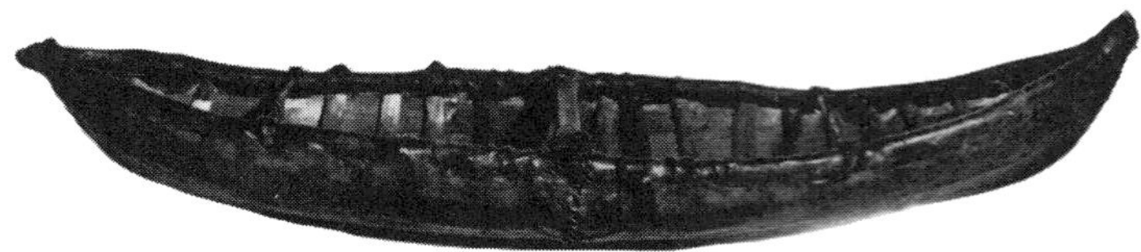

And this was a Malecite moosehide canoe—ninety-nine per cent function and one per cent form.

The sharp, pointed ends of this Malecite were ancient in design.

Finally, these two. They are both Malecite canoes; and they are the kind Henri Vaillancourt most often builds. They look much like the pair we traveled in through the woods of Maine. This one is the St. Lawrence River Canoe.

And this is the St. John River Canoe.

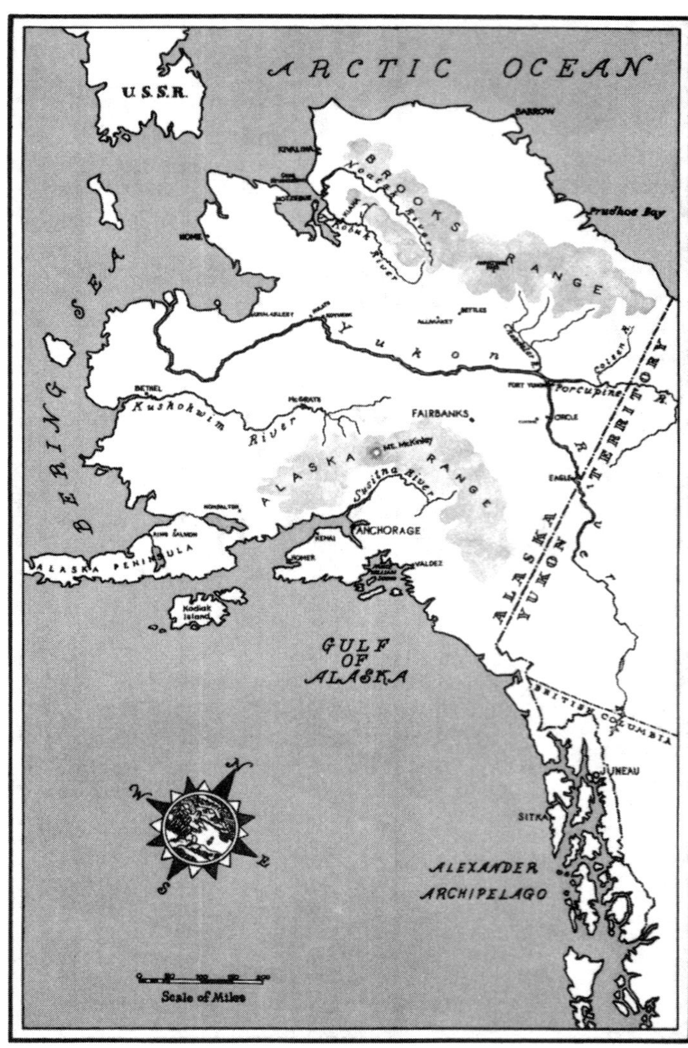

ARCTIC OCEAN
U.S.S.R.
BARROW
BROOKS RANGE
Noatak River
Kobuk River
Prudhoe Bay
NOME
BERING SEA
Yukon R
BETTLES
Chandalar R.
Coleen R.
Porcupine R.
FORT YUKON
CIRCLE
EAGLE
FAIRBANKS
BETHEL
McGRATH
Kuskokwim River
Mt. McKinley
ALASKA RANGE
Susitna River
ANCHORAGE
KENAI
HOMER
VALDEZ
KING SALMON
ALASKA PENINSULA
Kodiak Island
GULF OF ALASKA
ALASKA
YUKON TERRITORY
BRITISH COLUMBIA
JUNEAU
SITKA
ALEXANDER ARCHIPELAGO
Scale of Miles

COMING INTO THE COUNTRY

For Martha

Contents

BOOK I

AT THE NORTHERN TREE LINE

The Encircled River

BROOKS
RANGE
N
W
E
S
Noatak River
Squirrel River
Salmon River
Qalugruich paanga
Kobuk River
KIANA
KOTZEBUE
NOORVIK
SELAWIK
ARCTIC CIRCLE
5 0 5 10 15 20 25
SCALE OF MILES

MY BANDANNA is rolled on the diagonal and retains water fairly well. I keep it knotted around my head, and now and again dip it into the river. The water is forty-six degrees. Against the temples, it is refrigerant and relieving. This has done away with the headaches that the sun caused in days before. The Arctic sun—penetrating, intense—seems not so much to shine as to strike. Even the trickles of water that run down my T-shirt feel good. Meanwhile, the river—the clearest, purest water I have ever seen flowing over rocks—breaks the light into flashes and sends them upward into the eyes. The headaches have reminded me of the kind that are sometimes caused by altitude, but, for all the fact that we have come down through mountains, we have not been higher than a few hundred feet above the level of the sea. Drifting now—a canoe, two kayaks—and thanking God it is not my turn in either of the kayaks, I lift my fish rod from the tines of a caribou rack (lashed there in mid-canoe to the duffel) and send a line flying toward a wall of bedrock by the edge of the stream. A grayling comes up and, after some hesitation, takes the lure and runs with it for a time. I disengage the lure and let the grayling go, being mindful not to wipe my hands on my shirt. Several days in use, the shirt is approaching filthy, but here among grizzly bears I would prefer to stink of humanity than of fish.

Paddling again, we move down long pools separated by short white pitches, looking to see whatever might appear in the low hills, in the cottonwood, in the white and black spruce—and in the river, too. Its bed is as distinct as if the water were not there. Everywhere, in fleets, are the oval shapes of salmon. They have moved the gravel and made redds, spawning craters, feet in diameter. They ignore the boats, but at times, and without apparent reason, they turn and shoot downriver, as if they have felt panic and have lost their resolve to get on with their loving and their dying. Some, already dead, lie whitening, grotesque, on the bottom, their bodies disassembling in the current. In a short time, not much will be left but the hooking jaws. Through the surface, meanwhile, the living salmon broach, freshen—make long, dolphinesque flights through the air—then fall to slap the water, to resume formation in the river, noses north, into the current. Looking over the side of the canoe is like staring down into a sky full of zeppelins.

A cloud, all black and silver, crosses the sun. I put on a wool shirt. In Alaska, where waters flow in many places without the questionable benefit of names, there are nineteen streams called Salmon—thirteen Salmon Creeks, six Salmon Rivers—of which this one, the Salmon River of the Brooks Range, is the most northern, its watershed wholly above the Arctic Circle. Rising in treeless alpine tundra, it falls south into the fringes of the boreal forest, the taiga, the upper limit of the Great North Woods. Tree lines tend to be digital here, fingering into protected valleys. Plants and animals are living on margin, in cycles that are always vulnerable to change. It is five o'clock in the afternoon. The cloud, moving on, reveals the sun again, and I take off the wool shirt. The sun has been up fourteen hours, and has hours to go before it sets. It seems to be rolling slowly down a slightly inclined plane. A tributary, the Kitlik, comes in from the northwest. It has formed with the Salmon River a raised, flat sand-and-gravel mesopotamia—a good enough campsite, and, as a glance can tell, a fishing site to exaggerate the requirements of dinner.

There are five of us, four of whom are a state-federal study team. The subject of the study is the river. We pitch the tents side by side, two Alpine Draw-Tite tents, and gather and saw firewood: balsam poplar (more often called cottonwood); sticks of willow and alder; a whole young spruce, tip to root, dry now, torn free upriver by the ice of the breakup in spring. Tracks are numerous, coming, going, multidirectional, tracks wherever there is sand, and in gravel if it is fine enough to have taken an impression. Wolf tracks. The pointed pods of moose tracks. Tracks of the barren-ground grizzly. Some of the moose tracks are punctuated with dewclaws. The grizzlies' big toes are on the outside.

The Kitlik, narrow, and clear as the Salmon, rushes in white to the larger river, and at the confluence is a pool that could be measured in fathoms. Two, anyway. With that depth, the water is apple green, and no less transparent. Salmon and grayling, distinct and dark, move into, out of, around the pool. Many grayling rest at the bottom. There is a pair of intimate salmon, the male circling her, circling, an endless attention of rings. Leaning over, watching, we nearly fall in. The gravel is loose at the river's edge. In it is a large and recently gouged excavation, a fresh pit, close by the water. It was apparently made in a thrashing hurry. I imagine that a bear was watching the fish and got stirred up by the thought of grabbing one, but the water was too deep. Excited, lunging, the bear fell into the pool, and it flailed back at the soft gravel, gouging the pit while trying to get enough of a purchase to haul itself out. Who can say? Whatever the story may be, the pit is the sign that is trying to tell it.

It is our turn now to fish in the deep pool. We are having grayling for dinner—Arctic grayling of firm delicious flesh. On their skins are black flecks against a field of silvery iridescence. Their dorsal fins fan up to such height that grayling are scale-model sailfish. In the cycles of the years, and the millennia, not many people have fished this river. Forest Eskimos have long seined at its mouth, but only to the third bend upstream. Eskimo hunters and woodcutters, traversing the Salmon valley, feed themselves, in part, with grayling. In all, perhaps a dozen outsiders, so far as is known, have travelled, as we have, in boats down the length of the river. Hence the grayling here have hardly been, in the vernacular of angling, fished out. Over the centuries, they have scarcely been fished. The fire is high now and is rapidly making coals. Nineteen inches is about as long as a grayling will grow in north Alaska, so we agree to return to the river anything much smaller than that. As we do routinely, we take a count of the number needed—see who will share and who can manage on his own the two or three pounds of an entire fish. Dinner from our supplies will come in hot plastic water bags and be some form of desiccated mail-order stew—Mountain House Freeze Dried Caribou Cud—followed by Mountain House Freeze Dried fruit. Everyone wants a whole fish.

Five, then. Three of us pick up rods and address the river—Bob Fedeler, Stell Newman, and I. Pat Pourchot, of the federal Bureau of Outdoor Recreation, has not yet cast a line during the trip. As he puts it, he is phasing himself out of fishing. In his work, he makes many river trips. There will always be people along who want to fish, he reasons, and by removing himself he reduces the number. He has wearied of take-and-put fishing, of molesting the fish, of shocking the ones that, for one reason or another, go back. He says he wonders what kind of day a fish will have after spending some time on a hook. John Kauffmann has largely ignored the fishing, too. A National Park Service planner who has been working for five years in Arctic Alaska, he is a New England mastertouch dry-fly fisherman, and up here his bamboo ballet is regarded as effete. Others taunt him. He will not rise. But neither will the grayling to his Black Gnats, his Dark Cahills, his Quill Gordons. So —tall, angular—he sits and observes, and his short gray beard conceals his disgust. He does agree to time the event. He looks at his watch. Invisible lines, glittering lures go spinning to the river, sink in the pool. The rods bend. Grayling do not sulk, like the salmon. They hit and go. In nine minutes, we have our five. They are seventeen, eighteen inches long. We clean them in the Kitlik, with care that all the waste is taken by the stream. We have a grill with us, and our method with grayling is simply to set them, unscaled, fins intact, over the fire and broil them like steaks. In minutes, they are ready, and beneath their skins is a brown-streaked white flesh that is in no way inferior to the meat of trout. The sail, the dorsal fin, is an age-old remedy for toothache. Chew the fin and the pain subsides. No one has a toothache. The fins go into the fire.

When a lure falls into the water, it can become arrested at the bottom, and you tug and haul at the line and walk in an arc, whipping the rod, four-lettering the apparent snag that has spoiled the cast and is stealing your equipment. Tug some more. Possibly a small boulder or a sunken log has stopped the lure. Possibly not, too. You may have a pensive salmon. He contemplates. He is not yet ready to present his response. Not long before this river trip, I was fishing in lake-and-stream country northwest of Anchorage and the line became snagged in a way that to me suggested big things below. When I tugged, there was a slight movement at the other end, a gesture in my direction, the signal—obviously—of an irritated salmon getting ready to explode. I strained the line. It moved a bit more in my direction. A couple of minutes later, I landed a Safeway Stores Cragmont orange-soda can, full of silt and sand.

Over the fire now, I tell that story, and Bob Fedeler responds that that country near Anchorage, where many people have summer cottages, has long since been virtually fished out and is now supplied with stocked rainbows from a state hatchery. "That is the myth of Alaska," he says. "The myth is that in Alaska there's a fish on every cast, a moose behind every tree. But the fish and the moose aren't there. People go out with high expectations, and they're disappointed. To get to the headwaters of a river like this one takes a lot of money. The state needs to look to the budgets and desires of people who cannot afford to come to a place like this."

John Kauffmann, sitting on the ground and leaning against his duffel, shifts his weight uncomfortably. "You can charter a lot of aircraft time for the cost of summer cabins and Winnebagos," he says, and he bangs his pipe on a rock.

Fedeler shrugs. He scratches his cheek, which is under a mat of russet beard. He is compact, sturdy, not particularly tall, with a wide forehead and intelligent brown eyes. He would resemble Sigmund Freud, if Sigmund Freud had been a prospector. Fedeler says that he and his wife, Lyn, almost left Alaska during their first year, because they saw so little, and could afford so little, of the outdoors, of the wild—let alone of wildlife. In 1972, he took an advanced degree from South Dakota State and straightaway headed for Alaska. To support themselves, he and Lyn found jobs in Anchorage. He worked at McMahan's Furniture. He is a wildlife biologist. The state work he sought was given preferentially to people who had been resident in Alaska for at least a year. Meanwhile, in Anchorage—a city sealed away by water and mountains, a city that would be right at home at the west end of the George Washington Bridge—he had to go to the movies to see anything wild. He did not have the hundred dollars an hour needed for air charter. He did not have a hundred dollars. He knew the wilderness was out there—several hundred million acres of it—but he lacked the means to get to it, and his soul began to stale. Fortunately, he stuck out the wait, went on shoving McMahan's furniture around. At last, he got the work he wanted, his present job as a wildlife biologist with the Alaska Department of Fish and Game, based in Fairbanks.

Pat Pourchot, of Anchorage, puts in that he finds plenty to do near home. He climbs cliffs. He kayaks on fast white rivers.

Stories emerge about others like Fedeler—for example, a young man I know from Arkansas, who came to Alaska a year and a half ago specifically to fish and hunt. Where he could afford to go he found no fish and nothing much to hunt. He drove a cab in Anchorage until he couldn't stand it anymore. Taking a two-month vacation, he went home to Mountain Home. Then he came back to Alaska and his taxi. "It was the prettiest spring I've ever seen," he reported. "The dogwoods and redbuds blossomed and they just stayed and stayed. I got all the fishing I wanted, in Arkansas. You need the bucks for the good hunting and fishing up here. Fishing is supposed to be, you know, so out of sight here. It really *is* out of sight for me. I haven't made the bucks."

People from outside write and say to friends in Alaska that they want to come stay with them and fish. "Fine," says the return letter, "but you'll have to charter. Air charter." "No," says the next letter. "We just want to stay at your place and fish from there." Urban Alaskans shake their heads at such foolishness and say, typically, "These people in the Lower Forty-eight, they don't understand."

Something in the general drift now has John Kauffmann on his feet and off to the river. He assembles his trout rod, threads its eyes. Six feet three, spare, he walks, in his determination, tilted forward, ten degrees from vertical, jaws clamped. He seems to be seeking reassurance from the river. He seems not so much to want to catch what may become the last grayling in Arctic Alaska as to certify that it is there. With his bamboo rod, his lofted line, he now describes long drape folds in the air above the river. His shirt is old and red. There are holes in his felt hat and strips of spare rawhide around its crown. He agitates the settled fly. Nothing. Again he waves the line. He drops its passenger on the edge of fast water at the far side of the pool. There is a vacuum-implosive sound, a touch of violence at the surface of the river. We cheer. For two minutes, we wait it out while Kauffmann plays his fish. Adroitly, gingerly, he brings it in. With care, he picks it up. He then looks at us as if he is about to throw his tin star in the dust at our feet. Shame—for our triple-hooked lures, our nylon hawsers, our consequent stories of fished-out streams. He looks at his grayling. It is a twenty-five-ounce midget, but it will grow. He seems to feel reassured. He removes the fly, which has scarcely nicked the fish's lips. He slips the grayling back to the stream.

Grayling are particularly fast swimmers. In Arctic Alaska, where small rivers like this one for the most part freeze solid, grayling can move big distances rapidly to seek out safe deep holes for winter. They are veterans of runs for life. They are indices, too, of the qualities of a stream. They seek out fast, cold, clear water. So do trout, of course, but grayling have higher standards. Trout will settle for subperfect waters in which grayling will refuse to live.

The sun, which two hours ago was behind the apex of a spruce across the Kitlik, is now far to the right of that and somewhat closer to the ground. All day, while the sun describes a horseshoe around the margins of the sky, the light is of the rich kind that in more southern places comes at evening, heightening walls and shadowing eaves, bringing out of things the beauty of relief. It is ten-thirty, and about time for bed. Everything burnable—and more, too—has long since gone into the fire. We burn our plastic freeze-dry bags and we burn our Swiss Miss cocoa packets. If we have cans—devilled ham, Spam—we burn them, until all hint of their contents is gone. This is in part tidiness. Everything the fire does not consume is later put into bags that will go with us all the way through and out of these tens of thousands of square miles of wilderness. Nothing is buried. Also, the burning of the cans is an expression of regard for bears. The scent of the food is scorched away. It is not necessary for us to string up our meat high in the air. What meat we have is either dried or canned, and is presumably without odor. I can think of places where all these foil-lined packets and plastic containers might be an affront to the woods, but in Alaska their advantage is great. They are a way to move through bear country without drawing bears. More accurately, I should say "without in all likelihood drawing bears." Unopened cans of sardines have been found in the scat of grizzlies.

Bear stories, for a time, traverse the campfire. John Kauffmann remembers when Ave Thayer, the refuge manager of the Arctic National Wildlife Range, surprised a grizzly one day and when the bear charged stood his ground. In a low voice, Thayer said, "Shoo!" The grizzly stopped short. The two faced each other ten feet apart, neither making a move. Thayer cautiously stepped backward. The grizzly slowly advanced. Thayer said, "Shoo!" The grizzly stopped. Thayer walked backward, with no sudden starts. The grizzly followed. In such manner, Thayer walked backward about two hundred yards. Then the grizzly moved off a distance and walked parallel to him all the way—a mile or so—to his camp, where it lost interest and turned away.

Fedeler makes the point that grizzlies in general will avoid people and people should avoid them, by not foolishly getting in their way—by not, for example, pitching a tent on a bear trail. Once, not long ago, a writer visiting Alaska pitched his tent on a bear trail. A bear removed the writer from the tent, ate him, and left nothing much but the pencil.

"All right, that's enough!" decrees Pat Pourchot, official leader of the trip. "No more bear stories. It is never a good idea to tell bear stories at night. I've known people to wake up screaming in their sleeping bags."

As it happens, there is behind the tents a dry channel, a braid of the river when the river is in flood, and now a kind of corridor that comes through the woods and past the tents to the river. Tracks suggest that it is something of a trail. I am mildly nervous about that, but then I am mildly nervous about a lot of things. We get into the tents and zip them up. Mosquitoes, while not overwhelming, are much around. We slap a few inside, and prepare for sleep. In moments, nearly everyone else is snoring. I look up through the mesh of the tent window past spruce boughs and into the sky. Twilight sky. The sun is down. It is falling nine minutes earlier per day. In three months, it will have ceased to rise. Now, though, in the dead of night, the sky is too bright for stars. I cannot quite read by the light at two.

7 A.M., and the water temperature is forty-four, the air fifty-six, the sky blue and clear—an Indian-summer morning, August 18, 1975. Pourchot, after breakfast, goes off to measure the largest of the spruce near the campsite. He finds a tree

twenty-two inches in diameter, breast high. Most of the spruce in this country look like pipe cleaners. The better ones look like bottle washers. Tough they may be, but they are on the edge of their world, and their trunks can grow fifty years and be scarcely an inch through. Yet here is a stand of trees a foot thick. A specimen nearly two. Pourchot says he will write in his report that there is *one* tree of such girth. "Otherwise, the Forest Service might think there's timber here."

Two of our boats—the kayaks—are German. They can be taken apart and put back together. They were invented long ago by someone known as the Mad Tailor of Rosenheim. The Mad Tailor, at the turn of the century, was famous for his mountain-climbing knickers and loden capes. It was in 1907 that he went into naval architecture on a diminutive scale. Every major valley in Bavaria had a railroad running through it. The forests were laced with small white rivers. It was all but impossible to get boats to them, because boats were too bulky to accompany travellers on trains. Wouldn't it be *phantastisch*, thought the tailor, if a boat could fit into a handbag, if a suitcase could turn into a kayak? His name was Johann Klepper. He designed a collapsible kayak with a canvas skin and a frame of separable hardwood parts. In subsequent manufacture, the boat became an international success. Klepper might have stopped there. Not long after the First World War, he designed a larger version, its spray cover apertured with two holes. Where the original boat had been made for a single paddler, this one was intended for a team. We have with us a single and a double Klepper. The smaller one is prompt, responsive, feathery on the stream. The double one is somewhat less maneuverable than a three-ton log. Stell Newman, of the National Park Service, began calling it Snake Eyes, and everyone has picked up the name. Snake Eyes is our *bateau noir*, our Charonian ferry, our *Höllenfahrt*. Throughout the day, we heap opprobrium on Snake Eyes.

Pourchot and I have the double Klepper this morning. The ratio of expended energy to developed momentum is seventy-five to one. This is in part because the bottom of Snake Eyes at times intersects the bottom of the river, which is shallow at many of the riffles. The hull has become so abraded in places that it has developed leaks. The Grumman canoe is wider, longer, more heavily loaded. It carries at least half of all our gear. Nonetheless, it rides higher, draws less water, than Snake Eyes. Fortunately, the pools are extensive here in the lower river, and are generally a little deeper than a paddle will reach. Pockets are much deeper than that. Miles slide behind us. A salmon, sensing the inferiority of Snake Eyes, leaps into the air beside it, leaps again, leaps again, ten pounds of fish jumping five times high into the air—a bravado demonstration, a territorial declaration. This is, after all, the salmon's eponymous river. The jumper moves on, among its kind, ignoring the dying. These—their spawning done—idly, sleepily yield to the current, their gestures slow and quiet, a peaceful drifting away.

We have moved completely out of the hills now, and beyond the riverine fringes of spruce and cottonwood are boggy flatlands and thaw lakes. We see spruce that have been chewed by porcupines and cottonwood chewed by beavers. Moose tend to congregate down here on the tundra plain. In late fall, some of the caribou that migrate through the Salmon valley will stop here and make this their winter range. We see a pair of loons, and lesser Canada geese, and chick mergansers with their mother. Mink, marten, muskrat, otter—creatures that live here inhabit the North Woods across the world to Maine. We pass a small waterfall under a patterned bluff—folded striations of schist. In bends of the river now we come upon banks of flood-eroded soil—of mud. They imply an earth mantle of some depth going back who knows how far from the river. Brown and glistening, they are virtually identical with rural stream banks in the eastern half of the country, with the difference that the water flowing past these is clear. In the sixteenth century, the streams of eastern America ran clear (except in flood), but after people began taking the vegetation off the soil mantle and then leaving their fields fallow when crops were not there, rain carried the soil into the streams. The process continues, and when one looks at such streams today, in their seasonal varieties of chocolate, their distant past is—even to the imagination—completely lost. For this Alaskan river, on the other hand, the sixteenth century has not yet ended, nor the fifteenth, nor the fifth. The river flows, as it has since immemorial time, in balance with itself. The river and every rill that feeds it are in an unmodified natural state—opaque in flood, ordinarily clear, with levels that change within a closed cycle of the year and of the years. The river cycle is only one of many hundreds of cycles—biological, meteorological—that coincide and blend here in the absence of intruding artifice. Past to present, present reflecting past, the cycles compose this segment of the earth. It is not static, so it cannot be styled "pristine," except in the special sense that while human beings have hunted, fished, and gathered wild food in this valley in small groups for centuries, they have not yet begun to change it. Such a description will fit many rivers in Alaska. This one, though, with its considerable beauty and a geography that places it partly within and partly beyond the extreme reach of the boreal forest, has been thought of as sufficiently splendid to become a national wild river—to be set aside with its immediate environs as unalterable wild terrain. Kauffmann, Newman, Fedeler, and Pourchot are, in their various ways, studying that possibility. The wild-river proposal, which Congress is scheduled to act upon before the end of 1978, is something of a box within a box, for it is entirely incorporated within a proposed national monument that would include not only the entire Salmon River drainage but also a large segment of the valley of the Kobuk River, of which the Salmon is a tributary. (In the blue haze of Interior Department terminology, "national monument" often enough describes certain large bodies of preserved land that in all respects except name are national parks.) The Kobuk Valley National Monument proposal, which includes nearly two million acres, is, in area, relatively modest among ten other pieces of Alaska that are similarly projected for confirmation by Congress as new parks and monuments. In all, these lands constitute over thirty-two million acres, which is more than all the Yosemites, all the Yellowstones, all the Grand Canyons and Sequoias put together—a total that would more than double the present size of the National Park System. For cartographic perspective, thirty-two million acres slightly exceeds the area of the state of New York.

Impressive as that may seem, it is less than a tenth of Alaska, which consists of three hundred and seventy-five million acres. From the Alaska Purchase, in 1867, to the Alaska Statehood Act, of 1958, Alaskan land was almost wholly federal. It was open to homesteading and other forms of private acquisition, but—all communities included—less than half of one per cent actually passed to private hands. In the Statehood Act, the national government promised to transfer to state ownership a hundred and three million acres, or a little more than a quarter of Alaska. Such an area, size of California, was deemed sufficient for the needs of the population as it was then and as it might be throughout the guessable future. The generosity of this apportionment can be measured beside the fact that the 1958 population of Alaska—all natives included—was virtually the same as the population of Sacramento. Even now, after the influx of new people that followed statehood and has attended the building of the Trans-Alaska Pipeline and the supposed oil-based bonanza, there are fewer people in all Alaska than there are in San Jose. The central paradox of Alaska is that it is as small as it is large—an immense landscape with so few people in it that language is stretched to call it a frontier, let alone a state. There are four hundred thousand people in Alaska, roughly half of whom live in or around Anchorage. To the point of picayunity, the state's road system is limited. A sense of the contemporary appearance of Alaska virtually requires inspection, because the civilized imagination cannot cover such quantities of wild land. Imagine, anyway, going from New York to Chicago—or, more accurately, from the one position to the other—in the year 1500. Such journeys, no less wild, are possible, and then some, over mountains, through forests, down the streams of Alaska. Alaska is a fifth as large as the contiguous forty-eight states. The question now is, what is to be the fate of all this land? It is anything but a "frozen waste." It is green nearly half the year. As never before, it has caught the attention of conflicting interests (developers, preservers, others), and events of the nineteen-seventies are accelerating the arrival of the answer to that question.

For a time, in the nineteen-sixties, the natives of Alaska succeeded in paralyzing the matter altogether. Eskimos, Indians, and Aleuts, in coordination, pressed a claim that had been largely ignored when the Statehood Act was passed. Observing while a hundred and three million acres were legislatively prepared for a change of ownership, watching as exploration geologists came in and found the treasure of Arabia under the Arctic tundra, the natives proffered the point that their immemorial occupancy gave them special claim to Alaskan land. They engaged attorneys. They found sympathy in the federal courts and at the highest levels of the Department of the Interior. The result was that the government offered handsome compensations. Alaska has only about sixty thousand natives. They settled for a billion dollars and forty million acres of land.

The legislation that accomplished this (and a great deal more) was the Alaska Native Claims Settlement Act, of 1971. Among events of significance in the history of Alaska, this one probably stands even higher than the Statehood Act and the treaty of purchase, for it not only changed forever the status and much of the structure of native societies; it opened the way to the Trans-Alaska Pipeline, which is only the first of many big-scale projects envisioned by development-minded Alaskans, and, like a jewel cutter's chisel cleaving a rough diamond, it effected the wholesale division, subdivision, patenting, parcelling, and deeding out of physiographic Alaska.

Because conservationists were outraged by the prospective pipeline, Congress attempted to restore a balance by including in the Native Claims Settlement Act extensive conservation provisions. The most notable of these was a paragraph that instructed the Secretary of the Interior to choose land of sufficient interest to its national owners, the people of the United States, to be worthy of preservation not only as national parks and national wild rivers but also as national wildlife refuges and national forests—some eighty million acres in all. Choices would be difficult, since a high proportion of Alaska could answer the purpose. In the Department of the Interior, an Alaska Planning Group was formed, and various agencies began proposing the lands, lakes, and rivers they would like to have, everywhere—from the Malaspina Glacier to Cape Krusenstern, from the Porcupine drainage to the Aniakchak Caldera.

Congress gave the agencies—gave the Secretary of the Interior—up to seven years to study and to present the case for each selection among these national-interest lands. Personnel began moving north. Pat Pourchot, for example, just out of college, had taken the Civil Service examination and then had wandered around the Denver Federal Center looking for work. He had nothing much in mind and was ready for almost any kind of job that might be offered. He happened into the Bureau of Outdoor Recreation. Before long, he was descending Alaskan rivers. He had almost no experience with canoes or kayaks or with backpacking or camping, but he learned swiftly. John Kauffmann (a friend of mine of many years) had been planning new Park System components, such as the C.&O. Canal National Historical Park and the Cape Cod National Seashore. Transferring to Alaska, he built a house in Anchorage, and soon cornered as his special province eight and a third million acres of the central Brooks Range. When confirmed by Congress, the area will become Gates of the Arctic National Park. It is a couple of hundred miles wide, and is east of the Salmon River. For five years, he has walked it, flown it, canoed its rivers—camped in many weathers below its adze-like rising peaks. Before he came up here, he was much in the wild (he has been a ranger in various places and is the author of a book on eastern American rivers), but nonetheless he was a blue-blazer sort of man, who could blend into the tussocks at the Metropolitan Club. Unimaginable, looking at him now. If he were to take off his shirt and shake it, the dismembered corpses of vintage mosquitoes would fall to the ground. Tall and slim in the first place, he is now spare. After staring so long at the sharp, flinty peaks of the central Brooks Range, he has come to look much like them. His physiognomy, in sun and wind, has become, more or less, grizzly. Any bear that took a bite of John Kauffmann would be most unlikely to complete the meal.

Now, resting on a gravel island not far from the confluence of the Salmon and the Kobuk, he says he surely hopes Congress will not forget its promises about the national-interest lands. Some conservationists, remaining bitter about the pipeline, tend to see the park and refuge proposals as a sop written into the Native Claims Settlement Act to hush the noisome ecomorphs. Those who would develop the state for its economic worth got something they much wanted with their eight hundred miles of pipe. In return, the environmentalists were given a hundred and thirty words on paper. All the paragraph provided, however, was that eighty million acres could be temporarily set aside and studied. There was no guarantee of preservation to follow. The Wilderness Society, Friends of the Earth, the Sierra Club, the National Audubon Society, and other conservation organizations have formed the Alaska Coalition to remind Congress of its promise, of its moral obligation, lest the proposed park and refuge boundaries slowly fade from the map.

The temperature is in the low seventies. Lunch is spread out on the ground. We have our usual Sailor Boy Pilot Bread (heavy biscuits, baked in Tacoma), peanut butter, jam, and a processed cheese that comes out of a tube—artifacts of the greater society, trekked above the Arctic Circle. Other, larger artifacts may be coming soon. The road that has been cut beside the Trans-Alaska Pipeline will eventually be opened to the public. Then, for the first time in human history, it will be possible to drive a Winnebago—or, for that matter, a Fleetwood Cadillac—from Miami Beach to the Arctic Ocean. Inevitably, the new north road will develop branches. One projected branch will run westward from the pipeline to Kotzebue and Kivalina, on the Chukchi Sea. The road alignment, which Congress could deflect in the name of the national-interest lands, happens to cross the Salmon River right here, where we are having lunch. We are two hundred and fifty miles from the pipeline. We are three hundred and fifty miles from the nearest highway. Yet here in the tundra plain, and embedded in this transparent river, will stand perhaps, before long, the piers of a considerable bridge. I squeeze out the last of the cheese. It emerges from the tube like fluted icing.

There is little left of the river, and we cover it quickly—the canoe and the single kayak bobbing lightly, Snake Eyes riding low, its deck almost at water level. The meanders expand and the country begins to open. At the wide mouth of the Salmon, the gravel bottom is so shallow that we get out and drag Snake Eyes. We have come down through mountains, and we have more recently been immured between incised stream banks in the lower plain, and now we walk out onto a wide pebble beach on the edge of a tremendous river. Gulfs of space reach to horizon mountains. We can now see, far to the northeast, the higher, more central Brooks Range, blurred and blue and soft brown under white compiled flat-bottomed clouds. There are mountains south of us, mountains, of course, behind us. The river, running two full miles to the nearest upstream bend, appears to be a lake. Mergansers are cruising it. The

Kobuk is, in places, wide, like the Yukon, but its current is slower and has nothing of the Yukon's impelling, sucking rush. The Yukon, like any number of Alaskan rivers, is opaque with pulverized rock, glacial powder. In a canoe in such a river, you can hear the grains of mountains like sandpaper on the hull. Glaciers are where the precipitation is sufficient to feed them. Two hundred inches will fall in parts of southern Alaska, and that is where the big Alaskan glaciers are. Up here, annual precipitation can be as low as fifteen inches. Many deserts get more water from the sky. The Arctic ground conserves its precipitation, however—holds it frozen half the year. So this is not a desert. Bob Fedeler, whose work with Alaska Fish and Game has taken him to rivers in much of the state, is surprised by the appearance of the Kobuk. "It is amazing to see so much clear water," he says. "In a system as vast as this one, there is usually a glacial tributary or two, and that mucks up the river."

Standing on the shore, Fedeler snaps his wrist and sends a big enamelled spoon lure, striped like a barber pole, flying over the water. Not long after it splashes, he becomes involved in a struggle with something more than a grayling. The fish sulks a little. For the most part, though, it moves. It makes runs upriver, downriver. It dashes suddenly in the direction of the tension on the line. His arms now oscillating, now steady, Fedeler keeps the line taut, keeps an equilibrium between himself and the fish, until eventually it flops on the dry gravel at his feet. It is a nine-pound salmon, the beginnings of dinner. Stell Newman catches another salmon, of about the same size. I catch one, a seven-pound adolescent, and let it go. Pat Pourchot, whose philosophical abstinence from fishing has until now been consistent, is suddenly aflush with temptation. Something like a hundred thousand salmon will come up the Kobuk in a summer. (They are counted by techniques of aerial survey.) The Kobuk is three hundred miles long and has at least fifty considerable tributaries—fifty branching streams to which salmon could be returning to spawn—and yet when they have come up the Kobuk to this point, to the mouth of the Salmon River, thirty thousand salmon turn left. As school after school arrives here, they pause, hover, reconnoitre—prepare for the run in the home stream. The riffles we see offshore are not rapids but salmon. Pourchot can stand it no longer. He may have phased himself out of fishing, but he is about to phase himself back in. Atavistic instincts take him over. His noble resolve collapses in the presence of this surge of fish.

He borrows Fedeler's rod and sends the lure on its way. He reels. Nothing. He casts again. He reels. Nothing. Out in the river, there may be less water than salmon, but that is no guarantee that one will strike. Salmon do not feed on the spawning run. They apparently bite only by instinctive reflex if something flashes close before them. Pourchot casts again. Nothing. He casts again. The lure this time stops in the river as if it were encased in cement. Could be a boulder. Could be a submerged log. The lure seems irretrievably snagged—until the river erupts. Pourchot is a big man with a flowing red beard. He is well over six feet. Blond hair tumbles across his shoulders. The muscles in his arms are strong from many hundreds of miles of paddling. This salmon, nonetheless, is dragging him up the beach. The fish leaps into the air, thrashes at the river surface, and makes charging runs of such thrust that Pourchot has no choice but to follow or break the line. He follows—fifty, seventy-five yards down the river with the salmon. The fish now changes plan and goes upstream. Pourchot follows. The struggle lasts thirty minutes, and the energy drawn away is almost half Pourchot's. He wins, though, because he is bigger. The fish is scarcely larger than his leg. When, finally, it moves out of the water and onto the gravel, it has no hook in its mouth. It has been snagged, inadvertently, in the dorsal fin. Alaska law forbids keeping any sport fish caught in that way. The salmon must take the lure in its mouth. Pourchot extracts the hook, gently lifts the big fish in his arms, and walks into the river. He will hold the salmon right side up in the water until he is certain that its shock has passed and that it has regained its faculties. Otherwise, it might turn bottom up and drown.

If that were my fish, I would be inclined to keep it, but such a thought would never cross Pourchot's mind. Moreover, one can hardly borrow the rod of a representative of the Alaska Department of Fish and Game, snag a salmon while he watches, and stuff it in a bag. Fedeler, for his part, says he guesses that ninety-five per cent of salmon caught that way are kept. Pourchot removes his hands. The salmon swims away.

Forest Eskimos, who live in five small villages on the Kobuk, do not tend to think in landscape terms that are large. They see a river not as an entity but as a pageant of parts, and every bend and eddy has a name. This place, for example—this junction of rivers—is Qalugruich paanga, which, tightly translated, means "salmon mouth." For thousands of years, to extents that have varied with cycles of plenty, the woodland Eskimos have fished here. The wall tent of an Eskimo fish camp—apparently, for the time being, empty—stands a mile or so downstream. We find .30–'06 cartridge cases sprinkled all over the beach, and a G.I. can opener of the type that comes with C rations. With the exception of some old stumps—of trees that were felled, we imagined, by a hunting party cutting firewood—we saw along the Salmon River no evidence whatever of the existence of the human race. Now we have crossed into the outermost band of civilization—suggested by a tent, by some cartridge cases, by a can opener. In the five Kobuk River villages—Noorvik, Kiana, Ambler, Shungnak, and Kobuk—live an aggregate of scarcely a thousand people. Kiana, the nearest village to us, is forty miles downstream. In recent years, caribou and salmon have been plentiful nearer home, and the people of Kiana have not needed to come this far to fish, else we might have found the broad gravel beach here covered with drying racks—salmon, split and splayed, hanging from the drying racks—and people seining for the fish going by.

We get back into the boats, shove off, and begin the run down the Kobuk. Paddling on a big lake is much the same. You fix your eye on a point two miles away and watch it until it puts you to sleep. The river bottom, nearly as distinct as the Salmon's, is no less absorbing. It is gravelled, and lightly covered with silt. In shallow places, salmon leave trails in the silt, like lines made by fingers in dust. Eskimos know that one school of salmon will follow the trails of another. In shallow bends of the river, fishing camps are set up beside the trails. "We must have fish to live," the people say; and they use every part of the salmon. They eat the eggs with bearberries. They roast, smoke, fry, boil, or dry the flesh. They bury the heads in leaf-lined pits and leave them for weeks. The result is a delicacy reminiscent of cheese. Fevers and colds are sometimes treated by placing fermented salmon on the skin of the neck and nose. A family might use as many as a thousand salmon a year. To feed dogs, many salmon are needed. Dogs eat whole fish, and they clean up the fins, intestines, and bones of the fish eaten by people. Dog teams have largely been replaced by snowmobiles (or snow machines, as they are almost universally called in Alaska), and, as a result, the salmon harvest at first declined. Snow machines, however—for all their breathtaking ability to go as fast as fifty miles an hour over roadless terrain—break down now and again, and are thus perilous. A stranded traveller cannot eat a snow machine. Dog teams in the region are increasing in number, and the take of salmon is growing as well.

Now, for the first time in days of river travel, we hear the sound of an engine. A boat rounds a bend from the west and comes into view—a plywood skiff, two women and a man, no doubt on their way from Kiana to Ambler. A thirty-five-horsepower Evinrude shoves them upcurrent. They wave and go by. There are a few kayaks in the villages, small ones for use in stream and lake hunting, but the only kayaks we are at all likely to see are the one-man Klepper and Snake Eyes.

Four miles from Qalugruich paanga, it is five in the day and time to quit. We are, after all, officially an extension of bureaucracy. Walking far back from the water, Kauffmann picks tent sites on beds of sedge. A big cottonwood log, half buried in sand, will be a bench by the fire. Mosquitoes swarm. They are not particularly bad. In this part of Alaska, nearer the coast, they sometimes fly in dense, whirling vertical columns, dark as the trunks of trees. But we have not seen such concentrations. Kauffmann talks of killing forty at a slap in the Gates of the Arctic, but the season is late now and their numbers are low. I slap my arm and kill seven.

The temperature of the Kobuk is fifty-seven degrees—so contrastingly warm after the river in the mountains that we peel off our clothes and run into the water with soap. However, by no possible illusion is this the Limpopo, and we shout and yell at the cold water, take short, thrashing swims, and shiver in the bright evening sun. The Kobuk, after all, has about the same temperature—at this time of year—as the coastal waters of Maine, for which the term most often heard is "freezing." Wool feels good after the river; and the fire, high with driftwood, even better; and a dose of Arctic snakebite medicine even better than that. In a memo to all of us written many weeks ago, Pourchot listed, under "optional personal equipment," "Arctic snakebite medicine." There are no snakes in Alaska. But what if a snake should unexpectedly appear? The serum in my pack is from Lynchburg, Tennessee.

The salmon—filleted, rolled in flour, and sautéed on our pancake grill—is superb among fishes and fair among salmon. With few exceptions, the Pacific salmon that run in these Arctic rivers are of the variety known as chum. Their flesh lacks the high pink color of the silver, the sockeye, the king salmon. Given a choice among those, a person with a lure would not go for chum, and they are rarely fished for sport. After sockeyes and humpbacks, though, they are third in the commercial salmon fishery. Many millions of dollars' worth are packed each year. Athapaskan Indians, harvesting from the Yukon, put king salmon on their own tables and feed chum salmon to their dogs. Hence, they call chum "dog salmon." Eskimos up here in the Arctic Northwest, who rarely see another kind, are piqued when they hear this Indian term.

We look two hundred yards across the Kobuk to spruce that are reflected in the quiet surface. The expanded dimensions of our surroundings are still novel. Last night, in forest, we were close by the sound of rushing water. Sound now has become inverse to the space around us, for we sit in the middle of an immense and almost perfect stillness. We hear the fire and, from time to time, insects, birds. The sound of an airplane crosses the edge of hearing and goes out again. It is the first aircraft we have heard.

Kauffmann says he is worried, from the point of view of park planning, about the aircraft access that would probably be developed for the Salmon River. "It's not a big world up there. I'm not sure how much use it could take."

This reminds Fedeler of the cost of travel to wilderness, and makes him contemplate again who can pay to get there. "The Salmon is a nice enough river," he says. "But it is unavailable to ninety-nine point nine per cent of the people. I wouldn't go back to Fairbanks and tell everybody that they absolutely *have* to go and see the Salmon River."

"It's a fine experience."

"If you happen to have an extra six hundred bucks. Is the Park Service going to provide helicopter access or Super Cub access to some gravel bar near the headwaters?"

"Why does there have to be access?" Pourchot puts in.

"Why do there have to be wild and scenic rivers?" Fedeler wants to know. "And why this one—so far up here? Because of the cost of getting to it, the Salmon Wild River for most people would be just a thing on a map—an occasional trip for people from the Park Service, the Bureau of Outdoor Recreation, and the Alaska Department of Fish and Game. Meanwhile, with pressures what they are farther south, the sportsman in Alaska is in for some tough times."

"His numbers are increasing."

"And his opportunities are decreasing, while these federal proposals would set aside lands and rivers that only the rich can afford."

"The proposals, up here, are for the future," Kauffmann says, and he adds, after a moment, "As Yellowstone was. Throughout the history of this country, it's been possible to go to a place where no one has camped before, and now that kind of opportunity is running out. We must protect it, even if artificially. The day will come when people will want to visit such a wilderness—saving everything they have in order to see it, at whatever cost. We're talking fifty and more years hence, when there may be nowhere else to go to a place that is wild and unexplored."

I have a net over my head and cannot concentrate on this discussion, because something worse, and smaller, than mosquitoes—clouds of little flying prickers that cut you up—are in the air around us now and are coming through the mesh of the head net. They follow us into the tents, ignoring the netting there. They cut rashes in our faces all through the night.

For two days, we stare at the hypnotizing vistas of the Kobuk, while its spacious novelty wears off. Uncannily, the river comes in almost precise two-mile segments, bend to bend. We move downstream a little more than twenty miles one day, only sixteen the next, in part because of stiff western headwinds. Having had one bad night with insects, we next choose to pitch our tents far out on a gravel point, on a dry part of the riverbed, two hundred yards from the nearest blade of vegetation, confident that the water will not rise, and preferring anyway to be drowned outright than consumed piecemeal. The instant the bows touch shore, mosquitoes in grosses try to settle upon us. As we finish putting up the tents, a light rain begins to spit. The sky is slate gray in the east. We are camped on an island, and we fish the slough that goes behind it. Nothing there but six-inch grayling. Kauffmann and I try to walk around the island, but it is bigger than we imagined. Moreover, the beach runs out some distance down the slough. Plowing on through dense willow and alder, soaking wet, we give up the circumambulation and traverse the island to return to camp. We see wolf tracks seven inches long—amazing size, but there is a tape measure in my pocket and that is what it says. Less than a yard separates one set of prints from another —the tracks of a slow loper. Earlier in the day, fishing by the mouth of the Kallarichuk tributary, we saw wolf tracks intricately intertwined with the tracks of a running moose. There were changes of direction, overlapping circles. No other sign. The calligraphy seemed to report some unresolved encounter —unless two extremely odd animals had been through there at different times. Now, after dinner, in light rain, we look upriver and see a cow moose walk out of willows. She drinks from the river. She stands, for a while, immobile, and stares across the water. Slowly, she retreats into the thicket. Moose are so numerous now in this part of northwest Alaska that it is difficult to imagine them absent, but they have been here scarcely fifty years. The patterns of other creatures—the bear, the fish, the caribou—run in long cycles over time, cycles of waxing, cycles of waning; but they have been in the region for ten thousand years, and when they have locally been gone for a time they have always returned. In the case of the moose, though, there is no evidence that they were ever here before the early part of this century, and now they are established in the milieu and in the native economy.

Eight boats, outboard-powered, going upriver, passed us in the course of the day—all with at least three people in them, some with children. Four have come back, and passed us again, during the evening. It seems to be the rhythm of the Kobuk that Eskimos go by about once an hour—at least on this part of the river, many miles from the nearest village. I remember Bob Waldrop saying how he counts on random Eskimos to pick him up near the finish of certain trips he makes. Waldrop is a Brooks Range guide, who leads long journeys, mainly on foot, on both sides of the Arctic Divide. Much of the time, he does not know exactly where he is. Maps lack detail, he explains; many mountains are unnamed. He generally has a fair idea of his position, within eight miles or so, but he finds it impossible to plan things more precisely than that, and people who expect to know just where they are and to follow an exact schedule, who are (in his words) "set in their ways," are likely to be unhappy on such trips, and unenjoyable company. Waldrop, like Kauffmann, does not want his Brooks Range any other way. He wants it imprecise. He wants to preserve its surprises. When he goes up nameless mountains and finds on their summits containers identifying someone or other as the first visiting conqueror, he puts the containers in his pack and hauls them out. If you say to him, "You're altering history," Waldrop says, "The people were altering history who put the registers there." When Waldrop comes out of, say, the Sadlerochit Mountains, and makes his way across the wet tundra toward the Arctic Ocean, he has no idea when or where he will come to the water; nevertheless, he relies on "flagging the nearest Eskimo" for a ride to Barter Island, where mail planes land. An hour here, a day there, he waits with patience until one comes along.

The Eskimos on the Kobuk never seem surprised when they come upon us, as if nothing could be less extraordinary than the Grumman canoe, the small blue single kayak, and Snake Eyes—all afloat under five white faces. And now, as we watch from our campsite, another skiff approaches, coming downriver. It passes the sandspit where the moose was standing. A couple of hundred yards from us, a heavyset man in the stern cuts the motor. There are three people—two men and a woman. They drift and observe us. The woman is wearing a long calico dress, fringed at the bottom, rubber boots. The men are wearing short parkas with fur ruffs. There is an exchange of waves. At length, the man in the stern picks up an oar and sculls the boat toward the edge of the river. The boat is plywood, about eighteen feet long, apparently homemade, with a flat bottom, a square stern, and a thirty-five-horse Evinrude. The woman jumps out, into a couple of feet of water, where she firms the skiff against the current. She acts as an anchor while the heavyset man—her husband—talks with us. His name is Clarence Jackson, and he is from Noorvik. The other man is his uncle. In the boat is a full cartridge belt and a .45-calibre pistol. This is their annual trip upriver, he says, to visit his great-grandmother's grave. We ask about fish, and he says the runs have been mediocre this season. He says the caribou were plentiful near Kiana. He smiles amiably, somewhat diffidently, as he speaks. He wonders if we happen to know anything about a party of white people, far down the Kobuk, who had no boats, and who summoned a young Eskimo to shore and when he got out of his boat were extremely rough with him. We are surprised, and as dismayed as Clarence Jackson. He says, grinning, that if he had not seen our boats he would not have come so close. Up in the country where we have been no one much goes in summer, but Kobuk people sometimes hunt there in winter, he says, his friendly tone unaltered. His wife gets back into the boat. With toothy smiles, they say goodbye and move on down the river.

The people of the Kobuk are among the few Eskimos in Alaska whose villages are well within the tree line. They have a culture that reflects their cousinship to Eskimos of the coast and that borrows also from the Indians of the Alaskan interior. The combination is unique. At first glance—plywood boats, Evinrudes—they may seem to be even more a part of the world at large than they are of this Arctic valley. Much of their clothing is manufactured. They use rifles. They ride on snow machines. They seine whitefish and salmon with nylon nets that cost upward of four hundred dollars. Now and again, they leave the valley in search of jobs. They work on the pipeline. Without the river and the riverine land, though, they would be bereft of most of what sustains them. Their mail-order likeness to the rest of us does not go very deep. They may use Eagle Claw fishhooks from Wright & McGill, in Denver, but they still know how to make them from the teeth of wolves. They may give their children windup toys, but they also make little blowguns for them from the hollow leg bones of the sandhill crane. To snare ptarmigan, they no longer use spruce roots—they use picture wire—but they still snare ptarmigan. They eat what they call "white-man food," mainly from cans, but they also eat owl soup, sour dock, wild rhubarb, and the tuber *Hedysarum alpinum*—the Eskimo potato. Some of them believe that Eskimo food keeps them healthy and brown, and that too much white-man food will turn them white. Roughly half their carbohydrates come from wild food—and fully four-fifths of their protein. They eat—and, more to the point, depend on—small creatures of the forest. Rabbit. Beaver. Muskrat. Thousands of frozen whitefish will be piled beside a single house. At thirty below, whitefish break like glass. The people dip the frozen bits in seal oil and chew them. From fresh whitefish, as they squeeze, they directly suck roe. They trade mud-shark livers for seal oil from the coast. Mud sharks are freshwater, river fish, and for maritime Eskimos the liver of the mud shark is an exotic and delicious import. The forest Eskimo has a reciprocal yen for seal oil. When a Kobuk woman goes "fishing for seal oil," mud sharks are what she is after. Loon oil is sometimes substituted for seal oil, there being a great deal of oil in a loon. Sheefish, rare in the world and looking like fifteen-pound tarpon, make annual runs up the Kobuk. They are prized by the people.

On nothing, though, do the forest Eskimos depend so much as on caribou. They use the whole animal. They eat the meat raw and in roasts and stews. They eat greens from the stomach, muscles from the jaw, fat from behind the eyes. The hide goes into certain winter clothing that nothing manufactured can equal. Toward the end of the nineteenth century, the number of available caribou gradually declined in the Kobuk valley. Why the herd avoided the region perhaps had to do with climatic cycles and their effect on vegetation, but nobody knows. From the turn of the century until about 1940, people of the Kobuk had to go into the Brooks Range to find caribou, making prodigious journeys in winter, and feeding much of the kill to their dogs, on which they depended for the trip home with essential skins and sinew. In the nineteen-forties, the herd began to return—in numbers that increased each year. The caribou cycle—dearth to plenty and back again—seems to close itself in sixty to a hundred years. The Arctic herd numbered two hundred and forty thousand a few years ago, and has been fast decreasing. Some fifty thousand come over the mountains now.

With the rise and fall of such cycles, the people of the Kobuk from earliest times expanded and contracted over the riverine lands. Whenever caribou were plentiful, people were able to congregate in relatively large winter villages. Where caribou were scarce, people had to spread out—up and down the river in small family groups—for hunting small game and for fishing through the ice. Pursuit of furs for trading purposes tended to disseminate them as well. The arrival—seventy, eighty years ago—of white missionaries, schools, and trading posts tended to force the Eskimos together in places like Noorvik and Kiana, but Kobuk River people have not traditionally thought of their homes as permanent in location. Through much of their history, they built new houses—on sites shiftingly appropriate—each fall. With their Evinrudes and their Arctic Cat snowmobiles, their range has been extended—they can cover more miles from a fixed base—but cycles of climate, of salmon, of caribou cannot be levelled by gasoline. In order to continue existence as they have known it, the forest Eskimos must follow where the cycles may lead. So they are worried. It is difficult to see how the essential flexibility of their history is going to be advanced by the Alaska Native Claims Settlement Act and the so-called national-interest lands. By the terms of the law, the Eskimos must choose specific land—to become theirs according to the settlement—and the land must, by and large, be contiguous to the villages. When a boundary is established around native land, what if the caribou go somewhere else? Suppose the caribou concentrate for a time in the Kobuk Valley National Monument? Hunting is not permitted in national parks. Oh, but exceptions will be made in Alaska, where people can hunt on their traditional grounds. A tradition of 1920 may not be a tradition now, but will be again, in all likelihood, some decades in the future. The government understands that. The government may understand that today, but officials change, regulations change. Will the government understand in 1990? The Eskimos undeniably got a good deal in the Native Claims Settlement Act, but it was good only insofar as they agreed to change their way—to cherish money, and to adopt the concept (for centuries unknown to them) of private property. "No Trespassing" signs have begun to appear up here, around villages where those words would once have not been understood. Boundaries now have to be adjusted, adjudicated, where boundaries never existed. Kobuk societies once functioned like the clans of Scotland. Terrain was common to all. Kinship patterned things; ownership did not. Use determined use. If you had been using a place—say, a fishing spot—it was respected as yours while you used it. Now the enforced drawing of lines on the land has created tensions among the Kobuk villages that did not exist before. Under the ingratiating Eskimo surface is a sense of grave disturbance.

There is, as well, an added complication. In 1906, the Native Allotment Act provided that any Alaskan native could file a claim for a hundred and sixty acres of Alaska. This meant next to nothing to the people of the Kobuk valley, since they were not attracted to private ownership, and, in any case, could make little use of such a minuscule amount of land. Few people bothered to file. When the Native Claims Settlement Act came along, however, a final deadline was set for native allotments, and many people, thus pressed, decided to register claims after all. They took the allotments in violation of their own customary principles. Bad feeling inevitably followed and to some extent soured their society.

The sense of private property that has been jacketed upon them is uncomfortable, incompatible with subsistence harvesting and its changeful cycles. It is ironic that while the land-claim settlement is being effected relative plenty has been close to the villages. In 1900, the people could easily have shown that they needed a vast area in which to subsist. Of late, they have needed less. They will need more again. It is impossible to draw lines around a situation like this one, but the lines are being drawn.

The people of the National Park Service, for their part, seem to be amply sensitive to the effects their efforts might have. They intend to adjust their own traditions so that Alaskan national-park land will not abridge but will in fact preserve native customs. Under the direction of Douglas Anderson, of the Department of Anthropology at Brown University, an anthropological team commissioned by the Park Service has recently described and voluminously catalogued what must be every habit, tic, and mannerism, every tale and taboo—let alone custom—of the Kobuk River natives. The anthropologists make a convincing case for helping the people preserve their modus vivendi, but the most vivid words in the document occur when the quoted Eskimos are speaking for themselves:

> Eskimos should make laws for those people outside. That would be just the same as what they try to do to us. We know nothing about how they live, and they know nothing about how we live. It should be up to us to decide things for ourselves. You see the land out there? We never have spoiled it.
>
> Too much is happening to the people. Too many outside pressures are forcing in on us. Changes are coming too fast, and we are being pushed in all different directions by forces that come from someplace outside. People thought that the land-claims settlement was the end of our problems, that it meant the future was secure; but it was only the beginning. Even before the lands were all selected the government wanted pipeline easements and road corridors right through our territory. These would take away strips miles wide, cutting right across our land. And instead of open access to the land, the Eskimos might be surrounded by huge pieces of country that are declared national resources for all the people. Land that has always belonged to the natives is being parcelled up and divided among the takers.

The forest Eskimos' relationship with whites has made them dependent on goods that need to be paid for: nylon netting, boat materials, rifles, ammunition, motors, gasoline. Hence, part of the year some Eskimo men leave the river to find jobs. These pilgrimages to the wage economy are not a repudiation of the subsistence way of life. They make money so they can come back home, where they prefer to be, and live the way they prefer to live—foraging the wild country with gasoline and bullets. If subsistence living were to be, through regulation, denied to them, the probable result would be that the government would have to support them even more than at present—more aid to dependent children, more food stamps —for they would not be able to find sufficient work, at home or on seasonal trips outside, to support their families.

> As long as I have the land and nobody tries to stop me from using it, then I'm a rich man. I can always go out there and make my living, no matter what happens. Everything I need —my food, clothes, house, heat—it's all out there.
>
> And another thing, too. If we have nothing of our Eskimo food—only white-man food to live on—we can't live. We eat and eat and eat, but we never get filled up. Just like starvation.

Breakfast in the frying pan—freeze-dried eggs. If we were Kobuk people, one of us might go off into the watery tundra and find fresh eggs. Someone else might peel the bark from a willow. The bark would be soaked and formed into a tube with the eggs inside, and the tube would be placed in the fire. But this is not a group of forest Eskimos. These are legionaries from another world, talking "scenic values" and "interpretation." These are Romans inspecting Transalpine Gaul. Nobody's skin is going to turn brown on these eggs —or on cinnamon-apple-flavored Instant Quaker Oatmeal, or Tang, or Swiss Miss, or on cold pink-icinged Pop-Tarts with raspberry filling. For those who do not believe what they have just read, allow me to confirm it: in Pourchot's breakfast bag are pink-icinged Pop-Tarts with raspberry filling. Lacking a toaster, and not caring much anyway, we eat them cold. They invite a question. To a palate without bias—the palate of an open-minded Berber, the palate of a travelling Martian —which would be the more acceptable, a pink-icinged Pop-Tart with raspberry filling (cold) or the fat gob from behind a caribou's eye?

It is raining. A wind is rising and pushing back a morning fog. The air—fifty-four—is cooler than the Kobuk. We have twenty miles to cover, downriver to Kiana. Each of us has put in identical time in the various boats, so now we draw lots to see who goes where, and Fedeler and I are the losers. We draw Snake Eyes. Even before we shove off, whitecaps have formed on the river, and waves two feet high. They are coming from the west, and that is where we are going. As we pack up, Fedeler and I are subjected to intense gratuitous ridicule because we are condemned to Snake Eyes; and, indeed, a chill wet day on a half-sunk log is about all we can expect. So we plow westward, into the waves, and the wind is so strong it brings tears to the eyes. They mix with the rain and the spray of the river. The length of a mile varies. These are three-league miles. The current flows west, the wind and waves come east, and they more than cancel the force of the river. To stop paddling is to move backward. The waves are so big they wash over the bow of the Grumman. Light and bobbing in its ride down the Salmon, the canoe here is too much up in the wind. John Kauffmann and Stell Newman have to bend their paddles on every stroke. The single Klepper, with Pourchot in it, is better off, but not much. It is so light that he has to strain to drive it. Snake Eyes, however, is thirty per cent submerged in its own leakings, another third by the natural depth of its draft. Snake Eyes is in and of the river. The wind cannot get to Snake Eyes, because the wind can't swim. The waves that wash over us roll over the deck, asserting an upstream thrust of zero. Snake Eyes, property of the United States government, is today straight out of Groton, Connecticut—a nuclear-powered submarine. Fedeler and I, the nuclei, begin to suffer in a way unimaginable before. We become chilly, and a little stiff, waiting for the others—idling at the river bends, scanning the gray river through its flying spray to see where the others might be. After six or eight miles, we are so cold we stop. We build a bonfire of drifted cottonwood, and stand downwind of it at the edge of the flames.

The wind gradually subsides through the afternoon, and the low gray sky begins to pull itself apart. The weather here is like the weather in Scotland. It can change so abruptly—closing in, lifting, closing in again—that all in an hour, let alone a day, wind-driven rain may be followed by calm and hazy sunshine, which may then be lost in heavy mists that soon disappear into open skies. We pass under a high bluff and go around a final bend; then the water spreads open before us in a three-mile reach to Kiana. The village is quite lovely from this perspective, lifted on its own high bluff above a confluence of rivers—the Squirrel and the Kobuk—and with a European compactness of buildings that contributes emphasis and irony to the immense wilderness in which it is a dot. We stop three miles away and camp on a flat gravel bar. The sky over supper is shot with color—with washes of salmon light on accumulating clouds. Their edges are gray to black, growing heavy. To the north, we hear thunder and see lightning. Such storms are rare in much of Alaska, but they are common here. This one rolls on into the Brooks Range and leaves us bright and dry. The talk over the campfire is entirely about Alaska. We are at the end of this trip now, and from the moment it began no one has once mentioned anything that did not have to do with Alaska.

In the morning—cool in the forties and the river calm—we strike the tents, pack the gear, and move on down toward Kiana. Gradually, the village spreads out in perspective. Its most prominent structure is the sheet-metal high school on the edge of town. Dirt-and-gravel streets climb the hill above the bluff. Houses are low, frame. Some are made of logs. Behind the town, a navigational beacon flashes. Drawing closer, we can see caribou antlers over doorways—testimony of need and respect. There are basketball backboards. We are closing a circuit, a hundred water miles from the upper Salmon, where a helicopter took us, from Kiana, at the start. Under the bluff, we touch the shore. Kiana is now high above us, and mostly out of sight. The barge is here that brings up supplies from Kotzebue. The river's edge for the moment is all but unpopulated. Fish racks up and down the beach are covered with split drying salmon—ruddy and pink. We disassemble the Kleppers, removing their prefabricated bones, folding their skins, making them disappear into canvas bags. I go up the hill for a carton, and return to the beach. Into envelopes of cardboard I tape the tines of the caribou antler that I have carried from the mountains. Protecting the antler takes longer than the dismantling and packing of the kayaks, but there is enough time before the flight to Kotzebue at midday. In the sky, there has as yet been no sound of the airplane—a Twin Otter, of Wien Air Alaska, the plane that brought us here to meet the chopper. Stell Newman has gone up the beach and found some people at work around their fish racks. He now has with him a slab of dried salmon, and we share it like candy.

Children were fishing when we were here before. They yanked whitefish out of the river and then pelted one another with the living fish as if they were snowballs. Women with tubs were gutting salmon. It was a warmer day then. The sun was so fierce you looked away; you looked north. Up at the airstrip behind the town—a gravel strip, where we go now with our gear—was the Grumman canoe. It had been flown in, and cached there, long before. The helicopter, chartered by the government and coming in from who knows where, was a new five-seat twin-engine Messerschmitt with a bubble front. On its shining fuselage, yellow-and-black heraldry identified it as the property of Petroleum Helicopters, Inc. The pilot removed a couple of fibre-glass cargo doors, took out a seat, and we shoved the canoe into an opening at the rear of the cabin. It went in halfway. The Grumman was too much for the Messerschmitt. The canoe was cantilevered, protruding to the rear. We tied it in place. It was right side up, and we filled it with gear. Leaving the rest of us to wait for a second trip, Pourchot and the pilot took off for the Salmon River. With so much canoe coming out of its body, the helicopter, even in flight, seemed to be nearing the final moment of an amazing pregnancy. It went over the mountains northeast.

There was a wooden sign beside the airstrip: "WELCOME TO THE CITY OF KIANA. 2nd Class City. Population 300 . . . Establish 1902 . . . Main Sources: Bear, Caribou, Moose, Geese, Salmon, Shee, Whitefish, Trout." The burning sun was uncomfortable. I walked behind the sign. In its shadow, the air was chill. I dragged the helicopter seat out of the sun and into the shade of a storage hut, sat down, leaned back, and went to sleep. When I woke up, I was shivering. The temperature a few feet away, in the sunlight, was above seventy degrees.

What awakened me were the voices of children. Three small girls had followed us up from the Kobuk, where we had watched them fish. They had crossed the runway and picked blueberries, and now were offering them from their hands. The berries were intensely sweet, having grown in the long northern light. The little girls also held out pieces of hard candy. Wouldn't we like some? They asked for nothing. They were not shy. They were totally unself-conscious. I showed them an imitating game, wherein you clear your throat—hrrrum—and then draw with a stick a figure on the ground. "Here. Try to do that." They drew the figure but did not clear their throats. "No. That's not quite right. Hrrrum. Here now. Try it again."

They tried twice more. They didn't get it. I sat down again on the chopper seat. Stell Newman let them take pictures with his camera. When they noticed my monocular, on a lanyard around my neck, they got down beside me, picked it off my chest, and spied on the town. They leaned over, one at a time, and put their noses down against mine, draping around my head their soft black hair. They stared into my eyes. Their eyes were dark and northern, in beautiful almond faces, aripple with smiles. Amy. Katherine. Rose Ann. Ages nine and eleven. Eskimo girls. They looked up. They had heard the helicopter, and before long it appeared.

I sat in the co-pilot's seat, others in the seat I had been napping on. We lifted off, and headed out to join Pourchot, who was waiting on a gravel bar in the upper Salmon. The rotor noise was above conversation, but the pilot handed me a pair of earphones and a microphone. He showed me on a panel between us the mechanics of communicating. I couldn't think of much to say. I was awed, I suppose, in the presence of a bush pilot (mustache akimbo) and in the presence of the bush itself—the land and the approaching mountains. I didn't want to distract him, or myself. He kept urging me to talk, though. He seemed to want the company. His name was Gene Parrish, and he was a big man who had eaten well. He smoked a cigar, and on the intercom was garrulous and friendly.

Before us now was the first ridgeline. Flying close to ground, close to the mountainside, we climbed rapidly toward the crest, and then—crossing over it—seemed to plunge into a void of air. The ground ahead, which had been so near, was suddenly far below. We soon reached another mountainside, and again we climbed closely above its slope, skimmed the outcropping rocks at the top, and jumped into a gulf of sky.

Parrish said, "Y'all ever seen these mountains before?"

Some of the others had, I said, but I had not.

"Me, neither," he said. "Aren't they fabulous? Alaska is amazing, isn't it? Wherever you go, everything is different. These mountains sure are fabulous."

Indeed they were something like it—engaging, upsweeping tundra fells. They were not sharp and knife-edged like the peaks of the central Brooks. They were less dramatic but more inviting. They looked negotiable. They were, as it happened, the last mountains of the range, the end of the line, the end of a cordillera. They were, after four thousand miles, the last statement of the Rocky Mountains before they disappeared into the Chukchi Sea.

Parrish went up the side of a still higher mountain and skimmed the ridge, to reveal, suddenly, a drainage system far below.

"Is that the Salmon River?" I said.

"Oh, my, no," he said. "It's a ways yet. Where y'all from?"

"I'm from New Jersey. And you?"

"Louisiana."

He said he had come to Alaska on a kind of working vacation. At home, where his job was to fly back and forth between the Louisiana mainland and oil rigs in the Gulf of Mexico, he seldom flew over anything much higher than a wave. Because the Messerschmitt had two engines, he said, he would not have to autorotate down if one were to fail. In fact, he could even climb on one engine. So it was safe to fly this way, low and close—and more interesting.

We flew up the sides of mountain after mountain, raked the ridges, fluttered high over valleys. In each new valley was a stream, large or small. With distance, they looked much alike. Parrish checked his airspeed, the time, the heading; finally, he made a sharp southward turn and began to follow a stream course in the direction of its current, looking for a gravel bar, a man, a canoe. Confidently, he gave up altitude and searched the bending river. He found a great deal of gravel. For thirty, forty miles, he kept searching, until the hills around the river began to diminish in anticipation of—as we could see ahead—the wet-tundra Kobuk plain. If the river was the Salmon, Pourchot was not there. If Pourchot was on the Salmon, Parrish was somewhere else.

The Salmon had to be farther east, he guessed, shaking his head in surprise and wonder. We rollercoasted the sides of additional mountains and came upon another significant drainage. It appeared to Parrish to be the right one. This time, we flew north, low over the river, upstream, looking for the glint of the canoe. We had as much luck as before. The river narrowed as we went farther and farther, until it became a brook and then a rill, with steep-rising mountains to either side. "I don't believe it. I just *can't* believe it," Parrish said. There was nothing much below us now but the kind of streak a tear might make crossing a pilot's face. "This just isn't right," he said. "This is not working out. I was sure of the heading. I was sure this was the river. But nothing ever is guaranteed. Nothing—nothing—is guarandamnteed."

He turned one-eighty and headed downstream. Spread over his knees was a Nome Sectional Aeronautical Chart, and he puzzled over it for a while, then he handed it to me. Maybe I could help figure out where we were. The map was quite wonderful at drawing straight lines between distant airstrips, but its picture of the mountains looked like calves' brains over bone china, and the scale was such that the whole of the Salmon River was only six inches long. The chopper plowed on to the south. I held the map a little closer to my eyes, studying the blue veiny lines among the mountains. The ludicrousness of the situation washed over me. I looked back at Kauffmann and the others, who seemed somewhat confused. And small wonder. A map was being handed back and forth between a man from New Jersey and a pilot from Louisiana who were amiss in—of all places—the Brooks Range. In a sense—in the technical sense that we had next to no idea where we were—we were lost.

There are no geographical requirements for pilots in the United States. Anyone who is certified as a pilot can fly anywhere, and that, of course, includes anywhere in Alaska. New pilots arrive steadily from all over the Lower Forty-eight. Some are attracted by the romance of Alaska, some by the money around the pipeline. The Alyeska Pipeline Service Company, soon after it began its construction operations, set up its own standards for charter pilots who would fly its personnel—standards somewhat stiffer than those of the Federal Aviation Administration. Among other things, Alyeska insisted that applicants without flying experience in Alaska had to have fifty hours of documented training there, including a line check above the terrain they would be flying.

One effect of the pipeline charters has been to siphon off pilots from elsewhere in the Alaskan bush. These pilots are often replaced by pilots inexperienced in Alaska. Say a mail pilot quits and goes off to fly the pipeline. His replacement might be three days out of Teterboro. The mail must go through. Passengers in such planes (passengers ride with bush mail) sometimes intuit that they and the pilot are each seeing the landscape in a novel way. Once, for example, in the eastern-Alaska interior, I rode in a mail plane that took off from Fairbanks to fly a couple of hundred miles across mountains to Eagle, a village on the upper Yukon. It was a blustery, wet morning, and clouds were lower by far than summits. As rain whipped against the windshield, visibility forward was zero. Looking down to the side, the pilot watched the ground below —trying to identify various drainages and pick his way through the mountains. He frequently referred to a map. The plane was a single-engine Cessna 207 Skywagon, bumping hard on the wind. We went up a small tributary and over a pass, where we picked up another river and followed it downstream. After a time, the pilot turned around and went many miles back in the direction from which he had come. He explored another tributary. Then, abruptly, he turned again. The weather was not improving. Soon his confidence in his reading of the land seemed to run out altogether. He asked in what direction the stream below was flowing. He could not tell by the set of the rapids. He handed the map to a passenger who had apparently visited the region once or twice before. The passenger read the map for a while and then counselled the pilot to stay with the principal stream in sight. He indicated to the pilot which direction was downhill. At length, the Yukon came into view. I, who love rivers, have never felt such affection for a river. One would not have to be Marco Polo to figure out now which way to go. I had been chewing gum so vigorously that the hinges of my jaws would ache for two days. We flew up the Yukon to Eagle. When we landed, a young woman with a pickup was waiting to collect the mail. As the pilot stepped out, she came up to him and said, "Hello. You're new, aren't you? My name is Anna."

That was a scheduled flight on an American domestic airline. The company was Air North, which serves many bush communities, and its advertising slogan was "Experience Counts." Another Air North pilot told me once that he liked being a bush pilot in Alaska—he had arrived from New York several months before—but he was having a hard time living on his pay. He said there was better money to be made operating bulldozers on the pipeline than operating planes for Air North. As a result, experienced, able pilots had not only been drawn away to fly pipeline charters; experienced, able pilots were also flying bulldozers on the tundra.

Some people I know in the National Park Service who were studying a region near the upper Yukon chartered a helicopter in an attempt to find the headwaters of a certain tributary stream. When they had been in flight for some time and had not seen anything remotely resembling the terrain they were looking for, they grew uneasy. When they looked ahead and saw the bright-white high-rising Wrangells, mountain peaks two hundred miles from where they were going, they realized they were lost. The pilot, new in Alaska, was from Alabama. "This is different, unique, tough country," a pilot from Sitka once told me. "A guy has to know what he's doing. Flying is a way of life up here, and you have to get used to it. You can't drive. You can't walk. You can't swim."

In Anchorage, John Kauffmann had introduced me to his friend Charlie Allen, a general free-lance bush pilot with a wide reputation for having no betters and few peers. From the Southeastern Archipelago to Arctic Alaska, Allen had been flying for twenty-five years. He was dismayed by the incompetence of some people in his profession, and was not at all shy to say so. "Alaska is the land of the bush pilot," he said. "You have to think highly of this bush pilot, because he's dirty, he has a ratty airplane, and he's alive. It's a myth, the bush-pilot thing. It's 'Smilin' Jack.' The myth affects pilots. Some of them, in this magic Eddie Rickenbacker fraternity, are more afraid of being embarrassed than they are of death. Suppose they're low on gas. They're so afraid of being embarrassed they keep going until they have no recourse but to crash. They drive their aircraft till they cough and quit. Kamikaze pilots. That's what we've got up here—kamikaze pilots from New Jersey. Do you think one of them would ever decide the weather's too tough? His champion-aviator's manhood would be impugned. Meanwhile, he's a hero if he gets through. A while ago, some guy ran out of gas at night on the ice pack. He had been chartered for a polar-bear hunt. He chopped off his fuel tanks with an axe and used the fuel tanks as boats. He and the hunters paddled out. He was then regarded as a hero. He was regarded as Eddie Rickenbacker *and* Smilin' Jack. But he was guilty of outrageous technical behavior. He was the fool who got them into the situation in the first place.

"Aircraft-salvage operators have a backlog of planes waiting to be salvaged in Alaska. Helicopters go out for them. In the past year and a half, I have helped salvage six planes that have been wrecked by *one* pilot. Don't identify him. Just call him 'a government employee.' Why do passengers *go* with such pilots? Would they go to the moon with an astronaut who did not have round-trip fuel? If you were in San Francisco and the boat to Maui was leaking and the rats were leaving, even if you had a ticket you *would not go*. Safety in the air is where you find it. Proper navigation helps, but proper judgment takes care of all conditions. You say to yourself, 'I ain't going to go today. The situation is too much for me.' And you resist all pressure to the contrary."

Allen paused a moment. Then he said, "You don't have to run into a mountain. Only a pilot is needed to wreck an airplane."

Of reported accidents, there have lately been something like two hundred a year in Alaska. Upwards of twenty-five a year produce fatal injuries, killing various numbers of people. Another fifteen crashes or so produce injuries rated "serious." The figures seem to compliment the fliers in a state where a higher percentage of people fly—and fly more often—than they do anywhere else in the United States. Merrill Field, a light-plane airfield in Anchorage, handles fifty-four thousand more flights per year than Newark International. On the other hand, if you get into an airplane in Alaska your chances of not coming back are greater by far than they would be in any other part of the country. Only Texas and California, with their vastly larger populations, consistently exceed Alaska in aircraft accidents. Government employees in Alaska speak of colleagues who have been lost "in line of duty." In air accidents during the past two years, the Bureau of Land Management has lost four, Alaska Fish and Game has lost one, U.S. Fish and Wildlife has lost three, the U.S. Forest Service has lost five, and the National Park Service has lost seven (in a single crash). A gallery of thirteen of the great bush pilots in the history of Alaska was presented in an Alaska newspaper not long ago. Of the thirteen, ten—among them Carl Eielson, Russ Merrill, Haakon Christensen, Big Money Monsen—died flying. I dropped in at a bar one day, in a small Alaskan town, where a bush pilot had one end of a plastic swizzlestick clamped between his teeth and was attempting to stretch it by pulling the other end. He had apparently been there some time, and he was challenging all comers to see who could stretch a swizzlestick the farthest. Jay Hammond, governor of Alaska, was himself a bush pilot for twenty-eight years, and a conspicuously good one. In an interview with him, I mentioned the sorts of things that cause disgust in pilots like Charlie Allen, and Hammond said, "There is nothing you can do by statute to assure competence." I wondered if that was altogether true—if, at the very least, regulations such as Alyeska's regarding pilots who come in from outside could not be extended to the state at large.

All this applies, of course, only to bush pilots and not to the big jet-flying commercial carriers, whose accidents are extremely rare and are not outstanding in national statistics. As we flew from Fairbanks to Kotzebue to begin the trip to the Salmon River, we were in a Boeing 737 of Wien Air Alaska. One Captain Clayton came on the horn and said he would be pleased to play the harmonica for us as soon as he had finished a Fig Newton. A while later, he announced that his mouth was now solvent—and, above clouds, he began to play. He played beautifully. The speaker system in that particular aircraft seemed to have been wired especially to meet his talent. He played three selections, and he found Kotzebue.

"This is not right. This just is *not* right," Gene Parrish said again, giving up on still another river and moving (west this time) to try again. Apparently, one of the streams he had passed over was, in fact, the Salmon. "I do my best," he said. "I do my best. I had the right heading—I'm certain of that. I do my best, but there ain't no guarangoddamntee." Of the next river he looked over perhaps twenty miles, without success. Then he began to mention fuel. He thought we should go back to Kiana and tap a drum. So he continued west, and crossed another mountain. Now he flew above a stream with a tributary coming into it that had a pair of sharp right-angled bends that formed the shape of a staple. Pictured on the Nome Sectional Aeronautical Chart was a staple-shaped pair of bends in a tributary of the Salmon River. The stream on the map and the stream on the earth appeared to be the same, but there was no guarangoddamntee. Forgetting Kiana for the time being, Parrish headed up the river. Down near the spruce, swinging around the bends, we hunted the gravel bars, looking for the shine of metal. There was much gravel but no aluminum. He turned once more for Kiana. There had been a hill on our left, and according to the map there should have been another tributary coming in on the far side of the hill. If the smaller stream was there, this was surely—so it seemed—the Salmon. Parrish could not resist having a look. He turned again, and flew north of the hill, which sloped down to the right bank of a tributary stream. We went on up the river. "This *must* be the Salmon, but it sure don't look right," Parrish said, and in the same instant Pourchot and the Grumman came into view. The chopper set down so near Pourchot it almost blew him over. We pulled out our gear, and wished Parrish well in his continuing tour of Alaska. In a whirling dust storm, the Messerschmitt took off, spattering us with sand and flying bits of dry debris. The dust would take a lot longer to settle than the laws of physics would suggest. Now we were alone between fringes of spruce by a clear stream where tundra went up the sides of mountains. This was, in all likelihood, the most isolated wilderness I would ever see, and that is how we got there.

The river was low, and Pat Pourchot had picked a site as far upstream as he judged we could be and still move in boats. We were on an island, with the transparent Salmon River on one side—hurrying, scarcely a foot deep—and a small slough on the other. Deeper pools, under bedrock ledges, were above us and below us. We built our fire on the lemon-sized gravel of what would in higher water be the riverbed, and we pitched the tents on slightly higher ground among open stands of willow, on sand that showed what Bob Fedeler called "the old tracks of a young griz." We would stay two nights, according to plan, before beginning the long descent to the Kobuk; and in the intervening day we would first assemble the kayaks and then be free to disperse and explore the terrain.

There was a sixth man with us, there at the beginning. His name was Jack Hession, and he was the Sierra Club's only salaried full-time representative in Alaska. Pourchot had invited him as an observer. The news that he was absent at the end of the trip could instantly cause hopes to rise in Alaska, where the Sierra Club has long been considered a netherworld force and Hession the resident Belial. Hession, though, was not going to perish on the Salmon. Pressures from Anchorage had travelled with him, and before long would get the better of him, and in cavalier manner—in this Arctic wilderness—he would bid us goodbye and set out early for home. Meanwhile, in the morning sun, we put together the collapsible kayaks—two single Kleppers and Snake Eyes. Hession's own single was the oldest of the three, and it had thirty-six parts, hardware not included. There were dowels of mountain ash and ribs of laminated Finnish birch, which fitted, one part to another, with hooks and clips until they formed a pair of nearly identical skeletal cones—the internal structures of halves of the boat. The skin was a limp bag made of blue canvas (the deck) and hemp-reinforced vulcanized rubber (the hull). The concept was to insert the skeletal halves into the skin and then figure out how to firm them together. We had trouble doing that. Hession, who ordinarily used rigid boats of fibre glass in his engagements with white water, could not remember how to complete the assembly. Stiff toward the ends and bent in the middle, his kayak had the look of a clip-on tie, and would do about as well in the river. We all crouched around and studied amidships—six men, a hundred miles up a stream, above sixty-seven degrees of latitude, with a limp kayak. No one was shy with suggestions, which were full of ingenuity but entirely failed to work. By trial and error, we finally figured it out. The last step in the assembly involved the center rib, and we set that inside the hull on a tilt and then tapped it with a rock and forced it toward the vertical. When the forcing rib reached ninety degrees to the longer axis of the craft, the rib snapped into place, and with that the entire boat became taut and yare. Clever man, Johann Klepper. He had organized his foldboat in the way that the North American Indians had developed the construction of their bark canoes. Over the years, the Klepper company had simplified its process. Our other single kayak, the more recent model, had fewer and larger skeletal parts, and it went together more easily; but it was less streamlined than the first. Snake Eyes, for its part—all eight hundred dollars' worth of Snake Eyes—was new and had an interior of broad wooden slabs, conveniently hinged. Snake Eyes had the least number of separate parts (only fifteen) and in the way it went together was efficient and simple. Its advanced design had been achieved with a certain loss of grace, however, and this was evident there on the gravel. The boat was lumpy, awkward, bulging—a kayak with elbows.

Toward noon and after an early lunch, we set off on foot for a look around. Pourchot went straight up the hills to the west, alone. Stell Newman and John Kauffmann intended lesser forays, nearer the campsite. I decided I'd go with Bob Fedeler, who, with Jack Hession, had the most ambitious plan. They were going north up the river some miles and then up the ridges to the east. I hoped my legs would hold up. I didn't want to embarrass myself, off somewhere in the hills, by snapping something, but I could not resist going along with Fedeler. After all, he was a habitat biologist, working for the state, and if the ground around here was not habitat then I would never be in country that was. The temperature had come up to seventy. The sky was blue, with moving clouds and intermittent sun. We stuffed our rain gear into day packs and started up the river.

Generally speaking, if I had a choice between hiking and peeling potatoes, I would peel the potatoes. I have always had a predilection for canoes on rivers and have avoided walking wherever possible. My experience, thus, was limited but did exist. My work had led me up the Sierra Nevada and across the North Cascades, and in various eras I had walked parts of the Long Trail, the Appalachian Trail, trails of New Hampshire, the Adirondacks. Here in the Brooks Range, of course, no one had been there clearing the path. A mile, steep or level, could demand a lot of time. You go along with only a general plan, free lance, guessing where the walking will be least difficult, making choices all the way. These are the conditions, and in ten minutes' time they present their story. The country is wild to the limits of the term. It would demean such a world to call it pre-Columbian. It is twenty times older than that, having assumed its present form ten thousand years ago, with the melting of the Wisconsin ice.

For several miles upstream, willow and alder pressed in on the river, backed by spruce and cottonwood, so the easiest path was the river itself. Gravel bars were now on one side, now the other, so we crossed and crossed again, taking off our boots and wading through the fast, cold water. I had rubber-bottomed leather boots (L.L. Bean's, which are much in use all over Alaska). Fedeler was wearing hiking boots, Hession low canvas sneakers. Hession had a floppy sun hat, too. He seemed to see no need to dress like Sir Edmund Hillary, or to leave the marks of waffles by the tracks of wolves. He was a brief, trim, lithe figure, who moved lightly and had seen a lot of such ground. He stopped and opened his jackknife, and stood it by a track in sand at the edge of the river. Other tracks were near. Two wolves running side by side. He took a picture of the track. We passed a deep pool where spring water came into the river, and where algae grew in response to its warmth. Grayling could winter there. Some were in the pool now—bodies stationary, fins in motion, in clear deep water as green as jade. Four mergansers swam up the river. We saw moose pellets in sand beyond the pool. I would not much want to be a moose just there, in a narrow V-shaped valley with scant protection of trees. We came, in fact, to the tree line not long thereafter. The trees simply stopped. We took a few more northward steps and were out of the boreal forest. Farther north, as far as land continued, there would be no more. I don't mean to suggest that we had stepped out of Sequoia National Park and onto an unvegetated plain. The woods behind us were spare in every sense, fingering up the river valley, reaching as far as they could go. Now the tundra, which had before been close behind the trees, came down to the banks of the river. We'd had enough of shoelaces and of bare feet crunching underwater stones, so we climbed up the west bank to walk on the tundra—which from the river had looked as smooth as a golf course. Possibly there is nothing as invitingly deceptive as a tundra-covered hillside. Distances over tundra, even when it is rising steeply, are like distances over water, seeming to be less than they are, defraying the suggestion of effort. The tundra surface, though, consists of many kinds of plants, most of which seem to be stemmed with wire configured to ensnare the foot. For years, my conception of tundra—based, I suppose, on photographs of the Canadian north and the plains of the Alaskan

Arctic slope—was of a vast northern flatness, water-flecked, running level to every horizon. Tundra is not topography, however; it is a mat of vegetation, and it runs up the sides of prodigious declivities as well as across the broad plains. There are three varying types—wet tundra, on low flatland with much standing water; moist tundra, on slightly higher ground; and alpine tundra, like carpeted heather, rising on mountains and hills. We moved on, northward, over moist tundra, and the plants were often a foot or so in height. Moving through them was more like wading than walking, except where we followed game trails. Fortunately, these were numerous enough, and comfortably negotiable. They bore signs of everything that lived there. They were highways, share and share alike, for caribou, moose, bears, wolves—whose tracks, antlers, and feces were strewn along the right-of-way like beer cans at the edge of a road. While these game trails were the best thoroughfares in many hundreds of square miles, they were also the only ones, and they had a notable defect. They tended to vanish. The trails would go along, well cut and stamped out through moss campion, reindeer moss, sedge tussocks, crowberries, prostrate willows, dwarf birch, bog blueberries, white mountain avens, low-bush cranberries, lichens, Labrador tea; then, abruptly, and for no apparent reason, the trails would disappear. Their well-worn ruts suggested hundreds of animals, heavy traffic. So where did they go when the trail vanished? Fedeler did not know. I could not think of an explanation. Maybe Noah had got there a little before us.

On the far side of the river was an isolated tree, which had made a brave bid to move north, to extend the reach of its progenitive forest. The Brooks Range, the remotest uplift in North America, was made a little less remote, fifty years ago, by the writing of Robert Marshall, a forester, who described several expeditions to these mountains in a book called "Alaska Wilderness." Marshall had a theory about the tree line, the boundary of the circumboreal world. He thought that white spruce and other species could live farther north, and that they were inching northward, dropping seeds ahead of them, a dead-slow advance under marginal conditions. Whatever it may have signified, the tree across the river was dead, and out of it now came a sparrow hawk, flying at us, shouting "*kee kee*

kee," and hovering on rapidly beating wings to study the creatures on the trail. There was not much it could do about us, and it went back to the tree.

The leaves of Labrador tea, crushed in the hand, smelled like a turpentine. The cranberries were early and sourer than they would eventually be. With the arrival of cold, they freeze on the vine, and when they thaw, six months later, they are somehow sweeter and contain more juice. Bears like overwintered berries. Blueberries, too, are sweeter after being frozen on the bush. Fried cranberries will help relieve a sore throat. Attacks in the gall bladder have been defused with boiled cranberries mixed with seal oil. The sedge tussocks were low and not as perilous as tussocks can be. They are grass that grows in bunches, more compact at the bottom than at the top—a mushroom shape that can spill a foot and turn an ankle. They were tiresome, and soon we were ready to move upward, away from the moist tundra and away from the river. Ahead we saw the configurations of the sharp small valleys of three streams meeting, forming there the principal stem of the Salmon. To the east, above the confluence, a tundra-bald hill rose a thousand feet and more. We decided to cross the river and go up the hill. Look around. Choose where to go from there.

The river was so shallow now that there was no need for removing boots. We walked across and began to climb. The going was steep. I asked Jack Hession how long he had been in Alaska, and he said seven years. He had been in Alaska longer than two-thirds of the people in the state. He was from California, and had lived more recently in western Washington, where he had begun to acquire his expertise in boats in white water. Like Fedeler—like me, for that matter—he was in good condition. Hession, though, seemed to float up the incline, while I found it hard, sweaty work. From across the river it had looked as easy as a short flight of stairs. I went up it a trudge at a time—on reindeer moss, heather, lupine. The sun had suddenly departed, and a cool rain began to fall. At the top of the hill, we sat on a rock outcropping and looked back at the river, twelve hundred feet below. Everywhere around us were mountains—steep, treeless, buff where still in the sun. One was bright silver. The rain felt good. We nibbled M&M's. They were even better than the rain. The streams far below, small and fast, came pummelling together and made the river. The land they fell through looked nude. It was all tundra, rising northward toward a pass at the range divide. Looking at so much mountain ground—this immense minute fragment of wilderness Alaska—one could wonder about the choice of words of people who say that it is fragile. "Fragile" just does not appear to be a proper term for a rugged, essentially uninvaded landscape covering tens of thousands of square miles—a place so vast and unpeopled that if anyone could figure out how to steal Italy, Alaska would be a place to hide it. Meanwhile, earnest ecologues write and speak about the "fragile" tundra, this "delicate" ocean of barren land. The words sound effete, but the terrain is nonetheless vulnerable. There is ice under the tundra, mixed with soil as permafrost, in some places two thousand feet deep. The tundra vegetation, living and dead, provides insulation that keeps the summer sun from melting the permafrost. If something pulls away the insulation and melting occurs, the soil will settle and the water may run off. The earth, in such circumstances, does not restore itself. In the nineteen-sixties, a bulldozer working for Geophysical Service, Inc., an oil-exploration company, wrote the initials G.S.I. in Arctic Alaskan tundra. The letters were two hundred feet from top to bottom, and near them the bulldozer cut an arrow—an indicator for pilots. Thermokarst (thermal erosion) followed, and slumpage. The letters and the arrow are now odd-shaped ponds, about eight feet deep. For many generations that segment of tundra will say "G.S.I." Tundra is even sensitive to snow machines. They compress snow, and cut off much of the air that would otherwise get to the vegetation. Evidence appears in summer. The snow machines have left brown trails on ground they never touched.

Both sunlight and rain were falling on us now. We had a topographic map, of the largest scale available but nonetheless of scant detail—about five miles to half a thumb. Of the three streams that met below us, the nearest was called Sheep Creek. A rainbow wicketed its steep valley. The top of the arch was below us. The name Sheep Creek was vestigial. "Historically, there were Dall sheep in these mountains," Fedeler said.

"What happened to them?"

"Who knows?" He shrugged. "Things go in cycles. They'll be back."

Alders had crept into creases in the mountainside across the Salmon valley. I remarked on the borderline conditions in evidence everywhere in this spare and beautiful country, and said, "Look at those alders over there, clinging to life."

Fedeler said, "It's hungry country, that's for sure. Drainage and exposure make *the* difference."

We ate peanuts and raisins and more M&M's—and, feeling rested, became ambitious. On a long southward loop back to camp, we would extend our walk by going around a mountain that was separated from us by what looked to be the fairly steep declivity of a tributary drainage. The terrain sloped away to the southwest toward the mouth of the tributary. We would go down for a time, and then cross the tributary and cut back around the mountain.

We passed first through stands of fireweed, and then over ground that was wine-red with the leaves of bearberries. There were curlewberries, too, which put a deep-purple stain on the hand. We kicked at some wolf scat, old as winter. It was woolly and white and filled with the hair of a snowshoe hare. Nearby was a rich inventory of caribou pellets and, in increasing quantity as we moved downhill, blueberries—an outspreading acreage of blueberries. Fedeler stopped walking. He touched my arm. He had in an instant become even more alert than he usually was, and obviously apprehensive. His gaze followed straight on down our intended course. What he saw there I saw now. It appeared to me to be a hill of fur. "Big boar grizzly," Fedeler said in a near-whisper. The bear was about a hundred steps away, in the blueberries, grazing. The head was down, the hump high. The immensity of muscle seemed to vibrate slowly—to expand and contract, with the grazing. Not berries alone but whole bushes were going into the bear. He was big for a barren-ground grizzly. The brown bears of Arctic Alaska (or grizzlies; they are no longer thought to be different) do not grow to the size they will reach on more ample diets elsewhere. The barren-ground grizzly will rarely grow larger than six hundred pounds.

"What if he got too close?" I said.

Fedeler said, "We'd be in real trouble."

"You can't outrun them," Hession said.

A grizzly, no slower than a racing horse, is about half again as fast as the fastest human being. Watching the great mound of weight in the blueberries, with a fifty-five-inch waist and a neck more than thirty inches around, I had difficulty imagining that he could move with such speed, but I believed it, and was without impulse to test the proposition. Fortunately, a light southerly wind was coming up the Salmon valley. On its way to us, it passed the bear. The wind was relieving, coming into our faces, for had it been moving the other way the bear would not have been placidly grazing. There is an old adage that when a pine needle drops in the forest the eagle will see it fall; the deer will hear it when it hits the ground; the bear will smell it. If the boar grizzly were to catch our scent, he might stand on his hind legs, the better to try to see. Although he could hear well and had an extraordinary sense of smell, his eyesight was not much better than what was required to see a blueberry inches away. For this reason, a grizzly stands and squints, attempting to bring the middle distance into focus, and the gesture is often misunderstood as a sign of anger and forthcoming attack. If the bear were getting ready to attack, he would be on four feet, head low, ears cocked, the hair above his hump muscle standing on end. As if that message were not clear enough, he would also chop his jaws. His teeth would make a sound that would carry like the ringing of an axe.

One could predict, but not with certainty, what a grizzly would do. Odds were very great that one touch of man scent would cause him to stop his activity, pause in a moment of absorbed and alert curiosity, and then move, at a not undignified pace, in a direction other than the one from which the scent was coming. That is what would happen almost every time, but there was, to be sure, no guarantee. The forest Eskimos fear and revere the grizzly. They know that certain individual bears not only will fail to avoid a person who comes into their country but will approach and even stalk the trespasser. It is potentially inaccurate to extrapolate the behavior of any one bear from the behavior of most, since they are both intelligent and independent and will do what they choose to do according to mood, experience, whim. A grizzly that has ever been wounded by a bullet will not forget it, and will probably know that it was a human being who sent the bullet. At sight of a human, such a bear will be likely to charge. Grizzlies hide food sometimes—a caribou calf, say, under a pile of scraped-up moss—and a person the bear might otherwise ignore might suddenly not be ignored if the person were inadvertently to step into the line between the food cache and the bear. A sow grizzly with cubs, of course, will charge anything that suggests danger to the cubs, even if the cubs are nearly as big as she is. They stay with their mother two and a half years.

None of us had a gun. (None of the six of us had brought a gun on the trip.) Among nonhunters who go into the terrain of the grizzly, there are several schools of thought about guns. The preferred one is: Never go without a sufficient weapon —a high-powered rifle or a shotgun and plenty of slug-loaded shells. The option is not without its own inherent peril. A professional hunter, some years ago, spotted a grizzly from the air and—with a client, who happened to be an Anchorage barber —landed on a lake about a mile from the bear. The stalking that followed was evidently conducted not only by the hunters but by the animal as well. The professional hunter was found dead from a broken neck, and had apparently died instantly, unaware of danger, for the cause of death was a single bite, delivered from behind. The barber, noted as clumsy with a rifle, had emptied his magazine, missing the bear with every shot but one, which struck the grizzly in the foot. The damage the bear did to the barber was enough to kill him several times. After the corpses were found, the bear was tracked and killed. To shoot and merely wound is worse than not to shoot at all. A bear that might have turned and gone away will possibly attack if wounded.

Fatal encounters with bears are as rare as they are memorable. Some people reject the rifle as cumbersome extra baggage, not worth toting, given the minimal risk. And, finally, there are a few people who feel that it is wrong to carry a gun, in part because the risk is low and well worth taking, but most emphatically because they see the gun as an affront to the wild country of which the bear is sign and symbol. This, while strongly felt, is a somewhat novel attitude. When Robert Marshall explored the Brooks Range half a century ago, he and his companions fired at almost every bear they saw, without pausing for philosophical reflection. The reaction was automatic. They were expressing mankind's immemorial fear of this beast—man and rattlesnake, man and bear. Among modern environmentalists, to whom a figure like Marshall is otherwise a hero, fear of the bear has been exceeded by reverence. A notable example, in his own past and present, is Andy Russell, author of a book called "Grizzly Country." Russell was once a professional hunter, but he gave that up to become a photographer, specializing in grizzlies. He says that he has given up not only shooting bears but even carrying a gun. On rare instances when grizzlies charge toward him, he shouts at them and stands his ground. The worst thing to do, he says, is to run, because anything that runs on open tundra suggests game to a bear. Game does not tend to stand its ground in the presence of grizzlies. Therefore, when the bear comes at you, just stand there. Charging something that does not move, the bear will theoretically stop and reconsider. (Says Russell.) More important, Russell believes that the bear will *know* if you have a gun, even if the gun is concealed:

> Reviewing our experiences, we had become more and more convinced that carrying arms was not only unnecessary in most grizzly country but was certainly no good for the desired atmosphere and proper protocol in obtaining good film records. If we were to obtain such film and fraternize successfully with the big bears, it would be better to go unarmed in most places. The mere fact of having a gun within reach, cached somewhere in a pack or a hidden holster, causes a man to act with unconscious arrogance and thus maybe to smell different or to transmit some kind of signal objectionable to bears. The armed man does not assume his proper role in association with the wild ones, a fact of which they seem instantly aware at some distance. He, being wilder than they, whether he likes to admit it or not, is instantly under even more suspicion than he would encounter if unarmed.
>
> One must follow the role of an uninvited visitor—an intruder —rather than that of an aggressive hunter, and one should go unarmed to insure this attitude.

Like pictures from pages riffled with a thumb, all of these things went through my mind there on the mountainside above the grazing bear. I will confess that in one instant I asked myself, "What the hell am I doing *here*?" There was nothing more to the question, though, than a hint of panic. I knew why

I had come, and therefore what I was doing there. That I was frightened was incidental. I just hoped the fright would not rise beyond a relatively decorous level. I sensed that Fedeler and Hession were somewhat frightened, too. I would have been troubled if they had not been. Meanwhile, the sight of the bear stirred me like nothing else the country could contain. What mattered was not so much the bear himself as what the bear implied. He was the predominant thing in that country, and for him to be in it at all meant that there had to be more country like it in every direction and more of the same kind of country all around that. He implied a world. He was an affirmation to the rest of the earth that his kind of place was extant. There had been a time when his race was everywhere in North America, but it had been hunted down and pushed away in favor of something else. For example, the grizzly bear is the state animal of California, whose country was once his kind of place; and in California now the grizzly is extinct.

> The animals I have encountered in my wilderness wanderings have been reluctant to reveal all the things about them I would like to know. The animal that impresses me most, the one I find myself liking more and more, is the grizzly. No sight encountered in the wilds is quite so stirring as those massive, clawed tracks pressed into mud or snow. No sight is quite so impressive as that of the great bear stalking across some mountain slope with the fur of his silvery robe rippling over his mighty muscles. His is a dignity and power matched by no other in the North American wilderness. To share a mountain with him for a while is a privilege and an adventure like no other.
>
> I have followed his tracks into an alder hell to see what he had been doing and come to the abrupt end of them, when the maker stood up thirty feet away with a sudden snort to face me.

> To see a mother grizzly ambling and loafing with her cubs across the broad, hospitable bosom of a flower-spangled mountain meadow is to see life in true wilderness at its best.

If a wolf kills a caribou, and a grizzly comes along while the wolf is feeding on the kill, the wolf puts its tail between its legs and hurries away. A black bear will run from a grizzly, too. Grizzlies sometimes kill and eat black bears. The grizzly takes what he happens upon. He is an opportunistic eater.

The predominance of the grizzly in his terrain is challenged by nothing but men and ravens. To frustrate ravens from stealing his food, he will lie down and sleep on top of a carcass, occasionally swatting the birds as if they were big black flies. He prefers a vegetable diet. He can pulp a moosehead with a single blow, but he is not lusting always to kill, and when he moves through his country he can be something munificent, going into copses of willow among unfleeing moose and their calves, touching nothing, letting it all breathe as before. He may, though, get the head of a cow moose between his legs and rake her flanks with the five-inch knives that protrude from the ends of his paws. Opportunistic. He removes and eats her entrails. He likes porcupines, too, and when one turns and presents to him a pygal bouquet of quills, he will leap into the air, land on the other side, chuck the fretful porpentine beneath the chin, flip it over, and, with a swift ventral incision, neatly remove its body from its skin, leaving something like a sea urchin behind him on the ground. He is nothing if not athletic. Before he dens, or just after he emerges, if his mountains are covered with snow he will climb to the brink of some impossible schuss, sit down on his butt, and shove off. Thirty-two, sixty-four, ninety-six feet per second, he plummets down the mountainside, spray snow flying to either side, as he approaches collision with boulders and trees. Just short of catastrophe, still going at bonecrushing speed, he flips to his feet and walks sedately onward as if his ride had not occurred.

His population density is thin on the Arctic barren ground. He needs for his forage at least fifty and perhaps a hundred square miles that are all his own—sixty-four thousand acres, his home range. Within it, he will move, typically, eight miles a summer day, doing his travelling through the twilight hours of the dead of night. To scratch his belly he walks over a tree—where forest exists. The tree bends beneath him as he passes. He forages in the morning, generally; and he rests a great deal, particularly after he eats. He rests fourteen hours a day. If he becomes hot in the sun, he lies down in a pool in the river. He sleeps on the tundra—restlessly tossing and turning, forever changing position. What he could be worrying about I cannot imagine.

His fur blends so well into the tundra colors that sometimes it is hard to see him. Fortunately, we could see well enough the one in front of us, or we would have walked right to him. He caused a considerable revision of our travel plans. Not wholly prepared to follow the advice of Andy Russell, I asked Fedeler what one should do if a bear were to charge. He said, "Take off your pack and throw it into the bear's path, then crawl away, and hope the pack will distract the bear. But there is no good thing to do, really. It's just not a situation to be in."

We made a hundred-and-forty-degree turn from the course we had been following and went up the shoulder of the hill through ever-thickening brush, putting distance behind us in good position with the wind. For a time, we waded through hip-deep willow, always making our way uphill, and the going may have been difficult, but I didn't notice. There was adrenalin to spare in my bloodstream. I felt that I was floating, climbing with ease, like Hession. I also had expectations now that another bear, in the thick brush, might come rising up from any quarter. We broke out soon into a swale of blueberries. Hession and Fedeler, their nonchalance refreshed, sat down to eat, paused to graze. The berries were sweet and large.

"I can see why he's here," Hession said.

"These berries are so big."

"Southern exposure."

"He may not be the only one."

"They can be anywhere."

"It's amazing to me," Fedeler said. "So large an animal, living up here in this country. It's amazing what keeps that big body alive." Fedeler went on eating the blueberries with no apparent fear of growing fat. The barren-ground bear digs a lot of roots, he said—the roots of milk vetch, for example, and Eskimo potatoes. The bear, coming out of his den into the snows of May, goes down into the river bottoms, where overwintered berries are first revealed. Wolf kills are down there, too. By the middle of June, his diet is almost wholly vegetable. He eats willow buds, sedges, cotton-grass tussocks. In the cycle of his year, roots and plants are eighty per cent of what he eats, and even when the salmon are running he does not sate himself on them alone but forages much of the time for berries. In the fall, he unearths not only roots but ground squirrels and lemmings.

It is indeed remarkable how large he grows on the provender of his yearly cycle, for on this Arctic barren ground he has to work much harder than the brown bears of southern Alaska, which line up along foaming rivers—hip to hip, like fishermen in New Jersey—taking forty-pound king salmon in their jaws as if they were nibbling feed from a barnyard trough. When the caribou are in fall migration, moving down the Salmon valley toward the Kobuk, the bear finishes up his year with one of them. Then, around the first of November, he may find a cave or, more likely, digs out a cavern in a mountainside. If he finds a natural cave, it may be full of porcupines. He kicks them out, and—extending his curious relationship with this animal—will cushion his winter bed with many thousands of their turds. If, on the other hand, he digs his den, he sends earth flying out behind him and makes a shaft that goes upward into the side of the mountain. At the top of the shaft, he excavates a shelf-like cavern. When the outside entrance is plugged with debris, the shaft becomes a column of still air, insulating the upper chamber, trapping the bear's body heat. On a bed of dry vegetation, he lays himself out like a dead pharaoh in a pyramid. But he does not truly hibernate. He just lies there. His mate of the summer, in her den somewhere, will give birth during winter to a cub or two—virtually hairless, blind, weighing about a pound. But the male has nothing to do. His heart rate goes down as low as eight beats a minute. He sleeps and wakes, and sleeps again. He may decide to get up and go out. But that is rare. He may even stay out, which is rarer—to give up denning for that winter and roam his frozen range. If he does this, sooner or later he will find a patch of open water in an otherwise frozen river, and in refreshing himself he will no doubt wet his fur. Then he rolls in the snow, and the fur acquires a thick plate of ice, which is less disturbing to the animal than to the forest Eskimo, who has for ages feared—feared most of all—the "winter bear." Arrows broke against the armoring ice, and it can be heavy enough to stop a bullet.

We moved on now, in continuing retreat, and approached the steep incline of the tributary valley we'd been skirting when the bear rewrote our plans. We meant to put the valley between us and him and reschedule ourselves on the other side. It was in fact less a valley than an extremely large ravine, which plunged maybe eight hundred feet, and then rose up an even steeper incline some fifteen hundred feet on the other side, toward the top of which the bushy vegetation ceased growing. The walking looked promising on the ridge beyond.

I had hoped we might see a den site, and this might have been the place. It had all the requisites but one. It was a steep hillside with southern exposure, and was upgrown with a hell of alders and willows. Moreover, we were on the south side of the Brooks Range divide, which is where most of the dens are. But we were not high enough. We were at something under two thousand feet, and bears in this part of Alaska like to den much higher than that. They want the very best drainage. One way to become a "winter bear" is to wake up in a flooded den.

The willow-alder growth was so dense and high that as we went down the hillside we could see no farther than a few yards ahead. It was wet in there from the recent rain. We broke our way forward with the help of gravity, crashing noisily, all but trapped in the thicket. It was a patch of jungle, many acres of jungle, with stems a foot apart and as thick as our arms, and canopies more than twelve feet high. This was bear habitat, the sort of place bears like better than people do. Our original choice had been wise—to skirt this ravine-valley—but now we were in it and without choice.

"This is the sort of place to come upon one of them unexpectedly," Hession said.

"And there is no going back," Fedeler said. "You can't walk uphill in this stuff."

"Good point," Hession said.

I might have been a little happier if I had been in an uninstrumented airplane in heavy mountain cloud. We thunked and crashed for fifteen minutes and finally came out at the tributary stream. Our approach flushed a ptarmigan, willow ptarmigan; and grayling—at sight of us—shot around in small, cold pools. The stream was narrow, and alders pressed over it from either side. We drank, and rested, and looked up the slope in front of us, which must have had an incline of fifty degrees. The ridge at the top looked extremely far away. Resting, I became aware of a considerable ache in my legs and a blister on one of my heels. On the way uphill we became separated, Hession angling off to the right, Fedeler and I to the left.

We groped for handholds among bushes that protruded from the flaky schist, and pulled ourselves up from ledge to ledge. The adrenalin was gone, and my legs were turning to stone. I was ready to dig a den and get in it. My eyes kept addressing the ridgeline, far above. If eyes were hands they could have pulled me there. Then, suddenly, from far below, I saw Jack Hession lightly ambling along the ridge—in his tennis shoes, in his floppy cotton hat. He was looking around, killing time, waiting up for us.

Things seemed better from the ridge. The going would be level for a time. We sat down and looked back, to the north, across the deep tributary valley, and with my monocular tried to glass the grazing bear. No sight or sign of him. Above us now was a broadly conical summit, and spread around its western flank was a mile, at least, of open alpine tundra. On a contour, we headed south across it—high above, and two miles east of, the river. We saw what appeared to be a cairn on the next summit south, and decided to go to it and stand on it and see if we could guess—in relation to our campsite—where we were. Now the walking felt good again. We passed a large black pile of grizzly scat. "When it's steaming, that's when you start looking around for a tree," Hession said. This particular scat had sent up its last vapors many days before. Imagining myself there at such a time, though, I looked around idly for a tree. The nearest one behind us that was of more than dwarf or thicket stature was somewhere in Lapland. Ahead of us, however, across the broad dome of tundra, was a dark stand of white spruce, an extremity of the North American forest, extending toward us. The trees were eight hundred yards away. Black bears, frightened, sometimes climb trees. Grizzlies almost never climb trees.

At seven in the evening, after wading up a slope of medium to heavy brush, we came out onto more smooth tundra and reached the hilltop of the apparent cairn. It was a rock outcropping, and we sat on it in bright sunshine and looked at the circumvallate mountains. A great many of them had such outcroppings projecting from their ridges, and they much resembled the cairns shepherds build on bald summits in Scotland. For that matter, they suggested the cairns—closer to the Kobuk—that forest Eskimos once used in methodical slaughter of caribou. The cairns were built on the high tundra in a great V, open end to the north, and they served as a funnel for the southbound herd. To the approaching caribou, the cairns were meant to suggest Eskimos, and to reinforce the impression Eskimos spaced themselves between cairns. At the point of the V, as many caribou as were needed were killed and the rest were let through.

Before us now, lying on the tundra that stretched away toward the river we saw numerous caribou antlers. The Arctic herd cyclically chooses various passes and valleys in making its way south across the range, and of late has been favoring, among other places, the Salmon and Hunt River drainages. Bleached white, the antlers protruded from the tundra like the dead branches of buried trees. When the forest Eskimo of old went to stalk the grizzly bear, he carried in his hand a spear, the tip of which was made from bear bone or, more often, from the antler of the caribou. A bearskin was the door of an Eskimo's home if the occupant had ever killed a bear, for it symbolized the extraordinary valor of the hunter within. When the man drew close and the bear stood on its hind legs, the man ran under this eave of flesh and set the shaft of the spear firmly on the ground, then ducked out from under the swinging, explosive paws. The bear lunged forward onto the spear and died.

Eskimo knife handles were also made from caribou antlers, and icepicks to penetrate the surface of the river, and sinkers for the bottoms of willow-bark seines, and woodsplitting wedges, and arrowheads. All caribou, male and female, grow antlers. The horns of sheep, cattle, buffalo consist of extremely dense, compactly matted hair. The antler of the caribou is calcareous. It is hard bone, with the strength of wrought iron. Moving downhill and south across the tundra, we passed through groves of antlers. It was as if the long filing lines of the spring migration had for some reason paused here for shedding to occur. The antlers, like the bear, implied the country. Most were white, gaunt, chalky. I picked up a younger one, though, that was recently shed and was dark, like polished brown marble. It was about four feet along the beam and perfect in form. Hession found one like it. We set them on our shoulders and moved on down the hill, intent to take them home.

We headed for the next of the riverine mountains, where we planned to descend and—if our calculations were accurate —meet the river at the campsite. The river, far below us, now and again came into view as we walked abreast over open tundra. Fedeler, even more alert than usual, now stopped and, as before, touched my arm. He pointed toward the river. If a spruce needle had been floating on the water there, Fedeler would have seen it. We saw in an instant that we had miscalculated and were heading some miles beyond the campsite and would have come eventually to the river not knowing —upstream or downstream—which way to go. Fedeler was pointing toward a gravel bar, a thin column of smoke, minute human figures near the smoke, and the podlike whiteness of the metal canoe.

Another two miles, descending, and we were barefoot in the river, with pink hot feet turning anesthetically cold. We crossed slowly. The three others were by the campfire. On the grill were grayling and a filleted Arctic char. The air was cool now, nearing fifty, and we ate the fish, and beef stew, and strawberries, and drank hot chocolate. After a time, Hession said, "That was a good walk. That was some of the easiest hiking you will ever find in Alaska."

We drew our route on the map and figured the distance at fourteen miles. John Kauffmann, tapping his pipe on a stone, said, "That's a lot for Alaska."

We sat around the campfire for at least another hour. We talked of rain and kestrels, oil and antlers, the height and the headwaters of the river. Neither Hession nor Fedeler once mentioned the bear.

When I got into my sleeping bag, though, and closed my eyes, there he was, in color, on the side of the hill. The vision was indelible, but fear was not what put it there. More, it was a sense of sheer luck at having chosen in the first place to follow Fedeler and Hession up the river and into the hills—a memento not so much of one moment as of the entire circuit of the long afternoon. It was a vision of a whole land, with an animal in it. This was his country, clearly enough. To be there was to be incorporated, in however small a measure, into its substance—his country, and if you wanted to visit it you had better knock.

His association with other animals is a mixture of enterprising action, almost magnanimous acceptance, and just plain willingness to ignore. There is great strength and pride combined with a strong mixture of inquisitive curiosity in the make-up of grizzly character. This curiosity is what makes trouble when men penetrate into country where they are not known to the bear. The grizzly can be brave and sometimes downright brash. He can be secretive and very retiring. He can be extremely cunning and also powerfully aggressive. Whatever he does, his actions match his surroundings and the circumstance of the moment. No wonder that meeting him on his mountain is a momentous event, imprinted on one's mind for life.

In the night, the air and the river balanced out, and both were forty-six at seven in the morning. Walking in the water promised to be cold, and, given the depth of the river at the riffles, that was apparently what we were going to do. We took a long time packing, as anyone would who apparently had twenty per cent more cargo than there was capacity in the boats. Duffel was all over the gravel bar. I had brought my gear in a Duluth sack—a frameless canvas pack in every way outsized. It had a tumpline and shoulder straps, all leather, and, stuffed to the bulge point, it suggested Santa Claus on his way south. My boat for the day was one of the single kayaks. I spread out the gear on the gravel beside it, turned the empty Duluth sack inside out and rolled and trussed it so that it was about the size of a two-pound loaf of bread. This went into the bow of the kayak. I poked it up there with a stick. Anyone with a five-foot arm could easily pack a Klepper. The openings in the rib frames were less than the breadth of two spread hands. Stowing gear fore and aft was like stuffing a couple of penholders, but an amazing amount went in. All excess was taken by the canoe, and it was piled high—our aluminum mule. I tied the caribou antler across the stern deck of the kayak, and we moved out into the river. The current was going about four miles an hour, but we travelled a great deal more slowly than that, because we walked almost as far as we floated. If we had a foot of water, we felt luxuriously cushioned. Often enough, we had an inch or two. Pool to riffle, pool to riffle, we rode a little and then got out and walked, painters in our hands. The boats beside us were like hounds on leashes, which now and then stopped and had to be dragged. Getting into a kayak just once is awkward enough, let alone dozens of times a day. You put your hands behind you on the coaming, then lower yourself into place, all in the same act removing your legs from the river and shaking off water. Hession, at the start, showed me how to do this, and then he sat down lightly in his own kayak and floated away. I flopped backward into mine and nearly rolled it over; but the day would hold, if nothing else, practice in getting in and out of a kayak. When the boats scraped bottom at the tops of riffles, we got out, sought the channel of maximum depth, moved the boats through, and then got back into them where the water was fast and deepening in the lower parts of the rips. The problem of getting in was therefore complicated by generally doing so in the middle of rapids. In the first such situation, I lost all coördination, lurched backward onto the boat, nearly sat in the river, and snapped a toe, ripping the ligaments off the second joint. By noon, however, I was more or less competent, and further damage seemed unlikely.

I was not disappointed that the Salmon was low. In a lifetime of descending rivers, this was the clearest and the wildest river. Walking it in places made it come slow, and that was a dividend in itself. A glance at the gravel bars, ledges, and cut banks told where the river at times would be—high, tumbling, full of silt, and washing down. I would prefer to walk in water so clear it seemed to be polished rather than to ride like a rocket down a stream in flood. For all of that, another two inches would have helped the day.

The water was cold by anyone's standards, for had it been much colder it would not have been water. Pourchot and Hession were wearing sneakers, and I did not envy them. Fedeler and Newman wore hip boots. Kauffmann and I had wet-suit boots—foam-rubber socks, more or less, that keep wet feet completely warm. The water that is arrested in the foam takes on the temperature of blood. I had on thick wool socks as well, and my feet were never cold. The sun was circling a cloudless sky, and needles of light came flashing off the river. The air went into the seventies. We walked along in T-shirts—feet warm, legs cool in soaking trousers, shoulders hot in the Arctic sun.

A couple of tributaries came into the river, the first from the east, the second from the west, and they deepened the pools and improved the rips. Somewhere up the easterly stream, said Pourchot, nineteen placer gold claims had been filed in 1968. The claims had not been kept up with yearly "assessment work," however. No mining had begun, and now would not begin as long as the claims were in national-interest land. This was not important gold country. Perhaps the most unusual event in the experience of the forest Eskimos was the arrival in 1898 of more than a thousand prospectors who had heard glistering rumors about the Kobuk valley. They looked around, did not find much, and lasted, for the most part, a single winter. About ten years later, gold of modest but sufficient assay was discovered on a creek near Kiana. Claims there were worked by placer mining—sluicing gravels, flushing out the gold. Where gold is mined in Alaska now, bulldozers, for the most part, move the gravels. The clear water that comes in from the upstream side goes on its way—brown and turbid—with a heavy load of fresh debris. Early in Fedeler's time with the Habitat Section of the Alaska Department of Fish and Game, he was shifted from pipeline surveillance to gold-mining surveillance—going from one site to another to check effluent standards in placer operations. He might better have waltzed with grizzlies than approach some of the miners, who told him to pack up his permit applications and get the hell off their claims. So what if some fish got a gutful of silt? Fedeler was only a few short years from his family's farm in Iowa, his master's thesis on the life cycle of pheasants, but he was quickly learning the folkways of Alaska. "Get out!" the miners suggested. "We've always done things when we want to, where we want to, how we want to, and that is what we're going to do now."

The forest around us, to the extent that it could be called forest, consisted of bands of spruce and cottonwood. Occasionally, it made sallies up the hillsides onto protected slopes or into dry ravines, but mainly it pointed north like an arrow, and gradually it widened as we moved downstream. Close to the river edge, much of the way, were clumps of willow and alder, backed by the taller trees, which in turn had bands of alder backing them, before the woods gave way altogether to open, rising ground—to the lichens, the sedges, and mosses of the high tundra. The leaves of alder, chewed to break out the sap, relieve itching when rubbed on mosquito bites. The forest Eskimos make red dyes from alder bark—American green alder, the only species that grows so far north. Willow, as a genus, is hardier. The Sitka spruce is the state tree, in recognition of its commercial distinction, for Sitka spruce is the most negotiable thing that grows from roots in Alaska. It grows only in the south, however, and while the Sitka spruce goes off to the sawmill, the willow vegetates the state. There are only a hundred and thirty-three species of trees and shrubs in all Alaska, and thirty-three of those are willows. Before the importation of nylon, fishnets were made from willow—from long pliant strips of the bark, braided with the split roots of spruce. Rope, dog collars, and hunters' bows were made from willow, and snares for small game and birds. Willow still goes into snowshoe frames, and fish traps, and wicker baskets. Young leaves, buds, and shoots of willow are edible and nourishing. The inner bark, chewed like cane, is full of sugar. Willow sap, scraped together with a knife, is sweet and delicious. At least twelve kinds of willow were growing along the Salmon—among them little-tree willow, halberd willow, netleaf, skeleton-leaf, and diamond-leaf willow, Arctic willow, barren-ground willow, Alaska bog willow. Oranges are easier to tell apart. We called all willows willows. The wood was agreeable in fires, and became almost as hot as the coals of alder.

On a broad acreage of gravel, we stopped now for lunch, and built a fire of willow and alder. The sun was hot to the point of headache, but there was a factor of chill in the day. Gradually the kayaks were acquiring water, dripping from us as we got out and in. One's buttocks, after several hours in cold kayak bilge, began to feel like defrosting meat. However warm one's head and shoulders might have been, a shiver went into the bones. The fire was piled high with wood that had bleached on the gravel in the sun, and a light breeze tilted the flame. Standing in the downwind heat was like standing in the Grand Canyon on a summer day. In a few minutes, our clothes had dried.

Three more tributaries came into the river, and its navigable stretches lengthened through the afternoon. Still, though, we did a lot of walking. Mergansers—a mother and six—fled ahead of us, running on the water like loons. Now and again, big ledges of bedrock jutted into and under the river, damming water, framing pools. Below one ledge, where water ran white from a pool, we stopped to fish. Stell Newman caught an Arctic char. Bob Fedeler caught another. They were imposing specimens, bigger than the Salmon's salmon. They were spotted orange and broad-flanked, with lobster-claw jaws. Sea-run Arctic char. They could be described as enormous brook trout, for the brook trout is in fact a char. They had crimson fins with white edges and crimson borders on their bellies. Their name may be Gaelic, wherein "blood" is "*cear*." The Alaska record length for an Arctic char is thirty-six inches, and ours were somewhat under that. I tossed a small Mepps lure across the stream, size zero, and bringing it back felt a big one hit. The strike was too strong for a grayling—more power, less commotion. I had, now, about ten pounds of fish on a six-pound line. So I followed the fish around, walking upstream and down, into and out of the river. I had been walking the kayak all day long, and this experience was not much different. After fifteen minutes or so, the fish tired, and came thrashing from the water. I took out my tape and laid it on him, from the hooking jaw to the tip of the tail. Thirty-one and a half inches. Orange speckles, crimson glow, this resplendent creature was by a long measure the largest fish I had ever caught in fresh water. In its belly would fit ten of the kind that I ordinarily keep and eat. For dinner tonight we would have grilled Arctic char, but enough had been caught already by the others. So, with one hand under the pelvic fins and the other near the jaw, I bent toward the river and held the fish underwater until it had its equipoise. It rested there on my hands for a time, and stayed even when I lowered them away. Then, like naval ordnance, it shot across the stream. The best and worst part of catching that fish was deciding to let it go.

Floating for a time, we moved on downstream. When Eskimos returning from long summer hunting trips rode down the Salmon River, they travelled on rafts. In June, when they had established their seine-fishing camps along the Kobuk, the men left the women and went off into the mountains in small groups to spend the summer killing creatures whose skins were needed for winter—marmots, lone caribou, caribou fawns (for undergarments). The hunters had long hours of leisure, and they sat around campfires, as we do, telling tales. They repeated the narratives night after night, yet no one ever told someone else's story; a sense of copyright was inherent, and plagiarism was seemingly unknown. Sons inherited stories from their fathers. Needless to say, many tales had to do with the hunt—hunting the wolf, hunting the caribou, fall and winter hunting the bear. Tramping up the mountains on snowshoes, they searched for signs of denning—watching, in otherwise uniform snow, for a glaze of ice, the product of the vapors of breath. Finding such evidence, they carefully removed the ice, quietly, gingerly, revealing a vent hole. An exploring spear was inserted in the hole and moved about until it touched something soft. Resting there, the spear would slowly move up and down. The hunter then rammed it home, and leaned on it with all his weight as the bear heaved in torment, lifting the hunter off the ground. The modern method is to poke for the bear with a long rod and when contact is established place a rifle by the rod and fire. When the bear is still, the hunters go into the den. Sometimes, living bears are in there, too—new cubs, or full-grown cubs, or a living mother and a dead cub. There is no need for fear, the hunters say, because a bear will not fight in its den. The bear is the animal whose intelligence they respect above all others', and around which they have spun over centuries skeins of ritual and taboo. In times past, the skull of a killed bear was ceremonially touched to the bear's heart and was then placed atop a living spruce and left in the forest with its eye sockets facing north.

With signs of autumn, hunters came down from the mountains to the upper waters of the river. They cut dead spruce, built their rafts, and piled them high with fur. In the upper river, in shallow water, rafts consisted of just a few logs, tied together with thongs of bear hide. The narrow ends of the logs all faced downstream; the wide ends formed the stern. Thus, the raft was a wedge, pointing down the river. Afloat, it was guided with a spruce pole at the bow. When it ran aground, it was dragged, like a Klepper, through the shallow rips. As the river deepened, the rafts of two or more parties were joined together. The bigger the river, the bigger the total raft—a stable vessel anytime, even in thundering flood.

Some of the wood in the rafts was for winter fires, but most was used for housing, a need that has waned on the Kobuk. Houses now come from the government, in three choices—A, B, and C—at so much a month for twenty years. They are frame structures, gabled, nondescript. They could be garages with windows. In winter the walls sweat, and show a frost line four feet high. Their exterior sheds are not large enough for the storage of meat and equipment. There is a new house today in Kiana made of river-floated logs.

We stopped for the night below a bedrock pool, pitching the tents on a sandy bank under woolly mountains whose ridgelines were a couple of thousand feet above the river. The forest now filled in most of the valley floor and went up the slopes maybe three hundred feet. Bear tracks in the sand by the river were eleven inches long, six inches wide. We fished—take-and-put—catching and releasing half a dozen grayling and several char. Eskimos, on their journeys, now cook char in aluminum foil, which is what we did. The pink flesh steamed in its own moisture, and each of us ate at least two pounds. Looking up from dinner, we saw a black bear, long and leggy, crossing a steep hillside at a slow lope. It stopped to graze for a time, and then, apropos of nothing, suddenly ran and took a crashing leap into a stand of willow and alder, breaking its way through, coming out the other side onto a high plain of pale-green caribou moss.

In the morning there was wind. A front as dank as an oyster was moving in over the eastern mountains. Rain was coming—an uninviting day to frog kayaks in the river. We ate oatmeal, and then, after coffee, Jack Hession said he thought he'd be going. He had deadlines to meet and simply had to get back to the office. The office—in Anchorage—was six hundred miles away. If there was a wild place in the United States, we were in it, and Hession was about to take off on his own, pressed for time. Terribly sorry, he said. He would have enjoyed staying with us, but he had pressures from home. He had decided to make the trip with us more or less at the last moment, and now he was deciding to leave at the last moment plus one. He would take the mail plane from Kiana, which was something like ninety miles downstream. With a packet or two of freeze-dry and six pieces of pilot bread, he got into his single Klepper and bobbed down the river. The two blades of his paddle wagged like a semaphore, and he was gone. He had no tent. Rain fell through much of the day, and all through the night.

Hession told us, many days later, stories of his solo run. Not long after he left us, he became preoccupied with his thoughts and overshot a channel in a riffle. Near the far ends of pools, where loose-stone deposits had built up as dams, the river would characteristically become fast and shallow and would tumble to one side over a brink of gravel—racing white toward a lower pool. The knack of navigation was to read the riffle, sense the heaviest flow there, and get into it before the broad general current could take the boat a little farther and run it aground; for while much water went down the riffle even more simply disappeared into the earth, passing into the porous basements of high, dry bars of gravel. Often enough, there was just a narrow slot, angling left or right, through which the kayak could proceed, and now Hession had missed such a place, so he would have to backferry—moving, stern first, across the stream, to realign his course and shoot the rip. He was close to a bank. Realizing his mistake, he reached backward with his paddle. He happened to look up as well. On the bank above him were a sow grizzly and a huge two-year-old cub. Across a distance of no more than fifteen feet Hession and the mother grizzly looked each other in the eye. Staring steadily at her, he slowly moved the paddle, retreating at an angle to the current. He felt helpless, because he could think of nothing to do if the bear attacked. He thought of turning the boat over in order to disappear beneath it, but there was nowhere to hide in less than a foot of water. Therefore, all decisions belonged to the bear. Hession kept on gazing fixedly into her eyes, making no gesture of fear or flight. The bears themselves retreated. But after a few steps they turned, and both stood up on their hind legs, squinting. Hession thought they were going to come for him, after this second look. But they dropped down, turned, and went. He told this story without modulation, without a hint of narrative excitation; and in the same flat manner he went on to say that he had later seen a pair of sandhill cranes and, some time after that, a golden eagle. It was all wildlife to him. When you are the Sierra Club's man in Alaska, the least of your problems is bears.

That evening, when he decided it was time to sleep, the rain was steady and miserable, and he looked around for shelter. He looked for big driftwood. He finally came to an uprooted spruce, washed downriver probably in June. Resting on its root structure, it was partly off the ground. He tipped the kayak so that it leaned against the tree, and put his sleeping bag in the space formed between them. (As an alternative, he might have cut a number of young spruce and arranged them in a circle with their tips together at the top—a form of tepee that the forest Eskimos call "poor people's camp.") Hession slid himself into place. The rain fell on the boat and tree. "I passed out," he said, "and the next thing I knew it was morning." When he arrived at the confluence of the Salmon and the Kobuk, two Eskimos were fishing there. They shared their boiled salmon with him, in a sauce of seal oil. Their Evinrude took him to Kiana.

John Kauffmann and I paddled Snake Eyes the day Hession left, and we spent a lot of time in the river beside it, making Klepper trails in the gravel. We had to bail frequently, because water was accumulating inside the hull not only from the rain and from our dripping boots but also through leaks in the vulcanized rubber. The shallow river was grinding Snake Eyes down. The hull, advertised to be as "strong as a heavy-duty conveyor belt," was losing its capability to convey us. We were coming into many deep pools and fine stretches of water now, but the momentum and response of Snake Eyes afloat were not much better than of Snake Eyes aground, so the others—in their maneuverable, shallow-draft canoe and light kayak—often had to wait. On the slope above the left bank we saw a lone grizzly walking north in the rain. Since the river was narrow and bending, the boats were sometimes out of sight from one another. Fedeler, in the single Klepper, saw a grizzly that was gone when the rest of us came along. There was no telling how many bears we may have failed to notice—or, for that matter, how many bears we may have seen twice. The Nikok, a tributary, came into the Salmon from the west, and we stopped for lunch beside it, and cast lures from smooth ledges into deep holes that were clear and green.

After the Nikok, there was more river to float us. The rain turned to mist and put a soft gray light on the hills. No matter what the weather might be, Kauffmann said, the Brooks Range for him was the best of Alaska—in the quality of its light, in the clarity of its flowing water, in the configuration of its terrain. He did not much care for the glacier country—the south. "It's too raw," he went on. "Up here in the north, you have all the effects of the glacier land forms without the glaciers themselves. You have clear streams." Studying the Salmon as a national wild river had been Kauffmann's idea. If Kauffmann could have his way, at least a quarter of Alaska would be held as wilderness forever. After his five years of study and planning for Gates of the Arctic National Park—an area twice as large as the state of Hawaii, four times the size of Yellowstone—odds seemed favorable that it would be congressionally confirmed. Kauffmann's total plans for the park's development—his intended use of airstrips, roadways, lodges, lean-tos, refreshment stands, trash barrels, benches—added up to zero. The most inventive thing to do, as he saw it, was nothing. Let the land stand wild, without so much as a man-made trail.

Kauffmann, among Alaskans, represented only a small arc or two in a wheel of attitudes toward the land. For one thing, he was a "fed" and thus an "outsider," who—in the view of some—was trying to "grab" and "lock up" prime terrain. Yet he was also an Alaskan. In a state largely populated by aggressive transients, he was at least as Alaskan as most. He had built a home and had become an earnest Alaskan citizen. As such, and not merely as a fed, he did indeed favor locking up land, if that meant saving it for the future of the future.

In the time Kauffmann had lived in Alaska, the number of voters with views sympathetic to his own had risen from very low to modest. Yet the presence of this minority (backed by support from outside) had produced a tension that underlay much of what was happening in the state. It was tension over the way in which Alaska might proceed, tension somewhat reminiscent of the matters (water rights, grazing rights) that divided earlier pioneers. In its modern form, it was the tension of preservation versus development, of stasis versus economic productivity, of wilderness versus the drill and the bulldozer, and in part it had caused the portentous reassignment of land that now, in the nineteen-seventies, was altering, or threatening to alter, the lives of everyone in the state.

The federal government, long ago, used to watch over Alaska with one eye, and with so little interest that the lid was generally closed. In all that territorial land, so wild and remote, emigrants from the United States easily established their frontier code: breathe free, do as you please, control your own destiny. If you had much more in mind than skinning hares, though, it was difficult to control much of a destiny—to plan, for example, any kind of development on a major scale—since the federal government owned more than ninety-nine per cent of the land. The push for statehood was seen as a way to gain more control; but, to their frustration and disappointment, Alaskans found that the big decisions continued to be made (or postponed, as the case might be) in Washington. After some years, and under pressure to find new energy resources, the federal government awakened to the potentialities of Alaska. With the development of the oil field at Prudhoe Bay, state and federal interests at last seemed to complement each other. The discovery of oil felt like the discovery of gold, and the future seemed lighted from behind. With the pipeline, however, Alaska suddenly had more development than it could absorb. It suddenly had manifold inflation and a glut of trailer parks. It had traffic jams. You could pick up a telephone and "dial a date." In the reasonably accessible bush, fishing and hunting—the sorts of things many people had long sought in Alaska—became crowded and poor. A boom was on, money was around, and buildings were going up; but a dream may have come too true. Most of the money was passing over the heads of Alaskans long established in the state. Confused and disillusioned, many were forced to ponder if big-scale development meant bonanza after all.

The people's new hesitation about the wisdom of development was expressed in 1974 in the election, by a narrow margin, of Jay Hammond as governor. Hammond had homesteaded land in Alaska. His wife was an Alaskan native. His approach to Alaska's future was to attempt to go slow, to build with caution, to try to find a middle course—not only *between* conservation and economic development but *within* them as well. He appointed Robert Weeden, a wildlife biologist from the University of Alaska, as State Policy Development and Planning Director, and set him the task of drawing together a state proposal for the future of the designated national-interest lands. Unsurprisingly, the state soon informed Congress that it would like to participate in the management of these lands, and hence was willing to put some of its own land into the total. The state would like various options to be left open for the future and not to be written away in legislation. "We're interested in sharing in the decisions on federal lands forever," Weeden told me one day in the capitol, in Juneau. "The federal proposals reflect the territorial imperative of agencies rather than the long-term interests of the state as the nation relates to it. The state has gone from a development urge to development plus conservation, while the federal trajectory—in general—has been from neglect and preservation to exploitation of resources. We've almost changed roles. Meanwhile, federal agencies are scrapping among themselves. The National Park Service wants the land as it is, and the Forest Service and the Bureau of Land Management would like to see it exploited. The Fish and Wildlife Service is closer to the middle. Their lands are available for 'compatible uses.' For example, their Kenai National Moose Range has oil wells in it. The Moose Range was the first oil field in Alaska. The National Park Service and Fish and Wildlife are the conservationists' favorites. Developers favor the Bureau of Land Management. We need an additional approach. Suppose you have good parkland that also has minerals. You say a firm decision should not be made there—not right now. There are places where a reasonable man would not want to make decisions yet. Our position has been described by some as a middle-of-the-road stance. Perhaps so, but in this road all the traffic seems to be hugging the two ditches. These days, man should be somewhat humble about his *capacity* to make permanent decisions." On a wall in Weeden's offices, a sign said, "Earth, this is God. I want all you people to clear out before the end of the month. I have a client who is interested in the property."

I had lunch one day in Anchorage with an entrenched Alaskan boomer—Robert Atwood, editor and publisher of the Anchorage *Times*. If the state government and its Robert Weedens were about ninety degrees around from the attitude represented by John Kauffmann, Atwood was a hundred and eighty. "We should preserve wilderness only in areas that are without other resources," he said. "The U.S. needs our oil. We're not going to prevent it going. God damn it, they should take it. They need it. The ultimate destiny of Alaska is to help the nation be self-sufficient. We should bend and help, not tie the land up in a knot to save a tree or a bear or a fond dream. A state develops by developing its resources. Prudhoe Bay was a big start for this little state. Then what happened? The pipeline was stopped for years by conservationists. It was the first time in history that a state was told it could not take its resources to market. Some people think anybody who wants to do anything with a shovel is bad. They should see Prudhoe Bay. It's so damned clean and neat and sterile—with refrigerated pilings, so the tundra won't melt. The pipeline will be the biggest tourist attraction in Alaska. Caribou will move close to it for heat. Meanwhile, these wilderness buffs, like your friend Kauffmann, have an insatiable appetite for wilderness. They have drawn lines on the map according to what is best and beautiful from their point of view. What they are trying for is a land grab, but they see it as the last chance to preserve something. From their point of view, it *is* the last chance. But locking the land up is unfair to future generations. Nobody knows wholly what is under it, in coal or oil or minerals."

Alaskan natives, for their part, were somewhere on the way back to Kauffmann. They saw the federal park and refuge proposals as possibly—but not necessarily—the least disturbing of the changes that could come to, for example, the Salmon River and the Kobuk valley. Willie Hensley, an Eskimo leader, once described it this way for me: "If we can hunt, fish, trap, we're not concerned. We don't have that assurance yet. If we can't drive our boats up the river, we're going to have problems. If we can't take our dog teams or snow machines after caribou, we're going to have problems. Now is a time of transition for the native people. We have long used the land as if we owned it. We thought we *did* own it. We had lived here ten thousand years and assumed it was ours. But in the past we never had the political or economic clout to make a single bit of difference in Alaska. The Native Claims Settlement Act has given us a voice that we did not have before. It has also given us the problem of the national-interest lands. If these lands can be used for subsistence hunting, fishing, trapping, we don't have many qualms." No less wary of the coming of the parkland were any number of whites living in the bush, who had also been trapping and hunting and fishing for (in many cases) generations, and who now found themselves confronted with much the same worries the natives had—but without the incidental benefits of a billion dollars and forty million acres of land.

Paddling on through the light rain, Kauffmann now began to fulminate. He said he had once drawn up an Alaskan coat of arms, its shield quarterly gules and gold with a motto written in each quarter, expressing what he took to be the core attitudes of the people of Alaska toward—as the Aleut word "Alaska" means—"the great land." The motto written on one quarter of the shield was "Dig It Up." On another, "Chop It Down." On another, "Fish It Out." On the fourth, "Shoot It." He said the forty million acres involved in the Native Claims Settlement Act amounted to something over six hundred acres for each native. He said the Statehood Act had provided what now amounted to two hundred and fifty acres for each Alaskan. And that left roughly one acre of Alaska for each citizen of the United States as a whole—an amount he considered minimal. "People who have come to Alaska, worked hard, and grubbed out a living feel resentment toward people whom they call 'Lower Forty-eight meddlers,'" he went on. "People here take a proprietary attitude. They say, 'Don't tie our hands.' They forget that we *all* own Alaska. They call it their land, but it's everybody's land. Alaska is the last great opportunity this nation has to set aside adequate chunks of natural landscape for a variety of conservation purposes. The land is still open. It is uncommitted. Think what the East would look like if Thoreau had been heeded. Think of the rivers and lakes of New Hampshire and Maine—Lake Winnipesaukee, Moosehead Lake. The opportunity exists in Alaska on a scale incomprehensible to anyone who hasn't seen it. Local interests should be satisfied, certainly, and state interests as well—but so should *national* interests. This river, this land around us, is of national interest, and it belongs to everybody in the United States."

In part to make him paddle harder, I said, "Yes, but why do all you sneakerfaces, you ecocentrics, think you need so much of it? Why do you need eighty million acres?"

"Everything in Alaska is on a bigger scale," he said. "There is a need for a place in which to lose yourself, for more space than you can encompass. It's not sufficient just to set aside sights to see. We need whole ecosystems, whole ranges, whole watersheds."

"Entire mountain ranges?"

"We're going to have to live in close harmony with the earth. There's a lot we don't know. We need places where we can learn how. The carrying capacity for plants and animals is limited here. They need plenty of space and time. Think of the years it takes a grayling to grow. If we do our thing, if we exploit shortsightedly, we impoverish even the biggest landscapes. There is no such thing as superabundance. I think many people have come to realize this. A sense of spaciousness has shaped the character of this country. We don't want to let that sense entirely pass. The frontier society feels it is here to exploit the land, though—to grow, to build, to tame, to extract, to realize the wealth that is here. They don't like regulation. They don't like to be told they can't do something. They want to do what they want to where and when they please. Between their interests and the interests of the nation as a whole the Native Claims Settlement Act tried to strike a balance."

"Some balance," I said. "The map is covered with proposed parks."

"The parks are ten per cent of the state, God damn it. Tithed to the future. The proposals are not repetitious. They are different. They complement each other. This river and the Gates of the Arctic are at the wilderness end of the spectrum. This is the last big piece of magnificent mountain wilderness we have left. First it was the Appalachians, then the Rockies, then the Sierra Nevada, then Alaska, and this is the last part of Alaska. This is America's ultimate wilderness; it goes no farther. This is our last opportunity to provide, admittedly in a contrived way, the chance to go adventuring in country so wild that valleys and mountains are without names."

"But why lock it up forever?"

"It will *not* be locked up. The resources aren't going to go anywhere. In some dire situation, they are there. People say, 'Study it first.' This is a delaying tactic by people who want to exploit it later. There's always someone who wants another look. Meanwhile, the time has historically come for preserving major pieces of land in Alaska, to have the freshness of Alaska —large landscapes, habitats—perpetuated, not tarnished and degraded as man grubs his way along with awesome power. The locations of oil reserves are largely determined. The national-interest lands include very little oil. What the contention comes down to is mining. Nineteenth-century laws let the miner onto most government land, but the miner is no longer the quaint old man with the burro and the pick."

Having goaded him, I thought I should reward him. I said, "In Alaska, we appear to be recapitulating ourselves. This may be our last chance to suggest that we've learned anything at all." I felt the momentum of Snake Eyes perceptibly increase.

We came to the end of a pondlike pool, and Snake Eyes ran aground. Salmon were thrashing up the riffle there—backs exposed, sculling against water and stones. Toward the bottom of the rip, water collected, becoming heavy and white and two feet deep. The river then curved right—a bending chute with a cut bank on one side and an apron of gravel on the other. Over the cut bank a sweeper had recently fallen, a spruce whose trunk reached into the river. Its green boughs spread over the white water. The swiftest of the current went under the branches, so the problem presented to Kauffmann and me was to get into the kayak in fast water and then collect ourselves at once for a move around the tree. Sweepers tend to trap boats and hold them almost broadside to the current while the weight of the river rolls them over. Kauffmann and I attacked the situation with the same easy confidence we had displayed over the years on a number of analogous occasions, beginning with a near double drowning in 1955. Standing in the rain in the fast water, we settled into Snake Eyes and flew at the sweeper. In concept, we would skirt it to the right. In practice, we hit it dead center. Kauffmann was still reminding me that this was our last opportunity to save the final American wilderness when Snake Eyes bought the river. The thought occurred to me as I pitched head first into the rushing water that I had not often involuntarily overturned on a river trip, and that on almost all the occasions when I had the last thing I had seen on my way to the bottom was Kauffmann. Tact restrained me from mentioning this to him until he had come up out of the river. Meanwhile, I jumped to my feet. The water was waist deep, cold as a wine bucket. I retrieved Kauffmann's hat. Under the gin-clear water, his head, with its radical economy of hair, looked like an onion. Snake Eyes was upside down. I wrenched it right side up, then took its painter and hurried out of the river. From the moment we spilled until I was standing on dry gravel, scarcely fifteen seconds went by. Kauffmann was soaked, but I was not. My rain gear had been drawn tight at the neck and had elastic cuffs. I was half wet—in harlequin patches, and not much on the chest or the back. A piece at a time, we floated our duffel out of Snake Eyes—sleeping bags, clothes bags. Then we dumped out the water, repacked the duffel, and got back onto the river.

We were chilled, and that was a long cold afternoon. Snake Eyes continued to move downstream like a sea anchor, and in the miserable rain we chose not to stop and build a fire. A few hours later, we embraced the fire that ended the day.

Pourchot, after dinner in the bright evening light, began repairing the Kleppers. The hulls were so abraded, the damage so extensive, that he interrupted the job for his night's sleep and finished it after breakfast. Kleppers afloat, it is only fair to insert, are tough and sturdy boats; and, as someone pointed out, an almost identical twin of Snake Eyes in 1956 had crossed the Atlantic Ocean. "Good God!" Kauffmann said on receiving this news. But the Salmon River in low water—with its limestones, its dolomite, its sharp miscellaneous schists—was too much for the rubber-coated kayaks. Both had been leaking seriously, and as I watched Pourchot taping their hulls I could not help thinking that we would be a stone's throw from nowhere without them. He worked slowly, with fibre-glass tape, trying through applied friction to enhance the strength of the sticking.

"We're up some creek," I said, "without those boats."

Pourchot said, "I always pack an extra day's food in case everything does not go right."

Since he had advised bringing emergency rations, I had along a bacon bar, a can of mixed nuts, a bag of dried fruit, and half a dozen packets of M&M's. Their octane seemed low for a walk to Kiana. I had waterproof matches strewn around in various places in my pack. I asked Pourchot if he ever took along a radio, and he said no. He said there was a choice of two types and both were disadvantageous. One was an FM transmitter that was much like a walkie-talkie, but it worked only on line of sight, and, even from a ridge, would at best carry twenty miles. Twenty miles is not an impressive radius in Alaska. Anyway, almost no one ever monitored the frequency. On the other hand, if you had a single-side-band, you could, with a properly laid-out antenna, call anywhere in Alaska. But the single-side-band was big as a breadbox, bulky, heavy (thirty pounds), and extremely expensive. So Pourchot could not be bothered with that, either. We had no axes with us, which at least reduced chances of injury. Pourchot said he had brought along a ten-dollar first-aid kit, but it had no sutures and no prescription drugs, and "a doctor would laugh at it."

He cut a short piece of tape and laid it over a particularly open break in the hull of Snake Eyes, then put a longer strip over that. "These trips are not fail-safe," he went on. "You can get hurt and not get attention for several days. There's nothing you can do, short of staying home all the time."

"You come to the place on its terms," Kauffmann put in. "You assume the risk."

"When people come to Alaska, there's a sifting and winnowing process that follows," Pourchot said. "Some just make day trips out of Anchorage into the bush. Others go out for more than one day—fishing or whatever—but they stay in one place, at an established camp or lodge. After that come the hikers and canoers, and from them you get many stories of, say, the boat that breaks up and the guy who sits on the gravel bar for two weeks and walks out in five miserable days. He makes it, though. It's a rare day when somebody starves or bleeds to death. You're just not going to make a trip perfectly safe and still get the kind of trip you want. There are no what-if types out here. People who come this far have come to grips with that problem."

Pourchot was apparently unaware that he was addressing a what-if type—an advanced, thousand-deaths coward with oak-leaf clusters. If I wanted to, I could always see disaster running with the river, dancing like a shadow, moving down the forest from tree to tree. And yet coming to grips with the problem may have been easier for me than for the others, since all of them lived in Alaska. Risk is everywhere, but it is in some places more than others, and this was the safest place I'd been all year. I live in New Jersey, where risks to life are statistically higher than they are along an Arctic river.

Fedeler pointed out that on the back of Alaska fishing licenses are drawings of a signal system for people in trouble who are fortunate enough to be seen by an airplane. I looked at my license. It showed a figure holding hands overhead like a referee indicating a touchdown. That meant, "Please pick me up." A pair of chevrons, sketched on the ground, was a request for firearms and ammunition. An "I" indicated serious injury. An "F" called for food and water, and an "X" meant "Unable to proceed."

"To get a plane to see you, a big smoky fire will help," Fedeler said.

What had struck me most in the isolation of this wilderness was an abiding sense of paradox. In its raw, convincing emphasis on the irrelevance of the visitor, it was forcefully, importantly repellent. It was no less strongly attractive—with a beauty of nowhere else, composed in turning circles. If the wild land was indifferent, it gave a sense of difference. If at moments it was frightening, requiring an effort to put down the conflagrationary imagination, it also augmented the touch of life. This was not a dare with nature. This was nature.

The bottoms of the Kleppers were now trellised with tape. Pourchot was smoothing down a final end. Until recently, he had been an avocational parachutist, patterning the sky in star formation with others as he fell. He had fifty-one jumps, all of them in Colorado. But he had started waking up in the night with cold sweats, so—with two small sons now—he had sold his jumping gear. With the money, he bought a white-water kayak and climbing rope. "You're kind of on your own, really.

You run the risk," he was saying. "I haven't seen any bear incidents, for example. I've never had any bear problems. I've never carried a gun. Talk to ten people and you get ten different bear-approach theories. Some carry flares. Ed Bailey, in Fish and Wildlife, shoots pencil flares into the ground before approaching bears. They go away. Bear attacks generally occur in road-system areas anyway. Two, maybe four people die a year. Some years more than others. Rarely will a bear attack a person in a complete wilderness like this."

Kauffmann said, "Give a grizzly half a chance and he'll avoid you."

Fedeler had picked cups of blueberries to mix into our breakfast pancakes. Finishing them, we prepared to go. The sun was coming through. The rain was gone. The morning grew bright and warm. Pourchot and I got into the canoe, which, for all its heavy load, felt light. Twenty minutes downriver, we had to stop for more repairs to the Kleppers, but afterward the patchwork held. With higher banks, longer pools, the river was running deeper. The sun began to blaze.

Rounding bends, we saw sculpins, a pair of great horned owls, mergansers, Taverner's geese. We saw ravens and a gray jay. Coming down a long, deep, green pool, we looked toward the riffle at the lower end and saw an approaching grizzly. He was young, possibly four years old, and not much over four hundred pounds. He crossed the river. He studied the salmon in the riffle. He did not see, hear, or smell us. Our three boats were close together, and down the light current on the flat water we drifted toward the fishing bear.

He picked up a salmon, roughly ten pounds of fish, and, holding it with one paw, he began to whirl it around his head. Apparently, he was not hungry, and this was a form of play. He played sling-the-salmon. With his claws embedded near the tail, he whirled the salmon and then tossed it high, end over end. As it fell, he scooped it up and slung it around his head again, lariat salmon, and again he tossed it into the air. He caught it and heaved it high once more. The fish flopped to the ground. The bear turned away, bored. He began to move upstream by the edge of the river. Behind his big head his hump projected. His brown fur rippled like a field under wind. He kept coming. The breeze was behind him. He had not yet seen us. He was romping along at an easy walk. As he came closer to us, we drifted slowly toward him. The single Klepper, with John Kauffmann in it, moved up against a snagged stick and broke it off. The snap was light, but enough to stop the bear. Instantly, he was motionless and alert, remaining on his four feet and straining his eyes to see. We drifted on toward him. At last, we arrived in his focus. If we were looking at something we had rarely seen before, God help him so was he. If he was a tenth as awed as I was, he could not have moved a muscle, which he did, now, in a hurry that was not pronounced but nonetheless seemed inappropriate to his status in the situation. He crossed low ground and went up a bank toward a copse of willow. He stopped there and faced us again. Then, breaking stems to pieces, he went into the willows.

We drifted to the rip, and down it past the mutilated salmon. Then we came to another long flat surface, spraying up the light of the sun. My bandanna, around my head, was nearly dry. I took it off, and trailed it in the river.

BOOK II

IN URBAN ALASKA

What They Were Hunting For

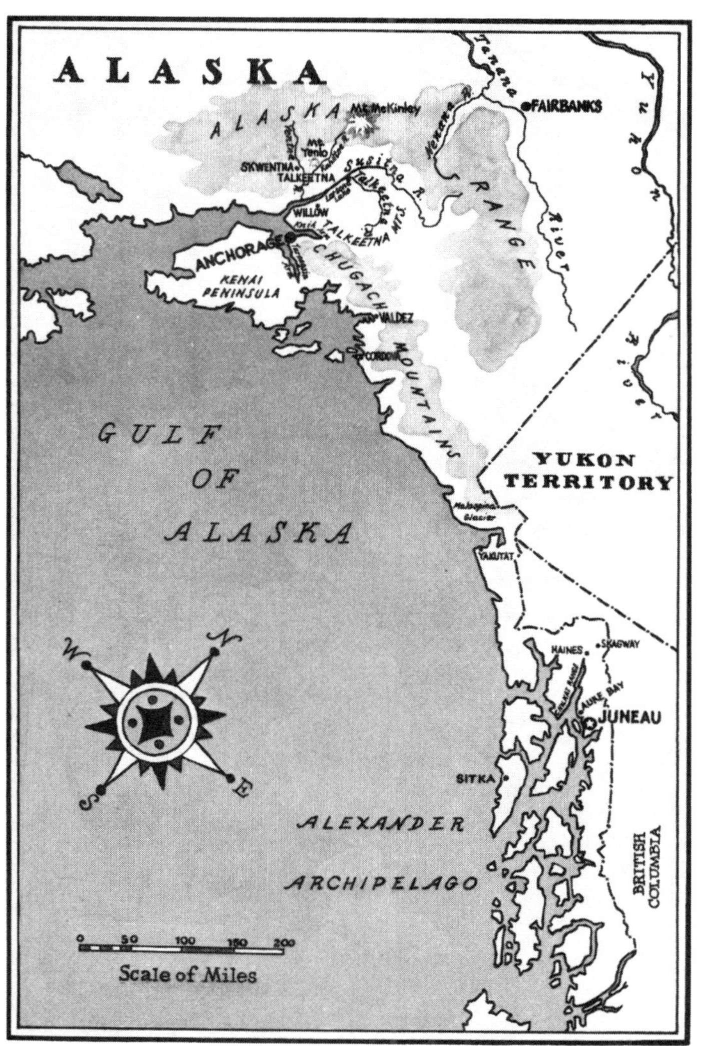
ALASKA
ALASKA
Mt. McKinley
FAIRBANKS
Tanana
Yukon
Mt. Tenio
SKWENTNA
TALKEETNA
Susitna R.
Talkeetna
WILLOW
TALKEETNA MTS.
ANCHORAGE
KENAI PENINSULA
CHUGACH
VALDEZ
CORDOVA
MOUNTAINS
RANGE
River
GULF OF ALASKA
YUKON TERRITORY
Malaspina Glacier
YAKUTAT
HAINES
SKAGWAY
AUKE BAY
JUNEAU
SITKA
ALEXANDER ARCHIPELAGO
BRITISH COLUMBIA
N
W
S
E
0 50 100 150 200
Scale of Miles

ONE MORNING in the Alaskan autumn, a small sharp-nosed helicopter, on its way to a rendezvous, flew south from Fairbanks with three passengers. They crossed the fast, silted water of the Tanana River and whirred along over low black-spruce land with streams too numerous for names. The ground beneath them began to rise, and they with it, until they were crossing broad benchlands and high hills increasingly jagged in configuration as they stepped up to the Alaska Range.

At about the same time, another and somewhat larger group took off from Anchorage in a de Havilland Twin Otter, and this sturdy vehicle, firm as iron in the air, flew north up the valley of the Big Su—Susitna River, a big river in a land of big rivers—and on up over alpine tundra that now, in the late season, was as red as wine. After moving over higher and higher hills, the plane moved in among mountains: great, upreaching things, gray on the rockface and then—above the five-thousand-foot contour and far on up, too high to see without pressing to the window—covered with fresh snow.

"Is the mountain out?" someone on the right side of the plane wanted to know. In so many mountains, there was one mountain. "Is the mountain out?"

"It surer than hell is."

"It never looks the same."

The mountain was a megahedron—its high white facets doming in the air. Long snow banners, extending eastward, were pluming from the ridges above twenty thousand feet.

"What would you call that mountain, Willie?"

"Denali. I'll go along with the Indians that far."

Everyone aboard was white but Willie (William Iġiaġruq Hensley), of Arctic Alaska, and he said again, "Denali. What the hell did McKinley ever do?"

The Twin Otter by now was so deep in the Alaska Range that nothing could be seen but walls of mountain in a pass. Then, finally, the pass widened the way to the north. Banking over terraces and high riverine bluffs—Nenana River—the plane landed on gravel near a small group of buildings, a mining town. The helicopter from Fairbanks was already there.

Handshakes all around. Brisk, nippy morning, right? Won't be long now. And then, in threes and fours, the group made successive flights in the small helicopter—down the right bank of the Nenana over the broad high benchland, back and forth in loosely patterned flight. Four grizzly bears—large and small, perhaps a ton or so of bear—were grazing a meadow below, eating blueberry bushes rich with fruit. The helicopter ignored the bears. It crossed the river and flew back to the north in vectors, as if looking for something. A small lake. Then a larger lake. This was indeed a hunt, and what the people in the air were hunting for was a new capital of Alaska.

When states move their capitals, as most of them have done at one time or another, the usual aim is to have a seat of government somewhere near the centers of geography and population—criteria that distinctly fail to describe Juneau. Juneau, capital of Alaska since 1900, is in the eccentric region that Alaskans call Southeastern—a long, archipelagic claw that dangles toward Seattle and is knuckled to the main body of Alaska by a glacier the size of Rhode Island. Southeastern Alaska reaches so far east that all the land north of it is Canadian. British Columbia. Yukon Territory. Juneau is two time zones from Anchorage, from Fairbanks, from the center of the state. It is twenty-five hundred miles from the other end of Alaska. Many Alaskans do not regard Southeastern as part of Alaska but, rather, as an appendage of inconvenience, because Juneau is there. Juneau is an outport—cannot be reached, or even approached, by road. Juneau was the site of a gold strike that attracted people enough to make a town, and the town's importance increased when strikes of bonanza quantity were made in mountains to the north, along the Klondike River and other tributaries of the upper Yukon. Juneau, already a mining town, was also a way station on trips to the Klondike, and it became—for the duration of the gold boom—a center of Alaskan commerce.

Anchorage is the commercial center now, and roughly half of political Alaska. As a result of a petition signed by sixteen thousand, an initiative appeared on the 1974 primary ballot through which the voters could indicate a wish to move their capital.

Similar initiatives in 1960 and 1962 had been defeated, perhaps in part because Alaskans elsewhere in the state did not want to see even more power concentrated in Anchorage. Anchorage, for its part, wished to yield nothing to Fairbanks. Their rivalry is intense to the point of unseemliness. So the 1974 initiative was written to exclude both cities—the new capital could not be within thirty miles of either one—and in strong majority (fifty-seven per cent) the voters went for it.

The state is more or less broke—if that term can be used to describe a budget that regularly expends a great deal more than it ingests. For this reason, it might seem an act of bravado to contemplate building anything at all, let alone a new capital city. Bravado, on the other hand, is a synonym for Alaska. A high proportion of the white people who have tried to make their way in Alaska have lived from boom to boom. The first boom was in fur, and then came gold, followed by war, and now oil. How could it matter that the treasury was atilt when the Alyeska Pipeline Service Company was moving toward completion of a tube that would draw so much oil out of the north of Alaska that the state government alone would collect in royalties as much as three and a half million dollars a day? Some Alaskans were already spending the money. Others were dreaming of ways to spend it. One of the dreams was of a new capital, in a wild setting, preferably within sight of the summits of North America's highest massif.

Following the terms of the initiative, the governor of Alaska appointed a Capital Site Selection Committee, most of whose nine members had been—like the governor himself—opponents of the initiative. One might think that only Gilbert and Sullivan could work out the story from there. The committee, though—representing a geographical spread of the state, including Southeastern—had taken up its work with a seriousness Alaskan in grandeur, and would spend well over a million dollars to narrow its choices down.

The move to move the capital has "bestirred the community," as one Alaska senator has put it, and from the community has come a chorus of comment. The dialogue assembled here contains voices from Seward, Sitka, Fort Yukon, Kotzebue, Fairbanks, Juneau, Anchorage.

"Despite the terms of the initiative, Anchorage is the logical place for the capital. The move would cost the least, and Anchorage would serve best. Anchorage should *be* the capital."

"There are more state-government employees in Anchorage now than there are in Juneau."

"Everyone is afraid of, and is envious of, Anchorage."

"Anchorage has got enough."

"People don't want the Anchorage scourge to spread."

"The initiative was a vendetta."

"The capital move started with people in Anchorage who thought they were getting screwed by the legislature in Juneau."

"Make no mistake. Anchorage wants the capital in Anchorage and will somehow get it."

"Anchorage works hard to get things from other towns. It has from the start. When Anchorage was just a few people in tents, they tried to take the headquarters of the railroad from Seward and the U.S. District Court from Valdez. In both instances, they succeeded. Recently, they have tried hard to take the university from Fairbanks. They have part of it already. They wooed the U.S. land office away from Juneau. 'Proud' is a word still used here in Alaska—but not about Anchorage."

A single voice can be particularly audible in Alaska, because there are so few people. Much is made of Alaska's great size. It is worth remembering, as well, how small Alaska is—a handful of people clinging to a subcontinent. There are nearly twice as many people in the District of Columbia as there are in the State of Alaska. In ten square miles of the eastern state I live in are more people than there are in the five hundred and eighty-six thousand square miles of Alaska.

"The capital must be a new city."

"Pipeline or no pipeline, the state would go broke buying land in Anchorage. On top of that, because everybody in Alaska hates Anchorage it is politically expedient to put the capital in a new place, an undeveloped place."

"The land out there is of no great value. It's just wilderness, standing there."

The committee's flight through the mountains that morning appeared to be, as much as anything else, a gesture of courtesy to Fairbanks, *de facto* capital of the terrain that is called the Interior. Fairbanks is the pivot from which travellers fan out to the north—the usual departure point for Arctic Alaska, and the departure point, as well, for mail planes and bush craft that serve the Interior villages. A look at a map would suggest a site near Fairbanks as an obvious capital for the state as a whole, because of Fairbanks' position near the center of the Alaskan mainland. There are drawbacks, however, in climate. The Interior is so named because it lies between the Brooks Range, which traverses the far north, and the Alaska Range, which is the climax of the mountain chain that comes up the Pacific coast and then bends across south-central Alaska to indicate the Aleutians. The Interior is the hottest region of Alaska. It is also the coldest. Temperatures there can go into the nineties in summer and into the minus-seventies in winter, and at times of deep cold large areas of the Interior will be palled with ice fog. Fairbanks has more motor vehicles per capita than does Los Angeles, and as the cars toot and tap bumpers on the long crawls through the ice fog the warm gases of their exhaust plumes seem to stick in the air close around them—an especially pernicious, carcinogenic subarctic variety of smog. This experience would suggest—too late to help Fairbanks—that it might be imprudent to plan deliberately to attract numerous vehicles to a single site in the Interior.

The capital committee got into the Twin Otter and flew back through the mountains toward the south. "A great place for grizzlies," said Willie Hensley, looking over his shoulder.

In its many months of sorting possibilities, the committee had discovered that there were few places in Alaska that could meet the criteria of the search. By law, resulting from the terms of the initiative, they had to find a hundred square miles of land somewhere near a road and a railroad and in terrain appropriate for a new airport that would consistently experience negotiable weather. The land had to belong to the state, or, in any case, to be available to the state for nothing. In addition, the committee and its consultants established standards of their own. Since weather and cold worsen with altitude, they would look for a site below two thousand feet. It should have, among other things, good soil, ample water, topography both practical and aesthetically appealing, relatively modest annual snowfall. It should not inconvenience resident wildlife—should not invade bear-denning grounds, salmon-spawning areas—and it should not be in zones of earthquakes or volcanism.

A simple task. In Indiana. Corydon was the capital of Indiana until a new-capital-site-selection committee drew a state-size X on the map and noted where the legs crossed. The spot was in deep forest. Indians owned the land. A treaty took care of them. Indianapolis, Indiana.

This was Alaska, though, where people are even more marginal than plants, and the choice was truly complex. About a third of Alaska is above two thousand feet. Something like two-thirds is demarcated for the natives and the federal government. It would be unwise to build in an area of permafrost. Two-thirds of Alaska is underlaid by permafrost. Alaska has two railroads. One is twenty-six miles long. The other runs four hundred and seventy miles, from Seward—a port on the Gulf of Alaska—through Anchorage and on to Fairbanks. The Alaska Highway comes into the Interior from Yukon Territory. The rest of the state's highway system principally consists of two roads. One goes from Fairbanks to Anchorage, and the other, by a newer and more westerly route, goes from Anchorage to Fairbanks. Roughly speaking, the land that has been built upon, pipelined, or otherwise trammelled in Alaska—all the land that is now taken up by towns, villages, cities, airports, trapper cabins, motels, roads—consists agglomerately of less than a hundred thousand acres. That leaves, untouched, nearly three hundred and seventy-five million acres. By almost any standards drawn from the North Temperate Zone, human settlement is still the next thing to nonexistent in Alaska. Juneau, a relatively small town of eighteen thousand, is Alaska's third-largest "city." The celebrated Trans-Alaska Pipeline is, in scale, comparable to a thread laid across Staten Island. With it, the "destruction of Alaska" may have begun, as some people will say, but utter wilderness—uncompromising, unhuman wilderness—is almost wholly what Alaska is now. So if a group of people had to choose a townsite near a road and a railroad, off permafrost and on fairly low but well-drained ground, and not inordinately far from the main pockets of existing population, nearly all of Alaska would recede from the conversation and by the facts the people would be ushered into the Susitna Valley.

The Twin Otter, coming out of the mountains, moved south above the Susitna, whose water, flowing swiftly, bore so much glacially pulverized rock that it was gray and glisteningly opaque, and appeared to be ready to set. The upper Susitna has cut a canyon—Devils Canyon—where rapids pile up almost to the scale of the Colorado; and then the currents spread out and braid their way among uncountable islands. The Susitna Valley—to a point more than a hundred miles above Anchorage—includes the most northerly penetration in Alaska of land that is generally free from permafrost. The Alaska Railroad goes up the valley, as does the Anchorage-Fairbanks Highway, which was opened in 1974—significant marks, to be sure, of advancing humanity, but from the low-flying plane they looked in the forest like a slim ribbon and a set of sutures. An occasional roadhouse, cabin, or clearing appeared along the highway, and there were other cabins beside streams splaying out from the railway. A train—Lionel in appearance among the black lowland spruce—was stopped near a stream in the undepoted wild. Someone was collecting supplies. Or getting off to go home. The railway serves many dozens of people who have abandoned the civilization the railway represents. The train, typically, drops them at a stream and they go in canoes or skiffs to cabins some miles away. They chose the cabin sites and staked them out as "Open to Entry" land, which was available for low sums until 1973, when the program was at least temporarily stopped, pending the resolution of all the major and interlocking events in the subdivision of Alaskan land: final selection by the state of the one hundred and three million acres allotted to it in the Statehood Act, in 1958; final designation of intended use—parks, refuges, national wild rivers—for vast segments of federal lands; and selection by the natives of the tracts to be deeded to them. When the Open to Entry program was set up, recreation was what its creators had in mind. But a number of people who staked lots went to live on them year round—to combat the winter, to live in wilderness, to kill and eat game, to trap fur, to simplify their lives and be relatively self-sufficient, albeit in some dependence on the Alaska Railroad. Making money was emphatically not their objective. They sought little more than permanent relief from the larger society. To place a city down among them would be to flick them from the earth. Willie Hensley and the committee, overhead, looked down over the spruce-and-hardwood forest. A couple of cabins were barely visible among the trees. Aspen leaves, yellow, were quaking in the fall air. "Too mundane," Willie Hensley said as the Twin Otter moved on toward Talkeetna.

A minor but handsome run of mountains—the Talkeetna Mountains—now framed the valley with a six-thousand-foot ridgeline to the east. To the west, the land was at first low and then rose toward mountains beyond which were only a few specks of settlement in the five hundred miles to the Bering Sea. To the north, roughly forty miles distant now, was the topographical mural that closed off the Interior. Mount McKinley, veiled in snow haze, was fast removing itself to obscurity. The big mountain, sometimes described as the Weathermaker, creates its own integument, because it is so high and cold that when it interrupts flows of warm and often moist summer air it causes violent reactions: roiling clouds that form in a moment, sudden storms, gale-driven blizzards. High up the mountain, the windchill—even during the elsewhere-warm Alaskan summer—can go down to (and beyond) a hundred below zero. From within its vapors, the mountain can emerge as swiftly as it disappeared, and when it is out only the distant curve of the earth can reduce its dominance, for it is the most arresting sight from forty million acres around. The Alaska Range elevates with a rapidity rare in the world. Its top is about two-thirds as high as the top of the Himalayas, but the Himalayan uplift is broad and extensive. If you were looking toward Mount Everest from forty miles away, you would lift your gaze only slightly to note the highest in a sea of peaks. Forty miles from McKinley you can stand at a bench mark of three hundred and climb with your eyes the other twenty thousand feet. The difference—between your altitude near sea level and the height of that flying white mountain—is much too great to be merely overwhelming. The mountain is a sky of rock, seemingly all above you, looming. Until it takes itself away, you watch it as you might watch a hearth fire or a show in color of aurorean light. The provocative immensity of Mount McKinley seems to symbolize Alaska to many Alaskans. No wonder they would have a capital with the mountain much in view. Some of those Alaskans, as it happens, are Athapaskans, and their regard for the big mountain is understandably deeper (in time, in metaphor, in spiritual mystery) even than the regard of white Alaskans. The Athapaskans are not much impressed that a young Princeton graduate on a prospecting adventure in the Susitna Valley in 1896 happened to learn, on his way out of the wilderness, that William McKinley had become the Republican nominee for President of the United States. In this haphazard way, the mountain got the name it would carry for at least the better part of a century, notwithstanding that it already had a name, for uncounted centuries had had a name, which in translation has been written, variously, as The Great One, The Mighty One, The High One. The Indians in their reverence had called it Denali. Toponymically, that is the mountain's proper name; and if a city were deliberately to seek the mountain and appear before it, the city might be Denali, too.

Talkeetna, the only community of any size in the upper part of the valley, voted sixty-nine to forty-two in favor of moving the capital. Talkeetna is a prime collecting point for climbers on their way to McKinley. I once saw a Japanese climber in Richard and Dorothy Jones's store there, buying a cabbage. It was a purple cabbage and somewhat larger than his own head, which was purple as well, in places, from contusions and sunburn, and probably windburn, suffered in his bout with the mountain. On his cheek was a welted wound, like a split in a tomato. Leaving the store, he walked out of town, ate his cabbage, and slept it off in a tent. I had asked Mrs. Jones what she thought of the idea of moving the capital away from Juneau, and she said she was all for it, but she did hope the new town would not be placed near Talkeetna. "Please may they leave this beautiful section of Alaska alone," she said. "Nature is part of us. We moved here for the out living—for the river. The capital has to have big buildings, a superhighway—and that takes care of the blueberry patches."

A genial person, easygoing and garrulous, she was somewhat beyond athletic weight. Her husband, wry and spare, smiled and nodded while she talked. "A new city, built from scratch in the bush, would be sterile," she said. "The state will probably sell off land to meet some of the cost. I can't see anything of value coming out of a place where people go in with speculation in mind. Meanwhile, we're so naïve we'd be stepped on like bugs. Like June bugs. We're all neighbors here, and together. Your neighbor might need you to help put out a fire in his cabin. But Anchorage and Fairbanks are crooked. If you don't wear pointed-toe boots and a Texas hat, you're not with it. And that is what would come with a capital here. The capital should go to Fairbanks or Anchorage. They're already ruined. But it goes in the bush because the cities are arch-rivals. If it comes here, it will be the end of this community as it stands."

Talkeetna was a random miscellany of log cabins, cabbage patches, some frame houses, house trailers, Quonsets, lettuce-onion-carrot gardens, two or three roadhouses, and an inn from the first part of the century, with a dusty moose rack in velvet on the wall and old colored-glass shades on the hanging lights above the bar. There were two hundred and fifty gold and silver claims around Talkeetna once. Talkeetna has a Historical Society. Dorothy Jones is on the board of directors. Unlike most of her neighbors, she grew up in Alaska. Her father homesteaded, in the Matanuska Valley, nearer Anchorage.

"I was brought up here, too," said her husband. "By Uncle Sam." He, also, was for moving the capital, but he seemed just a little less concerned than his wife did for the environs of Talkeetna. He was a disaffected fisherman. Things had been better when Talkeetna was more isolated, when it was served only by the railroad and bush aircraft; but now, with the new highway, and Anchorage only a little more than two hours away, the fish had been beaten down and you couldn't find a rainbow more than twelve inches long.

Looking down from the Twin Otter at Talkeetna—close by the confluence of three rivers, where the Chulitna and the Talkeetna pile into the Susitna—I could see the Joneses' place and, facing it, an old and ramblingly extended cottonwood-log cabin called the Roadhouse, and near that the small Quonset home of a bush pilot named Cliff Hudson. Climbers stay in the Roadhouse—gather there, go over and over their gear, and wait for the mountain to come out, or, at least, for weather promising enough so that Hudson (among others) can fly them to the Kahiltna Glacier, on the mountain's south side, landing on skis at seven thousand feet. A gravel airstrip runs from behind Hudson's Quonset on out to the edge of the Susitna. I had once flown with him, not to the glacier but into the country around Talkeetna, looking for the dragon's teeth of capitals. Hudson will take anything that comes along—trappers and miners to their cabins, hunters, Oriental alpinists. Bearded, bespectacled, with tousled thinning curly hair, Hudson flew in ten-inch boots and a brown wool shirt that had seen a lot of time on his back. In fact, he appeared to have been *in* the bush instead of flying it—to have lost his plane there and to have just walked out. In 1948, he had come to Alaska (from the Pacific "northwest") for all the great hunting and fishing, and he had become a bush pilot because it was "the only way you could get around." He was disappointed, bitterly, with Alaskan progress. Would he vote—now—for statehood? "Hell, no. They're ripping us off every way they can think of. It's bad enough just to have to *feed* all those politicians. We've got nine-tenths too many of them. They're a bunch of kids. It's just a big playpen —Juneau—at our expense. They argued once for eleven days over who would be the House Speaker." Flying me around the valley, bumping along on the wind over the spruce and the high tundra, he said he did not really care now if a capital were to come springing up from the land below. The plan was "ridiculous" and "expensive," but if a new city was to be built, it would be "O.K. anywhere." He said, "The game is all gone, anyway. Those asses in Juneau won't let us hunt wolves from airplanes anymore. Three packs of wolves roam this area in winter and kill at least three moose a week—sometimes that many in one day. The fishing is going downhill, too, like everything else up here. When I came up here, you could catch fish till your arm was tired. That's Montana Creek down there. Used to be good. The air is cooler beyond Montana Creek. If you're driving south in the winter and it's, say, ten below in Talkeetna, it's suddenly forty below when you cross Montana Creek, and you feel the car tighten up—the steering gets stiff. Talkeetna is a little higher and warmer than the lower part of the valley." Montana Creek, having unglacial waters, was pebbly clear. A day or two before, I had caught a four-pound humpback salmon there.

The Roadhouse was a good place to stay. Climbers on the mountain had returned to the glacier, and were waiting day upon day for clear enough sky to get off; meanwhile, the Roadhouse, except at mealtime, was quiet. It was run, somewhat stringently, by Carroll Close and his wife, Verna, with an unnegotiable ten-thirty curfew, and signs here and there to remind you that you were not in your own home. "DON'T TOUCH." "NOTICE: In meeting the public the proprietors of this Roadhouse do not employ profane or obscene language. We ask you to display similar restraint while quartered here." At seven in the morning in an upstairs room, cracks in the floorboards become fumaroles of coffee, and the scent draws you down from the summit. In the kitchen, under racks of utensils, is a big wood stove, and Verna Close is sprinkling salt on its hot iron surface. She is dour, silent, stolid as a ceramic cat. She places thick slices of bread over the salt to toast. Each day, she bakes forty-six loaves of bread. Carroll Close, who is in his seventies and has been out splitting spruce, brings a load of it in and commits some to the fire. He is thin, thewy, with snowy hair and eyes that flash. With his wife, he makes and serves the standard breakfast: a mound of potatoes fried in white lard, scrambled eggs, four thick hunks of buttered toast, juice, coffee, ham, jam. Only a long-distance run at fifty below zero could work down such a meal, but the temperature outside is in the easygoing seventies and for the future there is no hope. There is dinner. No one is allowed to be late for dinner, so throughout the hour beforehand, in twos and threes, people drift in. They come from Talkeetna and from down the valley. Weekends, they come from Anchorage. They wait quietly in the sitting room before the unlighted face of the television, gray like the river ("DON'T TOUCH"), and at six they file to the table, and Carroll Close tells them where to sit. Eighteen is the capacity. Eighteen are there—around an oilcloth-covered table. They will make friends quickly. They are, for the most part, long in Alaska. But they are relatively silent in the early minutes of the meal, passing platters and bowls of potatoes, rice, meat-loaded gravy, beans, salad, corned beef, fried chicken, carrots, peas, bread, jam, and butter, leaving room for cake. And all the while Close circles the table, alert, attentive.

He came to Alaska from Oregon when he was in his thirties. I asked him, one afternoon, why. "Poverty," he said. When the war came, he found work around Anchorage, and eventually he had enough money to move north and, with his wife, buy the original part of the Roadhouse. He had built the extensions. "People voted five to one for statehood," he said. "You weren't a good citizen if you were against it. It was a lost cause."

"You were against statehood?"

"Oh, sure. Oh, sure. Before then, three-quarters of the people here weren't here. Eight or nine hundred people ran the Territory. Ten thousand now run the state. Where it used to take one person to investigate you, it now takes two to four. The state spends too much. If a tree blows down, two guys from the state come with a chain saw. The state has sold the state out. To the unions. To the oil companies. The oil companies have more power than the legislature. The capital move is a lot of talk. That's all it is, a lot of talk. What we need is not a new capital but better legislators than we have. I'd say leave the capital where it's at. The state can't afford it. There *is* no economy. They're dreaming about all this oil money. You do more good with a letter into Juneau than going there, anyway. Up here, we have the severest winters this side of the range. This is no place for a capital. If it does move, the proper place for it is in Anchorage."

He opened the stove and flung in some spruce. Spruce tends to be tough, stronger than most people who try to split it. "Since statehood," he said, "this country's went sour."

The unofficial mayor of Talkeetna was Evil Alice Powell. She did not seem to mind her nickname. She had worked, years ago, for the Alaska Territorial Department of Health in Anchorage —inspecting bars, bakeries, groceries, private sewage systems —and the doctor she worked for gave her the title because she scoured Augean Anchorage as few people have ever done. Her husband had come to Alaska as a highway- and railway-bridge engineer, and they moved out to Talkeetna in 1960.

She ran a sort of roadhouse up the road from the Roadhouse, but she had attempted to upgrade it with the word "motel." I found her there, ironing linen, and she said, "It's reached the point now where if someone wants to see an old-timer they come to me." She looked the part and she didn't—in slacks and a sweater, white hair streaked blond. She was small, gentle, amiable, accommodating, grandmotherly. Evil Alice. She said yes, the capital should move, and move up here to the valley. On various private and public missions, she had had it with Juneau—too hard to get there, too much chance of being weathered in there. Anybody in Talkeetna with a little property was for the capital move. The people who were not for it were "food-stampers" and "welfarers" and some of the hippies up the track, in cabins in the woods north of town. "They have Mary Jane and hard stuff up there," she said. "Some of them are on welfare, too. If the capital came, there might be a job and they'd have to go to work. Some are on the God Squad. They got religion a while back—Mickey Mouse religion—and they spun off from the others. A number came down to Talkeetna to live. A few work for me. They're O.K. I don't have to worry. They won't rip off the cigarettes and the booze."

She knew where the capital should be, she said. She had the spot picked out. It was just a few miles east of town. Talkeetna's air facilities could be expanded. Road and rail service already existed. Hydroelectric power could come from Devils Canyon, up the Big Su. Money had already been appropriated for a study of a dam there. The capital site she had in mind was up near the headwaters of Montana Creek, in a lovely world of birches, on elevated ground, with an unimpeded view of the mountain.

Alice Powell might have been holding a forked stick that had just swung down. The terrain she described had become prominent on a list of what the Capital Site Selection Committee called "footprints"—feasible, desirable places to build. The capital would be a footprint in the wilderness. On an earlier outing, the committee had flown in a helicopter to the top of Bald Mountain, seven miles east of Talkeetna, and there, from a vantage altitude of thirty-six hundred feet, had looked down on everything that had been ordered but a gold dome. It was heavily wooded country with few muskeg pockets and good soil. Divisioning the woodland, clear streams ran down out of the mountains—Sheep Creek, Montana Creek, Sheep River, Talkeetna River—and at the time they were viscous with salmon. One stream was interrupted by a three-mile lake—Larson Lake—which was only six hundred feet above sea level, was surrounded by spruce-and-birch forest, and had behind it a rising slope that yielded a view over the lake to the big river valley overtowered by the imminent Denali. The mean January temperature at Larson Lake is nine degrees; July, fifty-seven. Here and there in sight was a strip of homestead plowing, but virtually all the land in the immediate area was still untouched. This was fine moose range, too. Moose are up in the mountains in the summer, and they go down toward the Susitna in winter. Whatever a capital might do for people, it would surely repel wolves and thus, to an extent, be good for moose. As had been learned when oil wells were drilled south of Anchorage, in the Kenai National Moose Range, moose get along with progress.

Now, off to the left of the Twin Otter, the Talkeetna Mountains, behind Larson Lake, were topped with a dusting of snow, and along the whole range the snowline was drawn absolutely level somewhere near five thousand feet, as if someone painting a wall had carefully cut in with a brush to whiten just the high part. Gradually, through the autumn, the level line comes down—down the sides of the Alaska Range, down the Talkeetnas, down the Chugach Mountains in view of Anchorage. It is watched like a river gauge: six thousand feet, five thousand, four thousand, three. Day by day, it is somewhat lower, until the mountains are totally white. The snow then comes over the people. Six months. Then Alaska turns green again: green in the Susitna Valley, green in the Interior, the Arctic green and reddish and buff. The snow stays only in the high cols of most of the mountain chains but all over the peaks of the Alaska Range.

The Twin Otter, some minutes later, gave up altitude toward the southwest and approached the gravel airstrip at Skwentna. Some forty miles from the highway over streams and muskeg bogs and island patches of black spruce, Skwentna was an air and river stopping place, remote, unconnected. Willie Hensley said, "When these people find out who we are, they will probably run us off. They don't want their homesteads ruined." But the population of Skwentna, Alaska 99667 (fifteen people), was otherwise occupied, and the airstrip, when the Twin Otter engines shut down, was a silent clearing in the forest. A large percentage of a moose, reduced to bloody chunks, with flies on the chunks like cloves in ham, lay waiting on the ground for its hunter to return and fly it away. By prearrangement—the better to present certain landscapes for scrutiny—a big Bell Huey, a kind of helicopter that carried troops in Vietnam, was waiting for the committee. Its transmission was in the middle of the fuselage and resembled a home oil-burner of the vertical type, covered with heavy padding. The ceiling and interior walls were covered with the same padding, as if heavy furniture were about to go up in an elevator. Passenger seats were in two benchlike rows, facing one another. The committee compacted itself into the chopper, knees touching: Cook, Bettisworth, Ward, Hensley, Sturgulewski, Kellogg, Corbus. A flying quorum. Only two members had failed to join the day—Guy Martin, Alaska's Commissioner of Natural Resources, and Dwayne Carlson, an Anchorage carpenter who had reached a high position in the Alaska State Federation of Labor. The big Huey took off in its own din, and headed miscellaneously east and north, tilting now and again to circle a footprint—a site by a lake on the valley floor, a site on a high slope, a site by a gold-claim creek. Much of the way, great fingers of muskeg reached through the spruce like fairways—soft, morassic, mosquito muskeg, virtually construction-proof. Someone cried out above the engine noise, "Corbus, you're looking better all the time! There's not enough land suitable for building!" William Corbus did not disagree. His home was Juneau. For the better part of two years, he had concentratedly fought the capital move. He had helped found, and was chief financial officer of, Alaskans United, a statewide organization dedicated to snuffing out the idea. And now that the state had voted to move the capital, Corbus, paradoxically, had become a member of the committee to pick the new site. The initiative required that two members be from Southeastern Alaska, and one of these could hardly *not* be from Juneau. So Corbus had agreed to serve. He saw himself as a kind of monitor, attempting to make sure that the committee as a whole was "straightforward as to how much it's really going to cost the state to make the move." A modest, self-effacing man—with a young face, wide-eyed, blue-eyed, and with bits of an almost-crew haircut sticking up here and there—he was given to gray suits and striped ties, and carried himself in a manner that suggested an Ivy League athlete still in shape twenty years after college. He had gone to the Tuck School of Finance, at Dartmouth, and had worked for Stone & Webster Securities Corporation, in Manhattan, before deciding, in 1970, that he wanted to move to, as he put it, "a place where you could feel you were playing a bigger role." The roles he was playing in separate aspects of the capital situation caused no apparent conflict within him; and, like everyone on the committee, he actually enjoyed the work and—all other considerations aside—felt caught up in "an interesting intellectual exercise."

Natchez and other towns were, in turn, the capital of Mississippi until a three-member site-selection committee chose the place where Jackson was cleared in the woods. Columbus, Ohio, was a forest, too. Detroit, for many years, was the capital of Michigan. Villages in the Michigan interior feared and resented what was known as the "Detroit influence." People were jealous, and thought Detroit had enough. Someone in the legislature proposed moving the capital to the township of Lansing. This was regarded as a joke. *Lansing*? "Amid choking miasma . . . where the howl of wolves and the hissing of massaugas, and groans of bull frogs resound to the hammer of the woodpecker and the solitary note of the nightingale?" Lansing? "A howling wilderness?"

The other member from Southeastern Alaska was C. B. Bettisworth, who came from Ketchikan, which is about as close to Seattle as you can get and still be in Alaska. Bettisworth represented Southeastern, but he had a particular interest in Fairbanks, because Fairbanks was his home town. When votes were taken in committee meetings, his tended to follow the Fairbanks view. A young man with a beard and boots and wide-wale trousers and tumbling light-brown hair, he had a backpackery, environmental look, a suggestion in his face of early Lincoln. (Young Lincoln's first successful activity as an Illinois legislator was the moving of the capital from Vandalia to Springfield.) By training, Bettisworth was an architect and planner, and he seemed much absorbed in the selection process, the sheer excitement of pressing the land and releasing a city.

Earl Cook, of Fairbanks, did not seem to relish being up in the air—a sane reaction in this machine, which shivered and lurched like a long-since-depreciated railroad car, occasionally spilling everybody sidewise for selected glimpses of prime terrain. The cockpit was partitioned off, and for the passengers there was no view forward. Cook's smile had thinned with altitude. He was a slim man, with receding hair combed straight back, a real-estate man, who somehow seemed formal in a Levi jacket and Levi pants and hiking boots. He had been in Alaska thirty-seven years. He was an advocate of the capital move, and he still held hopes for a site on the Fairbanks side of the Alaska Range. Among his six children was a young accountant who, opposing the move, had helped organize the Fairbanks chapter of Alaskans United. Like father and son, Fairbanks as a whole had split on the issue, and Fairbanks' vote on the initiative was almost a balance, with a slight tip toward the proponent side.

Austin Ward—more or less a unit vote with Cook—was the other Fairbanksan on the committee. He came from Pontiac, Michigan, and had lived in Alaska twenty-two years. Light and compact, a haberdasher (and now wearing bright-red-and-gray checked slacks), he looked jaunty—if anyone could, shaking in the air—and a great deal jauntier after the helicopter touched down for recess near the summit of a long loaf of tundra called Little Peters Hills. The committee and its consultants—Barry Quinn, a planner; William Pyle, a geologist—bent their heads under the rotors and ran away from the machine a hundred yards or so, to a swale of relative quiet, although the constant roar of the vehicle was practically inescapable, even with the help of a mountain wind. The altitude was two thousand feet, and the view to the east, toward Talkeetna, was over moist green tundra and high red alpine tundra, with gray bedrock sticking through. To the north, the big white peaks were now partly visible, but only careful study of the sky would suggest what was cloud and what was mountain. Over broad miles of nearby tundra, isolated spruce stood like incense cones. On the low eastern slope of the hill were a couple of homesteads, neat in appearance, neatly sculptured out of the forest, and a clear rainbow stream—Peters Creek—with the core of a capital city in contemplation beside it. The committee was not contemplating much of anything, though. Voluble after their release from the helicopter, the people smoked and chattered and took one another's picture eating bearberries and blueberries. Some of the tundra blueberry plants were so small that an entire bush might consist of one short stem, like a golf tee, with a single blueberry, much larger than the bush itself, resting upon it. "You stay out of my berry field," said Arliss Sturgulewski, and Bill Pyle—short, dark, bearlike—shifted his forage.

Pyle had been assigned to the capital project by Dames & Moore, international experts in geophysics. Looking up from time to time and across the valley, he offhandedly indicated moraines that had been bulldozed by advancing ice, silt deposits in what had been lakes, the pitted outwash plains of melted glaciers. He was like a radiologist reading a picture. There were in this area some beautiful sites, he said, for vegetation and topography, but there were problems, too: an uncomfortable level of seismic risk, for one thing, and a few too many bogs, and possibilities of permafrost. We were beyond the area that was usually free of it. Pyle had been in Alaska fifteen years. With his bald pate and handlebar mustache, he appeared to have been there since the discovery of gold. He spoke not just with knowledge but with ample affection for the Alaskan land. He had worked for a time in Chicago, and when he left for Alaska someone asked him why he was going. He said, "If you have to ask that question, you wouldn't understand the answer."

Louise Kellogg, of Palmer (thirty-five miles northeast of Anchorage), had been a vigorous proponent of the capital move—unlike most of the committee. And now she smiled and said to me, "Has Willie brainwashed you yet?"

I said, "How would I know?"

Beyond the big Huey, on down the ridge, Willie Hensley stood alone, looking southeastward over the valley. In time, I left the berry-picking and went to join him. In his Western boots, his dungarees, his bright-red down jacket with blue-banded shoulders, he seemed somewhat incongruous there—an Eskimo, many miles from home, dressed apparently for a rodeo or a basketball game in which he might star. He was slender, physically adroit, and his high Mongolian cheekbones, his soft black hair ruffling in the wind, his Asian-mynabird look all seemed to suggest that he had recently walked across the land bridge to have a look around. Willie in the committee was first among equals. The others had long since made him their chairman.

Willie Hensley was born in Kotzebue, in Arctic Alaska, and grew up some ten miles out of town in a kind of family commune, with uncles, aunts, and cousins all around him as well as his immediate family. In winter, they lived in an *ivrulik*, which was an *iglu* made of sod. "*Iglu*" means "house"—any kind of house—and the kind that is made of blocks of snow in the shape of a dome was unknown to Willie, the nearest one being in Arctic Canada, more than a thousand miles away. Kotzebue was distant, too ("It seemed like a thousand miles"), and during Willie's early youth the whole family went there only twice a year, at Thanksgiving and at Christmas, for dinners, pageants, and the communal opening of what he remembers as "a mountain of gifts." All this took place in Friends Church—a mission derived from Whittier, California—and Willie grew up a titular Quaker, but the most lasting impression he took away with him was of the great amounts of food there: seal oil, piles of frozen fish to dip into the seal oil, and pyramids of berries—altogether "so much you took it home." The sod house was across an arm of Kotzebue Sound of the Chukchi Sea of the Arctic Ocean, two hundred miles from Siberia, six hundred miles from Anchorage. In chicken-wire traps the family caught whitefish in the late fall, and stored them in gunnysacks outside for the winter. Later on, they netted sheefish under the ice and stacked them up frozen, like cordwood. In summer they moved upriver—up the Noatak—and lived in tents, and hunted ducks and muskrats. In early fall, toward the end of August, they gathered berries and took them by the barrel back home.

They had no radio, no magazines, and, in Willie's words, "formal education was not that critical." There was a Bureau of Indian Affairs school in Kotzebue, and when Willie learned about it he decided, on his own, that he wanted to go there. He remembers his mother saying, "Go ahead. Go ahead, then. Go to school." He stayed with relatives in Kotzebue, and worked his way through what he has called "a highly sporadic primary education"—as little as a month a year. As he grew up, he became the family scribe.

Kotzebue is in an election district that is larger than most of the states of the United States, yet its population warrants only one representative in Alaska's forty-member House. In 1966, Willie—age twenty-five—was elected to the job. Two years later, he was head of the Democratic Party in Alaska. In 1970, he was elected to the Alaska Senate. In all, he spent eight years—eight legislative sessions—in Juneau. He emerged with certain goods. He brought high schools to his district, and a radio station (KOTZ) to Kotzebue, and an old people's home. He made himself unpopular with the liquor lobby by sponsoring legislation that created municipally owned liquor licenses, with the idea that communities could derive money from liquor sales and use it to pay the costs that liquor incurs. He brought electric generators to small villages in the north. But with all this, he seldom brought himself. Juneau was a thousand miles from Kotzebue, and he could rarely afford the trip. Nonetheless, when the initiative to move the capital came along he decided that in the interests of the Alaskan treasury the capital should remain in Juneau.

In 1974, he ran for Alaska's single seat in the United States House of Representatives. The capital-move initiative had been on the primary ballot, and Hensley had spoken against it wherever he went. He thought that Alaska, whose budget had more than quadrupled in a few years' time, was heading for failure and could ill afford to crown it with a billion-dollar capital city. Privately, he regarded his achievements in the legislature as "crumbs" begged for and sent back to his people. If so much money were to go for a capital, he feared for the faraway villages. There would be funds not even for crumbs. "When there is a budget crunch, the bush loses," he said. He compared the capital-movers to a young couple whose eyes shine at the prospect of a new house but who find themselves unable to cope with the terms of the mortgage. A federal building then projected for Anchorage was going to cost at least a hundred million dollars. So how much would an entire city cost? If Alaska were to build a capital, state-federal sharing money would be applied to the airport, utilities, highways, housing —money that would otherwise go to existing communities. The capital-move prevailed, but Hensley lost. Before long, he found himself on the Capital Site Selection Committee, the lone native, the lone northwestern member.

I had met him for the first time some months after the election, quite by chance, in Kotzebue, where he was trailing a cone of dust from his Chevrolet pickup, in a town whose streets—four hundred miles from the nearest highway—were connected only to themselves. He stopped at the airfield to complete an errand, and I talked with him briefly and wondered if his attitudes about the capital had changed since the election. He said that, like everyone else on the committee, he had become caught up by the inherent excitement in the idea of creating a new town, but he was still a pessimist about the financial future of Alaska, and nothing had happened to alter that view. Kotzebue was almost painfully decibelled, Yamahas and Hondas ratchetting the air. I was struck, the more, by the lilting modulation of Hensley's voice, calm as (that day) the Chukchi Sea. Detached humor played across his eyes. He said he would like to see a new referendum on a future ballot presenting to Alaskan voters a more extensive set of choices. Choice No. 1: Juneau. Choice No. 2: Anchorage. Choice No. 3: A wholly new capital city, its cost realistically estimated and included on the ballot. Cost—the essential factor—was being too widely ignored, he said. "In Alaska, too many people seem to think they are floating to Heaven on a sea of oil."

If Boston was once the most provincial place in America (the story goes that after a six-megaton bomb exploded in Times Square a headline in a Boston paper would say, "HUB MAN KILLED IN NEW YORK BLAST"), Alaska, in this respect, may have replaced Boston. In Alaska, the conversation is Alaska.

Alaskans, by and large, seem to know little and to say less about what is going on outside. They talk about their land, their bears, their fish, their rivers. They talk about subsistence hunting, forbidden hunting, and living in trespass. They have their own lexicon. A senior citizen is a pioneer, snow is termination dust, and the N.B.A. is the National Bank of Alaska. The names of Alaska are so beautiful they run like fountains all day in the mind. Mulchatna. Chilikadrotna. Unalaska. Unalakleet. Kivalina. Kiska. Kodiak. Allakaket. The Aniakchak Caldera. Nondalton. Anaktuvuk. Anchorage. Alaska is a foreign country significantly populated with Americans. Its languages extend to English. Its nature is its own. Nothing seems so unexpected as the boxes marked "U.S. Mail." Alaskans talk and talk about their pipeline—about the big welders from Tulsa ("Animals, sheer animals"), whose power showdowns with the Teamsters so terrified the Teamsters that the Teamsters turned to petroleum jelly. Years in advance, they talked about the royalties the pipeline would bring them, and, to some extent, about the devastation it could bring to Prince William Sound, which, starred with islands, is one of the marine splendors of the subarctic.

"*There* is the real problem—not the possible spills on land but the spills that could happen in Prince William Sound."

In recent time, the entrenched, traditional boomers of Alaska, the develop-it majority, have been challenged by a growing body of people who wonder if the boom philosophy is good for the state. Fairbanks, under the impact of the pipeline, has become (in Willie Hensley's word) "scroungy"—prostitutes, Texans, ticky-tacky. Maybe Alaska should take a more circumspect look before entering such arrangements again. This was the novel body of thought that helped to produce the 1974 election victory of Governor Jay Hammond—fisherman, homesteader, wilderness man. Hammond was hardly a fierce and fighting conservationist. Alaska had not molted. But Hammond's prudent, balanced approach to things was an attempt to reconcile what his first Commerce Commissioner, Langhorne Motley, once called "the Sierra Club syndrome and the Dallas scenario." In the ongoing debate about the new capital, among all the varied reasons for and against the move, those two strands were prominently braided.

"The new capital will be a growth center for Alaska. It will take the pressure off Anchorage."

"In a state this size, if you put everything in one area you detract from the reasons we're all here. The new capital won't be all that far from Anchorage. You put all the people in one place, you create an unattractive state, and you pull out the employment from people who would like to live in the Juneau area."

"Juneau will die."

"The people of Alaska have mandated this, and the people of Alaska have darned good judgment."

"I don't think anyone is smart enough to plan a place like that. In Valdez, after the '64 earthquake, up we went and moved the city. Four or five miles, to a safer place. What a mess! The new Valdez is full of cul-de-sacs. What do you do with twenty-five feet of snow at the end of a cul-de-sac? A mess. And I was the mayor."

"Places like that are sterile. Salt Lake is the only planned city worth a damn. Have you ever seen a town planned by an American planner?"

"Savannah was sketched out in England."

"The purpose is better government. Move the seat of government to the Susitna Valley and seventy per cent of the population is within driving distance."

"Legislators could drive home for the weekend to Fairbanks, Homer, and anywhere between. To Anchorage they could drive home evenings."

"You want to drive home evenings at fifty below?"

"Try flying to Juneau. Socked in. You end up in Seattle."

"Lobby groups have an advantage in Juneau. They can afford to stay there, and they are unhampered by people coming down and butting in. They have the legislators to themselves."

"The highway people down there have to fly five hundred miles to see the roads they're working on."

"People voted for the move because they thought the money would be coming in. It won't be there. We have virtually already spent the money from the pipeline. To me, it's that bleak. The state has been taking in about three hundred million a year—from petroleum revenues, highway-fuel revenues, income tax—and it is spending five hundred million. By 1980, Alaska's annual expenditures will be around one billion.

The legislature spends money faster than they can get it, and nobody sees where it goes. To try to cover themselves, they hit the oil companies. They enacted a reserves tax on oil that is still in the ground, deductible from future royalties. I guess it's legal, but it sure doesn't sound moral."

"The state parking garage in Fairbanks cost four and a quarter million—or fourteen thousand dollars a parking slot. So who can pay for a city?"

"Having Juneau the capital provides one more reason for tourists to travel around the state."

"Putting it up here near Anchorage is like putting the barn close to the fields. Better, more responsible people would agree to be legislators. Doctors and lawyers are out of business when they're in Juneau."

"The new city would grow here, grow naturally, the way Alaska will grow."

"Not so fast! The flow of oil will not do everything. We'd better sit back and look at our hole card."

There are those who would say that tens of thousands of barrels of oil erupting from a break in the Trans-Alaska Pipeline would be the lesser accident if, at more or less the same time, a fresh Anchorage were to spill into the bush. While the dream of the capital city plays on in the mind, Anchorage stands real. It is the central hive of human Alaska, and in manner and structure it represents, for all to see, the Alaskan dynamic and the Alaskan aesthetic. It is a tangible expression of certain Alaskans' regard for Alaska—their one true city, the exemplar of the predilections of the people in creating improvements over the land.

As may befit a region where both short and long travel is generally by air, nearly every street in Anchorage seems to be the road to the airport. Dense groves of plastic stand on either side—flashing, whirling, flaky. HOOSIER BUDDY'S MOBILE HOMES. WINNEBAGO SALES & SERVICE. DISCOUNT LIQUORS OPEN SUNDAY. GOLD RUSH AUTO SALES. PROMPT ACTION LOCKSMITHS. ALASKA REFRIGERATION & AIR CONDITION. DENALI FUEL . . .

"Are the liquor stores really open Sundays?"

"Everything in Anchorage is open that pays."

Almost all Americans would recognize Anchorage, because Anchorage is that part of any city where the city has burst its seams and extruded Colonel Sanders.

"You can taste the greed in the air."

BELUGA ASPHALT.

Anchorage is sometimes excused in the name of pioneering. Build now, civilize later. But Anchorage is not a frontier town. It is virtually unrelated to its environment. It has come in on the wind, an American spore. A large cookie cutter brought down on El Paso could lift something like Anchorage into the air. Anchorage is the northern rim of Trenton, the center of Oxnard, the ocean-blind precincts of Daytona Beach. It is condensed, instant Albuquerque.

PANCHO'S VILLA, MEXICAN FOOD. BULL SHED, STEAK HOUSE AND SONIC LOUNGE. SHAKEY'S DRIVE-IN PIZZA. EAT ME SUBMARINES.

Anchorage has developed a high-rise city core, with glass-box offices for the oil companies, and tall Miamian hotels. Zonelessly lurching outward, it has made of its suburbs a carnival of cinder block, all with a speculative mania so rife that sellers of small homesites—of modest lots scarcely large enough for houses—retain subsurface rights. In vacant lots, queen-post trusses lie waiting for new buildings to jump up beneath them. Roads are rubbled, ponded with chuckholes. Big trucks, graders, loaders, make the prevailing noise, the dancing fumes, the frenetic beat of the town. Huge rubber tires are strewn about like quoits, ever ready for the big machines that move hills of earth and gravel into inconvenient lakes, which become new ground.

FOR LEASE. WILL BUILD TO SUIT.

Anchorage coins millionaires in speculative real estate. Some are young. The median age in Anchorage is under twenty-four. Every three or four years, something like half the population turns over. And with thirty days of residence, you can vote as an Alaskan.

POLAR REALTY. IDLE WHEELS TRAILER PARK. MOTEL MUSH INN.

Anchorage has a thin history. Something of a precursor of the modern pipeline camps, it began in 1914 as a collection of tents pitched to shelter workers building the Alaska Railroad. For decades, it was a wooden-sidewalked, gravel-streeted town. Then, remarkably early, as cities go, it developed an urban slum, and both homes and commerce began to abandon its core. The exodus was so rapid that the central business district never wholly consolidated, and downtown Anchorage is even more miscellaneous than outlying parts of the city. There is, for example, a huge J. C. Penney department store filling several blocks in the heart of town, with an interior mall of boutiques and restaurants and a certain degree of chic. A couple of weedy vacant lots separate this complex from five log cabins. Downtown Anchorage from a distance displays an upreaching skyline that implies great pressure for land. Down below, among the high buildings, are houses, huts, vegetable gardens, and bungalows with tidy front lawns. Anchorage burst out of itself and left these incongruities in the center, and for me they are the most appealing sights in Anchorage. Up against a downtown office building I have seen cordwood stacked for winter.

In its headlong, violent expansion, Anchorage had considerable, but not unlimited, space to fill. To an extent unusual among cities, Anchorage has certain absolute boundaries, and in that sense its growth has been a confined explosion. To the north, a pair of military bases establish, in effect, a Roman wall. To the west and south, fjordlike arms of the Pacific—Knik Arm, Turnagain Arm—frame the city. Behind Anchorage, east, stand the Chugach Mountains, stunning against the morning and in the evening light—Mount Magnificent, Mount Gordon Lyon, Temptation Peak, Tanaina Peak, Wolverine Peak, the Suicide Peaks. Development has gone to some extent upward there. Houses are pushpinned to the mountainsides—a Los Angelized setting, particularly at night, above the starry lights of town. But the mountains are essentially a full stop to Anchorage, and Anchorage has nowhere else to go.

Within this frame of mountains, ocean, and military boundaries are about fifty thousand acres (roughly the amount of land sought by the Capital Site Selection Committee), and the whole of it is known as the Anchorage Bowl. The ground itself consists of silt, alluvium, eolian sands, glacial debris—material easy to rearrange. The surface was once lumpy with small knolls. As people and their businesses began filling the bowl, they went first to the knolls, because the knolls were wooded and well drained. They cut down the trees, truncated the hills, and bestudded them with buildings. They strung utility lines like baling wire from knoll to knoll. The new subdivisions within the bowl were thus hither and yon, random, punctuated with bogs. Anchorage grew like mold.

WOLVERINE ALUMINUM SIDING. ALASKA FOUR-WHEEL DRIVE. JACK BENNY'S RADIO-DISPATCHED CESSPOOL PUMPING.

Low ground is gradually being filled. The bowl has about a hundred and eighty thousand people now, or almost half of human Alaska. There are some in town—notably, Robert Atwood, of the *Times*—who would like to see Anchorage grow to seven hundred thousand. Atwood is a big, friendly, old-football-tackle sort of man, with whitening hair and gold-rimmed glasses. Forty years on the inside, this impatient advocate of the commercial potentialities of Alaska is said to be one of the two wealthiest people in the state, the other being his brother-in-law. "Idealists here in town see a need for a park in every housing development," Atwood told me one day. "They want to bury utility lines, reserve green belts, build bicycle paths. With these things, the bowl could only contain three hundred and fifty thousand. They're making it very difficult for man, these people. They favor animals, trees, water, flowers. Who ever makes a plan for man? Who ever *will* make a plan for man? That is what *I* wonder. I am known among conservationists as a bad guy."

In Anchorage, if you threw a pebble into a crowd, chances are you would not hit a conservationist, an ecophile, a wilderness preserver. In small ghettos, they are there—living in a situation lined with irony. They are in Alaska—many of them working for the federal government—because Alaska is everything wild it has ever been said to be. Alaska runs off the edge of the imagination, with its tracklessness, its beyond-the-ridgeline surprises, its hundreds of millions of acres of wilderness—this so-called "last frontier," which is certainly all of that, yet for the most part is not a frontier at all but immemorial landscape in an all but unapproached state. Within such vastness, Anchorage is a mere pustule, a dot, a minim—a walled city, wild as Yonkers, with the wildlife riding in a hundred and ninety-three thousand trucks and cars. Yet the city—where people are, where offices are—is perforce the home address of wilderness planners, of wildlife biologists, of Brooks Range guides.

The first few days I spent in Alaska were spent in Anchorage, and I remember the increasing sense of entrapment we felt (my wife was with me), knowing that nothing less than a sixth of the entire United States, and almost all of it wilderness, was out there beyond seeing, while immediate needs and chores to do were keeping us penned in this portable Passaic. Finally, we couldn't take it any longer, and we cancelled appointments and rented a car and revved it up for an attempted breakout from town. A float plane—at a hundred and ten dollars an hour—would have been the best means, but, like most of the inmates of Anchorage, we could not afford it. For a great many residents, Anchorage is about all they ever see of Alaska, day after day after year. There are only two escape routes—a road north, a road south—and these are encumbered with traffic and, for some miles anyway, lined with detritus from Anchorage. We went south, that first time, and eventually east, along a fjord that would improve Norway. Then the road turned south again, into the mountains of Kenai—great tundra balds that reminded me of Scotland and my wife of parts of Switzerland, where she had lived. She added that she thought these mountains looked better than the ones in Europe. Sockeyes, as red as cardinals, were spawning in clear, shallow streams, and we ate our cheese and chocolate in a high meadow over a torrential river of green and white water. We looked up to the ridges for Dall sheep, and felt, for the moment, about as free. Anchorage shrank into perspective. It might be a sorry town, but it has the greatest out-of-town any town has ever had.

BIG RED'S FLYING SERVICE. BELUGA STEAM & ELECTRIC THAWING. DON'T GO TO JAIL LET FRED GO YOUR BAIL.

There is a street in Anchorage—a green-lights, red-lights, busy street—that is used by automobiles and airplanes. I remember an airplane in someone's driveway—next door to the house where I was staying. The neighbor started up its engine one night toward eleven o'clock, and for twenty minutes he ran it flat out while his two sons, leaning hard into the stabilizers, strained to hold back the plane. In Alaska, you do what you feel like doing, or so goes an Alaskan creed.

There is, in Anchorage, a somewhat Sutton Place. It is an enclave, actually, with several roads, off the western end of Northern Lights Boulevard, which is a principal Anchorage thoroughfare, a neon borealis. Walter Hickel lives in the enclave, on Loussac Drive, which winds between curbs and lawns, neatly trimmed, laid out, and landscaped, under white birches and balsam poplars. Hickel's is a heavy, substantial home, its style American Dentist. The neighbors' houses are equally expensive and much the same. The whole neighborhood seems to be struggling to remember Scarsdale. But not to find Alaska.

I had breakfast one morning in Anchorage with a man who had come to Alaska from The Trust for Public Land, an organization whose goal is to buy potential parkland in urban areas and hold it until the government, whose legislative machinery is often too slow for the land market, can get up the funds for the purpose. In overbuilt urban settings—from Watts to Newark and back to Oakland—The Trust for Public Land will acquire whatever it can, even buildings under demolishment, in order to create small parks and gardens that might relieve the compressed masses. And now The Trust for Public Land had felt the need to come to Anchorage—to the principal city of Alaska—to help hold a pond or a patch of green for the people in the future to have and see.

Books were selling in Anchorage, once when I was there, for forty-seven cents a pound.

There are those who would say that the only proper place for a new capital of Alaska—if there has to be a new one—is Anchorage, because anyone who has built a city like Anchorage should not be permitted to build one anywhere else.

At Anchorage International Airport, there is a large aerial photograph of Anchorage formed by pasting together a set of pictures that were made without what cartographers call ground control. This great aerial map is one of the first things to confront visitors from everywhere in the world, and in bold letters it is titled "ANCHORAGE, ALASKA. UNCONTROLLED MOSAIC."

To place its government nearer the center of things, Missouri moved its capital from St. Charles to Jefferson City; West Virginia from Wheeling to Charleston; South Carolina from Charleston to Columbia; North Carolina from New Bern to Raleigh. The first capital of California was San Jose. Then General Mariano Vallejo offered to underwrite a new capital in, as it happened, Vallejo. The capital soon moved to Benicia, to Sacramento. New York has moved its capital more times than can conveniently be counted. New York City, White Plains, Harlem, Fishkill, Kingston, Marbletown, Hurley, Poughkeepsie . . . When you have been espoused that often, you are possibly in no hurry to make matters legal the next time around. Such was the case with Albany. The legislation designating Albany the capital of New York was finally written and passed in 1971. Santa Fe became the capital of the Kingdom of New Mexico ten years before Plymouth Rock.

Now, from the Arctic to Southeastern, the committee had been holding "workshop hearings," inviting and even recruiting people to come and help "relocate" the capital of Alaska. The total attendance each evening would first be separated into small conversational units, and after an hour or so of that a mass parliamentary fracas would follow, during which the various groups reported what had turned up in their discussions.

"Our group is not really familiar with the Susitna area. To us, it's a swamp."

"A swamp is an appropriate place for government."

"Swamp or no swamp, get those legislators up here where we can watch them."

"Even if we don't go to see them many times during a session, just the thought that we can will keep them on their toes."

Maps were put up on the walls, and people were invited to offer their suggestions on the maps. Someone drew an X in the ocean near Anchorage and wrote, "Just the place for watered-down politicians."

Someone else said, "Put the capital on a barge. It can travel around the state."

Quickly the maps were covered with advice.

"Put the money into education."

"Why destroy one town and at the same time destroy more wild land to build another?"

"Don't mess up more of Alaska."

"I strongly suggest that the capital not be placed in a wilderness site. We are not Brazil. I don't think we need a new city in Alaska."

Brasília, unsurprisingly, had been much on the minds of Alaskans, and they tended to assess Brasília in the light of their opinions of the Alaskan initiative. Certain promoters of the new city recommended that the Capital Site Selection Committee go to Brasília to see a vital new capital at work. Others believed what they had read, and saw Brasília as an airplane (it is laid out in the shape of an airplane) that had made a long flight inland and crashed.

In one of the seminar discussions in a workshop hearing I attended, everyone kept nodding in agreement as grandiose assumptions circled the table.

"I don't know if anybody should even bother to figure the cost of something as important as this."

"We're going to be Arabs when the royalties come from the pipeline."

"Alaska will be another Saudi Arabia."

Then someone compared Anchorage to the slums around Brasília.

Someone else said, "Yes sirree. What we do not need is a Brasília in our wilderness."

And someone else said, "At least, we should profit by others' mistakes."

Whereupon a distinguished-looking gray-haired man, whose spine was straighter than a T-square, straightened it a little more and gave a short-bark cough for attention. He appeared to have received in his lifetime an unquestioning lot of attention. He said firmly that he felt the moment had come for him to make himself known. His name was B. B. Talley, he said, and he lived in Kenai and was a retired brigadier general in the United States Army Corps of Engineers. During the Second World War, he had built bases in Alaska. Later on, as a civilian contractor, he had been "in on the planning of Brasília from beginning to end." When building began, his company was the only foreign firm with a construction contract there. "We poured the concrete for Brasília."

He paused, and looked around the table. A woman across from him said, "Beg your pardon, sir. Are you bragging or complaining?"

General Talley went on to say that Brasília had been placed far out in the wilderness because various parts of Brazil despise one another and would agree only on a wilderness site. Surely, he said, that's not the case in Alaska.

"Begging your pardon, sir. It surely is."

Canberra, to a lesser extent, came into the workshop conversations. Canberra, set in the Australian bush between Sydney and Melbourne, had been designed in Chicago by Walter Burley Griffin and had won, through the years, the acceptance of Australians. A somewhat sterile place, undeniably attractive, it has tended to depress some visitors because it offers nothing but government, no relief from government.

In groups formal and informal, small and large, however, the city that was talked about more than any other was Juneau.

"Juneau will be decimated in its spirit as well as in its pocket-book."

"Juneau's fishing industry is almost gone. The gold mine closed thirty years ago. The logging industry is down—cut down by the Sierra Club. What a shame! The timber is rotting on the vine."

"The capital is Juneau's only economic base."

"They will move the capital over my dead body."

"That condition is acceptable."

"This move in effect puts up a fence across the hundred-and-forty-first meridian and says, 'We don't care what happens to you in Southeastern Alaska.'"

"Juneau snatched the capital from Sitka in 1900. They lobbied secretly in Washington."

"Anchorage thinks Juneau exercises an undue and malign influence over the entire state—in matters of money, land speculation, capital improvements."

"Juneau, with the legislature, has had more than its share of appropriated funds. People want to get the money up here in Anchorage."

"People maneuver, and they put on masks to cloak their maneuvers. Those behind the scenes don't really want to have the legislature close to the people, but that's been the way to peddle the move. What they want is the money."

"To make a power play work, you have to give lip service to the people."

"Juneau will survive. Many government employees will stay there in service jobs for Southeastern."

"Tourists will still come. Every spring, they can't wait, in Juneau, for the legislators to leave, so they can fill the houses with tourists."

"Juneau will just have to broaden its base."

"Long before Juneau was ever the capital, Juneau was making a living."

"They might even start digging some more gold out down there and spending it up here in Alaska."

Gold prospectors in the nineteenth century had little to go on except an association of gold with quartz and pyrite, and, since that required neither a great deal of intelligence nor academic training, many gold prospectors were the sort of people who had little to go on whatsoever. Two such were Richard Harris and Joe Juneau, whose most noted employer described Harris as "an inveterate drunkard" and said of Juneau, "Between hooch and squaws he never had a cent to get away on."

The employer was George Pilz, a mining engineer who set up a mill near Sitka to extract gold from bearing rock. Sitka, in the Alexander Archipelago, had been the Russian capital and was now the American capital of Alaska. The year was 1879, and three events of that season led, ultimately, to the moving of the capital away from Sitka. First, Kowee, principal chief of the Auks, travelled a hundred and fifty miles to Sitka to show the mining engineer certain rock he had collected along Gastineau Channel, near his home. Pilz had promised a hundred Hudson's Bay blankets and steady employment to any tribe that led him to a place where mining could successfully follow. Kowee wanted the work and the blankets. Then, by odd coincidence, the naturalist John Muir passed by on an eight-hundred-mile canoe trip. He reported that he had been through Gastineau Channel and had seen interesting mineralization there. And, third, Joe Juneau and Dick Harris—each about forty-five years old—came wobbling down a gangplank off a ship from Wrangell. They owed the purser and the captain for passage, and they were looking around for work.

There was no special hurry about checking out the leads of Muir and Kowee. Pilz had prospectors all over the archipelago—from the Taku Inlet to the Peril Strait, Admiralty Island, Chichagof Island—playing hunches or following the reports and hunches of others. He grubstaked prospectors and salaried them at four dollars a day. In return, he reserved the right to choose two claims from every three they might make. He himself was little more than a middleman. He had to go to the merchants of Sitka, or even to San Francisco, for money to keep all his prospectors active. In attempting to cover an archipelago four hundred miles in length, Pilz in his employment practices could not impose high standards. He took what came along. Joe Juneau and Dick Harris had been around mining camps much of their lives, and they had come along.

Harris had been educated—Girard College, Philadelphia. Juneau had avoided school. He had fished and hunted, and projected himself into later life able only to write a little French. Harris had a large nose and lenticular eye sockets and a certain look—in the wings of the mustache, perhaps—of the schemingly disenchanted. Juneau—slim, sad-eyed Juneau, lip hair tumbling, crown hair short and flat—appeared to be a Yonne Valley farmer, an eel fisherman, the mayor of an embarrassed village, a waiter in a one-fork brasserie. Actually, he was born near Quebec and raised in Wisconsin, where his uncle, Solomon Juneau, built the first cabin in what is now Milwaukee but did not have the honor of seeing his name transferred to the town. In July, 1880, Harris and Juneau set out from Sitka Harbor with three months' provisions. Following a northeasterly route, they panned streams here and there but came up with only "light prospects"—some float quartz and colors of gold, but not enough for a profitable claim. They had several Auks with them, who were guiding for one dollar, a few hardtacks, and a cup of seal oil per day. The Auks took Harris and Juneau to Auk Village, and the two prospectors then spent three weeks in a condition—even by the standards of the Indians who would tell the story—of total bibacity. The Indians of the archipelago distilled a drink they called *hoochinoo*. They were adding its first syllable to the American language, with the help of Harris and Juneau. The prospectors paid with equipment and grub, and to buy more drink, and squaw-pleasures as well, they gave up more food, more equipment, until, scarcely a month out of Sitka, their three months' supplies were all but gone. Moreover, they lost their boat. It floated away with the tide in mid-binge. So, having no alternative, they decided to return to Sitka. They paid the tribe a rifle to take them home. But first the Indians took them down Gastineau Channel to a small anchorage near the mouth of a stream.

Its water ran white over ledges of rock and down through the cleavage of two sheer mountains—mountainsides stiff with big Sitka spruce, rising on up to avalanchine balds with declivities so steep that brooks fell down them in veils. When you look up from the streets of Juneau, that is what you see, for Juneau is compacted where the mountains touch, and the mountains loom behind the town in shades of green with snow-covered summits and alpine ice. The channel, Gastineau, is deep-water and blue, three-quarters of a mile wide, nineteen miles long, mountainsided all the way. Big white ships come up the channel to the town. In the opposite direction, sometimes, travel the Taku winds—off Taku Glacier, some thousands of feet above—winds so fierce and flattening that in 1880 it was on some days impossible to build a fire, and tents were not up long before they blew away. A pedestrian today in Juneau, head down and charging, can be stopped for no gain by the wind. There are railings along the streets by which senators and representatives can haul themselves to work. In recent years, a succession of wind gauges were placed on a ridge above the town. They could measure velocities up to two hundred miles per hour. They did not survive. The Taku winds tore them apart after driving their indicators to the end of the scale. The weather is not always, or even generally, so bad; but under its influence the town took shape, and so Juneau is a tight community of adjacent buildings and narrow European streets, adhering to its mountainsides and fronting the salt water.

There is a characteristic, too, of frequent rain. It rains in Juneau about two hundred and twenty days a year. Clouds hang like bunting on the mountains. Many sidewalks of the town are covered with permanent roofs that are cantilevered from building sides and held in place by coupled rods. Houses go unpainted, because it is so hard to find an appropriate time to paint them. Old-timers, eating halibut cheeks in the City Cafe, talk about putting a dome over Juneau. Rain does not fall around the clock, however, and the weather will shift with tonic swiftness, the gray above the channel brightening to cotton and tearing apart to show blue sky, with tilted shafts of sunlight coming through, a rainbow forming.

There is no permafrost in Juneau. It is six hundred miles from the Arctic Circle. The temperature in winter seldom goes below zero, and in summer it holds under eighty. Out past the airport are forested bays that suggest Washington, Oregon, northern California, with the difference that the Mendenhall Glacier approaches them—all blue ice and powdered rock, like a huge white earth-fill dam. In streams near the glacier run cutthroat trout and Dolly Vardens two feet long. When the king salmon come into nearby waters they weigh as much as eighty pounds.

Juneau, bright at night from across the channel, is dense and galactic under the dark shapes of the mountains. From the same perspective in the day—with its ships at wharfside, its small-craft anchorage, its buildings all crowded before an uprising wilderness—it is a pocket city in a setting as wondrous as the setting of a city could ever be. Juneau is Alaskan, and American, and it has its oil-storage tanks in the heart of town. It holds its own in junk and crud. Gold Creek, the rushing stream that was named by Harris and Juneau, now runs through town in a concrete trough, a large storm sewer. The State Capitol is a six-story yellow brick-and-limestone building with big windows of the sort that are opened with a pole. In appearance, it is an abandoned junior high school. The governor's mansion is Southern and decadent, tired in its innards. On the edge of town is the abandoned mine—abandoned during the Second World War—of the Alaska-Juneau Gold Mining Company, a flooded ruin now, fronting the mountain like the façade of a theatre that has long since played its last show. From Calhoun Avenue to Willoughby Avenue, old wooden steps go far down the cliffside and around the new State Office Building, which soars into the air and goes down the hill, too. People approaching the building on the uphill side walk in on the eighth floor—into a high atrium of light and space, of glass-walled, unpartitioned offices that look down into the interior as well as out upon the mountains and the channel. A sign on the ground floor says, "POSITIVELY NO DOGS." So much for old Alaska.

After the United States bought the territory from Russia, Juneau was the first city to be founded there. Juneau was also the first city in Alaska to be founded in result of a discovery of gold.

Through the cleft in the mountains, the two prospectors went up the stream a mile and more, panning. They found promising color in their pans, and in the creek bed "very good float gold quartz." And, having done that and no more, they left. Back to Sitka went Richard Harris and Joe Juneau. They had staked no claims. They had gone only a short way upstream. They had only guessed at the gold beyond. Hungry, hung over, out of hooch and barter, they—prospectors!—had found the underbrush forbidding, the going too tough, so they had taken with them a hundred pounds of the river quartz and departed.

Chief Kowee, amazed, saw his chances for a hundred blankets going straight down the channel with these fools. So he chased after them to Sitka and complained to the mining engineer that Harris and Juneau had not been inclined to follow him far enough upstream, and he laid on the table some rich gold quartz as an example of what was there. Pilz arranged the grubstake for another expedition, and he paid for a canoe. For prospectors, now, in the fall, with the season running short, he had to use whatever he could find, and the pickings were limited to Harris and Juneau. After naming the canoe the Alaska Chief of Gold Creek, they started out in mid-September from Sitka.

Chief Kowee made extremely sure this time that they found the proper gold. En route, they prospected a stream or two that they had prospected before, apparently not remembering where they had been. But the guiding Indians firmly led them on to the small anchorage in Gastineau Channel near the stream they had named Gold Creek. This time they went for the headwaters, and the brush was indeed so dense that to get around it they went up a gulch—calling it Snowslide Gulch—and on up the mountainside to a commanding view of an El Dorado. It was a stream-sculptured dish of ground into which long eras of erosion—glacial, fluvial, ice-spall erosion—had (from the mineralized mountains) poured a deep filling of gravels of gold. "I broke some with a hammer and Juneau and myself could hardly believe our eyes. We knew it was gold, but so much and not in particles, streaks running through the rock and little lumps as large as peas or beans." (These quotations are from "The Founding of Juneau," a careful history by R. N. De Armond which was published in 1967 by the Gastineau Channel Centennial Association.) In days that followed, claims were staked in the names of Juneau and Harris and their assorted grubstakers, backers, and creditors. Harris called a meeting—consisting of himself, Juneau, and three Indians—to formalize a code of local laws, the usual procedure under the Mining Act of 1872. Harris took the power job—district recorder—and two hundred square miles around the discovery was designated the Harris Mining District. Then, beside Gastineau Channel, a townsite of a hundred and sixty acres was staked and claimed. The name given the town was Harrisburgh. Pressed, at a later date, for his reasons for choosing that name, Harris said he wished to honor the state of Pennsylvania. Five bona-fide miners—not two miners and three Indians—were by custom required for the approval of a code of laws; and as the gold rush developed in Harrisburgh other miners quickly challenged Harris's power and, in the process, relieved the town of his name. The honor was transferred to Juneau. In a dispute about overlapping claims, the new Alaska court system a few years later deprived Harris of nearly all his property in and around the town. He eventually died in a sanatorium in Oregon, his way there paid by friends. Juneau died in Dawson, in Yukon Territory, after a lifetime in the wild, always, but perhaps not primarily, in search of gold. It was his wish to be buried in Juneau, and four hundred dollars was raised there to bring the body south. In 1900, the year after he died, the town became the capital of Alaska.

The man who caused the initiative to select a new capital for Alaska to be placed on the 1974 ballot—the man who took up the idea and organized a group of volunteer workers and collected signatures and raised money and administered the entire successful procedure—was named, as it happens, Harris. He was not a descendant of the eponymous Harris of Harrisburgh. He had found his own lode in Anchorage in the nineteen-forties when he quit as a deliveryman for a dry-cleaning company and, with another driver, borrowed something over three thousand dollars and started the Alaska Cleaners, 610 Fireweed, Anchorage—a hanging-clothes forest, wherein someone presses a button and twenty miles of garments begin to move. Frank Harris is a lean man, bald, gentle in voice, with long jaws, an English face. He was elected to the Alaska State Senate in 1966, defeated in 1968. The urge to move the capital came over him during those two years. Sessions began in January and ran on at least three months (of late they have been extending through June), and Harris in Juneau developed what he called "a complete feeling of isolation—stuck there." He found Juneau "a dilapidated city, buildings unpainted, streets dirty, sidewalks crumbling," and could not imagine "people having pride in a state capital in such condition." He lived in a big concrete coop that was painted pink—the Mendenhall Apartments. The wind blew so hard it seemed to come through the paint. He covered his windows with sheets and masking tape, and, even so, he could not stay warm. "The Capitol Building was cold, too, if you could get to it, leaning into the Taku wind. The rain didn't bother me. I come from Oregon. I could not imagine how any place could be so isolated. People couldn't get at you. You were in a cage. You talked to the hard lobbyists every day. Every day the same people. What was going on there needed more airing." So he sponsored a bill to move the capital. The day he introduced it, the news went out over the radio, and when he went to have lunch in the Baranof Hotel a waitress refused to serve him. In the State Affairs Committee, a legislator from Juneau killed the bill. Each of the three times that a capital-move initiative has appeared on the Alaska ballot, it has been as a result of a people's petition. "The legislature could do it," Harris has explained, "but they don't have the guts."

In Minnesota, when a bill was introduced to move the capital from St. Paul to St. Peter, Joe Rolette, legislator and fur trader, disappeared with the bill itself until the legislature adjourned. In Nevada, when the count was shaping up as close, one delegate shot another, and Carson City became the capital by a single vote.

Harris, in his effort, was taking up an idea that had come from nowhere so concentratedly as from Robert Atwood, of the Anchorage *Times.* All through the statehood years, Atwood had been writing columns advocating that the capital be moved. Atwood had, in Harris's words, "always been ve-*he*-ment on the subject." When initiatives made the ballot in 1960 and again in 1962, Juneau taxed property owners to raise money to fight and defeat them. Twelve years went by, during which oil was discovered at Prudhoe Bay, in Arctic Alaska. Money was on the way. In the same period, the population of the Anchorage Bowl a great deal more than doubled. "Fairbanks and Juneau and the bush always combined and defeated the previous initiatives," Harris told me one day at the cleaners. "But now we had the votes."

The legislature, in the end, is to pick a name for the new capital. Meanwhile, astonishingly, almost no one shows interest in what the city might be like. I guess I have talked with several hundred Alaskans about the moving of the capital, and among them virtually no one has offered any concept, any vision, of how the new city might appear. Virtually no one but Harris. He had thought about it a lot—all through the Taku winds, the signature gathering, the days beyond the vote. "The capital should sit overlooking a lake," he said. "The lake should be large enough for float planes. You dock and walk to the Capitol. It is a rustic Capitol that fits the setting of the country. It is a state capital and a sports capital—winter and summer sports. From it you can see Mount McKinley. There is no big gold dome. That's of the past. It should be built of concrete and natural rock—something that will blend in with wilderness. Industry and farming will be all around it. It should be west of the Susitna, on the projected road to McGrath."

Willie Hensley, west of the Susitna, and high on the tundra of Little Peters Hills, looked down across the valley and said quietly that he hoped the work he was doing as chairman of the Capital Site Selection Committee would count for something, hoped the group was not wasting its time. Somehow, he made himself heard without raising his voice, despite the big helicopter standing by, shaking and muttering, a hundred yards away. "One wants to think that one's energy is concentrated on something worth doing," he went on. If the people insisted on a new capital in a wild site, at least he meant to find a good one. Six possible sites were visible from the hill—six "footprints" —including one on Blair Lake (in the low ground between the Chulitna and the Susitna), one along Deep Creek (below the Peters Hills), and one on Peters Creek (among swales of open spruce) right before him. Favorably impressed by this hill-and-river, rolling, forested land, he said as much, and added that, for all his travels, he had never been in this part of Alaska.

To borrow a term used by some Alaskans, Willie Hensley is a Brooks Brothers native. In recent years, a class of native has developed, or has at least increased, that has seen and experienced a much wider segment of the world than nearly everyone else in, say, Kivalina, Kotzebue, or Unalakleet. In an old military barracks below Mount Edgecumbe, across the harbor from Sitka, is a high school staffed by the Bureau of Indian Affairs, and that is where in Willie's time the qualified Eskimo children of Kotzebue would ordinarily be sent. That was far enough from home—eleven hundred miles—but Willie went off on an educational odyssey a great deal more exotic than that. Straight out of the sod houses and the riverine tent sites of Eskimo Arctic Alaska, Willie went to high school in Tennessee. To prepare him for the experience, he was indoctrinated —age fourteen, just off the plane from Kotzebue—in Myrtle, Mississippi. If he did not previously have what has become his outreaching sense of the absurd, he surely acquired it then. A town too small to be a crossroads, Myrtle was somewhere between Corinth and Oxford—in the northeastern corner of Yoknapatawpha. The first thing that struck him, of course, was the heat—the amazing, breath-stopping heat—and he wondered who could long endure such a climate. But before he had a chance to suffocate in that way he was smothered in another. He was given what he described years later as "a hell of a dose of Southern Baptist rural religious outlook." It was a Baptist preacher in Kotzebue who had arranged Willie's travels. The preacher's parents lived in Myrtle. They had agreed to take care of this fine young Eskimo and show him the ways of America. Anxious to please, Willie became, in his own phrase, "a temporary Southern white." "It was 1956. There was hardly a ripple of change yet—of desegregation. I knew no history of the black problem. I knew nothing about slavery. I couldn't understand the situation. I couldn't believe that people would work for three dollars a day in a field. I wanted to talk to them, but I got the impression I should not." Instead, he was exposed to a battery of preachers. Myrtle was "a preachin' center," and foremost among its congested clergy was the celebrated Brother Ray, who went around in a Cadillac and wore overalls. Brother Ray's fundamentalism overwhelmed Willie, and in a religious sense he has never recovered. He does not customarily go to church. "No." He grins. "But some of my best friends are preachers."

He went to Harrison-Chilhowee Baptist Academy, in eastern Tennessee. ("It was in the foothills of the Smokies and it was very beautiful. I couldn't believe such sculptured hills.") He saw Alaska—Kotzebue—only once in those four years. Then, in 1960, he entered the University of Alaska, in Fairbanks. Halfway through, he transferred to George Washington, in the District of Columbia, where he studied Russian (and managed to see Poland and Russia on a trip sponsored by the Experiment in International Living) and got his B.A. in political science. Doing summer work in Washington for the Bureau of Indian Affairs, he "met a lot of Lower Forty-eight Indians," and became interested in their legal relationship to their aboriginal land. It was a subject that had already been much on his mind in regard to Kotzebue. In the nineteen-fifties, the federal government had ruled off land there in lots and sold it at auction. Eskimos did not have enough money or understand auctions. Doctors, nurses, teachers, and Civil Aeronautics Administration personnel bought the property. "Eskimos had owned the property communally for ten thousand years. Now the C.A.A. types owned lots. That is how I got interested. Everybody had a way to get property but the native people." Missionaries, using church land, rented lots to the natives. "You are responsible for the hereafter, not profits," Hensley said to them. "Turn the land over to the natives." The missionaries had not acted on the suggestion.

Hensley did graduate work in business and took a course in Constitutional law at the University of Alaska. For the law course he wrote an extensive paper on who owned Alaskan land. Specifically, it was called "What Rights To Land Have The Alaska Natives?" and it traced from the Alaska purchase onward the uncertain title and unrealized claims of his people. The root question was, do the Alaskan natives, by dint of aboriginal use and occupancy, have special claim to Alaskan land, and, if so, how much land, and in how wide a range around their established villages? The 1867 purchase treaty and subsequent acts of the United States Congress did not ignore the point but left it in shadow. Now, in 1966, the Eskimos, Aleuts, and Indians of Alaska were increasingly demanding a settlement. Hensley wrote his paper in May of that year, and, drawn more than ever to the subject, inevitably became drawn into politics. He helped form the Alaska Federation of Natives, a group whose efforts were dedicated to a settlement of native claims. And that fall—age twenty-four—he ran for the state legislature and was elected.

Stewart Udall, Secretary of the Interior, reacted to the native-claims situation by suspending until the question was settled all transactions in land that was under his control. He controlled nearly all of Alaska. The U.S. Constitution and several hundred treaties made with natives elsewhere in the country tended to suggest that Congress was liable if native property was abridged. In order to be free of liability, Congress would have to extinguish native title, specifically and consciously. In days gone by, the way to do that was to extinguish the native. The treatment of Indians in the Lower Forty-eight was hardly forgotten, and among the factors that were gaining momentum in the Alaska natives' favor white guilt was not the least. Other points intensified, too. The State of Alaska, having been promised a hundred and three million acres of land in the act that made Alaska a state, needed the money that would be derivable from the land. The state wished to get on with the process of selection, but what land could it select with the native claims unsettled? Oil companies, pending native-claims settlement, had nine hundred million dollars' worth of questionable leases, cloudily titled. Moreover, to protect the native interest a court granted an injunction against the building of the Trans-Alaska Pipeline pending a settlement of native claims. Pressure for settlement then came from labor unions looking toward pipeline jobs. Conservationists got into it, too, because the matter of preservation of lands in Alaska was so close in nature to the native-claims question that it more or less had to be dealt with at the same time. These combined pressures, kept at the highest levels possible by the maneuvering of Willie Hensley and his native colleagues, yielded the Alaska Native Claims Settlement Act of 1971.

When the natives settled for one billion dollars and forty million acres of land—much of it likely to contain gold, silver, and other minerals, and oil and gas—their claims were thus extinguished. This was perhaps the great, final, and retributive payment for all of American history's native claims—an attempt to extinguish something more than title. The settlement suggests not only principal but interest as well on twenty decades of national guilt. The natives of Alaska were suddenly, collectively rich. Along tribal and cultural lines, the state was divided into twelve aboriginal regions, and in each a native corporation was established to hold and invest the new wealth. The Sealaska Corporation, for example, would handle the share of the Tlingit-Haida tribes, in the southeastern archipelago. Doyon, Ltd., would be the holding company for the Athapaskan interior. NANA Regional Corporation, which grew out of the Northwest Alaska Native Association, would direct the funds of the people of Kotzebue and of ten other villages in the Kobuk Valley. In the Alaska lexicon, a new synonym for "native" was "stockholder," and NANA's five thousand stockholders would receive in incremental payments sixty-two million dollars and 2.3 million acres of land. The jets of Alaska Airlines and Wien Air Alaska were soon a third to half full of natives zipping around the state on business—for nothing, of course, prevented one corporation from investing or operating in another's region. The corporations were, as Hensley put it, "mini-conglomerates." NANA, for example, set up a development corporation that started, among other things, a protection agency and a construction firm. They won a contract for all pipeline security north of the Yukon, another to supply labor to pipeline pumping stations, another to build a high school in Kivalina (on the coast of northwest Alaska), another to build a new control tower at Anchorage International Airport. Willie Hensley, it seems almost needless to say, became a founding member of the NANA board of directors, a member of the executive committee, and president of two of NANA's principal companies. That is what is meant by Brooks Brothers native. John Sackett, of Doyon. Roy Huhndorf, of Cook Inlet. They do not travel just in Alaska. They are often in San Francisco, New York, the District of Columbia. Needing expertise beyond the attorneys of Anchorage, they use the finest and dearest of Wall Street and Washington law firms to construct and straighten their affairs.

Jade Mountain, in the Kobuk Valley, belongs to NANA. Jade Mountain is a mountain of jade. One day in Anchorage, Hensley had strewn some before me on his desk in NANA's offices. It was exquisite stone (the state gem), polished, viridian, in blocks and wafers, from the NANA Jade Products Division. "I hope that this jade will be used liberally in the new capital," he said, and he added, with a subtle smile, "because it is so beautiful, not just because we own it." And now, as he stood on the hilltop looking east toward Talkeetna and places where his Alaskan jade city might rise, it occurred to me that Willie Hensley—sooner or later—might live in the new capital, in a jade-columned mansion near the center of the town.

If you order a glass of beer in Alaska, it is likely to be modest in all ways but cost, which can run upward from a dollar. If you order a couple of eggs with toast, the bill may be three dollars and fifty cents. If you order a new capital, just the choosing of a site for it will run you a million and a half dollars, but the price is in line with the beer and the eggs, and seems on the whole accepted. Words are what the money has bought, in the main—words by the troy ounce, delivered in Consultaspeak.

"East of Talkeetna, the cost impact will be impacted."

"The planning aspects are far more important than whatever the megastructure may turn out to be."

The prime consultant was CCC/HOK, an international planning and architectural firm, whose planners and architects —Ed Crittenden, Anne Kriken, Barry Quinn, Dan Gale—came from the company's Anchorage and San Francisco offices but had about them a certain quality of Eastern tweed. They, in turn, reached out for help to engineers, hydrologists, economists, botanists, biologists, meteorologists, geologists (notably Dames & Moore); and the general procedure was set up and coördinated by Leonard Lane, the Capital Site Selection Committee's full-time executive director.

"With McHargian geophysical determinants, we factor in the transportation and utility infrastructure."

"The approach, overall, is essentially McHargian."

Ian McHarg, the absent master, is a landscape architect and regional planner who teaches at the University of Pennsylvania and developed some years ago a technique for selecting the best new site or alignment for anything from a doghouse to a city of ten million. McHarg's method, in crude summary, was to take all relevant information—developed by his own research and that of his staff and consultants—and express it in the form of markings and shadings on clear plastic overlays that could be placed upon a map. One overlay might deal with, say, drainage, ground water, and additional hydrological considerations; another would shade in the extent of vegetation. Each criterion could be individually considered, then literally piled atop the others until an expert, peering down through the layers of plastic, could see on the map the best and worst sites for construction. McHarg had presented this to the world in a fountainhead treatise called "Design with Nature." McHarg was not connected with CCC/HOK, but when his name was mentioned its people tended to swivel and face Philadelphia.

They had buried the map of central Alaska under layers of acetate, and had eventually eliminated everything on it but the Susitna Valley. Under more overlays, the valley itself was graphically analyzed. The Land Status Acetate showed, in various colors, state ownership, borough ownership, federal ownership, and private ownership. The Natural Limitations

Acetate showed, in various patterns and colors, floodplains, bogs, muskeg pockets, swamps, steep slopes, alpine tundra, moose habitats, bear habitats, salmon spawning areas. "To develop our extensive sensitivity to wildlife," Leonard Lane reported, "we talked to thirty-one people in the Department of Fish and Game." The Existing Transportation Acetate showed two-lane roads, gravel roads, dirt roads, airstrips, railroad, airport sites. The Elevation Acetate included twelve altitudes. The Capital City Footprint Areas Acetate presented the regions of the valley that had shown up best under earlier fathoms of acetate. Within each footprint, or generally buildable area, was a "centroid"—the spot where buildings would most likely rise. Following this came more plastic, neatly sketched upon, plotted, shaded—criterion after criterion, layer upon layer: the View Aspect Acetate, the Degree of View Acetate, the Water Features Acetate, the Vegetation Types Acetate, the Landscape Features Acetate, the Background Features Acetate. The committee had to develop a talent for peering down through the plastic. The committee was like a crane standing on one leg staring into a pond.

Meanwhile, to make new photographic mosaics of the valley, the consultants ordered and the committee paid for twelve thousand dollars' worth of aerial pictures. Dames & Moore defended the need for this by pointing out—to some people's astonishment—that certain features of the topographic maps of the United States Geological Survey were only about sixty per cent accurate. Stream courses, for example, were often out of date. A stream course in Alaska, writhing like a firehose, can rapidly put a map out of date.

The consultants had been hired to envision a setting, not a city. The design of the community was specifically excluded from their procedure. They could not help but consider it, though, in the light of the question that was always with them: Is it possible to create an unsterile community that has only government there?

"I sure hope so," Barry Quinn said one day. "The capital has a lot going against it. Its economic base is government. There will not be much secondary employment. And diversity makes a community healthy." Quinn, from East Rochester, New York, had been working in Alaska off and on for nine years. He was young, with dark longish hair parted in the middle, his manner gentle, engaging. "It is difficult to initiate the incentives that create diversity," he went on. "They tend to evolve naturally. And industry is simply not going to spring up here. It's cheaper to process oil and timber elsewhere. The town's overall development will depend on the development of Alaska. It may not work for this generation but for the next. You can't create a Friday-night spot in a brand-new town."

Ed Crittenden, president of CCC/HOK, is an architect and city planner, trained at Yale and M.I.T., who has been in Alaska twenty-six years. Five of his six children were born in Alaska. His hair is graying and as long as the times. There is a pipe, a sports jacket, a blue button-down shirt, a knitted tie. I asked him one day how he saw the new city, and he said he deliberately tried to avoid thinking of that in order to play his role as written. Crittenden had done the new Federal Building, the BP Building, the Union Oil Building—some of the high-rising glass of Anchorage. Pressed to describe the new capital as it might appear in his private thought, he finally said, "Well, to tell you the truth, I would reverse all of the things that people come to Alaska to get away from. I would not go along with the I'll-build-my-cabin-where-I-damned-well-want-to syndrome. I would apply ideas from the Eastern United States—a central core, a central walking mall, a controlled environment. Living structures would be concentrated, and in modules of enclosed space. There would be modules for state and local government, and commercial modules, all concentrated, with plenty of open space around them—plenty of undisturbed, or almost undisturbed, Alaska." So saying, and in a cloud of pipe smoke, Crittenden departed for Siberia. An honored figure in the field of Arctic construction and Arctic community development, he was going there to participate in the first Soviet-American exchange on human environment in the north.

In recent years, certain construction has enhanced the weight of Juneau. Along Gastineau Channel, for example, runs a four-lane divided highway, engineered with the breadth and grandeur of an interstate—implying New York at one end, Chicago at the other. The road cost sixteen million dollars, and runs from Juneau out to Juneau Municipal Airport, and back—there being nowhere else to go. The new State Office Building, edificial focus of the town, has been complemented by a new courthouse and a multilevel parking garage. It is not a coincidence that so much construction came about at a time when Juneau was threatened by the movement to move the capital, and no one will argue about the fact that all this effort can be traced to one man. His name is Bill Ray. Nearly forty years ago, he turned up in Juneau after sleeping in his own blankets in the hold of the S. S. Baranof. From Wallace, Idaho, he had been driven north by the Depression, and had come to Juneau with his father to look for work. He began as a longshoreman, and, moving from job to job, he did about all there was to do in southeastern Alaska. He worked in canneries, on fishing boats, and as a deckhand on a canning tender. After the Second World War, he bought a liquor store in Juneau. He helped defeat the capital-move initiatives of 1960 and 1962. In 1964, he was elected to the Alaska House of Representatives, and eventually became chairman of its Finance Committee. In 1970 and 1974, he was elected to the Senate, where he also became chairman of the Finance Committee. As one of his constituents has said of him, "Hands down, Bill Ray brings home more bacon than anyone else in the legislature."

"They call me the lovable bandit," Ray told me one day, in his office in the Capitol. "I take everything that isn't nailed down. I admit it. Aren't you supposed to do what you can for your district? They say I have the guts of a second-story man and the brains of a Mafia chieftain." The second-story-man part was protruding under the hem of a jade-green polo shirt. Life had been good in Juneau. Ray appeared to be in his middle fifties. He had heavy eyelids, and was a little figgy in the jowls. Through his office window he gazed contemplatively at the State Office Building, whose eleven stories of airy glass were more than framed by ponderous abutments of sandstone, turreted and crenellated so that it looked something like a greenhouse prepared for war.

"That's my building there," he said. "They call that Fort Ray. It's no secret—it cost fifteen million dollars. We have thirty-five hundred government employees. That means more than ten thousand people—well over half the town—depend directly on the government. And now powerful forces are at play to kill us, all set in motion by a little clique in Anchorage."

"Clique?"

"Atwood, at heart. Atwood was here once, in Juneau, and didn't make it. Atwood has had gubernatorial ambitions, senatorial ambitions. When he looks in the mirror, he sees God. He's a brilliant man, but he has insulated his mind against reality. He misrepresents the truth. What they really want to do—the little clique that has been forcing this issue—is to put a legislative hall thirty miles outside of Anchorage, and that would be the head of the state government, but the heart and guts would be in Anchorage. What they sold the people was that the head, guts, and feathers—everything—would be in one place, and you can't do that thirty miles from Anchorage. They've done nothing but sell it on a lie. Lie No. 2: It won't hurt Juneau. They say Juneau has its cruise boats, and so on. Cruise boats? People get off the boat, look around, take a bus out to the glacier, and go back to the boat. They're visitors, not tourists. A tourist stays a week and drops four hundred dollars. A visitor comes with a shirt and a twenty-dollar bill and doesn't change either one."

"Shouldn't the state capital be near the population center?" I asked him.

"That argument doesn't hold. The spectrum of public pressure is larger where the people are. Can you imagine a march of *welfare* people? In Juneau, you don't have pressures like that. You can sit with a clear head and do your work."

I mentioned that Jan Koslosky, of Palmer, had told me that during his six years in the legislature he only went home once during a session. He said he had been a pilot for thirty years but did not like the flight into Juneau. He had had too many close calls trying to get in.

"Koslosky is a cautious man. I'll tell you this. You are safer coming into Juneau than elsewhere, because when you come into Juneau the pilot is flying the plane. The *captain* is flying the plane. He wants to be sure he gets here."

As an aircraft feels its way down toward an airport in weather, the pilot reads an instrument-approach chart, which indicates the distance and altitude from which the runway should be visible or the approach has been missed and the plane must climb out and perhaps have another try. For most airports, the missed-approach point is close to the runway, or even just above it. For Juneau Municipal, the missed-approach point is three and a half miles from the runway and fourteen hundred feet in the air. If you can't fly in visually from there, you immediately turn and rapidly climb. In all directions from the airport are mountains, and certain ones are close. As the Juneau approach chart presents the situation, "Any go-around commenced after passing the published missed-approach point will not provide standard obstruction clearance." In the legislature, quorums can erode when flights approach Juneau, fail to see the runway, and go off and land somewhere else.

An Alaskan pilot once advised me never to fly to Juneau. "It's a one-way shot," he said. "Once you get lined up on final, you're looking right at the rocks. Mountain goes straight up and down in back of it. The weather is notoriously poor. You have to have supreme confidence in all your instruments and in the F.A.A.'s instruments. The approach is relatively steep. You go from five thousand feet to sea level in fourteen-point-seven nautical miles. If you miss, you do a very steep, sharp climbing turn to avoid hitting something. An airplane is most inefficient when making a sharp turn and climbing. A mile from the runway you go over a five-hundred-foot hill, and the top has been cleared of trees so that planes will not hit them. Now, is that or is that not a little hairy? After crossing the hill, you have to make a dogleg to the right before touching down."

In September, 1971, a Boeing 727 of Alaska Airlines, with seven crew members and a hundred and four passengers, was coming in toward Juneau at an altitude considerably below the approach-chart minimum. Investigators are sure there was an error in the navigational equipment—either in the plane or on the ground. The pilot apparently thought he had passed a checkpoint he had not yet reached, and thought he was over Auke Bay. He was still in the Chilkat Range. In cloud, the aircraft flew among mountains, feeling its way down—forty-five hundred, thirty-five hundred, twenty-five hundred feet. The height of the last ridge—before the terrain would fall away to low ground and open water—was thirty-five hundred and nine feet.

Ray said he flew out to see the accident. "It was a terrible, terrible thing. The plane had split. It had been peeled like a banana, spewing people out both sides. But that is the only major accident we have had here. There are more accidents in Anchorage—more air traffic and more danger. And how many people get killed in Anchorage in car wrecks? What are the chances of getting *shot* in Anchorage—by some drug-crazed son of a bitch? Or getting acid thrown in your face? Compare *that* with Juneau. I can't even *remember* a murder in Juneau. I wonder if *anybody* remembers a murder here."

He got up, stuck his head out the door, and asked if anyone out there remembered a murder. Zero.

"I can tell you when the last one in Anchorage was," he went on, sitting down again. "It was last weekend."

"What do you suppose the new capital will look like?" I asked him.

"Personally, I think the capital's going to look like Juneau. Because it's going to *remain* in Juneau. But if there ever were a new capital, I'd want them to have a collection of buildings Alaska could be proud of, I'll tell you that—not a boxworks, not an Anchorage, not a glorified privy. Anchorage looks like Poppincorn, Iowa. There is nothing Alaskan about it. A new capital should look like Alaska."

"What sort of look is that?"

"I don't know. All I know is Anchorage stinks. The Anchorage strategy will be to piecemeal the capital. They'll peddle a temporary, functional capital to keep the cost-appearance down, and then they'll sock it to 'em, baby. At least a billion dollars. Oh, they're making a big effort, these Anchorage people, and to keep people trying that hard there's got to be, someplace, a dollar in the ground."

"So you built Fort Ray as an immovable object, a defense against the move?"

"Right."

"And the highway, too?"

"Right. God-damned right."

"And the courthouse?"

"Exactly!"

"And the garage?"

"You've got it!"

"All to turn millions into masonry that could never leave Juneau, all to stop the move?"

"That's it! That's what I did! With all that built, how *could* they move it?"

"What will you do when the capital moves?"

The Senator fell suddenly quiet, and for at least two minutes stared out his window and down the street to Fort Ray. "What *is* there to do?" he said, at last. "Just sit here and look at it, that's all. Juneau. Wiped out. With more than half of the work force gone, the city will fall dead. There won't be anything left. While the state squanders money on a new capital, Juneau will fall dead. And what will we gain? We don't—in Alaska—have money to run our schools."

He paused a moment, then went on, "Oh, we're steadily building up the University of Alaska's Southeast Branch here. We're building the fisheries-research program. There are some tourists. But, frankly, what are you going to do for tourists in the wintertime when the god-damned Taku wind is blowing fifty miles an hour and the windchill factor is sixty below?"

"Not to mention the rain."

"People make too much of the god-damned rain. There's more than average, but you kind of like it. It keeps you alert."

The Senator stood up, shook hands warmly, said he was sorry he had to go but he had a plane to catch, put on his coat, went to the airport, and flew to an apartment he maintains in Torremolinos, on the Costa del Sol, of Spain.

In Florida, in the nineteen-sixties, a movement stirred to have the capital shifted from eccentric Tallahassee to the center of the state, to Orlando. The legislature's direct response was to appropriate ten million dollars for new House and Senate office buildings and forty million for a new Capitol—in Tallahassee.

Seven per cent of Juneau's voters voted for the capital move. Some of these were government employees who had lived "up north" (as they say in Juneau) and were hoping to go back. Others were people who thought the state government had inflated the local economy. And another was Fishpole John. John Klett, from Meriden, Connecticut, was considerably more Alaskan than most Alaskans, in that he had been there more than forty years when he died not long ago. In an old shop on South Franklin, he meticulously fashioned salmon rods, and he sent them on order as far as Europe. He was a big man with stiff white bristles, a red knitted cap—and before anyone who cared to listen he would fulminate as he worked. "I voted to move it. I'm glad they're going to move the son of a bitch. Jesus Christ. It costs too much to keep the capital here. If the state government was out of here, this would be a better town. No matter where you've got a capital, you've got crime. This town is a rip-off town in a rip-off state. The dirty dozen —the people that runs Juneau—want to keep all the money to themselves, but a lot of people who don't have money get nothing and would like to see the capital go. The legislature voted themselves a raise this year—to fourteen thousand seven hundred dollars. What the hell do they do up there? Nothing. Everybody wants the legislature out of here. They're the biggest bunch of chisellers. They leave stores holding their personal checks. Sitka was the capital seventy-five years ago. Sitka is better off than we are now."

The mayor of Sitka happened to stop off in Juneau while I was there, and he did not disagree with Fishpole John. "We lost the capital, and nobody in Sitka regrets it," he said. "The government makes Juneau a rat race, where strangers come and go." The mayor of Sitka, John Dapcevich, had grown up in Juneau, had become an accountant, and had once been the state budget analyst. "Sitka is a bad place for the capital," he continued. "And so is Juneau. But it's stupid to move it. It's just a matter of economics. We can't afford this new utopia. The Boeing report was ridiculous—not even close to the picture."

Boeing—the aircraft company—has a computer-services subsidiary that will study just about anything for anybody, and in 1974 it analyzed for the government of Alaska the cost of moving the capital from Juneau. The cost turned out to be modest, according to Boeing. Some fifteen years in the future, the cost of having relocated the capital would exceed by only a hundred and ten million dollars the cost of the capital should it stay in Juneau, in part because the state would be spared the expense of refurbishing its older buildings there. Boeing also decided that so much matériel and manpower would be on hand as a result of the pipeline project that the new capital's building costs would be significantly reduced. The Boeing report could not help but influence the fate of the initiative on the ballot, and the report left Juneau particularly bitter. Juneau attorneys were quick to say that while the report depreciated the buildings of the old capital it did not depreciate the new buildings in the new location. Juneau rumbled about a lawsuit.

One of Juneau's responses to approaching catastrophe has been to suggest that people need not actually travel to the capital to watch, or even confer with, the legislature. In Alaska, in fact, the difficulty of bringing people together to make (and to influence the making of) laws is only one of countless problems in weaving an economic, political, and cultural fabric across a third of a billion acres of land. Alaska is attempting to solve the problem with RCA earth stations that are trained on satellites and patterned so that telecommunications and closed-circuit TV can tie any part of Alaska to any other. An earth station is functioning now in Talkeetna. Others are in place as well. The goal is a hundred and twenty-nine, all over the state. Using them, doctors in Anchorage are already treating patients lying in infirmaries in the bush. Juneau has pointed out that people in Bettles, Barrow, or Nome could go into a room in a state office building and watch, say, the House Resources Committee at work in Juneau. They could talk to the committee. They could even testify.

Rhode Island used to worry about its great size, too. In an area so large, one capital site could not serve all the people. So the legislature travelled from Newport to Bristol to East Greenwich to South Kingstown to Providence, and did not settle exclusively in Providence until 1901. Vermont's legislature travelled, too. Delaware, which is smaller than quite a few islands in Alaska, moved its capital from New Castle to Dover in order to have a central location. On the other hand, there have been capitals even more out of the way than Juneau. Of the three capitals in the history of Wisconsin, one was Burlington, Iowa. The Vermont state legislature once convened in Charlestown, New Hampshire.

Some of the people I met in Juneau were cultivating the hope that after the new capital site was chosen environmental-impact statements would show intolerable costs. The Trans-Alaska

Pipeline had been projected in 1969 as a nine-hundred-million-dollar project. Now the guess was that the pipeline would cost, in the end, something like eight billion.

Meanwhile, the dissident seven per cent still wanted the capital to go. Some people in Juneau felt that Juneau was more attractive as an old mining town than it would ever be with the development that would continue if the capital stayed. They had voted for the initiative. So had commercial fishermen, irritated by a boat harbor full of pleasure-fishing cruisers owned by state employees, by a clutter of sport fishermen, while the commercial catch declined. In the Juneau Cold Storage Company, in a big room full of running water and silver salmon in iced hampers, I watched rubber-booted men and women slicing the salmon clean. As he worked, a tall, strong, unreserved young man, a big man in thick wool trousers and two wool shirts, said, "I know a girl who works in the State Office Building, and she knits a sweater there every month. I hate those bureaucrats with a purple passion—the god-damned parasites, walking around doing nothing, sitting on their butts. They're wrecking the fishing for the commercials. I'd like to see them go. I'd like to see mosquitoes eat them. I'd like to see them up in the bush."

The big helicopter, in the air again with the Capital Site Selection Committee, moved generally southward in a loose, truffle-sniffing zigzag. In haze to the east we could barely discern the corridor line of the Anchorage-Fairbanks Highway. Someone remarked that the Matanuska-Susitna Borough had announced that it was going to put several dozen parcels of land on the market—land spaced through the valley from Willow to Talkeetna.

"Somebody's out for a land grab," said Louise Kellogg, and she volunteered to look into it and see what she could do to discourage feverish speculation. This was her district, her borough. She had come to it nearly thirty years before, and had long had a dairy farm near Palmer. The farm—a hundred and twenty-five cows—had been leased to a younger farmer. With a partner, she was now running an antique shop, whose contents discouraged her, she said, because so many items familiar to her when she was young had now become negotiable as antiques. When she was young, she had gone to Vassar. She had recently been to her fiftieth reunion there. She had been a member of the South Central District Republican Committee and a trustee of Alaska Methodist University. Small, gentle, white-haired, wearing trifocals, she may not have appeared to be particularly forceful, but no one seemed to doubt that she could deal with the borough. Its freeholders, like any number of other people, apparently wanted to test and sample the capital-engendered increase in the price of land. ("The capital has been located; located against the wish of the great majority of the people—located for the pecuniary and personal benefit of Tom Cuming and his brother bribers—located at a place without any natural advantages, and one totally barren of anything save whisky shops and drunken politicians . . . a place having no historic interest—simply because they could make a better bargain with the speculators," wrote the Nebraska *Palladium*, in 1855.)

Along the road near Talkeetna, some years ago, the state sold off ground for something like a hundred and twenty-five dollars an acre. Five thousand dollars will buy such an acre now. Under the aspens and birches by the roadside, fresh signs appear beside the unbuilt gates of unbuilt subdivisions—SPORTSMAN ACRES, RUSTIC WILDERNESS, TIMBER PARK—and into the woods run new roads with earth plowed up to either side like banks of brown snow. Parka Parkway. Lichen Drive. Grizzly Way. The new capital is not the only fetal town in the Susitna Valley. Where the committee hovers, speculation hovers as well.

It can be worth your life to visit such a place. Nose a car in under the cottonwoods, have a look around. Before you can back out, a salesman has appeared from behind a tree and placed you under house arrest. He has a contract in his hand, and the lots are going fast. "No" is a word he does not comprehend. He tells you—erroneously—that the man who owned the computer firm in Anchorage that did the feasibility study for the Capital Site Selection Committee sold the computer firm and bought lots in this beautiful subdivision, and so did eight others in the same office. Hurry, buy a lot, you may be too late. This little beauty is almost two-thirds of an acre, and the price is fourteen thousand dollars. The distance to Anchorage is eighty miles, but the distance to the capital of Alaska will be a great deal less than that. Meanwhile, consider the view. The lot is on a high escarpment above the Susitna, and beyond the river are broad spruce and muskeg barrens and beyond them the white mountains. That big one on the right is McKinley. The Indians called it Denali, which meant "You'll be sorry if you don't sign now." Would you like to see some wildlife? Let's go down to the airstrip. Take you up and show you a moose.

The salesman whose trap line I had happened onto one summer evening was named John Leifer. He had lived until recently in Juneau, he said, but had left because Juneau had had it. Juneau was dead. This was where things were happening now—up here in the Susitna Valley, where the capital would be. He had flown an air taxi in Juneau. "Just like a taxi-driver, but in a plane—under six-hundred-foot ceilings, two-hundred-foot ceilings. In Juneau, you fly them or starve. You get to know every curve in the shoreline." At full throttle, in a Stationair, he jumped off the airstrip and across the Susitna, and began to search its sloughs and its tributary streams for moose. Skimming trees, banking at such steep angles that his stall-warning horn was constantly sounding, he swooped and circled in the hunt for wildlife. Printed on his company's brochures were moose, beavers, bears, and wolverines, but there were none in sight beneath the plane. In wider and wider arcs, he expanded the search, diving, climbing, and repeatedly saying, "I can't understand it, I can't understand it. Where *are* all the moose?" Finally, in the arriving dusk, we flew over a black bear. Turning, making a tight one-eighty, he lined up the Stationair for a second view. He throttled back, and we glided silently down on the bear, which stood still, in nearsighted perplexity, wondering where the sound had gone. Then, suddenly, Leifer advanced the throttle and buzzed the astounded animal, which ran across the muskeg in a kind of rolling cringe as we passed over and then gained enough altitude to clear the trees.

I was to learn, much later, that John Leifer crashed and was killed close by the Susitna on the same autumn day that the

Capital Site Selection Committee was crisscrossing the skies above.

Earl Cook spotted a moose from the committee helicopter. It did not so much as lift its head—just stood there in its muskeg pocket like a horse in a pasture. We circled low over Amber Lake, a site under consideration, and then turned west and crossed wide stands of balsam poplar and broad muskeg meadows, beyond which, on a clear stream, were a couple of homesteads—one a crude assemblage of shacks, the other a tidy collection of small cabins, with a rectangle of timothy and an airstrip so short it looked more like a driveway. Homesteaders—with their big (hundred-and-sixty-acre) blocks of land—stood to make or lose the most if the capital should settle near them. They could lose their remoteness, with nowhere comparable to go; new homesteading in Alaska was shut off indefinitely in March, 1974. On the other hand, homesteaders in the Anchorage Bowl had sold out for many hundreds of thousands of dollars, and analogous deals might be offered in the Susitna Valley. Meanwhile, some homesteaders who had "proved up" on their land—that is, had lived on it for three years, built a habitable dwelling, and grown a crop on an eighth of the acreage—were already selling at prices that guessed the future. Only a few weeks before, a Susitna Valley homestead had sold for a hundred and forty-eight thousand dollars, and, like the ones we were flying over, it was many miles from the road.

A homestead on the highway system would be worth a great deal more than that. I had visited one, some miles south of Talkeetna, where a young couple, Don and Patty Bender, had moved onto the land in 1974 and had lived in a camper while they mixed concrete, poured a foundation, and, together, built a house. It was a small, handsome place, with a steel-drum wood stove and big windows of insulated glass. Mount McKinley was framed in one window. Sometimes bears were too. Don Bender had a .300 Magnum but had not yet used it on a bear. He used it for his annual moose, and through the winter he and his wife ate mooseburgers, moose sausage, moose steak. They had eggs, too, and bacon coming. Near the house was an A-frame combination coop and sty. A pig lived in one end, chickens in the other. On cold nights, the chickens found a way to get near the pig. The Benders were in favor of the capital move. "Juneau is too inaccessible," he said. "Therefore, many of our politicians have hidden from their constituents." They did not want to lose their homestead, though, no matter how much its value might appreciate. They said they hoped the new capital would "not destroy our personal place of life." Their property, theirs for living on it, would probably be worth half a million dollars by the time it was proved up. If the capital came near, that sum could multiply, and the Benders would feel some pressure to change their minds.

They had so far cleared ten acres, in conformity with the rules—dense, closed-forest acres of spruce, birch, aspen—and had planted timothy and oats. Although the homestead was in the Susitna Valley, the terrain was rough with sheer-sided hillocks, and the Benders' ten acres under cultivation looked less like a field than a bald lumpy spot on a high mountainside, the crops clinging to serpentine contours. The appearance of it all tended to suggest mockery of the Homestead Act, which was written to offer farmland to an expanding nation, and this minimal "farm" had been hacked absurdly from a steep subarctic forest. The Homestead Act, though, had a venerable history of mocking itself. It had worked well only east of the hundredth meridian, where there was enough rain to serve a farm, and homesteads in the range country and semideserts of the West had made, if anything, less sense than the homesteads of Alaska. In general, the Alaskan climate is not much more severe than the climate of, say, Montana, and the soil under Alaskan cottonwoods could be richly supportive of crops. The growing season is not prohibitively short —roughly mid-May to the first of September—and in various fruits and vegetables sugar content will build up to unusual levels in the cool air and the long northern light. A potato developed by Curtis Dearborn, at the University of Alaska's experimental farm in the Matanuska Valley, is eleven per cent sugar and can be eaten like an apple. Dearborn also developed the Alaska Frostless Potato, which survives frosting at twenty-seven degrees. Potatoes could be farmed very successfully as far north as the Yukon, and may be someday, if the idea ever takes hold. Agriculture, though, is among Alaska's foremost undeveloped assets. There is a so-called "farm loop" north of Fairbanks, with broad cleared fields and haystacks under tarps

—a Pennsylvanian scene, reminiscent of the mother country. Rampant subdivisions, of late, have been eating it up. The Trans-Alaska Pipeline winds among the farms. In the Matanuska Valley, which forms a V with the Susitna Valley around the Talkeetna Mountains, the soil—loess soil—has the color and consistency of Hershey's cocoa and is rockless two feet down. Farmers from the Middle West were brought to the Matanuska Valley during the Depression and, after a disorganized beginning, established successful farms. In many parts of the valley are fields and gambrel-roofed barns, with the Chugach Mountains rising to alpine snowfields beyond—a phenomenal sight from a farm. Matanuska notwithstanding, of arable Alaska not much is plowed—far too little to be expressed as a percentage. As Alaskan land, in huge segments, is divided up for various purposes, agriculture fails to make the list. But the strawberries are delicious enough to make you drunk—Susitnas, Talkeetnas, Matareds. You can grow carrots, beets, spinach, broccoli, rhubarb, cauliflower, Brussels sprouts, zucchini—all in the heart of Alaska—and wheat, barley, alfalfa, oats, and white sweet clover eight feet high. Peas are particularly sweet and aromatic. There is virtually no need for pesticides. Cabbages grow to be two feet in diameter and can weigh seventy pounds. They look like medicine balls. If Alaska would get up off its past (the boom philosophy), it could be the world center of sauerkraut-cabbage production. That sounds laughable, but the state might come out of it economically sound. The new capital city could be sterile and governmental and given to one purpose, or it could be an island in a sea of farms—the state of Alaska, from one end to the other, being green about half the year.

Exceptions are glaciers, but they are only three per cent of Alaska—the big ones close to the gulf coastline, which reaches down and east from Anchorage toward Cordova, Yakutat, Haines, and Juneau. Something like seventeen thousand square miles are permanently under ice, while the rest of Alaska melts. Ninety-seven per cent—half a million square miles—melts. Even the great ice sheets of the glacial ages did not cover Alaska. An arm of the Laurentide covered the Brooks Range. The Cordilleran Glacier Complex, which covered the Canadian Rockies and the chains of the Pacific coast, reached out over the Alaska Range and across all the land between the mountains and the gulf. But the Interior and the Arctic Slope and all the west coast were bare. While much of New Jersey was covered with ice, most of Alaska was not.

The truly immense glaciers might be down in the southeast, but the glacier that was off to our right just now was in no sense modest. The helicopter had crossed Shulin Lake, and had circled it, tilting far over so the committee members could hang by their seat belts for a plan view, its big rotor blades biting the air with the sound of a working axe. Level again, it was proceeding west toward the Kahiltna River, the source of which, off to the north, was almost as preëminent as the mountains above. It came down out of the Alaska Range like a great white tongue. It came—the Kahiltna Glacier—from eleven thousand feet, from a high saddle between the peaks of Foraker and McKinley. And two, three, four miles wide all the way, it flowed fifty miles south into the valley, where it finally turned into river at an altitude of scarcely a thousand feet. This was the big glacier the climbers land on—and the fact that they land at the seven-thousand-foot contour has nothing to do with the strategies of the sport. They do so because airplanes are not permitted to land in Mount McKinley National Park, and the park boundary happens to cross the glacier at that level. The river below us was the product of the sun, and even in autumn and from the helicopter's high perspective it was awesome to see. Most fast rivers are white, smooth, white, smooth—alternating pools and rapids. This one was white all the way, bank to bank, tumultuous, torrential, great rushing outwash of the Alaska Range. With so many standing waves, so much white water, it appeared to be filled with running sheep. The color of the water, where it was flat enough to show, was actually greenish-gray, and its clarity was nil. It carried so much of what had been mountains. Glacier milk, as it is called, contains a high proportion of powdered rock, from pieces broken off and then ground by the ice. The colors of outwash rivers are determined by the diets of the glaciers—schist, gneiss, limestone, shale.

Glacial erratics were all over the valley, and there was one below us now. The ice in the past had nosed southward these huge monoliths—supermagnified boulders—which had rafted along on the advancing terminus and had not become caught and ground. The one beneath us appeared to be as large as a three-story building, weirdly standing in the forest. It was so big that soil had formed on its upper surface, and trees grew from it like hair.

We crossed Lake Creek, which was not a glacial stream and was running so clear we could see its gravels. Ahead was Mount Yenlo, a four-thousand-foot rise in the western Susitna Valley, and the helicopter set down there, on a southerly slope of the mountain, to release the committee. Just below, and beside the clear stream, was the most remote site under consideration for the capital—thirty-five miles from the highway and undeniably as beautiful a setting as could possibly exist in the valley. It was high grassland—under, but approaching, a thousand feet—with white birches and white spruce scattered through it, big trees for this part of the world, almost a foot in diameter. The mean January temperature was ten degrees, July fifty-six. The summit of Yenlo was above the site, to the immediate northwest, and due north, close across fifty miles, was the palpable McKinley. The committee spread out through berry fields, these laced with stands of fern. There was sign of moose and caribou. There were depressions in the grass where bears had slept.

In Alaska, when you ask people if they know a certain place—a river, a lake, a hill, a valley—they often say, "I've flown it, but I've never been on the ground there." Alaska is too big to be broadly inspected in other ways, but looking at something from the air is nonetheless an inadequate perspective. Dimensions tend to be removed. There is no substitute for being on the ground, for experiencing a landscape close at hand, for feeling the earth underfoot. And this was frustratingly apparent now, for the helicopter had spilled us suddenly into a three-dimensional wilderness world—for a ration of tangibility, to last fifteen minutes. Its lights blinking, its engine guttural, it sent out signals of impatience. Waiting to take us away, it took away something of what it had brought us to see.

Arliss Sturgulewski, offering berries from her hand, said as much, and shook her head, and looked long at the splendid landscape—the city site—sloping down to the stream. "We need the right kind of planning before Dollar One is spent on the ground," she said. "We need to take advantage of views

—of the uniqueness of the setting—and then see to it that the capital is not just another place. You've got to take everything that you've learned and absorbed and make something out of it. You can't just quantify it. You need a gut feeling, and at least we get something of that standing here. I'm wondering who, in the end, will run this capital. What will the land use be, the zoning, the planning? Government is the catalyst at the beginning, but then may lose control."

Loose flakes of gold hung in a clear amulet around her neck. Over her blouse was a Levi jacket. She was tall, large-boned, attractive, blond. She came from the mountains of northern Washington and had been in Alaska—in Anchorage—almost twenty-five years. Her husband had died in an F-27 propjet on its way to King Salmon, and, in the seven years since, she had immersed herself in civic affairs, most notably as a member of the Greater Anchorage Area Planning and Zoning Commission. Like the Mrs. Partington who tried to fight the Atlantic Ocean with a mop, she had watched, and she had fought, the splurge of Anchorage.

Control had been lame as it followed development, she said. "Lots were ruled off on paper that for one reason or another could never be developed. Soil testing, the presence of adequate utilities were not required. For a long time, there was no control. When efforts at control came, they lacked force and lagged behind. There were no building codes. We finally got some codes, but not until 1972. There was no floodplain ordinance until 1975. There are sixty streams and rivers in the Anchorage Bowl. Before this year, there was development in the floodplains, and even in the floodways! Authorities had to approve development that was already built. The planning commission had no power. We were only advisory. We did get some positive things. We got bike trails. But in a boom situation your development really gets away from you. Twelve thousand new people have come to Anchorage in the past year. The streets are falling apart. We were unprepared for the impact of the pipeline. When a boom comes along, you don't have strong enough rules. You can't keep up. Now look at this place—how beautiful it is. Can you imagine what could happen out here? Alaskans don't see the value of order, don't see the value of looking to the future."

We were about forty-five minutes from Anchorage, and the helicopter had forty minutes of remaining fuel—a condition that would hardly arouse the interest of many Alaskan pilots, but ours was particularly careful, and he landed again at Skwentna, where he had a cache of fifty-five-gallon drums. The bloody moosemeat we had seen there earlier was gone. The gravel airstrip was as silent as it had been before. Out of a stand of fireweed, the pilot, Bill Brandt, rolled two drums. He set them on end by the helicopter. He knocked out a bung and smelled the contents. Never knew what might get into these barrels, he remarked, and he inserted a high-vacuum hand pump and began to work. He pumped hard. With beavery sideburns and a billowing glory of a mustache, he looked like an antique Alaskan, and all the more incongruous there pumping Chevron Jet Fuel into a big chopper. He grew tired, and Willie Hensley took over, pumping in an easy rhythm and half as hard.

In the air again, we flew southeast and soon over Bulchitna Lake, a capital-site possibility, its water so clear that we could see, in places, its white sand bottom, and blue-green fathoms where the sand was below the reach of light.

"Is that Bulchitna?" said Arliss Sturgulewski.

"Bulchitna, Alaska," said Willie Hensley. "I propose that as the name of the capital."

It was a lovely lake in a closed spruce-hardwood forest, and I would much have liked to see it from its shore, but the helicopter did not set down by it, or even give up altitude. C. B. Bettisworth said he thought the surrounding terrain too flat, and Earl Cook said he agreed. A pair of eagles flew out from the shoreline trees.

We flew on over a water-dispersed country of ponds and beaver houses, bogs, muskeg fairways, and across the big rivers —Kahiltna, Susitna—to an even greater spread of lakes. These, near Willow, had become a summering world for people from Anchorage—ice out in May and swimming by July—many of whom were now experiencing their own private spasms of the Alaskan paradox, the Dallas scenario versus the Sierra Club syndrome. They worried about their country retreats while they watched the values rise. For beyond Willow, on the upland toward Hatcher Pass, in spruce-and-birch forest that gives way in a dramatic treeline to moors of alpine tundra, was a capital site perhaps more likely than all others to be the ultimate choice of voters. Its temperatures and altitude were much the same as they were at remote Mount Yenlo. Its views—of the valley and of the Alaska Range to the north—were almost as good. The railroad and highway were close. A five-thousand-foot gravel airstrip, built for B-29s, stood ready for facilities and tarmac. And—point of points—Anchorage was scarcely thirty miles away.

Willow is still a hamlet—three hundred people—with potatoes growing in surrounding clearings and tomato vines five feet high: the sort of place where it is not unknown, in the dead of winter, for an old moose hunter to die in his cabin and be brought into town frozen solid. I had stayed in Willow for a night or two, in a cabin that had no windows. Wadded paper filled the gaps in the logs. Twenty dollars a night, with heat. In the Willow Trading Post one morning, a man in a baseball suit was tending bar, and people sitting on stools there were talking about the five acres they had bought for two thousand dollars and how they had recently been offered fifty thousand dollars but were waiting for seventy-five. "OUR COW IS DEAD," said a sign above them. "WE DON'T NEED YOUR BULL." Just up the track was another, somewhat newer sign: "WILLOW BROOK ESTATES, A QUALITY DEVELOPMENT BY LANDAK, INC."

In its meetings in following weeks, the committee would finally reduce its list to three sites that would appear on Alaskan ballots, and the three it would choose would be Larson Lake, near Talkeetna; Mount Yenlo, in the western valley; and the heights to the east of Willow. The site attracting the most votes would be the site of the new capital of Alaska, and when the election came, the emphatic preference of the voters would prove to be Willow. By the terms of the initiative, the move was to begin by 1980. Opponents of the move would go on clinging to the hope that, come groundbreaking day, the money would not be there. Meanwhile, the big helicopter flew on into rain and falling darkness, down the short run to Alaska's principal city—over Knik Arm, into the Bowl. The rain blurred the windows. Through them, the streets and buildings below appeared to be lying under ten layers of acetate. The chopper touched down. Earl Cook, who had left his home in Fairbanks at six in the morning, unbuckled his seat belt with a terminal sigh. "That . . ." he said. "That's a hell of a way to get to Anchorage."

BOOK III

IN THE BUSH

Coming into the Country

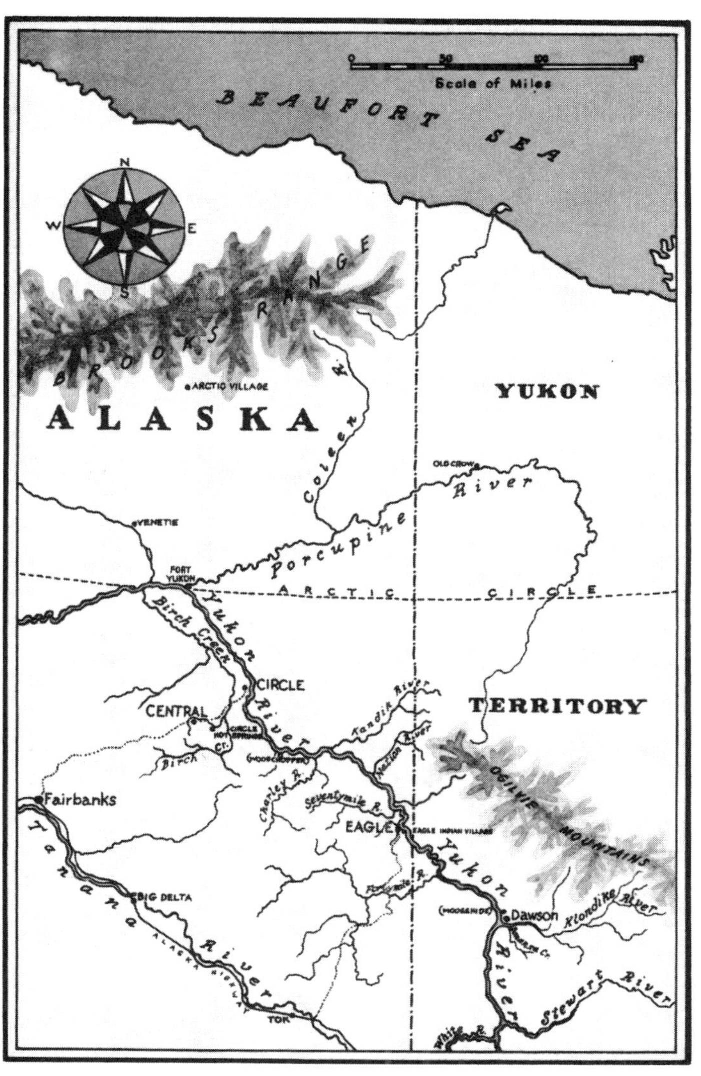

0
50
100
150
Scale of Miles
BEAUFORT SEA
N
W
E
S
BROOKS RANGE
ARCTIC VILLAGE
ALASKA
YUKON
Coleen R.
OLD CROW
River
Porcupine
VENETIE
FORT YUKON
ARCTIC CIRCLE
Birch Creek
Yukon
CIRCLE
River
Kandik River
TERRITORY
CENTRAL
CIRCLE HOT SPRINGS
Cr.
Nation River
Birch
(WOODCHOPPER)
OGILVIE MOUNTAINS
Charley R.
Fairbanks
Seventymile R.
EAGLE
EAGLE INDIAN VILLAGE
Yukon
Tanana River
Fortymile R.
BIG DELTA
(MOOSEHIDE)
Dawson
Klondike River
ALASKA HIGHWAY
River
Stewart River
TOK
White R.

WITH A CLANNISH sense of place characteristic of the bush, people in the region of the upper Yukon refer to their part of Alaska as "the country." A stranger appearing among them is said to have "come into the country."

Donna Kneeland came into the country in April, 1975. Energetically, she undertook to learn, and before long she had an enviable reputation for certain of her skills, notably her way with fur. Knowledgeable people can look at a pelt and say that Donna tanned it. In part to save money, she hopes to give up commercial chemicals and use instead the brains of animals—to "Indian tan," as she puts it—and she has found a teacher or two among the Indian women of the region, a few of whom remember how it was done. The fur is mainly for sale, and it is the principal source of support for her and her companion, whose name is Dick Cook. (He is not related to Earl Cook, of the Capital Site Selection Committee.) A marten might bring fifty dollars. Lynx, about three hundred. Wolf, two hundred and fifty. They live in a cabin half a dozen miles up a tributary stream, at least forty and perhaps sixty miles from the point on the border meridian where the Yukon River leaves Yukon Territory and flows on into Alaska. The numbers are deliberately vague, because Cook and Kneeland do not want people to know exactly where the cabin is. Their nearest neighbors, a couple who also live by hunting and trapping, are something like twenty miles from them. To pick up supplies, they travel a good bit farther than that. They make a journey of a couple of days, by canoe or dog team, to Eagle, a bush community not far from the Canadian boundary whose population has expanded in recent years and now exceeds a hundred. For three-quarters of a century, Eagle has been an incorporated Alaskan city, and it is the largest sign of human material progress in twenty thousand square miles of rugged, riverine land. From big bluffs above the Yukon—five hundred, a thousand, fifteen hundred feet high—the country reaches back in mountains, which, locally, are styled as hills. The Tanana Hills. The tops of the hills are much the same height as New Hampshire's Mt. Washington, Maine's Mt. Katahdin, and North Carolina's Mt.

Mitchell. Pebble-clear streams trellis the mountains, descending toward the opaque, glacier-fed Yukon, and each tributary drainage is suitable terrain for a trapper or two, and for miners where there is gold.

For Donna Kneeland, as many as five months have gone by without a visit to Eagle, and much of the time she is alone in the cabin, while her man is out on the trail. She cooks and cans things. She grinds wheat berries and bakes bread. She breaks damp skins with an old gun barrel and works them with a metal scraper. A roommate she once had at the University of Alaska went off to "the other states" and left her a hundred-and-fifty-dollar Canadian Pioneer parka. She has never worn it, because—although her cabin is in the coldest part of Alaska—winter temperatures have yet to go low enough to make her feel a need to put it on. "We've had some cool weather," she admits. "I don't know how cold, exactly. Our thermometer only goes to fifty-eight." When she goes out at such temperatures to saw or to split the wood she survives on—with the air at sixty and more below zero—she wears a down sweater. It is all she needs as long as her limbs are active. Her copy of "The Joy of Cooking" previously belonged to a trapper's wife who froze to death. Donna's father, a state policeman, was sent in to collect the corpse.

Donna is something rare among Alaskans—a white who is Alaska-born. She was born in Juneau, and as her father was biennially transferred from post to post, she grew up all over Alaska—Barrow, Tok, Fairbanks. In girlhood summers, she worked in a mining camp at Livengood, cooking for the crew. At the university, which is in Fairbanks, she majored in anthropology. In 1974, she fell in love with a student from the University of Alberta, and she went off to Edmonton to be with him. Edmonton is Canada's fourth-largest city and is the size of Nashville. "In Edmonton, every place I went I could see nothing but civilization. I never felt I could ever get out. I wanted to see something with no civilization in it. I wanted to see even two or three miles of just nothing. I missed this very much. In a big city, I can't find my way out of a paper bag. I was scared to death of the traffic. I was in many ways unhappy. One day I thought, I know what I want to do—I want to go live in the woods. I left the same day for Alaska."

In Alaska, where "the woods" are wildernesses beyond the general understanding of the word, one does not prudently just wander off—as Donna's whole life had taught her. She may have lived in various pinpoints of Alaskan civilization, but she had never lived out on her own. She went to Fairbanks first. She took a job—white dress and all—as a dental assistant. She asked around about trappers who came to town. She went to a meeting of the Interior Alaska Trappers Association and studied the membership with assessive eyes. When the time came for a choice, she would probably have no difficulty, for she was a beautiful young woman, twenty-eight at the time, with a criterion figure, dark-blond hair, and slate-blue, striking eyes.

Richard Okey Cook came into the country in 1964, and put up a log lean-to not far from the site where he would build his present cabin. Trained in aspects of geophysics, he did some free-lance prospecting that first summer near the head of the Seventymile River, which goes into the Yukon a few bends below Eagle. His larger purpose, though, was to stay in the country and to change himself thoroughly "from a professional into a bum"—to learn to trap, to handle dogs and sleds, to net fish in quantities sufficient to feed the dogs. "And that isn't easy," he is quick to say, claiming that to lower his income and raise his independence he has worked twice as hard as most people. Born and brought up in Ohio, he was a real-estate appraiser there before he left for Alaska. He had also been to the Colorado School of Mines and had run potentiometer surveys for Kennecott Copper in Arizona. Like many Alaskans, he came north to repudiate one kind of life and to try another. "I wanted to get away from paying taxes to support something I didn't believe in, to get away from big business, to get away from a place where you can't be sure of anything you hear or anything you read. Doctors rip you off down there. There's not an honest lawyer in the Lower Forty-eight. The only honest people left are in jail." Toward those who had held power over him in various situations his reactions had sometimes been emphatic. He took a poke at his high-school principal, in Lyndhurst, Ohio, and was expelled from school. In the Marine

Corps, he became a corporal twice and a private first class three times. His demotions resulted from fistfights—on several occasions with sergeants, once with a lieutenant. Now he has tens of thousands of acres around him and no authorities ordinarily proximitous enough to threaten him—except nature, which he regards as God. While he was assembling his wilderness dexterity, he spent much of the year in Eagle, and he became, for a while, its mayor. A single face, a single vote, counts for a lot in Alaska, and especially in the bush.

The traplines Cook has established for himself are along several streams, across the divides between their headwaters and on both banks of the Yukon—upward of a hundred miles in all, in several loops. He runs them mainly in November and December. He does not use a snow machine, as many trappers in Alaska do. He says, "The two worst things that ever happened to this country are the airplane and the snow machine." His traplines traverse steep terrain, rocky gullies—places where he could not use a machine anyway. To get through, he requires sleds and dogs. Generally, he has to camp out at least one night to complete a circuit. If the temperature is colder than thirty below, he stays in his cabin and waits for the snap to pass. As soon as the air warms up, he hits the trail. He has built lean-tos in a few places, but often enough he sleeps where he gets tired —under an orange canvas tarp. It is ten feet by ten, and weighs two and a half pounds, and is all the shelter he needs at, say, twenty below zero. Picking out a tree, he ties one corner of the tarp to the trunk, as high as he can reach. He stakes down the far corner, then stakes down the two sides. Sometimes, he will loft the center by tying a cord to a branch above. He builds a lasting fire between the tree and himself, gets into his sleeping bag, and drifts away. Most nights are calm. Snow is light in the upper Yukon. The tarp's configuration is not so much for protection as to reflect the heat of the fire. He could make a closed tent with the tarp, if necessary. His ground cloth, or bed pad, laid out on the snow beneath him, is the hide of a caribou.

He carries dried chum salmon for his dogs, and his own food is dried moose or bear meat and pinole—ground parched corn, to which he adds brown sugar. In the Algonquin language, pinole was "rockahominy." "It kept Daniel Boone and Davy Crockett going. It keeps me going, too." He carries no flour. "Flour will go rancid on you unless you buy white flour, but you can't live and work on that. I had a friend who died of a heart attack from eating that crap. It's not news that the American people are killing themselves with white flour, white sugar, and soda pop. If you get out and trap thirty miles a day behind dogs, you can damned well tell what lets you work and what doesn't." From a supplier in Seattle he orders hundred-pound sacks of corn, pinto beans, unground wheat. He buys cases of vinegar, tomato paste, and tea. Forty pounds of butter in one-pound cans. A hundred pounds of dried milk, sixty-five of dried fruit. Twenty-five pounds of cashews. Twenty-five pounds of oats. A forty-pound can of peanut butter. He carries it all down the Yukon from Eagle by sled or canoe. He uses a couple of moose a year, and a few bear, which are easier to handle in summer. "A moose has too much meat. The waste up here you wouldn't believe. Hunters that come through here leave a third of the moose. Indians don't waste, but with rifles they are overexcitable. They shoot into herds of caribou and wound some. I utilize everything, though. Stomach. Intestines. Head. I feed the carcasses of wolverine, marten, and fox to the dogs. Lynx is another matter. It's exceptionally good, something like chicken or pork."

With no trouble at all, Dick Cook remembers where every trap is on his lines. He uses several hundred traps. His annual food cost is somewhere under a thousand dollars. He uses less than a hundred gallons of fuel—for his chain saws, his small outboards, his gasoline lamps. The furs bring him a little more than his basic needs—about fifteen hundred dollars a year. He plants a big garden. He says, "One of the points I live by is not to make any more money than is absolutely necessary." His prospecting activity has in recent years fallen toward nil. He says he now looks for rocks not for the money but "just for the joy of it—a lot of things fall apart if you are not after money, and prospecting is one of them."

In winter on the trail, he wears a hooded cotton sweatshirt, no hat. He does use an earband. He has a low opinion of wool. "First off, it's too expensive. Second off, you don't have the moisture problem up here you have in the States." He wears Sears' thermal long johns under cotton coveralls, and his feet are kept warm by Indian-made mukluks with Bean's felt insoles and a pair of wool socks. He rarely puts on his parka. "You have to worry up here more about overdressing than about underdressing. The problem is getting overheated." Gradually, his clothes have become rags, with so many shreds, holes, and rips that they seem to cling to him only through loyalty. Everything is patched, and loose bits flap as he walks. His red chamois-cloth shirt has holes in the front, the back, and the sides. His green overalls are torn open at both knees. Half a leg is gone from his corduroy pants. His khaki down jacket is quilted with patches and has a long rip under one arm. His hooded sweatshirt hangs from him in tatters, spreads over him like the thrums of a mop. "I'll tell you one thing about this country," he says. "This country is hard on clothes."

Cook is somewhat below the threshold of slender. He is fatless. His figure is a little stooped, unprepossessing, but his legs and arms are strong beyond the mere requirements of the athlete. He looks like a scarecrow made of cables. All his features are feral—his chin, his nose, his dark eyes. His hair, which is nearly black, has gone far from his forehead. His scalp is bare all the way back to, more or less, his north pole. The growth beyond—dense, streaked with gray—cantilevers to the sides in unbarbered profusion, so that his own hair appears to be a parka ruff. His voice is soft, gentle—his words polite. When he is being pedagogical, the voice goes up several registers, and becomes hortative and sharp. He is not infrequently pedagogical.

A decade and more can bring deep seniority in Alaska. People arrive steadily. And people go. They go from Anchorage and Fairbanks—let alone the more exacting wild. Some, of course, are interested only in a year or two's work, then to return with saved high wages to the Lower Forty-eight. Others, though, mean to adapt to Alaska, hoping to find a sense of frontier, a fresh and different kind of life. They come continually to Eagle, and to Circle, the next settlement below Eagle down the Yukon. The two communities are about a hundred and sixty river miles apart, and in all the land between them live perhaps thirty people. The state of New Jersey, where I happen to live, could fit between Eagle and Circle. New Jersey has seven and a half million people. Small wonder that the Alaskan wild has at least a conceptual appeal to certain people from a place like New Jersey. Beyond Circle are the vast savannas of the Yukon

Flats—another world. Upstream from Circle are the bluffs, the mountains, the steep-falling streams—the country. Eagle and Circle are connected only by river, but each of them is reachable, about half the year, over narrow gravel roads (built for gold mines) that twist through the forest and are chipped out of cliffsides in high mountain passes. If you get into your car in Hackensack, Circle is about as far north as you can go on North America's network of roads. Eagle, with its montane setting, seems to attract more people who intend to stay. In they come—young people in ones and twos—from all over the Lower Forty-eight. With general trapping catalogues under their arms, they walk around wondering what to do next. The climate and the raw Alaskan wild will quickly sort them out. Some will not flinch. Others will go back. Others will stay on but will never get past the clustered cabins and gravel streets of Eagle. These young people, for the most part, are half Cook's age. He is in his middle forties. He is their exemplar—the one who has done it and stuck. So the newcomers turn to him, when he is in town, as sage and mentor. He tells them that it's a big but hungry country out there, good enough for trapping, maybe, but not for too much trapping, and they are to stay the hell off his traplines. He does not otherwise discourage people. He wants to help them. If, in effect, they are wearing a skin and carrying a stone-headed club, he suggests that technology, while it can be kept at a distance, is inescapable. "The question," he will say, "is how far do you want to go? I buy wheat. I use axes, knives. I have windows. There's a few things we've been trained to need and can't give up. You can't forget the culture you were raised in. You have to satisfy needs created in you. Almost everyone needs music, for instance. Cabins may be out of food, but they've all got books in them. Indian trappers used deadfalls once—propped-up logs. I wouldn't want to live without my rifle and steel traps. I don't want to have to live on a bow and arrow and a deadfall. Somewhere, you have to make some sort of compromise. There is a line that has to be drawn. Most people feel around for it. Those that try to be too Spartan generally back off. Those who want to be too luxurious end up in Eagle—or in Fairbanks, or New York. So far as I know, people who have tried to get away from technology completely have always failed. Meanwhile, what this place has to offer is wildness that is nowhere else."

A favorite aphorism of Cook's is that a farmer can learn to live in a city in six months but a city person in a lifetime cannot learn to live on a farm. He says of newcomers, "A lot of them say they're going to 'live off the land.' They go hungry. They have ideas about everything—on arrival. And they've got no problems. But they're diving off too high a bridge. Soon they run into problems, so they come visiting. They have too much gear and their sleeping bags are too heavy to carry around. They are wondering where to get meat, where and how to catch fish, how to protect their gear from bears. You can't tell them directly. If you tell them to do something, they do the opposite. But there are ways to let them know."

Cook seems to deserve his reputation. In all the terrain that is more or less focussed on the post office at Eagle, he is the most experienced, the best person to be sought out by anyone determined to live much beyond the outermost tip of the set society. He knows the woods, the animals, sleds, traps, furs, dogs, frozen rivers, and swift water. He is the sachem figure. And he had long since achieved this status when a day arrived in which a tooth began to give him great pain. He lay down in his cabin and waited for the nuisance to pass. But the pain increased and was apparently not going to go away. It became so intense he could barely stand it. He was a couple of hundred miles from the most accessible dentist. So he took a pair of channel-lock pliers and wrapped them with tape, put the pliers into his mouth, and clamped them over the hostile tooth. He levered it, worked it awhile, and passed out. When he came to, he picked up the pliers and went back to work on the tooth. It wouldn't give. He passed out again. Each time he attacked the tooth with the pliers, he passed out. Finally, his hand would not move. He could not make his arm lift the pliers toward his mouth. So he set them down, left the cabin, and—by dogsled and mail plane—headed for the dentist, in Fairbanks.

John Borg came into the country in 1966. He was a mailman, on vacation, and he pitched his tent by American Creek a mile out of Eagle. The Army had brought him to Alaska in the nineteen-fifties—just before Alaska became a state—and (in his phrase) "plain opportunity" was what had caused him to stay. He carried letters around Anchorage for a number of years while opportunity in other forms withheld itself. And then he found Eagle. From birth he had been at home among low populations in open settings. He had grown up in Spirit Township, in the hills of northern Wisconsin, and had gone to Rib Lake High School, thirteen miles away. Now here was a town smaller by far than any he had known—some log cabins and a few frame buildings aggregated on a high bank above a monumental river. It seemed to him beautiful in several respects. "The quality of the people who lived here at the time is what made it particularly attractive." In 1968, he and his wife, Betty, took over the Eagle Roadhouse, providing bunks and board for exploration geologists, forest-fire fighters, and anyone else who might happen into Eagle. Before long, they had the propane franchise; and Borg became, as well, the regional Selective Service registrar, and president of the Eagle Historical Society, and the local reporter for the National Weather Service, and the sole officer (at this river port of entry) representing the United States Customs Service, and—on the payroll of the United States Geological Survey—the official observer of the Yukon. Borg had left Anchorage because half of the people of Alaska lived there and that was "just too many." Now, hundreds of miles distant in the bush, he was on his way to becoming a one-man city. Inevitably, with his postal background, he also became the postmaster—of Eagle, Alaska 99738—and, as such, he is the central figure in the town. He is a slim, fairly tall man, who looks ten years younger in a hat. He was born in 1937. He has a narrow-brimmed cap made from camouflage cloth that, once on his head, is unlikely to come off, indoors or out, and gives him a boyish, jaunty air as he cancels stamps, weighs packages, and exercises his quick, ironic wit. There is a lightness about him, of manner, appearance, and style, that saves him from the weight of his almost numberless responsibilities. One place where the hat comes off is in the small log cabin called Eagle City Hall. Inside are a big iron stove, benches for interested observers, and a long table, where Borg sits with the Eagle Common Council. His bared forehead is a high one—an inch or two higher than it once was. His eyes seem lower beneath it. His regard is uncommonly stern. Shadows come into his mustache, which turns into an iron brush. The youth in the post office has been returned to sender. Behind the heavier demeanor at the head of the Council table is John Borg the Mayor.

The post office is in a small cabin about a hundred yards from the riverbank at an intersection of unpaved streets—the heart of town. Borg owns the building and rents it to the United States. He arrives there by eight in the morning, after checking the height of the river (when the river is liquid). Because this is where the Yukon enters Alaska, its condition at Eagle is of considerable interest to the two dozen villages in the thirteen hundred river miles between the Canadian boundary and the Bering Sea. Borg also reads instruments that react to the weather, and he turns on the Weather Service's single-sideband radio to attempt to send facts to Anchorage. Eagle is not in perfect touch with the rest of the world. Signals get lost. Fairbanks, urban center of the northern bush, would be the more appropriate place to call, because, among others, the bush pilots of Fairbanks want the information. But the radio gets through to Fairbanks only about one time in five. Success in reaching Anchorage is about eighty per cent. So Borg calls Anchorage, toward four hundred miles away, and the word—of the river, of the weather, of an emergency—is relayed back north to Fairbanks.

"KCI 96 Anchorage. KEC 27 Eagle. Clouds now, six to eight thousand feet. Visibility, fifteen miles. Winds, calm. River, thirty-eight and falling. Water temperature, thirty-six degrees." The air in the night went down to twenty-eight. Yesterday's high was fifty. Right now, the air is at forty-five on an uncertain morning under volatile skies—May 13, 1976. It is mail day, the country's substitute for organized entertainment, but there is no guarantee that the plane will come through. It comes two, three, occasionally four times a week. The weather is inconstant, mutable. Squalls of snow may be shoved aside by thunderheads that are soon on the rims of open skies. Borg's records show that on a July day in the nineteen-sixties the thermometer reached ninety-six. During a night in January, 1975, the column went down to seventy-two degrees below zero. Borg says the air was even colder by the river. While this is the coldest part of Alaska, it is also the hottest and among the driest. Less than four feet of snow will fall in all of a winter, and about a foot of total precipitation (a figure comparable to New Mexico's) across the year. There is a dusting of new snow, Borg comments, on the mountains down the river.

The foyer stirs. The post office has a miniature lobby, a loitering center, with a small grid of combination boxes, public notices, and a wicketless window framing Borg himself. Camouflage hat. Faded plaid shirt. "What can I do for you?"

Lilly Allen (in her twenties) has a cartful of textbooks to ship back to the University of Nebraska. High school in Eagle is by correspondence, and is controlled from filing cabinets in Lincoln. The teachers are in Nebraska. Lilly is the resident supervisor.

Jim Dungan comes in, slowly, hands Borg a letter, and makes no move to go. He leans forward on his crutches and draws on his pipe. Dungan has more time even than his fellow-townsmen do this year, as a result of an accident. He says, often, "I'll be off these crutches soon. I won't be wearing them all my life, that's for sure." There are lead weights on the crutches today. Borg asks about them, and Dungan says they are divers' weights, and that when his leg gets better he will slip them into pockets in his wet-suit when he dives for gold. One on each crutch, the weights total fifty pounds. They are not there to create a vanity of muscles but to build his stamina, to keep him in condition.

"It's easy to get out of condition," Borg remarks. "All you have to do is nothing."

Bertha Ulvi and Ethel Beck, Indian sisters, come in to mail raingear to Ethel's husband, who is working in the Arctic for the Alyeska pipeline consortium.

A plane goes overhead. Borg, busy at the scales, says it's not the mail plane—just Jim Layman in his Taylorcraft. A few minutes later, he hears another plane, and says, "No. That's not it. That's Warbelow, coming up from Tok." Borg doesn't have to go out for a look. From the sound alone, he can usually say where an aircraft is coming from, what kind it is, and who is flying it.

Eagle is a dry community. Its leading bootlegger comes in and posts a letter, followed by his closest competitor. They, in turn, are followed by Elva Scott, Sage Cass, Horace

Biederman, Sarge Waller (an alumnus of the Marine Corps), and Jack Boone. With dark furry hair and a dark furry beard, Boone appears to be part bear and part wolf. "You've got a bunch of weird individuals in this town," he observes. And he adds, "Me included."

On one wall of the post-office lobby is a thick sheaf of notices about fugitives all over the United States who are "WANTED BY FBI." They include descriptions, fingerprints, and pictures of people who appear to have arrived long since in Eagle.

Roy Miettunen comes in with a letter—a rare public appearance. He likes to talk, but he stays in his cabin; you have to go to him. In the warmer weeks of the year (a short season), he works his claim on Alder Creek, far out in the mountains, sluicing gold. He once prematurely used up his food, and he walked out in eleven days, eating squirrels. It takes more than squirrels to keep Roy Miettunen in form. He lost more than sixty pounds, and came out of the woods weighing two thirteen. He speaks slowly, firmly, attractively. With his great frame and his big head, his unfrivolous jaw, he looks more sergeant than Sarge. He was, long ago, of the Seattle police. In his cabin he has eighteen rifles, thirty-four pistols, and two swords.

A visitor from the state Department of Highways, concerned about the condition of a stretch of local road, comes in and speaks with Borg about the use of his Cat. The term Cat derives, of course, from the Caterpillar Tractor Company, of Peoria, Illinois, and, in the synecdochical way that snow machines in Canada are generally called Ski-Doos and snow machines in the Alaskan upper Yukon are called sno-gos, all bulldozers of any make or size are called Cats. John Borg's Cat is a forty-two-horse John Deere, with a seven-foot blade. Borg mentions forty dollars an hour as the asking price for his Cat—at work with him on it. The State of Alaska hems but does not completely haw. Borg nods at thirty-eight.

Anton Merly appears, and Jack Greene, followed by Ralph Helmer, who now runs the roadhouse. He has a letter for his grandmother near Spokane. She is in her eighties, and the letter is in acknowledgement of her birthday. He tells Borg that he lived for three years on her farm after his parents were divorced. "That was a very beneficial thing in my life, although I didn't realize it at the time." Helmer, about a dozen others, and the central buildings of the city of Eagle are supplied with electricity at thirty-five cents a kilowatt-hour by a private power company consisting of Charlie Ostrander and John Borg. They have two diesel generators, which can put out twelve kilowatts over an effective radius of a thousand yards. Borg sells power to the post office. But his home cabin, in the woods far back from the river, is out of range. He has a small generator there to run the washing machine and power tools, but the cabin does not use electric light.

Kay Christensen comes in. She has no letter. She wants to speak to Borg about plowing up her garden with his Rototiller. Borg accepts the job. In the eighteen-nineties, Jack McQuesten, a storekeeper celebrated in the country, used to plow his garden with a moose.

The sky was clear at 7 A.M. Then cumulus built up, and some rain fell, and now, at eleven, comes the dinning sound of hail. Dan Kees, a relative newcomer, talks about the hail in West Virginia, where he is from, and Borg listens. Borg is a member of the Bible Chapel, politically the strongest unit in Eagle, and Kees is his pastor. Kees wears a cowboy-style hat, so wide-brimmed it could be looked upon as a stunted sombrero. He is technically a missionary here. That is, the church headquarters at Glennallen, Alaska, pays him. His parishioners are referred to locally as "the bloc," "the group," "the Christians," "the fundamentalists." They also include the families of Ralph Helmer, Ron Ivy, the Ostrander brothers, and Roger Whitaker, the regional constable. In the spectrum of Eagle society, the fundamentalists are all the way over in the ultraviolet, beyond the threshold of visible light. Dick Cook and the young people of the river (the wheat grinders, meat hunters, trappers —liberal, certainly, and in some ways lawless) are at the opposite end, deep into the infrared. A few whites are married to Indians. The Indians number less than fifty, and almost all live three miles upriver, outside the plat of the town. Philosophically, they are as close to the river people as they are to anyone else. Across the middle span of the society are—among others —drifters, merchants, visionaries, fugitives, miners, suburbanites, and practitioners of early retirement. There is something of the rebel in everyone here, and a varying ratio between what attracts them to this country and what repels them in places behind. "Never put restrictions on an individual" is probably page 1, line 1 of the code of the bush. But people here encounter restrictions from governments state and federal, from laws to which they do not all subscribe, and—perhaps to an extent just as great—from one another. Compressed, minute, Eagle is something like a bathysphere, lowered deep into a world so remote it is analogous to the basins of the sea. The people within look out at the country. John Borg remembers regretfully when there was more room to move around inside.

He takes from a wall a photograph of someone in Eagle holding a gold pan full of hailstones the size of eggs, and shows the picture to Kees, possibly to imply that hail like that could destroy a place like West Virginia. The stones falling now are scarcely half an inch thick. Their clatter is considerable, but is not enough to kill the sound of a Cessna 207, up there in the storm with the incoming mail. Borg loads up a van and drives out to the airstrip, which is halfway between the town and the Indian Village. The strip, for the moment, is white as winter. The hail continues, but the skies are broken, and around the gray clouds are wide bays of blue. Borg has collected mail here at sixty below zero, coming out from town on a snow machine for half a ton of Christmas cards arriving one month late. The 207 flares, lands, and taxis up, its wings like snare drums under the pounding stones. The pilot gets out, catches some hail, and examines it. The stones, in shape, resemble Hershey's Kisses. He looks back into the storm and sees seven geese fighting their way through the same airspace he was in moments before. "How would you like to get *that* in the eyeballs?" he says, with feeling for the geese. The pilot, new in Alaska, is from New Jersey. There is a passenger or two. A small roll of chain-link fence comes off the plane. An Indian family is expecting it, and is on hand to pick it up. Borg stuffs the van with mailbags and cardboard cartons. The wing of the 207 is now coated with slush. "That will raise hell with the airfoil," says the pilot, and Borg produces a broom. He sweeps three hundred pounds of slush off the airplane, and the pilot returns to the air.

People throng the post office like seagulls around a piling, like trout at the mouth of a brook. Many, of both races, wear sweatshirts and windbreakers on which are stencilled the words

"Eagle, Alaska." Make what they will of the country, they seem to yearn for contact with the outside world. On days when the mail plane does not come, the human atmosphere is notably calmer than it is now. With a sheet of plywood against his postal window, Borg blocks himself away while he and his wife, whose head tops out at his shoulder blades, do the sorting. As letters go into the boxes, the doors open and slap shut. The babble declines. Many stand and read without dispersing to their cabins. Viola Goggans is baffled by something to do with wheel bearings. Borg gives her a short lesson in their function and potential flaws. Almost gingerly, he hands Lilly Allen a package that—as he knows from her many inquiries—contains a beautifully crafted dulcimer. He is obviously relieved that it has come at last. Sara Biederman, an Indian who lives in the town, is having trouble with the legal phraseology of a letter from Fairbanks. She comes to the window and hands the letter to Borg. "It says there's fourteen hundred and ninety-eight dollars due on your truck and if the money is not paid they will come and get the truck," he tells her. Michael David collects mail and packages, for himself and others in the Indian Village. He is young, slim, without expression. A headband holds his long black hair. Michael David is the Indian Village Chief. "He's got an awful uphill grade in front of him," remarks his counterpart, the Mayor.

Steve Ulvi wants to know if a fourth crate of bees, shipped from Navasota, Texas, has arrived for Dick Cook—and possibly a queen bee as well, due in from Louisiana. Borg shakes his head. The post office is, for the moment, innocent of bees.

Three crates arrived about a week ago, and Cook was here waiting for them, having travelled up the frozen river with his dog team to fetch them. While he waited, breakup came. It was early, and took him by surprise. He had intended to collect the bees and mush back down the Yukon to Donna and the cabin well before the ice would run. But then, one Sunday afternoon, the silent river began to move. Bank to bank fifteen hundred feet, the ice subdivided itself without particular spectacle, and, like an ore in motion on a giant belt, departed for the Bering

Sea. The Yukon is a practical thoroughfare in summer and in winter, but during its times of transition it becomes almost unapproachably inimical. Great floes coming on from upriver roll, heave, compile; sound and surface like whales. Many hundreds of millions of tons of ice, riding a water discharge of two hundred thousand cubic feet per second, go by Eagle at a speed approaching ten miles an hour. Looking at the river, you cannot help but recoil. In water that cold, a human being couldn't live much more than a few minutes—a benevolent brevity, the struggle being hopeless anyway against the current and the ice. The river's edges are lined with ice that is stationary—"shelf ice," "shore ice," the first to freeze at the start of winter and the last to go in spring. It is four feet thick, but will break apart under a stamping foot, shattering into columnar palisades, untapered icicles known as "needle ice" or "candle ice." The shore ice rests on rock and gravel, while only a step or two away is the riverborne ice, big masses pounding into one another with a sound like faraway thunder, or, often, like faraway surf. These are muted sounds. For all its weight and speed, the ice moves softly much of the time, fizzing like ginger ale.

The ice run will thin out now and again, nearly disappear. The river becomes clear of all but isolated floes. In another hour, or day, heavy ice is running again—wall to wall, crunching, jamming, lethal as ever. The ice comes segmentally from upriver and from the tributary rivers. The Yukon, even above Eagle, has tributaries four hundred miles long. When ice of the Yukon, ice of the tributaries comes free and begins to run, it does so in big units. People watch for ice from Dawson—which is about a hundred miles away, in Yukon Territory—and whenever barrels, garbage, foul debris go hurtling by on soiled floes, someone will grunt knowledgeably and say, "Dawson ice." The White, the Klondike, the Stewart, the Pelly, the Nordenskiöld, the Teslin, the Fortymile let go their ice arrhythmically and give it into the Yukon. Pelly ice. Stewart ice. Teslin ice. Fortymile ice. It takes two or three weeks for it all to go by a single point like Eagle. In weeks thereafter, it forms a temporary, bobbing delta spread miles out to sea.

With the ice comes wood. The breakup flushes out of Alaskan and Canadian uplands many millions of cords of forest debris. Trunks go by that are sixty and seventy feet long. Some ride just beneath the surface. They are called sleepers. The big logs rarely retain their branches, but many still have their root structures, and those that do are sometimes called preachers, because the roots ride down in the water while the upper trunk breaks through the surface at an angle, and bows and rises, bows and rises, as it glides by. Once in a while a big trunk will nosedive and stick like a javelin into the bed of the river. Then a following ice floe snaps it in half with the sound of a battleship gun. Sometimes the wood in the river seems as voluminous as the ice. The people of Eagle collect logs that have paused in eddies or have otherwise come near enough to shore. Firewood is worth sixty dollars a cord, and twice that in winter. People have to travel considerable distances—to forest burn areas, for example—to get it legally. So it is not just wood but a great deal of cash that is bobbing by on the Yukon. For the most part, the people can't do much, however, but wistfully watch it go. The big river delivers the wood to the Yupik Eskimos of the western coast, where there is no timber to speak of and where for ten millennia—before missionaries, books, schools, and visual aids—fires were made with fuel from a forest-mountain landscape that the Eskimos had never seen and could scarcely have imagined.

Cook was anxious to get back to Donna. So, less than a week after breakup, with ice running heavy, he borrowed a canoe and started for the river with his dogs. He might have used the quiet eddy at Eagle's boat landing, a short distance upstream, but that would have meant taking the dogs through town, and Cook did not wish to create a disturbance. Several dozen dogs are chained to stakes beside cabins throughout Eagle, and Cook's loose ones, running amok, could be counted on to start fights and drive the tied ones berserk. So Cook, whose base in Eagle is a shack on some land he owns, led his dogs through woods and down to the river just below the town. He met Steve Ulvi there, who meant to go downriver with him. Slipping, falling into crevices, they slid the canoe over high shelf ice and lowered it into a small indentation of water, a petty cove. This was at an outside bend, where current runs fast in a river. Flying ice chunks in tumbling hundreds pounded by. Big flat discs, called pan ice, their edges worn round, spun among the chunks. The canoe was a nineteen-foot Grumman aluminum freighter. Cook and Ulvi loaded it—three crates of bees, two hundred and fifty pounds of gasoline, an old outboard motor, the corpse of a great gray owl, a big wooden box of supplies, two rifles, a shotgun, a sixty-pound sack of sugar, and the five sled dogs (about four hundred pounds of dog). Steve sat in the bow. Cook, in the stern, made a few shifts for balance. Then he shoved the canoe out into the stream. The ice was so heavy and concentrated that the mean free path for anything attempting to move through to a safer part of the river would inevitably be extremely short. The canoe travelled about ten feet. It was on the current for perhaps two seconds when it was hit from behind and driven like a nail into the stationary ice. It might as easily have been upended, or pressed down into the water, or, most probable event of all, rolled over. But luck was running with the ice. Wedged there, stuck, protruding backward into the river, the canoe was at least upright. Blood ran out of Cook's face. His skin became as pale as the floes in the river. If more ice were to strike the canoe now, it could crumple it up like an aluminum can. Ulvi wrenched the bow free and shoved the canoe backward. Once more it floated among the ice. He and Cook, prying hard to get the bow around, were nudged but not hit. They tried an angling path toward the slower side of the river. Ahead of them to the end of the view was a thousand acres of ice-filled water. Beyond sight, it was impossible to guess the level of danger, for ice can jam at bends, entrapping with it anything that floats, while the weight of the river builds up behind until the force is sufficient to explode the ice free.

Sarge Waller—who is, among other things, a professional riverman—later commented on Cook and Ulvi's journey and described them as "yahoos." Sarge said, "Them ice floes could knock the boat over and wipe it out. They could get wiped out ten miles down. They could be dead now. Who would know?" And no one did know for a number of days—or think much about it, truth be told. Then Ulvi and the canoe reappeared in town. He looked tired, cold, gaunt, but, withal, intact.

Ulvi is a young, cinematically handsome man, with blond curls and blue eyes and a nineteenth-century drooping gold mustache. He came into the country when he was twenty-three, and has been here two years. He followed his brother

Dana, who first encountered Eagle as a stop on a Yukon raft trip, and who is now married to Bertha Paul, of the Eagle Indian Village. Harold Ulvi, an uncle, was the Northern Commercial Company's storekeeper here in Eagle twenty-five years ago. After growing up in California, Steve went to college briefly in Oregon. He backpacked all over the Western mountains. When he moved to the Alaskan bush (with his wife, Lynette Roberts), he had in advance some of the skills he would need. He had rebuilt every car and motorcycle he had owned. He knew cooking, carpentry, and more than a little about edible wild plants. Lynette and Steve, who expect a baby, have a cabin upriver near the international boundary and live there as much as they do in Eagle. "Dick Cook and I both hold in highest regard not the intellectual but the man of maximum practical application. Like Dick, I'm trying to be self-sufficient on this earth, to live successfully without altering the environment. Cook is not sucking on fossil fuels, and I don't want to, either. People say, 'If you feel that way, why don't you make candles out of bear fat?' But I'm not prepared to do that. It's all relative, of course. I do burn ten or fifteen gallons of kerosene a year for light, some white gas for my Coleman stove, some fuel for my kicker. But if everybody else did no more than that we would not have an energy problem. I learn things when I visit Dick. I go see him about his garden, for example. The most returns for the least effort—Dick is definitely interested in that. He has great perspective, a good body of working knowledge. He remembers when caribou were really running around here. He's been here long enough to cover a couple of the natural cycles. He knows a lot about guns. He hand-loads. I hand-load. He carries a 6.5 × 55 Swede military carbine. I carry a 7 × 57 Mauser. Some people like a high-speed bullet. Some like a big, slow bullet. They all kill. Dick goes for a long bullet at a moderate recoil. He believes that placing the shot is what matters most."

When the conversation in Eagle—outside the post office, inside the general store—concentrates, as it does sometimes, on Cook, not everyone is so admiring. In fact, as Lilly Allen's husband, Brad Snow, once said to me, "You will find it impossible here to say anything nice about anybody without considerable disagreement."

"Cook is a romanticist, fancies himself a latter-day Henry David Thoreau. There's not a hell of a lot of depth there."

"He's a patient hunter. He will sit half the night waiting for a beaver to come out of his house."

"He is a pontifical, messianic guru. He's no dummy. He likes all these young river buckos sitting at his feet while Donna works her tail off tanning a moosehide."

"It takes Cook two years to develop an idea."

"It took him *six* years to get himself together and get out to his cabin downriver. Ann, his second wife, was not a bush woman, and—like some other women in the country—was not willing to compromise."

"He's a wealth of information. If he's going to do something, he does it right. Build a sled. Snowshoes. Rifles. Gardens. Dogs. He's an excellent musher—as good at dogs as anybody."

"His dogs are no better than mine."

"He *is* self-sufficient. He is the closest to attaining the goals of all of the people of the river. He is the old man of the business, and he is making it work pretty well."

"He manages to suggest he knows the country, but he has never even seen the Charley River."

"Cook is not good at one-to-one relationships. So he's here in Alaska, here in the bush. We are all here for similar reasons. My mother would say we're all failures. That's not so. We are seeking alternatives."

"Cook does not want anyone else doing his thinking for him. He also does not want to let other people think. Donna is now learning and following. When Donna starts thinking for herself, there will be trouble."

Viola Goggans and her family came drifting into the country in a school bus a couple of years ago, with purpose ignited by the presence of gold. They stayed first in the drainage of the Fortymile River, and then shifted to Eagle. Because Communists would before long take over the nation as a whole, they reasoned, there could be "no future for the kids." Money would be "worthless," and "the only thing that will buy anything is gold." Tom and Vi Goggans were not in a position to hoard commercial bullion. They had entered Alaska some years before with a baby and a dime, and only the baby had substantially grown. If they wanted gold, they would have to separate it from placer ground.

The school bus was their mobile home. For its future they had imaginative plans. It was full size, yellow, the standard model, and they were going to convert it into a boat. They would then launch the bus on the Yukon and navigate downstream to a tributary river and up that to high creeks with promise of gold. To scoffers who cared to listen Vi was not reluctant to give details. ("They thought we was crazy. They thought we was going to drive out on the water. They was about ready to send a straitjacket down. We had 'em all confused.") People seemed to think that the Gogganses were going to seal the body, drive off the bank, and let the wheels spin in the river. Actually, they meant to slice the bus in half —the long way, under the windows and around the ends—and then flip over the top part and make it into a barge. The lower half would float upright on eight evenly spaced steel barrels, and, barge in tow, would be powered by the bus engine, with a propeller on the drive shaft. Old Cap Reynolds, long gone from Eagle now, once built his own miniature stern-wheeler. He took it down the Yukon a couple of hundred miles, and far up the Porcupine River. The school bus, for its part, never had a chance to prove itself one way or the other. The Gogganses had two partners, who got into money trouble and withdrew. Vi and Tom could not fund the adventure on their own. So Tom is off working on someone else's claim, and for months at a time Vi is alone with her children in a rented cabin in Eagle—a gold widow, showing visitors the few flakes and small nuggets that are the beginnings of the family's defense fund against the second coming of Russian America.

She is a small woman, not five feet tall, with a touching, uncalculating friendliness that would win her more friends almost anywhere than it has in Eagle. She says, "I'll play you a tune on this here, if you'd like it," and she picks up her Hohner accordion. Beth and Jimmy, seven and five, look on. She plays "You Are My Sunshine." It is the only tune she knows on both the piano and the chord sides. She plays it again. Intently, she tilts her head toward the keyboard. Her hair is tallowy blond. She has a narrow face, and many missing teeth, a prominent nose. She wears a red headband above blue denim. She is thirty-nine. Before Alaska, she lived all her life, and went for a time to grade school, in Havre, Montana. Asked for more, she plays "Roll Out the Barrel," apologizing for its incompleteness, for without the support of chords, she suggests, a barrel will not roll. Carrying a thermos of coffee, she goes to the Common Council meetings, where she is sure she has identified at least one pure Communist, albeit he is just an observer like herself and not a member of the Council. "I got a family now. I like to find out what's going to happen when they get older. I never been to a council meeting before I came to Eagle."

Jess Knight, thirty years ago, made a log raft, draped a car over the raft with paddle wheels in place of tires, and drove on the river a hundred and sixty miles to Circle. The school bus is still beside the Yukon but is hardly ready to go anywhere. It is beyond hope for road or river. It has no wheels, no motor, no seats—items sold to pay for food. The bus interior is utterly stripped out, and all the windows have been shattered—random targets of random bullets.

"I like Eagle, but not the people. They are either Bible thumpers or alcoholics. They try to rub the Bible on you. They don't like it that I won't go up in front of them and confess. If you confess, you confess in silence, before God, and not broadcastin' it. Leanin' on the Bible there, they can't stand up on their own two feet. They talk nice to you, and what they say about you hurts when they think you won't know."

At home, I spend much of my time looking out of windows, and in the cabin I am occupying here nothing changes the habit. Outside is First Avenue: mud and dust, pocked and gravelled, the principal thoroughfare of the city, where children go by in wagons harnessed to dogs, and old-timers in pickups cruise slowly back and forth—"trolling," as someone has put it, for conversation. The cabin is tight, comfortable, heated by an Ashley. It is said of a fine stove like this one that it "will drive you out of here at seventy below," a promise enhanced by bush architecture. Cabins are generally small, so the stove can retain command. My wife was here for a time. We slept in a loft just above the Ashley. Routines developed. Every other day, we sawed and split some wood, but, with the ice petering out on the river and the sun shining eighteen hours a day, we were soon using the stove for little more than to get our blood moving in freezing temperatures as the day began.

All water must be lugged from the community well house, which is up past the post office, in the center of town—drinking water, dishwater, bathwater. I prefer my scent. Under the eaves of the cabin, however, are barrels, buckets, tubs, which will occasionally catch enough water to wash and rinse a moose. In the rainwater, lather swells and crowns, forms pillows on the skin. The lather is a particular luxury in Eagle, where rain is fairly scarce and the well water is so hard it turns soap into stone. Eagle is directly over an old inactive fault, and its water rises through a fracture from an exceptionally deep source, bearing a taste of soda. There is a stream not far away called Champagne Creek. The ground that lies between the cabin and the outhouse is unvegetated glacial flour—fine-ground soil, soft as powdered talc, brought down by the Yukon from the ice fields of the high Wrangells and left here for aeons past. It sticks to shoes and is tracked in. Clothes become stiff with it, so they are washed in leftover bathwater—and, after that, in goes the odd pot or pan. Finally, the water washes the floor, where its arc of utility ends. What is left is carried to the riverbank and dumped over. A block of shore ice, at the same time, is chipped out with an axe in order to refill an insulated cooler.

A quart of milk in the cooler cost $1.36. It came from Visalia, California. It is neither condensed nor evaporated but "sterilized" whole milk, in a can, without preservatives. It is fine milk, but too expensive. Condensed milk, appropriately diluted, works out at 60¢ a quart, and powdered milk at half of that. Frozen steak costs $4.20 a pound, bacon $2.07, chicken $1.15, hamburger $2.10, cheddar cheese $2.35, butter $1.85—all this in Eagle's only store. Grapefruit cost 55¢ apiece, a cucumber 75¢, tomatoes and lettuce about $1.15 a pound. Fresh food, after travelling upward of two thousand miles, for the most part has jet lag. Campbell's soup is 51¢ a can, a dozen eggs $1.30. A standard box of Morton's salt costs 62¢. Much is said about the high cost of things in Alaska, but what seems remarkable is that prices are not much higher than these, since virtually everything arrives by truck, plane, or boat from the rest of the United States. The supply lines to Anchorage and Fairbanks are long and costly enough, but these prices —roughly half again as high as they would be in New Jersey— are set in Eagle, where nearly everything has been brought in light planes another two hundred miles over mountains. Dave McCall, the pilot-storekeeper, charges 19¢ a pound for flying things in. Hence the especially costly salt.

Outside the cabin window, a robin is hopping around with feathers fluffed up against the cold. The ice goes out. The birds come in. Transition is almost instant from winter to spring. It is curious to see these robins—big, tough robins—so far up here, so near the Arctic Circle, near the top of their range. They seem miserable, fluffing themselves up into balls in an attempt to make down jackets of their own feathers. Dozens of Lapland longspurs are jumping, pecking, jumping, pecking in the dust near the robins, and looking immeasurably more at home. We have seen warblers, juncos, blackbirds, gyrfalcons, a pair of golden plovers, an Arctic tern. A seagull sits on the outhouse, thirteen hundred miles upriver from the sea.

Twilight holds through the night now, and darkness has gone for the summer. There is little need of lamps, but when I want them to read or write by I fiddle with mantles and pump up pressures for intense white-gasoline light.

The dogs staked out all over town set up a chorus wail. They seem to be responding to direction from the sky, because their arioso howls begin with a simultaneity that has no explanation. There is a hint of wolf in some of these dogs, and the part that is wolf seems to be their voices. The wailing stops the way it starts—all at once there is silence, and no saying why.

In woods across from the cabin window, the remains are visible of two or three older cabins—moldering away, so far gone now they are barely discernible and have almost disappeared. A little to the right of them is Elmer and Margaret Nelson's new place, wood still shining from the saw. The neighborhood represents the rise and fall and rise of Eagle. The Nelsons have come here to retire, like one or two other couples in the town, which, as retirement centers go, is about as far as you can get from Sun City. Margaret Nelson is grandmotherly, with whitening hair, and Elmer is wiry, spare, and gray. She came to Alaska from the state of Washington in the thirties, worked for the Northern Commercial Company, and, during the war, wrapped parachutes in Fairbanks. He grew up on a homestead in Montana and has lived in Alaska fifty years. He built roads and he trapped. Deep among the mountains off the left bank of the Yukon, Nelson and a partner had a chartered airplane fly them around while they dropped packages. Eventually, they landed at a hand-dug airstrip. This would be in September most years. They would ask the pilot to return a day or two before Christmas. Then—without machines of any kind, without dogs—they would separate and cover country as rapidly as they could in an attempt to get to their dropped supplies in advance of foraging bears. They laid out patterned traplines —loops, cloverleafs. Every five days, they rendezvoused—each to see that the other was all right, and to pass on information. This was total wilderness. They were something over a hundred miles from Circle and eighty from Eagle and eighty from Big Delta, where the Nelsons lived at the time. In any kind of need, there was nowhere else to go. In discrete valleys were a few cabins, and they stayed in them or siwashed (camped on the trail). When they were picked up—after three months in there, generally apart and alone—they had collected a good share of their income for the following year.

The Nelsons' place is landscaped only by its woods. Neat, odd, it lacks the expectable outdoor furnishings of an Alaskan cabin. My side of the road makes up for that. A few feet away from me, in the direction of the center of town, is the cabin of Dale and Gloria Richert, who sell used snow machines, washing machines, sleds—examples of which are strewn about the space between the cabin and the road. The cabin is roofed with slit and flattened fuel cans. Richert had a store in Michigan not long ago. It was firebombed by hoodlums. This helped him decide that an appropriate community in which to seek a new life might be somewhere near the Arctic Circle. A sign among the used machines says "Eagle Sports Shop." Richert has lures, flashlights, tents, boots—a little L. L. Bean going on inside the cabin. In their regard for his goods, the river people call him Taiwan.

Close by me the other way are the yard and cabin of Louise and Sarge Waller. The remarkable propinquity of these dwellings is characteristic of nearly all settlements, large and small, in Alaska. In three hundred and seventy-five million acres—a sixth of the whole United States—so little property is available for purchase that conditions are as crowded as they are in Yonkers. A window of my cabin frames a postcard view of Sarge's yard, which, in no discernible geometric arrangement, contains boxes, tarps, stove parts, cans, buckets, Swede saws, washtubs, tires, sawhorses, fourteen fifty-five-gallon drums, and five snow machines in different stages of dismantlement. When you drive along an old back road in the Lower Forty-eight and come upon a yard full of manufactured debris, where auto engines hang from oak limbs over dark tarry spots on the ground and fuel drums lean up against iron bathtubs near vine-covered glassless automobiles that are rusting down into the soil, you have come upon a fragment of Alaska. The people inside are Alaskans who have not yet left for the north. An architect I know, who prefers to style himself an "environmental psychologist," once remarked to me, "Aesthetics are not compatible with survival." In any case, Sarge Waller's place is by no means atypical of the world he has taken for his own. He is out in his yard now, surviving. He is piling up wood. On his pickup—which has three spare tires, a gun rack, and a searchlight—is a load of driftwood he has collected from the boat-landing eddy. To get his cabin through a winter, he needs at least five cords. His cabin, exhaling smoke, is angular and miscellaneous. Sarge himself is less vulnerable to heat loss. He is a big man, with a girth approximating four feet. His arms are legs of lamb. His large, ovoid head is covered with Marine brush. In all this magnitude, his eyes, which are dark, seem small. Sarge is amiable, garrulous. In his house is a framed photograph of the younger Sarge, dimensions the same. He is dressed for battle, but not in his staff sergeant's uniform of the United States Marines. Instead, he wears the white robes of karate, cinctured with black. Sarge was tough. He has dragons on his skin, and snakes, and skulls—eleven tattoos, from as many parts of the world. He survived the battle of the Chosin reservoir, in Korea. He liked the Marine Corps as he found it in 1949 but not as he left it a decade later. He was a junior in high school when he joined up, and what the Marines had then, he says, was "spirit de corps." In the aftermath of Korea, the U.S. Marines, in his view, "turned into a Girl Scout troop." If a private first class became troublesome, a sergeant could no longer "punch him in the mouth." An increasing number of officers, at any rate, would not encourage or support such gestures. One day at Camp Lejeune, in North Carolina, a corporal in Sarge's unit had trouble with a private and the private was locked up in the brig. Sarge took justice literally into his own hands. He went to the brig, reached through the bars, grabbed the offending Marine private, and pulled him forward with such force that his face crashed into the bars and blood ran from his nose. Sarge explained why he had come, and left. In short order, his phone "jumped a foot off the desk." The chaplain wanted to see him. "This is no longer the old Marine Corps," the chaplain informed him, and warned him that a repetition of such behavior could cost him his stripes. He remained a sergeant, but such a disappointed, disillusioned one that he planned on quitting, and wondered what on earth he would do.

He had grown up in Massillon, Ohio. (His father was a conductor, brakeman, trainman on the Nickel Plate.) In Massillon, there was an old man with fur clothes and nuggets in his pockets—a living mothball from the far-northern rush for gold. He liked to talk to kids, and every Saturday he told them stories. He showed Sarge pictures of the wild north. Sarge took to trapping, hunting, and fishing until the truant officer was sent in search of him. When he was nine, he got his first rifle, and decided he would live someday in Alaska. All this came back to him as a depressed Marine—in 1959, the year the territory became a state. Sarge quit the Corps and moved north. It was another eleven years before he came into the upper-Yukon country. He lived meanwhile in Slana, on the "Nigger Highway"—that is to say, on a road that had been built by a black regiment of the Army Engineers. He married Louise there, a somewhat metropolitan woman, touched with glamour. She was an outback restaurateur. She had a daughter, and they had two more, and Sarge, all the while, had a vision. He was a riverman whose time had not yet come, and one day he would live, utterly on his own, on a big river in a big wilderness. To fulfill these requirements, he need not go far—not two hundred miles away. He arrived in Eagle in 1970 with two boats, a thousand feet of lumber, corrugated roofing and what he estimated to be a year's supply of food. It was a place "where a guy could branch out into the country." With his three daughters and his wife, he went fifty miles down the Yukon and built a cabin. Sixteen by twenty feet, with log walls, it was two stories high, and was thus unusual. Its upper level was a sleeping loft. Food ran low, and Sarge's hunting, much of the time, failed to make it up. On rabbit tacos, his waist shrank and shrank to a low of thirty-four. He trapped with some success. Meanwhile, his "womenfolks," as he lumps them, were not affectionate toward the cabin. They were lonesome, for one thing—miles from the nearest human being—and, for another, the cabin had not been designed by a heating engineer. The warmth of the wood stove collected against the roof, and the overall insulation was not adequate to keep much heat on the ground floor. The family was in the cabin all winter, 1970–71, and spent much of it up in the loft. There were times—too many times for the womenfolks—when the stove could not raise the temperature of the ground floor any higher than forty degrees below zero. In this situation, Sarge's vision, the dream of his life, froze solid. He saw himself as a man of the wild, but his family did not. Whatever else might happen to him, though, he was not about to lose his spirit de corps—and the corps, now, was his family. He retreated from the deep wild and settled with them back in Eagle. Louise, more at home, became the clerk of the city and in some ways its leading politician. Gracefully, she will still say of her husband, "He does not have blood in his veins—he has Yukon River water." Sarge has set himself up as a charter boatman, taking hunters and geologists downriver. He has established traplines near town. For the most part, though, he seems to enjoy himself talking; and he likes to say, "I did not come up here to work anyway. I don't work. And my family is happy."

Jim Dungan comes swinging up the road on his way from his cabin to the urn of coffee at the store, where he can sit on a stool and use up a part of his day. When he leaves, he will go down by the river and stare, leaning forward on his crutches, for as much as an hour at the flamelike, firelike movement of ice. Meanwhile, he greets Sarge. He waves in my direction, too. "Just call me Hopalong," he says. Visiting Jim's cabin now and again, I will have a drink of Postum or coffee and be let into his present and all but disoriented world, which has no walls of time. "I'll be off these crutches soon," he says, as if I had not previously heard him say it. "I won't be wearing them all my life, that's for sure."

When the crutches go, he wants to get out again into the wild with a suction dredge. Like Sarge Waller, Jim Dungan has dreamed of a life beyond community, a cabin somewhere up a faraway stream, an existence financed (in his case) not with furs but with gold. "Just to get out and live the way I figure a guy should. I didn't buy land here in Eagle because I like the town. I like the country. The dredge gives me a purpose out there. If you're not gettin' good color, you can shut down the dredge, take a pan, and go off prospecting for a couple of weeks. Set up a little lean-to. Find a better place. Get the dredge and work the better place."

Suction dredges are a modern vogue, and, if any comparison is valid, are miniature versions of the old gold dredges —the shiplike, company-owned floating units that elsewhere in Alaska still eat whole streams. Suction dredges are portable, cheap, irresistible to a certain class of lone, adventuring miner. They are floating units, using inner tubes or Styrofoam blocks. Typically, they will have a seven-horsepower engine and a short, narrow sluice box. The whole unit can be dragged about by someone in a wet-suit, holding a long hose that sucks up stream-bed gravel. *Alaska* magazine advertises a "high-impact Jet Age plastic" sluice box that sells for $39.95, a Gold-Vac dredge for $295. Dungan prefers somewhat better gear, and figures that thirteen hundred dollars would equip him. Generally, the miner kneels in the river, its riffles driving at his chest, but he can go down eight, ten feet, if he knows what he is doing, and draw gravels from crevices in rock. The hoses are usually about four inches in diameter, and can swallow stones almost as large. Rocks, sand, gold, and gravel go into a hopper, then on through the sluice box, which catches the gold. That is what Jim Dungan came into the country to do—in 1968, with a partner called Polack Joe. Dungan was an experienced diver. ("I used to be able to hit sixty feet free-diving with no air.") The partners first worked the Bottom Dollar, a small tributary in the Birch Creek mining district, upward of a hundred miles west of Eagle. In one six-day period, they got forty-seven ounces of gold, worth about two thousand dollars. They left Alaska, but came back for good in 1970 and worked the Fortymile River, near Eagle. "We were living all over the Fortymile. We'd find an old cabin, and dry off, and then get back on the river. We caught grayling, shot rabbits. Me and Joe. It's a different way of life, not the rat race you got down there. That's all it is down there that I can see. Up here, a person is as good as he's going to make it. A guy's freer in this country. Down there, you're so restricted. Up here, they ain't gettin' you for spittin' on the sidewalk."

A flood on the Fortymile for the time being killed the good life. It might have killed the partners. It utterly destroyed their suction dredge. The partnership broke up; Dungan went to Fairbanks and took a job. He planned to work until he had bought a truck, a cabin in Eagle, and a new dredge. First as a cook and later as a jug-hustler, chain man, and shooter, he worked for Geophysical Service, Inc., using seismic instruments in the search for oil. From the air, six months of the year, large parts of the green surface of Alaska appear sutured with seismic trails. A jug is a geophone, and as many as two thousand may be set in the ground, usually in straight lines, to monitor the waves from dynamite blasts as they reflect from underground formations. After each blast, jugs from the rear are moved to the front. Day after day—usually in winter, to reduce damage to the terrain—the procession moves cross-country. Dungan worked on seismic crews from the North Slope to southeastern Alaska—walking a hundred and ten miles once in the Arctic in winter, calling in helicopters to drive off grizzlies in summer, and saving the money he earned. He once worked a line down the Susitna Valley, and on winter nights could see the lights of Anchorage. He went no closer. "Jesus Christ, you go in there and there goes your winter's paycheck. I just stayed in camp." He saved enough to buy his cabin in Eagle and, later, a three-quarter-ton green Ford pickup. He was about ready to buy his new suction dredge when he came back to Eagle on leave from a job in the Brooks Range, May 14, 1974.

He got drunk that night with a celebrational friend, and the next morning, feeling drier than the town itself, he decided to take a ride over the mountains to a roadhouse where he could see some friends, drink a beer or two, and buy some booze for fresh reunions. The pickup spat and sputtered. It was just a year old and in powerful shape, but had been idle all through the winter. He reasoned that its engine was full of carbon, so he went into the hills burning it out with speed. He was found two hours later. The truck had rolled three times. He had broken all his left ribs and both legs. The right leg was not so much broken as shattered. Pieces of the bone were never found. Eagle's satellite radio called for help. Thirteen hours after the accident, Dungan reached the hospital in Fairbanks, two hundred miles away. In the years since, he has been given skin grafts, bone grafts, a steel plate, and seven pins that look like wood screws. "They said I didn't have much chance of keeping my leg after the bone graft and the plate, but I fooled 'em. I still have the leg." The plate is to come out when the bone graft is solid, but the plan is not working well, because a hole will not close in the leg above the plate. "Sometime next winter, I should be working. After the cast comes off, I can walk with a shoepac and a cane. I'll be off these crutches soon. I won't be wearing them forever."

His cabin, where he does most of his waiting, is eight feet by twelve—not quite three steps by four. He sits at a table, and I sit on his bunk. The stove fills the rest of the room. The previous owners were a family named Waite—trappers, now gone from the country. Four of them—two girls and their parents—lived in the cabin two years. With a tar roof and board siding, it is lined with aluminum foil and looks like a baked potato experienced from the inside. There is one small window, with two panes, presenting a view of stacked cordwood—birch and spruce. When I first called on Dungan, in the course of a trip through the country in 1975, he said he was disturbed about his wood stove, because it was not airtight and had been hard to control. When the temperature outside was sixty below zero, the stove had driven the temperature up to a hundred and thirty degrees, and Dungan was besaunaed in his own steam. He has since replaced the stove. I remember, too, that he had a glass jar full of king salmon preserved in rock salt. He said he was saving it for his Christmas dinner.

I ask him now about the salmon, and he tells me that it spoiled. He spent Christmas in the hospital. He still has the bad salmon. "When my leg heals, I'll use it for bear bait."

His green pickup, its roof crushed down, now sits in front of Dan Kees' house, next door. Kees bought it for parts, and the hulk is there for Dungan to stare at, which he often does. Dungan is thirty-nine. His dark hair is receding. He has a quietly modulated voice, and the wide stare of a wounded creature. He grew up mostly in Wisconsin, stepson of a railroad switchman, and went to Cudahy High School, in Milwaukee, and straight into the U.S. Marines. He worked for eight years on the assembly line at American Motors. "That's enough to drive a man completely insane." It drove him, at any rate, to Vietnam—as a reënlisted Marine. "That's one place I'd rather forget, to tell you the truth. I hear all this petty-ante bitching around here, and I think, They should really have something to bitch about. This town is divided between the outlaws and the do-gooders. I don't give a damn about their stories about each other. I try to stay out of it. This is just like every other bush town. If I could be, I'd be in the high country, or on the Yukon River."

A quiver of arrows hangs from a rafter. Tacked to another rafter is an emblem that says "GSI ARCTIC OPERATION 1969–70." A note on a wall calendar under January 17th says "SUN—frist time sence Nov. 21." There are pictures on the table and the windowsill. One is of his stepfather, recently dead, others of a child or two. There are six pictures in all, of the family of his only, and older, brother. "My brother, Bob, was killed in 1972 in a light airplane in the Lower Forty-eight. That's him. That's his little girl there. She got run over by a car."

"Have you ever been married?"

"No. I've always been just kind of a bum."

Joseph Hajec, Polack Joe, also worked for American Motors. Dungan tried decking on car ferries and driving spikes in the railroad yard before the two of them left for Alaska. "We were working the whole god-damned year to get two weeks' vacation. Then we'd head for open country. Then back to work for eleven and a half months to get back to the country. Some people get a good job at American Motors and think they've got it made. If you can go out and enjoy the country—to me, that's the life. My reason for being up here is basically a guy can be an individual. In Milwaukee, we had armed robberies, murders, rapes. There's no crime in Eagle. I didn't feel safe walking a country road in Wisconsin. I feel safe going down here to the store."

In Dungan's cabin are two pistols, two shotguns, and three rifles. He keeps a pistol and a shotgun always loaded. "Bears come right into town here. You never know. The first night I ever spent in Eagle, I was sleeping in a tent. I had two Eskimo women with me and a case of booze. When I was sleepin', I had a four-hundred-pound black bear lookin' me in the face. Dave Crump, who was there, shot him under the chin with a .30–'06. You never know. Besides, I've got a philosophy. I let the people know the guns are loaded. I've always kept a gun. I kept a .38 in Wisconsin. There are no bears there. But there are jealous husbands. I'm not exactly an angel."

He lights his pipe. It is long and low and looks somewhat Sherlockian and even more like a toilet bowl. He wears a cotton sweatshirt, corduroy trousers. His toes look like dead wizened tubers protruding from the cast. "I'm hopeful that in a matter of weeks they'll cut this cast off and say, 'Dungan, put on a shoe.' That damned life goes by too quick. You look back and say, 'Where'd that go to?' If this hole's healed up by summer, I'm going to go for gold. Everybody says a suction dredge is just a god-damned toy. But I'm going up there as a way of being independent, as a way of making a winter's grub. These guys who go out trapping—Cook, Edwards, Potts—they could make five times as much on the pipeline. But they're independent. I'll use all the proceeds from dredging first to buy a snow machine to take food and equipment in winter to the dredging sites—spare parts, gasoline, case lots of bacon, beans, and rice. Up in the Fortymile country, I got a couple of places picked out. It's high country, closer to bedrock. I'll stake no claims. I'll just go for the gold."

"What would you do if you got a hundred thousand dollars' worth of gold?"

"Put it in the bank."

"How would it change your life?"

"It wouldn't."

Wyman Fritsch, a conventional placer miner, has a nugget larger than his thumb. He found it in the Discovery Fork of American Creek, some ten miles out of Eagle, and he says it is by no means the largest one he has taken from that stream. He has been mining there for fifty years. He was a boy when he came into the country. He is currently known as The Man with the Big Nugget. He showed it to me the other day, so that I could hold it in my hand and rub the genius of the gold. It was lumpy, pitted, pocked, rough, ugly—an apparent filling from the tooth of a Sasquatch. The marvel of it—as the earth's elements go—is that when Fritsch came to it with his mining equipment, scraping up the deep gravels of American Creek, it was there as nearly pure metal. Gold is not merely rare. It can be said to love itself. In the idiom of science, it is, with platinum, the noblest of the noble metals—those which resist combination with other elements. It wants to be free. In cool crust rock, it generally is free. At very high temperatures, however, it will go into compounds; and the gold that is among the magmatic fluids of interior earth may be combined, for example, with chlorine. Gold chloride is "modestly" soluble, and will dissolve in water that comes down and circulates in the magma. The water picks up many other elements, too: potassium, sodium, silicon. Heated, the solution rises into fissures in hard crust rock, where the cooling gold breaks away from the chlorine and—in sizes ranging from specks to the eggs of geese—falls out of the water as metal. Silicon precipitates, too, filling up the fissures and enveloping the gold with veins of silicon dioxide, which is quartz.

Gold can be taken from such veins with dynamite blasts, pneumatic drills. But that requires the funds and efforts of a large corporation. The deepest mine in the Western Hemisphere —the Homestake gold mine, in Lead, South Dakota—goes down into the earth more than a mile and a half. Its capital cost to date has been upward of a billion dollars. Alaskan lone miners—people who have, or who have had, names like Pete the Pig, Pistolgrip Jim, Groundsluice Bill, Coolgardie Smith, Codfish Tom, Doc La Booze, the Evaporated Kid, Fisty McDonald, John the Baptist, Cheeseham Sam, The Man with the Big Nugget—prefer to wait for God to break open the rock, to lift up and expose something like the Sierra Nevada and with epochal weathers blast it and spall it and tear it apart until the gold rolls out into the rubble of the streams. Placer mining —separating gold from stream gravels—is difficult work, but beside any other method it is comparatively easy. "*Placer*," in Spanish, means "pleasure."

This is the country that Arthur Harper came into in 1873. The journey itself—two thousand miles, a large part of it on scarcely charted Arctic rivers—was an accomplishment in exploration, but to Harper that was incidental. A native of Ireland —intelligent, intense—he was a big bull-shouldered man with an H-beam jaw and a look so glazed it correctly suggested a quest. He had spent a lot of time in American goldfields, and he had what the geologist Alfred Hulse Brooks later described as "a conception of the broader orographic features of the western cordillera." That is to say, Harper had noticed that the important gold discoveries of North America had occurred in the Western mountains, and that the mountains went a great deal farther north than did—at that time—the discoveries. This suggested to him that as the highlands traced their way around the basin of the Yukon River, in Canada and in Alaska, their contributive streams in all likelihood contained undiscovered deposits of gold. Always confident that this was true, he searched with only modest results for upward of twenty years. Elusive stories were already in the air. An itinerant missionary named Robert McDonald, eleven years ahead of Harper, was said to have found a stream in the country where gold was so concentrated he picked it up with a spoon. There was no saying where, except that it was probably a tributary of Birch Creek. The strike in 1880 at what became Juneau was far to the south but was nonetheless encouraging. It was the northernmost discovery in North America to date. Harper tried Birch Creek, the Fortymile, the White, the Stewart, the Tanana, and myriad branching streams. He went to some of the right rivers and looked in all the wrong places. The luck of the Irish he had left at home. He killed and ate game along streams near the mouth of the Tron-diuck, missing the gold below. Here and there, with his pan, he did find enough color to support his conviction. With Leroy Napoleon (Jack) McQuesten, who came into the country by the same route in the same year, he sent back the word that drew prospectors northward in numbers sufficient to favor a find. And so—in a broad orographic way—he was the discoverer of the gold of the Yukon.

McQuesten, from Maine, was no less a believer than Harper, but it was McQuesten's way to support the search rather than pursue it. He took furs downriver and returned with goods. Representing the Alaska Commercial Company, he set up trading posts—for example, Fort Reliance (1874), forty miles up the Yukon from what came to be known as the Fortymile River. The posts were served by stern-wheeled steamers arriving from the Bering Sea. McQuesten grubstaked prospectors—in many cases, for penniless year after penniless year—with a generosity that would have bordered on charity were it not for his merchant's instinct that when the dust at last came out of the streams it would settle in the merchant's safe. The first major strike in the region was made on the Fortymile in 1886, when prospectors named Harry Madison and Howard Franklin—acting on suggestions made by Harper—went twenty-five miles up the river, dug to bedrock, and found coarse gold. Just before freeze-up, they emerged with the news. After volunteering to relay it to the outside world, an Alaska Commercial Company river pilot named George Williams made an overland trip and raced the coming winter. He almost survived the trip. Of exhaustion and cold, he died like Pheidippides delivering his message. McQuesten, who was in San Francisco buying supplies, bought more supplies. He need hardly bother to help spread the word. Along the two thousand miles of the Yukon, a dozen whites had lived before. They would now be coming in many hundreds, and soon in many thousands. Harper and McQuesten had spent thirteen years preparing the way—developing transportation, gathering detailed geographical and geological information. Needless to say, they readily established a trading center where the Fortymile goes into the

Yukon. Shovels and flour, picks and pans were for sale there. Advice was plentiful and free.

For seven years, the Fortymile—yielding as much as eight hundred thousand dollars in a season—was the focus of attraction in the mining of Yukon gold. The drainage was almost wholly in Alaska but ran a few miles into Canada—dissecting a high plateau immediately to the south of what is now Eagle. In 1893, excitement shifted to a relatively distant part of the country. McQuesten grubstaked two prospectors named Pitka and Syroska, sending them downriver and into the hills to have another look for the Reverend Mr. McDonald's legendary spoonfuls of gold. Pitka and Syroska made their strike at a fork of small streams some fifty miles from the Yukon, in a world of mica schists and quartz intrusions, of sharp-peaked ridges, dendritic drainages, steep-walled valleys, flat spurs, and high, isolated mountains locally known as domes. While find followed find, small brooks acquired their ultimately storied names—Mammoth Creek, Mastodon Creek—and since all of them drained into Birch Creek, the area became known as the Birch Creek mining district. Hundreds of miners left the Fortymile to rush to the new discoveries. McQuesten, of course, followed, and built a store. Because miners were so scattered in the hills, McQuesten established his trading post at the river port that supplied them, which had been named Circle City in the mistaken belief that it was on—and not, as it was in fact, fifty miles below—the Arctic Circle. Quickly becoming the foremost settlement on the Yukon, it proclaimed itself "the largest log-cabin city in the world." By 1896, there were ten thousand miners in the district. The resident population of Circle was twelve hundred. Works of Shakespeare were produced in its opera house. It had a several-thousand-volume library, a clinic, a school, churches, music and dance halls, and so many whorehouses they may have outnumbered the saloons. Then certain fresh information came floating down the river from the half-abandoned settlement at the mouth of the Fortymile.

Two men known for their low credibility had walked into Big Bill McPhee's Caribou Saloon, at Fortymile, and announced a new find upriver. Scarcely an eyelid moved. One of the men, Tagish Charlie, was an Indian. The other was Lying

George Carmack. Lying George said they had found pay on a small stream off the Tron-diuck, where a third member of their party, an Indian named Skookum Jim, had remained to guard their claims. The saloon was full of miners. No one was much impressed. For every worthwhile tip that might ever come along there were dozens upon dozens of meretricious leads to feverish diggings and dismal disappointment. Moreover, Carmack had a reputation for tall tales and short accomplishments. He was also the victim of their prejudice, for he was the white husband of a Tagish squaw. He had gone so native he actually wished to be chief. He encouraged himself with a double dram of whiskey. It mattered a great deal to Carmack that these skeptics believe him. He felt, he said later, as if he had dealt himself "a royal flush in the game of life." He and his companions had staked all the ground the law allowed them, and now he earnestly sought the respect that might come to him if he made these beggars rich. He finished his whiskey, and he took a used rifle cartridge from his pocket and turned it upside down. Gold is characteristic of the stream it comes from—the shape of the nugget, the rustlike shadings of the flake. Flat, rough, oblong, tear-shaped, round, smooth—bits of gold are the consistent signatures of the source placer. An experienced miner can look at a nugget and name the stream. A crowd drew in around Carmack's gold. Only a small amount was there, but no miner in the saloon had seen its like before. They fell silent. The surveyor William Ogilvie, who was working out of Fortymile at the time, made the quiet observation that, in effect, the gold could not have fallen from the sky. Faking nonchalance, miners melted away. The claims of George Washington Carmack, Skookum Jim, and Tagish Charlie were recorded, and soon the stream where they had staked them was named Bonanza Creek. It is the richest placer stream that has ever been found in the world. The discovery claim was ten miles above the Tron-diuck—an Athapaskan phrase meaning "hammer water." (Fish traps made of stakes had been driven into its bed.) Tron-diuck, alchemized into English, became Klondike.

I cannot resist a digression into the fate of Big Bill McPhee, who was apparently generous with his cache in a way that any number of his clansmen are not. One person who asked for his help after Carmack's visit to the saloon was Clarence Berry, a young man from California who was eager to stake his own claims and who had all the determination and physical strength required in a miner but had come to Fortymile with no money, no food, no supplies of any kind. McPhee told Berry to go out to the cache and take whatever he needed. Berry's claims, as things proved out, were among the richest on Bonanza Creek, and they led to the development of a widespread mining conglomerate and, later, to added fortunes in California oil. Big Bill, for his part, settled in Fairbanks. One day his home and saloon there burned to the ground, destroying all of his assets in the world. Berry, in California, heard of this through his company and at once sent a message north: Rebuild, restock, restore everything; have all accounts sent to me.

The fact that a hundred and fifty million dollars was awash in the drainages of the Klondike diminished but did not extinguish the goldfields of the Alaskan Yukon. Circle City declined by eighty per cent but did not ghost out. Enough miners remained in the Birch Creek district to remove half a million dollars' worth of gold in the season after the Klondike strike. The Fortymile region was drained of talent, but not necessarily of the best talent. Established miners continued to work its streams. For the majority, certainly, the years around the turn of the century were ones of rushing to and fro, impelled by the brightness of news. Miners of the Alaskan gold country went into the Klondike with the advantages of propinquity and experience over the green multitudes coming up from the United States, most of whom found every stream that showed any color completely staked. The Klondike was in Canada. Ninety per cent of the miners were American. The Crown imposed a heavy tax on wealth drawn from Her Majesty's placers. The Royal Canadian Mounted Police, understaffed and apprehensive, sent a letter to Ottawa setting forth the possibility that the Americans might by force attempt to move the international boundary far enough east to comprehend the Klondike. But, without violence, many of them just went quietly "home," crossing the line to Alaska, to settle in places—and to work streams—that often flaunted remarkably patriotic names: Eagle, Star City, Nation, American Creek, Washington Creek, Fourth of July Creek. In 1900 came the rush to the beaches of Nome. Eight thousand left Dawson, the instant city where the Klondike meets the Yukon, and conspicuous among them all was Ed Jesson, who came walking into Eagle carrying a bicycle. Riding down the frozen river, he had thirteen hundred more miles to go, but for the time being he was going nowhere; his bearings were cold and stiff. When the temperature went up enough, he rode away. Meanwhile, someone else on his way to Nome went by on ice skates. Populations halved in Eagle and Circle, but, as before, miners by no means disappeared from the country. Nor have they ever. Birch Creek and the Fortymile, where the Yukon mining began, have always since discovery had miners on their creeks.

The principal technique of placer mining is to wash gravel through a long, narrow sluice box, its bottom ribbed with partitions that simulate the riffles of a stream. Gold and heavy sands settle among the riffles, while stones and boulders move on through the box and out the far end as "tailings." The pioneers, with their picks and shovels, could move about five cubic yards of gravel a day. Before long, these individual prospector-miners were outdone by small groups who could collectively move more stone—for example, with mechanical scrapers—and who could greatly increase available water by building elaborate wooden flumes. Giant, high-pressure hoses were developed as well, with dug reservoirs feeding mountainside ditches from which water would fall through pipe to emerge from nozzles with power enough to excavate gravels to bedrock. Inevitably, big dredges were built, too—by companies that bought up claims and worked entire streams. The dredges floated on ponds of their own making and on capital from cities months away.

Notwithstanding all this, the individual miner persevered. Quite apart from the major strikes, a kind of life had been discovered that to some—to Axel Johnson, for example—was no less alluring than the gold. Johnson was a Swedish fisherman who came into the country in 1898 and built a cabin, dug a garden at the falls of the Seventymile River. He worked Big Granite Creek, Alder Creek. He "sniped" a lot of his gold—just took it from likely spots without settling down to the formalities of a claim. He would go to the deep holes of stream rapids and periodically clean them out with a large instrument that resembled a spoon. Or he might take, say, eighteen hundred dollars out of a little bench of gravel, working it by hand. When he came into Eagle for mail and supplies, he sniped as he travelled, and once picked up sixty-seven ounces on the way. He trapped; and below his falls he caught Arctic grayling in such quantities that he had enough to dry and keep for winter. He lived well. He died in his cabin, in 1933. The life that attracted him, with its great liabilities and its great possibilities, has gone right on attracting others, and has been enhanced occasionally by a fresh sense of boom. There have, in fact, been three boom eras in the gold streams of Alaska. The second came in the nineteen-thirties, when the price of gold doubled. During the rushes of the eighteen-nineties, the price had been about seventeen dollars an ounce—a figure that remained essentially steady until 1934, when the government raised it to thirty-five. Lonely miners out on the creeks were suddenly less lonely. Fresh activity was encouraged as well by the almost simultaneous advent of the bulldozer, which could push around roughly four hundred times as much gravel per day as an old-timer with a pick and a shovel. The third Alaskan gold boom began in the early nineteen-seventies, when the United States allowed the price to float with the world market and announced that American citizens, for the first time in forty years, would be allowed to buy gold and save it. The price giddied. It approached two hundred dollars an ounce. Then it settled back to present levels—around a hundred and fifty.

New miners come into the country every year—from Nevada, Montana, Oregon, wherever. They look around, and hear stories. They hear how Singin' Sam, on Harrison Creek, "hit an enrichment and took out nuggets you wouldn't believe." They hear about "wedge-shaped three-quarter-inch nuggets just lying there where water drips on bedrock." They hear about a miner in the Birch Creek district pulling nuggets from the side of a hill.

"I have always been mining, always preparing ground. I'm not telling you how much money I've got ready to dig up. She's in the bank. Trouble is, there's too much gravel with it."

In tailing piles left behind by dredges, people hunt for nuggets that were *too big* to get stopped in the sluice boxes and went on through the dredge with the boulders. People reach into their shirt pockets and show you phials that are full of material resembling ground chicken feed and are heavier than paperweights. Man says he saw a nugget big as a cruller tumbling end over end in the blast from a giant hose. It sank from view. He's been looking for it since. Man on Sourdough Creek, working for someone else, confessed he had seen a nugget, and reached to pick it up, and found it was connected by a strand of wire gold to something much larger and deeper. He broke off the nugget and reported nothing. He could hardly mark the spot. Later, he went back to try to find what was there—he knew not where.

To stories of such nature Stanley and Ed Gelvin have not always been immune. Son and father, deep-rooted in the country (the one by birth, the other since long before statehood), they live in Central, a community with a Zip Code and a population of sixteen, so named because it was the point on the Birch Creek supply trail from which the miners fanned out to the gulches. Some went surprisingly far. Both Stanley and Ed Gelvin are, among other things, pilots, familiar with the country from the air; and some years ago they became more than a little interested in certain conjunctive stream courses in high remote terrain, where they saw aging evidence of the presence of miners. The site is—they request that I not be too specific—somewhere in the hundred-plus miles of mountain country that lies between Eagle and Central. Along a piece of valley floor more than three thousand feet high they noticed, among other things, a wooden sluice box weathered silver-gray, a roofless cabin, a long-since toppled cache. The old-timers did not build cabins, caches, and sluice boxes just in hopes of finding worthwhile concentrations of gold. Having found it, however, they lacked the means to remove anything like the whole of what was evidently there, even when they dug down in winter into places where flooding would stop them in warmer weather—thawing frozen deep gravels with fires and hoisting it up in buckets for sluicing in the spring. Under the stream beds were soaked unfrozen depths known as live ground, where the old-timers could not have worked at all. While some Alaskan streams freeze solid, most continue to run all winter under phenomenally increasing layers of ice and snow. The phenomenon is overflow, which has so often been lethal to people travelling streams on foot—soaking themselves, freezing to death. Water builds up pressure below the ice until it breaks through a crack and spreads out above. When the pressure is relieved, the flow stops and the water becomes a layer of ice. Before long, snow falls, and compacts. More pressure builds, and water again flows out on top. Through a winter, these alternating layers of snow and ice, white and blue, can build up to great confectionery thicknesses—but the stream below remains liquid to bedrock. With appropriate earthmoving equipment, Stanley pointed out, a guy could go into that live ground and scrape up what lay on the rock. No such machine had ever reached these alpine streams, as a glance at their unaltered state confirmed. They were much too far from the mining road and the dredged and bulldozed creeks of the district. It was almost too bizarre to imagine—a bulldozer in the roadless, trail-less wilderness of those mountains. The price of gold, on the other hand, had lately quintupled. Maybe going in there was worth a try. Over the Gelvins' kitchen table, father and son kept talking, and a program gradually evolved. Attention became focussed on the family backhoe. The first necessity would be to sample the deep gravels and see what was there. That long steel arm and big steel bucket could reach many feet into the bottom of a stream. If a guy wanted to have a look at what was lying on the bedrock, that backhoe would be the thing. Maybe a guy could fly it up there. The backhoe was a modified tractor that had once belonged to the United States Air Force and had hauled bombers around in Fairbanks. It weighed five thousand seven hundred pounds. A guy could take it apart. Reduce it to many pieces. Fly it, in the family airplanes, like birds carrying straws, nut by bolt in fragments into the hills.

When I first met the Gelvins, in the early fall of 1975, pieces of backhoe were strewn all over the ground beside the airstrip behind their cabin. The machine itself was still recognizable but was fast melting away under the influence of the wrench. The airstrip looked like a dirt driveway scarcely ten feet wide, with weeds upgrown on either side almost to the level of a Cessna's wings. The runway had a dogleg. Every so often, Stanley or Ed would stuff some parts into an airplane, roll off in a plume of dust, disappear around the bend, and reappear eventually, rising, to clear a backdrop wall of spruce. Stanley—tall, lanky, still in his middle twenties—being of the country, was a gold miner almost by nature. His father, Ed Gelvin, was more diversified. Over the years, he had become, it seems safe to say, as much as anyone in Alaska an example of what Steve Ulvi has in mind when he speaks so admiringly of "the man of maximum practical application." Mining, as it happened, was what first drew Ed and his wife, Ginny, into the country. In the early nineteen-fifties, he worked some claims on Squaw Creek, near Central. He moved a lot of gravel but not a lot of gold. They liked the country, turned to other things, and stayed. Trapper, sawyer, pilot, plumber, licensed big-game guide, welder, ironworker, mechanic, carpenter, builder of boats and sleds, he suffered no lack of occupation. I once asked him if there was anything that could go wrong around his place that would cause him to seek help from elsewhere. He looked off into the distance and carefully thought over the question—this compact and gracefully built man of fifty or so with thick quizzical bifocals, a shy smile, a quiet voice. Finally, he said no, he guessed there wasn't. Ginny hunted with him, and ran the traplines as well. They raised a son and three daughters, who were so fond of moose and caribou they never much cared for beef. Over all the years, meanwhile, and despite the multifarious activities which followed that first attempt at mining, Ed had more trouble getting gold out of his mind than he had had getting it out of Squaw Creek. He had contracted gold fever, the local malaria; and he passed it on to Stanley.

If they were teased by the sight of the old relics they saw in that high nameless valley, there were stories around that were stimulating, too. Old miners in the district said they had always heard it was shallow ground up there, with good colors near the surface—and not much developed by the real old-timers. It had been the valley of, among others, Pete the Pig. That would be his cache lying on its side. Pete the Pig Frisk was a savvy prospector, an efficient miner, not one to waste his time where there was no pay. He found a good pay streak there, and not a few bears. He was a clean, attractive man, Pete the Pig

—but he grunted while he worked, while he rooted for gold. When he opened his mouth to speak, he grunted first. When he got old, he went to the Sitka Pioneers' Home. From time to time, the miners out in the country saw a published list of who was there. One year, Pete Frisk's name was gone from the list. In 1962, a man named Brown—from Oregon or "somewhere down near there"—had had himself flown to Pete Frisk's valley in a helicopter. He had a partner with him, two pet Airedales, and a set of miniature sluice boxes that were innovative and effective as tools for prospecting. He also had a .357 Magnum for grizzlies, of which he killed three. When the partners left, they attempted to walk out, by crossing mountains to the Yukon. Because the creeks and streams of Alaska have a geminate quality that can fool even people who know them well, the two men thought they were on Coal Creek headed for the big river when in fact they were on Hanna Creek headed somewhere else. Brown's partner came out weeks later, with an injured leg, floating on a raft he had made on the Charley River. Brown, for his part, "stayed" in the high country; that is, he apparently died there. He was never heard from again. His partner said they had separated after the injury, as Brown went on for help. All that was ever found was the carcass of an Airedale, butchered out as for the table, but uneaten. Possibly, a bear ate Brown. His widow suspected something worse. She thought there had been more than just colors found up there in Pete Frisk's valley.

A dozen years later, Stanley Gelvin, in his Aeronca Champ with its dunebuggy tundra tires, flew so low he skimmed the dwarf willows, hunting the valley for a place to land. Thirteen treeless summits, each about the height of the high Adirondacks, surrounded the three confluent streams there, and down from this nippled coronet ran sweeping tundra fells deceptive to view. They appeared to be as smooth as fairways, but with their sedge tussocks and fissured soils they were in fact as rough as boulderfields. Flying near stallout speed, Stanley followed one creek and another, studying the ground. Finally, he saw a place he thought he could get out of if he were to set the plane down. The walk would be long if he couldn't—not to mention what to do about the plane. Rising, circling, returning, he gingerly put his wheels on the ground and jumped back at once into the air. Felt pretty good. He circled again. He rolled his wheels on the tundra twice more. It was thumping rough, but it seemed negotiable. He set the Aeronca down.

Taking off successfully, he went home and told his father, and they began to advance their plans. First, they should improve the landing place. They had a little Ranger—a diminutive tractor, like a Cub Cadet—which they had used to like purpose when they built a cabin on the Charley River years before. Ed cut the Ranger in half. They flew it to the mountains, and he welded it back together. The backhoe before long followed, and when it was at last reassembled they scooped into the center of a stream. Bedrock was eight feet down. Even at six, they panned the colors they had hoped to see.

They had intended to spend the whole of the following season ranging with the backhoe around the claims they had made, trying out pieces of seven miles of streams, but early results were so encouraging that they sharply foreshortened the tests. To put it conservatively, a pay streak appeared to be there, and what was needed now—since the backhoe was just a fifty-seven-hundred-pound shovel—was a means of moving gravel in a major way. The Caterpillar Tractor Company produces the eponymous Cat in seven sizes—styled D3, D4, and so on to D9. Most gold miners use something less than the largest, but the Gelvins—forming a partnership with two friends in Fairbanks—decided to go all the way. The supreme Cat, twenty-seven feet long, eleven feet high, with a blade of fourteen feet, could sweep forty yards of gravel before it —possibly a hundred dollars a shove. Ed Gelvin went to Los Angeles to shop for a used D9.

With his partners in Fairbanks putting up the money in return for a half interest in the claims, he paid forty-seven thousand five hundred dollars for a ten-year-old machine—D9, Series G. In the fleets of general contractors, it had spent its lifetime ripping raw California land, making freeways, and preparing building sites on beaches and deserts. Who, watching it there—clanking, dozing, wheezing, roaring, grunting like Pete the Pig—could ever in farthest-fetched imaginings have guessed where it would go? It went to Seattle by train, and by barge to Whittier, in Prince William Sound. There the Alaska Railroad picked it up and took it to Fairbanks, where, in early

April, a lowboy hauled it up the dirt road north. Forty miles from Central, the haul stopped—blocked by the still unbroken winter snows. The road had been smothered since October. Ed Gelvin, who was observing from the air, landed on the road and with Stanley put the blade on the Cat. The weather in a general way was warming. Snow was melting. Ice was beginning to rot. If the D9 was going to move up frozen stream beds and climb into the mountains, it had to keep going now. If the road was closed, the Cat would open it.

When Stanley Gelvin was a small boy and did his elementary-school work by correspondence from the kitchen table in Central, he was from time to time required to draw a picture. When the choice of subject was his to make, he always drew a Cat. He operated one before he drove anything else. Now, with a Cat all around him, he knew where things were. He sensed like an athlete the rhythm of the parts—the tilt cylinders, the blade-lift arms. A good Cat skinner is a Cat mechanic, and, from the torque converter to the sun-and-planet gears, he knew what was making the moves. "I know what's inside the thing—everything—and what makes it work. My father knows how the stuff goes together, too. If the thing needs work, we do it."

The snow-obscured road leading on toward Central was—even at its best, in summer—a tortuous trail. In several high places, it traversed the flanks of mountains as a fifteen-foot shelf with no rail of any kind and a precipitous plunge on the outboard side. On the last of these mountain passes, twenty miles from home, Stanley encountered drifts that were thirty feet deep. To keep going, he had to bite into the snow, doze some to the brink, send it avalanching down, then turn and bite some more—all the while feeling for the road, feeling with his corner bits (the low tips of the blade) for the buried edge where the road stopped and the plunge began. A D9 is in some ways the most difficult Cat to operate. "You've got so much iron in front of you you can't see what you're doing." It is also his favorite size, because it is so big it does not bounce around. This one weighed a hundred and ten thousand pounds. Its balance point was ten feet back of the blade. Repeatedly, Stanley moved the blade eight feet over the edge. He knew where it was. If he had gone off the mountain, he would have raised one fantastic cloud of snow. Instead, he trimly dismantled the prodigious drifts and dozed on down to Central.

To the pads of the track Ed Gelvin welded ice grousers. They would keep the Cat from sliding. They were small pieces of steel, protruding like hyphens from the tracks. Ed and Stanley had built a steel slick plate and a steel sluice box, and Ed had rearranged them as a huge loaded sled—eight feet wide and twenty-four feet long: I-beams, H-beams, three-sixteenths-inch plate. He had made a thousand-gallon fuel tank. It was full and on the sled. Here and there, he slipped in snowshoes, gold pans, a two-hundred-amp generator, a welding tank and torch. Finally, he secured to the top of the load a plywood wanigan—that is, a small hut, with three bunks, propane, and a cupboard full of food. The rig, composed, weighed about twelve tons. When it was hooked to the D9, Stanley left for the mountains.

He crossed low terrain at first. His mother rode with him. His father hovered in the air. Then he changed passengers, taking on a friend named Gary Powers, and they began to move up Woodchopper Creek. His altitude at the start was nine hundred feet. The highest point on the trip was well above four thousand. They travelled five days, fourteen hours a day. There was plenty of wind. The highest temperature they experienced was zero. They stopped to cut their way through trees with a chain saw (fearing to doze them because the wanigan might be crushed). The Cat fell twice through rotting ice. With no difficulty, it climbed out of the water. There was some luck in the conditions, but not much. With less ice in Woodchopper Canyon, Stanley might have been stopped. But successive overflows on the creek had built the ice thickness in places to thirty feet. Nearing the head of Woodchopper, he moved the Cat slowly up a steep slope of ice, slid back, crept again, slid back, and thought for a while he wouldn't make it. Without the grousers, the big rig would have been stopped, but they held just enough, and gradually he crawled out of the head of the creek—only to move into snow so deep the D9's steel tracks spun out. Stanley thought it wise to stop for the night. For one thing, all this was happening in a blizzard. Next day, the sky was clear, the air colder, and Stanley moved on a contour through the deep snow until he found an uphill route. Steadily, he climbed ridges, sometimes in little snow, sometimes in seven-foot drifts. At one point, the going was so steep that he disengaged the sled and tried first to clear a trail. "I knew that ridge was too steep to go over, because it was almost vertical. So I went around to the right. Without them ice grousers, the machine would have slid sideways and straight to the bottom as if it was on skates. Gary was scared to death. I went real slow now, and slipped some, and then went down to a dead crawl. I had it idled as low as it would go. I went on a half a mile or so. When I saw it was possible, I went back for the sled."

Landing on skis, his father would fly him out, and the D9 would sit idle in the mountains until summer. Meanwhile, there was one last ridge to cross. "One side was sheer, and the other had deep snow and was very steep. It must have been forty-five degrees. A guy could have maybe gone around one side—if you'd left the wanigan, dug the snow, and plowed a road. But I didn't want to make a horrible-looking mess. I moved slowly up. The track did spin a bit. I couldn't go straight up. It was too steep. I couldn't go sideways too well. I couldn't go back, because I had the sled. I'd have been afraid to back down. You can cut a road into the side of a mountain if you want to with a Cat like that, but I just inched up the thing, and over. I didn't want to dig up the country."

Brad Snow and Lilly Allen came into the country in 1974. They were twenty-six and twenty-one. Their route had begun in New Hampshire and had included Anchorage, where they took jobs to collect enough money to venture into the bush. Like many other young couples who wished to get past the turnstiles of urban Alaska, they studied the map and guessed at the merits of this or that possible destination. Many people they encountered seemed to be headed for McGrath and Bethel and points between on the Kuskokwim River. Allen and Snow therefore looked the other way. "None of those people even knew where Eagle *was*. We figured it was the place to go."

They arrived in a pickup—with their axes and hammers, drill bits and drawknife, whipsaw; their new, lovely, seventeen-foot

Chestnut Prospector canoe. They were exploring in more ways than the geographical. They were looking for a milieu—and a manner of developing their lives. For necessary money, they could work from time to time in Fairbanks—and, possibly, in Eagle. But they hoped to live much of the year apart from any community. "I reject suburbia," Snow was not shy to explain. "I reject crowds. I do not want a new car, a fancy house. They are not worth working for. In the Lower Forty-eight, economic pressure made it impossible for me to have the land and space I would like to have without spending twenty years to get it and then being surrounded by box houses. In order to get anything like what I wanted, in New Hampshire, I would have had to deal in large figures. I was unwilling to complicate my life to get those figures."

What he and Lilly sought was terrain where the individual spirit might be confined only by the metes and bounds and rules of nature. They meant to go down the Yukon, whose banks were just the beginnings of millions of acres of wilderness. They asked around—of others, like Dick Cook, who had pursued the same idea—and they discovered the country's code of seniority right. Tributary rivers were prime locations. There was someone already living on each incoming stream for a considerable distance below Eagle. The first vacancy was the Nation River, forty-six miles away—a little far, but it would do. Snow had brought with him a sense of impending catastrophe, in large part because he had staked his plans on the character of the Yukon without even knowing if it was safely navigable or a boiling flume of rapids. When he had become assured that for all its great power the big river ran smooth, his confidence improved. He felt expansive as he loaded the canoe with seven hundred pounds of grain.

He was an electrician by trade—a fact of no value on the Nation. He was good at carpentry, though, and he was a sharpshooter—skills enough for a beginning. Seven miles up the Nation, he and Lilly built a ten-by-fourteen-foot cabin of unpeeled, saddle-notched logs. It had two windows, paned with soft clear plastic. It was chinked with moss. Its roof consisted of layers of sod, moss, and plastic. It was a tight, well-made, neatly made cabin. Its door, for some months, was nothing more than a hanging blanket, but even on nights at thirty-five below zero the cabin was so warm that the blanket was kept to one side. They had an airtight heat stove ("a poor man's Ashley"), and their cookstove was a sheepherder's unit, its firebox scarcely a cubic foot. With the whipsaw, Snow made boards for a bench and a table. From dry spruce he made dowels, which he tapped into holes drilled in the wall logs, and on these he set shelves for their pinto beans and bulgur, their whole-wheat-soy ribbon noodles, their cherry butter and corn-germ oil, rolled oats, popcorn, brown rice, and wheat berries. He killed a moose, and they hung strips of the meat from the ridgepole to dry. They preserved blueberries, cranberries, rose hips. In the clear Nation, they fished for grayling and northern pike.

They had only two dogs with them, and one night Miki, a Siberian husky, was off scenting the neighborhood when Snow and Allen heard the nearby howl of a wolf. Snow took a shotgun and walked in the direction of the sound. He came back with Miki on a stick. The wolf had ripped the dog's throat. The winter was otherwise safely uneventful, with the exception that Snow one day decided he had appendicitis and took off for Fairbanks, leaving Lilly Allen behind. For five weeks, she was there alone, more than fifty miles from Eagle, with no idea if he was dead or alive. In the end, it was Snow's woman, and not his appendix, that was inflamed.

Not many months before, they had made a trip to Basking Ridge, New Jersey, to be married. The bride's father wore lilies of the valley. He is an Exxon exxecutive. Lilly went to Ridge High School and for one semester to the University of Arizona. She was working as a waitress on Route 16 outside Conway, New Hampshire, when Snow came into her life. She wanted someday to own fields of sheep, she told him, because she was "into spinning and weaving." He wanted to go where even fleece would freeze. He was from Reading, Massachusetts, had studied some at the Universities of Massachusetts and Hawaii, and had been to trade school, but he had found a deeper interest working in New Hampshire forests for the Appalachian Mountain Club. A lithe man of middle height, he has a big brown beard, a tumble of shining brown hair, a serious turn of mind. Lilly Allen—handsome, unadornedly feminine—is facially Puritan, sober, with a touch of anachronism about her, as if on Sundays somehow she occupies a front pew, listening to Cotton Mather.

"We came here to get away from lots of people, lots of machines, and into a simpler way of life," she will say. "Everybody in Eagle says they came here 'to get away from it all.' We found 'it all' in Eagle. We came here to do without unnecessary things, to live out, to deal with the land in a more natural way."

In the vernacular of the river people, hunting moose, caribou, porcupine, duck, bear, rabbit is known as "getting your meat," and for Snow the task was complicated from the beginning by more than the problems of stalking and marksmanship. He had trouble, sometimes, pulling the trigger on a wild creature. "I hunt for meat, but I don't really enjoy hunting," he confesses. "It comes down to having or not having a spirit of predatorship. If Dick Cook or Charlie Edwards sees a goose, he doesn't hesitate. Bang. But I stop and admire the goose, and then I think of the gun. When I shoot a moose, I walk up to it with profound reverence—this beautiful beast that I, a scrawny little thing, am destroying. The last time I shot my moose, I cried. I really sympathized with him. I don't know how to put it. Having shot the animal—and seeing it lying there, dying—shakes me up."

In their search for ways to make a living in the country, Snow and Allen avoided trapping altogether. "I would do that if I had no other way to get money," he explains. "But I don't want to kill animals up here to clothe fat whores in New York. I don't mind wearing furs, but I prefer not to sell them." Meanwhile, there was money to be made fighting fires—in a smoking forest with a water bag on his back—and from two such experiences he earned a thousand dollars, or more than half of what they needed for a year.

They were still tasting their new and more natural life when Lilly's parents arrived for a visit in Eagle. In two canoes, the four went down the Yukon for a few days, just to have a look at the cabin on the Nation. The journey was more than Lilly's mother could complete, but Snow and his father-in-law left the women camped behind and tracked the Chestnut up the stream. It was a laborious effort, and they had been at it several hours when a helicopter suddenly came over the trees and passed them. Just the sight of it angered Snow, because—fifty miles from civilization—it ruined the wild scene. The two men tracked on, forgot the chopper, and finally arrived at the cabin. It had a door now, and an ingenious Oriental-puzzle sort of lock, which Snow had devised. Scarcely had he brought out some gear to air when the helicopter returned. It circled, landed on a gravel bar. "Let me do the talking," said Snow.

The pilot got out, and so did a man with a federal patch on his shirt. He was a short, slight, briefcase of a man. "Hello," he said. "I'm Dave Williams, of the Bureau of Land Management. You're on a canoe trip. I'm very sorry to disturb your wilderness experience. We're just checking here. Do you mind if we look around? This isn't your place, is it?"

Snow was noncommittal, but he became increasingly irritated as Williams went into the cabin and rummaged among its goods. The pilot said, "Really nice place here—nice, well-built cabin. This your place?"

Brad and Lilly own a framed copy of a celebrated photograph made by Dorothea Lange in Kern County, California, in the nineteen-thirties, which shows a compressed-air pump at a rundown rural filling station and two prominent signs—one saying "AIR," the other saying "This is your country. Don't let the big men take it away from you."

"Yes, it's *my* place," Snow blurted.

Williams reappeared like a genie. "Did you say *your* place?" he asked.

"Those are my things in the cabin," Snow said. "I'd rather you didn't go through my things."

"I said, 'Is this your place?'"

"You seem to think it's yours."

As he left, Williams said, "The cabin is in trespass. Very likely you'll be hearing from me in a short while. This is now the twentieth century. You can't just do what you want to do. You cannot play with the wilderness."

Snow was shortly given written notice that the cabin was on federal ground, that its presence conflicted with "the necessary and appropriate use of said land," and that if he left his personal property there it would be removed and stored at his expense. Lilly Allen was mentioned only as "any and all other persons." Alaska had attracted them. The United States had rebuffed them. Sarge Waller got a notice, too, about his cabin at the Kandik. Other notices went down the river. In the hundred and sixty miles between Eagle and Circle, the exact small number of people living on or near the Yukon had always been indeterminate, and as the scrutiny of the Bureau of Land Management drew closer the number became even less determinate than before. Under blue wisps of smoke separated by pieces of land the size of Eastern counties, people did what they could to remain invisible, knowing they were in trespass on federal land.

From time immemorial until the nineteen-seventies, anyone who had the drive and spirit to build a cabin in this northern wilderness was not restrained from doing so. For a long time, gold was the almost exclusive draw, and, as Lieutenant Frederick Schwatka had observed when he was sent to scout the region in 1883, "the discovery of gold in paying quantities is probably the only incentive for men to enter the country, and were it not that indications are seen all along the river, white men would probably never venture in." In more recent times, though, as the pressure of population in the Lower Forty-eight increased toward critical levels, a quite different incentive presented itself as well. Some of the hardiest people in the society were drawn to bush Alaska in search of a sense of release—of a life that remembered the past. The Alaskan wild was, as advertised, the last frontier—where people willing to combat its cold and run its risks could live an existence free from supererogatory rules as long as they did no harm to one another. The government did not interfere, and through the Homestead Act and other legislative provisions it even assisted this dream; but, with the discovery of oil at Prudhoe Bay on the edge of the Arctic Ocean, events began to occur that would change, apparently forever, the use and demarcation of Alaskan land. Meanwhile, certain long-established forms of freedom would disappear—the sort of freedom that drew a family like the Gelvins a generation earlier into the country, the sort of freedom envisioned by young people who set off to live in the wild of the upper Yukon. If the oil had never been discovered, there would not have been an eviction notice prepared for Brad Snow.

The discovery of the oil was in 1968, and after it became clear that there would be no pipeline until the land claims of the natives were satisfactorily extinguished, the United States Congress (attempting to satisfy not only the natives but at the same time the conflicting ambitions of conservationists and developers; attempting to promote the economy, protect the ecology, and respond multifariously to the sudden demand for this long-ignored but now prime segment of American national real estate) got together in a single bill the mighty ziggurat of legislation within which the catalytic pipeline would seem, while important, almost minor. Long after the publicity had receded and the pipeline had become as little discussed as the Big Inch, the social and political effects of its progenitive congressional bill would still be poignantly felt. Everyone of any race in all Alaska would be affected by the Alaska Native Claims Settlement Act. In elemental respects, the character of Alaska would change.

The natives would be afforded some variety in the choosing of their forty million acres of land, but much of it would be close to established villages. Included, meanwhile, among the epic consolations given the conservationists—the big pieces of land that were to be set aside for consideration as national parks, forests, rivers, wildlife refuges—were more than two million acres along the Yukon between Eagle and Circle. Many millions of additional acres—including the valley where the Gelvins legally staked gold claims—were to be closed to all but those in pursuit of "metalliferous minerals." Meanwhile, the State of Alaska was still choosing the hundred and three million acres awarded to it in the Statehood Act. It had until 1984 to complete the selection, and for the time being the land under scrutiny would remain—to the individual—beyond reach. When one adds in the existing parks, government forests, and wildlife refuges and a vast federal petroleum reserve in the north, not much remains, so it is one of the ironies of Alaska that in the midst of this tremendous wilderness people consider themselves fortunate to have (anywhere at all) a fifty-by-a-hundred-foot lot they can call their own.

Meanwhile, down below, outside, people who sit on sidewalks wearing Italian hiking boots and machine-faded jeans imply an extremity somewhere else. Surely, some of them will stand up and leave town, and when they leave they will go toward the wild—probably to the nearest mountain. Some will keep going to an even wilder place. Some will go farther than that. The logical inevitability for this chain of beings is that the ultimates will appear in Eagle (or Circle or Central or somewhere else in Alaska)—where civilization stops. And a very few will then jump free, going deep into the roadless world. By the time they reach Eagle, their momentum is too great to be interrupted by an act of Congress, even if they know of it and understand what it says. What the law now calls for is the removal of the last place in the United States where the pioneer impulse can leap from confinement. It is in the character of the impulse that the impulse will leap anyway—so the Bureau of Land Management, custodian of all the huge acreages under shift and selection, is charged with driving the trespassers away. Whites feel sold out and shoved under by the settlement of the native claims. Reticence has never been a characteristic of people attracted to this kind of terrain. They howl their upset, its focus the B.L.M.

"You can't go out and build a cabin and live in the goddamned woods, which people have been doing since the country was founded. Nobody argues with a few parks, but such a big percentage of the land is too much."

"It's not as if we're building fifty-thousand-dollar houses with asphalt driveways and stinking cesspools."

"Our cabins are more like tents than like most people's homes. They are made with native materials—white spruce, earth, moss. They are biodegradable. When they are abandoned, trees thirty feet high grow up out of the sod on their roofs. Eventually, the cabin collapses and disappears into the ground."

"Most people felt if we became a state we'd get rid of some of this federal control, and actually it's got worse."

"Alaska's ruined by this native-land deal that's went through. You could build a cabin anywhere, and mine anywhere, when I came. Now Alaska is going to be just like every other state."

"What bugs me is that when decisions are made about Alaska, people from Texas and Ohio, California and New York carry more weight than people from Alaska."

"Why should people be hassled for building cabins out here? What harm are they doing? Why should they be bothered? Why destroy a life simply because it exists? Slap a mosquito, yes. But if a life is not harming, why destroy it? Every species of animal has a wide genetic base, or they don't exist. Our living out here is a widening of the genetic base. I think the government people are fools to wipe us out."

"It's public land. We're the public."

"Down at the North Fork are twelve cabins. Mostly, the sites have been in use since the turn of the century, maintained and repaired by trappers and prospectors. Now the B.L.M. wants to kick these people out. It tells them they can never go to those cabins."

"Why should they drive us away? They ought to pay us to be out here—just to keep these places in good shape and well supplied."

"There are emergencies in this country, and when they happen sometimes cabins are needed."

"More than one life has been saved when someone in trouble has come upon a cabin."

The country is full of stories of unusual deaths—Old Nimrod Robertson lying down on a creek in overflow and letting it build around him a sarcophagus of ice; the trapper on the Kandik who apparently knocked himself out when he tripped and fell on his own firewood and froze to death before he came to—and of stories also of deaths postponed. There are fewer of the second. I would like to add one back—an account that in essence remains in the country but in detail has largely disappeared.

On a high promontory in the montane ruggedness around the upper Charley River lies the wreckage of an aircraft that is readily identifiable as a B-24. This was the so-called Liberator, a medium-range bomber built for the Second World War. The wreckage is in the dead center of the country, and I happened over it in a Cessna early in the fall of 1975, during a long and extremely digressive flight that began in Eagle and ended many hours later in Circle. The pilot of the Cessna said he understood that the crew of the Liberator had bailed out, in winter, and that only one man had survived. I asked around to learn who might know more than that—querying, among others, the Air Force in Fairbanks, the Gelvins, various old-timers in Circle and Central, some of the river people, and Margaret Nelson, in Eagle, who had packed parachutes at Ladd Field, in Fairbanks, during the war. There had been one survivor—everyone agreed. No one knew his name. He had become a symbol in the country, though, and was not about to be forgotten. It was said that he alone had come out—long after all had been assumed dead—because he alone, of the widely scattered crew, was experienced in wilderness, knew how to live off the land, and was prepared to deal with the hostile cold. Above all, he had found a cabin, during his exodus, without which he would have died for sure.

"And the government bastards try to stop us from building them now."

"Guy jumped out of an airplane, and he would have died but he found a cabin."

If the survivor had gone on surviving for what was now approaching thirty-five years, he would in all likelihood be somewhere in the Lower Forty-eight. When I was home, I made a try to find him. Phone calls ricocheted around Washington for some days, yielding only additional phone numbers. The story was just too sketchy. Did I know how many bombers had been lost in that war? At length, I was given the name of Gerard Haselwander, a historian at the Albert F. Simpson Historical Research Center, Maxwell Air Force Base, Alabama. I called him, and he said that if I did not even know the year of the crash he doubted he could help me. Scarcely two hours later, though, he called back to say that he had had a free moment or two at the end of his lunch hour and had browsed through some microfilm. To his own considerable surprise, he had found the survivor's name, which was Leon Crane. Crane's home when he entered the Army Air Forces had been in Philadelphia, but Hasselwander had looked in a Philadelphia directory and there was no Leon Crane in it now. However, he said, Leon Crane had had two brothers who were also in service—in the Army Medical Corps—during the Second World War. One of them was named Morris. In the Philadelphia directory, there was a Dr. Morris Crane.

When I called the number, someone answered and said Dr. Crane was not there.

I asked when he would return.

"I don't know" was the reply. "He went to Leon's."

The Liberator, making cold-weather propeller tests above twenty thousand feet, went into a spin, dived toward the earth, and, pulling out, snapped its elevator controls. It then went into another spin, and the pilot gave the order to abandon ship. There were five aboard. Leon Crane was the copilot. He was twenty-four and he had been in Alaska less than two months. Since the plane was falling like a swirling leaf, he had to drag himself against heavy centrifugal force toward the open bomb bay. He had never used a parachute. The outside air temperature was at least thirty degrees below zero. When he jumped, he forgot his mittens. The day was December 21st.

The plane fiercely burned, not far away from where he landed, and he stood watching it, up to his thighs in snow. He was wearing a hooded down jacket, a sweater, winter underwear, two pairs of trousers, two pairs of socks, and felt-lined military mukluks. He scanned the mountainsides but could see nothing of the others. He thought he had been the second one to go out of the plane, and as he fell he thought he saw a parachute open in the air above him. He shouted into the winter silence. Silence answered. Months later, he would learn that there had been two corpses in the aircraft. Of the two other fliers no track or trace was ever found. "Sergeant Pompeo, the crew chief, had a hell of a thick set of glasses. He must have lost them as soon as he hit the airstream. Without them, he really couldn't see. What was he going to do when he got down there?"

For that matter, what was Crane going to do? He had no food, no gun, no sleeping bag, no mittens. The plane had been meandering in search of suitable skies for the tests. Within two or three hundred miles, he had no idea where he was.

Two thousand feet below him, and a couple of miles east, was a river. He made his way down to it. Waiting for rescue, he stayed beside it. He had two books of matches, a Boy Scout knife. He started a fire with a letter from his father, and for the first eight days he did not sleep more than two hours at a time in his vigilance to keep the fire burning. The cold awakened him anyway. Water fountained from a gap in the river ice, and that is what he lived on. His hands, which he to some extent protected with parachute cloth or in the pockets of his jacket, became cut and abraded from tearing at spruce boughs. When he spread his fingers, the skin between them would split. Temperatures were probably ranging between a high of thirty below zero and a low around fifty. The parachute, as much as anything, kept him alive. It was twenty-eight feet in diameter, and he wound it around him so that he was at the center of a great cocoon. Still, he said, his back would grow cold while his face roasted, and sparks kept igniting the chute.

He was telling me some of this on a sidewalk in Philadelphia when I asked him how he had dealt with fear.

He stopped in surprise, and looked contemplatively up the street toward Independence Hall, his graying hair wisping out to the sides. He wore a business suit and a topcoat, and he had bright, penetrating eyes. He leaned forward when he walked. "Fear," he repeated. "I wouldn't have used that word. Think about it: there was not a hell of a lot I could do if I were to panic. Besides, I was sure that someone was going to come and get me."

All that the search-and-rescue missions had to go on was that the Liberator had last been heard from above Big Delta, so the search area could not be reduced much below forty thousand square miles. Needless to say, they would not come near finding him. He thought once that he heard the sound of an airplane, but eventually he realized that it was a chorus of wolves. In his hunger, he tried to kill squirrels. He made a spear, and threw it awkwardly as they jumped and chattered in the spruce boughs. He made a bow and arrow, using a shroud line from his parachute, but when he released the arrow it shot off at angles ridiculously oblique to the screeching, maddening squirrels. There was some rubber involved in the parachute assembly, and he used that to make a slingshot, which was worse than the bow and arrow. When he fell asleep by the fire, he dreamed of milkshakes, dripping beefsteaks, mashed potatoes, and lamb chops, with lamb fat running down his hands. Awake, he kicked aside the snow and found green moss. He put it in his mouth and chewed, and chewed some more, but scarcely swallowed any. Incidentally, he was camped almost exactly where, some twenty-five years later, Ed and Virginia Gelvin would build a cabin from which to trap and hunt.

Crane is a thoroughly urban man. He grew up in the neighborhood of Independence Hall, where he lives now, with an unlisted number. That part of the city has undergone extensive refurbishment in recent years, and Crane's sons, who are residential builders and construction engineers, have had a part in the process. Crane, more or less retired, works for them, and when I visited him I followed him from building to building as he checked on the needs and efforts of carpenters, bricklayers, plumbers. He professed to have no appetite for wild country, least of all for the expanses of the north. As a boy, he had joined a city Scout troop, and had become a First Class Scout, but that was not to suggest a particular knowledge of wilderness. When he flew out of Fairbanks that morning in 1943, his lifetime camping experience consisted of one night on the ground—with his troop, in Valley Forge.

He decided on the ninth day that no help was coming. Gathering up his parachute, he began to slog his way downriver, in snow sometimes up to his waist. It crossed his mind that the situation might be hopeless, but he put down the thought as he moved from bend to bend by telling himself to keep going because "right around that curve is what you're looking for." In fact, he was about sixty miles from the nearest human being, almost a hundred from the nearest group of buildings large enough to be called a settlement. Around the next bend, he saw more mountains, more bare jagged rock, more snow-covered sweeps of alpine tundra, contoured toward another river bend. "Right around that curve is what you're looking for," he told himself again. Suddenly, something was there. First, he saw a cache, high on legs in the air, and then a small cabin, with a door only three feet high. It was like the lamb chops, with the grease on his fingers, but when he pushed at the door it was wood and real. The room inside was nine by ten: earth floor, low ceiling, a bunk made of spruce. It was Alaskan custom always to leave a cabin open and stocked for anyone in need. Split firewood was there, and matches, and a pile of prepared shavings. On a table were sacks of dried raisins, sugar, cocoa, and powdered milk. There was a barrel stove, frying pans on the wall. He made some cocoa, and, after so long a time without food, seemed full after a couple of sips. Then he climbed a ladder and looked in the cache, lifting a tarp to discover hammers, saws, picks, drills, coiled rope, and two tents. No one, he reasoned, would leave such equipment far off in the wilderness. "I figured civilization was right around the corner. I was home free."

So he stayed just a night and went on down the river, anxious to get back to Ladd Field. The moon came up after the brief light of day, and he kept going. He grew weak in the deep cold of the night, and when the moon went below the mountains he began to wander off the stream course, hitting boulders. He had been around many corners, but no civilization was there. Now he was sinking into a dream-hazy sleepwalking numbed-out oblivion; but fear, fortunately, struck through and turned him, upriver. He had not retraced his way very far when he stopped and tried to build a fire. He scraped together some twigs, but his cut and bare hands were shaking so—at roughly fifty below zero—that he failed repeatedly to ignite a match. He abandoned the effort, and moved on through the snow. He kept hitting boulders. He had difficulty following his own tracks. He knew now that he would die if he did not get back to the cabin, and the detached observer within him decided he was finished. Left foot, right foot—there was no point in quitting, even so. About noon, he reached the cabin. With his entire body shaking, he worked at a fire until he had one going. Then he rolled up in his parachute and slept almost continuously for three full days.

In his excitement at being "right around the corner from civilization," he had scarcely looked in the cache, and now he found rice, flour, beans, powdered eggs, dried vegetables, and beef—enough for many weeks, possibly months. He found mittens. He found snowshoes. He found long johns, socks, mukluks. He found candles, tea, tobacco, and a corncob pipe. He found ammunition, a .22. In the cabin, he mixed flour, peas, beans, sugar, and snow, and set it on the stove. That would be his basic gruel—and he became enduringly fond of it. Sometimes he threw in eggs and vegetables. He covered his hands with melted candle wax, and the bandage was amazingly effective. He developed a routine, with meals twice a day, a time for hunting, a fresh well chopped daily through the four-foot river ice. He slept eighteen hours a day, like a wintering bear—not truly hibernating, just lying there in his den. He felt a need to hear a voice, so he talked to himself. The day's high moment was a pipeful of tobacco puffed while he looked through ten-year-old copies of *The Saturday Evening Post.* He ransacked the magazines for insights into the woods lore he did not know. He learned a thing or two. In a wind, it said somewhere in the *Post*, build your fire in a hole. He shot and ate a ptarmigan, and had the presence of mind to look in its stomach. He found some overwintering berries there, went to the sort of bushes they had come from, and shot more ptarmigan. Cardboard boxes, the magazines, and other items in the cabin were addressed to "Phil Berail, Woodchopper, Alaska." Contemplating these labels, Crane decided that Alaska was a fantastic place—where someone's name and occupation were a sufficient address. One day, an old calendar fell off the wall and flipped over on its way to the floor. On the back was a map of Alaska. He stared at it all day. He found Woodchopper, on the Yukon, and smiled at his foolishness. From the terrain around him, the northward flow of the stream, the relative positions of Fairbanks and Big Delta, he decided—just right—that he was far up the Charley River. The smile went back where it came from.

He decided to wait for breakup, build a raft, and in late May float on down to the Yukon. After five or six weeks, though, he realized that his food was going to give out in March. There was little ammunition with which to get meat, and he had no confidence anyway in his chances with the rifle. If he stayed, he would starve. He felt panic now, but not enough to spill the care with which he was making his plans. He had set off willy-nilly once before and did not want to repeat the mistake. He patched his clothes with parachute cloth, sewing them with shroud lines. He made a sled from some boards and a galvanized tub. He figured closely what the maximum might be that he could drag and carry. On February 12th, he left. The sled would scarcely budge at first, and snow bunched up before it. Wearing a harness he had made, he dragged the sled slowly downriver. Berail's snowshoes had Indian ties. Try as he would, he could not understand how to secure them to his feet. The snowshoes were useless. Up to his knees, and sometimes to his hips, he walked from dawn until an hour before dark each day. He slept beside bonfires that burned all night. Blizzards came up the river some days, and driving williwaws —winds of a force that could literally stop him in his tracks. He leaned against the wind. When he could, he stepped forward. Once, at the end of a day's hard walking, he looked behind him—on the twisting mountain river—and saw where he had started at dawn. The Charley in summer—clear-flowing within its canyon walls, with grizzlies fishing its riffles, Dall sheep on the bluffs, and peregrines above it in the air—is an extremely beautiful Alaskan river (it has been called the loveliest of all), but for Leon Crane it was little more than brutal. He came to a lead one day, a patch of open water, and, trying to use some boulders as stepping stones, he fell in up to his armpits. Coming out, barging through snowdrifts, he was the center of a fast-forming block of ice. His matches were dry. Shaking as before, he managed this time to build a fire. All day, he sat steaming beside it, removing this or that item of clothing, drying it a piece at a time.

After a couple of weeks on the river, he found another cabin, with a modest but welcome food cache—cornmeal, canned vegetables, Vienna sausage. He sewed himself a backpack and abandoned his cumbersome sled. Some seven or eight days on down the river, he came around a bend at dusk and found cut spruce tops in parallel rows stuck in the river snow. His aloneness, he sensed, was all but over. It was the second week of March, and he was eighty days out of the sky. The arrangement of treetops, obviously, marked a place where a plane on skis might land supplies. He looked around in near darkness and found a toboggan trail. He camped, and next day followed the trail to a cabin—under smoke. He shouted toward it. Al Ames, a trapper, and his wife, Neena, and their children appeared in the doorway. "I am Lieutenant Leon Crane, of the United States Army Air Forces," he called out. "I've been in a little trouble." Ames took a picture, which hangs on a wall in Philadelphia.

Crane remembers thinking, Somebody must be saving me for something, but I don't know what it is. His six children, who owe themselves to that trip and to Phil Berail's fully stocked Charley River cabin, are—in addition to his three sons in the construction business—Mimi, who is studying engineering at Barnard; Rebecca, who is in the master's program in architecture at Columbia; and Ruth, a recent graduate of the Harvard Medical School. Crane himself went on to earn an advanced degree in aeronautical engineering at the Massachusetts Institute of Technology, and spent his career developing helicopters for Boeing Vertol.

"It's a little surprising to me that people exist who are interested in living on that ground up there," he told me. "Why would anyone want to take someone who wanted to *be* there and throw them out? Who the hell could *care*?"

Al Ames, who had built his cabin only two years before, harnessed his dogs and mushed Crane down the Yukon to Woodchopper, where a plane soon came along and flew him out.

Crane met Phil Berail at Woodchopper, and struggled shyly to express to him his inexpressible gratitude. Berail, sixty-five, was a temporary postmaster and worked for the gold miners there. He had trapped from his Charley River cabin. He was pleased that it had been useful, he said. For his part, he had no intention of ever going there again. He had abandoned the cabin four years before.

The river people refer to seasons of their year with names like "ducks" and "fish."

"We'll be in Eagle soon after fish."

"There's not a lot to do before ducks."

They hunt ducks in May, and work on things that are needed for the coming winter—a new toboggan, for example, so it will age all summer and be slippery and hard in the fall. New cabins are started, and repairs are made on others. In July, nets are put out for king salmon. There is some use of fish wheels—postcard symbols of the Yukon. A fish wheel is a revolving trap that was invented by a white man but is generally associated with Indians. The big kings weigh as much as sled dogs. Their dense ruddy flesh—baked, smoked, or canned—is one of the supreme gifts of nature. The river people are less interested in kings than in the chum salmon that follow, for while king salmon may be luxuries on the human palate, chum—dried or frozen—are year-round staples for dogs. They are, in effect, gasoline. A team consumes at least a thousand a year. The river people believe that the health of a sled dog can be measured by the proportion of fish in its diet. When they happen to do odd jobs for one another or engage in barter, they like to be paid in dog salmon. Lilly Allen has given fifty salmon for a quarter of a bear. You try to get your meat around the first week of October, hunting moose and bear while they are still fat. "This is a fat-starved country. This is not the coast. You'll look a long while before you'll see a seal in the river." You see ice instead, coming down in the middle of the month. At the sight of it, harnesses are brought out and repaired. The ice is light at first, and goes tinkling by, but with advancing cold the floes increase, harden, crash, thunder—until one day a startling silence replaces the sound. Trapping begins, and lasts off and on until April. The Indians used to follow this cycle more than they do now. The river people have taken up where the Indians left off. April is a lag month—not a lot to do before ducks. April is a good time to go out of the country and work on the pipeline, or on something else that yields money for wheat berries, ammunition, and fuel.

Spread out they may be, but the river people are social and gregarious. News moves quickly of a reason to convene. Dick Cook shot a wolf near Eagle not long ago and stewed it in a twenty-one-quart pressure cooker. His ilk in eager numbers gathered around the pot and ate twenty-one quarts of wolf. Not all gatherings are impromptu. To celebrate the 1976 vernal equinox, for example, the river people held a tribal convention just below the mouth of the Nation. It was planned many months in advance and went on for nearly a week. To them, the vernal equinox is a more important date than Easter, just as December 21st is a more important date than Christmas, and in each case by a factor so large it tends to dismiss the comparison. The vernal equinox is the fulcrum of light and dark which holds the promise of warmth to come, of the summer fish runs and garden harvests, the growth of Brussels sprouts and Mary Jane. Nearly everyone grows the latter. The law does not frown upon the practice in Alaska. In the long northern light, the compound serrate leaves will rise on tall stems to the height of a man, and as whole stands come together, enmeshing, interdigitating, they form colonies of such spiky luxuriance that small segments of the banks of the Yukon appear to have been painted there by Henri (le Douanier) Rousseau.

The specific site of the river people's equinoctial gathering was the abandoned camp of Jim Taylor, who went out of the country in 1933 to die of cancer. By the evidence of what he left behind, he was a far-northern Crusoe. He could have earned an advanced degree in log architecture. He failed at mining, working the gold-bearing placers off the left bank of the Yukon, but he loved the country so much he stayed on, and he paid off his debts trapping. On the right bank near the Nation, he built a cabin that included a dumbwaiter, which served as a refrigerator when it was lowered into a spring. There were two rooms, full of period "Alaska furniture" made from orange crates, Blazo boxes, and egg crates. He built other cabins for shopwork and storage. Where most people chain their dogs to trees or to stakes in the ground, separating them in short-radius confinement, Taylor built long, palisaded, individual dog runs, each including a log kennel and a fragment of a running brook. For times of severe weather, he built an entire cabin exclusively for dogs. It has six rooms, three on either side of a central corridor, and appears to be a small, comfortable jail. Taylor could pull a lever from outside and release simultaneously six chattering huskies. Taylor had the first radio in the country, and miners would come down their streams and cross the Yukon to visit him and hear it. He was a big man, and is remembered as a "good guy." Surely he would have been flattered that his like in the nineteen-seventies chose to gather in his compound. The main cabin burned some time ago, but the rest is there, intact, the sod roofs shaggy with growing spruce.

It was a council of war and a party, too—a time of talk and music, no booze—a way to keep contacts, to exchange opinions and information.

"The economy's got to go eventually, because they're into using minerals and resources way too heavy."

"Keep a cache of ammunition. You can't survive without a rifle."

The ground was white, the brooks and rivers frozen. The people slept for the most part in tents. They strategized about the federal bureaucracy—how to oppose it, how to melt out of its way. They planned a network of cabins for winter travel. They tried, with no success, to agree on a communal bulk food order, and on a way to administer common ownership of a truck for use in Eagle. Their desire to be "tribal" does not approach in strength their need to be self-reliant. For all their garrulity, they are not compact. As they always do, they talked in loops without end about hunting, fishing, trapping, and dogs; knives, axes, the kerf-width of saws; mortises, tenons; steel-cut oats; oars, poles; sleds, toboggans; aluminum boats; trail sets, visuals, tracks on the pan; single trees, spreaders; the collars of stoves; what sort of pups a certain bitch might throw; shelter, clothing, death, and marten bait (grouse wings versus salmon skins versus strawberry jam); and as the talk curved through its long ellipses it turned and returned, as always, to the Yukon, to every gravel bar, rock, rip, eddy, and bend—free or under ice. They baked pies. They argued ethics. Is it wasteful to feed moose to dogs? They tacked up a moosehide. The girth alone covered thirteen cabin logs. There was a common hunt across the Yukon in the Fourth of July flats, and a common mush—a dog Olympiad—far up the Nation River. Competition, open or subtle, is in everything they say and do. Who—figuratively, physically—goes deepest into the wilderness? Who is the most established, the most "dug in"? Who takes the highest percentage of his food from the land? Who has been caught in the deepest overflow? Who has the oldest whipsaw, the oldest bench screw? Who has the best woman?

A good woman is a subservient woman, or so it seems to the alien eye. As Brad Snow has explained to me, "Women's lib doesn't survive very well in the bush. There's a bunch to do—and responsibility has to be delineated where it fits. The meal has got to get cooked. The meat has got to get found." Snow, nonetheless, prepares about half of the meals he shares with Lilly Allen. Charlie Edwards, while a star of a hunter, grinds grain and bakes bread at home. But those are exceptions. Cook cooks nothing. By and large, the men seem to be waited upon to an extent that even our forefathers might not have known.

In a good fish year, two moose, two hundred ducks, and seventy-five quarts of king salmon will be plenty for one river couple. The upper Yukon now is considered "full," saturated with settlers, all space reserved—roughly one person for every five miles. Not everyone on the river gathers for the equinox. Some are not tribally inclined. I was in the Yukon Trading Post in Circle one time when a man about forty came up over the riverbank and bought six bottles of Worcestershire sauce, twelve packets of yeast, a case of matches, some Spam, sardines, hot dogs, three pounds of tea, a hundred and fifty pounds of sugar, a hundred and fifty pounds of rice, fifty pounds of cornmeal, and two cigars. He counted out three hundred and forty-four dollars cash, laid it on the counter, and went back to the river without so much as a word about the weather. Frank Warren—pilot, trapper, keeper of the Trading Post—remarked that he had happened by that man's cabin one day and had thought to pay a visit. It was a small cabin, eight by ten, without windows. As Warren approached, he heard a voice. The man was telling himself a joke. Reaching the punch line, he erupted in laughter. Warren tiptoed away.

Of Cook's mentees, Charlie Edwards seems to be the most wild, in the extent that he prospers away in the woods. As energetic as he is successful, he lives on his rifle for months at a time. "I get so high being out in the woods it's like doing acid," he says. "I get high just being straight. I'm happy. I never wanted to work for anybody but myself. I wanted a country big enough so I could move into the woods. I can live good in the woods here on two thousand dollars a year." He makes that much trapping. His wife, Cheryl, brings back fifteen hundred dollars more from seasonal work in Fairbanks. He saves money by assembling his own ammunition. They live at a creek mouth under twenty miles from Eagle because Cheryl is less comfortable farther away, and, as Charlie elaborates, "It's a hell of a lot nicer when you got an old lady than when you ain't." They make candles from the wax of their own bees. When they take a moose, they use everything. Cheryl sews Charlie's clothes. He wears moosehide trousers, mukluks of moosehide and fur, a marmot vest, a patchwork parka of beaver, caribou, wolverine, and wolf. "If I get myself another bear, I'm going to have fur pants," he told me once, and the next time I saw him his pants were hairy and black. He is twenty-five or so and comes from a well-to-do family in Fairfield, Connecticut. He went for a time to Suffield Academy, in Connecticut, where he is remembered (by a faculty member) as "a renegade of tremendous aggressive energy—really into the music of the time. He baked his hash in those little ovens, you know. He was into philosophy, as I recall. He left of his own accord." Cheryl is dark and slight, and also from Connecticut. Edwards is of middle height, strong, with missing teeth, and a golden ponytail flying behind. They are well dug in. They have a good cabin, a log sauna, and impressive caches, impressively filled. "I couldn't ask for any more out of life," he says. "I don't care if there's a life after life. I'm having an awful good time in this one."

From Eagle, Circle, Central—the communities of the country—the river people are watched with absorption, not to mention awe and envy, admiration, contempt, and fear. They are widely looked upon with high esteem, and the reverse, too, since almost no one in the country is shy to put the slam on any being that heaves into sight, let alone the people of the river. That is to say, some who would not advance a toe into the wilderness will travel any distance by tongue.

"Alaska was one of the few places left where you could do this sort of thing. There is room enough in Alaska. What harm have they done to the country? They trap a little. They put up fish. They're not hurting anything."

"They're a generation too late."

"They are unrealistic romanticists, and some are just plain stupid. They are devoid of values—materialistic, selfish people. We are constituents of a society grounded in law. They flout the law to live their romantic life style. They harvest moose, bear, fish—whatever they can get their hands on that they can fit into a pot—without regard for seasons or for sex, or for the law. Anything that walks, crawls, flies, or swims is fair game to them. They are interlopers. Every time they kill a moose or bear and toss it into the pot to feed their dogs, they deprive me of the opportunity to see that moose or bear. When I see something, I leave it to the person after me to see. Frankly, it just tees me off. I consider them to be a god-damned curse."

"They're a public nuisance."

"English common law used the term 'public nuisance' to refer to, for example, a slaughterhouse upwind. The people had the right to abate such a public nuisance. These people on the river are not a public nuisance. Hell, no. If I were twenty-one, I'd build there, and if the United States marshal came after me I would kill him. People should not have to live in ghettolike shacks they can control you in. The prime urge of all life is for an exclusive domain. Each human being needs that. These kids are trying to get away to a place of their own."

"I've got a .357 Magnum. If someone tried to kick me out of my cabin, there'd be a murder in defense of my home. Instead of landing in that helicopter and driving Brad Snow off his place, the government should have given him patent to five acres of land and said, 'You've done a good job. You're not a god-damned parasite living on others.'"

"That helicopter. If I was Snow, I'd have set her afire."

"These river people couldn't make it if it weren't for the present accident of the high price of fur. Some hapless lynx comes along and stumbles into their trap. The three hundred dollars you can get from a lynx is what is keeping them alive."

"I can't stand them—they're so sociable."

"I don't believe—and I don't think any other Indian believes—that these young people down the river are harming anyone. But I don't believe they have a right to be there. They don't own the land. Really, they got no home. They got nothing. They live pretty tough. They learn fast, but I don't think they are as well prepared as older pioneers. One man up in the Seventymile last winter lost his toes. He got caught in overflow."

"They come and they go. It takes a peculiar type person to live in this country. The winter usually weeds them out."

"Several who came in last spring went out again in the fall, satisfied in their own minds that this is no country for them, and we are of the same opinion," wrote Gordon Bettles the better part of a century ago. "When we old prospectors jump off, there won't be any tough fellows to go in there and go through the hardships we went through. There's a future in Alaska for the young man with the right kind of stuff."

"A blue column of smoke, faintly rising from the spruces of some lonely gulch, guides one to the lonely camp of some pioneer who has been in Alaska since the first discovery of gold," said a United States government bulletin describing this country in 1905. "Over a cup of coffee, prepared in an old baking powder can, one is made to understand the important part these men have played in the development of this portion of our possessions and their reasons for having learned to call it home . . . men who have labored hard in a quiet way to satisfy the craving for individual independence and have gained through hardship something that is worthwhile even if their hopes are not yet realized."

Dick Cook, in his generosity, lifts from his plate a small gob of muskrat fat and gives it to me. The fat is savory, a delicacy. The lean of the "rat" could be taken for dark, strong chicken.

He is saying, "There's a pride to doing something other people can't do. My life style is what so many people dream about. What they don't dream is that it took six or eight years of hard work to get it. A lot of these people who keep coming into the country don't belong here. They have fallen in love with a calendar photo and they want to live under a beautiful mountain. When they arrive, the reality doesn't match the dream. It's too much for them. They don't want to work hard enough; they don't want to spread out—to go far enough up the streams. This is relatively poor trapping country. You need a twenty-mile radius. But they won't move away from the Yukon. My cabin is the farthest off the river. Have another cup of tea."

Tea strong enough to blacken tin. Hanging over the campfire is a No. 10 can, coated with carbon from the fire, and even blacker within, its bottom a swamp of leaves. To use his own term for what he is doing here, Cook is on vacation. In cool spring weather toward the end of ducks, we are close by three lakes near the Yukon, far downriver from Eagle. He is here to hunt. The vacation is from the weight of tasks at home, which is ten miles away. His shelter is only his orange canvas tarp, one side strung between spruce, the opposite staked in the sphagnum. He finishes his duck-and-muskrat stew, and stretches out under the tarp, head propped up, taking his ease. He remarks that Nessmuk could not stand the confinement of an A-shaped or wall-sided tent and neither can he.

Cook's knowledge of wood lore is encyclopedic. Impromptu, he can, and readily will, give a thirty-minute lecture on just about any aspect of it from wolf dens to whetstones, so it is no surprise—except in a geographical way, far off in the Alaskan bush—to hear him invoke the pen name of the nineteenth-century Eastern writer George Sears, called Nessmuk, whose "Woodcraft," published in 1884, was the first American book on forest camping, and is written with so much wisdom, wit, and insight that it makes Henry David Thoreau seem alien, humorless, and French. Donna Kneeland is beside the fire, her legs folded straight beneath her. She adds wood. She is attempting to dry, possibly repair, a boot that has a two-inch rip near the sole. A parabola of wire crosses the top of the No. 10 can. She lifts it. With a short stick in her other hand, she tilts the bottom, pouring tea into my cup. I welcome it, to defray the chill, which neither Dick nor Donna seems to notice. Staked out in the woods around us are seven sled dogs. They, too, are on holiday.

When new people come in, Cook continues, he recommends that they rent a cabin in or near Eagle, somewhere close to civilization, and spend a winter there first—with the wilderness a quarter of a mile away. "That leaves some unburned bridges. Try trapping, hunting meat, getting some skills together—setting yourself up. Money will not accomplish it, but money is important. You need axes, splitting mauls, rifles, saws, winter clothing. The average person brings—or buys within a couple of years—at least ten thousand dollars' worth of gear. It helps to have a truck at the post-office town. A small boat with a kicker costs twelve hundred dollars. Bring a two-year supply of food. You won't learn enough in a year."

Donna, looking up from her boot, says, "Steve Ulvi, when he was here last week, wanted to know what traps to buy, and he—"

"He asked a lot of things, but that is his business," Cook says, with such sharpness that Donna falls silent.

"Why do people live in Eagle?" I ask him.

"I don't know," he says. "I've always wondered. Some of them came with the intention of going on into the bush and have never carried it out. One person in Eagle has tried three times. But a lot of people come with a desire not to work—just to be there and not to work. I've never understood that. The country and the weather are too hard just to sit."

He draws an analogy between what he has done and what the early Western settlers did. They dug makeshift houses into the dirt while concentrating on the clearing of fields and the construction of barns. That was the way settlement had to take place. "If you built a nice house first, your livestock would die." Dogs, in Cook's case, were his livestock, so fishnets came first. Then he planted a garden. Then he set traplines. He learned sleds and mushing from Indians. "There were several of the old ones around who knew what they were doing and were still sober enough to talk about it." He has continued to learn, he says, just by observing other people along the river. "Charlie Edwards *does* things. I sit and think them out. I've learned more from his mistakes than I've learned from my own. I feel at home now, after twelve years—at home on water, in the woods, in summer, in winter. I feel a part of what is here. The bush is so far beyond what anybody has been taught. The religious power here is beyond all training. There are forces here that a lot of people don't know exist."

"What are they?"

"They can't be articulated. You're out of the realm of words. You are close to the land here, to nature, to what the Indians called Mother and I call Momma. Momma decides everything. The concept is still here, but the Indians have given it up. They say the Indians now have rights to land in which to do their subsistence hunting and trapping. That is ridiculous. It is about time the whites got it equally. There is just no land, no legal place to go, in Alaska. If they wipe out the white people who are living in the bush, they wipe out the native culture."

He shifts his weight, and for a moment I can see his arm. There is a chamois-cloth shirt under his cotton pullover, but both are so shredded and rent with holes that the arm is visible behind its curtain of rags. The skin is as white as paper. A skull and crossbones is tattooed there. A dagger sunk into the skull from above protrudes from the chin like an iron Vandyke. It is flanked by the letters US and MC. "I grew up in Lyndhurst, Ohio. My father was in the commercial-industrial air-conditioning business. I helped pay my bills at the Colorado School of Mines by going into the mountains with dynamite, blasting open pegmatite dikes and selling the crystals. Students then all had dynamite in the trunks of their cars—like nowadays they all wear Vibram soles and carry sheath knives." Cook's first wife was a model. She left him, and for a time he looked after his two infant children. When she divorced him, he lost in court a case for custody. "Since then, I have never understood trees," he says. "They put down roots." He has not seen his children in a great many years. One is eighteen, and has a child of her own.

There is a small, square-ended aluminum boat—dragged in here over riverine muskeg and rammed through hells of willow. In it now is an armory of guns, one of which belonged to Dick's father and grandfather. The lakes are small. Quietly, we paddle across one of them, leave the boat, and creep through the woods. We avoid a mound of bear scat—fairly, but not acutely, fresh. It glistens but has stopped smoking. Approaching the shore of the next lake, Dick motions us to get down, and we crawl toward the water without damaging the silence. The forest cover extends to the edge. We lie there, behind trees, looking out. Dick lifts a shotgun. In the beginnings of the twilight, a pair of loons are cruising. They are beyond range. Their heads are up. Their bodies float high. They sense no danger. Their course is obliquely toward the gun. Now we can distinguish the black-and-white shingling on their necks. Silently swimming, they come nearer still. Loons. They are quick. Diving, they can suddenly be gone. He fires. He fires again. The loons elect to sprint down the surface—cacophonous, flailing—their splayfeet spading the water. A pellet or two may have touched them, but it seems unlikely.

Dick hands one of the guns to Donna and says that he is going to skirt the lake. If the loons return, she is to fire.

Silently, he is gone. We hear nothing of his movements among the trees. He is gone an hour. Donna, whispering, asks me if I know much about this gun.

"Nothing," I tell her.

"Nothing?"

"Nothing."

"Neither do I. Those loons will have to come pretty close before I'll try to hit them."

A single loon now tests that distance. It comes swimming around a peninsula of sedge and adopts a path that leads directly toward the muzzle of the gun. Serene in its ignorance, it glides steadily onward without even a slight change of course until, with the distance nearly closed, its breast seems a yard wide. Still it has not seen us. The gun is aimed and ready. If the bird swims any farther, it will hit the shore. Donna blasts. The loon's move is too quick to be called a dive. It is a complete and instant disappearance. There is no commotion, no blood in the water, no loon.

We whisper through the time. At length, more shots ring out, down the lake. It is the sound of Cook, missing. Eventually, he comes back. We now try another lake—creeping the final dozen yards through the forest to its shore. "Wait here," Cook says, and he leaves the .22. "Kill a rat if one goes by." Meanwhile, he will circle the shoreline. This lake has rats for sure, and there—he points to a far cove and a barely visible line of darning-egg heads—are ducks. In the unending twilight, another hour passes. At various distances and times, we hear half a dozen sharp reports. "You can be active in a job in town, but it doesn't seem as important," Donna whispers. "Here the important thing is—well, getting your meat." She mentions that she was a stewardess once for Reeve Aleutian. A muskrat rounds a clump of sedge, swimming before us, left to right. Donna follows it with the rifle and fires. The water jumps a foot. We cannot see the spent bullet, sinking like a pebble toward the bottom of the lake, but the muskrat probably can. There was something she particularly liked about Reeve Aleutian. The airline was always ready to ignore its schedules and serve as an emergency ambulance service for the entire island chain. And so the work was, as she phrases it, "more interesting than just coffee, tea, or me." Winds blew seventy miles an hour over the islands sometimes. A DC-3 would try to touch on a runway and have trouble setting down because its wings wished to stay in the air. In an Electra once, she was approaching Adak, winds in the seventies. Suddenly the turbulence increased and the Electra overturned. It was not just steeply banked—it was flying upside down. Donna noted with interest the silence of the passengers. She had thought that in such a situation people would scream. Objects fell to the ceiling. Toilets spilled. The plane crossed the island, and slowly rolled upright. Its second approach was successful. On the ground, after thanking the passengers for flying Reeve and wishing them a pleasant stay on Adak, Donna suggested to the other stewardess that they have a drink. "That is the only time in my life I have ever done that," she whispers now—"taken a drink, you know, in order to relax." Intense firing breaks out far down the shore, a Boone and Crockett sonata. When Cook appears again beside us, he has nothing in hand and nothing to retrieve. He says, "One trouble with this type of life is you can go hungry when you screw up." This is true in two ways, for cartridges cost a few cents apiece and shotgun shells a quarter. In effect, he has been firing grocery money into the lake. We return to the sled dogs and the lean-to, but soon Cook, frustrated, says, "If we don't get something, we're not going to eat," and, cursing Momma, he takes off once more, for a final walking circuit of the shore.

By the fire, Donna sews a patch on a pair of Dick's trousers, and remarks to me that for an Easterner I seem to be surprisingly dressed, in that my boots and vest and general gear are the sorts of things she associates with Alaska. I explain to her about the Wild East, and how I like to go out when I can, and that I always have. "But I'll tell you the difference, Donna. The difference is that pile of bear sign back there, and the absence of trails, and . . ." My thoughts race ahead of what I am trying to say. The difference is also in the winter silence, a silence that can be as wide as the country, and the dreamy, sifting slowness of the descent of the dry snow. If there were only twenty-five people in the state of New Jersey, they would then sense the paramount difference, which is in the unpeopled reach of this country. I may have liked places that are wild and been quickened all my days just by the sound of the word, but I see now I never knew what it could mean. I can see why people who come to Alaska are unprepared. In four decades of times beyond some sort of road, I never set foot in a place like this. It is in no way an extension of what I've known before. The constructions I have lived by ought not, and do not, apply here. Left on my own here, I would have to change in a hurry, and learn in a hurry, or I'd never last a year.

For a time, the only sound is the fire. The dogs are asleep. There's no wind. The forest is as quiet as it was, a month before, under snow. Donna tightens the thread. She says, finally, "I know what you mean. When I first came out here, I felt the same way. I saw what it was like and I thought, I'll never survive."

What would she do in a medical emergency, like a simple case of appendicitis?

"I hope this doesn't sound corny," she answers, "but things are living and dying out here all the time. If I got appendicitis, I would just die."

Cook, in half an hour's absence, fires one shot. When he comes back, he drops a muskrat on the ground with a hole above its ear. Donna says, "They're hard to skin when they've been shot in the head." She skins it out neatly, and covers the pelt with salt. The inner rat goes into the pot.

We roll out our sleeping bags side by side, remove our boots, settle in. I have before now lacked the courage to reach into my pack and take out a thing for which I feel a great need. Antithetical forces are in strife within me. What I want is my pillow. Its capacity to soften the coming sleep is perhaps not as great as its capacity to humiliate me before these rugged pioneers. Shame at last loses out to comfort. My hand goes into the pack. The pillow is small and white. The slip is homemade, with snaps at one end, so that it can contain a down jacket, which it does. I mumble an explanation of this, saying that nonetheless I feel a touch ridiculous—in their company, in this country—reaching into my gear for a pillow.

"Don't apologize," says Cook, getting up on one elbow to admire the pillow. "As Nessmuk said, we're not out here to rough it. We're here to smooth it. Things are rough enough in town."

Rich Corazza came into the country in 1974. In Wyoming and Colorado, he had worked in the open, and the attraction held for him by the upper Yukon was unarguably succinct: "There ain't no barbed wire up here." Trapping in winter, gold-mining in summer—he would try whatever the country might offer, but not to take and go. He did not seek a living so much as a life. He was twenty-three, and he was in love with a woman named Sara, but she was thousands of miles away—outside—and, while he fervently hoped she would join him, she was, for the time being, less appealing than the Yukon. In the fall of 1975, he learned of a cabin where he might spend the approaching winter. It had been built by Sarge Waller, who had used it one winter and decided not to do so again. Waller's cabin is just upstream of where the Kandik River, coming in from Canada, gives itself up to the Yukon. Corazza would be alone there, but he would not be entirely without neighbors. There were three occupied cabins within a quarter of a million surrounding acres.

After hitching a boat ride or two, he finished his journey on foot. Walking upriver, he came to the Kandik on the seventh of October, late in the day. The Kandik surprised him—too big and fast to ford. So he slept where he was, his dog, Molly, beside him. When he woke, his bag was covered with an inch of snow. He built a raft and crossed the river.

For several months, he kept company with a journal, written on loose sheets of ruled yellow paper.

> *Thursday, Oct 9 . . . Seen a white weazel right outside the cabin, his nest is in the dog house. Plan to cut wood tomorrow, seems like Molly and I are just waiting for winter. Things are pretty well straightened up at the cabin and damn it sure feels like home. Wish we had a moose! Good night, Sara.*

The writing atrophied when perhaps he felt even more at home. The seasons changed, and he went elsewhere in the country to mine gold. Behind him he left only two signs of his occupancy: beaver castors hanging from a beam, and, up on one wall, the record of his novice days.

> *Friday, Oct 10 . . . I have 3 Swede saws here and the biggest works the best, it is a 5 footer. After a hardy breakfast, I will now attempt to secure the winter's wood.*

One day in June, I stopped in at the cabin, on my way by canoe downriver. The mouth of the Kandik is roughly halfway between Eagle and Circle, the upper and lower gateways of the country. The mountainous land between them comes to an end with a final bluff near Circle. Beyond that bluff is another world, an almost oceanic peneplain known as the Yukon Flats. Brad Snow had never been near this natural boundary, and was interested in expanding his knowledge of the river. He had the canoe. For my part, I was on my way to a lengthy visit with Ed and Virginia Gelvin, in Central, and with miners of the Birch Creek district, and was only too pleased to be able to make the journey in Snow's nineteen-foot Grumman freighter. We left Eagle in what was locally termed a heat wave—seventy degrees. Steve Casto, standing on the high bank watching us go, said it was too hot a day to drink coffee.

. . . Sure is nice to come into a warm cabin. As Sally once wrote, "It's never too cold to cut wood when you're out of fire."

Saturday, Oct 11 . . . Just a skiff of snow on the ground, the Yukon isn't flowing ice yet, but I think maybe she will shortly. Driftwood really burns good and there is a load of it about 100 yards from the cabin. It's rough cutting but I'll get after it today. Good morning, Sara!

Sunday, Oct 12. Cut wood & hauled it for 5 hours yesterday, good thing too on account that the ground is white this morning and still snowing, good day to set by the stove. 37° and windy on the Yukon.

Didn't get much accomplished today. It snowed off and on again, dropped to about 30° and is hanging there. I went hunting near a lake about a mile from here. No sign of anything except squirrel, of which I shot one and boiled it up for Molly, she's looking awful thin. It would be nice to throw her a moose bone (me too).

Just as the country ends with an isolated bluff, it was thought once to begin with one—a high, mansarded prominence that looms above Eagle. When Lieutenant Frederick Schwatka, U.S. Army, was sent to look over the area in 1883, he was instructed to determine, roughly, where the Yukon came into Alaska. Rafting hundreds of miles through Canadian mountains down the giant bending river, he noted shifts in its direction, guessed distances, guessed current velocities, ran the data through his mind, and what is now named Eagle Bluff he called Boundary Butte. It was some guess—like a sailor's fixing his position by the feel of it—for the hundred-and-forty-first (boundary) meridian was scarcely twelve miles upstream, and, by air line, six miles away. William Ogilvie, sent by Ottawa, surveyed the border four years later. Eagle, Alaska, looking east from a bend in the river, has all before it a sweep of boundary ridgelines, and behind them rise the Ogilvie Mountains, Yukon Territory. The international boundary is now absurdly shaved. Trees are levelled and brush kept cut in a thirty-foot swath.

Monday, Oct 13. 28° and wintery at 8 this morning. My wood supply looks meager for the weeks of cold weather ahead. (So does my meat supply.) Keeps me on the ball.

When Brad Snow's canoe went out past Eagle Bluff, the buildings of the town diminished behind until the white ones looked like dentils against the pale green of birch and aspen that were just coming into their leaves. There were blocks of shelf ice still along the shore. Belle Isle, in the river at Eagle, was a dark loaf of spruce. American Summit, the southern backdrop, and the Ogilvies, to the east, were dusted white. I was wearing a T-shirt in the bright June sun, but I soon put on a sweater. The temperature of the river was forty-six, and the air close above it was cool. Six miles downstream, I had added a down vest, a 60/40 windbreaker, and a rain suit, hood to heel. Brad Snow was in a rain suit, too. We were driving into a head-on squall, and there were whitecaps on the river. Another bend and there was sun again; another bend, more rain.

. . . Met Harold today, he is Fred's partner. They're pretty much "hippies" it seems to me but real nice fellas. Found out he is the one who came down on the raft with all the supplies for he and his new found gal from Kentucky. Strange world, but I remember the time I resorted to offering a gal life in the woods. How can an adventurous young thing resist?

Some of the people who live together in remote settings along the river refer to themselves not as couples but as units.

It happens at times that two half-its will decide to form a new unit. Or one might go out to Fairbanks and come back with someone new. The country is not without its citadels of righteousness, wherein certain burghers seem to look with disdain upon what they refer to as "river people's morals." They have possibly forgotten that this river is not the St. Mary, the Ste. Anne, the St. Croix, and does not flow uphill or in any sense suggest detachment from the functions of the earth. In their disdain, they overlook tradition. Beside the Yukon, a young woman of indisputable appeal once presented herself to a saloonful of miners and auctioned herself to the highest bidder. She offered fair terms. If she were to back out at any time within six months, he would get a complete refund. If he backed out, she would keep the money. All right, now, get up your pokes, boys. Who's the first bidder? There were bidders enough, and she brought down the gavel for a pretty sum. So far as is known, she stayed with the winner forever.

When people seeking gold first came across the high southeastern passes to the headwater lakes of the river, they hewed boats out of the forest and took them down the Yukon in small, inexperienced navies. One young wife fell out of a boat and appeared on her way to drowning. She thrashed and bobbed and went under at least twice, while her husband anxiously watched. At length, another man in another boat saved her. When her husband rowed over to pick her up, she demanded instead her duffel. Then and there, she formed a new unit.

Tuesday, Oct 14. 21° . . . Walked through the spruce and hit the Kandik about 1½ miles up. It's pretty well froze in places. A guy couldn't even line a canoe up for the ice. . . . Still no ice on the Yukon . . . I only been wearing longhandles and a wool shirt and I've been sweating at times.

Wednesday, Oct 15. 28°. Sunny. Prettyful.

Thursday, October 16. Fred came down yesterday, left a dog here overnight, and said that some people on the river will be meeting for the spring equinox at Nation (the old Taylor place).

Sun. Oct 19 . . . Beaver is one of the best tasting meats I've ever had—fatty and kinda naturally sweet. I got the castors and am soaking the oil glands in water for scent.

> *Sun Oct 26. 20°. Windy. Still snowing. About 6–8 inches on the level. This morning big sheets of ice were flowing on the sides of the river, and by now (11:45 A.M.) there is ICE all the way ACROST. BIG sheets 40–50 ft long and they just keep packin' together, fusing to the sides (banks) or just keep flowing downstream, quite a site.*

Brad Snow said that if the canoe were to tip over, it would have to be abandoned, because the river, even now, in June, was too cold to allow the usual procedure of staying with the boat and kicking it to shore. "Keep your clothes on in the river. They provide some insulation, and you will need them later on. It's a good idea to have some matches tucked away in a dry container. We would need a drying fire." With luck, and fair probability, the canoe would go into an eddy, he said, and might be recovered there.

Nothing much was going to turn us over, though. Only at one or two points in a hundred and sixty miles did we see anything that remotely suggested rapids, and these were mere drapefolds of white in the otherwise broad, flat river. Sleepers were in the water—big logs flushing down out of Canada and floating beneath the surface—but they were going in our direction and were much less dangerous than they would have been had we been heading upstream. The great power of the Yukon—six and more fathoms of water, sometimes half a mile wide, moving at seven knots—was unostentatiously displayed. The surface was deceptively calm—it was only when you looked to the side that you saw how fast you were flying.

From the hull, meanwhile, came the steady sound of sandpaper, of sliding stones, of rain on a metal roof—the sound of the rock in the river, put there by alpine glaciers. Dip a cupful of water and the powdered rock settled quickly to the bottom. At the height of the melting season, something near two hundred tons of solid material will flow past a given point on the riverbank in one minute. Bubbling boils, like the tops of high fountains, bloomed everywhere on the surface but did not rough it up enough to make any sort of threat to the canoe. They stemmed from the crash of fast water on boulders and ledges far below. Bend to bend, the river presented itself in large segments—two, three, six miles at a stretch, now smooth, now capped white under the nervously changeable sky. We picked our way through flights of wooded islands. We shivered in the deep shadows of bluffs a thousand feet high—Calico Bluff, Montauk Bluff, Biederman Bluff, Takoma Bluff—which day after day intermittently walled the river. Between them—in downpourings of sunshine, as often as not—long vistas reached back across spruce-forested hills to the rough gray faces and freshly whitened summits of mountains. Some of the walls of the bluffs were of dark igneous rock that had cracked into bricks and appeared to have been set there by masons. Calico Bluff—a sedimentary fudge, folded, convoluted in whorls and ampersands—was black and white and yellow-tan. Up close it smelled of oil. It was sombre as we passed it, standing in its own shadow. Peregrine falcons nest there, and—fantastic fliers—will come over the Yukon at ballistic speeds, clench their talons, tuck them in, and strike a flying duck hard enough (in the neck) to kill it in midair. End over end the duck falls, and the falcon catches it before it hits the river. As we passed the mouth of the Tatonduk, fifteen ducks flew directly over us. Brad Snow reached for his shotgun, and quickly fired twice. Fifteen ducks went up the Tatonduk. Above the Nation, steep burgundy mountainsides reached up from the bright-green edges of the river, then fell away before tiers of higher mountains, dark with spruce and pale with aspen, quilted with sunlight and shadow. Ahead, long points of land and descending ridgelines reached toward one another into the immensity of the river, roughed now under a stiff wind. Filmy downspouts dropped from the clouds. Behind the next bend, five miles away, a mountain was partly covered with sliding mist. The scene resembled Lake Maggiore and might have been the Hardanger Fjord, but it was just a fragment of this river, an emphatic implication of all the two thousand miles, and of the dozens of tributaries that in themselves were major rivers—proof and reminder that with its rampart bluffs and circumvallate mountains it was not only a great river of the far northwestern continent but a river of preëminence among the rivers of the world. The ring of its name gave nothing away to the name of any river. Sunlight was bright on the mountains to both sides, and a driving summer rain came up the middle. The wind tore up the waves and flung pieces of them through the air. It was not the wind, though, but the river itself that took the breath away.

Mon Oct 27. Good morning, Sara! 6° . . . The water froze in the water buckets and I slept good. . . . The river is really flowin' a lot of ice, but it is still moving—ripping and tearing at the shelf ice on the banks.

Wed Oct 29. −20° this morning, clear as a church bell and feels good. Got a ruffed grouse and a squirrel yesterday, also set some rabbit snares.

Rain gone, and in sun again we could hear the consumption of an island. Large pieces of the bank fell thunderously into the water, because the Yukon had decided to yaw. We passed a deep fresh indentation in the shore where a dozen tall spruce had plopped at once. They were sixty-foot trees, and so much of the ground that held them had fallen with them that they now stood almost vertically in thirty feet of river. Ordinarily, as a river works its way into cut-bank soil the trees of the bank gradually lose their balance and become "sweepers"—their trunks slanting downward, their branches spread into the water. The islands of the Yukon have so many sweepers that from a distance they look like triremes. The river roars through the crowns of the trees with a sound of heavy rapids.

Fri Oct 31. −32° & clear. Thank God for wood!

Sat Nov 1. −33°. It sure got to cracking and buckin' last night. She is really still out this morning. It took 8 days to freeze since the ice started flowing. The Yukon is froze solid.

Often, after the general freeze-up, there is a lead in the left-bank bend beside Eagle—the current keeping open a patch of river long after the rest is ice. It can stay open for more than two months. A cold snap—reaching, say, seventy below zero—will finally close it.

Barney Hansen, who came into the country fifty years ago to mine gold, says he once watched a file of thirteen caribou pick their way down Eagle Bluff to drown in the river lead. The bluff approaches sheer, and its face is rough with crags and ledges and plunging tight ravines. Slowly, surely, the thirteen creatures descended, almost every move a feat of balance and decision. Poised there, each avoiding a fall to destruction, they gave Hansen and whoever else may have been watching plenty of time to wonder why they had chosen that route. They could readily have swung wide of both the town and the bluff. Finally, they reached the ice and started across the river. Everywhere around the lead, the ice was solid to the farther shore. Yet the thirteen caribou one after another jumped into the open water. The current drew them to the downstream end, where it sucked them under the ice.

In May, when big floes begin to move downriver like ships, caribou have been observed upon them. Caught crossing the river when the ice moved, they now stand in huddled helplessness, riding to certain death as the support beneath them crashes, cracks, diminishes in size, and ultimately rolls over.

Sun Nov. 2. −35° . . . Beautiful, clear day. Still no moose sign. Lots of overflow on the Yukon. I set out some traps and snares tonight, feels good to be runnin through the woods lookin for them little critters.

Mon Nov 3. −38°. Still and clear.

Wed Nov 5. −31°, still clear and I still love Sara a bunch. Today is woodchoppin day, so I et 3 lbs. of taters, a pound of spam, and a gallon of coffee. I'm not full, but it'll have to do.

Thur Nov 6. −30 . . . Seen a fresh cat track today where the lynx had bedded down right beside a rabbit run. Twice he had picked himself a good spot to lay in readiness for a meal.

Sun Nov 9. −24°. Reset some traps. Got a lynx comin to one of 'em. Put some squirrels in a couple for marten bait. Did a lot of snowshoeing & breakin trail and am tuckered out.

Mon Nov 10. −12° cloudy and may snow. Today is the anniversary of being in Alaska for exactly one year now. Quite a lot has happened and if I had Sara now it would be the end of a near perfect year. Still, it was the best decision I ever did make, and am very glad things worked out. If I was religious, I might say, "Thank you, Lord." Amen.

Approaching the mouth of the Kandik, Snow and I maneuvered among shoals and heavy driftwood in an attempt to get to shore, going in for an assessive look at our friend Sarge Waller's cabin. We went up the bank. Snow gave the cabin a long, professional sniff—a construction worker's frank inspection. "This," he said finally—and paused a moment to mortise the words—"this is the most poorly built cabin you ever will see." The walls were convex. The foundation was not banked. The roof was virtually without insulation. The corners were mail slots for the wind. The loose sheets of Corazza's journal were held by a metal clip hanging on a wall. I took them down and riffled through them.

The journal was roughly four thousand words. (Only fragments are here.) The author's name was nowhere on it so far as I could see. It had been left in an empty cabin, in near-absolute wilderness, on land that belonged to the people of the United States, of whom I was one. If ever a piece of writing was born in the public domain, surely this was it. Yes—but it seemed private. It wasn't like food in a cache, to take and later replace. I returned it to the wall.

A few weeks later, I was sitting in the roadhouse in Central talking with a man who was down from the mining claims on Porcupine Creek. He was young, dark-haired, strongly built. Like most bush Alaskans, however new to the bush they might be, he had greeting in his face. In the course of a second beer, he mentioned that he had spent the winter in a cabin near the mouth of the Kandik.

I surprised him by telling him I had glanced at his journal, and had wished I could someday read it. He said he had a little time off and had been thinking of going up there anyway; he would see me again in a few days. He went eighty miles up the river and brought back the journal.

> *Wed Nov 12. −3° cloudy & snowing. Molly of the North, great Alaskan cat hound, says she likes this turn in the weather. She has put on considerable weight and looks real strong.*
>
> *Saw a gyrfalcon today. Flew right over my head clippin along at a pace so fast it sounded like a jet. Almost white bird. Could have been a female, it was pretty good size. Also saw a bird killed hare yesterday near the cabin. Bet it's that gyr's meal. This country is neat.*

We carried mail with us downriver, and now and again Brad would, in effect, toss it into the woods. There were people in there who would read it. The names on the packages and envelopes were not familiar to me. Snow said, "There are those on the river who are discreet and those who are not. People like Dick Cook and Charlie Edwards need to talk and be chatty in Eagle. Others come into town rarely, say nothing much, and leave."

We stopped one morning in a hidden slough with letters for Jan Waldron. She was slender, lankily built, with long blond hair, a quick and friendly smile. She ran down the bank and fairly jumped into the canoe. "Gosh, it's so good to see you." Her husband, Seymour Abel, had been away many days. Their home was a wall tent on supporting courses of logs, with a door that was more like a window. We crawled in. She and Seymour were just camping in this tent, she explained, and opened some beer she had brewed there. She pointed proudly to a cavity in the earth at her feet. To surprise and please Seymour, she had passed the time removing a stump. I remembered meeting Seymour, briefly, in Eagle, where we had talked about bears, and the pros and cons of carrying a protective gun. "If you're going to get et, you're going to get et," he had said, conclusively, and, repeating himself, "If you're going to get et, you're going to get et, whether you have a rifle or not." Seymour came into the country from Tennessee. Jan is a born Alaskan. "I'm so glad to see you," she said again, and opened another beer. The top of the tent was lined with Styrofoam. In the gable was a shelf of books. There was a plank table, a Singer sewing machine, a banjo, a guitar, a violin. There was a barrel stove. The chimney, where it poked through the tent, was flashed with a two-gallon can. Dark-haired sled dogs were staked outside. A day or so before, they had raised a great clamor. To Jan, it signalled the nearness of a bear. Carrying clothes for washing to a small clear stream, she took along a gun because of the bear. "Are you sure you have to go?" she said as we stood up. "It's so good to see you. Why go?"

Around the turn of the century, when dog teams travelled more frequently on the river, there was an isolated roadhouse not far from where Jan lives now. The woman who ran it would shoot at people who tried to go by without stopping.

Fri Nov 14. −28°. Clear. I have become pretty well used to the cold now and can get a roarin fire going awful quick these days. Caught a hare and one beautiful red fox today. The fox had been caught in a trail-set about a mile from where I crossed his tracks. She had broken the wire I had tied to the trap chain. I followed her to the river and then ran up to within shooting distance. She was moving pretty good with a #3 double spring on her front paw. I shot her right below the eye at 100 ft. with the pistol (Ruger). She sure is pretty and would make Sara a nice hat.

Sun Nov 16. Full moon, *and the Yukon is in party dress. Everything is lit up just prettiful. . . . I jumped a bunch of grouse (ruffed) roosting. Got 5 with the pistol and about 18 shots. Could have got more but I run plumb out of shells. I sure do love that grouse meat.*

The moon cycle is funny up here. It starts waxing in a small arc through the southern sky, then day by day it gets brighter and the arc gets higher and longer till it's full moon almost overhead and stay light all night. Just magnificent!

2 of them grouse I got at 40 yds with that little Ruger (makes a guy proud). Wish Sara would fix em up for us.

We passed fish camps all down the river, for the most part established by Indians and abandoned now—places that once netted as much as thirty tons of salmon a year. At one fish camp stood the biggest cache I have seen in Alaska, virtually a full-size cabin in the air, resting on columnar stilts. All it contained was a beaver's forepaw.

Tues Nov 18. −22°. The other day when I got them grouse, a funny thing happened. The last grouse was perched in the top of an alder about 30 ft high. I shot at it twice from about 35 yds and thought I'd missed it. But it stayed up there. I snuck up to about 20 yds from it and emptied the pistol. It still sat there. It was gettin dark and I was out of shells. I figured that that grouse wouldn't be a meal for me. Then all of a sudden I got MAD, went over to the tree, shook it, and yelled, "Get outa there you son of a bitch." Well, down comes a blanket of snow on my head—but also Mister Grouse, who is only winged. He scooted along the ground for awhile and then just disappeared! By God, he was gone just like that. Then I flashed to a memory that Dad had told me a story of a grouse he had winged and the dog pointed at a bunch of leaves. Finally he seen a feather stickin out of the leaves, took off his hat and caught him a grouse in it. Well, I seen where he last was and used my mitten (it was 20 below and didn't want to take off my hat) to clamp down on the snow and by Jesus if I didn't come up with another supper in my hands. Made me laugh just a bit to think that my anger had been changed so fast into a memory. Had some grouse gumbo last night. Ummm!

The brilliance of this north country under the full moon is dazzling to say the least. At midnight the sky is still a deep *blue with the twinkling of many bright stars. Moon shadows of the tall spruce are everywhere and the Yukon River lays quiet and white. This moon seems to stand guard on this country.*

There has long been talk of a tourist road connecting Eagle and Circle. Running for the most part beside the river, it would "open up" what is generally regarded as the handsomest stretch of the Yukon in Alaska. The longest piece of road along the Yukon now runs three miles upriver from Eagle to Eagle Indian Village. On the river near that road, I have paddled more than once in dust that was thicker than smoke.

Mon Nov 24. −6°. Plan to go upriver.

Tues Nov 25. −4°. On the way up, Bob's lead dog got caught in one of Fred's Conibears. Boy it was a mad scramble for Bob and I to get to the front of 9 dogs and prise the jaws apart on that trap. The dog acted like nothing had ever happened and went right on again. Could have been tragic but it turned out funny. . . . Found out that Thanksgiving is on the 27th. . . . It was fun to run them 9 dogs all strung out single. Bob and I took turns as it was a rough run over the muskeg and the sled was loaded heavy (probably 500 lbs +). It tipped over 5 or 6 times but things went smooth. Both of us were wore plumb out. . . . I fell through the ice 2 or 3 times yesterday, & ran around with wet pacs. Feels like I frosted the ends of my big toes a bit, but they're far from my heart, so I'll keep on truckin.

We stopped one night at an abandoned cabin, containing so much clutter of junk debris that we decided to sleep outside. Mosquitoes were dense there but tolerable—not yet coming in clouds. In the Yukon Flats, beyond the mountains, were thirty-six thousand lakes and ponds, with geese, canvasbacks, scaup, cranes, swans, teal, and widgeons in millions, and mosquitoes in numbers a physicist would understand. But we were still upriver, and only five or six thousand of them were now close around us. I asked Brad if he would like to share my netted tent. Inside it moments later, he told me how his wife plays what she calls Revenge. In the security of a tent, she places near the netting an example of her flesh until it drives to frenzy the singers in the night. A truly ambitious mosquito will soon thrust its proboscis through the net. She then seizes the proboscis and yanks the bugger inside. For my part, I mentioned that when mosquitoes seek human blood they are fulfilling their sexual cycle, doing what nature is instructing them to do, and therefore an authentic conservationist will never react unfavorably to the attentions of a mosquito. This simple test—a way of telling the phonies from the truly committed—I had first come upon long ago in the Lower Forty-eight. Gradually in Alaska, however, I had come to realize that an Alaska mosquito is not a Lower Forty-eight mosquito that has moved north. Before getting into the tent, I had slapped my leg, turned the palm up, and counted seventeen corpses in my hand.

Sat Dec 13 . . . The weather has been −50 or lower (−60 was the lowest) for 12 days but this morning the wind started blowing and the weather warmed up some 40° to −8. I ran the dogs down across the river to get a load of fish yesterday. Saw fresh moose sign and Errol & I spent all day today hunting. Lots of sign but no luck. I haven't checked my line since the new moon and it's already past half. Tomorrow will be the day. There seems to be more cat around since it got cold.

Sun Dec 21 . . . Errol and I were hunting cause the 2 moose were staying in this area. Errol ran into them and got us both of them, by God! We eatin high nowadays. Moose liver and steak for breakfast. Hmm! We had a real chinook for a few days and the temp went up to 39° above. Couldn't believe it.

Mon Dec. 22. Zero. Oboy! Biscuits gravy & moose steak this fine day. Yepper, sure wish Sara were back home where she belongs.

Tues Dec 23. Zero and clear . . . Made a few more cat sets today in the slough. Missed a cat in one of my cubbies.

A "cat" is a lynx. A "lynk" is also a lynx. Nine times out of ten, people who say "lynk" are trying to sound like trappers.

Mon Dec 29. +15° . . . Walked up to 3 Mile today with Molly on a lead rope (she was leading me). We didn't hit a fresh track till after dark on the way back. She struck out on the cat's trail but didn't run it very far, it was in thick alders. She sure wanted to though.

Jan 7. −40. I've had some bad luck. Molly run off about 3 days ago at 25 below. I could hear her howling bloody murder from the cabin here. I'd just got a fire started after a 6 mile hike down river. Well, I figured, she got herself in a trap, so I went to looking for her. Found her 3 hours later, almost to Errol's cabin with her right front paw in a number 4 doublespring. It was frozen solid. My lantern had run out of fuel and there was no moon. We ran to Errol's cabin where I soaked her paw in lukewarm water for about an hour. It swelled plumb up as big as a cat track, but today it started to blister and I think it may heal. The swelling's gone down a bit. Poor ole Molly Blue!

Jan 8. −40. Red is the color of my barrel stove when it's 40 below, when it's 40 below! A bit nippy these last few days, but it's nice to set by a roarin stove.

Snow and I lingered at the mouths of tributary streams, and went miles up the Charley, the river of Leon Crane. Logs cruised toward us like alligators, and with the same stately glide. We surprised ravens, geese, a bald eagle, which lumbered into flight. It slowly achieved altitude, its wings barely recovering from flap to awkward flap. Peregrines, which nest on bluffs above the Charley, can pin down one of these eagles and keep it where it is indefinitely—the falcons diving, pecking, strafing, dominating, while the symbol of national grandeur cowers on the ground, a screaming eagle. After nine or ten miles, the Charley, with riffles, increased its gradient rise, and the immense, confining forest began to open to big, long-distance views. Far up the corridor of the river were white-patched mountains, and far behind them more and higher mountains totally covered with newly fallen snow. We tied up in an island slough and climbed the steep face of a bluff—loose, flaky shale; no trees; not much to hang on to—and when we had worked our way upward five hundred vertical feet I looked back at what seemed a straight plunge to the river. It was a bluff of swallows and lupine, blueberries and bears. We saw only sign of the bears. Brad was carrying his rifle. He remarked that his friend David Evans, who has been in the country about as long as he has, apparently rejoices in a nearly perfect state of "anestrophic anticipation." Asked to explain what that is, Snow said, "You have no sense of catastrophe. You walk through the valley of the shadow of death and you fear no evil—not because you are fearless but because you have no awareness of what may happen. David walks miles and miles, unarmed, and doesn't seem to understand that there's a chance of being mauled."

We sat down and ate berries, looking up frequently at many hundreds of square miles of dark broadloom forests curling at the edges into rising tundra fells, which ended in mountain rock. Through the mountains came the clear river, often deep within its peregrine bluffs, which were pinpointed white with visible Dall sheep and darkened by invisible bears. It was landscape uncompromised, under small white cumulus by the tens of dozens evenly spaced to the corners of the sky. I remembered Frank Warren, in Circle, talking about the Park Service's yen for the Charley, and saying, "What can you do to improve an area that is perfect? What possible satisfaction could a hiker ever get walking on a man-made trail?" We descended the bluff and descended the stream, stopping at the cabin built by Al Ames, where the government had posted a sign beside the door forbidding habitation.

We drifted down the Yukon through a windless afternoon. The fast-flowing water was placid and—with its ring boils—resembled antique glass. Down one long straightaway, framed in white mountains, we saw ten full miles to the wall of the coming bend.

> *Fri Feb 6. Been traveling this ole Yukon from Sam Creek (at times to Coal Creek) all the way to 20 miles this side of Eagle. Not much cat sign anywhere . . . Molly is healed up pretty good.*

> *Sat Feb. 7. −37° before sunrise, now an hour later it's −40 and droppin fast, looks like another snapper! Beautiful light show last night . . . Sara, where are you?*

Stanley Gelvin grew up in the country, and therefore has no capacity to see it as exotic. He has sampled other worlds, which have failed to attract him—Fairbanks, mainly, and a visit or two outside. He has spent most of the nights of his life in sleeping bags. When he sleeps in a bed with sheets and blankets, he turns, tosses, and flips until the bedding is out of tuck and is composed in mummy shape around him. While Stanley was growing up, Central, Alaska, with its population under twenty, did not offer him a large reserve of playmates. Instead, he had engines. Getting to know them, he acquired a primary skill of the country, and now has almost a maker's sense of their design and function. In mining, hunting, trapping, ice fishing, he and his family used everything from rasping little two-cycle chain-saw engines to the turbocharged diesel of the D9 Cat. They have pumps, generators, airplanes, snow machines, washing machines, automobiles, pickups—and when you are well over a hundred miles from the corner garage you do not go there to have someone listen to what seems to be wrong. Stanley, in his middle twenties, has never known that sort of dependence. Like his father, Ed Gelvin, he routinely works on the pumps, the saws, the cars, the planes. "Living in the bush, you have to," he says. "I don't know anything different. You just have to be a good mechanic. You have to modify machinery until you get the imperfections out. I never found nothing I couldn't fix."

From early youth onward, Stanley's gold fever has been chronic, running along steadily a few degrees above normal. As a child, he made little rocker boxes and took them out to Deadwood Creek to separate from its gravels its cereal flakes of color. As he moved through the boxes small heaps of pebbles and sand, the point was not lost on him that a guy could move a whole stream bed with a big machine, and when that day came a guy would have to be able to maintain the machine. For ten dollars, he bought from a neighbor a pre-Second World War Chevrolet. It was long since dead on the road. He sent off for piston rings and gaskets from Sears in Philadelphia. The bearings were babbitted and could not be replaced, so he took out the shims and adjusted them for proper clearance. He was seven years old. He had a book on auto mechanics. He did a valve job. He installed the new gaskets and rings. The engine sat up in its coffin.

Ed and Ginny Gelvin ran the Central roadhouse for a time. To drivers who had made the long trip from Fairbanks up the dusty seasonal road Stanley was generous with alarming advice. "Why don't you turn that bearing over? If you don't, you'll be sorry." A truck driver came in once, hauling supplies to Circle, and before he could fairly sip his coffee he was confronted by this little kid telling him his differential was in bad trouble. "Don't worry about it, son. It always sounds like that," the driver said, departing. Thirty miles up the road, the truck went around a curve, and the wheels tried to turn—as they are wont to on curves—at varying rates of spin. The differential failed to see the difference anymore. The breakdown was complete.

The mining season ordinarily is short. It can be even shorter when a stream remains "glaciered" until the middle of July. A bush Alaskan—miner, trapper, whatever his interests may be—is particularly secure if he carries a union card and can go out part of the year for extra money. Stanley belongs to 302—the Fairbanks local of the Operating Engineers' union. In Fairbanks, in the cabs of cranes, he sometimes sets steel for ironworkers—an extremely delicate job. "One slip and you can kill someone. You work in fractions of an inch, making bolt holes line up. You're swinging all the time. It's harder to operate equipment than to fly." After growing up on the seats of Cats—plowing snow, skidding logs—he went out to work on the Chandalar Shelf, the Dietrich River, Galbraith Lake, running his first D9s, building the pipeline road. He prefers to be in Central. In 1975, in Greenhorn Gulch, ten miles up a creek from home, he set up a twenty-four-foot wooden sluice box that took in nearly a hundred and fifty dollars' worth of gold in every hour it ran. Unfortunately, it ran only twenty-four hours (an aggregate of short bursts), because water was scarce in the gulch. The experience, however, was anything but discouraging. Thirty-five hundred dollars will fuel a fair amount of living in the bush. With his infant son, Jimmy, and wife, Andrea, who is the daughter of a Fairbanks contractor, Stanley lives in a new cabin on his parents' property. He would have liked to build somewhere else, off in the hills or out near the Yukon, in an unneighbored place he could call his own, but, in the vastness of all the surrounding country, land was not available. That, for Stanley, has been a bewildering disappointment. When he was born, in 1950, the country was open and free. Expectations were that when he grew up he could live where he pleased.

Then Alaska became a state. Oil was discovered. Homesteading ended. In the great reapportionment of Alaskan land, the squares seemed to be moving as well as the checkers. Stanley, who had always been at ease with all aspects of this place and latitude, now found himself feeling more than uneasy. A government many thousands of miles away had "frozen" the land with printed words. It was settling forty million acres on Eskimos, Aleuts, and Indians, but for his future it offered little more than atrophy, a narrowing of what he once might have looked upon as his birthright opportunities. He could not comprehend this. He was a native, too.

When Stanley's mother was a girl, she lived in urban Pittsburgh, and she often said, "When I grow up, I'm going to live in a log cabin with a wolf hide on the wall." She read Louise Dickinson Rich ("We Took to the Woods"), Willa Cather ("O Pioneers!"), Jack London ("White Fang"), and works of Peary and Byrd. Her father, a carpenter, had a cottage about ninety miles north of the city. He took her there to fish for bass, perch, and bullheads, and to hunt rabbits, squirrels, and ducks. Driving home, she could smell Pittsburgh long before its stacks came into view, and she would begin thinking of the next trip to the cottage.

Ed Gelvin grew up on a small dairy farm a mile and a half out of Hartstown, Pennsylvania, in the northwestern corner of the state. There were eighteen cows, a hundred and some acres. Four generations of Gelvins had lived there. Ed's father, Stanley Gelvin, liked horses so much he did not buy a tractor until 1939, when Ed was fifteen. As a twelve-year-old, Ed plowed behind a team, and planted corn, wheat, and hay "in a little valley of real rich sandy loam." He milked, he fed the stock, and when his chores were done he hunted and he trapped. A skunk pelt was worth eight dollars, a muskrat three. He mailed them to Sears, Roebuck in Philadelphia, who sent him a check or credited the furs against items he ordered from their catalogue. He got to know Ginny when he was still in his teens. "Her Dad had this little cottage in a swamp, about a mile from our farm."

Ginny talked of "going somewhere"—a place where "you could make your own life." The Second World War interrupted the conversation. Ed apprenticed himself as an ironworker, helped build a defense plant near his home, and went into the Navy, which trained him as a shipfitter in Newport News. She joined the Women's Army Corps. They were married in 1946, and he went back to "putting up iron," while Ginny went back to thinking of a place where they could be more on their own. "I noticed a lot about this keeping up with the Joneses. Look-alike houses were starting. I couldn't see living like that. I couldn't see straining and striving to make a better can opener when all it does is open a can." She wrote a letter, and Ed signed it. "Department of the Interior, Washington, D.C. Dear Sirs: Would you please mail me any information you have on the Territory of Alaska."

They bought a new sedan (a naïve beginning) and started out in June, 1949. Neither of them had ever been west of the Mississippi. In Montana, they saw, for the first time, high mountains topped with snow. In Alberta, they began seeing moose racks on barns and houses. In British Columbia and Yukon Territory, they saw mud, and rain, and spruce. On the nineteenth of June, they crossed the hundred-and-forty-first meridian, and now "the roads were like crick beds, the rocks were like grapefruit"—Alaska! Not that they needed further proof of where they were, but they got it forthwith when they stopped at a roadhouse, three in the afternoon, and everyone in it was drunk. In Fairbanks, hungry, they cruised around looking for a place to eat, but all they could afford was soup and coffee, for two dollars and fifty cents. There were no hotel rooms. They slept in the car. Of the many hundreds of people they would come to know whose arrivals were similar to theirs, most—within days, a month, a year—would turn and go. The Gelvins sold the car and bought a pickup. Ed got a job in the railroad yard, and before long was building a school. One day in July, they went up the long dust trail to Central, to the domes of the Tanana Hills. Their purpose was to see caribou, and they stood on high passes and swept with their eyes the tundra fells. The nearest caribou was somewhere else. All they saw was the country.

If gold first drew them to settle here, the country itself is what kept them—the rivers, the mountains, this immense wild range lying open to anyone who could meet its climatic terms. In their first mining season on Squaw Creek, they made expenses and then some. After that, because of slow-melting stream ice, they barely made expenses. That is when they would have left if gold had been all they wanted, but they had chosen the country in the way that someone else would choose a career. Sense of place registered higher with them than a sense of accumulating wealth. They went to work at almost anything that might support them, and tried to stay where they were. They first lived in Circle Hot Springs, a clump of buildings around a natural phenomenon that fogged the winter air with warm steam and coated the spruce with ice. Central was eight miles away. It appealed to them because it was "less junky than most Alaskan towns." It was scarcely a town at all, had never had a school or a church—just a few cabins around the T in the road where a spur went off to the Springs. They took on the local mail run. They cut and sold cordwood and lumber. They ran the roadhouse for a year and a half. They shot wolves for the bounty, which was fifty dollars. The price of fur was too low at first to make other animals worth trapping, but as the price went up their lines went out, and fur eventually became their primary source of money. Meanwhile, Ed went off to construction jobs —a month here, six weeks there. In Arctic Alaska, in winter, he helped build stations of the DEW line. He built oil-drilling platforms in Cook Inlet and rigs on the North Slope. He was gone, in aggregate, no more than three months a year. Since 1970, the family has lived almost wholly on the possibilities of the country, and Ed has gone out for work only twice.

Stanley and then Betsy went to grammar school at the kitchen table. The material came by mail from Baltimore, and in the season when the sun was gone for upward of a month the children worked by kerosene light (or gasoline-generated electric light), while their mother watched over them and licked the stamps. When Stanley reached junior high, he went to school in Fairbanks, and was ahead of his peers by a couple of levels. Education as a whole, though, was a patchwork affair, a hazard of the bush—correspondence, boarding homes, shuttlings to an apartment in Fairbanks. The Gelvins' twins, Carol and Colleen, six years younger than Stanley, went to grade school in Fairbanks and high school by correspondence from Central—under the program run by the University of Nebraska. The course was "cattle-oriented," according to Ginny. While they might better have been studying, say, aviation and geology in addition to fundamental subjects, they sat at the table in their log cabin at fifty degrees below zero in the penarctic twilight studying animal husbandry. Colleen stayed the course, but Carol went off to Colorado to finish high school from the home of an uncle. Stanley matriculated at the University of Alaska, intending to become a mining engineer. He stayed two weeks, leaving when he discovered that he had to study English, too. Only Betsy, the middle child, went on through college. There was no television in Central. The children could watch it in Fairbanks if they wanted to—and, in their mother's words, "see the foolishness of it." But Ginny always felt relieved that Central was, as it still is, beyond TV's frontier. She had seen TV in a bar in Ohio in 1949 and had sensed what it could do to children.

For years, she kept a diary of the meals the family ate. Grouse, which she hunted with a .22, occasionally appeared in it, and beaver, lynx, mountain sheep, grayling, and pike, not to mention king salmon. But the main staple of the house was always moose, as a flip of the pages reveals. These were the features of consecutive winter nights:

Spaghetti with mooseburger.
Moose steak.
Omelet.
Moose steak.
Moose roast.
Pinto beans and cabbage.
Toasted cheese sandwiches.
Moose stew.
Moose meatloaf.
Leftover moose.
Leftover moose.
Sandwiches.
Spaghetti with mooseburger.
Swiss moosesteak.
Leftover moose.
Roast moose.
Moose steak.
Moose sandwiches and soup.

Mooseburgers.
Mooseburgers.
Clam chowder.
Fried moose liver.
Swiss moosesteak.
Ground moose in Spanish rice.

Looking up from this list when I read it, I asked her, "What are we having tonight?"

"Swiss caribou," she said.

With fair regularity, the family would listen—as they still do—to programs like "Tundra Topics" on KFAR, "Pipeline of the North" on KIAK, and "Trapline Chatter" on KJNP (King Jesus North Pole). As a public service in the absence of telephones, Alaskan radio stations spray messages around the bush. "To Brenda Carter. I'll be in late tomorrow night. I love you. John." "To Mr. O at Eagle from J.R. at Fairbanks. Please clean the snow off my roof." "To Martha Malcolm in Eagle. Angela Harper is in Fairbanks and O.K." "Passed police exam. Love, Jim." "Planning to have baby born at Lynette's cabin. Ellen and Jim Frazier. Eagle." "To Jan and Seymour on the Yukon from Mom in Anchorage. Are you there?" "To all my brothers and sisters in Anaktuvuk Pass . . ." "Please, Isaac, don't drink. We'll be getting married next week." "Chris is still hoping to make it out before breakup." These one-way communications are the only device to beat the mail. In recent times, the Gelvins' daughters have been working as bookkeepers and bull cooks on the Trans-Alaska Pipeline, and when they go out of Fairbanks to a new assignment or are coming home on leave they let their parents know by "Trapline Chatter." "Even when there's no message for us," their mother says, "it's a good way to keep up with what is going on around the bush."

The Gelvins bought their cabin from an old-timer who had once worked claims on Mastodon Creek. Gradually—as they added a room, razed a woodshed, built a porch—a new cabin evolved. It ate up and spit out its predecessor. In their sawmill, they cut their own lumber. Ed designed a gravity-feed system featuring the first flush toilet in the history of Central. It works much of the time. There is a supportive outhouse that is not always redundant. He dug Central's first year-round well. The kitchen sink is fed by a hand-cranked iron pump. Dishwater is heated on the stove. Ed designed and built the all-metal shop-garage, the one-plane hangar. He works with sheet metal like a tailor handling flannel, and has been called the best welder in Alaska. There are beautiful sleds in the shop and on the ground outside—Yukon sleds, basket sleds, racing sleds, freight sleds, bobsleds. He built them. He is the author of a laconically written booklet called "How to Build an Alaskan Dog Sled." The team is staked near the cabin. His lead dog, Tara, is fifty-percent wolf.

Gelvin is soft-spoken, clean-shaven. His construction shoes, his dark poplin work clothes, his visored cap do not suggest the extent to which he stands out against the landscape. Had he remained in the Lower Forty-eight, he would have gone on being an ironworker of the highest ability, but the geometry of his life, which in the far-northern bush is an ever-changing set of interlocking polygons, would have been less discernible—more like a faint straight line. Shy, quiet, admirably unassuming—whatever else he is up here, he is not anonymous.

"I worked with him on the Colville River. He knew what he was doing. Everything he did he did well and quickly. He is the most efficient man I've ever met."

"A lot of these bush Jacks-of-all-trades just want things to work out. Ed wants them right."

"He is the most capable man I've ever known. Every move he made he was doing something. There were no dead moves."

"The Gelvins are here thirty years and they attack any project with the enthusiasm of a newcomer."

"They leave a situation better than they found it."

"They are modern-type pioneers. They do things the old way, they do things the new way. They are the kind that built the country."

Ginny Gelvin is of middle height, with dark hair, dark quick eyes, and a skeptical corner-mouth grin. She wears jeans, usually with a wool shirt. She is comfortable in her surroundings, and is made nervous if she has to visit a populous place—even Fairbanks, a hundred and twenty-seven miles away, which she calls "town." She does not like, among other things, being dependent for water and power on sources outside her family's control. She has endured a flood in town, and the threat of earthquakes. At such times, she yearns for home. "Out here, anything can happen and it doesn't bother you. We have our own power system, our own well. We have double systems generally. We have kerosene and propane light when we don't want to run the generator." With temperatures that snap toward seventy below, they also have snows that close the road six months a year and bears that visit in summer. She looks up sometimes and sees wolves in the yard. She says, "In town, I always feel insecure."

Operating a sewing machine, her husband is, if anything, more able than she, at least when tailoring moosehide. With a rifle, she is the better shot. In two big gardens and a greenhouse, they grow most of their vegetables—tomatoes, peppers, cabbages, lettuce, kohlrabi, beans, cauliflower, celery, rhubarb, blood-red turnips a foot in diameter that resemble the hearts of bulls. They smoke salmon. They fly to Arctic lakes, drill holes in the ice with an auger attached to a chain saw, and pull out northern pike. Hunting game not just for food but for profit as well, Ed is the region's only registered big-game guide. For sums upward of two thousand dollars, he will take some cheechako up into the hills and glass and glass until he shows him a full-curl Dall ram or a grizzly big enough to carpet a hall.

The Gelvins have ten acres of land, an extraordinary spread for a family to own up here in ironic Alaska. A stream, Crooked Creek, runs along one side. Their compound has grown to sixteen buildings, nearly all of which are extremely small by any but local standards. Considerable safety is in these numbers—always somewhere to go, at fifty below zero, in the event of fire. There is a guest cabin, an eight-by-fourteen-foot wanigan (which is a habitable cabin in itself), a meat cache, a smokehouse, a toolshed. A "warehouse" contains sugar, flour, cornmeal, paper goods, coffee (things that can ignore the cold). Even the family's "attic" is a small freestanding building. Most of these structures are made from logs, and the scene might suggest an Eric Sloane book on Early American cabins were it not that the compound is for the most part arranged around one end of an airstrip. Your eye also rests on the fibre-glass greenhouse, not to mention the hangar and workshop. There are no anachronisms. All of it meshes in this place and time.

The main cabin is L-shaped, and its long sides are eighteen and thirty-two feet. Floor to ceiling, its height inside is ten courses of logs. There are many dozens of books, a core sample of which would be "Scotty Allan, King of the Dog Team Drivers," "Mining Engineers' Handbook," "Developing Gold Properties with Airplane Placer Drills," "The Home Physician and Guide to Health," "Yukon Women," "Fifty Years Below Zero," "Ancient Men of the Arctic," "The Call of the Wild," "The Wilderness Trapper," "The Trail Eater," "Grizzly Country," "Notorious Grizzly Bears," and "Return of the Alaskan." A waist-high bookshelf separates the kitchen area from the living room, where a couch and a couple of chairs—the walls, too—are draped and decorated with the long soft pelts of timber wolves. A full basement is below. There are five rooms in all. The wolf bitch Tara was not named for this house, but there is more analogy than meets the eye, for it is as handsome a cabin as there is in the country, and could be a setting to remember if the life here were to vanish with the wind.

When I have stayed with the Gelvins, I have for the most part occupied a cabin toward the far end of the airstrip—a place they acquired not long ago from an old-timer named Curly Allain, who was in his seventies and went south. He had no intention of returning, but he left his cabin well stocked with utensils, food, and linen—a tin of coffee close to the pot, fifty pounds of flour, five pounds of Danish bacon, firewood in three sizes stacked beside the door. Outside, some paces away, I have stood at a form of parade rest and in the broad light of a June midnight been penetrated in the most inconvenient place by a swarm of indecent mosquitoes, and on the same spot in winter, in a similar posture at the same hour, have stared up in darkness from squeaky snow at a green arch of the aurora, green streamers streaming from it all across the sky. At home, when I look up at the North Star I lift my eyes but don't really have to move my head. Here, I crane back, lift my chin almost as far as it will go, and look up at the polestar flirting with the zenith. The cabin is long and low, and its roof is loaded white —mantled eighteen inches deep. Its windows are brown-gold from the light of burning lamps. The air is so still I can hear the rising smoke. Twenty-two degrees below zero. Balls of ice are forming in the beard. I go back inside and comb it off, and jump into a bag of down.

The spruce in their millions are thick with snow, but not heavy snow—a light dry loaf on every bough, with frost as well, in chain crystals. Just touch one of these trees and all of its burden falls, makes craters in the snow of the ground. The load is so delicately poised a breath can break it, a mild breeze denude the forest. Day after day, the great northern stillness will preserve this Damoclean scene, while the first appearance of each February dawn shoots pink light into the trees, and colors all the blanketed roofs, the mushroom caps on barrels and posts. Overhead, sometimes, a few hundred feet above the ground stillness, the wind is audibly blowing.

I have flown with Ed in winter to this place and that, in his Bellanca Citabria, landing on frozen rivers and sloughs. The first time he set down, I did not know the plane had landed. The snow was so deep and so dry there was no feel of the skis touching. When we ran into some unseasonably warm air one day—a williwaw blowing over the mountains from the south—the Citabria's oil temperature began to climb toward an unacceptable level. He landed on the Yukon, got out, opened the engine cowling with a Phillips screwdriver, and removed a sheet of cardboard. He had put it there to block off the oil cooler, to keep it from doing too good a job. "When you bring an airplane into this country, you have to modify it in various ways," he said. "You prepare it for our kind of cold. Block off the oil cooler. Cut a bigger hole in the breather tube so it won't freeze up and blow your nose seal. Partly cover the bugeyes—the air intakes—on the cowling. You adapt for summer, too. When a new plane comes into the country, people say, 'It's still in wheel pants,' because wheel pants are the first things to come off. You put on tundra tires, and a big Scott tail wheel." The Citabria is built for short takeoffs, but, even so, when he bought it he replaced its fixed prop with a constant-speed prop, and he drooped the ailerons and adjusted the gap seals so he could get off the ground in two hundred feet (unloaded). "That's the way it is out here—you adapt things to the country. If something breaks down, you tear it apart and learn that way. Stanley is way better than I on airplanes. He built the new bungee-cord landing gear for his Champ. It originally had a sixty-five-horsepower engine. He took a ninety-five-horse engine from a wrecked 140, rebuilt it, replaced parts, put it in the Champ, and took off. Stanley can listen to an airplane from a distance and tell its horsepower, and with one glance he knows if it has a PA18 rudder, a PA11 horizontal stabilizer. I'd rather have him working on my airplane than just about any licensed mechanic I know." We got back into the Citabria and prepared to lift off from the river, but the snow was soft, the skis stuck, and the plane at full power plowed along well below takeoff speed. We were glued to the Yukon. Ed, though, had had this possibility in mind and had therefore chosen to land on a smoothly frozen segment of the river many miles long. He turned around and taxied back to where he had started, completing a large oval imprint, which suggested a race track. Then he went around and around it, packing and smoothing the surface until the plane began to move with increased speed and the skis at last came off the snow.

Ed did not know how to fly when he came into the country but inevitably took it up as an important skill of the bush. Since there are so few people in all Alaska, the coincidence is more commonplace than remarkable that he was taught by Don Jonz. Jonz, whose name had once been Jones, instructed in Fairbanks, and Ed remembers him as "a flippant, cocky sort of guy." He was the pilot of the Cessna 310 that disappeared on its way to Juneau in 1972 with Alaska's Representative Nick Begich and his Louisiana colleague Hale Boggs. The plane apparently iced up and fell into the Gulf of Alaska. As it happened, the issue of *Flying* magazine that was on newsstands at that time contained an article called "Ice Without Fear," by Don Jonz. "The thought of inflight structural icing inspires the crazies in a lot of airmen," he wrote. "In my opinion, most of it is a crock. . . . It's hard to convince some people that the sun is always shining on top. . . . If your bid for blue sky is unsuccessful, you have a monkey on your back. The trip down won't be pleasant. . . . Ice can be, and is, consistently deadly. An aircraft under severe ice loads suffers on both ends of its speed range. Stall goes up. Cruise goes down. When the two meet, the world comes to an end."

The Gelvins never fly anywhere without leaving a note on the kitchen table saying where they have gone and at what time, and giving a flight plan. They are known as people who will go out of their way to fly over someone's remote cabin to be sure that smoke is visible there, but the cabin will be in their flight plan. On long trips, if something of surprising interest attracts their attention—some digression they would like to make—they resist the temptation. They stay with their plan, because if searchers had to look for them they might look in the wrong place. Their planes have emergency-locator beacons, and each contains survival gear—an axe, a week's food, flares, a tent, two sleeping bags. Snowshoes are strapped to the wing struts. They haven't had much trouble. Stanley once had a rough landing at the family's cabin on the Charley River. The "airstrip" there is so short it looks like a helicopter pad, with a surface of grapefruit gravel. The plane came down short and hard, bending a strut to the point of fracture. The propeller was bent, too. Stanley and his father cut a spruce and wired it, as a splint, to the damaged strut. They removed the propeller and laid it across two big logs. With a third log, they pounded the prop until its gross disfigurement essentially disappeared. They put it back on the airplane, revved up, and flew away.

Ginny worries now and again about her husband and son. I remember her pacing around one day when they were two hours overdue from the mountains, where they had gone to work on the airstrip that would service the development of their gold claims. They were using Stanley's Champ. She kept watching the dogs outside, waiting for them to herald the plane, for they always hear it long before she does. She spoke of going to Circle, thirty-five miles away, to ask Frank Warren to fly reconnaissance with his plane to see if there was trouble, but first we would wait a bit longer, with a glass of MacNaughton's Canadian. "I'm not really worried," she said. "But I always get to thinking about it when they don't come home when they say they're going to." Tara at last delivered an annunciating howl. The other dogs joined in.

After the plane arrived, Stanley opened the cowling with a penny, poured in some oil, gassed up from a gravity-feed tank, got a towel and some soap, spun the prop with one hand to start the engine, ducked under a wing, climbed aboard, and flew eight miles to the Springs to take a shower. The planes are used more than the VW and the pickup. Flying is the talk of the table, when the talk is not about gold. Weather, parts, loads, structures—Stanley flips through aviation magazines and tells his father about stall-spin accident rates in various aircraft per thousand hours. Stanley was once cruising in the mountains looking for a place to fish, Ed has told me. He saw a gravel bar that looked negotiable, so he set the plane down, but the bar was rougher and shorter than he had thought. It was Mistake No. 1 to risk landing there. Now he made Mistake No. 2: he went fishing. The sun came out. The day warmed up. Warm air is less dense than cold air, and provides less lift. The warmer the air, the longer the run for takeoff. When Stanley tried to leave the gravel bar, he went off the end of it and almost into the river. The tail of the plane dragged in the water as he barely lifted away. "His legs were shaking," said his father. "He learned judgment there."

Ed is a careful and skillful pilot unendangered by bravado, and I would rest on his judgment wherever he thought he could go—all of which, I feel, is an essential preamble to going on to say that on the day I arrived from upriver, by canoe from Eagle, he cracked up the Citabria. The word the family used was "dinged." He dinged the airplane. Patricia Oakes, down the road, said "pranged." In a place where flying is in many situations the only means of travel, people are careful how they land certain words. Whatever happened, no one said that the plane had crashed. He had been up in the gold-claim valley, where still there was unmelted snow, on which he landed (with wheels). Rolling to a stop, he set the hand brake, so the plane would not slide in the breeze. When eventually he took off, he forgot the hand brake. Like skis, his oversize tundra tires, locked and rigid, slid along the snow. The Citabria got up all the speed it needed to lift into the air. Ed flew home with the brake still on. At the lower altitude of Central, the gravel runway was bare and dry. He came in on final, flared, and made a three-point full-stall landing. When the wheels touched, they grabbed the ground. The Citabria did a forward flip. Ed hung there for a moment in a ganglion of straps. Then he disengaged himself and finished his trip on foot. The extent of his physical injury was a cut on one hand, but his pilot's pride was pranged. For the plane's part, the prop was bent, the windshield was smashed, a wing member was cracked, a strut was gone, the fuselage was dented, the tail was crumpled. Ed got out his Buck knife, his welding torch, his hacksaw. He cut away fabric. Carrying parts into the shop, he repaired the plane. He figured the job would cost at least six thousand dollars in Fairbanks, so clearly he was making money. A guy seizes an opportunity when it comes, in the bush. "Drive a car long enough and you'll have both minor and major scrapes," he said, straightening with force of muscle the rudder's tubular steel.

"That's the sort of thing they say in Eagle," I told him. "They say about the pilots there, 'You can't learn to ski without falling.'"

On a wall of the shop is a museum of traps—a catalogued collection of about a hundred and fifty, of various types and ages. Hanging opposite are some dozens of furs—wolf, fox, wolverine, lynx. Most will go to markets outside, but Ed and Ginny also sell quantities of wolf ruffs to regional Indians. Their snow machine—Ski-Doo Alpine—rests on the floor below the furs. It goes ten miles an hour on the trail, and the two of them ride it. Ed took me out with him once, and as we chugged along among the laden spruce at least a thousand trees thanked us for coming by dumping on our heads a tumult of snow. We collected a marten that had climbed up a pole-set for a grouse wing and was now hanging by a leg in a lifelike pose, frozen stiffer than taxidermy, its forepaws stretched as if leaping for prey, its eyes, at fifteen below zero, like white chick-peas. The coat was toast brown. We saw the scant remains of a wolf-killed moose, and a bowl in the snow full of feathers of grouse. A springing lynx had killed and eaten it. Amazingly, for a cat of such size—big as an ocelot, thirty pounds, with long dangling legs—its tracks were shallow in the deep dry snow. The pads of a lynx are like pancakes.

Ginny wears a one-piece snow-machine suit with a sewed-on wolf ruff, Ed a down parka with a wolf ruff and an Eddie Bauer down cap that he has trimmed with mink. Both wear mukluks with felt liners and felt insoles inside the liners and more felt between the liners and the soles. (Mukluks, with their soft moosehide bottoms, thin leggings, and layered contents of felt, are the lightest, driest, warmest, most comfortable things I have ever had on my feet. Water is their nemesis, so they function only in cold snow.) The Gelvins make their sets for the most part near lakes east of Central. They use single and double long-springs—the sort of trap that has a "pan" held by a "dog" (trigger), which releases snapping jaws. They use coil-spring traps and jump traps. They use Conibears—traps made of rectangles of heavy steel rods that are brought together with enough force to destroy vertebrae. The Gelvins might cut a hole in lake ice and dangle a snare that is baited with cottonwood. A beaver, caught in the snare, drowns. Most of their trap sets are cubbies, though—contrived shelters of cut boughs—with a grouse wing or a piece of lynx or beaver inside. They make rounds every three days. When they find, say, a lynx in a trap, the cat is generally just sitting there, patiently waiting for another surprise. They choke it with rope or wire. If a fox is alive, they rap the snout with a stick. The fox loses consciousness. Standing on its chest will cause its heart to stop. Mink and marten ordinarily freeze, but if one is alive it is taken in hand and squeezed. Caught in a Conibear, a wolverine or a fox is usually dead. If not, it is shot with a .22. (Some trappers shoot everything.) Wolves, standing in their double long-springs, are shot in the ear. Owls, hawks, and ravens occasionally get into the traps. Ginny tried to trap a bear once, within a few feet of their cabin in Central. She strewed grouse carcasses in a tempting circle. The bear sat on the trap, leaped six feet in the air, and ran off defecating cranberries. Despite such failures, the take of a typical recent season has been ten thousand dollars' worth of fur.

Ginny looks through *Alaska* magazine, where her attention is arrested by letters from the Lower Forty-eight. "'There was a time when man was justified in taking wildlife,'" she reads aloud, "'for then man's survival was at stake, but that time is long gone. What is left of wildlife now belongs to all of us, and not to a few.'

"'The Kodiak bear is brought back to the Lower Forty-eight to be mounted as lifeless trophies on rich men's walls.'

"'There is absolutely no defensible position for trapping.'

"'I would hope the day will come when men no longer want to kill everything that moves.'"

She slaps the magazine down on the table. "They don't understand," she says. "Trophy hunters go for big boars. That gives younger grizzlies a chance to breed, and makes for better breeding stock. These people who write these letters are not even rational. They say we're out to kill everything. People in the Lower Forty-eight do not understand Alaska."

"They have everything wrong," Ed inserts. "They think it's all ice and snow and igloos here."

Ginny continues: "They wonder how Alaskans get their mail, and what they do in winter. They can't believe anything can grow here. They're amazed we can't buy any land. They think Indians are Eskimos. They know nothing about Alaska, and yet they've been manipulating us for years. We thought statehood would put an end to that."

"They don't understand trapping. They don't understand the harvesting of animals," Ed says. "And they say that Alaska is 'fragile.' All this delicate-ecology business just kills me. How could it be so delicate if it has survived all these Siberian winters? Alaska would be O.K. as a state if the feds hadn't kept two-thirds of it. Now, under the native-land-claims act, they want to make eighty million acres into parks. My contention is that nothing stays the same in this earth. Everything changes. You can't keep anything. Even the vegetation changes. So all this preserving things—it doesn't work."

Ginny is still fuming at the magazine. "Oh well," she says, shoving it aside again. "The bad image of trapping has at least raised the price of furs. People down there are afraid they won't be able to get them."

Moose racks protrude from under the gables of buildings in the compound. It is important to the Gelvins, as to Alaskans generally, that this custom be seen as a symbol of respect—respect for the moose and for the needs of the people who use moose to sustain their lives. "If people had to buy meat and raise a family, it would be pretty rough," Ginny says. "It is a serious thing to get that meat. During the season, in the fall, people don't say 'Hello,' they say 'Did you get your moose yet?' We help each other out. People who don't get their moose will be given a quarter here, a quarter there, by others."

"The best way to shoot a moose is to be doing something else when he walks up to you," Ed says. "The best thing in the world to call a moose is to chop wood. When one comes near, I grunt like another bull, and he comes nearer."

The four dressed quarters of a good-size bull moose will weigh maybe seven hundred pounds. Deduct a little over a third for trim and bones, and what is left is upward of four hundred pounds of meat, or nearly enough in itself to see a family of six through a winter. Meanwhile, the competition for the meat moves in packs through the nearby terrain—the Preacher Creek pack, the Porcupine Creek pack, the pack near Medicine Lake, the pack between Central and Circle. Ed remembers a time when he was off working on a drilling rig somewhere and saw a copy of *Not Man Apart*, the journal of the conservation organization called Friends of the Earth. It contained an article on Alaskan wolves. "I couldn't believe the misconceptions. Some of the things it said were outright lies. It said wolves live on weak, sick, and crippled moose and caribou. That is not true at all. Do you think a moose that has run hard for many miles and has been encircled four or five times is weak, sick, or crippled? Sometimes you see a moose standing up with blood pouring out of it and big hunks of meat torn from its body. Would a sick moose be standing? There aren't that many sick moose in the country. Wolves seem to know when calves are coming. They hang around and grab them when they drop. Are the calves sick? They are certainly weak. People like the Friends of the Earth and the Sierra Club have the idea that we want to kill *all* the wolves up here. We like wolves. They're a part of everything else. People need their fur for ruffs. But they also have to be controlled if we are going to harvest game."

"I see a lot of women writing these articles," Ginny comments. "Seems kind of strange."

The State of Alaska has been auctioning the skins of wolves killed by the state in a program of wolf control. The program annoys the Gelvins. Wolves, they say, belong to the people, not to some government agency. For the state to—in effect—get into the fur business is a bad precedent. Hunters at present can shoot two wolves a year, and trappers can take all they want, but that does not keep the numbers sufficiently down. "In the forties, there was a situation like now," Ed Gelvin says. "Wolf were up. Caribou, moose, and sheep were down. A big poison and bounty-shooting program followed. By the sixties, things were just about right. There were plenty of wolves and moose and caribou and sheep. The bounty was still on, and we could hunt from planes. Then all these wolf-loving outfits came along. The outside pressure stopped aerial hunting. Wolves are high now and game is low."

Even Ginny's brother is sometimes "one of them that don't understand." In the same mail with the *Alaska* magazine was a letter from him saying that nature has its balance and advising her, "Don't fool with it."

"But it's not a balance," she says. "It's feast or famine. The cycles go up and down. Some years there are rabbits all over the road to Circle. Some years there are none. Nature can't cope with itself. Enough wolves should be shot to keep things even."

From the air, the Gelvins see the wolf-moose story in all its phases—the chase, the standoff, the kill, the sign. They see a ring of wolf tracks where a pack first encircled a moose, and a while later another ring, and then another, another. Each time, the moose fended off the wolves, recovered its wind, broke out, and ran on. Now the plane goes over the resting pack, perhaps five wolves. Not far away, the Gelvins will see the moose, its forelegs spread like an A-frame, its head down, its blood bright red on the snow. Returning later on, they see nothing where the moose was but a hoof and some hair, within a tracked circle. A sticker on the rear bumper of their Chevrolet pickup says "EAT MOOSE—10,000 WOLVES CAN'T BE WRONG."

A number of times a day, as I walk back and forth between Curly's cabin and the main one, I pass Tara, in her pen. Not only is she fenced in, she is also chained to a stake—a double precaution. I have spoken in a soft soothing voice in her direction for weeks on end, but I remain a stranger, and whenever I come near her she races around her stake in the tight circles it prescribes, while from her throat comes a threat so guttural and wild that it calls into question the strength of the chain and the fence. Her mother was pure wolf, from Anaktuvuk Pass, dug out of a den by Eskimos. Tara—pale, silken, a flowing runner when she pulls a sled—has the long legs of the timber wolf, and they fairly whirl her around the stake, a flying blur, but, as fast as they move her, her eyes are always on mine. Her eyes are ochre. She once got out, and slit the throat of Andrea's pet dog, Lazarus. Lazarus survived. But I have no doubt that if Tara were to come off that chain and out of that pen as I am passing by, there would be nothing much left of me but a rubber hoof and a little hair on the unencircled ground.

One summer day, Ed and I made a two-hundred-and-fifty mile run in the pickup to collect a shipment of dog food in Fairbanks. Not far from town, we came to the Trans-Alaska Pipeline, which descended a long incline like a pneumatic message system in an as yet incomplete department store. We pulled off the road to contemplate this wonder; and as we sat there Ed mentioned an oil-drilling rig he had helped assemble in the far north, years ago. It had a jackknife mast. "You do the work on the ground, and then the thing stands up—a hundred and fifty-seven feet high." He had done all of the welding, in winter, with temperatures at forty and fifty below.

"How was that?"

"Pretty cold, most of the time."

The rig drilled a dry hole, and then was moved sixty miles to try again. The second drilling found oil. It was the discovery well of the 1968 oil strike in Arctic Alaska, and was called Prudhoe Bay State No. 1.

Across a sea of fresh dirt, a D9 Cat with a side boom was holding a section of pipe in a sling. Welders, with their pinpoint fires, were beading away, making a butt-weld joint. We walked over for a closer look. With their face masks, their heavy suiting (against cold that did not happen to be there), they looked like astronauts. Ed said they had six passes to make, six revolutions of the pipe—the first bead, the hot pass, the filler (three times), and the cap. The pipe was no wider than the spread of a child's arms, but nonetheless the work seemed to me long and tedious. "To me it's not," Ed said. "You have to pay attention to see that the metal's going in there right." He spoke with the welders. He said he was surprised they weren't using low-hydrogen rods. The welders looked up with interest, and talked tensile strengths in Oklatexan accents. Unused rods were lying around in profusion on the ground. As we left, Ed picked up some, like a figure gathering flowers. One of the pipe welders—a big man in cowboy boots—called out,

"Hey there, y'all don't need to do that. Y'all just back your truck up here and we'll give you some." Ed responded to the suggestion. Into the back of the pickup the welders set several cylindrical cans full of high-tensile rods. Driving away, Ed said the hourly wage those men got was no more than it would be in a place like New York. What attracted them was the overtime—ten- to fourteen-hour days, time and a half Saturdays and Sundays. Some miles up the road, we stopped and looked at another pipeline, of larger diameter, built many years ago on an eighty-three-mile route to carry water to float gold dredges. Ed said he resented the long struggle carried on by environmentalists telling Alaskans they should not build their oil pipeline. The delays caused by the great battle had injured the state. "The pipeline is using resources," he said. "It's a way the state can pay their bills. It doesn't spoil the appearance of Alaska."

An hour later, we were looking from a summit pass long distances across the peaks of the country. We paused, taking it in, and he told me another story remembered from the North Slope. He and the others would now and again see a lone raven, flying over the flat tundra. It would fly on and on, close to the ground. Below the raven, almost always, was a running fox. Mile upon mile, the fox stayed under the raven. If the raven sped up a bit and settled to the ground, the fox then stalked the raven. When the fox sprang for the capture, the raven—at the last moment—would jump into the air, and fly on across the tundra, with the fox running below. The relationship was apparently static, a ritual equilibrium, a possible pantomime. One day, such a pair came flying and running almost into camp. The raven set down. The fox went into its assassin creep—one crafted step after another—and then made a sudden dash. The raven jumped into the air. After a short flight, it came down, and was again stalked and rushed by the fox. Again it made a short flight, and settled down, even closer to the crew. The fox renewed its subtle glide, this historically futile contest with the raven's eye. Once more came the move, the rush, the leap. The fox caught the raven, ate it on the spot, and left a pile of black feathers on the ground.

Joe Vogler came into the country in 1944. He was from Barnes, Kansas, near the Little Blue River, where he grew up on a farm that had been homesteaded by his grandfather. On a boyhood day that stands particularly fresh in his mind, he saw a guinea hen running around the farm in agitation and dismay. "I mean, she was a-talkin'. She was raising hell." Near her nest was a large bull snake, awkwardly out of streamline, with bulges below its neck. He feared serpents, but he killed this one with his corn knife, and cut off its head. "My goal in life is to serve a good purpose." From its tubular body he gently squeezed twenty-one eggs. He wiped each one with his handkerchief and returned it to the nest. The guinea hen eventually hatched twenty-one chicks. Joe had come along before the snake had a chance to crush the eggs.

He went to a one-room school. He bucked his teacher. He swam in the Little Blue, fished for bullheads and carp, and put out trotlines for channel cats. "We planted a hundred and eighty acres of corn one year and we didn't raise a cob as big as my finger. When it's dry, it's bad there. My mother and father are dead now. This is my country up here." As a result of the dry weather and agricultural depression of 1921, a number of neighbors had to give up their homes, and Joe formed a boyhood wish for enough gold dust to pay his taxes as long as he lived. He went to the University of Kansas and earned a law degree, and was admitted to the bar in the same year. It was 1934. There were no jobs, so he went home and put up the harvest. The Great Depression kept him on the farm, and he never really practiced. He was not much interested in the law anyway, but the general absence of opportunity embittered him. A few years later, he had a job with Dow Chemical in Texas, and he lost it—in large measure because he referred to Franklin Roosevelt as "a dirty rotten son of a bitch of a Communist traitor." It was an era of intense patriotism. It was the height of the Second World War. Vogler's remarks were not looked upon favorably by his superiors. His animosity toward President Roosevelt was grounded in the view that Roosevelt "put the government into the business of providing security instead of opportunity," and it seemed just a matter of time before a good part of the creative vitality of the American people would disappear into an absorption with security, a craven and self-defeating need. The Dow people told him he was unfit to work for Dow Chemical, unfit to get along in the American society. This was clear enough to him, and he left for Alaska. "The only two things I have ever been afraid of are snakes and claustrophobia," he likes to say. So he chose to live in a country where he had nothing to fear.

Vogler is a friend of the Gelvins, and I met him when he stopped by and exploded with pleasure at the sight of their infant grandson. I have seen a fair amount of ground with him since. He is a roamer, a garrulous companion, perhaps the most active prospector in the country, and least active miner, although he owns several patented claims, including Woodchopper, two hundred and thirty-three acres close to the Yukon. If the Gelvins, in their quiet and straightforward way, exemplify the versatility of people who are long established in the bush, Joe Vogler is a sort of cartoon Alaskan, self-drawn: a part-time politician with strong attitudes and a stronger, not to say incendiary, way of expressing them. In recent years, he has become a figure of some significance not only in the upper Yukon but all across the state—as an advocate of independence for Alaska.

"A colony is any people or territory separated from a ruling power but subject to that power," he says. "The United States has made a colony of Alaska. When they want something, they come and get it. We are their oyster. They open us when they need us. Under the flag, you've got to have uniformity of laws. They have laws in the Lower Forty-eight that protect their environment, their resources. They need those laws. The laws unfortunately apply to us, and we do not need them. They hinder us. We are a developing nation, like any developing nation in the world, and we cannot develop under American laws. They can take their Fourth of July and go to hell with it. They have their independence from Britain. We do not have our independence from them."

He is tall, weathered, rangy—now in his middle sixties—his features strong and handsome. His hair is sandy, and his clear blue eyes seem set in a permanent squint. His voice is husky, its register high. He wears khaki work clothes, and a dark visored cap, and on his hip, bouncing in rhythm as he hikes along, is a holstered Smith & Wesson .44 Magnum revolver, which he refers to as "the hog leg." One day when we were resting from the exertion of climbing a granite-pinnacled hill above his claims on Ketchem Creek, he leaned against a boulder, wiped his forehead with his cap, and said, "If we ever get a revolution going, I want to import a bunch of guillotines. Lots of black currants up here. If you're dying of thirst, you can get water out of those mossberries. My government is my worst enemy. I'm going to fight them with any means at hand."

"What are you going to do when the feds take away your hog leg?" I asked him.

"Ever see one of these little fellas?" he said, and he dug down deep in a trouser pocket for a derringer .22 Magnum. It was as small as the palm of his hand but had two barrels, one above the other. "When the bureaucrats come after me," he went on, "I suggest they wear red coats. They make better targets. In the federal government are the biggest liars in the United States, and I hate them with passion. They think they own this country. There comes a time when people will choose to die with honor rather than live with dishonor. That time may be coming here. Our goal is ultimate independence by peaceful means under a minimal government fully responsive to the people. I hope we don't have to take human life, but if they go on tramping on our property rights, look out, we're ready to die." (Vogler does not avoid confrontations. For example, he once said to the mayor of Fairbanks, "You son of a bitch, get ready to look at this town for the last time, because I'm going to close your left eye with one fist and your right eye with the other." Joe's violence was entirely in his rhetoric, though. His difficulty with the mayor led to a courtroom, where the mayor paid a fine.) "The czars exiled misfits to Siberia," he said. "The Soviets do that, too. The Siberian exiles will eventually break away. Alaska is the place for misfits from the Lower Forty-eight. And we will eventually break away. Alaskans are inheritors of determinative genes that took people out of Europe to the New World. Alaska attracts construction workers who are wild hairs, willing to take a chance. The Gelvins would be misfits somewhere else. They're doers. They don't destroy. They build. They preserve. They are conservationists in the true sense of the word. They have killed wolves right and left. They are responsible for many moose being alive today. That

Ginny—she's a hell of a gunner. She can take a Browning and shoot the hell out of wolves."

His voice lowering a bit, he said, "Ed is fortunate that Ginny likes it here. This is a hard country on women. That makes or breaks a man here—a woman." His own wife had left him, and gone outside, some thirty years before. "She did not like this country." His children were one and three when he put them on a plane with their mother and saw them for the last time. "My daughter, I think, is married to a professor in Manhattan. I would not know my children if I saw them right here on the trail."

The granite pinnacles were an enlofted Stonehenge, an alpine garden of standing rock. The views were of the local domes and the middle-distant bluffs of the Yukon. There were dwarf spruce and lupine. There were lovely young aspen, their leaves spinning like coins. "What do you think of my little private park? Isn't it nice?" Vogler said, and he called attention to the unusual size of the feldspar crystals in the granite, which could not have become so large unless they had cooled very slowly, so there had once been at least a mile of rock above the place where we stood, of which the pinnacles, with their big crystals, were a slowly uncovered vestige. "To me," he said, "that is the writing of God."

He had bulldozed the trail to the summit, on federal land —a mile and a half from his gold claim. He said, "God, I like to move dirt with a Cat. I may make another road up here from one set of pinnacles to another, just for my private use. I could level the top with dynamite, and build a cabin. Wouldn't that be a crow's roost? Parks should not be federal—that's where my bitch comes in. The federal government should have nothing to say. I'd like to have seen the natives get a hundred million acres—anything to get the land away from the federal government. They tie it up. They just set on it, making jobs for bureaucrats. They're going to destroy private ownership in Alaska."

He picked up and tossed idly in his hand a piece of dry wolf feces with so many moose hairs in it that it looked like a big caterpillar. "Greedy gut-ripping son of a bitch," he said. "Stinking dirty cowardly predator. I'd kill the last pregnant wolf on earth right in front of the President at high noon. People who are against killing wolves are sentimental idiots who don't live up here. If they came and lived here, I'd listen to them. If the majority here did not want to kill wolves, I would not want them killed. But the meat the wolves take is needed. I believe in my own kind. I believe in gold, I believe in yellow scrap iron, and I believe in my own kind."

"Yellow scrap iron?"

"Bulldozers. Cats. Earthmoving equipment."

Vogler travels the mining district in a big three-axle truck so much the worse for wear it appears to have been recently salvaged after a very long stay at the bottom of the Yukon. He drives it on what roads there are and, where roads do not exist, directly up the beds of rushing streams. Lurching, ungainly, it is a collage of vehicular components—running gear from one source, transmission from another—that Vogler selected and assembled to be "good in the brush." The front wheels are directly under the cab, and the engine mount (high off the ground) is cantilevered a full eight feet forward to become a projecting snout, probing the way toward gold. The cab and engine are military fragments, artifacts of the Second World War. The frame was taken from a twenty-five-year-old tractor trailer. A long flatbed reaches out behind and is towered over by a winch and boom. There are no fenders. Much of the engine's cowling is gone. The headlights, far out front by themselves, suggest coleopteran eyes. Enfeebled as the rig looks, it has six-wheel drive and, thunking up ledges and over boulders, is much at home in a stream.

With his colleague Wayne Peppler, Joe has been using the truck to transfer from one claim to another steel pipe to be used in hydraulic mining, and they have taken me with them on their long working days. There is no muffler system in Joe's truck, and most of the bulkhead is missing between the engine and the cab, so the full detonations of the engine come directly to the ears, enough to mask the sound of any roaring stream, to blot out everything but Joe, shouting, as he did one day, "Jefferson got away with the purchase of Louisiana. Seward did the same thing here. The purchase of Alaska was unconstitutional. There are only two clauses whereby Congress can purchase lands—for a seat of government, or for military forts, docks, arsenals, and magazines—unless you go to the common defense and general welfare, which is the trash bin of the Constitution. Since the Congress had no authority to buy Alaska, they in effect held the land in trust for the first legally constituted government to come along. The federal government should now, therefore, yield all the lands of Alaska to the state."

Since it seems unlikely that the United States will pursue such a course, Vogler would like to advance his cause by suing the federal government for violation of the statehood contract. In the Statehood Act of 1958, Alaska was given twenty-five years to select a hundred and three million acres, he pointed out, but thirteen years later, to clear the path for the removal of oil, Congress passed the Alaska Native Claims Settlement Act and gave forty million acres to the natives, while setting aside eighty million more as proposed federal wildlife and recreational reserves. The State of Alaska had by that time chosen only a small fraction of its promised land. Now, suddenly, its latitude of choice had been drastically narrowed, and he meant to sue. He would ask the court to set aside the statehood contract for substantive violation. After the case was decided, he said, he would like to see certain choices on the next Alaska ballot: (1) a return to territorial status; (2) reaffirmation of statehood, with appropriate damages; (3) commonwealth status; (4) independence.

Generous by habit, Joe brought lunch for the three of us in a brown paper bag, and as we gathered convivially he spilled the lunch onto the bed of the truck—Hershey bars, Butterfingers, Mounds, Bit-O-Honey. These candy bars were all we ate in seventeen working hours. Tearing off a Bit-O-Honey wrapper, he released it into the wind, saying, "We are totally controlled. We can't even kill our own wolves. The posy-sniffers yelp too loud. With statehood, we were supposedly given management of our game. Now they won't even let us do that. Our sole desire is, we'd like to run the show."

When I felt myself becoming sick on Butterfingers, I ate an antidotal Hershey bar, while Joe stayed with the Bit-O-Honey—agglutinated, Pre-Cambrian corn syrup that seemed peculiarly appropriate to the effort it was serving, which was, after all, the removal of gold.

"This ain't part of America. This is a foreign country," Wayne Peppler said.

"Just as removed as the Colonies were three hundred years ago," said Joe.

"People up here are running scared and bewildered," Peppler said. "They're afraid they ain't going to be free anymore."

Peppler is a lean, sinewy young man with dark, swept-back hair and a face that makes an angular silhouette. He came to Alaska more or less directly from a Los Angeles high school, because—as he remembers imagining—"the little guy could count for something here." In Alaska's 1974 gubernatorial election, he was the Alaskan Independence Party's candidate for lieutenant governor, a nominee by petition. The Party's candidate for governor was Joe Vogler, and his name appeared on the ballot with those of William Egan, the Democratic incumbent, and Jay Hammond, a Republican. In implication and influence, the results of Vogler's campaign were more sizable than anyone might have guessed. All told, just under a hundred thousand votes were cast. The number by which Hammond defeated Egan was only two hundred and eighty-seven. Almost five thousand people voted for Joe Vogler and his declarations of independence.

Vogler and I stopped by one morning, some fifteen miles up the road from Central, to say hello to Fred Wilkinson, a soft-spoken and retiring bachelor, whom Joe described as "a working fool." Wilkinson's grandfather staked claims to four miles of Miller Creek in 1903. His father and uncle also mined there, and Fred now works the same claims, living alone in isolation, with five pieces of heavy equipment, including two D8 bulldozers and a D9, with which he moves not only the gravels of the stream bed but also the gravels wherever the stream, in the shifting courses of its geologic history, has been. In a process analogous to the separation of isotopes, he goes through roughly forty thousand cubic yards of pay dirt a season and from it removes a handful of beautiful teardrop nuggets and several pints of flaky dust worth tens of thousands of dollars.

For a man who works in the summer sun, he looked remarkably pale this day, and in his rubber boots and torn brown denims seemed to have come out of a coal mine and not from a stream of placer gold. Solidly built, rugged, attractive, he seemed above all else grim. He soon told us he was feeling lonely and scared. Vogler, out of sheer good nature, had brought along some sandwiches and pie, and Wilkinson, as he sat at his table and ate, said that an International Scout belonging to the federal government had appeared there yesterday, with four men in it, one of whom had handed him some papers, which he now shoved across the table past the pie. They were from the Region X headquarters of the United States Environmental Protection Agency, in Seattle, and were titled "In the Matter of Fred Wilkinson, Alaska. Findings of Violation and Compliance Order."

"Somebody's got to go, Fred," said Joe.

Although Wilkinson had been advised nearly a year before of the requirements of the Federal Water Pollution Control Act, he had not applied for a National Pollutant Discharge Elimination System permit, the documents said, and he was forthwith to apply for one or incur fines up to ten thousand dollars a day. He was to dig settling ponds for all the mud stirred up on his claims. If the water five hundred feet downstream at any time contained more than twenty-five Jackson Turbidity Units above normal background levels, he was subject to penalties also at the rate of ten thousand dollars a day. If he had questions, he should call Area Code 206, in western Washington, 442–1275, and speak with an attorney there. The nearest telephone—not that Wilkinson would have hurried to pick it up—was more than a hundred miles away.

"The government swine," said Joe. "Hate 'em, hate 'em, hate 'em, Fred."

"Three of them were from the state," Fred went on quietly. "The federal man's name was Lamoreaux. He told Del Ackels, up Gold Dust Creek, that sulphides uncovered by his Cat were polluting the stream."

"I wonder what Lamoreaux is going to do when I jab him in the belly with my .357."

"He was just the man the government happened to send," Wilkinson said.

"If you step on a rattlesnake, does the rattlesnake go for you or for the man who sent you?" said Joe. "I am a rattlesnake, and I will sink my fangs into the ones that come. They're taking our country away from us, Fred. They're taking our country away. They're taking private property without due process of law."

Nearly all mining claims are on public land, but under the Mining Law of 1872, which remains in force, miners not only own a hundred per cent of the gold they extract but have traditionally been able to do almost anything they wished on the land, just as if they, and not the people of the United States, were the owners of the property. The pick-and-shovel miners of the gold-rush days started out with that understanding. Across the decades, hydraulic miners, dredgers, and Cat miners have all had a sense of uninhibited franchise, too. And now, after more than a century, Bill Lamoreaux, of the United States Environmental Protection Agency, Jeff Mach and Lance Elphic, of the Alaska Department of Environmental Conservation, and Bob Fedeler, of the Alaska Department of Fish and Game, had come to say that things had changed. Fedeler was worried about the grayling in the stream. The fish could not spawn up a tongue of mud. Wilkinson was ordered to "ensure that the receiving stream is not blocked to fish passage," or risk heavy fines for that, too.

"Ten thousand dollars a day," Vogler repeated. "You've got to kill for that."

(Vogler has actually taken a shot at a man only once in his life, but that was long ago in Texas and he missed.)

To Wilkinson's considerable surprise, there was a stir of arrival outside, and Bob Littlefield appeared in the door. Gold miners work backbreaking hours, seven days a week, and it is most unusual for one—let alone two—to appear on another's claim in the middle of a day. Littlefield is a short, pleasant, round-faced man with a beard and tortoiseshell glasses and a ready smile that was not ready just now. He had come over from his claim on Harrison Creek, about eight miles away, because he wondered if some government people had been to see Fred.

Wilkinson had thought he was alone—singled out by the government as an example to other miners. He felt some relief, he said, and his pallor began to recede. "What did you say to them?" he asked.

"I said, 'I ought to shoot the four of you and bury you with your car,'" Littlefield told him. "The fed, Lamoreaux, bragged that he was going to close down all miners who do not comply."

Vogler said, "I'm going to run over him with a Cat and turn mosquitoes loose on him while he dies."

"We're not polluting," Littlefield went on. "We're creating turbidity with what is already present—with rock, mud, and dirt. We don't do more than what Mother Nature does in spring or after a rain."

"It's the nationalization of gold."

"The mining law says the man below you has to put up with what comes down from above. Settling ponds won't work. They'll silt up in a week's time. Wildlife will get mired in them. The E.P.A. says we have to push the silt out, but that is unreasonable, expensive, hard on the equipment. In five feet of silt, most Cats would sink out of sight."

"It's a tragedy that we must live by their laws."

And now another figure appeared in the door (Joe Green, of Mammoth Creek), and another (Bob Sherwood), and another. Miners' meetings, at the turn of the century, were the courts of the country. They heard cases of every kind, and decided the fate of the accused. Whether they "blue-ticketed" an offender, exiling him or her forever, or merely levied a fine, it was a system of justice that worked. In Fred's place now, there was an iteration of the old way, and as the miners presented their cases to each other they made up in spirit what they had come to lack in authority.

"We're just trying to make a decent living, and the government won't let us."

"The reason they're after us is because they've received complaints from canoers on Birch Creek. They complain that the fish can't see the hook. Canoers stay a week and contribute nothing to the economy."

"They got a package, they throw it in the creek. They're here today, gone tomorrow. We're here. It's our way of life."

"Thomas Jefferson said you need a revolution every twenty years to keep the country in balance."

"These government people coming around amounts to harassment."

"I said to them, 'I'm going to go on mining—and mining here. Meanwhile, get your ass off this claim.'"

"Murder! Kill! Burn! Torture!"

"I've been working the same creek fifty years, and when I shut down for the day I always caught grayling for dinner until tourists started coming and fished out the stream."

"Settling ponds have to hold a full day's run through the box, which is impossible."

"They say miners resist change."

"Anyone's going to resist getting his head bashed in."

"They can't really pinpoint what damage we're doing."

"We're not damaging anything."

"We're not dumping acids—we're only stirring up what's there. The same laws that apply to Homestake and Kennecott apply to us."

"The posy-sniffers are behind all this."

"When John Seiberling, the congressman, came to the country, he saw the tailings at Woodchopper and Coal Creek, and he said, 'What a mess.' He's the same one that would ban all handguns in the United States. His family is from Akron, Ohio, and makes tires. His family has probably released more pollutants than have ever been released in all Alaska."

"He probably feels guilty about that."

"We are *improving* the creeks from the standpoint of game. After the bulldozer has cleared the overburden, redtop grasses grow up that harbor mice and small rodents. Ermines and foxes come in to eat the rodents. Then comes your willow brush, and that brings in your moose. Before, there were alders, which moose don't eat. So I say we are improving the creek."

"Kill!"

"It's an independent life. We keep our bills paid. We make a little money. We hurt no one—except maybe finer sensibilities who don't like to look at our tailing piles."

"We've left some passable road. We've left something to make up for the 'destruction' of the creeks."

"Henry Speaker has a lawyer in Portland. He's up in years, but he's good. He specializes in mining laws and defends small miners."

"I'll put in a thousand dollars for a lawyer," Wilkinson volunteered. "I'll go along with the rest of you. I'll do what the lawyer says, and I'll hope he's on the right side of the law."

When the others, including Vogler, prepared to disperse,

Wilkinson, still far from relaxed, decided to go over to the North Fork of Harrison Creek for an audience with Henry Speaker—the richest and oldest working miner in the district. I asked if I could go with him, and Wilkinson said he would be glad to have the company.

At speeds as low as five miles an hour, we moved south through the mountains in Wilkinson's pickup on a road roughly scraped into the tundra. It led first up Mammoth Creek to Independence Creek and Mastodon Creek, past huge hills of tailing gravel, where the C. J. Berry Dredging Company had mined in the nineteen-twenties and thirties. Wilkinson pointed up Mastodon as we went by its mouth, and said that the 1893 discovery, first in the district, had been just up there—"only one reef away." He noted, too, that wherever a creek would "rib in" to another the names of both tended to change. In the early days, miners could stake only one claim per creek, so they divided the waters with semantic abandon. Mammoth Creek was actually Independence below Mastodon; Crooked Creek was actually Mammoth below Porcupine; and the whole lot of them emptied into Birch Creek. We followed Independence Creek until it was a rivulet, and then moved up into high terrain and crossed a dome of alpine tundra that gave panoptic views of higher domes and more tundra, yellow and purple with avens and saxifrage. "Once you scrape it, it takes aeons to grow back," Wilkinson said. The tundra was in places moving on its own. Down the steep treeless mountainsides the surface soils were creeping—wet now in summer, heavy-liddedly sliding over the permafrost, forming semicircular folds like bunting on a bandstand. Solifluction. We crossed a divide and descended steeply to the North Fork of Harrison Creek, still another Birch Creek tributary, which had been evaluated by some professor, Fred said, at a million and a half dollars a mile. Henry Speaker was down there now, proving the professor right. Unhindered by the constant upkeep of bulldozers, unencumbered by a need to stockpile many drums of fuel, moving just as much gravel per season as the Cat miners and with a cost overhead ninety-seven per cent lower than theirs, he is a hydraulic miner, one of the last in the country of his kind. The drawback of the method is the need for ample water, which is not always there.

Speaker had begun his operation by building a reservoir a mile and a half upstream. Then, with a little Cat, he had cut a beautifully engineered minutely inclined ditch along one steep side of the V-shaped valley of the stream. The ditch, being almost on a contour with the reservoir, would carry water to a point some three hundred feet of altitude above the segment of the North Fork that he meant to mine. The water would then plunge down the mountainside from the ditch through iron pipe of decreasing diameter and come out through a giant nozzle with such force that from one established hosing position it could tear to bedrock more than a hundred thousand square feet of land. The giant, as such nozzles are in fact called, has the appearance of a naval cannon, is attached to the pipe with a ball socket, and is counterbalanced with a "jockey box" full of small boulders, the result being that, for all its power, it can be controlled with one hand. Speaker, a hand on the giant, stood almost literally astride the stream. Behind him, in the direction of the reservoir, open spruce forest ran down the steep slopes and across the valley floor, all but concealing the as yet unmined, meandering stream. The banks were still shelved with thick blue ice. In the other direction, in the range of the working giant, the valley had been torn apart from wall to wall. Every vestige of what had been there before—forest, tundra, soil, gravel—had been driven asunder, washed over, piled high, and completely changed. It was an exposed boulderfield, all its overburden flushed away. The nozzle opening was five inches, less than the spread of a hand. At a hundred and twenty-five pounds of pressure per square inch, though, the column of water shooting out of it had the hard, compact appearance of marble. Its great arc of power, as it trajectoried over the stream, seemed to subdivide into braided pulse units hypnotic to the eye. And where it crashed at the end of its parabola it sounded like a storm sea hammering a beach.

Henry Speaker is a little over five feet tall. Clear-eyed, firmly put together, in his seventies and obviously in fine condition, he appeared to have figured out how to extend beyond previous limits the so-called prime of life. The skin of his face was hickory brown—tight skin, across sharp peregrine features, wrinkled only with a welcoming grin. He wore hip boots, overalls, and gold-colored monkey-fist gloves. On his watchband were rubies embedded in an egglike field of placer gold. On his head was a brown Stetson—the only Stetson I've ever seen that was made of hard plastic. It had a crack in it that was patched with grout.

He said the horsepower of a D9 Cat was about half the horsepower he had coming out of that hose—look out, you could burn your fingers on the water. To be burned by water seemed irresistible. I put my fingers on the solid ice-cold projectiling cylinder a few inches out from the nozzle tip, and pulled them away in an instant, burned. Speaker suggested that I toss a rock into the water jet to see what would happen. I lobbed up a big one. It intersected the jet about a foot from the nozzle, shot through the air like a discharged ballistic shell, and smashed into a pile of tailing boulders several hundred feet away. There was an eternal rainbow under the jet. The air around it swirled with mist and spray. Speaker said he had been operating giants for sixty years—in Oregon before Alaska—and he had once seen a jet of water (out of control) go straight through the body of a distant grazing cow.

Nearly three hundred feet from the nozzle was a sluice box with wide wooden "wings" that helped funnel the gravels through. The art of the giant, Speaker said, was to clean all the gravel off the bedrock without digging into it holes that could entomb the gold. With only a slight miscalculation, an error of timing and the eye, the jet could destroy the wooden sluice box, which was forty-eight feet long and five feet wide. To build up water for the sluicing, he drove gravels before the hose, causing them to heap up and dam the stream. He waited twenty minutes for a pond to fill. Then he aimed the giant at the dam, played the jet up and down, and cut a deep aperture directly in front of the box. Water and gravels roared through —a roiling brown inferno.

Speaker soon built another dam, swishing the jet carefully from side to side, piling up gravel and rocks. Certain small boulders struck by the jet leaped ten feet into the air. While he waited for the pond to fill again, he went up his pipe to check his ditch. The whole mountainside system consisted of four thousand feet of steel pipe, eleven inches in diameter at the lower end, increasing up the slope to twenty-two inches at the top, where it came out of the ditch. "Notice how much harder it is underfoot near the bottom," he said as he briskly walked up the pipe in perfect balance, his voice as pantless as if he were sitting in a chair. I had to run to hear him—struggling the while not to fall. Near the top, he said, "The pipe is not quite full up here, you can feel it jumpin' yet." It was studded with pressure valves and ringed with slip joints. Without the valves, he said, changes in pressure could "suck the pipe flat." Without the slip joints—sleeves made from fifty-five-gallon drums—the pipe could expand and buckle in the sun. He had taught himself to weld, and had built the system alone, for less than twenty thousand dollars. At the top, he checked the level of the water in the ditch, the rate of its flow into the orifice of the pipe. "This ditch is seven thousand six hundred feet long, and I built it in eight days," he said. "How's that for bulldozin'? I guess that's the record, ain't it? See the grass here. Moose and caribou come to this ditch and graze here, the full length of it. This ditch is just a flower garden when the flowers are in bloom."

Speaker had crawled across the mountains with his wife, Lora, in a twenty-thousand-dollar Winnebago—his cabin. He winters in Oregon. Rejoining Fred Wilkinson, we went into the Winnebago for a cup of coffee. On the door was a decal that said "Sheriff's Posse Comitatus," and one with a sketch of a Colt .45 over the message "Warning. Intruders and Trespassers Beware. This Property Protected by Armed Citizen." Speaker sat Wilkinson down and told him not to worry about the government invaders, with all their compliance orders and threats of fines, because what they were doing was unconstitutional. "The Constitution protects you and I," he said. "Our forefathers saw to it that our government, just like the King of England, can't harass the citizens. The government cannot harass the individual. I've been studying the Constitution now for two years. The people is the master, Fred. The government thinks they are. They've just turned that right around and they've made the people believe it. The Bureau of Land Management and the Office of Environmental Quality say they are concerned here, but two branches of government enforcing the same law is unconstitutional. In fact, government agencies are unconstitutional, because they infringe on your constitutional rights. They're trying to kill private enterprise, but don't worry. Your livelihood is guaranteed by the Constitution."

Wilkinson wanted to know what Speaker had said when the four men in the government Scout appeared on his claim. "I said to them, 'You go harassing me and I'll be looking at you through bars. I will put you in jail.'" To back up his threat, he had handed them a printed document with big block letters that said "LEGAL NOTICE: To federal officers of the IRS, HEW, HUD, Environmental, Health, and other unconstitutional agencies . . . WARNING! If two or more persons conspire to injure, oppress, threaten, or intimidate any citizen in the free exercise or enjoyment of any right or privilege secured to him by the Constitution . . . they shall be fined not more than $10,000 or imprisoned not more than ten years."

"Their complexion just changed when they saw that," Speaker reported. "I told that Lamoreaux he should be ashamed of himself, for he was killing private enterprise, and when it is dead, people will accept Communism. No law is constitutional that says you're guilty before you do something. The people on their property's got the right to choose to do as they please. Now government agents are coming to tell us what we can't do, but don't worry, the laws they are going by are in violation of the Constitution and are therefore ultured virus and not law. Now, that's right in the god-damned book. That's the law." He picked up a copy of the United States Constitution and held it out for Fred and me to see. "Boy, this is exciting to read," he went on. "It's too bad when our own people wants to sell our country out. Pretty near every law in the books is unconstitutional, because they conflict with protected rights. I'm afraid we're going to have to fight now for our freedom."

Lora Speaker, who lacked her husband's lean, smiled amiably, nodded agreement, and, at a gesture from Speaker, brought out of a cupboard an economy-size Jif creamy peanut-butter jar in which was twenty-five thousand dollars' worth of gold. It was so heavy I thought it would break the glass. It was all dust and small flakes, and had with the greatest of patience been separated—most of it by Lora—from the black and ruby sands (magnetite, hematite, scheelite, garnet) that are heavy enough to stay down with the gold all through the sluicing and the cleanup. Some miners nudge the sand aside by letting the mixture fall through the wind. Some use electric fans. Most wash it free with water in a gold pan. Some gold is so fine that on the water's surface tension it will float. Wilkinson mentioned that he sprays his gold with Windex as a means of keeping it down.

Speaker said he was "ratholing" the Jif jar. He was not ready to pay the Internal Revenue Service any portion of the gold's value (his privilege until it is sold). Cradling the jar like a sixteen-pound shot, he said, "The United States government has two ships out on the ocean right now looking for new sources of gold. They got a source of gold right here, and they want to shut it down. How god-damned crazy can those god-damned guys get? According to the Constitution, our money is supposed to be gold and silver. That's the way our forefathers set it up. Paper backed by paper is worth nothing. With gold from California we paid our debts to England—gold that came from our soil. It should be like that yet."

Some days later, I met Bill Lamoreaux, of the United States Environmental Protection Agency, and I asked him about his trip in the Scout to see the recalcitrant miners. Lamoreaux seemed easygoing and calm. Sandy hair. Brown beard. Twenty-nine years old. He had degrees in sanitary engineering from San Jose State. He said he had found the miners, on the whole, an amiable and agreeable lot—not bristly and tough, as he had expected them to be. In his travels among them, there had never been a threat of violence. He had found Wilkinson confused but apparently eager to do right. Littlefield had said he would soon build settling ponds. Speaker had been friendly and polite, even while explaining to Lamoreaux that "everything since the 1872 mining act is unconstitutional" and saying that he was going to take the case to court and personally fine Lamoreaux ten thousand dollars a day for trying to enforce unconstitutional laws. Most of the miners in the country had applied for permits. "They can appeal permits. They can work within the law. They have real good attitudes generally. That Joe Vogler keeps his mind right on what he's talking about. There's a hell of a lot of nice people out there. I enjoy them. They're some of the most straightforward people you'll ever meet. They don't beat around the bush."

Earl Stout, who was teen-age and full-grown before Henry Speaker was born, is too old to be concerned with settling ponds or enforcement orders or turbidity units in any form. He worked Sly Creek, Fourth of July Creek—and in 1959 he retired to his cabin on Crooked Creek, in Central. He eats potatoes. They are the fundaments of his breakfasts, his lunches, and his dinners. "I ain't too heavy on the meat situation. I never was. I get my outfit in the fall of the year. Potatoes." He is in ruddy health, white-haired, of medium height, a little stooped—eighty-five years old. He smokes a pipe. In his cabin are three calendars and three clocks. He gets up at exactly five-thirty every morning. Evenings, just before he goes to bed at nine, he goes to the calendars and crosses off the day.

This is a Friday in winter, as it happens. Sometime this morning, he filled his gas lantern. That is about all he has accomplished today. "In fact, I ain't done a whole lot since I retired in '59," he says, and in the silence that follows the ticking of his clocks sounds like the puffing of locomotives. There is an iron bed, a couple of chairs, and a big galvanized tub full of melted stream ice. When he needs more, he will cut it out of Crooked Creek and haul it on a go-devil behind his old Oliver Cat. In his Bean's boots, open wool shirt, and gray trousers, he sits and sleeps and reads—*Newsweek*, *Popular Science*, *National Geographic*, *Prevention*. On a shelf beside him is a book called "Upper Tittabawassa Boom Towns," in a couple of which (Hope and Sanford, Michigan) he grew up. He came to the upper Yukon fifty years ago.

On Fridays now, at precisely four o'clock, he goes down the road to collect his mail. He could run this errand at almost any time and on almost any day. In good weather, the mail plane arrives three times a week. But Earl Stout likes to gather mail in weekly units. "What's the use of getting it," he explains, "before it's all in?" Saturday nights, he used to play pool at the Central store—stick in hand, cigar in mouth, brandy on the cushion. "That was until the old Chevy went out. Now I stay home. All the years I was on the Yukon, there was no place to go. The nearest person was five miles away. You got to get used to staying home." He sorely misses Bob. A black, short-haired mongrel, Bob was for many years Earl's only companion. Five wolves running on the creek overtook Bob not long ago. They left his collar and a small piece of his tail. After finding the blood and the fragments, Earl drank a bottle of rum. It is 3:45 P.M. He gets up and pulls denim overalls over his trousers. He ties strings around the ankles. He puts on mittens and a wool cap, and he says, "I can't take the cold the way I used to." The air outside is ten below zero. I make a move to leave. "You don't have to go," he says. "It isn't time yet. There's still ten minutes." He waits until the clocks say four. "Now," he says, "it's time to go."

For all its miners and trappers and conjugal units on the river, the country seems to have an even higher proportion of people who prefer to be surrounded by but not actually to be in the wilderness. To describe Eagle, for example, the last word that I would once have imagined ever coming to mind is the one that comes to mind now: Eagle, in its way, is suburban. This remote cluster on the Yukon, two hundred air miles from Fairbanks, is as good a place as any to avoid being too much on your own if you wish at the same time to draw a circle around yourself a very great distance from the rest of your life. In all directions from Eagle are tens of thousands of square miles of deep and total wild, into which a large part of the town's population—living in dependence on supplies from cities—rarely sets foot.

Jack Boone came into the country in 1973. "Basically, I'm a square," he says, and in Eagle he has built an octagonal cabin. He makes no effort to conceal his justifiable pride in his work. The cabin is a log structure of clean lines and apt proportions —as apparently durable as it is imaginative. "I have the ability to earn my living completely with my brain, but I don't want to," Boone remarks, making an instant friend of the visiting writer.

He sits at dinner, three children around him—Margaret, Cindy, and Daniel Boone. His wife, Jean, is in Anchorage, five hundred miles away, with a fourth child, who was in need of medical attention. Lacking money to pay for the journey, Boone went down by the river to the cabin of Jim Scott, explained the situation, and sold Scott two cords of firewood as yet uncut. "I don't believe in welfare, in assistance of any kind," Boone says. "There have been times when economic circumstances have forced me to take a small amount of it. Some people here make it a way of life. The poverty level for a family of six is eight grand. I made four grand last year. I do not constitute the way I am living as poor."

He is a big man, whose woolly beard and woolly crewcut surround pale-blue penetrating eyes. There is often a bemused smile. His voice is smoothly rolling and timpanic. He seems to drive it, like a custom-built car, to play it like a slow roll of drums. "You may have noticed my speech is not perfect," he says. "That is deliberate. My language was once a distinct liability. I have had to alter it over the years to get along with the people I have worked with."

I remark that in his conversation there is an indelible aura of culture and education, whether he likes it to be there or not.

"I am putting that on for you," says Boone, opening a quart of homemade beer. "Fifteen years ago, I spoke perfect English. I deliberately destroyed that capability. Every beer drinker in this town has drank this product, admired it, tried to duplicate it, and failed. I can still write perfectly, with no difficulty."

"Why have you come here?"

"The advantages of modern civilization do not impress me."

He grew up in Oroville, in northern California, and for a time studied electronics at Caltech, but had no desire to join the surrounding society. "I do not like the forcing of the individual toward a high-expense manner of living," he explains. "I do not like restrictions placed on one's life just because of close proximity to several million people." He is a direct descendant of Daniel Boone, on what he refers to as "the squaw side." First, he migrated to Juneau, and set up a marine-electronics business, but, as small as Juneau is, even Juneau was too restricting for him. So he chose a town on the Alaskan Yukon, where there was more elbowroom than he would ever care to explore, and not a great deal of employment opportunity. "Those who are trying to live an independent life style in the country are paying a very high price for it," he says. "Unless one's name is John Borg, it is difficult to find much of a job —indeed, any job—in Eagle." Boone eventually found one

—as a seasonal laborer with the local road crew. And so did his neighbor Jack Greene. Working together all day, the two scarcely speak. It is a feud of buried origins, apparently deep, a feud not dissimilar from all the countless crosshatching cabin-fever feuds of Eagle, in some measure having to do with the general fierceness of competition for the few available jobs, in some measure with rivalry over the building of their cabins, but mainly as a casualty of place—a community deeply compressed in its own isolation, where a cup of borrowed sugar can go off like a grenade. The Boones and the Greenes live on Ninth Avenue, a euphemism for a pass a bulldozer once made through woods at the uphill end of town, about half a mile from the Yukon. Outside Boone's cabin is a sign that reads "Welcome to Those Who Wish Us Well, and the Rest of You Can Go to Hell." Boone means what it says. "Anyone who walks past that sign is probably broadminded enough that I can get along with them," he explains. "Diana Greene will not walk past that sign."

Diana Greene is a doctor of philosophy in classical literature, her husband an electronics engineer. Their awareness of Boone's sign is in the sub-basements of subliminal. They came into the country in 1974—on a ten-thousand-mile journey in search of a place to build—to create a life exotic to the ones they had known before, and a cabin to contain it. He was from Greene, New York, she from Long Island. They had met in Boulder, where she was in graduate school and he with the National Bureau of Standards. He was her first husband, she his second wife. In the course of their quest, Eagle seemed the only choice. ("Everywhere else we went in Alaska, people were really rowdy—no couth.") By mail from Colorado, they later bought a building lot at auction, and, starting with a big wood-sided flatbed Chevrolet truck, began assembling things for Alaska. They bought a two years' supply of food—fifty pounds of rice, fifty pounds of rye, two hundred pounds of wheat, a hundred pounds of salt, and so on to twelve pounds of almonds and twenty-five pounds of black-eyed peas. They packed up their cellar of homemade wines. He built five cabin windows. Each was three panes thick, all quarter-inch glass, heavy as a desk top, set in a redwood frame. The first and third panes were sealed with synthetic rubber, while the inner one gapped an eighth of an inch from the bottom, so air could circulate to either side. This would be a tight cabin. They also piled onto the truck a double bed, a couch, chairs, a rolltop desk, two stoves, chain saws, a generator, a washing machine, a Louis Quatorze boudoir dresser with a mirror that might once have framed Marie Antoinette. With this altitudinous load, they backfired downhill into Eagle one spring day, and braked to a halt at the roadhouse. "I'm embarrassed to say this," said Greene to Ralph Helmer, "but I've come here to build a cabin and I don't know where my land is." Helmer pointed back up the hill.

Greene is as good with his hands as Boone. Their cabins were begun at about the same time, with exchanges of beer and wine. There was a tacit race—to the ridgepole, to completion. The Greenes won, three months to seven. Between them, the two families cut upward of three hundred logs, finding them dead on an old burn forty miles down the road, where the Bureau of Land Management would permit the cutting. The Greenes' cabin is eighteen by twenty-four, with attached foyer, long-lash eaves, and big overhangs at either end supported by a ridgepole thirty-eight feet long. Greene's brother-in-law was with him at the time, and the two of them twitched the big logs out of the forest with rope and brute effort. Boone concluded that he could not do that. He decided that logs twelve feet long were all his daughters could manage. Therefore, he would build an octagonal cabin.

For ceiling poles, the two families cut and peeled an aggregate of five hundred three-to-four-inch green spruce. Each of them also set ten fifty-five-gallon drums, filled with gravel and punctured at the bottom, gingerly into the ground—twenty separate excavations, dug carefully so as not to melt or break away the permafrost. Building his floor, Greene used the shiplapped boards from his truck body—and two kinds of insulation. Boone chinked his walls and insulated his floor and ceiling with moss collected by his children, planning to supplement it with cement and lime, while the Greenes used fibre glass between their logs. With their heating stove and cooking stove, the Greenes had powerful defenses against the coming cold, almost enough to drive them out into the snow, because if their cabin was handsome, it was ten times as snug. A lighted match could make it warm. The Greenes burn wood at the rate of four cords a winter. The Boones, with their larger cabin, use fifteen.

Jack Greene has built an efficient cistern, with an adroit plumbing system that services a kitchen sink and a solar-heated shower. His cabin's interior, while not as soaringly airy as Boone's, is spacious and, like the Greenes themselves, is amply touched with elegance. He is blond, with a strong and handsome face that would not be out of place on an old coin, she light and slim, with brown, quick, smiling eyes. Around their table pass sparkling cherry wine, additional wines from varietal grapes, wines they have made from berries in Eagle, wild-cranberry ketchup, baked salmon, mincemeat made from moose. From under the gable at one end of the cabin protrudes a pair of moose antlers fifty-six inches tip to tip, truly a mighty rack. Greene was humming along in his orange Volkswagen bug one day when the moose stuck its nose out over the road. He has shot spruce grouse from the VW, opening the door and firing a .22. In like manner, with a .30–'06, he dropped the big moose.

"They will not live long here," Boone says of the Greenes. "You have been there. How would you describe their cabin?"

"Very nice."

"It is very fancy, I would say. They serve gourmet meals. No one in Eagle will ever appreciate that. None of us slobs will notice. She's a Ph.D. Between her and this town there's a sociocultural gulf."

Boone rolls himself a smoke while I make a trip to his outhouse. On its interior walls are a set of rules for displaying the flag of the United States. Boone's octagonal cabin, from the outside, has enough grace of line to be saved from resembling a military blockhouse. He is building an identical structure close by, as a garage and shop. The ceiling of the main cabin is eighteen feet high, and there are two balconies, with two children bunked on each balcony. A footbridge runs between. From window to window, the logs of the walls are horizontal, while above and below the windows the logs are vertical, creating an unusual and effective symmetry. "I'm kind of anti-money," Boone says. "I don't hardly believe in the stuff, but in Auke Bay, near Juneau, I built a place for two thousand dollars that was appraised when I left at forty-three. I'm an accomplished scrounger." He and his tall, sharply intelligent wife are also accomplished teachers. Their children are educated at home, and in national testing place as high as five years ahead of their ages.

He opens another quart of beer. It is brewed in a plastic garbage can, in which the Boones mix twelve gallons of water, ten pounds of sugar, a tablespoon of yeast, and forty-eight ounces of hop-flavored extra-pale malted barley syrup, yielding the equivalent of a six-pack a day, or a little over five cases every three weeks, saving themselves approximately two thousand dollars a year against the twenty-four dollars a case charged by Eagle bootleggers. Moreover, it is fine beer. One would have to bypass Milwaukee and St. Louis and scour Europe to find its peer. It may be getting to me. Boone says not to worry: "I have drank it for years and never had a hangover." Close by him is a gun rack with three rifles. He sees me looking at them and says they are loaded. "Hunting season comes in the fall, and the fall is the busiest time of year for anyone who is trying to live any kind of subsistence life style," he says, apropos of nothing much, since the season just now is spring.

"Do you hunt a lot?" I ask him.

"No. I cannot say I am a hunter. I have not hunted anything in the three years since we came to Eagle. The purpose of the rifles is protection."

"Do you fish?"

"We buy our salmon."

"Do you use the river?"

"We have a small boat and a kicker but have not yet been out on the Yukon. We have not had time."

"Have you travelled some on foot in the country?"

"Since I've been here, I've done very little that did not have a purpose. I'm not really sure that I could enjoy trekking ten miles without a goal. I don't think I would defend that position. It's probably wrong. It's how I am. I know I'm a freak. That's why I moved to Eagle." He rolls another cigarette. He lights it thoughtfully. He spreads a screen of smoke through the octagon. "If you live in this country awhile," he says at last, "you really get to appreciate a stove and four walls."

Boone's forked message of warning and welcome—the sign on the path to his cabin—is by his report an effective deterrent to virtually every member of the Eagle Bible Chapel, known to the laity as the fundamentalist bloc. "They are here for the religious climate," says Boone. "I don't go to church. I'm not a religious man. I wouldn't go to church *here* if I was. We are moving closer to anarchy now, but the bloc still controls every winter paying job but schoolmaster. Eagle is excellent for unemployment, incidentally. If you work part of the year, it's a good place to be sure of not being offered a job. On public assistance, people can live quite well here. Even members of the bloc take food stamps, unemployment, and welfare, in various combinations. They are very social. They have dinners, prayer meetings, men's Bible study and women's Bible study once a week. They have a sewing circle that is open to Indians. Indians do come. Social relationships between the bloc and the Indians are good but condescending. To the best of my knowledge, no one in the bloc touches alcohol. In Eagle, there is one lush. Also, there are five or six people who live in the town because it is dry—who go out of their tree when a bottle appears. None of these are in the bloc. Those of us who are not in the bloc are rugged individualists, and we can't get along with each other. When I was elected to the city council a couple of years ago, I had eight friends. After six months, I had two. This does not happen among the Christians. They sit down and pray about it and decide it isn't worth it. In Eagle, there are many arguments, many short-term enemies, but few permanent enemies. The bloc will forgive and forget—the day after they have screwed you."

Eagle has upward of fifty registered voters. Roughly twenty are in the bloc. Not long ago, when the population was smaller and the bloc was proportionately larger, most of the city council was of the religious group. Eagle was their town. The landscape is what lasts around here. The people huddled upon it are—in the long span of things—as rootless as the wolves. The religious bloc, already losing its political grip, has been a factor in the town for less than a decade—its existence dating to the arrival in the late nineteen-sixties of Betty and John Borg. Other couples soon moved to join them, their common affiliation being a relationship with the

Central Alaskan Mission, in Glennallen, with which the Eagle group has since relaxed its ties. While the rugged individualists went on being rugged and individual, the people of the bloc helped each other in the finding and swapping of jobs, and they cornered the job market: fire-control officer, school-bus driver, school custodian (the grammar school is three miles away, in the Indian Village), teacher's aides, preschool program, and on down a list that attained to much length through the many positions—postmaster, weatherman, customs officer, and so forth—of John Arthur Borg, the mayor. The group's minister, for a time, was Roger Whitaker, who resigned to become constable. "The whole bloc is a Communist front," commented one resident observer. "First, they get to the kids. Then, when they feel the time is right, they take over the police power."

Resident observers have a great deal to say about the bloc, which has harvested in Eagle the timeless fruits of hegemony, the ripest of which is gossip:

"They feel threatened at every turn. They are frightened, terrorized."

"They came not with a sense of mission but to seek a protected enclave. Religiously, they keep to themselves. Politically, they want to control the town. They preferred it here when everybody knew everybody—knew what everyone was up to. Everybody let everybody else know what they were doing. Now they see rigs going through town and they don't know who is in them. They don't like that."

"They have dug a hole in the world and are trying to stay in it."

"They have a map of Eagle with flags on the cabins of sinners. They invite one sinner a week to dinner, and attempt a conversion."

"On the school bus, their children sing hymns, recite the Twenty-third Psalm, and tell other children, who are not 'saved,' that they are damned forever to Hell."

(On December 12, 1917, at a meeting of the Eagle Common Council, a citizen complained that Miss Owen, the teacher, was compelling her pupils to pray in school.)

"Neither the religious people nor the river people have any interest in seeing Eagle develop economically. In that one respect, we see eye to eye."

"They were against the federally funded alcohol program, because there was nothing in it for them. The money bought a pool table, card tables—alternatives to booze."

"It was all for the natives. Alcoholism is widespread among the whites, too. But they don't show up as well against the snow, you see, as these buggers with the dark skin."

In 1898, in Eagle, small building lots sold for a thousand dollars. In 1947, thirty dollars would buy an entire acre—a price that reached two hundred by 1967 and two hundred and fifty by 1971. By then, however, some outsiders were beginning to ask not so much about the price of land as about the legality of the manner in which lots were sold.

"If you went to their church and were one of their kind, you could buy land. But if you were a drinker—that is, not one of them—they wouldn't talk to you. You couldn't get nothing."

"They were five out of seven on the city council. It was the city council that sold the undeveloped city lots. If you were not acceptable to them, you were turned down."

"Man named Carr, from Anchorage, owned eight or ten lots here, and wanted to sell them. He arrived one day with letters he'd received from people in Eagle. He went into the roadhouse—some Christians were in there, and Sarge Waller—and asked where he could find Jo and David Barnett. The Barnetts were living in a tent, hoping to get land for a cabin. No one said a word. The man repeated his question. Where could he find the Barnetts? Finally, Sarge said, 'Well, God damn it, I know where they are if nobody else does.' And he went and got the Barnetts."

In the fall of 1973, a majority was elected to the city council which was—in the adroit parlance of this community—unchurch. Within a year, the town held its first public-land auction of modern times—and now the way was open to the Greenes, the Boones, the Vandals, the Visigoths. The invaders had to pay, of course. Here in a wilderness that reaches out beyond comprehension, two thousand dollars became a going price for less than an eighth of an acre.

"The do-gooders used to control the town, but at last they are being outvoted."

"They really blowed their cools when I got this place."

While other things erode, John Borg remains the focus of Eagle. Because of his power and positions, he is the focus of the tattle as well. In a community of palavered reputations, no one is so thoroughly discussed as Borg. First, there are the usual and expectable patterns:

"Borg is confused, conservative."

"He professes to be quite Christian, but his religion is shallow."

"He's an opportunist."

"He hasn't missed any bets around here to date, but he is basically honest."

"He gravelled his road at the city's expense."

But even more of what is said about him is confided almost in whispers:

"I don't want you to say who said this. Do you promise not to mention my name?"

"Yes. Tell me what you like. It will not be attributed to you."

"Is that a promise?"

"So help me."

"Well, I think he's one of the finest persons in town. He's always willing to help anyone. He's friendly. He keeps his likes and dislikes to himself. His religion is his personal concern. He doesn't try and force it on anyone else. He is one of the few people in Eagle who is willing to do things. He keeps the well house going. He tills people's gardens."

"He is the one person in his group that tolerates the river people."

"In general, he has tried to help us, has tried to help the Indian community."

"He has a lot of energy, and he lives in a place where there are limited outlets for such energy, and that's why he holds so many jobs."

"He is a leader, a goer, a doer. At thirty below zero, he will get on his snow machine and go fifty miles—for a reason. At zero, he will go for no reason. During the winter we lived at Gravel Gulch, he was the only one who came to pay a visit. John could live in this country on his own. He could do it without the group. Most of the others never leave their stoves in winter."

"Even if I don't like their ways, I still talk to him. He's good."

Borg insists that he has no ambition to run the town he runs. He implies that he does so by default. "I would be tickled to death if someone would take over some of these jobs—*and* do them," he told me one day when I was helping him lug cartons off the mail plane. "I'm certainly not trying to build a kingdom around me. I have accepted these responsibilities not because I think no one else can do them. I do the weather job, and the U.S.G.S. river job, and the U.S. Customs work because they interest me. People say I'm trying to build me an empire in Eagle, but I don't think they'd be breaking down the door to ask for these jobs if I were to leave."

Like Boston and Chicago, Eagle seems to foster strong central figures. Bob Steele, whose daughter Roberta still lives in town, once ran the roadhouse and the post office and was, as well, United States Commissioner and United States Deputy Marshal. Esther and Anton Merly, now for the most part retired, preceded Borg in various positions, including the weather, the customs, the roadhouse, and the post office.

"When the Merlys turned their jobs over to John, they were looking for someone they could control."

"Borg wouldn't say yea, boo, or nay without consulting the Merlys."

"In this town, they are the puppeteers, Borg the puppet."

"The Merlys began the 'right people' idea long before the Borgs came into the country. Anton once said to me, 'It used to be so good when everybody thought alike here.' I said to him, 'How dull life must be for you.'"

Anton Merly is a tall man, bald, approaching seventy at apparent full strength. Esther has a shrewd and watchful look. She is dour and apronly and has a warm smile not easily won. For all the gossip they draw in parts of the white community, it is worthy of note that they enjoy high respect—for their understanding and compassion—among the Indians. When they were children, the Merlys grew up five miles apart on homesteads in North Dakota. Their parents had arrived there in wagons. "The winters we remember in North Dakota were worse than any we have known here," Esther has told me, and Anton explained: "In North Dakota, it blows pretty near all the time. Here, the wind doesn't blow. In North Dakota, we had thirty-five-mile winds at thirty below. Here, you go out and you can see where you're going, and there is no danger. There, if you went out and a blizzard came up you were lost, unless you had a fence or a good horse that could take you home."

They came to Alaska in 1949 and to Eagle in 1955. "We could see there was a future here, with places so cheap—as low as a hundred and fifty for a cabin and a lot." They bought seven lots and four cabins as a start. "You're crazy," an old-timer said to them. "The town is dying." In 1959, the year of statehood, the population of Eagle was nine. Almost the entire city was on the city council. The Merlys took turns as mayor. Inevitably, they all but cornered the paying jobs, and were only too glad, they say, to pass them on, when they could, to Borg.

"Borg may be independent of the Merlys by now."

"No. The Merlys are the land barons here, the manipulators of everything that goes on behind the scenes."

"When I came into the country, I asked the Merlys if they knew of a cabin for rent. They said no. We talked awhile, and discovered we had a mutual acquaintance in Tok. The Merlys suddenly remembered a cabin that was vacant. It was far out of town and had no door. We talked some more, and it turned out I knew a friend of theirs who lives somewhere near Big Delta. Anton then remembered an empty cabin close to Eagle with a door but no windows. Later, when we hit on the name of a really good friend we have in common, I ended up with a fine cabin in the heart of town."

"Make no mistake—the seat of government of Eagle, Alaska, is Esther Merly's kitchen."

It is a spotless room, a Midwestern farm kitchen with a big wood stove and, of all things, a big white refrigerator. Anton established the first generator in Eagle, and later sold it to Borg. The Merlys now buy their power from him.

Borg has no specific trade or skill, but he feels that he could support his family anywhere, because "jobs exist if you are willing to do the work." Among his constituents are those who may sit around and disagree, but no one, at least, will ever say of Borg that, given a task to do, he is not willing. He is up at 6 A.M., twiddling shortwave dials. He listens, some days, to news on the BBC. His cabin is on Third Avenue, in deep woods. A fresh black bearskin is nailed to an outside wall. Borg does not welcome the bears that come to town. He shot one not long ago on Jefferson Street, near the post office, after children came running to tell him it was there. This one was near his own door. He seldom goes out of town to hunt, and describes himself as "not much for fishing." He gets a few grayling each year. Neat as he is in person, his yard is a scavenger heap of fuel drums and machine fragments—a true Alaskan ornamental garden. He has three snow machines, a pickup, and a Mercedes-Benz, which appears to have left Germany during the Weimar Republic and to have been driven across Canada without reference to roads. There is a hutch of rabbits, which he calls his Arctic chickens—two fat bucks and a bordello of does. "This type of life style isn't all that severe," he says. "The severity of it is a state of mind. You have your basic cabin, and you need water and wood. It is easy to get wood. Certain people, that's all they do. They live on money they earned elsewhere. When I have absolutely nothing to do, I'm just driven up the wall. I don't know what I'd do if I didn't have something to get me up in the morning. So I open my mouth and get another responsibility." Some people in Eagle don't even haul wood. Borg hauls it for them—for twenty dollars an hour or fifteen per cent of the wood. He takes his Cat across the river ice, two bobsleds riding behind him, and goes three miles through the spruce to the site of an old forest burn.

A trail leads from his cabin to his post office through a beautiful grove of aspens. To keep in close touch with his home and his bloc, he has a battery-operated field-telephone system of the type that contributed to battle tactics in the Second World War. As the resident officer of the United States Customs Service, he pretty much lets the business come to him. He is responsible for anything that comes floating or flying out of Canada, but problems are almost nil. Around the turn of the century, there was a certain amount of waltzing with customs. A boat built in Canada with Canadian trees was a "British bottom," and by the rules of U.S. Customs had to pay a handsome fee to continue downriver past Eagle. The duty on Canadian sawboards was negligible. So Canadian crews arriving in Eagle would unload their boats, unscrew the decks, totally disassemble the hulls, and pay duty on a rick of Canadian lumber. Then they would put it all together again and shove off into Alaska. Monitoring something like that kept customs men busy, but what Borg sees now are mainly homemade rafts, many of which are barely afloat, having disassembled themselves while still in the river. He examines gear, checks identification, asks people where they're from and where they are going. "I don't sit on the riverbank. The people come to me. I've never made a seizure." Occasionally, the Brainstorm arrives—a small barge that hauls fuel and building materials from Dawson, in Yukon Territory, down the Yukon into Alaska and up the Porcupine River back into Canada, to Old Crow, an aggregate five hundred miles. Borg does the customs paperwork, and says it is no less voluminous than it might have been for the Queen Mary. With regard to aircraft, "most pilots are aware of the fact that they are in bad trouble if they have not reported to customs somewhere along the way." So they seek him out, too.

("I have wondered whether the customs collection at Eagle pays for itself nowadays, or whether the salaries and other expenses of collection do not exceed the revenue," wrote Hudson Stuck, the Archdeacon of the Yukon, in 1917.)

In the small, seventy-five-year-old log-cabin city hall, Borg runs his council meetings with a skepticism (he is now the only member from the bloc) that is muffled toward his colleagues and less so toward the language of state and federal statutes. "All this government talk is so many big words," he says. Federal funds are contributing to the restoration of the courthouse, near the center of town. Wearily, Borg explains that careful archeological excavations must be performed with "magic wands and metal detectors" or the federal money will not be forthcoming. He calls it a "federal fiasco." He refers repeatedly to the Eagle Historical Society as "the Eagle Hysterical Society." He does not appear to be fond of history, but he is the president of the society. Councilman Horace Biederman, pressing for his dream of a new community center (also to rise on federal funds), mentions HUD and "what they call a block-type grant."

"Who is Hud?" asks Borg, and moves on to new business: the dumping of trash. A sign on the wall says "Get Into America."

At home in his cabin after a long complex day, the Mayor will sometimes relax with cassettes he owns of radio serials from the nineteen-thirties and forties. He leans back, presses a lever. The tape rolls. There is a sound of whistling gales. An announcer, urgent and stirred, says, "Now, as howling winds echo across the snow-covered reaches of the wild northwest, the Quaker Oats Company, makers of Quaker Puffed Wheat [sound of rifle shot] and Quaker Puffed Rice, the delicious cereals shot from guns [sound of rifle shot], in coöperation with the Mutual Broadcasting System presents 'Sergeant Preston of the Yukon' [sound of howling husky]. It's Yukon King, the swiftest and strongest lead dog of the northwest, breaking a trail for Sergeant Preston, of the Northwest Mounted Police, in his relentless pursuit of lawbreakers. [Voice of Preston: 'On, King! On, you huskies!'] Gold. Gold, discovered in the Yukon, a stampede to the Klondike in the wild race for riches. Back to the days of the gold rush and the adventures of Sergeant Preston and his wonder dog, Yukon King, as they meet the challenge of the Yukon."

There is a sewing machine in the post office. Betty Borg works there when John—hauling wood, plowing gardens—is away. Dark-haired and bright-eyed, she is petite, and as trim as he. They have one child, Barbara, whose advance upon the years of secondary education has presented a dilemma to the Borgs. They feel that the supervised high-school work available to her in Eagle is more than a match for academic programs elsewhere, but they worry that she will be deprived socially, that she will suffer for lack of activities with others. Yet to leave the country in search of a high school is to give up what they have here. "I've got the most secure economic situation in Eagle," he says. "I've got it made here. To move means cashing it in, means starting all over again." A boarding school is not, apparently, in the conversation, but how about a high school in Anchorage or Fairbanks, where she might be able to live with friends?

"The life style is unacceptable there," says Borg.

"Unacceptable?"

"Too much garbage." He refers to drugs in Anchorage high schools and police having to keep order there, teachers smoking in the classroom, a grade-school teacher using *Playboy* as a textbook—an overall atmosphere "where kids' rights reign supreme."

"Politically, most of us are conservative," Borg says of the bloc. "We have a common denominator, the church. We are the largest mutual-admiration society in Eagle. There's some truth in some of the gossip about the group. But we have a basis for conversation, a common spirit about many things. Others are interested in drinking. We are not. They gripe and bellyache. The problem is, so few people here have a steady job. They complain at council meetings, and when I assign them to a committee to look into their own complaints they can't back away fast enough. If you have a solid group, outsiders will chip away at it. When people say we don't want them, it's their rationalization, not ours. We haven't closed doors to anybody, and aren't about to."

When Borg ran the roadhouse, he tried to get the Common Council to advertise Eagle on the radio. He would hardly do that now. When he had been here four years, the population was thirty-six, and—in the flux that is the way of things with the careers of white Alaskans—he and his family were by then the fifth-longest continuing residents of the town. The river people soon arrived, and the Wallers, and whatnot. In a couple of years, the population more than doubled. "I don't say they'll have to sharpen my head and plow me into the ground to get rid of me," Borg says now. "Too many people, and I would want to leave. If you double your population, you geometrically square your problems. With a thousand people, Eagle would not be the same."

"It would be like the eighteen-nineties."

"Only worse. You don't need a vacation from Eagle to get yourself together again. People are not assigned here. They live here by choice. When the road closes in the fall, we are not snowed in. Other people are snowed out."

On the twelfth of June, 1950, there was a motion before the Common Council of Eagle, Alaska, that "a mowing machine" be acquired "to clean the streets." Seconded. Carried. As bush communities in Alaska go, Eagle is a trig town. It has a reputation for grace and beauty. This is not always evident to the eye of the outsider, which tends to alight on yards full of old tires, fencing, caribou racks, dogsleds, snowshoes, lynx pelts, pole wood, fifty-five-gallon drums, cans, kayak frames, kerosene heaters, cast-iron grain mills, tarpaper, fuel cans, six-cell batteries, corrugated roofing material, and rotting fish compost in open pits. The inhabitants have the aesthetic disadvantage of being human beings. Where people exist, things are gross. In Short Hills, New Jersey, and Greenwich, Connecticut, the lovely creatures on the combed lawns are spared their own grossness because they pay not to see it, they do not picnic at the town dump. There are community dumps in Alaska, too, but much of what might go there lingers in the yard because one day it could be needed. If, to some extent, the people of the bush array themselves in squalor, it surely does not exceed what everyone creates but most don't see.

The center of town, in fact and in function, is the well house, because few people have their own water. It is a white frame blockish structure, taller than wide or deep, with a pagoda roof, and a firebell cupola up against the sky. The windmill standing beside it has a long history of lassitude, a record expressible in revolutions per month. March 26, 1951: "Tank very low but today some wind arrived allowing an extra half-foot of water to be collected." November 26, 1917: "No wind during past month and tank dry." In present times, the windmill sings castrato. A Jacuzzi submersible pump, hidden in the well house, tops up the twenty-thousand-gallon cedar tank. Water comes out of a hose and nozzle of the type used for pumping gasoline. Firefighting equipment is piled up in the well house, and so are kerosene pots for mercy flights (for spacing around the airfield to light emergency landings). The outer door opens out, and shuts like a book with an inner door that opens in. After these two comes a small foyer, then another door, which leads to the water. All this to keep back the cold. The deep cold comes in waves, spells, snaps—and really long ones are rare. From late in December, 1917, until early in February, 1918, the air was never warmer than forty-six below. If you want to be very sure of encountering someone, know his habits and meet him at the well house. A prominent citizen of Eagle (the description will not reveal him, because in Eagle there is no other kind) recently did just that, with intent to take advantage of the complex doors. A's wife was in B's cabin. B kept a 12-gauge shotgun, loaded with rock salt, leaning by the door. A knew about the salted shotgun. He studied B's habits, and when B went to the well house A locked him in with three doors. Then A, picking B's cabin lock, recaptured his wife,

> who walked down the street with
>   him hand in hand,
> enjoyin'
>   the sportin' life.

Killing frosts can come at any time of year. Vegetable gardens will have bonfires along all four sides. Up the Yukon five miles and behind the first bend, the tributary Eagle Creek cuts a wide V into the jagged mountains. One distant peak—without a name, like the others—sits exactly in the trough of the V: a sort of gunsight mountain. Even in the floodings of solstitial light, it will turn, from time to time, pure white. If Eagle is, as it has been said to be, the best-looking town in Alaska, it is infinitely outclassed by its setting—high on its bend in ten visible miles of river, among heathery soft and purplish stands of cottonwood, stream-course white spruce, and, on the uplands, black spruce only eight inches in diameter but two and a half centuries old. Near the summit of Eagle Bluff, soaring fourteen hundred feet above the town, the flag of the United States flies eight thousand seven hundred and sixty hours a year. A huge rugged cross was hauled up there and erected, but it lacked the endurance of the flag and lies toppled on a ledge below.

The city's budget this year is thirty-seven hundred dollars. That should mow a lot of streets. There are people, as in any town, who wonder where it all could go. Its highest and best use is self-preservation, for the courthouse (1901), the well house (1903), the old log church (1900) are settling with dignity into their own foundations, and while state and federal money might help with the larger places, any number of cabins and buildings are of similar age. Eagle was the first incorporated city in interior Alaska, and Theodore Roosevelt's picture is on the courtroom wall, because he signed the papers that made it so. Eagle was a city before Fairbanks was a tent. Anchorage was thirteen years unborn. On the bench in Eagle, James Wickersham, United States District Judge, presided over three hundred thousand square miles of land. Eagle may have an A-frame here and there, two gas pumps, and a couple of picture windows looking out past biffies at the Yukon, but in many of its essentials its appearance is long unchanged. It much resembles itself in, say, 1905.

Leaflets were tacked up around town that year showing a resolute character holding a pistol aimed at the viewer. They were titled "Western Philosophy," and said, in intimidating black-letter type, "LIVE EACH DAY SO THAT YOU CAN LOOK EVERY DAMN MAN IN THE EYE AND TELL HIM TO GO TO HELL." The intent may have been to buck up the miners, a few of whom had hearts of gold but in other respects were equally yellow and soft. "O T T & SCHEELE, General Merchandise," said a big sign over the door of what is now the Eagle Roadhouse. At the top of a post in front was a kerosene lamp. The North American Trading & Transportation Company did business out of a corrugated-tin building put up in 1899. A store of the rival Northern Commercial Company (a structure now vacant) was just up the street from the Riverside Hotel, the Coffee House, the Laundry and Baths, the Olympia Bar, and Henry Raymond's combined Saloon and Chamber of Commerce. On May 22, 1905, there was a motion before the Common Council that women be prohibited from frequenting saloons. Seconded. Carried. The women wore long dresses with full sleeves, pinned their hair up, and sometimes carried parasols. The men, with any sense of occasion, wore ties and vested dark suits. There were many sod-roofed log cabins. Three hundred people lived in the town. The Merlys' place was here, and the Ivys', the Stouts', George Beck's. The hall of the Improved Order of Red Men, which still stands on Third Avenue, was the scene of the gatherings and dances and assorted activities of "acknowledged conservators of the history, the customs, and the virtues of the original American people." The Improved Order of Red Men was dedicated to "friendship, brotherly helpfulness, fraternal love, and good fellowship," and was for whites only. Its charter purpose was that the "memory of primitive red men will be preserved to the latest period of recorded time." On November 27, 1905, an ordinance was passed by the Common Council "to restrict and regulate the disposition of intoxicating liquors within the town of Eagle." Everyone voted aye. The community had a handwritten newspaper, the *Eagle City Tribune*. The first typewriter arrived that year. Lumber was cut for the making of culverts. An ordinance forbade throwing garbage over the riverbank. (It remains, by and large, in force.) The Heath Hotel was near the Grotto Restaurant was near the United States Customs House. The customs agent is preserved in a photograph that looks very much like John Borg.

The log church, close by the river, was the purview of the Reverend and Mrs. James Woolaston Kirk, who came into the country in 1899. Their first services were held in a saloon. Their first pulpit was covered with wolfskin. They brought with them a bell cast in Albany. (It is still here.) They did not espouse the Western Philosophy. They were from Philadelphia, and they meant to put some of Rittenhouse Square down on the bank of the Yukon. Dr. Kirk was tall, with opalescent eyes under brows that lifted like spires. Mrs. Kirk was spruce and petite and from the front row of a good long history of choirs. When the couple arrived in Eagle, the miners took one look and instantly got the picture, warning each other that the "minister" and his wife were obviously professional grafters. Mrs. Kirk was forming her impressions, too. She wrote that she was "heartsick when I saw those bold, degraded persons, calling themselves women, who were in the place bent on lowering all standards of morality. I never before saw iniquity in its unblushing hideousness, for wickedness does not stalk abroad in the big city, where the law protects the safety and morality of its citizens." (In December of the following year, Margaret Johnson was fined a hundred and fifty dollars "for the crime of keeping a Bawdy House," and put in jail until all was paid—"not to exceed eighty-five days.") Mrs. Kirk had with her a foot-pumped organ. She could swell a room with hymns. She also had the first dustpan and brush ever seen in the Interior. She had crystal and china and napkin rings. When miners came into her cabin, tears sometimes collected in their eyes. The miners were homesick. Winter and summer, life in the gold camps and on gold claims was spare and sometimes bitter. They came to her, confided in her, and asked her to play the hymns. "Once, I was worth three hundred thousand dollars, had a fine home and a noble wife," one miner told her. "All are gone and I am here to get money enough to educate my two daughters, but if the whole camp was compelled to put up ten dollars in gold dust or be shot we would all have to die." Mrs. Kirk prayed and played for him. A young man came to her once depressed and suicidal. She played the intermezzo from "Cavalleria Rusticana," and after a time he got up and went back to work feeling better. "Although the Fortymile and Birch Creek districts are among the oldest of the gold-placer producers of Alaska," Alfred H. Brooks was reporting at the time, "investigations show that they are by no means exhausted and that, with the introduction of improved methods of mining, they will continue to yield good returns." Brooks, whose name would rest in the Brooks Range, was the U.S.G.S. Geologist in Charge of the Division of Alaskan Mineral Resources, and he was quite right, of course, but the good returns did not apply to all. While Brooks was fostering new successes, the failures went off to Mrs. Kirk.

When miners and prospectors, in the eighteen-nineties, had begun appearing in the country in rush quantities, there was —on the American side of the boundary—little order and less law. The War Department, imagining a need for both, sent Captain P. H. Ray on a journey of reconnaissance in 1897. Ray travelled up the Yukon on a cargo-carrying riverboat that was hijacked when it reached Circle City. The miners took the supplies, because they were otherwise going to starve, and they scrupulously paid a price they thought fair. (The boat had been saving its goods for Dawson, in Canada, which glittered with economic inflation.) Ray continued upriver. When he wrote his report, he said there were eighteen thousand people in the region, "which on our side of the boundary is without semblance of law, civil or military." There was a need for Army installations, he said. "A turbulent element is coming into the country that will have to be controlled." He recommended, among other things, a military garrison at the mouth of Mission Creek. It was a good site—fairly level and well-wooded ground on a high bank of the Yukon—close to the international boundary. Ray had scarcely left the country when twenty-eight miners platted a townsite on the same bend of the river where he had said the fort should be. If they were not the first real-estate speculators in the Territory of Alaska, they were somewhere high on the list. They might have called the place, say, Rustic Wilderness, but they happened to glance up at the white-headed birds that lived on the river bluff that would dominate the town, and decided to name it for them.

For a hero dead in the Philippines, the Army base was called Fort Egbert. Police work became the least of its preoccupations. The Army Signal Corps wanted to extend its great web to cover all America, including the upper Yukon. Communications in Eagle were nothing to write home about. After the Eagle post office was established, in 1899, the Post Office Department, in Washington, decided to establish a winter mail route across the Alaska Range from Valdez, on Prince William Sound, to Eagle, on the Yukon. A carrier, with eleven horses and a sack of mail, set out in October for the north. Eleven horses died. The carrier kept going, of course, and in the dead of winter he finally came walking into Eagle. The trip had cost the government three thousand dollars. In the sack were three letters. The Signal Corps meant to improve on that with instantaneous messages, by overland wire, from Eagle to all the world. Laying the wire was a project weirdly analogous to the building of the Trans-Alaska Pipeline, in that it required the clearing of a tortuous route north from Valdez (now the pipeline's southern terminus), with camps set up along the way and crews working the equivalents of overtime and double time. The crews were soldiers, earning thirteen dollars a month. Their boss was Lieutenant William Mitchell, twenty-one years old. He was on his way to fame in the air, to a court-martial, to a vindicating posthumous medal, but this was two years before Kitty Hawk, and all he had on his mind was how to move men and materials through several hundred wilderness miles where men and mules carrying heavy loads sank deep into muskeg. Mitchell's solution was to transport in winter what he would build in summer—a procedure new to the Army, and requiring Mitchell to become an expert in everything from Arctic clothing to the efficacy of sled runners. To protect morale, he prohibited thermometers. Work proceeded even at forty and fifty below. Mitchell was not lacking in flair. He was a Crockett on snowshoes, a beardless Boone. Travelling the line from crew to crew, he wore fringed hide clothing trimmed with extensive beadwork. His rifle was kept in a beaded sheath. He devised a parka of stuffed mattress ticking. He wore a beaver hat.

Poles were set, and wire strung, in summer. Repair cabins were built at regular intervals, relay stations where necessary. Finally, in June of 1903, the project was complete. Mitchell before long departed. His construction was fated for brief use and long desuetude. Isolated bits of wire still hum in the wind. Cabins here and there remain intact. For the time being, though, in 1903, a town that would celebrate its nation's Bicentennial beyond the reach of television and telephone—without public utilities of any kind—had a telegraph line from which word of great moment could go in an instant around the earth.

"Have Charly Harper in custody."

"Get typewriter from clerk's office and ship to this office."

"Pawn takes pawn."

"Queen to King's Bishop Four."

"Knight to King Six. Check."

"Ascertain if Alexina Byron is a proper person to conduct a barroom. The Judge is adverse to granting liquor licenses to women."

The date of that last message was the eighth of August, 1905—a wet summer in much of the country, very good for mining but with less rainfall locally and, in the Fortymile, consequent despair. In the desk of John Robinson—Deputy United States Marshal, Eagle, Alaska—was a letter from an agent of the White Pass & Yukon riverboat company in Dawson, Yukon Territory, that said, "Dear Sir: I have your letter of May 31 advising me of four insane persons coming up on the Lavelle Young en route to the outside. I may say that we have no regular place for the accommodation of insane people; however, we have often taken out batches of insane people for the Northwest Mounted Police here, and if they are violent or apt to annoy passengers we construct cages for them on the main deck." Robinson presumably shipped them out. After at least a dozen telegrams went up and down the country, Alexina Byron got her license to operate a barroom, although women were not to be served there. Eugene Miller was jailed that fall for indecent exposure, Frank Van Norstran for cursing and swearing and making unnecessary noise. Winter came down particularly hard. A few days after the first of December, Berber the tailor froze to death. On about the same day—at any rate, on December 5, 1905—a stranger appeared on a sled on the Yukon, came up the bank, and mushed into town. The temperature was sixty degrees below zero. He was of modest height, with a wiry spareness that was somehow evident within his abundant furs. His hair was thin and was beginning to recede. His glance was level, prosaic. He asked where he could send a telegram. His voice was accented, attracting no interest, for half the Tower of Babel was already in the goldfields. In the telegraphy office, he sat and wrote for some time. The moment did not call for a ten-word cryptogram. Nothing had been heard from him for two and a half years. He wrote, actually, a thousand words. Addressing the message to Dr. Fridtjof Nansen, in Christiania, Norway, he signed it "Amundsen." The essence of what he had to say was that he had discovered the Northwest Passage.

His sloop, Gjöa, was frozen in sea ice nearly four hundred miles north. To get from the ship to Eagle, he had travelled a great deal farther than that: over passes among mountains of nine thousand feet, then following the routes of frozen rivers —the Coleen, the Porcupine, and two hundred miles on southward up the Yukon. An Eskimo man and woman travelled with him as far as Fort Yukon, and a whaling captain whose ship was so badly damaged that he was on his way to San Francisco for another. Amundsen stayed in Eagle two months, going like everyone else to the well house for his water, and waiting for mail from home. His men were provisioned and safely encamped, and for him, meanwhile, Eagle was more comfortable than the shore of the Beaufort Sea. Neither in "The North West Passage" nor in "My Life as an Explorer" does he say what he thought of Eagle's collective cupboard, but he would have had his Alaska strawberries, his bacon, doughnuts, condensed milk, sweet chocolate. Butter cost as much as four dollars a canned pound, oranges about fifty cents apiece. A hundred pounds of sugar was thirty dollars, a hundred pounds of flour fifteen. The cost of a breakfast of ham, eggs, bread, butter, and coffee approached three dollars. At the Eagle Roadhouse all these years later, the cost of the same breakfast has gone up fifty cents. Alaska strawberries were dried beans.

The nine officers and the hundred and thirty-eight enlisted men of Fort Egbert apparently gave him an awestruck, warm reception. His tenth day in Eagle was December 14th. It would be the date, six years later, of his unprecedented arrival, with associates and dogs, at the South Pole. Meanwhile, though, he had tales enough to tell. He had determined, on his voyage, the exact location of the North Magnetic Pole—the other, and more scientific, purpose of his trip. He had spent two winters frozen in ice. He had come near burning the Gjöa to a crisp. In August, less than four months before, he had been trying to pick his way westward through shallow water that had never been sailed, and he felt such stress that he could not eat or sleep. One sounding would be more discouraging than the last. The bottom was a lethal maze. The hull barely slid above it, once with an inch to spare. The Gjöa thus crept westward, and on the western horizon one day there was a sail. "A sail!"

> It meant the end of years of hope and toil, for that vessel had come from San Francisco through Bering Strait and along the north coast of Alaska, and where its deep belly had floated, we could float, so that all doubts of our success in making the Northwest Passage were at an end. . . . Instantly, my nerve-racking strain of the last three weeks was over. And with its passing, my appetite returned. I felt ravenous. Hanging from the shrouds were carcasses of caribou. I rushed up the rigging, knife in hand. Furiously I slashed off slice after slice of the raw meat, thrusting it down my throat in chunks and ribbons, like a famished animal, until I could contain no more. Appetite demanded, but my stomach rejected, this barbarous feast. I had to "feed the fishes." But my appetite would not be denied, and again I ate my fill of raw, half-frozen meat. This time it stayed by me, and soon I was restored to a sense of calm well-being.

The sighted ship was a whaling vessel, and when the whalers met with the company of the Gjöa they guessed that Amundsen was at least fifty-nine and possibly as much as seventy-five years old. From the age of fifteen, he had had what he described as "a strange ambition" to "endure . . . sufferings" at extreme latitudes: "Perhaps the idealism of youth, which often takes a turn toward martyrdom, found its crusade in me in the form of Arctic exploration." He was thirty-three years old.

The Arctic tree line in Alaska and Canada does not even closely follow a degree of latitude but is a jagged graph made by the digital extremities of the boreal forest as they reach with varying success into Arctic river valleys. Amundsen's route from the Gjöa to Eagle happened to go up the valley of what has since proved to be the northernmost extent of trees. As he travelled southward (for the most part on skis), he was impatient to glimpse the beginnings of the forest, for he had not seen a tree in two and a half years.

> I . . . knew that on this day we should reach the wooded district, and I was very excited at every turn in our course. When at length the first fir tree stood out against the sky up on the ridge—a very diminutive, battered little Christmas tree, hanging out of a crevice—it produced a wonderful sensation, reminding me that we were now out of the Polar regions and on more homely human ground: at that moment I could have left everything that was in my charge and scrambled up the rock to catch hold of that crooked stem and draw in the scent of the fir trees and the woods.

Amundsen remembered his two months in Eagle as a "cherished" and "pleasant" time. The cabin he lived in belonged to Frank Smith, the manager of the Alaska Commercial Company store. It is still here. The main part is only twelve feet wide and fourteen deep, with two extensions out the back that make it long and narrow, like the Gjöa. Only the name of the street it is on has changed. The cabin is just off First Avenue, on Amundsen.

Amundsen had heroes, his own capacity for awe. He met such a person on his way back to his ship. He departed Eagle February 3rd (leaving Fix, one of his sled dogs, behind, because Fix had gorged himself on the provender of Eagle and was a useless ball of fat). He retraced his route, rejoined his two Eskimo companions in Fort Yukon, and had gone maybe a hundred miles up the Porcupine when he saw one day a dark, solitary speck on the distant snow. It moved toward him. An hour later, the gap closed, and he met a man named Darrell, who was hauling a small toboggan by hand. Darrell worked for the Hudson's Bay Company, and he was carrying mail. He had come from the Arctic Ocean and had crossed the mountains alone, because an unusually heavy snowfall on the North Slope was too deep for dogs. "I could not believe my eyes," Amundsen wrote in one book. "Here was a man, hundreds of miles from the nearest human being, with not a soul to aid him in case of illness or accident, cheerfully trudging through the Arctic winter across an unblazed wilderness, and thinking nothing at all of his exploit. I was lost in admiration." And in another book he said, "I stood looking after him as he disappeared from view, and I thought, if you got together a few more men of his stamp, you could get to the moon."

The riverboats that stopped at the port of Eagle were sternwheelers of the Mississippi style, with curtained saloons and decks for strolling and wood piled high on their bows. They burned a cord an hour. They ran until mid-century. "It's a dirty shame they ever stopped," says Barney Hansen, who well remembers them. "If they'd quit giving so much money to foreign countries and kept the steamboats on the river for God's people to run in, it would have been wonderful, but they didn't." The Sarah, the Yukon, the Lavelle Young—there were dozens of them, and they tied up at Eagle, their company flags and thick smoke flying, intense in their competition: Northern Commercial versus North American Trading & Transportation. They could be heard miles away, their big pistons thumping. Al Stout, who now works claims on American Creek, came into the country working on such a vessel, and it cured him of riverboats forever. His bunk was in the stern, directly above the thump. He worked six hours on and six off, with additional duty at every wood stop and every port. He fell asleep in any slack moment, wherever on the boat he might be. His pay was two dollars a day. He got off at Eagle, and stayed off, to become a miner—a relatively easeful occupation.

One-way tickets on the steamers were blue. They were not always bought by the people who used them. They were sometimes bought by the community. In Council meeting on December 13, 1909, for example, the "matter of relieving the town of Otto Strom was generally discussed and it was arranged to start him down the river." His offense was assault and battery—obviously even a heavier crime than prostitution, for no blue ticket had been forthcoming when the Fort Egbert surgeon, earlier that year, discovered that Gertrude Carson was suffering from v.d. The commanding officer requested that the community banish Ms. Carson, because she was a menace to the health and discipline of the troops. Two months later, though, she was allowed to reopen, provided she keep "sober and clean, and a respectable place in her line." Her cabin was in the western half of Block 18 on C Street, where, in a move to clean up First Avenue, all prostitutes had been consigned a year before (and where all the cabins are gone and a grove of aspens quakes today). Those were milestone times for Eagle. The windmill was shipped in, with a bill for almost twelve hundred dollars. And a package arrived that killed Fort Egbert dead. In it was a wireless transmitter, and all the work of Billy Mitchell, five years after its completion, was in the instant obsolete.

By 1910, nothing was going out on the wire. In 1911, the War Department closed the Army post. Forty-five buildings had been built, and a water-supply line from American Creek. At intervals through the woods, this water line passed over fires that kept it fluid twenty-four hours a day. The soldiers burned three thousand cords of wood a year. When they departed forever, Eagle was balder than Kansas, and six thousand stacked cords stayed after them to rot. Regulations prohibited the departing soldiers from giving or selling materials to local people, so they ignited a pyre of coonskin coats—two hundred coonskin coats—and they threw their rifles into the Yukon.

A few years ago, Tom Scott, of Eagle, took a job in the Washington office of Alaska's Senator Mike Gravel. On a lunch hour, he happened into the Library of Congress, and could not believe what he saw—"all that material there to be used." He looked up "Fort Egbert" and was soon directed to the National Archives, where he found plats and photographs and records—a trove unknown in Eagle. Much of Fort Egbert had long since disappeared—the gymnasium, with its basketball court; the post exchange and commissariat; the veranda-bordered barracks, so odd and Southwestern—but the N.C.O. quarters were still standing, and the enormous mule barn, the quartermaster warehouse, the granary, the water-wagon shed, not to mention various ruins with outlines intact. Scott called a friend named Gerald Timmons in the Bureau of Land Management. What could be done in the way of restoration and preservation? Timmons told him to write certain letters on Gravel's stationery and ask Gravel to sign them. The first letter went to the Bureau of Land Management. As a citizen of Eagle, and without revealing his employment with Gravel, Scott went to Senator Ted Stevens, of the opposite party. The Senator asked Scott, who was twenty years old, what a hundred and fifty thousand dollars could do. "We were so naïve. With a hundred and fifty thousand, we figured we'd have a Williamsburg here." The Fort Egbert restoration was soon in the B.L.M. budget for seventy thousand dollars, to be repeated annually. To preserve buildings in the city, twenty-five thousand was provided by the state and matched by the National Park Service—a deal engineered by "Gravel." The Seabees were sent in to work on the mule barn. They were transported by the National Guard. Eagle is indeed becoming a far-northern Williamsburg, to the particular wonder of young Tom Scott, who says, "It's just amazing. I can't believe it. So many resources are *available*."

When Jim and Elva Scott, Tom's parents, came into the country to settle, in the early nineteen-seventies, they paused on the hill above Eagle and reminded each other that they had lived in many Alaskan bush communities, and with regard to this one they wished to share a firm resolution: in its politics they would not become involved. A couple of years later, he was impeached as mayor. The tattle says "impeached." The word is a shade strong. He resigned, at any rate, in foul humor, and a majority of the Council enthusiastically approved. His initial act had been to kill the opening prayer. It was while he was on the Council that the preponderance of the religious bloc came to an end. When members of the Bible Chapel hopefully asked him if he would come to a Scripture reading, he mentioned his atheism and said he might have "little to contribute." His principal offense, though, if such it was, seems to have been the advice and support he gave his son in the effort to preserve and restore the fort and the town.

"They made deals with the government—him and Tom—regarding the designation of historic sites, which require approval by the city. None was given."

"Eagle was in the National Register of Historic Places for two years before the city found out it was."

"When Eagle was changed from a First Class to a Second Class City, he executed the papers without notifying the Council. He did not acquaint the people with appeals procedures."

"Recently, he has said that the city should be abolished, due to excessive taxation. He says the public well should be closed and abandoned."

"He thinks the Bureau of Land Management could run Eagle better than the Council."

"I don't like his ways. He wants the town government out of here. He's a Communist."

"Show me the card. But I'll buy Socialist—and I don't think we need any in Eagle."

"He's such a wide person. He has so much of everything. But at times he does not listen to other people's ideas."

"The people of the Indian Village respect him. I respect him."

Jim Scott is a big man, angry and funny, his face alive with wit. He is a forester, now retired from long federal service. He is the salt and the pepper of Alaska. He is my neighbor, and, while I am here, my landlord. The two cabins are back to back. We split our wood against the same log. I watch from my window to encounter him there. He sets the axe down, puts a boot up, looks out over the Yukon, and says, "When I came here, I was, in effect, seeking the philosophical outlook of our Founding Fathers—you know what I mean?—here in this great and glorious community." He lifts the axe. "The town is corroded with ne'er-do-wells," he says. Chop. "It is, in effect, Forest Lawn for the living." Chop. Chop.

His eyes are owlish, because snowlight blinded him once, burned his corneas. He has a beardless, broad face, suggesting honesty—the face of an overweight hawk. I remember thinking when I first saw him that he looked a lot like George Washington—a Washington caught by a cannier Peale, with a slicing edge in his demeanor, as if someone had just put a question to him concerning his expense account. As an "administrative forester," he made patterned journeys across hundreds of miles of Territorial Alaska, by float plane, by canoe, by snowshoe. In his "idiot bag" he carried forms and applications —for homesteads, cabin sites, "headquarters sites" for bush endeavors—and he tried to educate people in the responsibilities of living on public estate, so they could stay within the rules, legalize their occupancy, prove up. He became their friend. He willingly brought them supplies—hams, snares, traps, shells, sugar, flour, medicine—when they sent him lists and asked the favor. He ate and slept in their cabins, and he always paid. He paid five or six dollars to roll out his sleeping bag, and two for any meal. There were no exceptions. "I didn't want so much as a piece of pie hanging over my head." Chop.

For a time, the family's cabin was in Homer, on Kachemak Bay. He would fly to Kenai, and walk the roadless miles home—seventy by airline, upward of a hundred on foot. One night, after snowshoeing a good distance at thirty below zero, he stopped at a cabin, tired. He said he would sleep on the floor, but the people insisted that he sleep in a bed with their children—a small boy and a small girl. The boy wet the bed all night. His sister kept warning him he was going to get spanked. Jim just lay there between them, floating on his back in a lake of urine, saying nothing. "It beggared description" is what he says now. "In effect, it was enough to pale the Pope." He uses exactly the same terms to summarize his experiences on the higher levels of bureaucracy.

When he had risen in the world, up out of the fun and into the shuffling paper—when he had become district manager, based in Anchorage, and in charge of half Alaska—he dealt regularly with, among others, people of the petroleum industry. They invited him for cocktails. "I never darkened their door. I avoided them like the bubonic plague. It made it so much easier to deal with the sons of bitches." It seems possible that if Jim Scott had ever cut down a cherry tree, he would have reported it, and would not have had to be asked.

He was born in Appleton, Minnesota, on the Pomme de Terre, commencing a lifelong passion for rivers. It culminates now with the Yukon. The river is why he is here. He has a twenty-foot Chestnut freighter canoe. He has been a canoeman from his earliest youth—on the Pomme de Terre, the Red River of the North, the Minnesota, the Otter Tail. He was in Alaska as a bachelor before the war. Elva, just graduated from Berkeley and a registered nurse, met him when he went through California on his way—as things eventuated—to

Britain and France with the Army. Since his return, they have lived in Alaska.

He worked for the Bureau of Land Management, but does not adopt a B.L.M. attitude toward the river people, who are, by and large, his friends. He is, in his way, as vehement as they. He says he had hopes for the work and future of the bureau in the days of President Kennedy (the B.L.M. has caretaker responsibility for most of the land of Alaska), but things later slid in an erosive way, and now the B.L.M., by his description, "has reverted to being a national grab bag surrounded by people in sharkskin suits." Scott is nothing if not verbal. He loves, and sometimes makes, words. He rolls words on his tongue with such savor that certain ones—"gymanastics," "mythyology"—would appear to have an extra syllable; he seems to like them so much that he is reluctant to let them go without a bonus.

He despises exploitation of the mythology of Alaska. When he is in the summer Arctic and sees Eskimos hurrying in parkas and mukluks to beat drums before tourists, he wishes he had enough money to pay them all to stay home. He is a xenophile. He is interested in high-latitude peoples, and has travelled from one country to another completely around the Arctic world. The State Department has sent him abroad, exporting his knowledge of northern vegetation. He praises the way things are ordered and organized in Lapland, Iceland, Finland, Soviet Siberia. For Russian conservationists he has particularly admiring praise. "And they are the supposed barbarians. We are the ones who are barbaric."

"He's a Communist. He's an out-and-out Communist."

"Show me the card."

He describes the building of the Trans-Alaska Pipeline as "a frenetic exercise, reactionary in character," and explains, "Ten per cent of the world's population is using sixty per cent of the world's resources. The inevitable result of that is conflict. Whenever a society puts all its chips on depletables, it's in trouble. We should socialize base minerals and hydrocarbons. It's the only way the public interest can in truth be served."

"I'll buy Socialist."

He says that the deals and the legislation that enabled the construction of the pipeline "constitute a scandal exceeding Teapot Dome—so corrupt and immoral it beggars description."

The eighty million acres of proposed parks and reserves which were a "tradeoff" for the petroleum industry's exploitation of the land are not only an example of "national vanity" but collectively a poor one at that, because "the best parts of Alaska" (from an economic as well as an aesthetic point of view) are not marked for preservation. He has in mind, among other places, sections of the Wrangells, of Wood River, of the Brooks Range. "They have been sold out, and the people of the United States sold short, to the merchants."

By the terms of the Statehood Act, Scott remembers, the hundred and three million acres that the state was to choose as its share of the land were meant to be entirely below a line formed by the Porcupine, the Yukon, and the Kuskokwim Rivers—the so-called PYK Line, a bend sinister across interior Alaska. North Alaska was to be a national-defense zone. "Anxious to please mercantile interests, the government ignored the PYK Line, but it was never revoked, and Prudhoe Bay really belongs to all the people. The merchants got the pipeline without much of a god-damned ripple, really. They'll get anything else they want, too—through cheap tradeoffs among politicians. All high-latitude areas are seen as places to be exploited. It fries my fanny." It would seem to be—chop—enough to pale the Pope.

One sometimes gets the impression that Scott lives in Eagle so he can contemplate Canada. His picture windows look east across the Yukon into Yukon Territory. "That's God's country there," he says, with a sweeping gesture over his home-caught, homegrown, homemade American dinner—his king salmon, his tomato salad, creamed corn, lowbush-wild-cranberry sauce on yogurt, cranberry brandy. In the view's right-middle ground is Eagle Creek, where he and I once fished for grayling. It is in the United States, and if it is not God's country, God should try to get it, a place so beautiful it beggars description—a clear, fast stream, which on that day was still covered on both sides and almost to the center with two or three feet of white and blue ice. The steep knobby hills above were pale green with new aspen leaves; there were occasional white birch, dark interspersed cones of isolate spruce, here and again patches of tundra. Overhead was a flotilla of gray-hulled, white-sailed clouds. Fresh snow was on the mountains in the distance. The

Scotts have all that framed in their Thermopane—a window that could have been lifted from a wall in Paramus and driven here, to the end of the end of the road. The window is synecdoche, is Eagle itself—a lens, a monocular, framing the wild, holding the vision that draws people up the long trail to the edge of things to have a look and see.

Out the other way, past my place, is the town. Scott is its conscience, if no longer its mayor. He does not miss the Council meetings or any opportunity to pull the trigger of his .45-calibre principles. Tonight is not an exception. All are present: Borg, with his toothpick; Sarge Waller, hatless, his fringe of hair cut crew; Junior Biederman; Dave McCall; Taiwan Richert, with his cigarette papers, his corncob pipe; Dave Roy; Steve Casto. The Common Council of Eagle, Alaska. Louise Waller sits as city clerk. A dozen observers fill the benches by the walls: Diana Greene, crocheting; Elva Scott, doing needlepoint; Viola Goggans, with her headband and her thermos. T. J. Voithoffer calls attention to the town's bank account, which is above fifteen thousand dollars. He says that Eagle has become "a regular greedy overtaxed municipality, like all the ones we escaped." The figure has long since irritated Scott, for in the most recent tax assessment Scott's assessment proved to be a full twelfth of the town's budget. ("You can imagine how this titillated my Celtic sensitivities," Scott told me. He went to the tax-assessment-equalization meeting and made no comment about his own situation but inquired into the criteria the assessor had used. When he found that there were no criteria—except what the town thought the payer could pay—his Celtic sensitivities went critical, and his tax bill atrophied as well.) Voithoffer's complaint is noted. Scott lets it pass.

Waller takes the floor. "In the minutes, April 26, which I was not here," he begins. . . . Jim and Elva Scott had said they wanted it recorded that they saw a conflict of interest in Sarge Waller's being a Council member while Louise Waller was a city clerk, and in Sarge Waller's being a Council member and also being given a job in the courthouse restoration, where jobs are awarded by the Common Council. Just what is the problem, Waller wants to know—what do the Scotts want to prove?

"Who hires the workers on the building—the city or the B.L.M.?" Scott asks.

"The city."

"How many applications were there beyond the number hired?"

"Three."

"Therefore, Sarge voted for a job for himself, and that is conflict of interest. The state has a conflict-of-interest law. Eagle is big enough not to have a councilman whose wife is clerk, a councilman who is employed as a result of a Council vote. We wish to have that point recorded in the minutes. There are no personalities in this."

"I think there *are* personalities!" Louise Waller shouts, and delivers a statement of the devotion to the United States felt by the Wallers, with undertone implications that the Scotts are Communists.

Sarge is shouting. Scott is repeating himself, also in high throat: "The *state* has a conflict-of-interest law."

Sarge now bellows out, "You came here saying you were retired and were just going to build your house, and you have been doing nothing but stir up trouble ever since."

The debate has gone up out of the larynx and into the bulging eyeball. An Eagle mayor once died in Council meeting. Through it all, Elva Scott is as calm as a gavel. When the Wallers shout questions at her, they get polite, quiet replies, without interruption of her moving needle. She is sharp, forensic, clever—politically very able. She is a medical person, interested in the damage, not the fight. Gradually, with a few references to Scott's memorable mayoralty, the thunder recedes.

The Scotts and the Wallers are next-door neighbors. Walking home, I ask Elva how such a great and angry confrontation will affect Jim's relationship with Sarge. "Jim doesn't have a relationship with Sarge" is Elva's reply. "Therefore, it can't be affected."

Elva has long-lashed gray-blue eyes that are as smiling as they are shrewd. Her insights seem to begin where many people's bottom out. Decades ago, she was diagnosed as having Hodgkin's disease, from which her oldest son, who shared it, is dead. She does not seem to be much affected by the tumult of the world. She is above average in height and in the strength of her frame, and she has the open, handsome face, the look of reposed affection that one associates with the exemplar Scandinavian women. Her name was Nelson, and she grew up in San Fernando. She has a master's degree in education from the University of Alaska. For many years, she ran the school-district health program in Anchorage. In Eagle, she runs, in effect, a clinic in her kitchen. She does preventive work that is paid for by the state, but most of her effort is donated. With a health aide in the Indian Village, who has had six weeks' training, Elva has all of the medical experience that is available in Eagle. The hospital in Fairbanks is three hundred and eighty miles away by road, an hour and twenty minutes through the air. When Charlie Juneby, in the Indian Village, had an emergency last year that resulted in a kidney transplant in Seattle, a red signal was sent out of Eagle on the medical satellite system, interrupting an agricultural program coming in from New Zealand. Fairbanks failed to catch the signal, but someone in Hawaii did, and telephoned Alaska. In the black of night, a plane came from Fairbanks, and Eagle was ready with flares all around the landing strip and headlights at either end. Juneby was in Seattle nine hours after the signal.

People like to sit and listen to the satellite—to the medical problems of all of Alaska. Their own they take to Elva. Her couches and chairs are often filled with fundamentalists, river people, bootleggers, and Indians. Old Sarah Malcolm sits there—with moosehide in her lap, sewing—absorbing at least ten times what she pretends to understand. Louise Paul, short and solid, saying nothing, is said to be the matriarch of the Indian Village. Archie Juneby—tall, slender, handsome, with a dark ponytail—drank too much last night with his brothers and smashed up Max Beck's boat. They come to Elva. Elva goes to them. She knits her day through the Village and the City. Mental health and alcoholism are the principal problems. "In the Village, children's ears run so much the people once thought that was normal and healthy," she has told me. "People come in off the river with blood infections, red streaks up their arm. They get cystitis from not enough water. They come down from Dawson with v.d. We don't have laboratory tests. We treat on symptoms. An outboard motor chewed on a guy's legs awhile. We sewed him up. I tell everyone, 'I don't mind helping you out. Just don't use me.' We don't want to be awakened for nothing, for someone who is merely drunk. For gunshot wounds and stabbings I of course get up. Oh, we have enough of that sort of thing. Yeah. You betcha. We're getting ready to have dinner with company and they come in and bleed all over the sink. Who needs TV in Eagle? We've got action enough in the streets."

Guns blazed in Eagle a short time ago—a row at Y's, big pistols cracking in the night; no casualties.

G's first wife died giving birth to H. G married N, who died in two years. G then married W, who was half his age. H, now fourteen, became pregnant, no one knows by whom, and gave birth to Z. Z is now one year old. Her mother has gone to Fairbanks and has disappeared. W has left G. He approaches sixty. He is alone with the infant Z.

When D's cabin caught fire, D was out of the country. Half the town—Christians and drinkers alike—came out to fight the fire and loot the cabin. There were individual piles of loot, and fights over the piles. "That's my pile." "The hell it is, it's mine."

M has requested that if his cabin ever smolders in his absence people please stay away and let it burn to the ground.

C drinks gin, Listerine, rubbing alcohol, and vanilla extract.

A's wife went off with X to one of Billy Mitchell's old telegraph cabins forty or fifty miles into the mountains. Writing out a false but wholly effective message, A chartered an airplane and dropped the message near the cabin: "Your brother is dead. The funeral is on Friday. Come in."

TV.

By a campfire near the boundary—the north-south Canadian boundary—Michael John David reads aloud to me and to his brother from "Lame Deer Seeker of Visions." It is one of several books he carries in his pack. Around us are tall spruce that Michael means to cut and float six or eight miles down the Yukon to become the walls of his new cabin. He is the chief of Eagle Indian Village. "'I think white people are so afraid of the world they created that they don't want to see, feel, smell, or hear it,'" he reads. He has turned with no searching to what is obviously a favorite passage. "'The feeling of rain and snow on your face, being numbed by an icy wind and thawing out before a smoking fire, coming out of a hot sweat bath and plunging into a cold stream, these things make you feel alive, but you don't want them anymore.'" He pauses to chuckle, to flash a grin. "Do you like this?"

I tell him he hasn't read enough of it to me. The book was written by John Fire/Lame Deer and Richard Erdoes, and is dedicated to Frank Fools Crow, Pete Catches, George Eagle Elk, Bill Schweigman, Leonard Crow Dog, Wallace Black Elk, John Strike, Raymond Hunts Horse, Charles Kills Enemy, and Godfrey Chips. Such names are as unfamiliar to Michael as they are to me, for they belong to the Minneconjou Sioux, in the Lower Forty-eight, and he is of the Hungwitchin of the Athapaskans. His family came into the country in immemorial time. Long before their settlement became known as Eagle Indian Village, it was known as David Camp. David, Juneby, Malcolm, and Paul are the four major families of the Village now. Michael throws a stick onto the fire and continues: "'Living in boxes which shut out the heat of the summer and the chill of winter, living inside a body that no longer has a scent, hearing the noise from the hi-fi instead of listening to the sounds of nature, watching some actor on TV having a make-believe experience when you no longer experience anything for yourself, eating food without taste—that's your way. It's no good.'" He laughs aloud—a long, soft laugh. His voice is soft, too—fluid and melodic, like nearly all the voices in the Village. The contrast with my own is embarrassing. No matter how I try to modulate it, to experiment with his example, my voice in dialogue with Michael's sounds to me strident, edgy, and harsh. He is twenty-five years old. His body is light, his face narrow, his nose aquiline. His hair, black and shining, passes through a ring behind his head and plumes between his shoulder blades. He wears a khaki jacket, patched pink denim trousers, leather boots, a belt-sheathed jackknife. He may be an Indian, but he looks like a Turk. On his head is a fur hat that has the shape of an inverted flowerpot—a long-haired fez. His thin, Byzantine mustache droops at the wing tips. He has a miniature beard, scarcely a quarter inch long, tufting from the point of his chin.

His brother, Minicup, teen-age, wears blue-jeans, a red headband. Minicup is taciturn but obviously interested and even inquisitive, his eyes moving back and forth between Michael and me. He was baptized Edward David. Minicup is a name he gave to himself years ago.

We are finishing dinner, a common enterprise. It began, after making camp, with a mutual presentation of what each of us had to offer. Michael and Minicup set out Spam, Crisco, Sanka, fresh carrots, onions, and potatoes. I set out tins of beef stew, and corn, tea, sugar, raisins, nuts, chocolate, and cheese. Michael, opening the Spam, said, "I remember when it cost a dollar." Between us there has been a certain feeling out of ways and means. It is my wish to follow Michael's lead, to see how he will go about things in the woods. To some extent, he seems to want to do the same with me. It was he who chose this campsite—a couple of hundred yards into the forest and away from the Yukon's right bank, on flat ground covered with deep sphagnum, close to the edge of a small, clear stream. Wicked thorns grow out of the moss on long roselike stems. We hacked at them with our knives until we had cleared an area big enough for my small nylon A-frame and the brothers' wall tent—an orange Canadian affair that Michael, for privacy, often stays in at the Village. Before building the fire, he turfed out the moss, cutting eight inches down and removing a five-foot square. Even so, he did not get to the bottom of the moss. I then, automatically, without pausing to think, went off to the river for rocks. I brought back two or three in my arms, like loaves of bread, and dropped them on the moss. I returned to the river. The brothers followed. We all collected rocks and carried them back into the woods—gathering, in several trips, more than enough for a fireplace. I was about to begin building one but checked myself and relinquished the initiative. Why should I build the sort of three-walled fireplace I would make in Maine? I wanted to see what they would do. I fiddled with my pack and left the rocks alone. Michael and Minicup laid them out singly—one after another, scarcely touching—in the closest thing possible to a perfect circle. I could not see what the purpose of such a circle might be. It could not shield the fire from wind, nor could it support the utensils of cooking. Possibly it was to retain the spread of smolderings through the moss, but it seemed awfully large for that. Why had they made it, unless purely as an atavistic symbol, emplaced by what had by now become instinct?

Now Michael, finishing his dinner, has a question for me. He says, "Why did you go get the rocks?"

I mention fireplaces I have made on lakes and rivers in Maine.

"Maine?" he says. The word "Maine" seems to excite him. "Have you been to L. L. Bean? I sometimes send for shirts and pants from there, and boots similar to yours."

Through the late but barely graying evening, we walk a couple of hours beside the Yukon, going upstream at first, within sight of the shaved incongruous border, which, on the far side of the river, comes up from the south and plunges down a ridge to the water. For the most part, we walk by the river, but we make occasional penetrations through alder hells and into the woods to assess the trees. In many places we see upheavals where bears have dug roots. The ground appears to have been plowed. Bear tracks, heading upriver and down, are in sand at the edge of the water. Michael tells of a couple of tourists who were approaching Eagle not long ago when they saw a grizzly chasing a black bear. The grizzly caught the black bear, tossed it around, broke its neck, and started to eat the warm carcass. The people got out of their car with cameras and moved toward the feast. The grizzly charged them. They were lucky. They made it back to their car.

Resting on Michael's shoulder is his .30–'06. After a time, we turn around, retrace our tracks, and then go on for some miles downriver. We pass the high stump of a white birch, eight inches in diameter. Inside is nothing. The wood, over many years, has completely disintegrated and disappeared. The bark—firm, unaltered, and solid—stands like a stovepipe on its own. Michael stops, and lifts his rifle as if he is about to fire. He moves it slowly, pointing along a bend of the river. He does not intend to shoot. He is using the rifle's six-power scope as if it were a monocular. He often raises the gun just to look around, to look at anything at all—the better to examine it, through the scope. This is more than a little disconcerting when he happens to be looking at you. Lowering the gun, he says, "Is 'Robinson Crusoe' fiction?"

I tell him it is, and ask why he wants to know.

He shrugs, and says he has always wondered. A scattering of feathers attracts his eye. He picks one up, saying, "A hawk killed a robin." He says he once climbed Eagle Bluff for a peregrine chick, trained it, and later let it go. We come upon a set of amoeboid tracks ("Porcupine") and grapelike clusters with star points in the sand ("Fox"). That brown object in the brush —what is that? "A garbage bag from Dawson."

I ask Michael where he earned the money for his 1967 Oldsmobile Vista-Cruiser.

"The Slope," he says. As an apprentice heavy-equipment operator, he has two thousand hours to his credit. Operating a bulldozer, he helped build the haul road that accompanies the Trans-Alaska Pipeline.

"Thanks to you, people will drive from the Caribbean Sea to the Arctic Ocean," I remark.

"Caribbean Sea?" he says. "Where is that? Is it far from New York?"

"It would be like going from here to Adak."

"Pretty far," he says, and after a moment mentions that one of his boyhood friends in Eagle Indian Village was sent off to be raised in New York. The boy's mother and father and his Uncle Pete mixed grape juice with wood alcohol from the school duplicating machine and drank it. The father went blind. Uncle Pete and the mother died. "The kids were not fed three times daily after that. Their home was upside down." It was arranged, somehow, for one boy to go off and live with a family in New York. "When he came back, years later, he knew nothing," Michael says. "He knew white things but not Indian things. He punched holes in foil in which meat was roasting. The same with potatoes. He saw a porcupine and thought it was a raccoon. He knew nothing." Michael walks in silence for a while, and then, as if trying the words on his tongue, he repeats, "Caribbean Sea."

Beside us now is a slough. It separates the Yukon's right bank from what Michael calls Old Man Clark's Island. "We have rabbit drives there. Drive the rabbits from one end of the island to the other and kill them. Not now, though. They go through a cycle. Now there are no rabbits." He has on occasion come to this side of the river to hunt sheep. "When you can barely see a sheep," he says, "the sheep can count your fingers.

That's how sharp eyes they got." We see a cottonwood that has been chewed by a beaver. We see, moments later, the beaver. Michael raises his rifle and follows it through the scope. Head up, swimming, it cuts a straight wake in the almost still water of the slough. Michael chooses not to shoot but to save the beaver. He will shoot it in time. He looks up from the gun. "This place compared to a city is—well, pretty nice," he says. "We have a little bit of everything—animals, fish, mountains, forest. Even people down the river envy what there is in this country." With a slap on the water, the beaver is gone. A light, cold rain begins to fall. We return upriver to the campsite and the tents.

A few days ago, when I heard that Michael was going up the Yukon for cabin logs, I went to ask if I could join him. In a canoe, I approached the Indian Village, which sits on the left bank—twenty, thirty feet above the river. It is a linear community: cabins spaced along the river a third of a mile, facing, across the water, a six-hundred-foot bluff. In front of each cabin, the steep slope of the riverbank glitters with broken glass—micaceous flakes, the Indian midden. I kept the canoe close under the bank, sliding below the Village. When the youth above are drinking, they like to shoot over the river at the bluff—a .30-calibre declaration of joy. That is what they were doing at the time, so it was prudent to be under the bullets. Harm, of course, was not intended. In 1898, one Angus, who lived up there, organized what he hoped would be a massacre of the whites of Eagle, but, like many projects that have got started in the Village, it was not carried out, it was merely conceived. The Hungwitchin appear to be characteristically passive. When and if they do go on what Michael likes to call "the warpath," their preferred weapons are legal briefs and lobbies—supplied by the native regional corporation that stands behind them. I went up the bank and found Michael alone in a cabin, sober and disconsolate, sitting in a chair, looking straight ahead. His face seemed less alive than cast. The cabin was spotless and almost empty, with psychedelic posters on the walls. It is shared by Village bachelors, of whom he is one. He was anxious to go upriver and to get back well in advance of the next session of the Village Council, he said. It would be of great importance to him, because it would have to do with control of alcohol. When I left him there, he was still staring straight ahead, listening to the reports of the rifles.

A door or two away was the cabin in which Michael grew up. Like most cabins in the Village, it is essentially one room, twenty by twenty feet, with a storm vestibule full of dog harnesses, guns, mukluks, parkas. In the main room, all furniture is against the walls, which are insulated with carton cardboard ("Burger King Frozen Shoestring Potatoes"). There are three beds, a bench and a table, a tall oval heat stove, a propane oven and range. Cordwood, stacked waist-high, is inside the cabin as well. Yet the first two impressions the cabin gives are a sense of neatness and a sense of space. Michael, three brothers, and two sisters are grown and away now, if not altogether gone. So his parents, Bessie and Harry David, have only four children at home with them still. The beds touch like dominoes. The three youngest sleep in one, parents in another, Minicup in the third. Clothes are in boxes under the beds. A broom hangs by the door. Coming inside in winter, you sweep your legs free of snow before it melts.

No one seems to knock. People just come in and sit down and don't say much until something occurs to be said. Harry, on the bench by the table, may be slowly sharpening a saw, Bessie pouring cups of tea. A radio plays rock. Charlie Juneby, big as a bear, comes in with a frozen mop, and without explanation sits and drinks tea. He is joined later on by his brother Isaac. Stay in one place long enough and almost the whole Village appears and visits and goes. If consumed time is the criterion, visiting is what the Hungwitchin mainly do. They tell about hunting. Jacob Malcolm impressively describes himself stalking moose on snowshoes—successfully running them down. In the phenomenal stillness of the winter air, he lights a match to see how the flame may bend, then he chooses his direction of approach. Jimmy David comes in, and drops a pair of bloody white ptarmigan on the floor, presenting them to his mother. A fresh snowshoe hare already hangs from a wire on the wall. Bessie wears slacks, has a ready grin. Her hair is tied behind her head. Her oldest child is in his thirties, her youngest is eleven. She is some years younger than Harry. Harry is as trim as a coin. He is short and gray-haired, wears glasses. He is intense, and is known for working hard. "I work hard, come in, take a god-damned good shot before I eat. I like coffee, too, soon as I get up." Harry is the kind of man who shakes Tabasco on his beans. "At home, I'm kind of hazy like, don't feel very good, no satisfaction with anything. I enjoy myself outside, across the Yukon River, feel fine, feel full of hell and vinegar, full of life, energy—lots of energy." So saying, one February day he went out of the cabin and walked seven miles in the snow. I went behind him, in his tracks. We are the same size; he has a rolling gait, a shorter stride than mine, but he made the going easier for me. He wore rubber boots, rubber trousers, a blue down jacket, a dark-brown leather hat. In his cheek he had a dip of Copenhagen snuff. When he stood still, to talk, he leaned forward. We walked some distance on the Yukon River, which, under the snow, was now smooth and now mountainously jagged where the ice floes at freeze-up had jammed. Gradually, we crossed over, and then went up a crease in the bluff—Harry without the slightest pause, as if he were ascending stairs, when in fact the snow on that precipitous ground was underlaid with ice, and a slip could mean a long fall down. He carried a stick. "This is a good place to go up from the Yukon River," he said, reaching back for me with the stick. Beyond the top, he had cut a maze of trails, miles through a forest burn. He works six and seven days a week cutting cordwood for sale. He does not use a power saw. "John Borg lost his way one time, coming to get some wood, and he said, 'God damn it, Harry, you got too many trails up here'—but he got a good trail to here, don't kick about that." We passed a large pile of whole spruce trunks—up to thirty feet long, their bark blackened—that Michael had cut and had stacked by himself. "He's a young boy. By God, he handle it," Harry said. "He's a well-liked boy. The girls are crazy for him. He is the chief. He has done his country good. By talking, you know—making everything go nice. I think he's got a little college in him. He studies the right way for his people. He like to see people get along together, make no enemy with nobody."

Fifteen years ago, Harry was the chief. "Anyone interfere with our country, we got a right to pitch in and kick like hell about it. You white people butt in, take our traplines, our fishing. That's what we try to stop."

"How do you feel about independence for Alaska, Harry?"

"That's the best way to look at it."

Making a long loop through the burn, we came out eventually at the highest part of the bluff, directly opposite the Village: a panoptic aerial view, of such height and distance, taking in so much river and mountain land, that it emphasized the isolation and the elongate symmetry of the Village by the river and—what is not apparent up close—its beauty. For Harry, this was obviously the supreme moment in the country—the sight of his village from the air. He was born, he said, far down the Yukon River, at the mouth of the Kandik, in 1913. "They kept on moving in those days. They don't stay one place. They lived off the country. They lived in tents, ten by twelve, the biggest they ever had. They just keep on moving. They don't stay in town all the time, like we do." Harry's father, Old David, died when Harry was six, and he was raised for a time by Chief Alec, at Fortymile, but when "the flu came up the river" Chief Alec died, and so did his wife, Mary Alec. Harry was returned to his mother, at Eagle, and lived with her until she died. In the same year, his stepfather drowned. Harry was by now a young man. He hauled wood for the riverboats, and he worked aboard them, too, until they stopped running, "when the Jap tried to take Alaska." At Moosehide one time, near Dawson, he met Bessie. "She is what they call a Crow, I think. One day, I bought two bottles of Hudson Bay rum—a hundred and fifty proof—and a keg of beer, and I married her." Looking across at their cabin, in miniature, in the third of a mile of cabins all touched with smoke, he said he had cut its logs by Eagle Creek and floated them down the Yukon River. For a time, he made his living as a trapper and in summer fished, with a wheel, on Goose Island. He pointed. "That is Goose Island, in the Yukon River—there." He soon went to work, seasonally, for the gold-mining operations at Woodchopper, Coal Creek, and Chicken. "For many years, my work and unemployment just connected." His and Bessie's children were born in the cabin—Michael in 1951, "clever, too, just like Howard, quick." Harry pointed toward the school, at the upstream end of the Village, and said Bessie taught Han there. Han is the language of the Hungwitchin. There are about thirty people in the world who speak it. A few are upriver, in the area of Dawson, but virtually all of them are in Eagle Indian Village. Han is one of the smallest subdivisions of the great Athapaskan language family, which reaches contiguously from Nulato and Koyukuk, in western Alaska, to southern Alberta and east to Hudson Bay—and makes a surprising jump, as well, across twelve hundred miles to the isolated Southwestern enclave of the Apache and the Navajo, which, among Athapaskans, are by far the most numerous. High on a pole outside the school we could see a small, dark movement—the flag of Alaska flying. The flag, as it happens, was designed by a native. It is lyrically simple, the most beautiful of all American flags. On its dark-blue field, gold stars form the constellation of the Great Bear. Above that is the North Star. Nothing else, as the designer explained, is needed to represent Alaska. It was the flag of the Territory for more than thirty years. Alaskans requested that it become the flag of the new state. The designer was a thirteen-year-old Aleut boy.

Michael went to high school in Tok, and he was "clever for anything," his father said. "With no trouble, he got into the Army. One day, he said, 'Dad, I'm going far to Anchorage with my friend.' He went far to Anchorage with his friend, and he got through the examination clean as a dollar. He went to California." Michael spent almost all of his two service years at the Presidio of San Francisco, where it never snowed, and he missed the winter. He also missed Sophie Biederman. She was a tall, slim, beautiful girl in brightly beaded moccasins. She had an outreaching smile, black hair, a complexion light and clear, notwithstanding that she went around with a can of soda pop almost constantly in her hand, and—eating virtually never—seemed to live on Coca-Cola alone. Harry told her she smoked too much marijuana. (Harry, for his part, does not even smoke tobacco.) Sophie's childhood had been roiled in her parents' troubles with alcohol. Nonetheless, she emerged with a joy in living, a fondness for excitement, a love of games. Her life and Michael's seemed to be spiralling upward through the summer of his return. Spilling Coke, she would dash into his arms. They planned a wedding, and he went to the North Slope to collect money to begin their married life. While he was there, she died of a gunshot wound, an apparent suicide. "Michael got broke down over her."

Through the night, the rain becomes heavier—a long, unremitting spring rain—and in the morning it is a downpour. Michael and I and Minicup make no effort to get up—just lie half asleep under the big dripping spruce as if there were no today. In an important sense, there isn't, because Michael, coming up the river to fell trees for his new log cabin, discovered that while he brought a chain saw he forgot gasoline. The temperature is less than ten degrees above freezing. The brothers have only one sleeping bag and a lightweight blanket. Michael has spent the night in the blanket. Toward noon, the rain has somewhat diminished. Michael gets up and builds a fire. His first gesture of the day is to make a cup of Sanka and carry it to Minicup, who is awake but has remained in the sleeping bag. "Nights out in a wall tent at sixty below, you just get up in the morning, throw everything into the sled, and move," Michael remarks. "In two hours, you might be warm. When I trap, I still use dog teams—not snow machines. You can't find a gas station out there. I trapped two years ago at Champion Creek with Jacob Malcolm. Wolves. Wolverines. Martens mostly. Lynx. Mink. We got seventy martens. We tan moose and caribou hides. From the caribou hides we make babiche to make snowshoes." Of all the whites who have come into the country, he prefers by far the young ones who live out on the river. "They believe more like an Indian believes," he says. "They believe in living like an Indian. They have dog teams. They fish. They hunt. They live in the woods. They tan hides, make dog harnesses, trap, use animal furs. They get to know the forest. They make sleds of birch. They survive in the woods with nothing, hardly. They are a good thing, going back to Mother Earth—just as long as they don't build on Hungwitchin lands."

With a cup of his own, he sits in the rain and makes an entry in a notebook. He tells me that he has been studying law, in a program offered by the Tanana Chiefs Land Claims College. A college education in earlier years was not possible for him, because he lacked the money, but now, as chief, he regards his present courses as imperative. "Other village corporations have gone bankrupt," he explains. "I would hate to see that happen to ours. The study of law is hard for me. It is hard for an Indian to understand contracts and corporations."

I ask if I may look at the notebook. He hands it to me, and I flip it open. "Judicial Department. Marbury v. Madison. Judges review, concept," says the first note I see. "Supreme Court don't make law but change them, and protect us from the government."

"The government wants to make a park down the river," Michael says. "Some of the best hunting grounds are down that way. It puts our native-land selections in a tight squeeze. I don't care very much for parks. I like to go into lands and check them out, not to be told what to do. But there is another side. If the government does not keep the land, someone will take over. I am against development in this country. Without the pipeline—without the Native Claims Act—I'd feel freer. The Alaska population is bigger now, because of the pipeline. I don't like a lot of people. I like the lands. If the land-claim settlement did not exist, you could go anywhere and build a cabin. If we strike oil in this country, we'll all be very rich, because it's on our land. But I don't want to see that. With a lot of money, people get into trouble. Where money is, more people will come. There will be a new pipeline, through here. I don't think I want to be rich."

In the pre-white epoch, the Hungwitchin's Chief Charley led his people from the Charley River up the Yukon to Mission Creek, where they lived in houses of skin. In small increments thereafter, they moved their principal settlement on up the left bank of the Yukon. In the eighteen-eighties, they were about a mile from their present site, and lived in six log cabins with interdigitating roof poles that stuck up like sawbucks against the sky. Michael whimsically suggests that the Village should move once more. "Move it a few miles on up the river," he says. "Into Canada. Nice people there. They are different—more mellow. They don't have no pipeline."

From their log houses in the nineteenth century, the Hungwitchin went out for moose and mountain sheep, rabbits and caribou. Women sat on the bank and watched for salmon. When they saw the barely discernible ripples, they pointed them out to men by the water, who went after the fish in bark canoes. They had dip nets in their hands. They wrestled the big kings to land. They smoked them. They trapped wolverines for ruffs. They hunted game with bows and arrows. They used sheep-horn spoons, and made birch-bark pots, and cooked by dropping hot rocks into water-filled baskets woven of spruce roots. Family by family along the river, they had long-established fish camps, which were jealously defined, as were their hunting and trapping grounds. When people of another tribe happened into the country and killed game, they could eat the meat but they had to surrender the hide.

That was the general ambience that has since become encapsulated within the word "subsistence." They subsisted in the country, almost independent of the rest of the world. Even before the gold rushes, there were touches of the coming difference. They enjoyed the tea and the tobacco they got from white traders, the novelty of guns. When the miners came in great numbers, and the freight of white supplies, the dress and the diet of the Indians began to change. Subsistence from the country somewhat declined. It would decline more as a result of the job economy of the Second World War, and still more following the discovery of oil. Alaska's booms denature the natives. The Yukon River fish camps that were symbols of the working unity of Indian families have gradually been abandoned.

Meanwhile, to assist the natives in their adjustment to the new social order, federal programs administered by the Bureau of Indian Affairs have long provided support of various kinds, from food and clothing subsidies to social services—a tradition of plausible generosity that reached its supreme expression in the Alaska Native Claims Settlement Act of 1971, widely described as the most openhanded and enlightened piece of legislation that has ever dealt with aboriginal people. While giving them a tenth of Alaska and about seventeen thousand dollars for each man, woman, and child, the act created a dozen regional native corporations to hold and invest roughly half the money, and to distribute the rest, on established schedules, to individuals and to village corporations. Doyon, Ltd., is in area the largest of the regional corporations, covering the whole of the Athapaskan interior and including about nine thousand people in thirty-four native villages, among them the Hungwitchin, each of whom is a Doyon stockholder. Doyon's fine new headquarters in Fairbanks are spread out and spacious, and resemble the headquarters of almost any large Eastern company that has just moved to a meadow in Connecticut. It is Doyon that is drilling for oil in the upper-Yukon region—within a hundred miles of Eagle. Two wells have proved dry, at nine and eleven thousand feet, but Doyon is undissuaded.

The disposition of Native Claims Settlement land begins with the villages, which get acreages related to population, and village choices must start with the ground around them. Michael David is the land-selection agent for the Hungwitchin. Because there are certain absentee stockholders, who belong to the community but live elsewhere, Eagle Indian Village qualifies for 92,160 acres. The selections will run from the Canadian border past Eagle and about thirty miles down the river, stopping at the edge of the large area the National Park Service hopes will become Yukon-Charley National Rivers (also as a result of the Native Claims Settlement Act). Eagle City, on its one square mile, and almost wholly white, has thus become an island in the Indian ocean. People in the city believe that the terms of the Settlement Act give Eagle the right to retain a two-mile "buffer zone" on all its sides. While the Indian Village is three miles upriver from the white community, it is less than two miles from the city line. Thus, the whites' buffer zone would overlap most of the Indian Village. This situation, while not the largest of the difficulties between the City and the Village, has touched off an example of what Michael David calls "modern-day Indian warfare." The Village would like to own land right up to the city line and give the city compensating acreage somewhere else. The Department of the Interior has rejected this. The Hungwitchin Corporation, with the help of Doyon lawyers, has taken the matter to the Alaska Native Claims Appeal Board and may take it to court. Michael calls this "a pretty deep question," and goes on to say, "Sometimes I wish the native land claims and the pipeline were not here. I could do a lot of things I want to do. I don't even know why they say 'own' land. You use land. You can't own land." As a result of the Native Claims Settlement Act, his sense of land —his people's sense of freedom of land—after ten thousand years is archaic and obsolete. Michael is a stockholder now, a landowner, a capitalist, a conscribed component of a distant system. For all its overt benefits and generous presentations, the bluntest requirement of the Alaska Native Claims Settlement Act was that the natives turn white.

When the whites of Eagle talk about the Indians, almost nothing of what they say is flattering—and why would it be? For, as Michael puts it, "they are always knocking each other." Within the flow of general disdain, about all that seems interesting is the recurrent implication that the troubles and shortcomings of the Indians are based on their not adequately thinking or acting white.

"They live day to day out there, whereas the white philosophy is 'progress.'"

"Time means nothing to them. There is no future. Today is today is today."

No one—at least, no one I have heard—brings forth the remark that there is much to be envied in such an approach to one's day. No doubt it accounts for the easygoing grace, the humor, the companionability of the Hungwitchin, not to mention the lilting, unbusinesslike way they speak—a primal outlook, so durable that, for all its beauty, it is perhaps unfortunate that it has survived while superficial facts have changed. The Hungwitchin may look upon a wristwatch as "the sun's heart," but they know what time it is, and they work on the pipeline. They seem to hang suspended between a fast-fading then and a more than alien now. Meanwhile, their failures to adjust are much noted by the whites.

"They've been hitting the booze since the nineteen-thirties. They've pretty much hurt their heads. They don't care."

"They all wish they were something else. They have come to hate the fact they're an Indian. They have adopted cowboy boots, of all things. They put cowboy boots on their kids."

"They have difficulty coping with the regimented life style that the capitalist system imposes upon them."

"Boys do not develop ambition. They don't want to get married."

"The Indian man has been emasculated by the whites. Indian women want to marry whites."

"The people are soft. They have no discipline. They have a job, and if it's difficult, they say, 'It's too tough.'"

"The Village Council does not get things done."

"Now that Michael is the chief, nothing ever will get done."

"A settlement should be a settlement. They still get transportation, medical, dental, free snow machines, chain saws—anything they want. Handouts. If you make a settlement, that should be that. The Native Claims Act should have made the natives like everybody else."

"The sums that have so far come down through Doyon and into individuals' pockets have amounted to less than eighty dollars a year. There are many resources elsewhere for the natives. They work as firefighters. They work on the pipeline. They come home and collect unemployment compensation—two hundred and more a month. They work on local road maintenance and do miscellaneous labor. They join the crews of exploration geologists. Moreover, the Native Claims Settlement Act has not put the Bureau of Indian Affairs out of business in Alaska, and a native can still turn to the B.I.A. for many kinds of grants and relief. With other Indians of the upper Tanana, they belong to the United Crow Band, which, under contract, distributes money for the B.I.A. for everything from fishing boots to Indian welfare checks to Indian relief checks. Welfare and relief money is available from the state as well. Three hundred to six hundred dollars a month is available in Aid to Families with Dependent Children. Nearly all health costs are paid by the Alaska Native Health Service. People over sixty-five not only draw Social Security but also receive an Alaska Longevity Bonus—a hundred and twenty-five dollars a month for anyone who has been in Alaska twenty-five years. No wonder all they do out there is visit."

That anyone in the Indian community might regret the events of the past century is not an insight that floats about on the surface of white conversation, but now and again it does rise.

"Michael David is a fine chap, slightly confused. He is a completely acculturated Indian, now trying to find his way back into the wigwam—a classic example of the 'advances' made in educating the Indian. He has assessed the world around him. He is not enamored of technology. So he affects the long hair and the headband. Given a chance, Michael would be a real good Indian. He would be a hopeless failure as a white man.

He is forthright. He does not speak out of both sides of his mouth. He is very honest."

I ask Michael, "What do you do as Village chief?"

He grins widely, and says, "What do I do as chief? Ha! Ask them in Eagle what I do. When I was elected chief, Louise Waller said, 'Now that Michael David is the chief, nothing is going to get done.' They are different people in Eagle. They don't understand us. We don't understand them. The town is Christians and bootleggers, and they fight between each other. They once had twenty preachers there. My people were happier before those people were ever here. The Indians did more things for themselves than they do now. I would like to have a post office in the Village, and a store of our own, run by Hungwitchin. I am working on the winterization program and improvements to the road around the Village. For Doyon, I am studying proposed easements to Doyon land. I am trying to get more jobs for Village people. Last year, the B.L.M. station-manager job went to a white who had been here six months. No one in the Village was given a chance even to apply. Oliver Lyman, of the Village, was fired as janitor of the school, and Charlie Ostrander was hired instead of a Village person."

"Who had the say?"

"I don't know who—but the town had the influence. Every year, it seems like the town's moving closer to the Village, and the town is half bootleggers. I hate the bootleggers. The constable makes twelve hundred dollars a month, and they bootleg right under his nose. The most important thing I try to do something about is the drinking in the Village. We get some help from the Alaska Native Commission on Alcoholism and Drug Abuse. Drinking is a sickness. I'm glad the town is dry. At this next meeting of the Village Council, there will be a big decision about alcohol. That is why the meeting is so important to me."

He speaks for a time of Tony Paul, who died recently of pneumonia complicated by cirrhosis of the liver. Admired for his intelligence, his energy, and his education, he was the brightest light of the Village. He was married and had a nine-year-old son, whom he often took camping. Tony was not yet thirty when he died. Larry Juneby, of Eagle, went out of a bar in Fairbanks and into the Chena River last week. Searchers are still dragging for the body. To drink, Michael says, Village people will sell their chain saws, their winter's wood—anything at all. On Easter, in bright sun by the white frozen river, they hold sawing contests, bag races, and tea races (make a fire from scratch, melt snow, and make tea), but such wholesome scenes are increasingly rare. Money was once collected for a Village well only to be spent on liquor. In various elections over the years, the white community has voted itself in and out of prohibition. It has been dry since 1967. Bootleggers get upward of two hundred dollars a case for blended whiskey—eighteen dollars a quart. "One of them did not like being wakened in the night," Michael tells me. "So he told the people just when to come around. He did that, really. He's bootlegging, and he's got hours."

I mention that I have asked Mayor Borg why the town did not stop the bootleg traffic, and Borg said, "Apathy. People don't want to become involved by signing a complaint. Reams of evidence would be needed before there could be an arrest. Meanwhile, the Village has been without any moral leadership for so long that there's very little sense of responsibility. It's each person for himself there, and alcoholism is widespread. They give young children booze. No one is there to say they shouldn't. A strong Village Council would prevent that."

Michael makes no comment. He says that in Venetie and Arctic Village, Athapaskan communities to the north, mailplane passengers and baggage and cargo are searched on arrival. Bottles are smashed. People actually drunk are returned to Fairbanks. "They get things done in those villages," he goes on. "They tan hides. They make babiche." By contrast, there are people of Eagle Indian Village who on arriving in Fairbanks are routinely detained and sent back to Eagle.

Last week, Michael went to see the most active bootlegger in the white community. He asked him to stop selling liquor to Village people, and mentioned that in his capacity as chief he might go to state authorities and seek their help in enforcing the local law. The bootlegger urged him not to do that but to put the matter before his own council instead. "If they vote that they want me to quit," said the bootlegger to the chief, "I'll quit."

Outside my cabin window, on First Avenue, Eagle City, the afternoon's entertainment is Horace (Junior) Biederman, who ambles up and down with a beer can in his hand, inviting Eagle to care. He is muttering. I can hear him through the open door. "I don't know if this here town wants to live in the past, or what it's trying to do. It's the right of the people to drink—to do anything. I don't mind packing it up or down the street—a beer in my hand. I don't give a damn who sees me."

Horace (Sophie was his cousin) is three-quarters Indian and seems to hang suspended between the Village and the town. His father ran the store that his grandfather took over from the Northern Commercial Company, and Horace grew up in the white community, where he still lives. The whites regard him as an Indian, the Indians regard him as white. "Junior Biederman has never been able to make up his mind which he would rather be," says Jack Boone. "He is not faithful to either community. He lives in the town like an Indian, in squalor. He never has more than two days' wood supply. He never plans ahead. That is the Indian way." Michael David's opinion is even lower than Boone's. He refers to Biederman as "a half-breed who is stuck in the middle, a bootlegger, and a husband and father who provides no wood." Biederman's wife, Sara, grew up a Juneby. Their marriage is a local dramatic series, one of Eagle's preoccupying events. He is said to be an effective hunter, knowledgeable in the ways of moose and caribou, but of Horace in Eagle about the highest praise one hears is "We sure did have a lot of hopes for Junior."

Odd, then, that he has been elected and reëlected to the Common Council of the city of Eagle. Something deeper than gossip makes a vote. Officially a white oligarch, he is a heavy-set, swarthy man with black curly hair. He may be called Junior, but there is nothing of the child in his appearance. He looks like a Mexican insurrectionist ten years after the coup. He stops by occasionally to share a bit of time, and he comes in now with his beer. His voice is a light one. It sounds like falling sand. "I don't think the people in this town have grasped what is happening," he says.

"What is happening?"

"The native people are coming into their own."

His mother, like Bessie David, was a Crow from Yukon Territory. His grandfather carried mail with dogs on the river —more than three hundred miles round trip to Circle—and lost toes to frostbite, even pieces of his feet. Horace is a Cat skinner. He has made $13.43 an hour when he has gone out to work on the pipeline or at the drilling sites of Doyon. During the king-salmon run when he was young, his family regularly occupied a fish camp, abandoned now.

"I'd like to see everyone acknowledge that it is one town, and get along," he remarks—an earnest, if lonely, wish. "I do care about my town." When he says that, he—uniquely—means all of Eagle, Village and City, white and Indian. He has taken a course in municipal government. He has been a vice-president of the Tanana Chiefs Conference, which is concerned with social welfare in the Doyon region. Even so, he confesses that he feels that the people of the Village do not wholly trust him. ("When Junior goes to the Tanana Chiefs, he is just there for the per diem and the trip," Michael has said to me.) "I'd like to see this Eagle become a stable town," Junior continues. "Not a modern city, with paved streets, but a growing town. I'd like to be able to live here and support my family without leaving. With the two communities together, there'd be opportunities for a utility company. I'd like to have lights."

"And running water."

"I don't really care about that. But we need a community center, a gym. The pipeline isn't going to go on and on, and without it people will need work. The town has got to grow, so somebody can support somebody. Right now, the major source of employment is firefighting for the B.L.M., because no one has figured out how to stop lightning. It's a hell of a note when your major part of your working force in your town is waiting for your country to burn up. In 1905, Amundsen came here to send a message to the world. Now you can't even call Tok. Something went haywire."

He falls silent and pensive, then suddenly changes direction. "My father was building the steeple for the church here in the city when he heard that I was born. My father was married in the church. He went through the door there on his last journey. Now the Bible group wants the church. The church belongs to all of us. I couldn't see trading it to a group that made me unwelcome. These people came here as missionaries for their own kind of Christianity, but they have not had much luck, particularly with me. As a group, they have not helped Eagle. They keep the town dry. That is not the way to deal with the problem of alcohol. The only way is through regional school boards, through education—teaching in the classroom what alcohol does to you. If a town votes dry in Alaska, it applies for five miles around. The Village is three miles. The people there are outside the city limits and can't vote here in town. After the last vote, the boozers—we thought the votes got miscounted. We'd have still lost, but it would have looked a little better. I don't believe that everyone who comes here from now on is going to be a religious type. Eagle may become a wet town soon. Then I really think the amount of drinking might go down. You heard what happened today? There was going to be a vote on alcohol in the meeting of the Village Council, but the meeting had to be cancelled, because almost everyone but Michael David was drunk."

Mike Potts, who is white and from Iowa, lives in Eagle Indian Village and is married to Adeline Juneby. He first saw the country in 1971, when he was twenty. His father flew him in here in his Comanche 400. Approaching Eagle in early summer, they looked down on the headwaters terrain of the North Fork of the Fortymile, and Potts, impressed, asked his father to fly low. They crossed spruce forests and clear, dendritic streams—Happy New Year Creek, Eureka Creek, Bear Creek, Comet Creek, Champion Creek, Slate Creek, a great many more without names. All around were mountain summits. Without circling twice, Potts decided that he had at last found his own territory, the piece of the world he had dreamed of, and he laid claim, in his plans and in his imagination, to something over a million acres, over two thousand square miles of land, in which, from the air, he could see no evidence of humanity. In half a dozen years that followed, he would encounter only two people there—and they prospectors, passing through, not to return.

When Potts was seven, he saw a picture in an encyclopedia of a trapper on a trapline, and decided he wanted to be a trapper, too, and live off wild country. He grew up in West Des Moines—in a big, comfortable house on twenty acres of well-kept grounds—and went in summer to Vermilion Lake, in the Quetico-Superior. He became a hunter, a canoer. In his early teens, he put up on his bedroom walls sectional aeronautical charts that covered the north of North America from Labrador to Alaska. "I would sit there for hours and dream, thinking where I was going to go." His heroes by that time were the mountain men of the eighteen-twenties and thirties. He had begun to collect a small library on them—"Bill Sublette, Mountain Man," "The Fur Hunters of the Far West"—and the same books are now in his cabins. He has read them all four times. The day after his high-school commencement, he left West Des Moines for Alaska. He was scarcely seventeen. He had a pickup, given him for graduation. His driver's license was five days old. ("I was one scared kid.") He had six hundred dollars, five hundred of which his sister had paid him for a quarter horse he owned. He had a couple of guns, his books on the mountain men, and little more. ("I was not loaded up with supplies.") He stayed scared, he says, for one day. He spent a year in southeastern Alaska and two in the Wrangells, trapping, looking after horses, working for big-game guides. Eventually, he heard things that attracted him to the upper-Yukon country. His father, a real-estate appraiser, happened to come to Anchorage on a business trip and flew him north to see it.

In Eagle, Potts learned that the last trapper who had worked his utopian drainage had left it ten years before. He quickly made friends in Eagle Indian Village, and—not an easy thing for a white to do—found a place where he could stay there. The Junebys took to him—in a sense, adopted him. Soon he went into the mountains, to prepare for the trapping life. He fixed up a cabin forty miles from Eagle. In the fall, he killed a moose and cached it for the winter. It gave him a sense of plenty. A bear took the moose. He killed rabbits, but there were not enough. As the cold weather came on, he lived for weeks on flour, rice, and beans. He set out traps, but nothing much entered them. Three hundred and fifteen dollars would be his income for the winter. All but one of his dogs died. "It took me time to catch on to the country. It is always difficult when you are learning. I was trying to learn to live like an Indian, and do things better than most. My basic mountain education fell in that year. Bob Stacy, one of the older men in the Village, went out there with me for a while. I owe him a lot. A white man thinks he's great in the woods—and he brings his snow machine. Indians live with the woods instead of fighting it. The white man thinks he has to pack everything in there. An Indian will pack very little and use the woods. The old people in the Village say, 'The driftwood sleeps at night.' They see everything as alive."

Potts saw himself as "in college." He almost took his final exam one night that first winter. Making a trip alone across a high divide, he overestimated the distance he could cover and had to stop far short of a cabin in which he meant to stay. He had shot a wolf and skinned it out. Considering himself to be in no hurry, he used up the light of the day. The sun set at four. The best route to the divide climbed two thousand feet in the two and a half miles before him. Slowly, on snowshoes in the dark, he attacked the steep ascent. His dogs had very little "go power." They were "half sick and half starved." He was hungry, too. He had no food with him and had not eaten all day. He was counting on the cache at the cabin. He decided, finally, that he would have to stay where he was. He had no tent. The temperature was twenty below zero. He saw a thick drift of snow against a clump of stunted spruce. He dug a kind of grave in the snow, almost down to the ground. He lined the bottom with spruce boughs and placed over them the pelt of the wolf. He took his lead dog in with him, leaving the others in harness. Across the top of his excavation he placed his snowshoes, which more than reached from side to side. Over the snowshoes he spread his tarp. He had a few candles. He lighted them, and melted some snow. The water was his dinner.

Potts, who is now established and successful, with cabins all over his trapping estate in addition to his principal home at the edge of the Village, told me that story in response to a question. I asked him if in all the seasons he had spent in that wilderness he had ever been afraid. "Yes—once," he said, and added at the end of the tale, "There was some uncertainty there. But I wasn't frightened to where I didn't have my head."

Potts is a big man, attractive, not wiry but hard. Now that he is twenty-five, his hair is disappearing on the top but hangs in long strings on either side. His eyes, bright and a rich blue, are so alert and dilated that they suggest anxiety until you hear the voice that calmly and confidently follows their gaze. His jacket is of fringed and beaded moosehide. His skin, where it shows, is as tan as his wife's. She is short and roundly soft in form. Her voice is light and slow.

Potts feels a world of difference between him and the whites of the river. While they are his good friends, his regard for them does not always stop shy of contempt. He will eat their boiled wolf and listen to their stories, but he is of the mountains and they are of the river, and "to get things to their cabin all they have to do is float them down." He continues, "In this day and age, few people would make the effort to go out where I go, to the North Fork. It is mountainous country. It isn't the Yukon, where you've got snow machines and a lot of people using the route. The mountain country is a lot tougher—and just myself breaking the trail. Long ago, when more people were out there in the mountains, it was a different type of man. There was no welfare and Social Security type stuff then. Nowadays, even on the river, people give up. They go hungry for a day and they quit. If it looks too hard, they can give it up and try something else: be a bum, like a lot of these people in Eagle."

Dick Cook, acknowledged high swami of the river people, does not share Potts' view of Potts. "He feels that he is living in the bush," Cook says. "But really he is living in town. All he has out there in the mountains is a few traps, and airdrop supplies." Cook is eating his breakfast, which begins with slices of moose sausage in bear casing, set in a bed of fried rice, prepared and served to him by Donna Kneeland. He sits in the larger of two chairs in his cabin, vaguely fifty miles into the wild from Eagle, and points out that we are as remote as we would be if the cabin were on Potts' trapline. We are nearly six miles from the Yukon as well.

The chairs are side by side, like thrones, against a windowless wall. I sat in Dick's chair once, and Donna warned me off it. Now I am in the other. With her plate in her lap, Donna is on the floor before us. Outside where Donna saws wood is a nine-pound maul, which she uses to split green spruce for her sheepherder's stove. In its tiny oven she bakes bread and pies.

"In this country, two people are necessary for each other," she says. "There is a purpose in what I do here. When Dick comes home, I have fixed his food."

"Out here, Donna is needed. Women in town are useless," says Cook.

"Women's lib, that's not me. Women's lib is women being like men. They are barking up the wrong tree. I'm helping Dick, not doing these things for the sake of being like a man. I can't be like a man. I couldn't haul a soaked moosehide out of the river. It's too heavy. But I haul fish. I cut and sew caribou socks. I train the puppies to pull a sled. Are we going to start planting the garden today?"

"I'll decide that this afternoon."

Clamped to a shelf is a hand-cranked grain mill, an import from Latin America, which carries in raised letters its own identification: "Molino Corona—Landers Mora & Cia., Ltda." Many people in the country have mills like this one. A young woman in Eagle said to me that because her mill came from Latin America she found the C.I.A. part "spooky." Making flour by stone friction is tough on the arm, a prizefighter's exercise, Donna's job. She seems amused when I take it over.

On the stove is a tin can full of simmering tea, under a sheet-metal lid that is a piece of a fuel can with a scorched clothespin clipped to it as a handle. Steam meanders upward past a slot window, low and wide, covered with clear soft plastic. The view is of segments of tree trunks. The cabin is on an island in a white rushing stream and stands in a grove of what for this country are specimen spruce. Some approach six feet in girth. For logs and lumber, Cook has selected the trees in a way that preserves the aesthetic of the grove. The cabin logs are not peeled—a practice he looks upon as repellently suburban.

The shanty that Dick and Donna use on stopovers in Eagle is only a little up from squalid. Old mattresses drape its roof, old wolf gristle lies on the cluttered floor, and many tons of junk are in profusion on the ground. Their fish camp down the Yukon can be discouraging, too—a dirty, fetid, lightless cabin astink in aging salmon. These more manifest habitations long ago earned Cook a reputation as a sloven—among people who have never been here. This secluded cabin (his home of homes) is neat and tidy—in fact, trig. For years, he was content with half of it, with ten by ten feet. Now, with Donna, he has added a second room, which is two steps lower—split-level. Down there is the bed, made of rough planks covered with the hide of a moose. They ate their Thanksgiving dinner sitting on the bed—roast of moose he had shot, with a sauce of cranberries she had picked, potatoes and rutabagas they had grown, alfalfa sprouts with vinegar and oil, "pumpkin" pie from Hubbard squash. Visitors sleep on the floor. The dogs, on their chains, are spaced among the spruce. They are usually quiet, but we hear them yelp, howl, or mutter from time to time. Curving overhead near the ridgepole is a curing pair of sled shoes, made from white birch. In very deep cold, steel runners stick to snow as if they were crossing sand. The cabin door is covered with a moosehide. Under the eave and the window, outside, is a workbench equipped with carpenter's tools and construction implements of high quality and extensive choice, all of them neatly, not to say meticulously, arranged. Around the cabin are Swede saws, a whipsaw, steel barrels, snowshoes, sleds, a shovel, a rake, a pickaxe, wedges, a crowbar, a hand sledge, axes, traps, the "Alaska Maytag" (basically a tub and plunger), a wall tent, a construction wheelbarrow with inflated tires, and any number of dozens of other things. We are as far down the Yukon from Eagle as New York City is down the Hudson from West Point, and the largest vehicle that can carry things the six miles up this tributary stream is a canoe. Dick means to bring a full-size cookstove soon, and an antique Singer sewing machine that belonged to his grandmother in Ohio. He says that half the work he has done, over the years, has been "hauling things in."

An amazing percentage of the cargo stands on the cabin shelves. Books everywhere. Books on carpentry, blacksmithing, metalcraft, guns, leather, taxidermy, trapping, woodcraft. "American Indian Medicine." "The Sacred Mushroom and the Cross." "A Room of One's Own." "A Field Guide to Animal

Tracks." "The Harvard Brief Dictionary of Music." "Desert Solitaire."

I tell him I like that one very much.

"You have a right to your opinion. The author's mistake is that he tries to express the meaning of nature. When you are writing about nature, you are writing about God, and it cannot be put into words."

"Shooter's Bible." "The Holy Bible."

"Meat killed first three days after full moon said to keep better," says a note neatly written on a wall calendar. "Harvest roots and fruit in third to fourth quarter. Mushrooms best on full moon."

When Dick and Donna are away, the cabin door is always left standing wide open. Blankets are tacked across the windows. Breakable objects are put under the floorboards, in a small cellar. Roughly half the times they are gone, they return to evidence of the presence of bears. Donna picks up a can of Crisco that a bear examined on a recent visit. As the bear held the Crisco and studied the label, a claw punched through the side of the can. The hole is of the diameter that would be made by a .45-calibre bullet. "When you live with nature, you have to share with nature, whether you like it or not," says Cook. "The cabin is bear bait. Bears know when we're not here, because the dogs are gone. The damage bears do is part of living here." Since breaking and entering is their most expensive habit, the cost is lowered by masking the windows and opening the door, suggesting to a bear the best way in and out, so the bear will not demolish the cabin.

Bears are on my mind today, because tomorrow I have to walk out of here alone and I hope for no encounters on the way. I have arranged with Sarge Waller to come down the Yukon in his boat and meet me at Cook's fish camp. The six miles from here to there have been travelled enough to create a sporadic trail—segments of beaten thoroughfare that tend to disappear, now into sedge tussocks, now into knee-deep muskeg, now into heavy thickets. As Nessmuk said, "The trail . . . branched off to right and left, grew dimmer and slimmer, degenerated to a deer path, petered out to a squirrel track, ran up a tree, and ended in a knot hole." Getting lost will not be possible, though—not with a wall of hills on the right and the stream on the left and less than a mile of ground between. My apprehension is focussed wholly on bears, of which I am more wary than I was at one time. A while back, I confided this fear, in a general way, to Jim Scott in Eagle. I told him I had heard John Ostrander saying how bears are not long out of their dens these days and are walking around mean and vicious. "Don't listen to these terrorized people," said Scott. "Don't let them spoil your fun, you know what I mean? When you walk out from Cook's cabin, your chances, in effect, of encountering a bear will be roughly equivalent to your chances of encountering Jesus Christ."

Jack Greene strongly counselled me not to go into the woods without a gun, and offered me one of his. I thanked him but refused. Having never hunted, I have almost no knowledge of guns. Arriving here, I came in with Dick and Donna from the fish camp, backpacking, the sled dogs running circles around us in the woods—a noisy, armed safari. Snoopy—brother of Chipper, the lead dog—had a forty-pound pack on his back, too. When Dick put it on him, he at once walked into the Yukon. We had come perhaps three-quarters of a mile when we passed a big mound of scat. "Maybe we'll get a bear!" Donna said. "It can happen anytime." The thought seemed to quicken their appetites. Like a traveller checking his wallet, Cook instinctively felt for his rifle. He had left it at the fish camp. He dropped his pack and returned for the gun. Donna and I sat down by the spoor. "A woman needs a lot of confidence in the man she is living with out here," she said. "I have superconfidence in Dick. When I wanted to go out with a man and live in the bush, I wasn't about to go out with someone from a university. The trouble with some people living out here together is that neither of them knows a whole bunch." When Dick returned and we proceeded, we soon passed another pile of bear scat, fairly new—and, a half mile later, one that was even fresher. Now, on the morning before I leave, every bear story I know keeps running through my mind, every newspaper headline—"HIKERS DRIVE OFF BEAR SUSPECTED IN EARLIER DEATH," "RIFLE OFFERS PROTECTION FROM BEARS"—and every bearchew feature in *Alaska* magazine, with color pictures of discharge day at Anchorage hospitals, people's eyes awry, their faces like five-year-old baseballs. When I told Tom

Scott of my own travels in the Brooks Range, with unarmed but ecologically experienced companions (Sierra Club, Bureau of Outdoor Recreation, National Park Service types), he said, "Pardon my saying so, but those gentlemen are fools. Alaskans are thought of as being gun-happy, and maybe that is what they are, but nearly everyone carries a gun in the woods"—including his father, he went on to say, regardless of Whom he might expect to meet there. And here I am about to walk through the woods the distance merely from Times Square to LaGuardia Airport and I am ionized with anticipation—catastrophic anticipation. I may never resolve my question of bears—the extent to which I exaggerate the danger, the extent of the foolishness of those who go unarmed. The effect of it all, for the moment, is a slight but detectable migration of my internal affections from the sneaker toward the bazooka, from the National Wildlife Federation toward the National Rifle Association—an annoying touch of panic in a bright and blazing day.

I profoundly wish it were winter. The country has seemed more friendly to me then, all the bears staring up at the ceilings of their dens. The landscape is softened, in illusion less rough and severe—the frozen rivers flat and quiet where the waves of rapids had been. Dick goes out on the levelled stream and lays down harnesses on the snow. The sled is packed, the gear lashed under skins. Everything is ready for the dogs. They are barking, roaring, screaming with impatience for the run. One by one, Donna unchains them. Out of the trees they dash toward the sled. Chipper goes first and, standing in front, holds all the harnesses in a good taut line. Abie, Little Girl, Grandma, Ug—the others fast fill in. They jump in their traces, can't wait to go. If they jump too much, they get cuffed. Wait another minute and they'll have everything so twisted we'll be here another hour. Go! The whole team hits at once. The sled, which was at rest a moment before, is moving fast. Destination, Eagle; time, two days.

The bluff above the stream is pastel tan, the sky rich blue. "Great day!"

"The snow could be a little drier!" Cook shouts. "In this god-damned country, no matter what the conditions are you wish you had something else!"

With a bit of time behind them, the dogs steady down. Gradually, Little Girl's tail comes up, begins to wag. She is goldbricking. Richard O. Cook stops his team. He walks up and down the line. "All right, you all know what is happening. You know who I'm after. You all know who I mean. No, not you, Grandma. You're O.K., girl. You are doing your work. You have not yet started to fake. No, not you, Chipper. You, either, Ug." He comes to Little Girl. "*You* know who I mean. *You* know what is going on," he says, and whumps her very hard on both sides of her butt. Dick does not pull back when he hits his dogs. He really belts them. But he is never cruel, he would not gratuitously beat them down. They are all exuberant animals, not a chronic cringer among them, and the full warm context of his relationship with them is something wonderful to see. The sled moves again. Little Girl's tail is low and wagless, and her chest is on the leather.

"Females are temperamental, flighty, not nearly as steady as males," he says. "I have two. If I didn't need them for breeding purposes, I would have none in my team."

Dick has sometimes handed the sled over to me for two and three miles at a time, he and Donna walking far behind. On forest trails, with the ground uneven, the complexity of the guesswork is more than I'd have dreamed. We come to, say, a slight uphill grade. I have been riding, standing on the back of the sled. The dogs, working harder, begin throwing glances back at me. I jump off and run, giving them a hundred-and-fifty-pound bonus. The sled picks up speed in reply. Sooner or later, they stop—spontaneously quit—and rest. Let them rest too long and they'll dig holes in the snow and lie down. I have learned to wait about forty-five seconds, then rattle the sled, and off they go. I don't dare speak to them, because my voice is not Cook's. If I speak, they won't move at all. There are three main choices—to ride, to run behind, or to keep a foot on the sled and push with the other, like a kid propelling a scooter. The incline has to be taken into account, the weight of the sled, the firmness of the trail, the apparent energy of the dogs, the time since they last rested, one's own degree of fatigue. Up and down hill, over frozen lakes—now ride, now half ride, run. Ten below zero seems to be the fulcrum temperature at which the air is just right to keep exertion cool. You're tired.

Ride. Outguess the dogs. Help with one foot. When they're just about to quit, step off and run. When things look promising, get on again, rest, look around at the big white country; its laden spruce on forest trails; its boulevard, the silent Yukon. On a cold, clear aurorean night with the moon and Sirius flooding the ground, the sound of the sled on the dry snow is like the rumbling cars of a long freight, well after the engine has passed. According to Harry David, dogs run faster in moonlight, because they are trying to get away from their shadows.

Now, at Cook and Kneeland's cabin, with the snow off the ground and the bears upon it, I am too abashed to confess my fright, although Cook, I have noticed, is rarely unarmed. Donna works at a muskrat skin. Dick assembles bee frames at his workbench. His hives look like cabinets and were made from the trees above. I examine his .22. "Is it loaded?"

He says, "Every gun here is loaded. A baseball bat is better than an unloaded gun."

And Donna says, "You may not get your meat if you're not ready."

Cook's bees gave him a heavy stinging last week, when he was already suffering from abscesses around his teeth. So, for the first time in twelve years, he prescribed for himself a course of penicillin. His first-aid supply also includes ammonia inhalers, a thermometer, tape, gauze, a scalpel, hemostats, sutures, Empirin Compound with Codeine No. 4, Darvon, paregoric, Pontocaine, and morphine.

One knee of his trousers has ripped out, possibly for the hundredth time. His long johns poke through. "We'd better learn to Indian tan or we're not going to have any clothes."

"I didn't even know how to split wood when I came out here," Donna says. "In this country, you can't afford the luxury of sitting around waiting for a man to cut firewood, of not being able to do it yourself. Someday he may be late."

"Someday he may not come back," Dick reminds her.

"I know. I think that every time you go out."

Donna hangs up some skins for airing—moose, caribou, two bearskins. One bear was shot by a stream near here, the other down at the fish camp. She hangs up the pelt of a wolverine. "The wolverine is the most verbally abused animal in the country," Dick says as he works on his bee frames. "And unjustly so. It's one of the finest animals out here. People say a wolverine is 'ornery,' 'mean,' 'vicious,' 'worthless.' They say it can't live with another wolverine. No animal is considered lower. My experience is entirely different. The wolverine is powerful. It hunts with its mate. If one is injured, the other will stick by it. Wolves are affectionate, too. They are really beautiful animals. I have come to know and love them. This year, I have a mating pair on my line. Two years ago, I had a whole pack. The nonbreeders pack up, so they won't get in the way of the sex game. Around the first of March, twenty-five of them went right by the cabin here. Wolves are easy to shoot in mating season. They're in love, I guess. They run in pairs. They don't pay attention to what they're doing. Indians call animals their brothers. You soon realize here that your life is no more important than the animals'. Animals give up their lives, and you will, too. You can't have life without death."

Through apertures in the tall spruce I can see far down the stream course, and even to the low hills on the opposite side of the Yukon. They are blue with distance. I wish I could jump that distance. It is the whole of the walk out of here, and then some. The hills appear to be on the outskirts of Mexico City.

Toward 6 P.M., Donna serves creamed squaw candy (smoked salmon) on whole-wheat biscuits. Resuming his work, Dick soon discovers that he is running out of foundations—the sheets of wax on which bees build their combs. He must have more foundations, he says, and the nearest supply is in Eagle.

"Come with me and Sarge tomorrow!" I tell him, the idea striking like sunlight. I can already see him on the trail before me, his rifle gently bobbing on its sling. Cook begins to think out loud. He must have the foundations. He must also plant his garden. He cannot go to Eagle and leave behind him an unplanted garden. This near the Arctic Circle, the margins of germination, growth, and harvest are extremely narrow. Even a couple of days can make a fatal difference. He and Donna live, in significant measure, on their crops. On the other hand, the bees have come all the way from Texas and are not easily replaced. He needs the honey. Possibly, enough of the more critical seeds and plants could be put into the soil tonight, and even early tomorrow morning, to free him to go with me and

Sarge. "I want to do that if I possibly can," he says, and my heart soars like a hawk. "But we will have to work like bastards planting the garden tonight."

Cook's approach to high-latitude agriculture is detailed and scientific. His garden is twenty-five hundred square feet, and he has planned it to the half inch. He carries a thick notebook. The notes reflect research on the chances and characteristics of many hundreds of varieties of berries, vegetables, and flowers. A Norman monk would not have styled a neater arrangement. Asters, pansies, cress, nasturtiums, burdock, dill, sage, cabbage, savory. Some are this year's experiments, some are tried and sure. The soil is black silt. Oriental poppies, beets, marigolds, grass, broccoli, endive, kale. Strawberries. Four kinds of peas. Potatoes. Lettuce. Cook is a one-man experiment station. Instead of hunting him down and trying to kick him out of here, the federal government should come and farm his genius. Subsidize him. Not that he would accept. Parsnips, cabbage, parsley, beans, onions, horseradish, Jerusalem artichokes, corn, clover, alfalfa, rhubarb. The evening is extremely feverish. The garden is close by the rushing stream, above a steep and mucky bank. I scramble up and down filling buckets with water. A thousand gallons may do. Sunflowers, calendula, radishes, rutabaga, shallots, turnips, tomatoes. Between buckets, I shovel compost, most of which is malamute-Siberian mongrel turd. Cucumbers. There is a small plastic-covered greenhouse, built by Donna, near the cabin. Cucumbers, tomatoes, and peppers are greenhouse crops in Alaska, as is Hubbard squash. Going away for a few days recently, Donna hid flats of green shoots in the cellar, so bears would not knock them over. Mice ate the young tomato plants and most of the Hubbard squash—next winter's "pumpkin" pies. Ermine, frequently, will inhabit the cabin like mice. Cook once had a pet weasel named Harriet that used to run on his table and knock off dishes and look at him with a weaselly smile. Harriet accidentally died in one of his traps.

Donna and I plant together, sliding opposite down the rows. We must slow up and be careful, or Cook, with his notebook, will find us at fault. Donna, in her generosity, seems as sensitive to my goals as to his, to feel my desire to get the seeds into the earth. Turnips form a four-inch grid. Radishes next. Beets.

There is a delaying search through the packet box for the right succession of varietal carrots. Cook advances to the new strawberry bed, at the far end of the garden. Donna and I talk. She mentions her honeymoon. When she married Bill Kneeland, an architect in Fairbanks, they went off to a cabin in the bush near Livengood that had been given her as a present. Her employer soon flew in after them. He said he was desperate, she had to come away and work. He ran an air-charter service in Fairbanks, and he needed her as a stewardess on a big, important job. What could she do, she wonders, giving a shrug, dropping carrot seeds into the ground. Leaving Kneeland in the cabin, she flew off with her boss.

After the honeymoon, she and the architect moved into a big house in Fairbanks, where she "was supposed to look pretty." She had nothing else to do. If she fulfilled the requirement by nature, she did not by predisposition. "That life was just not my style. I like it more here. It's more worthwhile. The satisfaction is in making your own living, as opposed to making money and buying your living—to have the garden all planted and a year's supply of salmon hanging on the racks. I get a lot of pleasure, too, out of having a nice piece of skin. When I tan it right, I feel good. I have sure learned a lot, stumbling around. In my first year, I broke two plates and several cups. I wouldn't do that now. I have a long way to go, though. I'm still not comfortable in boats."

To get over to their cabin when we arrived, we used Dick's canoe, which he had left in the mainland woods. First, we lined it up the shelf ice to a point opposite the island, where we would try to angle down the heavy rapids and get a purchase on the island side. The dogs, meanwhile, jumped in and swam. One was a seven-month-old pup, swimming a current for the first time in her life. The choppy torrent was sparkling with sun, and her head was hard to follow. She tried to swim straight upstream, and the river—thirty-three degrees—kept moving her backward. At best, she just held even. I thought she was going to die. Finally, a bit at a time, she ferried on the current, moved sidewise, and, after a very long baptismal swim, went shaking onto the bank. Now, in the canoe, we human beings shoved into the rapid. Dick had a pole and wanted no help. We bucked on into the haystacks. "That pup was really working," I said to Donna. "Quiet!" she replied. Her hands were wrapped around the center thwart, the knuckles white.

"I do worry a lot," Donna admits. "I worry about Dick. I worry about him and the river. I worry a whole hell of a lot when he is gone for weeks. I try to work on new skills. I'm learning to work with wood. I worked two months on a small wooden car for my son." The axles were of birch, the wheels of red alder, bound to the chassis with rawhide. The wheels had spokes of spruce. The body was cottonwood. The bumper was moose bone. The surface was finished with beeswax. Edward, Donna's son, is two. He lives in Oklahoma. His stepmother could not stand Alaska. Donna wrapped the finished car with extraordinary care and mailed it to Edward from Eagle, wondering to what extent he might sense that it had not come from a store.

It is 11 P.M. We have one section planted—roughly half a dozen to go. The strawberry bed is under way, and I help Dick there. It is his notion that strawberries in a depressed bed can survive a penarctic winter. So this bed will be six inches deep. A lot more than six inches has to be shovelled up and lugged away, though, because he has tons of compost for the bed.

By midnight, with half the excavation done, Dick straightens up and says he is ready to quit. He doubts he'll finish in the morning. So why not quit now? He enters a debate—with himself—aloud. Vegetables versus bees. Participation by others is not invited. He flings pros into the air like skeet, and one by one he shatters them with cons. He finally announces that he is not going to leave in the morning.

He has at least given me an evening off from my imagination. We go inside for a late dessert—cranberry shortcake with milk and sugar—and I pick at it while he reviews the sterner facts of nature. "In New York," he says, "people separate the concepts of life and death. In this country, their whole view of life and death would change. The woods are composed of who's killing whom. Life is forever building from death. Life and death are not a duality."

"These concepts aren't earthshaking," says Donna. "It's just that you can see it all here."

"You look at this country, it hits you in the face," Dick continues.

"What hits you in the face?"

"That life and death are not a duality. They're just simply here—life, death—in the all-pervading mesh that holds things together. Less than five minutes after a wolf stops chasing a moose, the moose is browsing. The wolf chases the moose again. Stops. Five minutes later, the moose is browsing. The moose does not go on thinking—worrying—about the wolf. Death is as much a part of life as breathing. People in cities seem to want life and death to remain at a standstill. Most people who are against killing are horribly afraid to die. They seem to think you can have life without death, and if so they have withdrawn from life. They seem to think the animals up here are smelling flowers. They use the word 'ecology' for everything but what it means. It means who's eating whom, and when."

I ask him what, if anything, makes him afraid.

"Uncontrolled fear and deep respect are two different things," he answers. "In one sense, there is nothing out here for me to fear. I'm going to die someday. I'll be food for somebody else. There are a lot of things up here that can kill you. You've got to have a healthy respect for the country."

I am supposed to meet Sarge at two in the afternoon. At ten-thirty in the morning, I ask Dick for a ride off the island. It took us four and a half hours to get up here, but I am sure I can get back in three, and I want some extra time in case I go astray. He poles me to shore. I jump out, thank him, and go up the bank. I go on up a rise, circle a swamp on a contour, and drop down among cottonwoods near the stream. I made notes coming in. "Go through sphagnum boggy open area after point of rock, hills to left, then into woods half a mile, then a quarter mile of tussocks, then by stream half a mile over gravel dry slough, then get up on bank and into willow." I attempt to follow this in reverse, and see nothing whatsoever that is mentioned in the notes. I am moving right along, though, finding here and there a bit of travelled path, here and there a sight of the stream. Animals use the same routes people do, especially where the way is narrow. The way is so narrow at times that the willow trunks simultaneously rub both ends of the rolled pad on the top of my pack.

Like an explosion in my face, a grouse starts up, two feet away, whirring. I break out in muskeg, back to heavy woods. I have a metal cup. I tap on it with a spoon. I pass bear scat, old and familiar. Tap. Now another mound. I have not seen that one before. Tap. Tap. In other words, never surprise a bear. One or two *must* be here somewhere. To make myself known, I deliver lectures to them in a voice designed to clear the hall. "Uncontrolled fear and deep respect are two different things," I explain to them. "You've got to have a healthy respect for what comes through the country."

An hour goes by, and more—fast-moving. I lose my way now, in dense alder. A path was clear before, but it is suddenly gone. With a couple of taps on the cup, I stand and wonder what to do. I go back, or what I think is back, but have lost where I have been. The brush is so dense I can't see the hills. I try moving laterally, toward and away from what I guess to be the direction of the stream. Now for some minutes I slowly walk in a rectangle, breaking branches to mark it, then build a larger one on that, and, while building a third one, come to beaten trail. In it is a mound of spoor. I recognize it as if it were a friend. It was the nearest defecation to the Yukon. Tap.

The trees finally end. I am pleased to see the big river. I make a bench of driftwood, eat cashews and apricots, and wait for Sarge. The walk took a little less than two hours. I don't feel elevated by that journey, nor am I shy to describe it—just happy that it is complete. I scarcely think I was crazy to do it, and I don't think I was crazy to fear it. Risk was low, but there was something to fear. Still, I am left awry. I embrace this wild country. But how can I be of it, how can I move within it? I can't accept anymore the rationale of the few who go unarmed —yet I am equally loath to use guns. If bears were no longer in the country, I would not have come. I am here, in a sense, because they survive. So I am sorry—truly rueful and perplexed —that without a means of killing them I cannot feel at ease. A punctual speck appears on the river. Staff Sergeant James Waller, United States Marine Corps, Retired. Tap.

I have been hired as scribe to Mike Potts. My ancestors in Scotland were scribes to the likes of Potts, so I feel an atavistic rightness in accepting the position. I won't take pay. He feeds me instead—a meal here and there, a little bread and moose. I enjoy Potts. Like Dick Cook, he has a certain picture of himself and he paints it every day—another daub, another skill, becoming more and more of what he once only dreamed. With John Gaudio, he now wishes to offer two-week dog-team trips to anyone willing to travel this far and pay him enough, and he needs, in effect, a brochure. He is a skillful editor. "Verbal" is not the word that Potts first brings to mind, but he senses how language might be cut to fit him. Taking hold of the text, he roughs it up. "Day 10: Cross over the divide into the Seventymile River drainage and camp at the headwaters of Mogul Creek (tent)."

The stipend on Potts' table tonight was perhaps more than I had bargained for. What we consumed, in the main, was fresh shoulder of grizzly—giving a new, unexpected, and grimly ironic turn to my evolving approach to this creature. Potts and Gaudio took a canoe down the Fortymile a few days ago. The Fortymile goes into the Yukon thirty miles above Eagle, in Canada. Heading back from there, they got into their sleeping bags in the canoe and drifted through the night. One woke the other when he saw the bear. It was on the right bank and close to the water. The canoe moved silently upon it. The bear was walking upwind, downriver, looking the other way—just on the Canadian side of the border. The two raised their rifles, fired, and knocked it into the United States. Halved at the waist, it has been hanging in Potts' butchery, a few steps from his cabin. The butchery, merely a roof on poles, is also his fish cache, and the shelter for his dog pot—half a fifty-five-gallon drum that sits like a caldron above a fire and is a pot-au-feu for huskies. Fish parts, bear gut, the voluminous udder of a moose —what goes in there is "anything you got," lamb's-quarters, too ("for roughage"). I have once or twice helped him feed the dogs, carrying buckets to their stakes behind the cabin. They scream and leap in frenzy and plunge their noses into the buckets and swallow gobs of viscera at a gulp, then sit down and pass the hours, bored at the ends of their chains. Burgundy is the color of the grizzly's flesh. With the coat gone, its body is an awesome show of muscular anatomy. The torso hangs like an Eisenhower jacket, short in the middle, long in the arms, muscles braided and bulging. The claws and cuffs are still there. A great deal of fat is on the back. The legs, still joined, suggest a middle linebacker, although the thought is flattering to football. The bear was two years old.

"*Shar-cho*," said Adeline Potts, means "big bear," means in her language the brown—the grizzly—bear. "Why don't you cook a bit?" said her husband. "I'm getting hungry." Across the grain, he had sliced a pile of steaks, and she cooked them in their own raging fat. The Potts' log cabin is fourteen feet square, no more, but "big enough, and not too hard to heat." A double bed, of planks, is in a corner, and above it the bunk of Adeline's three-year-old son. There is a small chest of drawers, a small cookstove, a half-drum heat stove, two benches, a table in a corner. Four rifles ride the ridgepole. The logs were cut in forests upstream, and yanked to the Yukon by Oddball and Patches, huskies who fill in as horses. Oddball is Potts' lead dog and is as white as a cue ball. The house in which Potts grew up, in West Des Moines, looks out from big Naugahyde chairs at handsome landscaping through picture windows. On the wall is a painting of snow-capped mountains—a stag in the foreground, its head held high. On the walls of Potts' cabin are posters of chiefs. "Tah-Me-La-Pash-Me. Dull Knife. Cheyenne. 1828–1879." "Oh-Cun-Ga-Che. Little Wolf. Cheyenne. 1820–1904." Adeline would not eat the bear. She cooked, in supplement, a platter of moose. She will eat lynx, she said, which is "just like turkey," and wolf, which recalls canned beef. But not this, never this meat. There might be taste but there was terror in the bear. Mike ate happily and hugely, fat and lean. "This is a fat-starved country," he said. "The Lower Forty-eight has to have cottage cheese, skim milk, and so on, because they have too much fat. The people there are fat. Up here, this is a fat-starved country, and you take fat when you can get it. I got five pounds of lard from this bear." The moose was tough. I ate little of it. The grizzly was tender with youth and from a winter in the den. More flavorful than any wild meat I have eaten, it expanded my life list—muskrat, weasel, deer, moose, musk-ox, Dall sheep, whale, lion, coach whip, rattlesnake . . . grizzly. And now a difference overcame me with regard to bears. In strange communion, I had chewed the flag, consumed the symbol of the total wild, and, from that meal forward, if a bear should ever wish to reciprocate, it would only be what I deserve.

Potts makes two thousand dollars in a winter's trapping. He has worked on the pipeline three weeks for the same. He prefers trapping. For $11.27 an hour, he once operated a chain saw that helped to clear the pipeline's right-of-way. When he goes out into the mountains, he is often accompanied by Michael David, who now runs lines in adjacent terrain. In the eyes of some people in the Village, including older ones, such endeavors in the wild are retrogressive. Adeline's father, Willie Juneby, is just amused. "My dad thinks we're crazy sometimes." The Hungwitchin have historically been nervous about certain high ground in the area where Potts goes to trap. They call it the Devil's Chair, and fear for Adeline if she is there. Septembers, Potts puts out nets for the running chum salmon. He dries them and packs them, and eventually has a chartered plane drop hundreds of pounds of fish in the mountains, where he caches them for his dogs in winter. The plane, out of Tok and costing eighty dollars a trip, also drops flour, salt, sugar, matches, candles, tea, coffee, tobacco, milk, baking powder, rice, Mapleine, jello, and canned goods in heavy double bags. Potts does not otherwise seek assistance. With sled and gear, moving up and over his mountains, he has broken trail for as much as nineteen straight hours through deep blown drifts at sixty below.

In spring, he puts out a net for pike and grayling, in an eddy up the Yukon where schools collect. His whole family gets into his canoe—a lovely eighteen-foot Chestnut—and goes up to discover the daily catch. Oddball pulls the canoe. He stands in harness on the edge of the river, and a long rope runs from the middle of his back over water to the bow quarter thwart. Potts speaks. Oddball advances. The canoe—carrying, say, five hundred pounds—begins to slide upstream. Steering with a paddle, Potts keeps the bow a few degrees off the grain of the current, maintaining tension on the rope. The mighty Yukon drives one way, mighty Oddball the other. Oddball defeats the river with ease. He jumps logs, he swims around sweepers—responding to remarks from Potts. The trip is not slow. The canoe fairly rips along. Caught by the gills, pike and grayling are waiting. ("Stay close to Potts," Jim Scott has urged me. "If for nothing else, for the northern pike.")

We cleaned them, late one evening, under a rainbow that vaulted from an orange northerly sky. Sonny Potts, half Eskimo, with wide soft eyes too deep to plumb, watched his adoptive father scaling a fish. "Is that a mother?" he asked. "Does it have beans in it?"

"We'll see," said Potts, a smile flapping the wings of his mustache. He slit the fish forward from the anus, spilling beans.

Sonny's father was Ray Foster, an Eskimo of Noorvik, who left a wife and many children to marry Adeline, and who now lives with the widow of Tony Paul. Potts was checking I.D.s and stopping fights as a temporary bouncer in a bar in Fairbanks when Adeline happened in, divorced and depressed. Mike talked her away from her troubles and the bar, and back to Eagle Indian Village. He is said to have stabilized her life. When he is in the Village, she is comforted and easy. He causes her to feel at home. She is not a little bitter. Of the whites of Eagle she has not much good to say. "They just want to cut us down. They gossip behind our backs. They feel superior. They give false grins." She is the first woman who has ever served on the Eagle Village Council. She has tacked a "Thanksgiving Prayer" to the rafters of her cabin. "Dear Lord, we thank You for poverty, starvation, infant death, a 44-year lifespan, diseases like smallpox, tuberculosis, diphtheria, and v.d. We thank You for alcoholism and suicide. . . ." She and Potts feel as strongly as Michael David about the white bootleggers of Eagle. They once attempted to "turn them in." The response in Eagle was an instant story that Mike Potts was a habitual user of the hardest kinds of drugs. "The truth is," he says, "I've never even bought a lid of grass."

He is subject to worse gossip than that, as are the three or four other whites who live in the Village and are married to Indians. The essence of what is said is that in marrying into the tribe they knew what they wanted, and that was franchise. With the Bureau of Land Management chasing people away from all parts of the federal domain, the choices for the arriving settler, for the would-be modern pioneer, are to live in trespass in defiance of the government, to make an arrangement with the Indians, or to fold one's tent and try to rent in Eagle. The Hungwitchin are reluctant to enter into most arrangements. Marriage is one they have to accept.

"You get the husky-dusky maiden, you see, and then you spin off the benefits from the native claims—the Village land selections, the corporate profit-sharing, the direct payments coming down from the Alaska Native Fund."

"We call them land-claim bridegrooms."

"They are romantics, too, remember. Back to Mother Indian. They love sleeping in dry caribou skin and eating jerky."

Mike Potts appears to be only mildly disgusted by all this. He came into the country for what is here; others have come for what is not. While he has been turning into a seasoned performer—relaxed in the pleasure of his chosen life—these others have been turning into hecklers. He shrugs them off and hits the trail. He is teaching his young brother-in-law Benny Juneby the skills of the woods, including the handling of dogs. (There are six dog teams in the Village, of which three belong to whites.) He divides his game with the Village. He has often shot a moose and ended up with the least of it. He is good at getting meat. Once, in the mountains, he shot three moose in a day. Two wolves were on the first moose, about to pull it down. Everywhere he looked he saw wolves, like shadows flying through the trees. When he fired, the wolves vanished. The moose staggered into the North Fork of the Fortymile. Potts was downstream, and the current delivered the meat. In the same area, a grizzly chased Oddball not long ago and was within ten feet of destroying him when Potts fired true enough to stop the chase. There is game, at times, much closer to the Village. The long tall bluff across the Yukon is a natural fence, and unfortunate is the animal that walks beside it. There is no good direction for escape. A black bear once came out of the woods between Potts' cabin and the Village school, went down to the river, and swam across. Michael David, Potts, and Tony Paul crossed the river in Tony's boat with a .44 handgun and a .30–'06. They were waiting onshore under the bluff when the bear came out of the water. Grizzlies have died the same way, and moose, and caribou. Caribou have been low in the country, have been all but gone in recent years, and Potts is restless to find them. He talks more and more of the Porcupine drainage, a hundred miles north, where the herds in the mountains move like rivers, thirty miles long.

"Potts' only problem is that he's white. He has difficulty coping with that. He fancies himself a male Sacajawea. He's not looking for monetary gain."

"He brings a lot more meat into that Village than he eats."

"He is from Des Moines, Iowa, and he keeps the Village Indian."

Now alone in mountains nearly a hundred miles west of Eagle and at least thirty from the nearest human being, I am puzzled by the hour of the day. I have no idea what it is. There has been no dark of night or visible sun. I don't wear a watch. I am like that Frenchman deep in the caves who hadn't a notion of the hour and slept and ate only according to need. I wonder: Could I have prepared and eaten three full meals in only two hours? In twelve? Fifteen? If I could see the sun, the sun would not help. I have neither a map nor a compass with which to assess its position, and now, at the summer solstice, it rides so low above the mountain ridges and dips so briefly behind them that 4 A.M. looks much like nine and noon. All of that is academic anyway. There is a leaden overcast, and the wind is driving a light, cold rain. Tracks are everywhere—wolf, grizzly, caribou. The mountainsides in surrounding view—sixteen doming tundra balds—are green and white, holding the winter and the summer in quilted fields of snow. In this remote landscape, as wild as any in the country—where not so much as a cabin stands in half a million acres around—my only companions are a backhoe and a bulldozer.

The nearest tree is a mile away. In fact, there is just one small colony of spruce in this otherwise treeless high terrain. The bowl the mountains form is a circumvallate world of what appear to be upsweeping lawns, and in fifteen or twenty square miles I can see—or, at least, I imagine I am capable of seeing—almost anything that moves. With my monocular I look around, scan the middle ground, glass the hills. "Schizomotive" is the word for this situation. I regularly check the landscape in hopes of seeing what I am reassuring myself is not there. Moving around from place to place, stopping to use the monocular, I am like a watchman with a Detex key. I would give a lot to see caribou, and more to see a wolf. I am content with the bears I have seen, and prefer that they keep their distance—notwithstanding this big fella on my shoulder, a Winchester .308.

At my request, Ed and Stanley Gelvin flew off and left me here in late afternoon, close to the confluence of two brooks in their gold-claims valley. They had things to do at home. They said they would return soon after eight o'clock this morning. (I am assuming this is morning.) I began listening for them while I was making breakfast. I have recently finished lunch. Since Stanley and his father are as punctual as they are industrious—and are never unmindful of the high investment and short season here at the claims—I have about concluded that I ate breakfast in the night in the belief that it was morning and have since had lunch for breakfast; they should be here anytime.

They have been working twelve hours a day. When they chose the site for the airstrip, the longest and naturally flattest place was across meanders of a stream. With the D9, Stanley set the stream to one side, gave it a straight new bed, and spread its gravels beside it for the runway. I have since caught many grayling in the new version of the stream, which has fine pools and flows clear. Removing the tundra from a wide swath of ancient channels, Stanley dozed more gravel onto the strip, then packed it down—seventeen hundred feet. Welding steel—using twelve-foot H-beams and angle irons—Ed created something that weighed a couple of tons and resembled a carpenter's plane. He dragged that up and down with the backhoe, making the runway smooth. There was not a lot I could do. I threw small boulders off the field. When it was complete, the Cessna 206, their single-engine workhorse aircraft, could land. It can carry, among other things, three or four fifty-five-gallon drums full of diesel fuel. Because the airstrip consists of stream-bed gravels, it contains, in all likelihood, gold. Long-range plans include another airstrip, to be made from tailings. Then this first airstrip can be run through the sluice box and deposited in a bank. There is a poplin wind sock, flying east. Ed sewed it at home. Its color is camouflage green.

Strewn around the wanigan, which is in effect a plywood tent, are tools, Blazo cans, propane tanks, the welding equipment, the generator—items no more congruous in this wilderness than the backhoe or the D9. A piece at a time, Ed and Stanley have disassembled the rig that Stanley hauled up here on his April journey over alpine snow and ice. The sled he dragged has become the slick plate—a couple of hundred square feet of half-inch-thick sheet steel, at one end of which Ed has fashioned and welded a steel mouthpiece to guide gravel into the sluice box. To carry water to the plate and box, he welded nine fifty-five-gallon drums end to end, forming a thirty-foot pipe. He used welding rods acquired from the Trans-Alaska Pipeline. Using a circular drum top, he made a valve for the pipe, and he fitted it with a handle that can regulate the flow of water. After assembling the steel sluice box, which is thirty-six feet long and four feet wide, he began to fill it with "riffles." Riffles vary considerably, and are the signature of the miner. Their general purpose is to create in the box a confined simulacrum of stream rapids, to intrude upon the flow of water so that it will leap, dive, tumble in souse holes, reverse itself in mid-torrent, rage forward, stack up, back up, and eddy out—just what happens when God welds a river. Prospectors in search of gold would try the deep, quiet pockets of rapids. In like manner, gold will collect in the deep, quiet pockets of the box. Most riffles are lengths of steel set perpendicular to the flow and only a few inches apart, ladderlike. They are set at various angles and spacings according to the theories of the miner. Some miners make riffles with wooden poles, wooden blocks, boulders. They even use slices of rubber tires. After Ed and Stanley had lowered into place all of their seventy calculated riffles—mostly three-sixteenths-inch angle irons, with a channel iron every four feet—they were ready at last to set up their mine.

They had decided to make the first cut half a mile below the airstrip, dozing wholly into the left side of the valley. "Them old-timers in the old days, they covered this country more thoroughly than you can imagine," Ed explained. "Up here, they worked only the left limit." Back from a hundred and fifty feet of stream (the basic dimension of the cut), Stanley scraped off the tundra in a swath that went out to "the width of pay"—to the margin, near the rising slope of the hillside, where a pan of gravel would no longer show colors of gold. His father worked with the pan, which was of a type called a grizzly, fitted with screens of varied mesh to simplify the job. Crouching in pools, he swirled sands and gravels until the pan smiled. In places it smiled wanly, in places not at all. He had found a few rough nuggets, he said. Not worn flat, they could not have travelled far. Adducing such evidence, he hoped to mine coarse gold.

The size of the cut was unusually large, but so was the size of the D9 Cat, with its fourteen feet of blade. For the sluicing operation, a reservoir was needed. Stanley built one, damming and diking the stream so that the reservoir stood beside the cut. He embedded the water pipe in the wall of the reservoir. It poked through to the low end of the cut. The idea was to position the slick plate under the pipe (with the sluice box adjoining), then doze heaps of placer onto the plate and turn on the water. First, however, there was a problem of drainage. The valley's natural gradient was slight, and the stream bed itself would not have been adequate. So Stanley dug a deep ditch and ran it out to contour, some four hundred feet downstream. There was a minor incident when he returned to the cut. He crushed his father's grizzly.

The sluice box should have a slope of exactly ten degrees. The D9—larger than most cabins, lurching over mounds of its own rubble—seemed an unlikely instrument for so precise a job. Stanley—in his high seat, hands and feet in rapid movement among the multiple controls—suggested a virtuoso on a pipe organ even more than a skinner on a Cat. Gradually, a smooth ramp appeared. He had wired a carpenter's level to the deck of the machine and had shimmed one end of it so the bubble would center when the Cat was on a slope of ten degrees. As he finished, and drove his fifty-five tons of yellow iron up the ramp, from bottom to top the bubble scarcely moved. Clanking off to fetch the sluice box, he hitched it to the rear of the big bulldozer, and pushed it backward down the narrow top of the dike. The sluice box weighs a couple of tons. He gently eased it down the ramp. Then he went and got the slick plate, and backed that down the top of the dike, too. He was grouchy—had been crabby all through the day—because he had no snoose. He was trying to quit, and had been six days without a dip of Copenhagen. Repeatedly, he shook his head in apparent dismay and made despairing remarks about the way things were going—heard mainly by the roaring Cat. The mouthpiece on the slick plate is nearly four feet wide and was designed to fit into the sluice box with very little clearance. Stanley backed the slick plate down the ramp. It weighs three tons, and he moved it steadily—without hesitation, without a pause for adjustment (just ran it downhill backward)—until the mouthpiece entered the box. It had not so much as brushed either side. The clearance was five-quarters of an inch one way and three-eighths of an inch the other. The day's work finished, father and son flew home.

Still no sign of them. The light rain is long since gone and the clouds are breaking. Even so, there is no sound, no distant approaching drone. Perhaps I did not sleep at all. Perhaps I just lay down for an illusory minute, then got up and sprinkled salt in the iron pan for toast. Collecting the only available firewood—the dead stems of dwarf willows, thinner than straws—I make a little blaze for warmth. The temperature is under forty. Once more I scan the mountains, where nothing is passing but the day.

I have fished, cooked, thrown rocks off the airstrip. Now I write a letter home. ". . . When the Gelvins departed, I was cleaning some grayling, five in all. I caught one with my fishing rod. The Cat caught the others. When Stanley dammed the river, and diverted it into the pipe, he took it out of its bed for a couple of hundred yards. Pools remained there, like low tide, and as they slowly drained they revealed the graylings' dorsal fins. I walked from pool to pool, trapping the fish with my hands. This pretty little stream is being disassembled in the name of gold. The result of the summer season—of moving forty thousand cubic yards of material through a box, of baring two hundred thousand square feet of bedrock, of scraping off the tundra and stuffing it up a hill, of making a muck-and-gravel hash out of what are now streamside meadows of bluebells and lupine, daisies and Arctic forget-me-nots, yellow poppies, and saxifrage—will be a peanut-butter jar filled with flaky gold. Probably no one will actually use it. Investors will draw it into their world and lock it in an armored cellar, while up here in these untravelled mountains a machine-made moonscape will tell the tale. Am I disgusted? Manifestly not. Not from here, from now, from this perspective. I am too warmly, too subjectively caught up in what the Gelvins are doing. In the ecomilitia, bust me to private. This mine is a cork on the sea. Meanwhile (and, possibly, more seriously), the relationship between this father and son is as attractive as anything I have seen in Alaska—both of them self-reliant beyond the usual reach of the term, the characteristic formed by this country. Whatever they are doing, whether it is mining or something else, they do for themselves what no one else is here to do for them. Their kind is more endangered every year. Balance that against the nick they are making in this land. Only an easygoing extremist would preserve every bit of the country. And extremists alone would exploit it all. Everyone else has to think the matter through—choose a point of tolerance, however much the point might tend to one side. For myself, I am closer to the preserving side—that is, the side that would preserve the Gelvins. To be sure, I would preserve plenty of land as well. My own margin of tolerance would not include some faceless corporation 'responsible' to a hundred thousand stockholders, making a crater you could see from the moon. Nor would it include visiting exploiters—here in the seventies, gone in the eighties—with some pipe and some skyscrapers left behind. But I, as noted, am out of sync with the day. Is it midnight? Is it morning? Is it late afternoon? Where on earth could the Gelvins be?"

The hum of Stanley's Aeronca Champion at last comes into the sky. He goes overhead with the wind, turns, lands, and when he cuts the engine I am under the wing. "I've been wondering what time it is," I tell him.

"What time do you think it is?"

"You said you were coming soon after eight in the morning. I suppose it is eight-fifteen."

Stanley smiles and withdraws his pocket watch. "The aircraft inspector showed up this morning. We didn't know he was coming. The time is three in the afternoon. Not a whole lot left of the day."

At the cut, Stanley shows disappointment with the velocity of the water as it comes through the pipe, falls to the plate, and races on through the box. It lacks power, he says, to move the material at the rate it should be moved. If a guy could expand the intake end of the pipe, where it sticks into the reservoir, the pipe would deliver more water. "Without a funnel effect, only so much will run in there. If a guy could make something like a funnel . . ." What is needed, as is so often the case, for thousands of purposes in Alaska, is a fifty-five-gallon drum. There are several near the wanigan, and Ed goes to get one while Stanley, with the Cat, opens the dam and lowers the reservoir enough to expose the pipe. With his torch, Ed cuts out the top and bottom of the drum and slits it down the side. At one end of the slit he pries the walls of the drum apart, making a V-shaped gap, which he fills in with scraps of steel. Attached —welded to the pipe—the new end flares like the bell of a trumpet, doubling the intake. Funnel effect.

A fifty-five-gallon steel drum is thirty-four and three-quarters inches high and twenty-three inches in diameter, and is sometimes called the Alaska State Flower. Hundreds of them lie around wherever people have settled. I once considered them ugly. They seemed disappointing, somehow, and I wished they would go away. There is a change that affects what one sees here. Just as on a wilderness trip a change occurs after a time and you cross a line into another world, a change occurs with these drums. Gradually, they become tolerable, and then more and more attractive. Eventually, they almost bloom. Fifty-five-gallon drums are used as rain barrels, roof jacks, bathtubs, fish smokers, dog pots, doghouses. They are testing basins for outboard motors. They are the honeypots of biffies, the floats of rafts. A threat has been made to use one as a bomb. Dick Cook, who despises aircraft of all types, told a helicopter pilot he would shoot at him if he ever came near his home. The pilot has warned Cook that if he so much as points a rifle at the chopper the pilot will fill a fifty-five-gallon drum with water and drop it on the roof of Cook's cabin. Fifty-five-gallon drums make heat stoves, cookstoves, flower planters, bearproof caches, wood boxes, well casings, watering troughs, culverts, runway markers, water tanks, solar showers. They are used as rollers for moving cabins, rollers to smooth snow or dirt. Sliced on the diagonal, they are the bodies of wheelbarrows. Scavenged everywhere, they are looked upon as gold.

With the dam resealed and the reservoir again full, Stanley, in the D9, lowers the blade into the cut and moves onto the slick plate a dark, high pyramid of gravel and sand. Ed opens the valve. Water thunders from the pipe, crashes onto the plate, seemingly melts the material, and drives it through the box. The lighter gravels roar along. The boulders bounce like balls. Some are so big they stick, attracting piles of gravel behind them, deflecting curtains of water into the air. Ed, with a rock rake, sends them tumbling on their way. To make the rake, he welded a bent reinforcing rod to a strut from his damaged plane. Stanley shuttles the big Cat back and forth from the top to the bottom of the box, now adding material to the slick plate, now clanking down to the lower end to doze aside the growing heap of tailings. A year in preparation, they are finally mining gold. Stanley is all pessimism, pondering the economics of the Cat. "It's in motion five times as much as it should be," he shouts as he goes by. He likes even less the proximity of the bedrock ("That shallow ground ain't worth a damn"), and he is down on the volume of the stream ("Another two weeks and we won't have enough water").

Ed, on the other hand, is obviously pleased. He grins as he works with his strut. "It's an odd way to make a living," he comments. "Just as it was for the old-timers. In winter, they'd go down in a frozen drift and shovel up gravel in the dark. They'd sluice in the summer, and then head into town with their poke, and some slick would come along and take it away. The same sort of thing happens now—to people coming off the North Slope."

At the end of the day, Stanley scoops a dark concentrate from the box. He puts it in a pan, partly submerges it, and swirls away the sand. Gradually, the pan's bottom begins to sparkle like a river under sun—flashing pinpoints, flickerings of yellow. Counting thirty-eight, thirty-nine, forty flecks of gold.

"Gold is like farming to me," Ed remarks. "One year, you don't have enough water. Another year, the Cat breaks down. You put more money in the ground than you ever take out. But I like the creeks. I like being out here in the country."

Stanley looks up from the pan. He says, "It cost fifty thousand dollars to get to this point. I'm sure glad to see that gold."

The last time I went through the country was in the winter, 1977, and a speakeasy had risen in Eagle. A large building by regional standards, it had blank walls on three sides and, around back, a single window that was the size of a hand mirror. A naked light bulb was outside the window, and, close by, there was a complicated foyer, wherein arrivals were processed through a double set of heavily hardwared doors. Stools and benches, rough spruce floor. A hundred-dollar bill had been inlaid in the bar. The first high school in Eagle's history had also been established, but the two teachers who had been sent to do the job had discovered an unusual P.-T.A., and had already announced their resignations, explaining privately that "picking on people" seemed to be Eagle's "winter sport." I saw a sled being pulled by an Irish setter, another by a mongrel collie, a third by a pedigreed scottie. Daniel Boone's descendant Jack Boone had at last set foot in the wild, taking a daughter down the river in summer and hiking in to Kneeland and Cook's. A geologist, about then, had been killed by a black bear up in Potts' trapping land between Eagle and the Charley River. He was using a magnetometer and could therefore carry no additional metal. A partner heard his distant screams and hurried to help him, but found him dead and partly eaten. Fur prices were up—up, for example, to four hundred and fifty for a top-grade lynx. Sarge Waller went out and got himself a top-grade lynx. A good marten was bringing a hundred and ten dollars. It was something of a trapping-world bonanza. When Jimmy Carter was elected, Horace (Junior) Biederman stepped out of his cabin into the snow with his Remington 12-gauge pump shotgun and blasted three holes in the air. He had been listening to KFAR. He wished there were some way to let the new President know that the Indians of Eagle were for him—all the Hungwitchin, the whole Village, en bloc. The white City, with few exceptions, went the opposite way. Some months earlier, at a community fête, Junior attacked Mike Potts with a club, and was himself subdued by Constable Whitaker, who was wearing a lead-filled glove. Now Junior had circulated a petition to the effect that Eagle did not require and therefore could ill afford a constable, and Whitaker was leaving town. Potts had been belatedly arrested by Alaska Fish and Game for failing to travel a hundred and fifty miles to submit, as the law requires, the skin of the grizzly that came close to killing Oddball. No one knew, for sure, who had turned Potts in. Viola Goggans was gone. Jim Dungan, after an at last successful operation on his leg, was away, working again for G.S.I. Michael David was on the North Slope.

The Hungwitchin had written to the Episcopal Diocese of Alaska asking for a minister, and the church had sent John Four Bear and his wife, Sandi. He is a ruggedly handsome man with a wide, strong build, and is only twenty-eight. He holds his services in the small drafty church in the Village, with its wooden benches and its rusted barrel stove, and he turns it into a cathedral. Danny David, Edward David, Isaac Juneby, Archie Juneby, Benny Juneby, Adeline Potts, Sonny Potts, Sara Biederman read together from the Book of Common Prayer. Firelight shows through a hole in the stove. In a congregation of thirty, perhaps a third are white—a fresh counterbalance for the Eagle Bible Chapel. John Four Bear has some regrets for the Indians of Alaska. He wishes that in their history they had chosen to resist the invader. He wishes they had a more compelling affection for their own culture and would not allow themselves to be bought white. John is a full-blooded Hunkpapa Sioux, who comes from Standing Rock, South Dakota. It is said of him in the Village, "He is the smartest Indian in Eagle, and he has to be a Sioux."

"I did not come here like a white missionary to rescue the heathen from the clutches of the Devil," he told me. "I came here to tell the word of God, and if they don't want to hear it that is up to them. It took some time, but the Village people have at last put a claim on me. They have said, 'This is our preacher.' When they said it a third time, I knew they meant it. I think I can help them some in the city. At least, I can deal with the white man on his own terms—which is not difficult in Eagle."

In a small cabin on the Seventymile River, I had a long talk with Brad Snow—nothing much to do, with time on our hands, but work out the fate of Alaska. He agreed that it is sheer foolishness to approach Alaska in terms of the patterned traditions of the Lower Forty-eight, and that this basic consideration—Alaska seen as a largely different country—should be Square One, should be the beginning of any plan made for Alaska by the federal government. Where this is not the case at present, the government should be urged to go back to Square One. In the society as a whole, there is an elemental need for a frontier outlet, for a pioneer place to go—important even to those who do not go there. People are mentioning outer space as, in this respect, all we have left. All we have left is Alaska, which, on the individual level, and by virtue of its climate, will always screen its own, and will not be overrun. If I were writing the ticket, I would say that anyone at all is free to build a cabin on any federal land in the United States that is at least a hundred miles from the nearest town of ten thousand or more—the sole restriction being that you can't carry in materials for walls or roofs or floors. Brad said he appreciated the thought but that specific numbers and written restrictions—however few or well-intentioned they might be—were anathema to him.

Mike and Adeline Potts were expecting a baby. Jack Boone's neighbor Jack Greene, worrying about the possible collapse of the economy, was investing his savings in gold. The Gelvins' D9 Cat, meanwhile, was collecting snow in the mountains. They planned to bring it out. It had made two cuts, and when the hundreds of tons of gravel had passed through the box the cleanup both times was disappointing. They had hoped for coarse gold, but were getting only fine. Mining money, they were not quite making it. They had no intention of quitting the claims. They would keep them, and bide their time, and watch the price of gold. Meanwhile, taking into account the current price, the cost of equipment and fuel, the amount of water, the quantity of ground to be moved, they folded their mountain show. A helicopter, taking off in Circle, tilted crazily and flew sidewise into Frank Warren's Citabria. The Gelvins—opportunistic—bought it from the insurance company for seven thousand dollars. They were fixing it to sell for fourteen. On an ice-fishing trip, Ed and Ginny, in their own repaired Citabria, were forced down by weather and, in "a squirrelly wind," smashed into a stand of trees. Well over a hundred miles north of home, they camped for three days and nights, wreckbound.

When they did not come back, Frank Warren went out and found them. They meant to salvage that plane, too.

Of the people I had seen coming into the country—particularly the young ones arriving in summer to seek the mountains and the river—the one I remembered best was an immense young man in a blue parka and blue rain pants and a wide-brimmed black hat, who walked up to me, total stranger, and said he had heard I had maps. Sure, I told him, and I took him into my cabin to a topographical stack. His beard was about a foot deep and his eyes were diamond blue. He was from southern California, he said, and he had "overwintered" down in southeastern Alaska—a preliminary and orientational kind of shakedown experience—and now he was ready for the Yukon. No one much remembered him in the winter. Not even John Borg had an idea where he might be. He was just one of the annual dozens who come into town preparing to try the country. He had been to the Eagle General Store, where he bought a standard gold pan and a length of gold nylon rope, which was coiled around his shoulder. He told me he had talked with someone named Cook and found him prickly. He took a close long look at the maps. He was as amiable as he seemed determined, and his manner suggested momentum—suggested that this was his time and his place and, from Doyon, Ltd., to the federal government, whoever didn't like it could step out of the way. Stuck in the band of his big black hat were a tall eagle feather and the dogtooth jaw of a salmon. I asked him where he meant to go.

"Down the river," he said. "I'll be living on the Yukon and getting my skills together."

I wished him heartfelt luck and felt in my heart he would need it. I said my name, and shook his hand, and he said his. He said, "My name is River Wind."

CHRONOLOGY

NOTE ON THE TEXTS

NOTES

INDEX

Chronology

1931 Born John Angus McPhee in Princeton, New Jersey, on March 8. His father, Harry Roemer McPhee, M.D., is a thirty-six-year-old associate professor of health and physical education at the university and the physician for the football team. His mother, Mary Ziegler McPhee, is a thirty-three-year-old former French teacher and the daughter of a Philadelphia publisher. Parents married in Philadelphia in 1921 and moved to Princeton in 1928, after several years in Iowa. McPhee has a six-year-old brother, Roemer, and three-year-old sister, Laura Anne.

1932–47 Grows up in Princeton, where he will live nearly all his life. Attends elementary school a few blocks from home, returning home each day for lunch. At six, spends his first of two summers at a Keewaydin wilderness camp off Cape Cod; is later a regular at Keewaydin in Salisbury, Vermont, returning as a camper for nine more years and for three as a swim instructor and canoe trip leader. Mother takes him to New York City each year for his birthday to see plays; one year, at ten or eleven, she accompanies him at his request to LaGuardia airport, where they watch takeoffs and landings. In November 1941, makes his first appearance in *The New Yorker* in a piece about football, as "the very small boy who runs out of the dressing room and onto the field with the Princeton team." During the Second World War, volunteers as an air spotter, scanning for enemy planes on a local hill and phoning in sightings; brother serves as a naval officer in the Pacific. McPhee attends Princeton High School beginning in 1944. Plays on the basketball and tennis teams—"all I cared about until I finished high school" was sports, he subsequently recalls. Is chosen as chief justice of the school's student court. Works part-time in a university lab: "my job was killing fruit flies after they finished experiments."

1948 Graduates from Princeton High. Later commends his English teacher Olive McKee for her excellent instruction in writing, and particularly in the finer points of structure.

Deferring admission to Princeton University, begins a postgraduate year at Deerfield Academy, a prep school in western Massachusetts, where he encounters a future subject, headmaster Frank Boyden. Writes for the *Deerfield Scroll.* Starts sending pieces to *The New Yorker.*

1949–52 Enters Princeton in the fall of 1949. Studies creative writing with R. P. Blackmur and Randall Jarrell, and majors in English. Plays freshman basketball. Becomes editor of *The Princeton Tiger*, a humor magazine that he helps remake into a general-interest publication somewhat resembling *The New Yorker.* Writes about student events for *The Princeton Alumni Weekly*, and about his famous roommate "Kaz"—Dick Kazmaier, winner of the 1951 Heisman trophy—for *The Nassau Sovereign.* Also publishes poems and short fiction in *The Nassau Lit.* Joins Cottage Club, an undergraduate eating club. Throughout his undergraduate years, commutes to New York once or twice a week to appear as a panelist on the television show *Twenty Questions*, hosted by Bill Slater. (YouTube features an episode with "Johnny McPhee, our teenaged student.")

1953–54 Graduates from Princeton in the class of 1953, with an AB in English literature. In lieu of an academic thesis, he completes a novel, "Skimmer Burns." Enters Magdalene College, Cambridge, in the fall, where he spends a year reading English literature. Joins the Cambridge University basketball team.

1955–56 Meets television producer Robert Montgomery through his brother Roemer, who is now working at the White House. Writes five dramatic scripts for *Robert Montgomery Presents* on NBC. Two of these—both based on short stories by *New Yorker* contributor Robert M. Coates—are finally produced, "In a Foreign City" in October 1955 and "The Man Who Vanished" in February 1956. Works as a corporate writer at W.R. Grace & Co., an industrial chemical firm. Continues to submit ideas and work to *The New Yorker* and receives a blizzard of rejection notes in return.

1957 Marries Pryde Brown, a recent graduate of Sweet Briar College, on March 16; they honeymoon in the Laurentians, and move to an apartment in Manhattan. They will have, in short order, four daughters: Laura McPhee (b. 1958), who becomes a photographer; Sarah McPhee (b. 1960), an art and architectural historian; Jenny McPhee

(b. 1962), a novelist and translator; and Martha McPhee (b. 1965), a novelist.

1958–61 Writes the first of what will be more than 500 stories for *Time*, without a byline and mainly for the "back of the book." His subjects include everything from *The Flintstones* to Beatlemania. Publishes cover stories on Mort Sahl, Alan Jay Lerner and Frederick Lowe, Jean Kerr, Jackie Gleason, Sophia Loren, Joan Baez, Richard Burton, and Barbra Streisand, winning not only the praise of his editors but the freedom, uncommon at *Time*, to report and write independently. His friends at the magazine include Calvin Trillin, John Gregory Dunne, Israel Shenker, Barry Farrell, and Michael Levitas, who would later edit *The New York Times Book Review*. In 1961, publishes a short story, "The Fair of San Gennaro," in *The Transatlantic Review*.

1962–63 Moves back to Princeton with his wife and growing family, commuting into the city. Toward the end of 1962, works on a piece about his experiences playing basketball for Cambridge University. Submits it to *Esquire*, where it is rejected, and then simultaneously to *Sports Illustrated* and to *The New Yorker*. Overjoyed when *The New Yorker* accepts it, he goes to *Sports Illustrated* to retrieve his story, inadvertently causing a scene: "Jack Tibby, who was assistant managing editor or something like that, turned into a cloud of fury when he heard my request. How dared I —a Time, Inc. writer—submit a piece to *The New Yorker*? *Sports Illustrated* might well want it, he added unconvincingly. This was a great breach of ethics and loyalty on my part. He was going to see to it that the episode was fully reported to Henry Luce and everybody else on the 34th floor, not to mention Otto Fuerbringer and the other powers of *Time*. Above all, he was going to see to it that the sale to *The New Yorker* was blocked. At this point, I interrupted him, saying, 'Mr. Tibby, I beg you not to do that.' I told him this was the most important moment of my professional life, that I had been trying to sell something to *The New Yorker* for thirteen years, that everything had failed until now, and I was begging him to hand me that story from the pile on his desk. Suddenly, he was quiet and his rage was gone. He found the story, gave it to me, and I never heard of or from him again." The piece, "Basketball and Beefeaters," appears in *The New Yorker* on March 16, 1963.

1964 Talks with the Princeton basketball player Bill Bradley in June, beginning work on a profile, "A Sense of Where You Are." Later that summer, on vacation from *Time*, visits Bradley's hometown—Crystal City, Missouri—gathering the impressions of those who know him. Finishes the piece in November, writing for *Time*'s show business section by day and about Bradley at night and on weekends. *The New Yorker* accepts the piece in mid-December. Visiting their offices, he meets editor William Shawn, who tells him, "This piece is not just acceptable. It is outstanding," about which he later remarks, "Concerning my work, nothing ever said to me before or since has had a greater effect."

1965 In January, writes a letter of resignation to Otto Fuerbringer, the managing editor of *Time*, saying he had "felt encouraged to experiment" as a writer there but that it was time to try writing longer things. "A Sense of Where You Are" published in *The New Yorker*'s January 23 issue. In September, Farrar, Straus and Giroux publishes the piece, in expanded form, as a book; he remains an FSG author to the present day. Determined to write more for *The New Yorker*, he visits the orange groves of Florida; what starts out as a sketch becomes a full-blown exploration of the history of the fruit and the world of growers, botanists, packers, pickers, and barons. Also starts research at Deerfield Academy for "The Headmaster," a portrait of Frank Boyden and the school.

1966 Becomes a prolific presence at *The New Yorker*, writing unsigned short pieces on all manner of subjects, from a Mensa convention to NBA All Star Oscar Robertson, in addition to his longer articles. The magazine publishes "Fifty-Two People on a Continent," a long fact piece about the M.I.T. Fellows in Africa program, and "The Headmaster." Struggles with his new editor, Robert Bingham, over the manuscript of "Oranges": Bingham initially cuts the piece by some 85 percent and ultimately restores many of these cuts only after five days of hard conversation. (The piece appears in May in two parts, and in extended form, as a book, the following year; Bingham becomes a close friend.) In the spring, summer, and fall, spends about eight months gathering information on the Pine Barrens of New Jersey, often making day trips to this little-visited region, or camping out. During an August trip to Hurricane Island, Maine, scouting a story on Outward Bound, he meets the forager Euell Gibbons. At Shawn's suggestion, he drops the Outward Bound idea—the group reminds Shawn of the Hitler Youth—and decides to take Gibbons as his subject. Finishes "The Pine Barrens" in September and October, writing against a rigorous schedule. In November, heads to Troxelville, Pennsylvania, for a journey down the Susquehanna River and along the Appalachian Trail with Gibbons. (His profile, "A Forager," will appear in 1968.)

1967 Works on "A Roomful of Hovings," a profile of Thomas Hoving, the head of the Metropolitan Museum. Spends the spring and summer in Scotland, England, and Spain with Pryde Brown and their four daughters. During that journey, he does research for a number of pieces that will appear over the next two years, including "The Crofter and the Laird," "Pieces of the Frame," "Josie's Well," "From Birnam Wood to Dunsinane," "Twynam of Wimbledon," and "Templex," a portrait of Temple Fielding, author and publisher of popular travel guides. In October, publishes a short story titled "Eucalyptus Trees" in *Reporter* magazine. "The Pine Barrens" appears in *The New Yorker* in two parts, toward the end of the year.

1968 Conspires with William Shawn, who is ordinarily indifferent to competition, to see to it that "Templex" is published in the January 6 issue, beating out a piece on the same subject in the works at *Life*. In October, begins travel and reporting for "Levels of the Game," a dual portrait of the tennis players Arthur Ashe and Clark Graebner. FSG publishes his first collection of pieces, *A Roomful of Hovings*. He also publishes what will be his last short story, "Ruth, the Sun Is Shining," in *Playboy*.

1969 Completes "Levels of the Game." In the spring, with old friend John Kauffmann, attends the Middle States Wildwater canoeing championships in the mountains of West Virginia. They spontaneously compete in a "non-expert" race, winning third-place medals. (His piece about the event, "Reading the River," appears in *The New Yorker* the next March.) Spends much of the year researching "Encounters with the Archdruid," a profile of the environmentalist David Brower and his confrontations with three ideological nemeses: a mineral engineer, a real estate developer, and a government commissioner who, unlike Brower, favors the damming of rivers. For the reporting, McPhee visits the Glacier Peak Wilderness in the North Cascades; Cumberland Island, Georgia; and the Colorado River in the Grand Canyon. Separates from Pryde Brown, who begins a career as a portrait photographer; they will divorce in 1972.

1970 Publishes "Josie's Well," about whiskey-making, in the January issue of *Holiday*, and "Pieces of the Frame" in *The Atlantic* the same month. His spirit flagging, he spends a lot of time on the telephone with Bingham talking through the challenges of "Encounters with the Archdruid"; reads him the entire manuscript aloud as he completes it, reassured by Bingham's attention and advice. Later that summer, begins research for "The Deltoid Pumpkin Seed," the story of Princeton classmate William Miller and his attempt to build the Aereon 26, an experimental wingless aircraft combining the qualities of an airplane and airship.

1971 From January to July makes road trips for "Travels in Georgia" and "The Deltoid Pumpkin Seed." "Encounters with the Archdruid" is published in three parts in *The New Yorker* beginning in late March and in book form later in the year. "Centre Court," an impressionistic piece about Wimbledon, appears in the June issue of *Playboy*. Spends much of the summer in northern New Hampshire, as he will for the next half dozen years.

1972 Marries Yolanda Whitman in March; she runs a houseplant business. In August starts research for "The Curve of Binding Energy," about nuclear physicist Theodore B. Taylor and the potential hazards of proliferating fissile materials. Also in late summer, reports and writes "The Seach for Marvin Gardens," a comic piece with an ingenious structure about Monopoly enthusiasts. In October, along with Whitman, visits Crystal City and St. Louis, Missouri, where they attend the Harry Truman Day Dinner, with Bill Bradley as master of ceremonies; this is one of Bradley's first political appearances. In the fall, travels widely with Theodore Taylor for "The Curve of Binding Energy."

1973 *The New Yorker* publishes "The Deltoid Pumpkin Seed" in three parts beginning on February 10. Takes six months to write "The Curve of Binding Energy" and publishes it in the magazine in three parts, in November and December;

it will be a finalist for the National Book Award. In summer visits Ruidoso Downs, New Mexico, to research "Ruidoso," a story on the quarter-horse All-American Futurity.

1974 In March, publishes "Sullen Gold," about the gold held in the Federal Reserve Bank of New York. Spends the spring and summer reporting a story about plans to build a floating nuclear power plant off the coast of New Jersey called "The Atlantic Generating Station." On July 15, in a "Talk of the Town" piece titled "Police Story," recounts an incident in which New York police officers come upon him and his wife attempting to break into their own car. In August, makes a journey of 150 miles with Henri Vaillancourt in bark canoes in northern Maine for "The Survival of the Bark Canoe." Along with "The Curve of Binding Energy" and his later "Basin and Range," the bark canoe piece is one of the most difficult of his career to write, "producing tears and continual anguish," as he later remembers it; "I nearly broke down." Offered a chance, in the middle of this difficulty, to teach at Princeton—replacing Larry L. King as Ferris Professor of Journalism—he instantly accepts: "No reflection. No hesitation. I sensed the possibility of balance in my overall writing pattern. I would lose money teaching but gain balance. That's just how it worked out."

1975 Spends most of the year reading and otherwise preparing for a major Alaska project that will be titled *Coming into the Country*. His friend John Kauffmann, now working for the National Park Service in Alaska, offers extensive advice and help. In February, begins teaching his first Princeton class, a writing seminar titled "The Literature of Fact." Later, the course is called "Creative Nonfiction"; he usually teaches one semester per year with every third year off. Over forty-five years he will teach nearly six hundred students, almost a quarter of whom will publish at least one book. They will include Peter Hessler, a staff writer at *The New Yorker*; Richard Stengel and Jim Kelly, both former managing editors of *Time*; Richard Preston, author of *The Hot Zone*; the novelists Jennifer Weiner and Akhil Sharma; Robert Wright, former editor and writer at *The New Republic* and other publications; and Eric Schlosser, author of *Fast Food Nation*. McPhee reads every paper closely, offering detailed, constructive, and sometimes unsparing critical comments that students remember decades later. Leaves for Alaska in August, spending two months there—the first of three extended trips.

1976 In September and October *The New Yorker* publishes "What They Were Hunting For," the first of his several Alaska pieces, about the search for a site for a new state capital. This is the first of the three simultaneously researched Alaska projects. FSG publishes *The John McPhee Reader*, with an introduction by McPhee's friend William Howarth, a professor of English at Princeton.

1977 Spends February and March living in cabins in eastern Alaska; journeys up the Yukon with a dog team. In May, the magazine publishes "The Encircled River," followed in June and July by the longest of his Alaska pieces, the four-part "Coming into the Country." In August investigates the workings of a New York City farmers' market. "The last thing I wanted to do was write," he later recalled. "So, I visited the Greenmarket for a couple of days, making a few notes. I went back a third time, and somehow I found myself wearing an apron and helping Rich Hodgson (Hodgson Farms, Newburgh, N.Y.) sell beans. I went back the next day and sold more beans—and eggs, and cucumbers, whatever there was to sell. We were in Harlem one day, Brooklyn the next, etc. Never in my life was I ever again going to have a time like this—selling beans on 137th Street in Harlem. I went every day, and brought out my notebook only when something irresistible took place. By a country mile, selling beans beats writing." *Coming into the Country* is published by FSG in December and becomes a best seller, eventually selling over a million copies. "Since it is a reviewer's greatest pleasure to ring the gong for a species of masterpiece," Edward Hoagland writes in *The New York Times*, "let me say he found it."

1978 Finishes "Giving Good Weight," about a day in the life of a New York Greenmarket; it appears in *The New Yorker* in July. *Casey's Shadow*, a film based on "Ruidoso" and starring Walter Matthau, opens in March to decent reviews, though throughout his career McPhee is wary of selling his work to Hollywood. Over the summer, writes "Brigade de Cuisine," about "a sort of farmhouse-inn that is neither farmhouse nor inn, in the region of New York City," which he declares has served him the best meals of his life—without revealing its name. (When the piece is published early the next year, there is a fuss: the *Times* quickly identifies the restaurant, unmasks its pseudonymous chef "Otto," and sneers at its food.) In October, sets out to write a short piece about a roadcut near New York City. It arouses an interest in geology that will become "an absorption for life" and the subject of many books to come (they are ultimately collected twenty years later, in *Annals of the Former World*). In November, with the geologist Kenneth Deffeyes, begins research for "Basin and Range," traveling from Salt Lake City to San Francisco in a pickup truck and investigating the Earth's ancient past. Other traveling and reporting companions, all recommended by Deffeyes, include the geologists Eldridge Moores, David Love, and Anita Harris.

1979 Travels through "Walker Percy country" in the spring with his daughter Sarah, who took a course on Percy at Harvard the previous semester. While in Louisiana they explore the Atchafalaya Basin, sparking an interest he will pursue a decade or so later, in *The Control of Nature*. ("There's nothing as catalytic as a kid in college," he writes a geologist friend.) As the geology project grows in scale, Shawn sees that the work will absorb McPhee and fill the magazine's pages for a long time to come; warns him, while extending his full support, that "readers will rebel."

1980 In May, while visiting the University of Alaska to receive an honorary degree, learns of a friend's efforts to bring telephone service to Circle City, Alaska (pop. 80). He lingers to make notes for "Riding the Boom Extension," which is published in three parts in the fall.

1981 In July, with Jenny, Sarah, and various Alaskan companions, takes a canoe trip from Bonanza Creek, Yukon Territory, to Circle City, Alaska, on the Yukon River, with a side excursion far up the Charley River, an itinerary of about five hundred miles. Begins work on a piece about the salmon run, but sets it aside at Shawn's request in deference to Edith Iglauer, who is writing about her recently deceased husband, an oceangoing salmon fisherman.

1982 Finishes "In Suspect Terrain" in April, writing and teaching his course at Princeton at the same time. Visits with Robert Bingham, who dies of glioblastoma, at fifty-seven, on

June 18. "I just took off," he later recalls, after learning of Bingham's death, heading to Blairstown in the Kittatinny Mountains of New Jersey. The next day, he meets with Pat McConnell, a wildlife biologist studying the state's bear populations; she has snared two bears to be examined and released, "including the first female trapped in the state," a sight he has been hoping for and that he knows Bingham would have celebrated with him. His obituary, "Robert Bingham—1925–1982," appears on July 5. Patrick Crow, a friend and fellow fisherman, becomes his new editor. "In Suspect Terrain" runs in three parts in September. In the fall, begins reporting for a piece on the Swiss army, "La Place de la Concorde Suisse."

1983 Visits Geneva, Lausanne, Epesses, Gruyère, Valais, and elsewhere for his Swiss army story; also spends time with daughters Jenny and Martha, the former living in Florence for a year and the latter in Varese. In August, begins reporting in Maine for "Heirs of General Practice," a portrait of young family physicians. On October 10 publishes "Open Man," about longtime friend Bill Bradley, now senator from New Jersey.

1984 Takes a field trip with David Love to Wyoming, Montana, and Idaho "to restore freshness and collect additional material for 'Rising from the Plains.'" Meets Yolanda in Salt Lake City; they tour Arches, Canyonlands, Mexican Hat, Monument Valley, Mesa Verde, the San Juans, the Black Canyon of the Gunnison, Grand Junction, and Colorado National Monument. In the fall, while in Maine, writes the beginning of "Rising from the Plains." Father dies in Maryland, at eighty-nine.

1985 Finishes "Rising from the Plains" in November; visits Jenny in Paris.

1986 Sees Paris, London, Devon, Cornwall, Somerset, Edinburgh, Caithness, Sutherland, and Argyll with Yolanda. In June conducts research for "The Control of Nature" in Los Angeles, Maine, Iceland, and Louisiana.

1987 Publishes "Atchafalaya" in *The New Yorker* on February 23, the first in the series called "The Control of Nature." The title is from a bas-relief on the front wall of the engineering building at the University of Wyoming: "Strive on—the control of nature is won, not given." In March, visits Hawaii to research plate tectonics and volcanism. In the spring he and Yolanda do a joint reading from "Rising from the Plains" for an audience at the residence of Princeton's president, William Bowen. Over the next fourteen years, they perform in twenty-two cities, "until Yolanda, whose part consisted of many passages from the Wyoming journals of the young Ethel Waxham, declared that she was too old to play a twenty-three-year-old anymore."

1988 "Cooling the Lava" is published on February 22. In May, McPhee is inducted into the American Academy and Institute of Arts and Letters and honored at a dinner given by Roger Straus, his publisher. In June, begins full-time research on the U.S. Merchant Marine for what will be "Looking for a Ship"; soon heads to Charleston, South Carolina, where he looks for a ship with second mate Andy Chase, and embarks on a voyage along the west coast of South America aboard the SS *Stella Lykes.* In October, visits Jacksonville and Savannah to talk with various crew members at home. Begins writing in November.

1989 In June, gives the completed manuscript of "Looking for a Ship" to Gottlieb and returns to work on his geology project with reporting in California. Settles down to write what he sometimes refers to as "Geology IV" and "Rocks IV": "It is going to be very difficult and it fills me with apprehension and gloom."

1991 Submits his geology manuscript on January 13; Gottlieb "reads manuscript overnight, accepts it warmly, hallelujah."

1992 In January, McPhee and Tom Wolfe are among the speakers at a black-tie dinner in honor of Roger Straus at the Lotos Club in Manhattan. In July, the owner of *The New Yorker*, S.I. Newhouse, announces that he will replace Gottlieb with *Vanity Fair* editor Tina Brown. Before Brown starts work in October, Gottlieb runs "Assembling California" in three parts.

1993 Writes a series of shorter pieces, including an obituary of his friend and subject Arthur Ashe, and "Irons in the Fire," a profile of a brand inspector in Nevada.

1994 With Yolanda, purchases and works on a house perched above the Delaware, on the Pennsylvania side. A lifelong fishing enthusiast, he is attracted to the spring run of American shad there. His fishing companions will include *New Yorker* staff writers Ian Frazier and Mark Singer, and his editor Pat Crow. In October, publishes "The Ransom of Russian Art," about Norton Townshend Dodge, a collector of Soviet dissident art that had been smuggled out of the country through a network of sources and CIA connections.

1996 Publishes pieces about a blizzard ("Other Snows") and forensic geology ("The Gravel Page"). *The Second John McPhee Reader* is published by FSG.

1997 For Mother's Day publishes a short piece about his mother, Mary Ziegler McPhee, "Silk Parachute." She dies in October, two months after her one-hundredth birthday, a grandmother of twelve children and great-grandmother of twenty-two.

1998 For *The New Yorker*, he publishes "Swimming with Canoes," about Keewaydin, and "Catch-and-Dissect," about a deep-sea fishing "rodeo" in Alabama. In *The Atlantic*, publishes "The Ships of Port Revel." In July, Tina Brown leaves *The New Yorker* to start a new magazine called *Talk*. Newhouse replaces her with a thirty-nine-year-old staff writer, David Remnick, who had been McPhee's student at Princeton. John Bennet becomes McPhee's editor at the magazine.

1999 Wins the Pulitzer Prize for General Nonfiction for *Annals of the Former World*, a seven-hundred-page omnibus that takes in all of his geology books and in which the reader learns how the continent came to be. ("At any location on earth, as the rock record goes down into time and out into earlier geographies it touches upon tens of hundreds of stories, wherein the face of the earth often changed, changed utterly, and changed again, like the face of a crackling fire.") Receives the President's Award for Distinguished Teaching from Princeton.

2000 "They're in the River," about shad fishing on the Delaware, appears in *The New Yorker* in April. Later shad pieces include "A Selective Advantage," "Absent Without Leave," and "Sapidissima."

2002 Collects his writings on American shad in *The Founding Fish*, published in October.

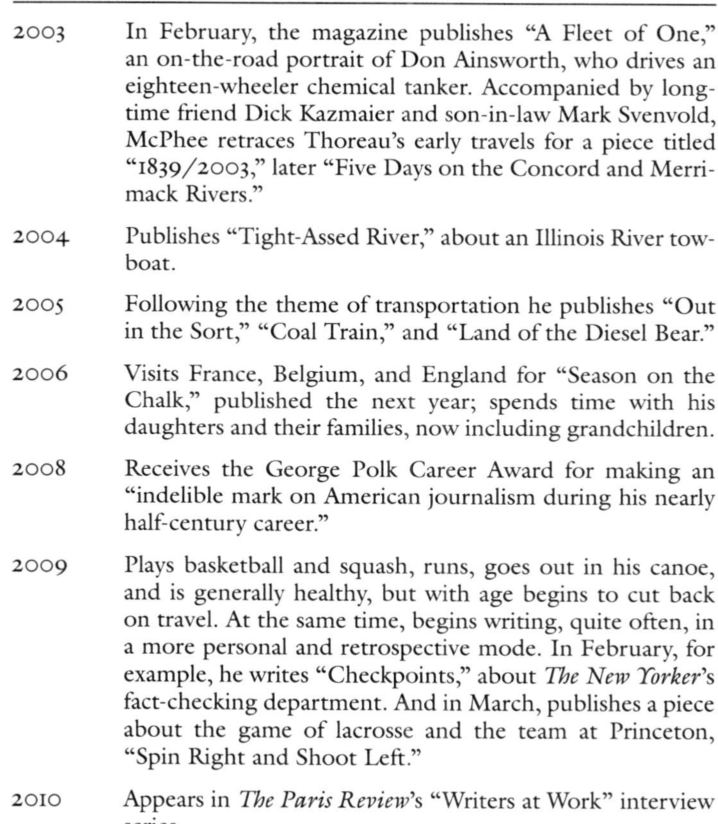

2003 In February, the magazine publishes "A Fleet of One," an on-the-road portrait of Don Ainsworth, who drives an eighteen-wheeler chemical tanker. Accompanied by longtime friend Dick Kazmaier and son-in-law Mark Svenvold, McPhee retraces Thoreau's early travels for a piece titled "1839/2003," later "Five Days on the Concord and Merrimack Rivers."

2004 Publishes "Tight-Assed River," about an Illinois River towboat.

2005 Following the theme of transportation he publishes "Out in the Sort," "Coal Train," and "Land of the Diesel Bear."

2006 Visits France, Belgium, and England for "Season on the Chalk," published the next year; spends time with his daughters and their families, now including grandchildren.

2008 Receives the George Polk Career Award for making an "indelible mark on American journalism during his nearly half-century career."

2009 Plays basketball and squash, runs, goes out in his canoe, and is generally healthy, but with age begins to cut back on travel. At the same time, begins writing, quite often, in a more personal and retrospective mode. In February, for example, he writes "Checkpoints," about *The New Yorker*'s fact-checking department. And in March, publishes a piece about the game of lacrosse and the team at Princeton, "Spin Right and Shoot Left."

2010 Appears in *The Paris Review*'s "Writers at Work" interview series.

2011 Pat Crow dies. McPhee is edited now by David Remnick, and occasionally by Deirdre Foley-Mendelssohn.

2017 Wins the National Book Critics Circle Award for lifetime achievement. Publishes *Draft No. 4: On the Writing Process.*

2018 Publishes *The Patch*, his seventh collection of essays.

2020 Retires from teaching at Princeton. Is now engaged in what he calls his "old person's project"—short, often autobiographical pieces written under the rubric "Tabula Rasa."

2023 *Tabula Rasa: Volume 1* appears in July.

2024 Pryde Brown dies in September.

2025 His fifth "Tabula Rasa" piece, subtitled "A project meant not to end," is published in *The New Yorker* in January. Donates current and future royalties from his book *The Pine Barrens* to the Pinelands Preservation Alliance.

Note on the Texts

This volume contains four books by John McPhee: *The Pine Barrens* (1968), *Encounters with the Archdruid* (1971), *The Survival of the Bark Canoe* (1975), and *Coming into the Country* (1977). All four were published first in *The New Yorker* and then by Farrar, Straus and Giroux in New York. At McPhee's recommendation, the texts of all four have been taken from the most recent FSG printings, which contain his latest corrections and revisions.

The Pine Barrens. McPhee sat down to begin *The Pine Barrens* at the end of the summer of 1966, and for two weeks or so found himself stuck. He had been visiting the region frequently for "about eight months," making day trips from Princeton and sometimes camping out for longer periods, and he had "assembled enough material to fill a silo," as he later recalled (*Draft No. 4: On the Writing Process*, 2017). Eventually, he realized he should foreground longtime "Piney" Fred Brown as the book's central character, around whom his miscellaneous notes and impressions might be organized, and he was able to start writing.

"The Pine Barrens" appeared in *The New Yorker* in two parts, on November 25 and December 2, 1967. A paragraph at the beginning of *The New Yorker*'s second installment of the piece, recapitulating what had come before, is omitted in *The Pine Barrens*, published by Farrar, Straus and Giroux on May 12, 1968, and in subsequent editions and printings of the book. Ballantine published a newly typeset edition, in paperback, in 1971. In 1981, FSG published a special edition featuring photographs by Bill Curtsinger and a brief afterword by McPhee describing his visits to the region with the photographer. Daunt Books published the book in London in 2018, using the original plates.

McPhee has occasionally made revisions and corrections to the text of the FSG edition, which has gone through numerous printings since 1968. The text of *The Pine Barrens* in the present volume is that of the most recent FSG printing, which contains McPhee's latest changes.

Encounters with the Archdruid. In 1969, McPhee accompanied the environmentalist David Brower on trips in the North Cascades of Washington State, to Cumberland Island, Georgia, and down the Colorado River through the Grand Canyon, reporting on Brower's meetings with three antagonists: a mining engineer, a real estate developer, and a dam builder. As he worked to describe these "Encounters with the Archdruid" for publication, he relied heavily on his *New Yorker* editor, Robert Bingham, reading him his entire 60,000-word first draft over the phone as he completed it and taking in Bingham's suggestions.

"Encounters with the Archdruid" appeared in the magazine in three parts, on March 20, March 27, and April 3, 1971. Later that year, on August 6, it was published as a book by Farrar, Straus and Giroux. In 1972, Ballantine reset the text for a paperback edition. The text of *Encounters with the Archdruid* in the present volume is that of the original FSG edition in its most recent printing, which contains McPhee's latest changes.

The Survival of the Bark Canoe. The 150-mile expedition through northern Maine recounted in *The Survival of the Bark Canoe* took place in August 1974. Back home, McPhee struggled to finish his account of the journey, fighting "tears and continual anguish" as he wrote, well into the new year.

"The Survival of the Bark Canoe" first appeared in *The New Yorker* in two parts, on February 24 and March 3, 1975. It was then published as a book—by Farrar, Straus and Giroux, on November 24, 1975—with the addition of an illustrated "Portfolio of the Sketches and Models of Edwin Tappan Adney (1868–1950)" depicting many of the canoes McPhee describes. Subsequent publishers, including Warner Books in New York (1975), MacFarlane, Walter & Ross in Toronto (1992), and the House of Lochar, on the Isle of Colonsey in Scotland (2000), used first-edition plates. The text of *The Survival of the Bark Canoe* in this volume has been taken from the most recent FSG printing of the original edition, which contains McPhee's most recent changes.

Coming into the Country. McPhee told friends "I'm going to Alaska!" in January 1975, and he then made three extended trips there, departing on the first in August of that year and returning from the last in March 1977. His accounts of these excursions appeared in *The New Yorker* in eight parts, under three separate titles: "What They Were Hunting For" on September 27 and October 4, 1976; "The Encircled River" on May 2 and May 9, 1977; and "Coming into the Country" on June 20, June 27, July 4, and July 11, 1977.

Coming into the Country, first published by Farrar, Straus and Giroux on December 1, 1977, gathers all three of these pieces, reversing the order of the first two and making each a "book" within the book, with a locodescriptive phrase added above each title ("At the Northern Tree Line" for "The Encircled River," "In Urban Alaska" for "What They Were Hunting For," "In the Bush" for "Coming into the Country"). Hamish Hamilton published the book in London at the end of 1978, using the original plates, and a newly typeset paperback edition from Bantam Books appeared in 1979. The text of *Coming into the Country* in the present volume is that of the original FSG edition in its most recent printing, which contains McPhee's latest corrections and revisions.

This volume presents the texts of the original printings chosen for inclusion here, but it does not attempt to reproduce features of their design and layout. The texts are presented without change, except for the correction of typographical errors. Spelling, punctuation, and capitalization are often expressive features and they are not altered, even when inconsistent or irregular. The following is a list of errors corrected, cited by page and line number: 82.38, short-leaf; 123.39, singlehanded; 131.32, *Anthocaris*; 172.13, Nevada ,; 262.33, Tusque; 708.17, '59;".

Notes

In the notes below, the reference numbers denote page and line of this volume (the line count includes headings but not blank lines). Biblical quotations are keyed to the King James Version. For further information about McPhee's life and works, and references to other studies, see Michael Pearson, *John McPhee* (New York: Twayne, 1997); Noel Rubinton, *Looking for a Story: A Complete Guide to the Writings of John McPhee* (Princeton: Princeton University Press, 2025); O. Alan Weltzien and Susan N. Maher, eds., *Coming into McPhee Country: John McPhee and the Art of Literary Nonfiction* (Salt Lake City: University of Utah Press, 2003).

The editor is grateful to John McPhee, who provided extensive notes during the preparation of this volume.

THE PINE BARRENS

2.1–3 *Pryde . . . Charles Mitchell Brown*] McPhee's wife, born Pryde Brown (1935–2024), and her recently deceased father (1902–1967), a former vice president of engineering for Western Union.

10.20–24 A framed poem . . . without pain.] These lines appeared in the longer poem "What God Hath Promised" by Annie Johnson Flint (1866–1932) in 1918, and circulated separately in newspapers, without attribution or title, at least as early as 1898.

11.3 up to Speedwell] Site of a late eighteenth-century sawmill and forge, south of Chatsworth, New Jersey.

20.8–9 an autobiography] See *Early Recollections and Life of Dr. James Still* (1877).

23.27 anconies] Large iron bars left unworked at each end.

27.11–15 In 1805 . . . *Shizaea pusilla*] *Shizaea pusilla*, sometimes described as "New Jersey's most famous plant," was discovered by Caspar Wister Eddy (1790–1828), John Le Conte (1784–1860), Charles Whitlaw (1771–1850), and Frederick T. Pursh (1774–1820) in 1805, and formally described by Pursh in his *Flora Americae Septentrionalis* (1814).

29.38–30.3 the colporteur records . . . barren sand."] See George Washington Newell's letter of March 17, 1846, in *Colporteur Reports to the American Tract Society, 1841–1846* (1940). A *colporteur* is a door-to-door seller of religious publications.

39.16–21 "I have been shocked . . . defectives."] Fiedler's remarks, made to the press at Brown's Mills Junction, New Jersey, were printed in the New York *Sun* on June 29, 1913, and in other papers (see "Gov. Fiedler Proposes to Segregate New Jersey's Degenerate Pineys—Finds Them a Menace to the State").

39.22–26 H. H. Goddard . . . a celebrated treatise] See *The Kallikak Family: A Study in the Heredity of Feeble-Mindedness* (1912).

40.24–33 Elizabeth Kite . . . people who live there."] Kite is quoted in Herbert Norman Halpert, "Folktales and Legends from the New Jersey Pines: A Collection and Study" (PhD diss., Indiana University, 1947).

52.30–31 Munyhon's cane . . . Toulouse-Lautrec's] The French painter Henri de Toulouse-Lautrec (1864–1901) owned a tippling cane, which one could unscrew to produce glasses and a flask.

70.34–35 the de la Huerta Rebellion] Adolfo de la Huerta (1881–1955) led an unsuccessful revolt against Mexican President Álvaro Obregón beginning in December 1923, after he was passed over as Obregón's successor. He went into exile in Los Angeles in March 1924, and some of the officers who supported him were executed.

86.14 pismire] Ant.

88.10 *Habenaria integra*] Now considered a species in the genus *Platanthera*.

92.21 fykes] Cylindrical or cone-shaped fish nets.

ENCOUNTERS WITH THE ARCHDRUID

110.1 *Robert Bingham*] Bingham (1925–1982) was McPhee's longtime editor at *The New Yorker*.

116.13 Stewart Udall] Udall (1920–2010), a three-term congressman from Arizona, served as secretary of the interior from 1961 to 1969, expanding protected federal lands and helping to pass major environmental legislation.

118.13 cirques] Amphitheater-like mountain valleys formed by glacial erosion.

119.26 tarn] A small mountain lake.

121.22 pirogue] A canoe hollowed out from a single tree trunk.

125.4 the Harz Mountains] Region in central Germany where mining has been a major industry since the Middle Ages.

133.5 the Willys Knight] A more expensive automobile than the family's former Maxwell; it was manufactured from 1914 to 1933.

138.20 lens] Also known as a lentil, an ore- or rock-body tapering at the edges and thicker at the center.

148.31–32 Lord Dewar . . . when they are open,"] Thomas Dewar (1864–1930), a Scottish whiskey distiller, is reported to have offered this witty aphorism in a speech at a London dinner in 1928; it circulated in newspapers without attribution during the prior year.

153.29 Antaeus] In Greek mythology, a giant of Libya who was invincible so long as he was connected to the earth (his mother Gaia); Hercules was able to defeat him by lifting him off the ground.

154.39 a biffy] An outhouse.

156.26–28 "We're not so poor . . . Newton Drury] Drury (1889–1978) served as director of the National Park Service from 1940 to 1951. The source of this quotation is unknown.

165.6–7 Nancy Newhall's . . . the future.] Newhall (1908–1974) was the author (with Ansel Adams) of the Sierra Club book *This Is the American Earth* (1960) and of other books on photography and on conservation. Her "definition" is not known to have appeared in print before the publication of *Encounters with the Archdruid* (1971).

170.35 John Brown] Brown (1800–1859), a radical abolitionist, was executed for treason for leading a raid on the armory at Harpers Ferry, Virginia, in which seven people were killed. He hoped to provoke and arm a slave revolt.

172.17–19 John Muir . . . the universe"] See *My First Summer in the Sierra* (1911); the text is adapted from Muir's journal of July 27, 1869.

172.19–21 Henry David Thoreau . . . put it on?"] From a letter to Harrison Blake dated May 20, 1860.

172.21–22 Buckminster Fuller . . . with less"] Perhaps a reference to Fuller's discussion of efficiency and "ephemeralization" ("doing more with less") in *Nine Chains to the Moon* (1938).

172.23 Pogo . . . he is us"] Pogo, the title character of a long-running comic strip by Walt Kelly (1913–1973), appeared under this slogan on a 1970 Earth Day poster Kelly designed, featuring Pogo in a trash-strewn forest.

176.5 Myres McDougal] McDougal (1906–1998), a longtime Yale law professor, was the author (with David Haber) of the casebook *Property, Wealth, Land Allocation, Planning and Development* (1948), among other books.

176.37 Taras] Tara is a fictional Georgia plantation in the Civil War novel *Gone With the Wind* (1936) by Margaret Mitchell (1900–1949).

178.1 Methuselan] Extremely old (after the biblical Methuselah, said to have lived for 969 years).

179.9 wan] Pale, weak, faint.

191.13–14 Robinson Jeffers . . . dropped from."] From Jeffers's poem "Pelicans," first collected in *The Women at Point Sur* (1927).

192.2–3 out of Chekhov . . . developer] See, for example, *The Cherry Orchard* (1904).

192.31–32 General Greene] Nathanael Greene (1742–1786), who served as commander of the Continental Army in the southern theater from 1780 to 1783.

193.27–28 a Deep South Lorca] Federico García Lorca (1898–1936), Spanish poet and playwright whose tragedy *Blood Wedding* (1933) and similar works may be alluded to.

197.32 Levittowns] Suburban housing projects developed by William J. Levitt (1907–1994) and his firm Levitt & Sons beginning with Levittown, New York, in 1947.

199.1 Zermatt] A mountain resort town in southern Switzerland.

199.2 Stehekin] A small community in the North Cascades of Washington State.

201.2 Arthur D. Little] A management consulting firm founded by Arthur Little (1863–1935) in 1886.

203.25 Senator Thurmond] Strom Thurmond (1902–2003), longtime Republican senator from South Carolina.

205.3–6 John P. Irish . . . cross of gold."] Irish (1843–1923) supported the gold standard, against which Bryan (1860–1925) was campaigning in his famous "cross of gold" speech at the Democratic National Convention on July 9, 1896.

205.27–28 Edna Ferber . . . beautiful but dumb] Perhaps a reference to a passage in Ferber's novel *Fanny Herself* (1927):

> "There is no describing a mountain. One uses words, and they are futile. And the Colorado Rockies, in October, when the aspens are turning! People who have seen an aspen grove in October believe in fairies. And such people need no clumsy descriptive passages to aid their fancies. You others who have not seen it? There shall be no poor weaving together of words. There shall be no description of orange and mauve and flame-colored sunsets, and sunrises and purple mountains. Mountain dwellers and mountain lovers are a laconic tribe. They know the futility of words."

205.35 an Agincourt . . . an El Alamein] Places where hard-pressed forces achieved unexpected and decisive victories: Henry V's army against the French in 1415, the Continental Army against the British in 1777, and the Allies against Rommel's German army in 1942.

206.8 Hannes Schneider] Schneider (1890–1955), an Austrian ski instructor who starred in more than a dozen alpine ski films in the 1920s and 1930s, emigrated to the United States in 1939, and opened a ski school in New Hampshire. After the U.S. entered World War II, he served alongside David Brower as an instructor in the 10th U.S. Mountain Division.

213.7–9 Joseph Conrad . . . inscrutable intention."] See Conrad's 1899 novella *Heart of Darkness*, chapter 2.

214.29–30 THE POPULATION . . . explosion] See *The National Review*, October 7, 1969.

214.40–215.1 the Leopold Report . . . Florida ecosystem"] See *Environmental Impact of the Big Cypress Swamp Jetport*, a 1969 report by hydrologist Luna Leopold (1915–2006) opposing the construction of a supersonic jetport in what subsequently became Big Cypress National Preserve.

215.20 "What makes Sammy run in the South?"] See *What Makes Sammy Run*, a 1941 novel by Budd Schulberg (1914–2009), adapted as a musical in 1965, about ambition and corruption in Hollywood.

223.26 the Corn-Hog Program] As part of the Agricultural Adjustment Act of 1933, implemented by Agriculture Secretary Henry A. Wallace (1888–1965), farmers were paid to reduce production of corn, wheat, hogs, and other commodities.

226.29 Alan Ladd . . . Jack Palance] Ladd (1913–1964) faced off against Palance (1919–2006) in *Shane* (1953), a classic Western, though not over water rights.

240.1–2 the Galloway-Stone expedition] Nathaniel Galloway (1854–1913) and Julius Stone (1855–1947) traveled from Green River, Wyoming, to Needles, California, in September–November 1909, in flat-bottomed boats of Galloway's design.

241.24–26 Edith Warner . . . past the mesas."] Warner (1893–1951) ran a general store and tearoom at Los Alamos, New Mexico, frequented by scientists at work on the Manhattan Project. The quotation is from a journal entry dated March 2, 1933.

243.35–36 the Order of DeMolay . . . Job's Daughters] Masonic youth organizations founded in 1919 and 1920.

247.8 *douane*] Customs house.

247.19–21 Marc Mitscher . . . Philippine Sea] Mitscher (1887–1947), a vice admiral, led the First Carrier Task Force from its flagship, the USS *Lexington*, against the Japanese fleet in the western Pacific on June 19 and 20, 1944, resulting in huge Japanese losses.

247.33–34 the day Major Powell . . . expedition] Lake Powell was formally dedicated on June 19, 1969, the date on which, a century before, Powell (1834–1902) reached the confluence of the Green and Colorado Rivers.

251.18 Caprian bays] Capri, off the coast of southern Italy, is known for its picturesque coastline and clear waters.

252.29–30 a Saranac, a Sunapee, a Mooselookmeguntic] Lakes in the northeastern U.S.: Saranac in the New York Adirondacks, Sunapee in New Hampshire, and Mooselookmeguntic in Maine.

258.12 Luna Leopold] Leopold (1915–2006), son of the writer and naturalist Aldo Leopold, was an expert hydrologist and geomorphologist.

258.31–32 draw a picture of a fish in the sand] A form of greeting among early Christians in times of persecution.

260.18 the defeat of John Muir] Muir's campaign to prevent the flooding of the Hetch Hetchy Valley, in Yosemite National Park, was defeated in 1913 with the passage of the Raker Act, authorizing the construction of a dam.

261.23 Pierce-Arrow] A luxury car, various models of which were produced from 1901 to 1938.

274.14–15 Wallace Stegner . . . Dam] See Stegner's essay "Glen Canyon Submersus," collected in *The Sound of Mountain Water* (1969).

276.15 monadnock] A hill, ridge, mountain, or other rocky projection rising in isolation from a surrounding plain; also known as an inselberg.

THE SURVIVAL OF THE BARK CANOE

286.1 *John Kauffmann*] Kauffmann (1923–2014) was one of McPhee's longtime friends; for further detail, see page 434 in the present volume.

289.11 tumplines] Slings used to carry a load on one's back, with a strap worn at the top of one's head.

293.6 a froe] Also known as a paling knife, an L-shaped tool for splitting wood.

309.20 *C'est dommage*] French: It's a shame.

316.40–317.1 He said . . . I expect."] Quoted in Thoreau's *The Maine Woods* (1864), "The Allegash and East Branch."

334.16 a churchwarden smoke] A churchwarden is a long-stemmed tobacco pipe.

339.22 Kordofan] A former Sudanese province, now the states of North Kordofan, South Kordofan, and West Kordofan.

343.1 Ain't he a James Dickey bird!] A *dickey bird* is a small bird or a thing of no consequence.

345.23–25 "The Indian . . . his journal] See Thoreau's journal for July 25, 1857.

350.11–21 Thoreau . . . wind increased."] From *The Maine Woods* (1864), "The Allegash and East Branch."

351.15 peaveys, pickpoles, pickaroons] Logging tools, the first two long-handled with a hook end used for rolling or pushing logs, and the last shorter-handled, used to pick logs up.

352.1 Jim Dickey house] *Dickey* can mean troublesome or in poor condition. See also note 343.1.

355.28 Patton . . . Hannibal?] George S. Patton (1885–1945), William Tecumseh Sherman (1820–1891), and Hannibal Barca (c. 247–c. 183 BCE), military leaders known for their long, wide-ranging campaigns.

367.33 *Tant pis*] French: Too bad.

369.30 Allagash-Ipswich] An "Ipswich clam" is a variety of soft-shelled clam (*Mya arenaria*) harvested in Ipswich, on the Massachusetts coast, or elsewhere in New England. Ipswich is claimed as the birthplace of the fried clam.

375.9 halazone] A chemical used to disinfect drinking water.

378.30 phreatophytic] Consisting of deep-rooted plants able to draw on groundwater and not exclusively reliant on rainfall.

383.1–2 the year Henri Vaillancourt was born] 1950.

383.23 a couple . . . 1900] "How an Indian Birch-Bark Canoe Is Made" (*Harper's Young People*, supplement, July 29, 1890) and "The Building of a Birch Canoe" (*Outing*, May 1900).

408.1 Têtes de Boule] French colonial name for the Atikamekw people of Quebec; literally, "ball heads" or "round heads."

COMING INTO THE COUNTRY

414.1 *Martha*] McPhee's daughter (b. 1965), now a novelist.

422.33 dewclaws] In moose, these are small digits behind the hooves; they may appear in tracks as dotlike dents beneath the larger hoofprints.

429.32–33 *bateau noir* . . . *Höllenfahrt*] French, ancient Greek, and German vessels suited for journeys to the underworld or Hell.

434.16–17 a book on eastern American rivers] See *Flow East: A Look at Our North Atlantic Rivers* (1973).

434.33 ecomorphs] In evolutionary biology, a species that is morphologically similar to, and that occupies the same ecological niche as, a phyletically distinct species. Used here euphemistically.

439.35 the Limpopo] A warm, slow-moving river that flows through southern Africa into the Indian Ocean.

440.6 Lynchburg, Tennessee] Home of Jack Daniel's distillery.

441.2 Super Cub] Small, single-engine plane manufactured by Piper Aircraft from 1949 to 1994 and often used in backcountry contexts.

456.1 Teterboro] Airport in the New Jersey Meadowlands used mostly for private and corporate flights.

457.27 Smilin' Jack] Title character of the aviation-themed comic strip *The Adventures of Smilin' Jack*, which ran from 1933 to 1973, initially in the *Chicago Tribune* and then in syndication.

457.28 Eddie Rickenbacker] Rickenbacker (1890–1973) was a celebrated World War I flying ace and a winner of the Medal of Honor.

461.7 Belial] In Christian tradition, a demon or personification of evil.

461.36 yare] Agile, easily maneuvered.

463.9 Sir Edmund Hillary] A New Zealand mountain climber, Hillary (1919–2008) reached the summit of Mount Everest on May 29, 1953.

463.10 the marks of waffles] A pattern on the soles of some running and hiking shoes.

471.18–34 The animals . . . wilderness at its best.] From *Grizzly Country* (1967) by Andy Russell (1915–2005).

471.29 alder hell] Alder thicket.

472.14 pygal] Of the rump or rear end.

472.16 porpentine] An archaic version of *porcupine*.

472.21 schuss] A straight, downhill ski run.

479.1–12 His association . . . mind for life.] From *Grizzly Country* (1967).

479.18 Duffel] A coarse cloth, named after the town in Flanders in which it was first manufactured, or, in informal North American usage, camping gear.

480.1 painters] Ropes attached to either end of a canoe or other boat for towing or other purposes.

481.5 the coaming] A raised border around a boat's hatch or cockpit.

485.18–19 take-and-put] A reversal of "put and take" fishing, where stocked fish are supplied for anglers to catch and keep.

492.15 gules] Heraldic red.

493.4 sneakerfaces] A pejorative term for environmentalists, perhaps of McPhee's invention.

505.31 McKinley] Denali was named Mount McKinley in 1896 after William McKinley (1843–1901), then a Republican candidate for the presidency and later president. See also note 513.11.

507.29–30 Gilbert and Sullivan] W. S. Gilbert (1836–1911) and Arthur Sullivan (1842–1900), whose comic operas often feature farcical, topsy-turvy plots.

513.11 a young Princeton graduate] William A. Dickey (1862–1939), who described his naming of the mountain in the New York *Sun* on January 24, 1897.

516.18 fumaroles] Cracks in the ground from which gases are vented.

516.25 thewy] Muscular, brawny.

519.3 muskeg] A term used in Alaska and Canada for arctic bog or peatland habitat.

530.5 Colonel Sanders] Harland David Sanders (1890–1980), founder and brand ambassador of the fast-food chain Kentucky Fried Chicken.

534.5 Sutton Place] A wealthy neighborhood on the east side of Manhattan.

538.23–25 most noted employer . . . get away on."] Attributed to Pilz in R. N. DeArmond's *The Founding of Juneau* (1967).

539.27–28 Yonne Valley] Yonne is among the least prosperous departments in France.

546.39 Yoknapatawpha] A fictional Mississippi county in the works of William Faulkner (1897–1962).

569.17–18 Mrs. Partington . . . mop] A resident of Sidmouth, England, whose struggle against a tidal flood, in the winter of 1824, was related by the cleric and wit Sydney Smith (1771–1845) in a political speech of 1831, and who has often since been referred to as a figure of comically futile effort.

595.22 kicker] A small outboard motor.

603.25 the Nickel Plate] A railroad network that connected various destinations between Buffalo, New York, and St. Louis, Missouri. Opened in 1881, it was absorbed as part of the Norfolk and Western Railway in 1964.

605.8 Postum] A roasted-grain beverage produced by the Post cereal company from 1895 to 2007 and popular as a coffee substitute.

606.25 jug-hustler, chain man, and shooter] A seismic field assistant, responsible for placing geophones or "jugs"; a surveyor; and an explosives technician.

607.27 shoepac] Heavy, waterproof laced boot.

611.21–23 Alfred Hulse Brooks . . . cordillera."] See Brooks's *Blazing Alaska's Trails* (1953).

612.31 Pheidippides] A semilegendary Greek herald (c. 490 BCE) said to have died from exhaustion after running from Marathon to Athens to announce the Athenians' defeat of the invading Persian army.

620.1 dogleg] Sharp bend.

621.13 geminate] Having a doubled or paired quality.

627.3 Ashley] A wood-burning stove brand introduced in 1905.

628.2 Cotton Mather] Mather (1663–1728) was a prominent New England Puritan minister and theologian.

630.16–21 Frederick Schwatka . . . venture in."] See *Report of a Military Reconnaissance in Alaska, Made in 1883* (1885).

631.15 the Big Inch] Pipeline from Texas to Illinois constructed to protect oil supplies from submarine attacks and completed in July 1943, at which time it was said to be the world's longest petroleum pipeline.

636.29 Big Delta] Alaska settlement at the confluence of the Tanana and Delta Rivers.

643.3 Mary Jane] Marijuana.

643.9–10 Henri (le Douanier) Rousseau] Rousseau (1844–1910), nicknamed "the customs officer," is known for his lush, dreamlike jungle scenes.

643.22 Blazo boxes] Various kinds of fuel were shipped to Alaska in cans and packed in wooden crates known as Blazo boxes. Blazo, manufactured by Chevron until the 1970s, was a fuel for portable lamps and stoves.

647.36–648.3 "Several who came . . . kind of stuff."] Bettles (1859–1945), a veteran fur trader and prospector, began writing for the *Yukon Press*, the region's first newspaper, in 1894. The source of the quotation is not known.

652.26 darning-egg] Egg-shaped tool used in the repair of socks or stockings.

652.40 coffee, tea, or me] Catchphrase associated with flight attendants; it was popularized by the fictional memoir *Coffee, Tea, or Me?* (1967), written by Donald Bain (1935–2017) and published under the names Trudy Baker and Rachel Jones.

655.35 beaver castors] Sacs near the anal glands that produce an oil called castoleum, used by the beaver for marking territory and by humans in perfumery.

657.17 dentils] In classical architecture, small decorative blocks under a cornice, resembling teeth.

658.6–7 the St. Mary . . . St. Croix] Rivers in northeastern North America named after Catholic saints.

660.28–29 Lake Maggiore . . . Hardanger Fjord] Lake Maggiore, in Italy and Switzerland, and the Hardanger Fjord, in Norway, are both famously picturesque.

666.17 *Conibears*] Animal traps designed by Frank Conibear (1896–1988) and manufactured beginning in the 1950s. See also page 685, lines 7–9, in the present volume.

669.3–4 You walk through the valley . . . no evil] Psalms 23:4.

672.16–17 works of Peary and Byrd] Polar explorers Robert Peary (1856–1920) and Richard E. Byrd (1888–1957); the former wrote *Northward over the "Great Ice"* (1898) and *The North Pole, its Discovery in 1909 under the Auspices of the Peary Arctic Club* (1910), among other books, and the latter *Little America: Aerial Exploration in the Antarctic, the Flight to the South Pole* (1930) and *Alone* (1938), among others.

674.22 the DEW line] The Distant Early Warning line, a string of Arctic radar installations designed to detect Soviet attack. It was built beginning in 1954; some sites were decommissioned in the 1980s and early 1990s while others became part of the currently operational North Warning System.

676.26–27 bull cooks] Camp helpers or kitchen assistants.

678.21 cheechako] Alaskan term for a tenderfoot or newcomer (from Chinook Jargon, "to come lately").

678.36 an Eric Sloane book] Sloane (1905–1985), a painter and illustrator, published several books evoking early American life and rural craftsmanship.

680.11 Damoclean] Damocles, in Greek legend, was a courtier to Dionysius I of Syracuse who praised his king's good fortune. Temporarily yielding his throne to Damocles, Dionysius hung a sword, by a thread, over Damocles' head, illustrating the perils to which he was subject as king.

693.12 derringer] A type of small handgun.

695.36 Seward] William H. Seward (1801–1872), who negotiated the Alaska Purchase as secretary of state, in 1867.

698.5 International Scout] An off-road vehicle manufactured by International Harvester from 1961 to 1980.

706.23–24 ultured virus] Possibly a malapropism for the Latin phrase *ultra vires* (beyond one's legal power or authority).

722.17–20 "I have wondered . . . 1917] See Stuck's *Voyages on the Yukon and Its Tributaries: A Narrative of Summer Travel in the Interior of Alaska* (1917).

724.35 trig] Having a neat or trim appearance.

728.21–27 She wrote . . . its citizens."] See James Wollaston Kirk and Anna L. M. Kirk, *Pioneer Life in the Yukon Valley, Alaska* (1935).

729.5 "Cavalleria Rusticana,"] 1890 opera by Pietro Mascagni (1863–1945).

729.8–11 Alfred H. Brooks . . . good returns.] From Brooks's "Letter of Transmittal," which prefaces *The Gold Placers of the Fortymile, Birch Creek, and Fairbanks Regions, Alaska* (1905), by Louis M. Prindle (1865–1956).

729.27–32 Ray continued . . . to be controlled."] Ray's reports—here, from a letter to the adjutant-general of the U.S. Army dated May 5, 1898—were presented to Congress on February 20, 1899, under the title *Letter from the Secretary of War, Making Report of His Action under the Act Authorizing Him to Assist in the Relief of People in the Yukon River Country.*

730.5–6 a hero . . . Egbert] Harry C. Egbert (1839–1899) died while leading a charge against Filipino forces at Malinta, now part of greater Manila.

732.14 Amundsen] Roald Amundsen (1872–1928), Norwegian polar explorer and author, among other books, of *The North West Passage; Being the Record of a Voyage of Exploration of the Ship "Gjöa"* (1908) and *My Life As an Explorer* (1927).

738.29 Forest Lawn] A name commonly given to cemeteries. The first Forest Lawn, opened in Buffalo, New York, in 1849, was part of the rural cemetery movement.

738.34 Peale] Charles Willson Peale (1741–1827), whose portrait *George Washington at Princeton* (1779) was originally commissioned for Independence Hall in Philadelphia.

740.40 Teapot Dome] A bribery scheme, made public beginning in 1922, in which Albert Fall (1861–1944), secretary of the interior under President Harding, secretly leased federal oil reserves in exchange for loans and gifts.

741.14 a bend sinister] In heraldry, a stripe across a shield, running from the viewer's upper left to the lower right.

742.2 Paramus] A suburban New Jersey town known for its shopping malls.

754.10–17 The flag . . . Aleut boy] The flag of the Territory of Alaska was designed by John Ben Benson Jr. (1912–1972), who won a contest in 1927. He was a member of the Qawalangin Tribe of Unalaska.

755.24 babiche] Strips of rawhide or sinew used as rope or string.

771.1–2 "Desert Solitaire."] *Desert Solitaire: A Season in the Wilderness* (1968), by Edward Abbey (1927–1989), recounts Abbey's experiences as a ranger at Arches National Monument in Utah.

771.36–39 As Nessmuk . . . knot hole."] See George Washington Sears's *Woodcraft* (1884), published under the pseudonym "Nessmuk."

774.3 goldbricking] Evading one's duties while appearing to perform them.

783.39 coach whip] *Masticophis flagellum*, a thin, nonvenomous snake found in the southern U.S. and northern Mexico.

787.14–15 that Frenchman . . . according to need] Michel Siffre (1939–2024), a French speleologist who undertook experiments in chronobiology beginning in 1962.

788.3 a Detex key] Until 2011, Detex Corporation manufactured watch clocks for use by security guards. Turning a key, guards logged their presence on their appointed rounds.

789.2 Blazo cans] See note 643.22.

793.28 the honeypots of biffies] Containers underneath the toilet seats of outhouses.

796.7 G.S.I.] Geophysical Service, Inc., an oil exploration firm.

Index

This book is set in 10 point ITC Galliard, a face designed for digital composition by Matthew Carter and based on the sixteenth-century face Granjon. The paper is acid-free lightweight opaque that will not turn yellow or brittle with age. The binding is sewn, which allows the book to open easily and lie flat. The binding board is covered in Brillianta, a woven rayon cloth made by Van Heek–Scholco Textielfabrieken, Holland.

Composition by Dianna Logan, Clearmont, MO.

Printing by Sheridan, Grand Rapids, MI.

Binding by Dekker Bookbinding, Wyoming, MI.

Designed by Bruce Campbell.